# THE BOOK OF HAGGAI

# SUPPLEMENTS

## TO

# VETUS TESTAMENTUM

EDITED BY
THE BOARD OF THE QUARTERLY

H.M. BARSTAD – PHYLLIS A. BIRD – R.P. GORDON
A. HURVITZ – A. van der KOOIJ – A. LEMAIRE
R. SMEND – J. TREBOLLE BARRERA
J.C. VANDERKAM – H.G.M. WILLIAMSON

VOLUME 91

TUTA SUB AEGIDE PALLAS · 1683 ·

# THE BOOK OF HAGGAI

*Prophecy and Society in Early Persian Yehud*

BY

JOHN KESSLER

BRILL

LEIDEN · BOSTON · KÖLN

2002

This book is printed on acid-free paper.

**Library of Congress Cataloging-in-Publication Data**

Kessler, John, 1951-
  The book of Haggai : prophecy and society in early Persian Yehud / John
Kessler.
      p.      cm. — (Supplements to Vetus Testamentum, ISSN 0083-5889 ;
      v. 91)
  Revision of the author's dissertation, Le rôle du prophete dans le livre d'Agée,
Sorbonne-Paris-IV and Institut Catholique de Paris, 1995.
    Includes bibliographical references and index.
    ISBN 9004124810 (cloth : alk. Paper)
    1. Bible. O.T. Haggai—Commentaries. 2. Yehud (Persian province).
I. Kessler, John, 1951- Rôle du prophete dans le livre d'Agée. II. Title
III. Series.

BS1655.53 .K47    2002
224'.97077—dc21                                                2002018319
                                                               CIP

**Die Deutsche Bibliothek – CIP-Einheitsaufnahme**

**Kessler, John:**
The book of Haggai ; Prophecy and Society in Early Persian Yehud / by
John Kessler. – Leiden ; Boston ; Köln : Brill, 2002
  (Supplements to Vetus testamentum ; Vol. 91)
  ISBN 90-04-12481-0

ISSN    0083-5889
ISBN    90 04 12481 0

PRINTED IN THE NETHERLANDS

*Dedicated to my parents,*

*Daisy Elizabeth Kessler (née Dyke)*
*1916–1987*

*and*

*Maurice Kessler*
*1916–1984*

*with profound and enduring love, admiration,*
*gratitude, and appreciation*

## TABLE OF CONTENTS

Preface and Acknowledgments ..................................... xi
Abbreviations ..................................................... xv

Chapter One. On Reading The Book of Haggai: Questions of
Method and Perspective .......................................... 1
  1.1. Introduction ................................................ 1
  1.2. Early Critical Evaluations of Haggai: Of What Value Is
     This Book? ................................................ 2
  1.3. Haggai and Second Temple Sectarianism: Whose Side Is
     Haggai on? ................................................ 12
  1.4. Theological Traditions and Literary Development: What
     Were the Theological Concerns of Haggai and His
     Editors? ................................................... 18
  1.5. Social Scientific Analyses of Early Persian Yehud .......... 22
  1.6. The Present Study: Purpose, Approach, and Structure ..... 25

Chapter Two. The Literary History of The Book of Haggai ...... 31
  2.1. Introduction ................................................ 31
  2.2. The Literary Development of The Book of Haggai ........ 31
  2.3. The Dating of the Redactional Framework ................. 39
    2.3.1. Evaluation of the Evidence for a Fifth- or
       Fourth-Century Redaction ........................... 39
    2.3.2. Evidence for a Late Sixth-Century Redaction ....... 41
      2.3.2.1. The Date Formulae ......................... 41
         2.3.2.1.1. Precision in the Date Formulae ... 42
         2.3.2.1.2. Form of the Date Formulae ....... 44
         2.3.2.1.3. The Designation of the Month ... 48
         2.3.2.1.4. The Date Formulae: Evaluation
              and Conclusions ................... 49
      2.3.2.2. Other Evidence for a Sixth-Century
         Redaction ..................................... 51

Chapter Three. Persian Rule and Yehud, 539–515: Critical Issues    59
  3.1. Introduction ...............................................    59
  3.2. The "Decree of Cyrus" and the Nature of the Early
       Restoration ...............................................    60
  3.3. Sheshbazzar ...............................................    63
  3.4. Zerubbabel ................................................    70
  3.5. The Political Status of Yehud, the Nature of its Leadership,
       and the Role of the Davidic Dynasty ......................    72
  3.6. The Second Year of Darius ................................    80
  3.7. The Impact of Persian Rule on Yehud from 538–515 .......    86
  3.8. The State of the Jerusalem Temple ........................    88
  3.9. The Population of Yehud ..................................    90

Chapter Four. Introduction To The Exegesis Of Haggai ...........    97
  4.1. Organization and Approach ...............................    97
  4.2. Theological Traditions in Haggai .........................    97

Chapter Five. Haggai 1: 1–15 ..................................    103
  5.1. Translation and Textual Criticism ........................    103
  5.2. Structural and Literary Considerations ..................    108
  5.3. Exegesis .................................................    114
  5.4. Rhetorical and Hermeneutical Use of Religious Traditions    153
       5.4.1. Tradition as a Basis for Understanding the Present    153
       5.4.2. Fusion of Independent Traditions and Extended
              Sphere of Application ..............................    155

Chapter Six. Haggai 2: 1–9 ....................................    159
  6.1. Translation and Textual Criticism ........................    159
  6.2. Structural and Literary Considerations ..................    161
  6.3. Exegesis .................................................    163
  6.4. Rhetorical and Hermeneutical Use of Theological
       Traditions ...............................................    183
       6.4.1. Tradition as Basis for Continuity with the Past .......    183
       6.4.2. Harmonization and Systematization of Traditional
              Elements ...........................................    186
       6.4.3. Adaptation of Tradition for the Needs of the Present    190
              6.4.3.1. Generalization .............................    190
              6.4.3.2. Focalization ..............................    192

Chapter Seven. Haggai 2: 10–19 ..................................... 197
   7.1. Translation and Textual Criticism .......................... 197
   7.2. Structural and Literary Considerations ..................... 201
   7.3. Exegesis ..................................................... 203
   7.4. Rhetorical and Hermeneutical Use of Religious Traditions  218

Chapter Eight. Haggai 2: 20–23 ..................................... 219
   8.1. Translation and Textual Criticism .......................... 219
   8.2. Structural and Literary Considerations ..................... 220
   8.3. Exegesis ..................................................... 222
   8.4. Rhetorical and Hermeneutical Use of Religious Traditions  239
      8.4.1. Generalization ........................................ 239
      8.4.2. The Conflation and Harmonization of Divergent
            Traditions ............................................. 240
      8.4.3. Tradition as a Basis for Continuity with the Past ..... 241
      8.4.4. Actualization of Religious Traditions ................. 241

Chapter Nine. The Book Of Haggai: Literary Synthesis .......... 243
   9.1. Introduction ................................................. 243
   9.2. The Form of Haggai ......................................... 243
   9.3. The Structure of Haggai ................................... 247
   9.4. *Leitwörter* And *Leitmotiven* in Haggai ...................... 251
   9.5. Characters and Action ...................................... 254
   9.6. Plot or Thematic Centre? .................................. 255
   9.7. The Central Theme of Haggai .............................. 256

Chapter Ten. Conclusions: Prophecy and Society in The Book of
   Haggai ......................................................... 259
   10.1. The Distinctive Perspectives of The Book of Haggai ....... 259
      10.1.1. Yehud and Persian Domination ..................... 259
      10.1.2. The Socio-Religious Portrait of Yehud .............. 262
      10.1.3. Prophecy and Yehud ............................... 265
         10.1.3.1. Titles and Designations .................. 265
         10.1.3.2. Social Location and Characteristic
              Behaviour .................................... 266
         10.1.3.3. Goals and Results .......................... 270
         10.1.3.4. Rhetorical and Hermeneutical Use of
              Religious Traditions ......................... 271

10.2. The Book of Haggai in the Socio-Religious Context of
      Early Persian Yehud .......................................... 275
10.3. Conclusions ................................................. 279

Selected Bibliography ............................................. 281
Indices ........................................................... 309

# PREFACE AND ACKNOWLEDGMENTS

The present volume is a complete revision and reworking of my dissertation, *Le rôle du prophète dans le livre d'Aggée* defended conjointly at the Sorbonne-Paris-IV and the Institut Catholique de Paris in January, 1995. My thesis directors were Professors Jean Lévêque (Institut Catholique de Paris) and Michel Meslin (Sorbonne-Paris IV). The other members of the examining committee were Professors André Lemaire, André Caquot, and Jacques Briend. This manuscript reflects both the suggestions made to me by the committee members, as well as the evolution of my own personal reflection on the issues under study. I completed this text during my sabbatical leave (2000–01) from my teaching responsibilities at Tyndale Seminary, Toronto.

The book of Haggai has held great interest for me since my attention was drawn to it as an undergraduate student by my former professor and present colleague, Dr. Donald Leggett. I continued my study of Haggai and the early Persian period, beginning in the early 1980s, at both the master's and doctoral level. In the last twenty years, the study of the Persian period in Palestine, including the biblical texts produced in it (whose alleged number is constantly increasing!), has undergone a remarkable transformation. This area has moved from its former position on the periphery of biblical studies to its present status as the object of profound scholarly interest (cf. my survey in ch. 1). I feel truly privileged to have been at work on Haggai during this most exciting period of transition, and to have met and dialogued with several of the key researchers in the area. One of the very real gains of this scholarly interest in the Persian period is the availability of a great body of excellent research which can help enable us to re-create the social, political, demographic and religious landscape which surrounded the production of the Persian period biblical texts. Now, more than ever, the necessity of an integrative, multi-disciplinary approach to the reading of these texts is evident. The present volume has sought to employ just such an approach. It reflects my ongoing reflection regarding the book of Haggai and its milieu of origin. Doubtlessly my thought will continue to evolve, however I feel quite convinced regarding the major lines of reflection presented here. In this study I have sought to enter into dialogue with the burgeoning, rich, and variegated bibliography which has emerged regarding Haggai and the early Persian period. Regrettably, P. R. Bedford's *Temple Restoration in Early Achaemenid Judah* (Brill, 2001) came into my hands too late for me to incorporate an analysis of it in these pages.

Thanks are due to the very many people who assisted me in my personal development as a researcher, and in the preparation of this text. At the masters level, the late Professor Thomas McComiskey encouraged me in my interest in the Persian period, and imparted to me many valuable insights into historical and exegetical investigation. Subsequently, my interest was nurtured and expanded by Professor Jean Lévêque, who graciously agreed to supervise my dissertation, and provided me with excellent suggestions, guidance, support, and criticism. Similarly, thanks are due to Professor Michel Meslin for his co-supervision, and his insights from the perspectives of religious anthropology. I am deeply grateful to the members of my examining committee, named above, for their invaluable suggestions. Special thanks are due to Professor André Lemaire for his extensive, careful, and detailed critique of my work, his encouragement to revise and publish my research, his careful reading of the manuscript, as well as for his numerous suggestions regarding content and bibliography. The warm and generous assistance which he has extended to me, as well as to a wide variety of students and scholars, is quite remarkable. I am also especially grateful to Arnaud Sérandour and the personnel at the library of the *Institut d'Etudes Sémitiques* in Paris for their helpful assistance and warm *acceuil*. I am also deeply indebted to Professor Charles Carter (whom I first met in 1990 through the kind introduction of Magen Broshi), who shared with me his ongoing demographic research, exposed me to various new avenues of approach to the study of the Persian period, and has provided ongoing interest and support. Thanks are also due to the Academic Dean, President, and Board of Governors of Tyndale Seminary, Toronto, for granting me this sabbatical year. Similarly I wish to thank Massey College in the University of Toronto, especially Mr. John Fraser (Master) and Ms. Ann Brummel (Registrar) for receiving me as a Senior Resident for the year. I also grateful for the availablitiy of the resources of the Tyndale College and Seminary library, and for the assistance of its librarians Mr. Sandy Finalyson and Mr. Hugh Rendle.

Many hands went into the production of this text and its predecessors. Here special thanks are due to Mr. Thomas Petter, Dr. Brian Irwin, Dr. Robert Webb, Rev. Michel Lemaire, Ms. Wendy Kirk, Ms. Chemaine Yin-Mei Chan, Ms. Allyson Lucas and Ms. Lynda Chantson. In addition to the individuals mentioned above, I wish to express my appreciation to those colleagues and friends who have provided support and advice. These include, to name only a few, Dr. Jeffrey Greenman, Dr. Cynthia Miller, Dr. Linda Oyer, Professor Ursula Franklin, Ms. Patricia Webb, Ms. Donna Petter, M. and Mme. Roland and Marianne Hattab, and Mlle. Claire Bedot. I hasten to add that the views expressed in this text, as well as any errors or inadequacies in it, are my own, and not those of the many people who have assisted me.

A final word of thanks goes out to my children Anna, Michael, Jeremy and Andrea whose encouragement, interest, and support has meant so much. This volume is dedicated to the memory of my parents, with deepest gratitude.

John Kessler
Toronto, August 26, 2001

# ABBREVIATIONS

## I. Journals, Series, Reference Works and Translations

| | |
|---|---|
| *AASOR* | *Annual of the American Schools of Oriental Research* |
| AB | Anchor Bible |
| *ABD* | *Anchor Bible Dictionary*, Edited by D. N. Freedman. 6 vols. New York, 1992. |
| ABRL | Anchor Bible Reference Library |
| AIONSup | *Annali dell'Instituto Orientale di Napoli*, Supplementary Series |
| *AJBA* | *Australian Journal of Biblical Archaeology* |
| *AJSL* | *American Journal of Semitic Language and Literature* |
| ATANT | Abhandlungen zur Theologie des Alten und Neuen Testaments |
| ATD | Das Alte Testament Deutsch |
| *BA* | *Biblical Archaeologist* |
| *BAIAS* | *Bulletin of the Anglo-Israel Archaeological Society* |
| *BAR* | *Biblical Archaelogy Review* |
| *BASOR* | *Bulletin of the American Schools of Oriental Research* |
| BDB | F. Brown, S. R. Driver, and C. A. Briggs, *A Hebrew and English Lexicon of the Old Testament*, Oxford: Clarendon Press, 1953. |
| BEATAJ | Beiträge zur Erforschung des Alten Testaments und des antiken Judentum |
| *BHS* | *Biblia Hebraica Stuttgartensia*, ed. K. Elliger and W. Rudolph. Stuttgart, 1984. |
| BibOr | Biblica et orientalia |
| BKAT | Biblischer Kommentar, Altes Testament |
| BL | H. Bauer and P. Leander, *Historische Grammatik der hebräischen Sprache des Alten Testamentes*. Hildesheim: Georg Olms, 1922. |
| *BN* | *Biblische Notizen* |
| *BT* | *The Bible Translator* |
| BWAT | Beiträge zur Wissenschaft vom Alten Testament |
| *BZ* | *Biblische Zeitschrift* |

| | |
|---|---|
| BZAW | Beihefte zur Zeitschrift für die alttestamentliche Wissenschaft |
| *CBQ* | *Catholic Biblical Quarterly* |
| CBET | Contributions to Biblical Exegesis and Theology |
| CEB | Commentaire Evangélique de la Bible |
| *CHJ* | *The Cambridge History of Judaism. Vol. 1 The Persian Period*, ed. W. D. Davies and L. Finkelstein, Cambridge: Cambridge University Press, 1984. |
| ConBOT | Coniectanea Biblica. Old Testament Series |
| COut | Commentar op het Oude Testament |
| DB | The Inscription of Darius I at Behistun |
| *DBS* | *Dictionnaire de la Bible: Supplément*, ed. L. Pirot and A. Robert, Paris: Letouzey & Ané, 1928- |
| DJD | Discoveries in the Judaean Desert |
| DMOA | I documenta et monumenta orientis antiqui |
| EtB | Etudes bibliques |
| ErIsr | Eretz-Israel |
| *ETL* | *Ephemerides theologicae louvanieneses* |
| *EThR* | *Etudes théologiques et religieuses* |
| *EvT* | *Evangelische Theologie* |
| *FO* | *Folia orientalia* |
| FOTL | Forms of the Old Testament Literature |
| FRLANT | Forschungen zur Religion und Literatur des Alten und Neuen Testaments |
| GKC | A. E. Kautzsch and A. E. Cowley, eds., *Gesenius' Hebrew Grammar*, 2nd. edtn., Oxford: Clarendon Press, 1910. |
| *HAT* | *Handbuch zum Alten Testament* |
| *HeyJ* | *Heythrop Journal* |
| HKAT | Handkommentar zum Alten Testament |
| HSM | Harvard Semitic Monographs |
| HSS | Harvard Semitic Studies |
| *HTR* | *Harvard Theological Review* |
| *HUCA* | *Hebrew Union College Annual* |
| IB | *The Interpreter's Bible*, ed. G. A. Buttrick et. al. 12 vols. New York: Abingdon, 1951–57. |
| *IBHS* | B. K. Waltke and M. O'Connor, *An Introduction to Biblical Hebrew Syntax*, Winona Lake: Eisenbrauns, 1990. |
| ICC | International Critical Commentary |
| *IDB* | *Interpreters Dictionary of the Bible*, ed. G. Buttrick, 4 vols., Nashville, 1962. |

| | |
|---|---|
| *IDB[S]* | *Interpreters Dictionary of the Bible:* Supplementary Volume. Edited by K. Crim. Nashville, 1976. |
| *IEJ* | *Israel Exploration Journal* |
| *Irén* | *Irénikon* |
| *Int* | *Interpretation* |
| IRT | Issues in Religion and Theology |
| ITC | International Theological Commentary |
| *JANES* | *Journal of the Ancient Near Eastern Society* |
| *JAOS* | *Journal of the American Oriental Society* |
| JB | Jerusalem Bible |
| *JBL* | *Journal of Biblical Literature* |
| *JETS* | *Journal of the Evangelical Theological Society* |
| *JJS* | *Journal of Jewish Studies* |
| *JNES* | *Journal of Near Eastern Studies* |
| *JQR* | *Jewish Quarterly Review* |
| *JSOT* | *Journal for the Study of the Old Testament* |
| JSOTSup | *Journal for the Study of the Old Testament.* Supplement Series |
| *JTS* | *Journal of Theological Studies* |
| *JTS, ns* | *Journal of Theological Studies, new series* |
| *Jud* | *Judaica* |
| KAT | Kommentar zum Alten Testament |
| KB | L. Koehler and W. Baumgartner, *Lexicon in Veteris Testamenti Libros*, Leiden : E. J. Brill, 1953. |
| KHC | Kurzer Hand-Commentar zum Alten Testament |
| LAPO | Littératures anciennes du Proche Orient |
| LD | Lectio divina |
| *LTQ* | *Lexington Theological Quarterly* |
| *MQR* | *Michigan Quarterly Review* |
| Mur | The scroll of the 12 Minor Prophets found at Murabba'ât |
| NAWG | Nachrichten der Akademie der Wissenschaften in Göttingen |
| NCBC | New Century Bible Commentary |
| NEB | New English Bible, 1970. |
| NICOT | New International Commentary on the Old Testament |
| NIV | New International Version |
| OBO | Orbis Biblicus et Orientalis |
| OBT | Overtures to Biblical Theology |
| OLP | Orientalia louvaniensia periodica |
| *OTE* | *Old Testament Essays* |
| OTG | Old Testament Guides |

OTL          Old Testament Library
*OtSt*         *Oudtestamentische Studien*
*PEQ*         *Palestine Exploration Quarterly*
POut         De Prediking van het Oude Testament
PTMS         Pittsburgh Theological Monograph Series
*RB*          *Revue biblique*
*REJ*          *Revue d'études juives*
*ResQ*         *Restoration Quarterly*
RGBA         F. Rosenthal, *A Grammar of Biblical Aramaic*. Fourth edtn.
             Porta Linguarum Orientalium, Weisbaden: Otto
             Harrassowitz, 1974.
*RHPR*        *Revue d'histoire et de philosophie religieuses*
*RHR*         *Revue de l'histoire des religions*
*RTR*         *Reformed Theological Review*
SB           Sources bibliques
SBLDS        Society of Biblical Literature Dissertation Series
SBLEJL       Society of Biblical Literature Early Judaism and its
             Literature
SBLMS        Society of Biblical Literature Monograph Series
*ScEs*         *Science et Esprit*
*SEÅ*          *Svensk Exegetisk Årsbok*
SemeiaSt     Semeia Studies
*Sem*         *Semitica*
*SJOT*         *Scandinavian Journal of the Old Testament*
SOSup        *Symbolae osloenses*, Supplement Series
SSN          Studia semitica neerlanica
SUNT         Studien zur Umwelt des Neuen Testaments
SVT          Supplements to *Vetus Testamentum*
*TD*          *Theology Digest*
*TDNT*         *Theological Dictionary of the New Testament*, ed. G. Kittel and
             G. Friedrich. Translated by G. W. Bromiley. 10 vols. Grand
             Rapids: Eeerdmans, 1964–1976.
*TDOT*         *Theological Dictionary of the Old Testament*, ed. G. J. Botterweck
             and H. Ringgren. Translated by J. T. Willis,
             G. W. Bromiley and D. E. Green. 8 vols. Grand Rapids:
             Eerdmans, 1974-.
*THAT*         *Theologisches Handwörterbuch zum Alten Testament* ed. E. Jenni
             and C. Westermann. 2 vols. Stuttgart, 1971–1976.
*Them*         *Themilios*
TOB          Traduction oecuménique de la Bible, 1973 and 1988.

| TOTC | Tyndale Old Testament Commentaries |
|---|---|
| *Trans* | *Transeuphratène* |
| TUGOS | Transactions of the Glasgow University Oriental Society |
| *TynBul* | *Tyndale Bulletin* |
| *TZ* | *Theologische Zeitschrift* |
| *VF* | *Verkundigung und Forschung* |
| *VT* | *Vetus Testamentum* |
| WBC | Word Biblical Commentary |
| Williams | R. J. Williams, *Hebrew Syntax: An Outline*, 2nd. edtn., Toronto: University of Toronto Press, 1976. |
| WMANT | Wissenschaftliche Monographien zum Alten und Neuen Testament |
| *ZAW* | *Zeitschrift fur die alttestamentliche Wissenschaft* |
| *ZDPV* | *Zeitschrift des Deutschen Palästina-Vereins* |

## II. Commentaries and Specialized Studies on Haggai Cited in Text by Author's Name

| Amsler | S. Amsler, *Aggée*, CAT XI-C, Genève: Labor et Fides, 1988. |
|---|---|
| Baldwin | J. Baldwin, *Haggai, Zechariah, Malachi*, TOTC, London: InterVarsity, 1972. |
| Barnes | W. E. Barnes, *Haggai and Zechariah*, Cambridge: Cambridge University Press, 1917. |
| Beuken | W. A. M. Beuken, *Haggai - Sacharja 1–8: Studien zur Überlieferungsgeschichte der frÜhnachexilischen Prophetie*, SSN 10, Assen: Van Gorcum, 1967. |
| Chary | T. Chary, *Aggée—Zacharie—Malachie*, SB, Paris: J. Gabalda, 1969. |
| Deissler | A. Deissler, *Les petits prophètes*, 2 vols., Paris: Letouzey et Ané, 1964. |
| Elliger | K. Elliger, *Das Buch der zwölf kleinen Propheten II*, 7th. edtn., ATD 25/2, Göttingen: Vandenhoeck & Ruprecht, 1964. |
| Floyd | H. M. Floyd, *Minor Prophets, Part 2*, FOTL 22, Grand Rapids: Eerdmans, 2000. |
| van Hoonacker | A. van Hoonacker, *Les douze petits prophètes: traduits et commentés*, EtB, Paris: J. Gabalda, 1908. |
| Horst | F. Horst, *Die zwölf kleinen Propheten II*, HAT 1/14, Tübingen: Mohr/Siebeck, 1964. |

Keil                    C. F. Keil, *The Twelve Minor Prophets, vol. 2*. Biblical
                        Commentary on the Old Testament, repr. edtn.,
                        Grand Rapids: Eerdmans, 1948.
Koole                   J. L. Koole, *Haggai* , Kampen: Kok, 1967.
Mason                   R. A. Mason, *The Books of Haggai, Zechariah, and
                        Malachi*, Cambridge Bible Commentary, New
                        York: Cambridge University Press, 1977.
Meyers and Meyers       C. L. Meyers and E. M. Meyers, *Haggai, Zechariah
                        1–8*, AB, Garden City: Doubleday, 1987.
Mitchell                H. G. Mitchell, *A Critical and Exegetical Commentary
                        on Haggai and Zechariah*, ICC, New York: Charles
                        Scribner's Sons, 1912.
North                   R. North, *Exégèse pratique des petits-prophètes
                        postexiliens: bibliographie commentée*, Rome: Biblico,
                        1969.
Nowack                  W. Nowack, *Die kleinen Propheten*, HKAT 3/4,
                        Göttingen: Vandenhoeck & Ruprecht, 1922.
von Orelli              C. von Orelli, *The Twelve Minor Prophets*, trans.
                        J. S. Banks, Edinburgh: T. & T. Clark, 1897.
Petersen                D. L. Petersen, *Haggai and Zechariah 1–8*, OTL,
                        London: SCM, 1985.
Redditt                 P. L. Redditt, *Haggai, Zechariah, Malachi*, NCBC,
                        Grand Rapids: Eerdmans, 1995.
Reventlow               H. G. Reventlow, *Die Propheten Haggai, Sacharja und
                        Maleachi*, ATD, vol. 2, Göttingen: Vandenhoeck &
                        Ruprecht, 1993.
Rudolph                 W. Rudolph, *Haggai, Sacharja 1–8, 9–14, Malachi*,
                        KAT XIII/4, Gütersloh: Gütersloher
                        Verlagshaus, 1970.
Sellin                  Sellin, E., *Das Zwölfprophetenbuch*, KAT XII/2,
                        Leipzig: Deichert, 1922.
Stuhlmueller            C. Stuhlmueller, *Haggai and Zechariah: Rebuilding
                        with Hope*, ITC, Grand Rapids: Eerdmans, 1988.
Verhoef                 P. A. Verhoef, *The Books of Haggai and Malachi*.
                        NICOT, Grand Rapids: Eerdmans, 1987.
Wellhausen              J. Wellhausen, *Die kleinen Propheten übersetzt und
                        erklärt*, Berlin: G. Reimer, 1898.
Wolff                   H. W. Wolff, *Haggai: A Commentary*, trans.
                        M. Kohl, Minneapolis: Augsburg, 1988.

# CHAPTER ONE

# ON READING THE BOOK OF HAGGAI:
# QUESTIONS OF METHOD AND PERSPECTIVE

## I.I. INTRODUCTION

The present study is premised upon the assumption that the book of Haggai has evidentiary value for the study of early Persian Yehud.[1] The principal objective of my inquiry is to examine the specific vision of prophecy and society portrayed in the book of Haggai set against the social context in which the book was produced.[2] However the book's evidentiary value can only be accessed when an adequate methodological approach to it is employed. Such an approach must include an understanding of the redactional history of the text, an analysis of the historical, political, sociological, economic, and demographic circumstances surrounding the oracular and redactional material in the book, due consideration of the ideological, literary, rhetorical, and theological orientation of the book, as well as a detailed exegesis of the text itself. The necessity of such a multi-disciplinary and integrative approach becomes evident when one considers various attempts to use the text of Haggai as an historical source, often with less than satisfactory results.

---

[1] Yehud is the commonly used English equivalent for the Hebrew *yᵉhûdâ* and the Aramaic *yhd* or *yhwd*. These terms were used in the Persian period to designate the administrative unit which comprised the former territories of Judah and Benjamin (though reduced in size). I will employ the term Judaea and Judah when I make reference to this region in other historical periods. I employ the term "early Persian Yehud" as a general designation of the early period of Persian rule in the West, approximately from Cyrus' conquest of Babylon in 539, to the beginning of the fifth century. All ancient dates are BCE. The designations BCE and CE will be employed only when potential ambiguity exists.

[2] I have adopted the following formal conventions in this study: Commentaries and major monographs on Haggai will be cited by the name of the author alone. A full list of such works is included with the abbreviations. In order to make this work as accessible as possible to all readers, in general, non-English works will be cited from their English translations, where such exist. Other non-English sources, where cited, will be translated. Where individual Hebrew and Aramaic words are cited for purposes of general historical and archaeological discussion, they will simply be transliterated. In the more detailed exegetical sections, the Hebrew characters will be used.

This introductory chapter will first examine a variety of approaches, methodologies, and perspectives relevant to the reading of Haggai, and assess their contributions and limitations. This survey will both introduce the reader to the critical discussion of the book, and set that discussion in an historical perspective. Subsequently I will outline my own methodological approach to the text, and explain how the present study will proceed.

## 1.2. Early Critical Evaluations of Haggai: Of What Value Is This Book?

The scholarly literature of the nineteenth to the first half of twentieth centuries quite frequently found the book of Haggai to be something of an embarrassment within the prophetic corpus of the Hebrew Bible. As early as 1912, H. G. Mitchell observed that it had "long been the fashion to disparage the book of Haggai."[3] Quite frequently, these negative evaluations of the book of Haggai were based upon the following supposed deficiencies: (1) the prophet's impoverished literary style and theological content; (2) the prophet's nationalism and exclusivism; (3) the prophet's narrow focus upon the reconstruction of the temple, and (4) the prophet's preoccupation with law, ritual, and ceremony, to the exclusion of any spiritual or ethical concerns.

Haggai's literary abilities were frequently disparaged. His vocabulary and style were described as "crabbed", "threadbare", and "poverty-stricken."[4] His book was described as "small and simple, without any passage of power and beauty."[5] Our prophet was said to lack the capacity for original thought and to have been content to borrow the ideas and words of his earlier counterparts. In 1893, A. Weiser concluded that Haggai was "an imitator of the prophets, one who stands closer to Judaism than to the old prophecies."[6] The label "epigon" (imitator) was

---

[3] Mitchell, p. 36. Mitchell specifically refers to Gesenius and de Wette, and cites a passage from the latter which includes comments by Marti and Reuss.

[4] Descriptions cited by G. L. Robinson, (*The Twelve Minor Prophets*, [Grand Rapids: Baker, 1953], p. 145) without indication of their source.

[5] J. A. Bewer, *The Literature of the Old Testament*, (rev. ed.; New York: Columbia University, 1933), p. 236.

[6] A. Weiser, *The Old Testament: Its Formation and Development*, (1893, Eng. tr. New York: Association Press, 1961), p. 268. J. Wellhausen, (*Prolegomena to the History of Ancient Israel*, [trans. Black & Menzies, Gloucester, MA: Peter Smith, 1883, repr., 1973], p. 410) appears to apply the term "Judaism" to everything written after the "pristine" period of prophetic religion.

one that would remain in the scholarly lexicon with reference to Haggai for quite some time. The expression was used of our prophet by G. Sauer[7] and G. Fohrer[8] but rejected by J. Lindbloom[9] and K. Beyse.[10] A more recent variation on this theme sees Haggai as relying heavily on the words of the classical prophets, and having an "access to Yahweh which appears limited when compared to that of the classical prophets."[11]

Not only was his style bereft of originality and interest, Haggai was said to be a zealous nationalist. In this regard, attempts were made to integrate Haggai's vision into the broader perspective of the Jewish attitude to the Gentiles at the beginning of the postexilic period. Some scholars posited a dialectic between a growing spirit of narrow exclusivism and a movement towards proselytism at that time.[12] It was maintained that the theme of the "pilgrimage of the nations to Jerusalem" was closely allied to the impulse towards proselytism.[13] Others spoke of "contradictory attitudes" within Israel with respect to the Gentile nations. Bright affirmed the existence of one theological understanding whereby Israel, as the servant of Yahweh, was called to suffer on behalf of the nations.[14] Yet he also maintained that at the same time there was

---

[7] G. Sauer, "Serubbabel in der Sicht Haggais und Sacharjas", in *Das ferne und nahe Wort. Festschrift Leonhard Rost*, (ed. F. Maass; Berlin: Töpelmann, 1967), p. 203.

[8] G. Fohrer, *Introduction to the Old Testament*, (1965, trans. D. Green; London: SPCK, 1970), p. 460.

[9] J. Lindblom, *Prophecy in Ancient Israel*, (1934, Eng. tr. D. M. Barton; Oxford: Basil Blackwell, 1962), p. 421.

[10] K. Beyse, *Serubbabel und die Königserwartungen der Propheten Haggai und Sacharja: Eine historische und traditionsgeschichtliche Untersuchung*, (Arbeiten zur Theologie 1/48; Stuttgart: Calwer, 1972), p. 65.

[11] B. D. Sommer, "Did Prophecy Cease? Evaluating a Reevaluation", *JBL* 115 (1996): 42–43. Interestingly, Sommer offers no evidence to support the claim regarding limited access as it relates to Haggai. In fact he admits that, unlike Zechariah, Haggai is addressed directly by Yahweh!

[12] In 1898, A. Selbie (s. v. "Gentiles" in *A Dictionary of the Bible dealing with its Language, Literature and Contents including the Biblical Theology*, [ed. J. Hastings; New York: Scribners, 1898], 2:149) stated, "Israel's attitude towards other nations ... underwent most important modifications in the post-exilic period. The reformation of Ezra deliberately aimed at fostering that spirit of exclusiveness which gave so much offense to the Gentile world. ... Side by side with this exclusiveness a proselytizing tendency was developed." E. J. Hamlin (s. v. "Nations", *IDB* 3:517) states, "The object of the (later postexilic) mission was to make Jews out of the people of the nations, to bring them to worship God at Jerusalem. It was closely linked with Jewish nationalism and legalism."

[13] So Hamlin, "Nations", 3:517.

[14] J. Bright, *The Kingdom of God*, (Nashville: Abingdon, 1953), p. 162. H. M. Orlinsky summarily dismissed such a notion. He riposted that "nothing could have been further

an eager desire for divine judgment against the nations.[15] The attempt
to distinguish "universalistic" from "particularistic" strands both in the
Hebrew Bible as a whole, and within prophetic literature, figured in
many analyses of Israelite religion produced in the earlier part of the
last century.[16] Deutero-Isaiah was seen as the parade paradigm of an
inclusive, universalistic, and non-legalistic religious approach, in contrast to such figures as Ezekiel, Ezra, and Nehemiah.

For several commentators, this tension between nationalism and universalism was to be seen in the differing attitudes of Haggai and Zechariah. Haggai, it was affirmed, was materialistic and bigoted. He displayed no interest in the salvation of the nations but was merely interested in their "subjugation and spoliation."[17] One very dim view of our
prophet's attitude regarding the Gentiles maintained that "Haggai's
picture of the future was narrowly nationalistic. [He] had no further
interest in the nations than to get hold of their money; for the rest let
them kill each other off and be done with it (Hag 2:22)!"[18] Zechariah,
by contrast, had a more nuanced perspective and favoured the conversion of the nations. This conversion was to be achieved through divine
intervention, rather than military devices.[19] Two elements in Haggai
have been traditionally cited as proof of that prophet's nationalistic
attitude. The first is the alleged exclusion of the Samaritans from the
rebuilding of the temple (2:10–14). The hypothesis that the priestly *torah*
of 2:10–14 became the basis for the exclusion of the Gentiles was for-

---

from the prophet's mind [i.e. Deutero-Isaiah] than that Israel was in existence for the
welfare of the nations, or that other nations could achieve equality with Israel in God's
scheme of things." (H. M. Orlinsky, "The So-Called 'Suffering Servant' of Isa 53", in
H. M. Orlinsky and P. A. H. de Boer, *Studies on the Second Part of the Book of Isaiah*, [SVT
14; Leiden: E. J. Brill, 1967], p. 36.)

[15] Bright, *Kingdom of God*, p. 165.

[16] See, for example, W. O. E. Oesterley and T. H. Robinson, *Hebrew Religion: Its
Origin and Development*, (London: SPCK, 1930), pp. 276–77, who begin their discussion
of the postexilic period with a section on "particularism and universalism." They see
the former as characteristic of the priests and the latter as present in the writings of
Deutero-Isaiah. See also J. Morgenstern, "Two Prophecies from 520–516 B.C.", *HUCA*
22 (1949): 365–431, who analyzes Isa 60 in terms of this motif. He distinguishes vv. 1–3
and 5–7 which are untinged by nationalism and reflect the voluntary submission of the
nations to Yahweh, from the rest of the chapter which manifests "a plain and assertive
nationalism. ... Yahweh's favor is for Israel alone; the nations of the world, He will
subject to Israel, that they may be exploited to the utmost by His people" (pp. 396–98).

[17] R. H. Pfeiffer, *Introduction to the Old Testament*, (New York: Harper and Bros., 1941),
pp. 606–7.

[18] F. James, "Thoughts on Haggai and Zechariah", *JBL* 3 (1934): 231.

[19] Pfeiffer, *Introduction*, pp. 606–7.

mulated by J. W. Rothstein.[20] E. Sellin proclaimed Haggai's decision to have been "the birthday of postexilic Judaism."[21] The second element is Haggai's alleged conception of Israel's position as a dominant world power following the destruction of the power of the nations (2:6–9, 20–23).

Closely linked to this nationalistic view of Haggai is the understanding of our prophet as one who actively promoted rebellion against the Persian empire. In an article published in 1957,[22] L. Waterman proposed the hypothesis of a rebellion attempt on the part of Zerubbabel, encouraged and supported by Haggai and Zechariah. Waterman's thesis was not new. For quite some time speculations had been made concerning the relationship of the rebellions in the Persian Empire to the oracles of Haggai.[23] James, Pfeiffer and Oesterley and Robinson[24] had already posited an independence movement under Zerubbabel which was supported by Haggai. The possibility of such a movement continues to be proposed as a viable hypothesis[25] although it is not widely accepted.[26] In a more nuanced manner, R. Mason discerns

---

[20] J. W. Rothstein, *Juden und Samaritaner. Die grundlegende Scheidung von Judentum und Heidentum. Eine kritische Studie zum Buche Haggai und zur jüdische Geschichte im ersten nachexilischen Jahrhundert*, (BWAT 3; Leipzig: J. C. Hinrich, 1908).

[21] Sellin, p. 413.

[22] L. Waterman, "The Camouflaged Purge of Three Messianic Conspirators", *JNES* 13 (1954): 73–78.

[23] Mitchell, p. 20; W. H. Bennett, *The Religion of the Post Exilic Prophets: The Literature and Religion of Israel*, (Edinburgh: T. & T. Clark, 1907), p. 74; J. M. Powis Smith, *The Prophets and their Times*, (Chicago: University of Chicago Press, 1925), p. 196.

[24] James, "Haggai", pp. 229–35; W. O. E. Oesterley and T. H. Robinson, *An Introduction to the Books of the Old Testament*, (London: SPCK, 1934), pp. 404–8; Pfeiffer, *Introduction*, pp. 602–4.

[25] Cf. J. Bright, *A History of Israel*, (2nd. ed.; Philadelphia: Westminster, 1972), p. 372; R. Carroll, "Prophecy, Dissonance and Jeremiah XXVI", *TUGOS* 25 (1973–74): 12–23; idem, *When Prophecy Failed: Reactions and Responses to Failure in the Old Testament Prophets*, (London: SCM, 1979), pp. 162–64. (Carroll sees the movement as essentially an attempt to restore the monarchy rather than an explicit attempt at rebellion against the Persians). H. J. Katzenstein, "Gaza in the Persian Period", *Trans* 1 (1989): 68–82, esp. p. 74 and even more recently J. Blenkinsopp, *A History of Prophecy in Israel*, (2nd. edtn.; Louisville: Westminster/John Knox, 1996), p. 203.

[26] Cf. the early criticism in A. Bentzen, "Quelques remarques sur le mouvement messianique parmi les Juifs aux environs de l'an 520 avant Jésus-Christ", *RHPR* 10 (1930): 493–503, followed by P. R. Ackroyd, "Two Historical Problems of the Early Persian Period", *JNES* 17 (1958): 13–27 and idem, *Exile and Restoration: A Study of Hebrew Thought of the Sixth Century B.C.*, (Philadelphia: Westminster, 1968), pp. 164–65. More recently see L. L. Grabbe, *Judaism from Cyrus to Hadrian*, (2 vols.; Minneapolis: Fortress, 1992), 1:128.

a strong political orientation in Haggai's oracles that the redactional framework attempts to attenuate.[27] Likewise, T. Chary does not hesitate (in contrast to Siebeneck[28] and van Hoonacker[29]) to affirm that Haggai could have "made Zerubbabel himself the bearer of the messianic hopes."[30]

Not only given to a nationalistic and particularistic attitude, Haggai was also viewed as a pragmatic materialist. This approach is purportedly seen in Haggai's understanding of the significance of the temple and his attitude toward the riches of the nations. According to the most extreme expression of this view, for Haggai the temple amounts to a kind of talisman.[31] Pfeiffer maintained that for Haggai, "the present prosperity and future glory of his people depended entirely on the rebuilding of the temple."[32] It was asserted that "Haggai's work ... was done when the work on the temple was revived. It was otherwise with Zechariah. ... He devoted himself to the spiritual edification of the community."[33] It was affirmed that, in Haggai's thought, the temple's reconstruction would act as a guarantee of blessing and fruitfulness. This interpretation of Haggai's view of the temple has remained influential in subsequent scholarship although it frequently appears in a more nuanced form. For example, Hanson[34] and Hamerton-Kelly[35] affirm that Haggai saw the rebuilding as a necessary prerequisite for the coming of the eschatological era, yet without being its guarantor. Haggai's view of the temple is said to be similar to his interest in the treasures of the nations (Hag 2:7). For James, Pfeiffer, and certain others, Haggai was interested in the Gentiles' riches on a purely material level. He simply wanted to "get hold of their money."[36] Furthermore, Haggai's emphasis on the temple was seen to belie an attitude which focused on ritual and ceremony, and was utterly devoid of ethical con-

---

[27] R. Mason, "The Purpose of the 'Editorial Framework' of the Book of Haggai", *VT* 27 (1977): 413–21, esp. pp. 420–21.

[28] R. T. Siebeneck, "The Messianism of Aggeus and Proto-Zacharias", *CBQ* 19 (1951): 314–15.

[29] Van Hoonacker, p. 526.

[30] T. Chary, *Les prophètes et le culte à partir de l'exil*, (Paris: Desclée, 1955), p. 134.

[31] James, "Haggai", p. 321.

[32] Pfeiffer, *Introduction*, p. 602.

[33] Barnes, p. xlv.

[34] P. D. Hanson, *The Dawn of Apocalyptic*, (Philadelphia: Fortress, 1975), pp. 248–49.

[35] R. G. Hamerton-Kelly, "The Temple and the Origins of Jewish Apocalyptic", *VT* 20 (1970): 1–15.

[36] James, "Haggai", p. 321.

cern. Pfeiffer states that Haggai's "great concern was not the moral and religious wickedness of the people, but adherence to rules of Levitical purity and the fulfillment of ritual acts."[37]

In sum, for certain scholars, Haggai was a key figure in the general movement away from the vital living "Hebraic" religion toward a "Jewish" system which was characterized by exclusivism and narrow particularism, and focused on ritual law and ceremony.[38] Powis Smith called Ezekiel the "father of Judaism" due to his "exaltation of ritualism and legalism" which "imperiled the ethical supremacy of the ethical element in religious life."[39] As noted, Sellin called Haggai's declaration (2:14) the birthday of postexilic Judaism.[40] In an essay published in 1961, F. Hesse stated, "Haggai was no precursor of Jesus Christ. He is one of the fathers of Judaism."[41]

Many contemporary readers will be taken aback by such statements. However such an approach to postexilic religious practice in general, and to postexilic prophecy in particular was quite common in the nineteenth and early twentieth centuries. Given the very different way in which the Persian period is treated in modern scholarship, I believe it to be worthwhile at this point to briefly describe the then-dominant perception of the period we are discussing. An illustration of how widely this reconstruction was accepted can be seen in the *Old Testament Theology* of Hermann Schultz (1836–1903).[42] Schultz dialogues with the lumi-

---

[37] Pfeiffer, *Introduction*, p. 603.

[38] Weiser, *The Old Testament*, p. 268.

[39] Powis Smith, *Prophets*, p. 175. Cf. the similar view of Ezekiel in H. P. Smith, *The Religion of Israel: An Historical Study*, (Edinburgh: T. & T. Clark, 1914), pp. 196–226, especially the chapter entitled "Legalism Triumphant."

[40] Sellin, p. 413.

[41] F. Hesse, "Haggai." In *Verbannunug und Heimkehr: Beiträge zur Geschichte und Theologie Israels im 6. und 5. Jahrhundert v. Chr. Festschrift Wilhelm Rudolph*, (ed. A. Kuschke. Tübingen: J. C. B. Mohr, 1961), pp. 109–134, esp. p. 129. It should be noted, however, that Hesse's purpose is to situate Haggai in his historical moment and, from that perspective (rather than some typological or Christological one), ascertain what kerygmatic value the text has within the church; cf. my earlier and more critical comments in J. Kessler, "Le rôle du prophète dans le livre d'Aggée", (Thèse de doctorat; Sorbonne-Paris IV, 1995), p. 10.

[42] Schultz was professor of theology at Göttingen. His *Old Testament Theology*, which ran four German editions, was translated into English and ran two editions (*Old Testament Theology: The Religion of Revelation in its Pre-Christian Stage of Development*, [2nd. edtn.; trans. J. A. Paterson; Edinburgh: T. & T. Clark], 1898). For an evaluation of Schultz's work, and a discussion of his importance see J. H. Hayes and F. C. Prussner, *Old Testament Theology: Its History and Development*, (Atlanta: John Knox, 1985), pp. 110–14. I have chosen Schultz's *Theology* for two reasons. First, as an OT theology, rather than a more specialized historical or exegetical study, Schultz's work presupposes certain historical

naries of nineteenth-century scholarship, such as Wellhausen, Keunen, de Wette and others, and his work provides a popular distillation of the OT scholarship of his time.[43] Schultz presents the following general scenario.[44] From the late seventh century, priestly legal pronouncements assumed greater importance than prophetic proclamation and the true prophetic spirit began to be lost (p. 321). During the exile Ezekiel and the priests constructed an idealized and logical system of ritual worship, that they attributed to Moses (p. 321). This approach made the older ideals of the prophets virtually inaccessible to the people. The majority of the exiles had become wealthy and at ease in exile, and "willingly and readily" adopted the religion of their conquerors (p. 322). However, a small and faithful believing community gathered around certain "prophets of the exile."[45] Schultz (following Josephus, *Ant.* 9.1.1f) then affirms that, had it not been for this prophetic remnant, Cyrus would have never issued his edict.[46] This exilic prophetic community without priest, king, temple, or worship found "its true life in the spiritual beauty of religion." Open hearted, it was ready to "receive the whole world into the new Israel." With the exception of the Sabbath, little attention was paid to outward forms. This small community returned to Jerusalem, but its spiritual uniqueness was soon lost. Under

---

assumptions to be past debate and therefore critically assured. Second, Schultz's *Theology* was highly influential, especially in that it sought to apply historical and critical judgments to broader issues of the theological meaning and value of the Old Testament. Hayes and Prussner (*Theology*, p. 110) describe Schultz as a "moderate conservative" who sought to "integrate critical scholarship with confessional orthodoxy." They note that his work had wide appeal and ought to be considered one of the most valuable OT theologies of the nineteenth century.

[43] See Schultz's own acknowledged debt to Wellhausen (*Theology*, 1:72).

[44] The following page references in the text are from his *Theology*, volume 1.

[45] Schultz affirmed that this faithful remnant had to endure suffering, not only because of the scorn of their negligent co-religionists, but also at the hands of their conquerors. "And as danger drew nearer Babylon, this faithful prophetic remnant naturally became the object of suspicion and hatred. They were regarded as natural allies of every enemy. ... [M]any doubtless died as martyrs" (p. 323). The more "worldly minded" Israelites, however, allied themselves with the Babylonians, and were thus able to enjoy the "peace and comforts" which they were beginning to obtain. The leaders of this remnant were not the priests, (who were wholly concerned with law), but prophets who demonstrated "unfettered faith and enthusiastic piety" (p. 324). Had it not been for this faithful remnant gathered around these prophets, Judah, like Ephraim, would have "perished in a world of heathenism without leaving a trace behind" (pp. 324–25).

[46] He states (*Theology* 1: 325) "It never occurred to him to dismiss to their homes the other nations that had been transplanted by their Assyrian or Babylonian conquerors. ... He acted as he did because ... restoration had been foretold and eagerly desired."

Zerubbabel, and with the prophetic support of Haggai and Zechariah, a new beginning was made. Things rapidly degenerated, however, for a number of reasons.[47] The temple, ruling Davidide, and prophets (presumably Haggai and Zechariah) were profoundly disappointing, mere shadows of that which had gone before (p. 327–28, 331). Schultz saw the postexilic prophets as "Epigonoi standing on the boundary line of mere learned imitation."[48] Faith was soon eclipsed by legalism.[49] A great turning point occurred with the emergence of Ezra, whose legalism and particularism brought an end to the vital, inclusive, non-legalistic movement begun during the exile.

> Israel, the people of God, became the people of 'the Jews'. ... The lofty enthusiasm, the joyous assurance that relied on the Divine Spirit without looking anxiously to a sacred book, was replaced by an inward weakness which leant all the more heavily on the former strength. Instead of inward religious assurance, the letter of the law governed the life of the people. ... Everything of true religious import that could be attained from an Old Testament standpoint, the prophetic age attained.[50]

Schultz maintains that in the years that followed, both the prophetic spirit and the legalistic approach remained among the people. The latter did serve to preserve the traditions of the earlier prophetic period. Thus, "this age led on, not merely to the Pharisaism that was hostile

---

[47] Schultz, (ibid., p. 326f.) opines that it had become impossible to live in peace with the Persian authorities, that provincial neighbours aroused the ill will of the Persians against the community, and that war with Egypt sapped the resources which were produced.

[48] Ibid., 1:327. In a similar vein, in 1892, C. H. Toy (*Judaism and Christianity: A Sketch of the Progress of Thought from Old Testament to New Testament*, [London: British and Foreign Unitarian Association, 1892], p. 53), summarized postexilic prophecy as follows, "The old prophecy had spent its strength; after the exile it was no longer what it had been, and in our period it is only the shadow of its former self. ... The great legal movement ... had superseded the old spontaneous utterance of prophetic men. ... Yet there still came occasionally the breath of the prophetic impulse, though in comparatively feeble form."

[49] Schultz comments, "There was among the returning exiles an overwhelming proportion of priests, men actually devoted to a religious career" (p. 328). These priests began to shape the life of the community. Due to the lack of a "healthy secular life" this led to an "unhealthy element akin to Pietism" which also attributed an "exaggerated importance to ritual." Methodologically this last comment is quite interesting in that Schultz perceives a common tendency in specific manifestations of Christian and Jewish religious expression, and evaluates them quite apart from any theological content (cf. modern religious anthropology), but with reference to their relative "health" as forms of spirituality.

[50] Ibid., 1:331.

alike to Christ and to the prophets, but also to those Israelites who
found in Jesus the fulfillment of their eager longings" (p. 332).[51] Thus
the negative evaluations of our prophet, cited earlier, stand within
a long line of scholarly opinion[52] which saw the Persian period as
characterized by the birth of Judaism and the decline of prophecy,
movements both reflected in Haggai.

It should be noted that these rather disparaging readings of Haggai
are not fully representative of the scholarly treatment of our prophet.
S. R. Driver, admitting that Haggai's style was "simple and unornate,"
saw him as a prophet "not devoid of force" whose words were shaped
in a way similar to that of Hebrew poetry.[53] Mitchell similarly defended
Haggai's literary abilities.[54] W. H. Bennett complained that it was "not
fair to contrast [Haggai's teaching on the temple] with the more ethical and spiritual messages of the earlier prophets. … The reasoning [in
Haggai] is an application of the doctrine of Ezekiel and the Deuteronomic writers, that material conditions are an index to the moral and
spiritual value of character and conduct."[55] S. Davidson saw Haggai's
eschatology as "defective; but right as far as it went."[56] The majority of the commentaries written on Haggai gave serious attention to
the book and its meaning, and avoided some of the hasty conclusions
reached on the basis of superficial readings.[57] Certain scholars challenged the assumption that Haggai, with Zerubbabel, was active in

---

[51] Cf. Hesse, "Haggai", p. 127–29.

[52] Such negative evaluations of Haggai in particular, and Judaism in general, raise
serious, broader issues regarding anti-Semitism and anti-Judaism. The citations presented above are neither intended to "label" their respective authors, nor to be viewed
as an indication of their personal attitudes to the Jewish communities of their day.
The quotations are simply meant to evoke the general scholarly ethos of the period.
See G. Vermes, *Jesus and the World of Judaism*, (London: SCM, 1983), p. 58f for a fuller
treatment of the issue of anti-Judaism and anti-Semitism in biblical scholarship. On
the diversity and complexity of the various attitudes to Judaism in nineteenth-century
Germany, with special attention to de Wette, cf. J. Pasto, "When the End is the Beginning? or when the Biblical Past is the Political Present: Some Thoughts on Ancient
Israel, 'Post-Exilic Judaism' and the Politics of Biblical Scholarship", *SJOT* 12 (1998):
157–202.

[53] S. R. Driver, *An Introduction to the Literature of the Old Testament*, (International
Theological Library; new ed.; New York: Charles Scribner's Sons, 1928), p. 344.

[54] Mitchell, p. 37.

[55] Bennett, *Post-Exilic Prophets*, p. 77.

[56] S. Davidson, *The Text of the Old Testament Considered*, (London: Longman et al.,
1856), p. 973.

[57] See the bibliography in Wolff, p. 23–24.

a rebellion against the Persian crown.[58] The interpretation whereby 2:10–19 referred to the exclusion of the Samaritans was deemed inadequate.[59]

One significant point, however, remains to be underlined regarding this "earlier" phase of criticism of the book of Haggai. Scholars of all stripes, even those most critical of Haggai from a stylistic, theological or religious point of view, agreed that the book was an excellent historical resource. J. Bewer commented, "He was no great prophet. ... His book ... is small and simple, without any passage of power and beauty. But for the history of our time *it is of the highest value*."[60] Pfeiffer agrees saying, "Negligible though the book appears from the point of view of literature and religion *it is of the greatest importance, together with Zechariah, as a historical source*."[61] Oesterley and Robinson conclude that the book is "of importance for the insight it gives of the early postexilic conditions in Palestine."[62] Torrey, in contrast to his characterization of the material in Ezra 1–6 as "untrustworthy" calls Haggai (and Zechariah) "*our first and only sure source of information* between Nebuchadnezzar and Nehemiah."[63] This notion of Haggai as a valuable historical source is intriguing, since it has, as we shall see, remained rather constant in historical reconstructions of the early Persian period. What is interesting in the literature just cited is that no precise definition was given regarding the *way* in which Haggai can be used as an historical source. Clearly, the use of any prophetic text for purposes of historical reconstruction is a complicated matter, and, what is more, such use will vary from text to text.[64]

The frequently one-sided and reductionistic approaches of this earlier period have been largely abandoned in recent literature. Nevertheless these studies did raise some important issues. Indeed, in a very real

---

[58] Bentzen, "Mouvement messianique", *passim*.

[59] So for example, A. Cody, "When is the Chosen People called a *gôy*?", *VT* 14 (1964): 1–7, and Chary, p. 31.

[60] Bewer, *Literature of the Old Testament*, pp. 235–36, emphasis mine, and in the following citations.

[61] Pfeiffer, *Introduction*, p. 603.

[62] Oesterley and Robinson, *Introduction*, p. 406.

[63] C. C. Torrey, *Ezra Studies*, (Chicago: University of Chicago Press, 1910), p. 303.

[64] On some broader issues of historiography cf. S. Japhet, "'History' and 'Literature' in the Persian Period: The Restoration of the Temple", in *Ah, Assyria...Studies in Assyrian History and Ancient Near Eastern Historiography Presented to Hayim Tadmor*, (Scripta Hierosolymitana 33; ed. M. Cogan and I. Eph'al; Jerusalem: Magnes, 1991), p. 174–88; cf. F. E. Deist, "The Nature of Historical Understanding", *OTE* 6 (1993): 384–98 and J. Elayi, "Réflexion sur la place de l'histoire dans la recherche sur la Transeuphratène achéménide", *Trans* 8 (1994): 73–80.

sense, the present study will re-examine many of the questions raised in this earlier body of literature. These include the approach of the book of Haggai to such issues as the significance of the temple, the nature of participation in the nascent community in Yehud, the relationship of that community to the Persian Empire, and, most especially, the nature of prophecy and the role of the prophet. However due to various crucial methodological inadequacies, most notably the lack of exegetical depth, a failure to recognize the ideological shaping of the text itself, as well as an inadequate grasp of the realities of the Persian period, these approaches produced images of Haggai which later scholarship tended to reject.

### 1.3. Haggai and Second Temple Sectarianism: Whose Side Is Haggai on?

In time a "second wave" of readings of Haggai emerged. These readings integrated two new factors into their analyses: (1) an awareness that aspects of the book may have been ideologically driven, and (2) a desire to relate the book's perspectives to the political, sociological, and religious landscape of the early Persian period. A foundational study of this type is O. Plöger's *Theokratie und Eschatologie* which appeared in 1959.[65] Plöger sought the origins of later Jewish sectarianism in the Persian period. However it was in the years of 1968–1973 that three detailed proposals were put forth which attempted to identify Haggai with one or another of the putative competing groups and factions within Second Temple Judaism. In his 1968 article and 1971 monograph, M. Smith theorized concerning the development of two competing theological groups from the ninth century through to the destruction of the Second Temple.[66] Smith claimed that three principal parties were to be found in Jerusalem in the postexilic period: (1) the descendants of those who remained in the land after the Babylonian conquest.

---

[65] O. Plöger, *Theokratie und Eschatologie*, (WMANT 2; Neukirch: Neukirchener Verlag, 1959); Eng. tr., *Theocracy and Eschatology*, (trans. S. Rudman, Oxford: Basil Blackwell, 1968).

[66] M. Smith, "Palestinian Judaism in the Persian Period", in *The Greeks and the Persians*, 1968, pp. 386–401; idem, *Palestinian Parties and Politics that Shaped the Old Testament*, (New York: Columbia University Press, 1971). For a summary of the major issues, see Grabbe, *Judaism*, 1:105–7. Cf. also S. Talmon, "The Emergence of Jewish Sectarianism in the Early Second Temple Period", in S. Talmon, *King, Cult and Calendar in Ancient Israel: Collected Studies*, (Jerusalem: Magnes /Hebrew University, 1986), pp. 165–201.

This group, called the ʿam hā ʾāreṣ in the literature of the period, worshipped Yahweh as well as other deities; (2) a first group of returnees, or běnê haggôlâ who were members of the former aristocracy and insisted on the worship of Yahweh alone. Zerubbabel was the leader of this group; and (3) a group of exiled priests who returned to Jerusalem. This group was under the leadership of Joshua. Some of these priests adhered to a "Yahweh-alone" position, whereas others were syncretistic.[67] Conflict arose over the reconstruction of the temple. The Yahweh-alone group wanted to exclude the syncretists from participation in the rebuilding project. The priestly group stood in the middle, and was able to turn the situation to its own advantage. An agreement was reached between the Yahweh-alone party and the priestly group. According to this agreement, the Yahweh-alone party under Zerubbabel would be recognized as the legitimate political authority, and would take control of the rebuilding of the temple. Furthermore, this group would provide financial support and encourage other exiles to return. It would also recognize Joshua's leadership of the Jerusalem cult. The priestly group, in return, agreed to adhere to the purity rules set down by the Yahweh-alone group. What is significant for our purposes is Smith's view of Haggai. On one hand the prophet is clearly to be allied with the Yahweh-alone group of returnees because of his declaration that Zerubbabel was the coming messiah, and his rejection of the syncretistic practices condemned by that group.[68] Yet, on the other hand, Smith views Haggai as something of a moderate in that he may have promoted a further compromise that would have allowed for the participation of the syncretistic group. This proposal, however, was quashed by Zerubbabel.[69]

In 1970, R. G. Hamerton-Kelly proposed an alternative social context for Haggai.[70] He maintained that Ezekiel and P were the fundamental sources for understanding the Second Temple. In his view, according to the Ezekielian tradition, the "genuine" temple existed in the heavens and would one day be revealed and descend to the earth. The precise moment of this great event had been determined by God. According to the contrasting priestly vision, however, even though the

---

[67] Smith, *Palestinian Parties*, pp. 107–8.
[68] Ibid., pp. 108–9.
[69] Ibid., pp. 112–13.
[70] Hamerton-Kelly, "Temple and Origins", *passim*. Hamerton-Kelly based his analysis upon von Rad's reconstruction of the principal theological traditions of the postexilic period, cf. *infra*.

"true temple" existed in the heavens, it was incumbent upon the people of God to build a replica below. Once it had become evident that
the glorious promises of Deutero-Isaiah were unlikely to be fulfilled in
the near future (promises that Hamerton-Kelly associated with the tradition of Ezekiel), the priestly group took over the leadership of the
nascent community. Its blueprint was Deuteronomy, and it had little or no eschatological interest. Postexilic apocalyptic expectation was
born out of a dissatisfaction with this lack of eschatological hope in the
priestly theology. The people's neglect of the temple (to which Haggai alludes, Hag 2:1–11), was not primarily due to their laziness. It was
rather the result of an ideological conflict. Haggai proposed a compromise by connecting the building of the temple to the coming of the
eschatological era. According to Hamerton-Kelly, this compromise was
rejected. The hierocracy won the debate, and the eschatological hope
concerning the new temple and the new Zion soon disappeared from
the official theology.[71] Again, in this reconstruction Haggai is a moderate who proposes a mediating position which is ultimately rejected by
the hard-liners.

In his work *The Dawn of Apocalyptic*, published in 1975, P. D. Hanson also attempted to provide a socio-theological explanation for the
origins of apocalyptic eschatology. A large portion of his analysis concerns the theological and sociological setting in Judah in 520. Hanson
presupposes a polarization of the community in two parties which he
calls "visionary" and "hierocratic." The first group was made up of an
alliance of various dissident alienated elements, especially those holding to the eschatological message of the prophets.[72] This group had
little political or religious power. The second group was composed of
Zadokite priests who had taken control of the temple, the priesthood,
and the local government. Hanson then seeks to apply to the sociological categories of K. Mannheim, M. Weber, and E. Troeltsch to
this polarized situation.[73] Contrary to Hamerton-Kelly's portrait, for
Hanson Haggai is associated with the Zadokite hierocracy. Ezekiel had
transformed the Zadokite ideal into a restoration programme. Haggai,
following Ezekiel, was interested primarily in the temple reconstruction. Those opposed to the Zadokites were not the disciples of Ezekiel
(as Hamerton-Kelly affirmed) but followers of Deutero-Isaiah, joined

---

[71] Ibid., p. 14.
[72] Hanson, *Dawn of Apocalyptic*, p. 217.
[73] Ibid., pp. 212–20.

by a large number of disenfranchised Levites.[74] According to Hanson, Haggai's compromise consisted of linking the rebuilding of the temple to eschatological hopes. This compromise was accepted by the people. After the completion of the temple, however, the eschatological aspect of Haggai's message was abandoned by the Zadokites. Haggai had in effect surrendered the impartiality of the prophetic office to the political prerogatives of the ruling elite.[75]

Hanson's judgment regarding Haggai and Zechariah is highly negative. In his view, Haggai and Zechariah placed prophecy at the service of the Zadokite hierocracy without reservation and without criticism. "In giving Yahweh's unquestioned sanction to a particular human institution, and to particular priestly and royal officials, they were wedding their fate to the fate of that institution and those officials, and were giving up the independent stance always maintained by the classical prophets vis-à-vis the institutions of the temple and royal court."[76]

A full analysis of Hanson's monograph is clearly beyond my purposes here.[77] Nevertheless, even apart from broader issues related to his methodology,[78] significant questions must be raised with reference to Hanson's treatment of Haggai. The first area of concern is his lack of a detailed analysis of the demography and economy of Yehud, or its

---

[74] Ibid., pp. 220–40.

[75] Ibid., p. 247.

[76] Ibid.

[77] The literature in response to Hanson's thesis is large and diverse. For an early critique see R. Carroll, "Twilight of Prophecy or Dawn of Apocalyptic?", *JSOT* 14 (1979): 3–35 and R. Mason, "The Prophets of the Restoration", in *Israel's Prophetic Tradition: Essays in Honour of Peter R. Ackroyd*, (ed. R. J. Coggins, A. Phillips and M. Knibb; Cambridge: Cambridge University Press, 1982), pp. 137–54, esp. pp. 138–46. For a recent challenge to Hanson's thesis relative to Isa 56–66 see B. Schram, *The Opponents of Third Isaiah: Reconstructing the Cultic History of the Restoration*, (JSOTSup 193; Sheffield: Sheffield Academic Press, 1995).

[78] Such questions would include: (1) can the undated oracles in Isa 56–66 be used in such a precisely detailed historical reconstruction? (cf. Carroll, "Twilight", pp. 24–25 and idem, "So What do We *Know* about the Temple? The Temple in the Prophets", in *Second Temple Studies 2: Temple Community in the Persian Period*, (JSOTSup 175, ed. T. C. Eskenazi and K. H. Richards; Sheffield: JSOT Press, 1994), p. 39. C. T Begg, (*CBQ* 54 [1992]: 514–15), discusses this question in his review of W. A. M. Beuken, *Jesaia*, (Deel III, POut; Nijkerk: Callenbach, 1989); (2) is it legitimate to set in total opposition the theological perspectives of Zech 1–8, on one hand, and Zech 9–14 and Isa 56–66, on the other? Can the theologies of Ezekiel and Isa 56–66 be so easily identified? (Cf. R. J. Bauckham, "The Rise of Apocalyptic", *Them* 3 [1977–78]: 11.) On the significant differences between Ezekiel and Zech 1–8, see Petersen, pp. 116–18.

status within the Persian Empire and its relationship to Persian imperial interests and goals.[79] This lack of historical rootedness is exacerbated by Hanson's use of the sociological methodologies of Mannheim, Weber, and Troeltsch[80] in that these approaches, formulated and elaborated in a European and "ecclesiastical" context[81] are applied to Yehud in 520 without adequate justification of the validity of such an approach.[82] Similarly, Hanson presupposes the division of the community between two and only two parties.[83] This would appear to be quite arbitrary, given the proliferation of sects and groupings that existed in other periods.[84] Furthermore, groupings and parties may be divided on certain points but in agreement on others.

Even more serious is the fact that Hanson's reading of Haggai is based on several unsubstantiated assumptions. First, he affirms that Haggai used "the visionary forms of the prophets"[85] (i.e. Deutero-Isaiah and his disciples) but without the perspective of a cosmic redemption that characterized their prophecies.[86] However Hag 2:6–9 and 2:20–23 use language found extensively in prophetic, eschatological traditions: the assault of the nations, the intervention of the divine warrior, the

---

[79] I have attempted to demonstrate the methodological importance of these kinds of considerations in J. Kessler, "Reconstructing Haggai's Jerusalem: Demographic and Sociological Considerations and the Quest for an Adequate Methodological Point of Departure", in *Every City Shall Be Forsaken: Urbanism and Prophecy in Ancient Israel and the Near East* (JSOTSup 330; ed. L. L. Grabbe and R. Haak; Sheffield: Sheffield Academic Press, 2001), pp. 137–58.

[80] Hanson neither evaluates the validity of their analyses nor provides a critical appreciation of their methodology, their classifications, and the success of their studies.

[81] Carroll, "Twilight", pp. 27–28.

[82] Carroll observes, "Anybody may use particular analyses but without a critical evaluation of the tools of analysis very little light is thrown on anything. The analogy between the settled empire life of Christianity and the struggles for community of the early postexilic period is too loose to be useful" (ibid., p. 28). On the broader issue of the use of sociological analogies in Biblical studies, cf. R. R. Wilson, *Prophecy and Society in Ancient Israel*, (Philadelphia: Fortress, 1980), p. 16. For a fuller discussion of the role of the social sciences in biblical studies, see C. E. Carter, *The Emergence of Yehud in the Persian Period*, (JSOTSup 294; Sheffield: Sheffield Academic Press, 1999), pp. 60–74 (with bibliography). See esp. p. 69, n. 143 and 144 with reference to the dangers of the applications of modern methodologies and analogies to ancient contexts.

[83] Hanson affirms, "In the realm of religious institutions, as in the realm of politics, the polarization tends to develop primarily between two forces." *Dawn of Apocalyptic*, p. 212. I do not perceive this to be true even from a contemporary political perspective.

[84] For a survey of the issue of sectarianism see Grabbe, *Judaism*, 1:103–11.

[85] Ibid., p. 245.

[86] Ibid., p. 17.

preservation of Jerusalem, and the cosmic renewal.[87] Hanson affirms the importance of these traditions for Trito-Isaiah and the "visionary" group, but ignores the presence and role of these themes in Haggai. He devotes 180 pages of exegesis to Isa 56–66[88] and five pages to the analysis of Haggai, without a single exegetical comment!

Hanson attributes a very pronounced political intention to Haggai. He speaks of Haggai's "masterful strategy" according to which "the detailed, pragmatic plans representing the interests of the hierocrats were cast into the visionary forms of the prophets, orchestrating the impulses of the visionaries and the realists into one passionate message."[89] But is it possible to affirm that this tactic (which, in the final analysis, is nothing but a ruse) was the prophet's intention? Nothing in the text appears to confirm such a motive. By contrast, Haggai appears to stand in the tradition of classical prophecy. He does not hesitate to confront the political and religious leaders, as well as people (Hag 1:1–2; 2:1–3, 12–14). Third, Hanson affirms that Haggai promised the people that the arrival of the eschatological era would accompany the rebuilding of the temple. However it is far from clear that such an affirmation is to be found in Haggai.[90]

In sum, like their earlier counterparts, the three reconstructions described above use Haggai as an historical source without much consideration of the basis upon which such use can be made. The book is assumed to provide great insight into the intra-communal conflict of the period.[91] Furthermore, the text of Haggai is not exegeted in great detail, but cited in passing, in the attempt to sketch the theological landscape of the period. Again, the questions and issues raised in these studies are valid ones. Yet the answers are frequently given without adequate methodological and exegetical support.

---

[87] This will be explored and developed in my exegesis of 2:6–9 and 2:20–23; cf. provisionally Chary, p. 33 and G. von Rad, "The City on the Hill", in G. von Rad, *The Problem of the Hexateuch and Other Essays*, (trans. E. W. T. Dicken; London: SCM Press, 1984), pp. 232–42.

[88] Carroll has suggested that Hanson's sympathies are with the visionary group, a suggestion which the latter denies ("Twilight", pp. 26–27).

[89] Hanson, *Dawn of Apocalyptic*, p. 245.

[90] This issue will be explored in my exegesis *infra*.

[91] For a survey of various reconstructions of this conflict, cf. Kessler, "Haggai's Jerusalem", p. 138–42.

## 1.4. THEOLOGICAL TRADITIONS AND LITERARY
## DEVELOPMENT: WHAT WERE THE THEOLOGICAL CONCERNS
## OF HAGGAI AND HIS EDITORS?

Another highly significant avenue of approach to the book of Haggai was developed by various scholars who sought to read the book in terms of its theological roots and its utilization of traditions found elsewhere in biblical literature.[92] Until quite recently, the application of this promising approach to Haggai has been rather limited. At times, exegetes noted the affinity between a certain tradition and a particular aspect of Haggai. Von Rad, for example, maintained that the motif of the pilgrimage to Zion, evident in other passages (Isa 2; Mic 4) was discernible in Hag 2:6–9.[93] He then attempted to elucidate the particular use Haggai makes of the tradition. While von Rad's analysis is highly insightful, and involves sound methodology and careful exegesis, its application to Haggai is limited. Only one section of the book is dealt with, and there is no attempt to establish the broader framework of religious traditions which form the wider backdrop against which the book of Haggai is to be understood. Furthermore, the presence of the idea of a pilgrimage to Zion in 2:6–9, which is central to von Rad's thesis, is rejected by certain exegetes. Such scholars see the passage in a more bellicose light, and view the treasures brought to Jerusalem as war booty or tribute.[94]

---

[92] This form of traditions analysis is not to be confused with either source criticism or *Überlieferungsgeschichte*, as practiced, for example, in Pentateuchal studies. This approach, sometimes called *Traditionsgeschichte*, consists of identifying the intellectual world (or *geistige Welt*), and the theological matrix of a text, with special attention to any innovative or distinctive usages of existing traditions. For an excellent discussion of the relationship between *Traditionsgeschichte* and *Überlieferungsgeschichte* see O. H. Steck, "Theological Streams of Tradition", in *Tradition and Theology in the Old Testament*, (ed. D. A. Knight; Philadelphia: Fortress, 1977), pp. 183–214. See also D. A. Knight, s. v. "Tradition History", *ABD* 6:633–38, and von Rad, "City", pp. 232–42. Von Rad speaks of certain concepts as being considered "axiomatic" by the prophets who draw upon these themes in their own proclamation.

[93] Von Rad, "City", p. 240f.

[94] P. D. Miller, *The Divine Warrior in Ancient Israel*, (Cambridge, MA: Harvard University Press, 1973), p. 135; F. M. Cross, *Canaanite Myth and Hebrew Epic*, (Cambridge, MA: Harvard University Press), p. 90; P. D. Hanson, "Zechariah 9 and the Recapitulation of an Ancient Ritual Pattern", *JBL* 92 (1973): 58–59; Petersen, p. 68 and idem, *Late Israelite Prophecy: Studies in Deutero-Prophetic Literature and in Chronicles*, (SBLMS 23, Missoula: Scholars Press, 1977), p. 17.

Various studies have sought to relate the religious traditions in Haggai to the various stages of the book's development. Frequently such approaches attempted to establish a distinction between the prophet's own theology and the theological perspective underlying the redactional framework through the analysis of the religious traditions present in the two sections. The studies of W. A. M. Beuken[95] and R. Mason[96] are cases in point. In Beuken's opinion, an editor working within a chronistic milieu reinterpreted, resituated, and actualized the prophet's oracles for the needs of a later period, primarily to justify the rejection of Samaritan cult practices.[97] An earlier collection of Haggai's oracles reflected an entirely different milieu of origin, theological vision, and future hope.[98] In a similar fashion, R. Mason maintained that the redactional framework attenuated the prophet's eschatological expectations, since these expectations had gone unfulfilled.[99] Both scholars attempted to differentiate these two distinct perspectives within the book on the basis of each section's idiosyncratic vocabulary, sociopolitical perspectives, or rootedness in a given theological tradition.[100] These pioneering studies have provoked lively debate[101] and set the tone for much of the subsequent discussion. More significant, however, than the accuracy of any particular conclusion is the use of religious traditions for an understanding of the redactional history of the book. This represents a clear departure from the more naïve use of the book as an historical source. Diachronic matters are introduced, and the book itself is subjected to analysis as a source. What remains to be seen, however, is whether the book does indeed belong to one or another of these proposed traditional matrices, whether the social location of these various theological tradents or communities can be determined, and, most crucially, whether a distinction in perspective can be

---

[95] W. A. M. Beuken, *Haggai-Sacharja 1–8. Studien zur Überlieferungsgeschichte der frühnachexilischen Prophetie*, (SSN 10; Assen: Van Gorcum, 1967).

[96] Mason, "Editorial Framework", pp. 413–21.

[97] Beuken (p. 72) discusses the redactional "actualization" in 2:14.

[98] Ibid., pp. 216–29, 334–37.

[99] Mason, "Editorial Framework", pp. 420–21.

[100] This has recently been undertaken by A. Sérandour, ("Les récits bibliques de la construction du second temple: leurs enjeux", *Trans* 11 [1996]: 9–32) who sees the oracles and framework as being distinguishable on the basis of their distinctive vocabulary and their view of dyarchic leadership.

[101] See, for example, Mason's critique of Beuken's "chronistic milieu" in "Editorial Framework", *passim*.

successfully established between the various constituent elements of the
book.[102]

Scholars have long been aware of the great diversity of theological traditions present in Haggai. Bright, for example, affirmed Haggai's thought to be steeped in Zion theology.[103] T. Chary declared that
"many already classical messianic expectations" were present in 2:6–
9.[104] The discussion of the theological motifs and traditions in the book
of Haggai has become a key element of most modern commentaries.
One may cite Petersen's analysis of Hag 2:20–23,[105] or Peckham's designation of Hag 2:5 as a "crasis of allusions."[106] It has furthermore been
observed that this presence of a variety of diverse and possibly disparate
traditions must be situated in the context of the movement toward the
collection and consolidation of religious traditions after the exile.[107]

As noted above, some earlier scholars saw this copious use of diverse traditions as evidence of the degenerate and unoriginal nature of
prophecy in Haggai.[108] More recent scholarship, however, has paid
significant attention to the theological motivation behind the particular
use of earlier traditions in the book.[109] One major work of this genre
is that of J. A. Tollington, published in 1993.[110] The book is devoted to
an analysis of various aspects of Haggai and Zech 1–8. With reference
to Haggai, Tollington discusses the date at which the book achieved

---

[102] For a broader discussion of this latter question, see R. Clements, "The Prophet
and His Editors", in *The Bible in Three Dimensions*, (JSOTSup 87; ed. D. J. A. Clines;
Sheffield: JSOT Press, 1990), pp. 202–20. This issue will be taken up in greater detail in
the following chapter.

[103] Bright, *Kingdom of God*, p. 165; idem, *History of Israel*, p. 371. See also, G. Fohrer, s. v.
"Σιων", *TDNT* 7:292–319.

[104] Chary, *Prophètes et culte*, p. 132.

[105] Petersen, pp. 98–105.

[106] B. Peckham, *History and Prophecy: The Development of Late Judean Literary Traditions*,
(ABRL, New York: Doubleday, 1993), p. 745.

[107] See for example, Wilson, *Prophecy and Society*, pp. 305–6; Mason, "Prophets of the
Restoration", p. 141; W. Zimmerli, "Prophetic Proclamation and Reinterpretation", in
*Tradition and Theology in the Old Testament*, (ed. D. A. Knight; London: SPCK, 1977),
pp. 69–100; P. D. Hanson, "Israelite Religion in the Early Postexilic Period", in *Ancient
Israelite Religion: Essays in Honor of Frank Moore Cross* (ed. P. D. Miller, P. D. Hanson, and
S. D. McBride; Philadelphia: Fortress, 1987), pp. 485–508.

[108] See *supra*, pp. 6–7XX.

[109] See, for example, the discussion of Haggai's use of the Davidic traditions in
S. V. Wyrick, "Haggai's Appeal to Tradition: Imagination Used as Authority", in
*Religious Writings and Religious Systems*, (vol. 1; ed. Jacob Neusner; Atlanta: Scholars Press,
1989), pp. 117–25.

[110] J. A. Tollington, *Tradition and Innovation in Haggai and Zechariah 1–8*, (JSOTSup 150,
Sheffield: Sheffield Academic Press, 1993).

its final form, the basis of the prophetic authority of Haggai, the way in which Haggai received his revelation, Haggai's view of leadership in the restoration community as well as the concepts of messianism, eschatology (specifically judgment), and the relationship between Israel, Yahweh and the nations of the world. It is primarily in connection with these latter, more theological themes, that Tollington discusses the use of earlier traditions in Haggai. She examines the use of various traditions in the book and the particular reasons why the traditions are so used. While in certain regards Tollington's work parallels my own, significant differences of focus, objective, and methodology exist.[111]

The nature and use of religious traditions has received attention from both religious anthropology and biblical scholarship. Most significant here is the growing awareness of the impact of the process of transmission (*traditio*)[112] on that which is transmitted (*traditum*).[113] M. Meslin rejects the notion of religious tradition as "the simple quasi-mechanical transmission of a lifeless and ossified deposit."[114] In his opinion such transmission is a "doubly living process" because of the "unceasing interaction" between the past and the present, between *traditio* and *traditum*. Transmission of tradition is thus essentially "dialogical and diachronic."[115] In a similar vein, Knight takes into consideration the notion of "*Vergegenwärtigung*" or the transforming process of interpretation and actualization which earlier traditions undergo when they are reformulated or reapplied in a later period.[116] Zimmerli[117] and Steck[118] employ

---

[111] These will become apparent as this discussion proceeds. The most significant is my discussion of the use of religious traditions. Furthermore, as I do not include Zechariah, much more attention can be allotted to issues more germane to Haggai. I will not only examine the nature and purpose of Haggai's use of earlier tradition, I will also inquire as to what the book as a whole, and the use of religious tradition in particular, can tell us about the role of the prophet in the early Persian Yehud. Furthermore, in order to do so, I shall take a more detailed look at several historical issues which greatly influence one's reading of the book.

[112] See, for example, J. Audinet, "Du transmettre ou la tradition comme pratique sociale", in J. Audeinet et. al. *Essais de théologie pratique: l'institution et le transmettre*. (Le Point Théologique; Paris: Beauchesne, 1988), pp. 109–15; and idem, "Dispositifs du 'transmettre' et 'confession de la foi'", in *Essais de théologie pratique: l'institution et le transmettre* pp. 166–205.

[113] D. A. Knight, s. v. "Tradition History", *ABD* 6:633.

[114] M. Meslin, *L'expérience humaine du divin. Fondements d'une anthropologie religieuse*, (Cogitatio Fidei 150; Paris: Cerf, 1988), p. 381.

[115] Ibid.

[116] Knight, "Tradition History", p. 634.

[117] Zimmerli, "Prophetic Proclamation", p. 76.

[118] Steck, "Streams of Tradition", pp. 183–98.

a similar methodological approach. What is significant in light of these recent studies, is that recontextualization of traditions is now accurately seen to be no neutral process, but rather a profoundly hermeneutical one.[119] It is essential therefore that an analysis of Haggai take into account this interpretive and hermeneutical activity—this *Vergegenwärtigung*—on the part of the prophet and his editors.

## 1.5. Social Scientific Analyses of Early Persian Yehud

Most of the recent analyses of early Persian Yehud and its literature employ social scientific methodologies, and seek to identify and describe the milieu of origin of the various relevant texts. The works of W. Robertson Smith, M. Weber, and E. Durkheim were foundational in this regard.[120] In more recent literature these methodological approaches have been utilised in several areas. Anthropological and sociological approaches have been applied to questions regarding the history of ancient Israel, aiming at the comprehension of its political origins and social structures.[121] Likewise, data drawn from the anthropological study of non-Western societies has been used to elucidate certain aspects of Israelite ritual.[122] More recently ethnoarchaeology,[123] a discipline that concerns the application of ethnographic studies to archaeological problems, has entered Syro-Palestinian archaeology and

---

[119] In a similar vein, B. Childs, (*Introduction to the Old Testament as Scripture*, [OTL; Philadelphia: Fortress, 1979], pp. 75–79) notes this hermeneutical activity in the redaction of prophetic texts.

[120] For a resumé of the influence of the social sciences in biblical studies, see C. E. Carter, *Emergence*, p. 60–70 and idem, "A Discipline in Transition: The Contributions of the Social Sciences to the Study of the Hebrew Bible", in *Community, Identity, and Ideology: Social Science Approaches to the Hebrew Bible*, (Sources for Biblical and Theological Study; ed. C. E. Carter and C. Meyers, Winona Lake: Eisenbrauns, 1996), pp. 3–36. Cf. also A. D. H. Mays, "Sociology and the Old Testament", in *The World of Ancient Israel: Sociological, Anthropological and Political Perspectives*, (ed. R. E. Clements; Cambridge: Cambridge University Press, 1989), pp. 39–63. I am indebted to Carter for much of the following overview.

[121] As for example in the work of Alt, Noth, Mendenhall and Gottwald.

[122] M. Douglas, *Purity and Danger: An Analysis of Concepts of Pollution and Taboo*, (London: Routledge & Kegan Paul, 1966), pp. 41–57; Meslin, *Expérience humaine*, pp. 66–80, 144–46; J. W. Rogerson, "Anthropology and the Old Testament", in *The World of Ancient Israel: Sociological, Anthropological and Political Perspectives*, (ed. R. E. Clements; Cambridge: Cambridge University Press, 1989), pp. 17–37.

[123] For a summary see C. Kramer, ed. *Ethnoarchaeology. The Implications of Ethnography for Archaeology*, (New York: Academic Press, 1977); cf. two recent volumes of *Near Eastern Archaeology* (63/1[2000] and 63/2 [2000]), both devoted to ethnoarchaeology.

the terms "new archaeology," "sociological archaeology"[124] or "contextual archaeology" are frequently employed.[125] These approaches seek to broaden the horizons of archaeology in order to integrate on the one hand, archaeological and textual data, and, on the other, questions relative to ecological, political, economic, and social conditions.[126] Particularly significant in this regard are the recent demographic studies of Palestine,[127] especially during the postexilic period.[128] Of a similar interest is the work of H. Kreissig and H. Kippenberg[129] on the economic situation in Judah after the exile as well as the analysis of its social structure, economic, and political situation elaborated by J. P. Weinberg[130] and D. L. Smith.[131] However, such approaches are not without limitations. A significant bibliography now exists on the limits[132]

---

[124] C. Meyers and E. Meyers, "Expanding the Frontiers of Biblical Archaeology", *Y. Yadin Volume*, (ErIsr 20; ed. A. Ben Tor, J. C. Greenfield and A. Malamat; Jerusalem: Israel Exploration Society, 1989), pp. 142\*-43\*.

[125] W. Dever, "Biblical Archaeology: Death and Rebirth", in *Biblical Archaeology Today, 1990: Proceedings of the Second International Congress on Biblical Archaeology*, (ed. A. Biran and J. Aviram, Jerusalem: Israel Exploration Society, 1993), pp. 706–22.

[126] Meyers and Meyers, "Expanding the Frontiers", p. 143. On this, cf. P. R. Davies, ed., *Second Temple Studies 1: Persian Period*, (JSOTSup 117; Sheffield: JSOT Press, 1991).

[127] M. Broshi, "Estimating the Population of Ancient Jerusalem", *BAR* 4 (1978): 10–15; idem, "La population de Jérusalem", *RB* 82 (1975): 5–14; R. Gophna and M. Broshi, "The Settlements and Population of Palestine during the Early Bronze Age II-III", *BASOR* 253 (1984): 41–53; idem, "Middle Bronze Age II Palestine: Its Settlements and Population", *BASOR* 261 (1986): 73–90.

[128] J. P. Weinberg. "Demographische Notizen zur Geschichte der Nachexilischen Gemeinde in Juda", *Klio* 54 (1972): 46–50.

[129] H. G. Kippenberg, *Religion und Klassenbildung im antiken Judäa. Eine religions-soziologische Studie zum Verhältnis von Tradition und gesellschaftlicher Entwicklung*, (SUNT 14; Göttingen: Vandenhoeck & Ruprecht, 1978); H. Kreissig, Die *sozialökonomische Situation in Juda zur Achämenidzeit*, (Schriften zur Geschichte und Kultur des Alten Orients 7; Berlin: Akademie Verlag, 1973).

[130] J. P. Weinberg, "Das *BEIT 'ABOT* im 6–4 Jh. v.u.Z.", *VT* 23 (1973): 400–414; "Die Agrarverhältnisse in der Bürger-Tempel-Gemeinde der Achämenidenzeit", *Acta Antiqua* 22 (1974): 473–85; "Zentral-und Partikulargewalt im achämenidischen Reich", *Klio* 59 (1977): 25–43; "*Netînîm* und 'Söhne der Sklaven Salomos' im 6.-4. Jh. v.u.Z.", *ZAW* 87 (1975): 355–71; "Transmitter and Recipient in the Process of Acculturation: the Experience of the Judean Citizen-Temple-Community", *Trans* 13 (1997): 91–105. Weinberg's major articles have been translated and are available as J. Weinberg, *The Citizen-Temple Community*, (JSOTSup 151; trans. D. Smith-Christopher; Sheffield: Sheffield Academic Press, 1992).

[131] D. Smith, *The Religion of the Landless*, (Bloomington: Indiana University Press, 1989).

[132] See, for example, N. P. Lemche, "On the Use of 'System Theory', 'Macro Theories' and Evolutionistic Thinking in Modern OT Research and Biblical Archaeology", *SJOT* 2 (1990): 73–88.

and on the validity[133] of such approaches, especially the use of analogies[134] to comprehend Israelite institutions. Valuable criticisms and
reservations have been expressed.[135]

Sociologists, biblical scholars and historians of Israelite religion have
found the phenomenon of prophecy and the nature of the prophetic
institution in Israel to be an area of common interest. A large number of introductions and specialized studies have described the evolution and history of Israelite prophetism, the various forms of prophetic
speech, the prophets' theological tendencies, and other issues related to
the phenomenon.[136] More recent studies of prophecy, which reflect the
influence of the social sciences, have followed several paths. Some have
attempted to analyze the mechanism of prophecy more closely. Others
have investigated the prophets' authority and the strata within society
that granted them their support.[137] Yet others have attempted to obtain
a comprehensive understanding of the prophet within society.[138] In this
connection, discussions of the prophetic role and the social location of
the prophet have become highly significant.[139] Interestingly, Haggai has
received little attention in this regard. He is at times considered to be

---

[133] See, for example, the review of Wilson, *Prophecy and Society* by G. E. Mendenhall
in *BA* 44 (1981): 189–90. In this vigourous critique of Wilson's work, Mendenhall
rejects the analogical use of African tribal groups for the understanding of Hebrew
prophetism. See also Lemche (n. 132) and J. M. Sasson, "On Choosing Models for
Recreating Israelite Pre-Monarchic History", *JSOT* 21 (1981): 3–24.

[134] Cf. Carter, *Postexilic Judah*, pp. 32–34.

[135] Ibid., also idem *Emergence*, pp. 68–70.

[136] The bibliography here is voluminous. For a general survey see J. Blenkinsopp, *A
History of Prophecy in Israel*, (2nd. edtn.; Louisville: Westminster/John Knox, 1996). See
also J. A. Soggin, *Introduction to the Old Testament*, (3rd. ed.; OTL; trans. John Bowden;
Louisville: Westminster/John Knox, 1989), pp. 239–81; L. Ramlot, s. v. "Prophétisme",
*DBS* 7 cols. 811–1222; R. E. Clements, *One Hundred Years of Old Testament Interpretation*,
(Philadelphia: Westminster, 1976), pp. 51–75; cf. also the earlier survey articles by
G. Fohrer in *Theologische Rundschau* 19 (1951): 277–346; 20 (1952): 192–271, 295–361; 28
(1962): 1–75, 235–97, 301–74; 40 (1975): 193–209, 337–77; 41 (1976): 1–12.

[137] B. O. Long, "Prophetic Authority as Social Reality", in *Canon and Authority: Essays
in Old Testament Religion and Theology*, (ed. G. W. Coats and B. O. Long; Philadelphia:
Fortress, 1977), pp. 3–20; idem, "Social Dimensions of Prophetic Conflict", *Semeia* 21
(1981): 31–53.

[138] Wilson, *Prophecy and Society*; D. L. Petersen, *The Roles of Israel's Prophets*, (JSOTSup
17; Sheffield: JSOT Press, 1981).

[139] Wilson, *Prophecy and Society*, p. 8f; D. L. Petersen, *Roles*; P. Berger, "Charisma and
Religious Innovation: The Social Location of Israelite Prophecy", *American Sociological
Review* 28 (1963): 945–50; J. Williams, "The Social Location of Israelite Prophecy",
*JAAR* 37 (1969): 153–65, (the last two are cited in Long, "Prophetic Authority", p. 7).
Blenkinsopp, *History*, pp. 26–39, with bibliography.

a "cult prophet,"[140] or associated with one or another of the various supposed theological and sociological groupings of the early Persian period. One article has been devoted to Haggai's role, but it only deals with Hag 2:10–14.[141] Closely related to discussions of the prophetic role and social location[142] is the issue of the fate of prophecy in the Persian period, especially its supposed cessation, a view which has been challenged in recent scholarly literature.[143] It seems judicious to affirm, with Petersen, that significant change did occur with reference to the prophetic office during the Persian period.[144] In this regard the book of Haggai does indeed contain valuable data about the nature and functioning of prophecy and presents the historian with a significant resource for understanding of the place of prophecy in early Persian Yehud.

## 1.6. The Present Study: Purpose, Approach, and Structure

The preceding survey of issues and approaches to the study of Haggai in its Persian context was intended to demonstrate that a fresh examination of the book and its social context is indeed warranted. This task is made all the more fruitful by the virtual explosion of publications dealing with our prophet, as well as the Babylonian and Persian periods in Palestine, which has occurred since 1980. Several major commentaries on Haggai have appeared, such as those of Amsler, Wolff, Petersen, Meyers and Meyers, Verhoef, and Redditt, as well as several

---

[140] Blenkinsopp, *History*, p. 201.

[141] E. M. Meyers, "The Use of *Tôrâ* in Haggai 2, and the Role of the Prophet in the Restoration", in *The Word of the Lord Shall Go Forth*: *Essays in Honor of David Noel Freedman in Celebration of his Sixtieth Birthday*, (ed. C. L. Meyers and M. O'Connor; Winona Lake: Eisenbraun's/American School of Oriental Research, 1973), pp. 69–76.

[142] Here see recently, J. Blenkinsopp, "The Social Roles of Prophets in Early Achaemenid Judah", *JSOT* 93 (2001): 39–58, with bibliography.

[143] See B. D. Sommer, "Did Prophecy Cease?" Sommer cites the relevant bibliographic data on both sides of the question (p. 31, n. 1 and 2). He personally concludes that prophecy did indeed cease in the Persian Period. Cf. also O. H. Steck, *Der Abschluss der Prophetie im Alten Testament*, (BthSt 17; Neukirchen-Vluyn: Neukirchener Verlag, 1991).

[144] D. L. Petersen, "Rethinking the End of Prophecy", in *"Wünschet Jerusalem Frieden"*: *Collected Communications to the XIIth Congress of the International Organization for the Study of the Old Testament*, Jerusalem 1986, (BEATAJ 13; ed. M. Augustin and K.-D. Schunck; Frankfurt am Main: Peter Lang, 1988), pp. 65–71. Cf. also his more recent articles, "Israelite Prophecy: Change versus Continuity", in *Congress Volume: Leuven, 1989*, (ed. J. A. Emerton; SVT 43; Leiden: E. J. Brill, 1991), pp. 190–203, and "Rethinking the Nature of Prophetic Literature", in *Prophecy and Prophets: The Diversity of Contemporary Issues in Scholarship*, (ed. Y. Gitay, Atlanta: Scholars Press, 1997), p. 23–40.

studies of Haggai in commentaries on the Minor Prophets, including those of Craigie, Achtemeier, Motyer, and Floyd. As Carter has noted, during the first three quarters of the last century, Yehud was generally treated peripherally in the context of larger works, or was the subject of shorter, more specific studies.[145] This situation no longer obtains. A major body of literature now exists on the Persian Empire.[146] We have a large and growing corpus of monographs and specialized studies on Syria-Palestine in the Persian period.[147] The journal *Transeuphratène* has contributed enormously to this literature, especially through its comprehensive bibliographic and review articles on disciplines such as archaeology, epigraphy, numismatics, and Old Testament.[148] The two recent bibliographic surveys and analyses published by P. Briant[149] that supplement the extensive bibliography in his *Histoire de l'empire perse de Cyrus à Alexandre*, as well as the related web-site,[150] have provided scholars with a regularly updated source of data on a variety of issues related to the Persian period. In comparison with the relative paucity of literature which existed as little as twenty years ago, we are now

---

[145] Carter, *Emergence*, p. 33.

[146] Cf. the work of the Achaemenid History Workshop, which has published 10 volumes to date. Of special importance due to its length and comprehensive nature is P. Briant, *Histoire de l'empire perse de Cyrus à Alexandre*, (2 vols., Achaemenid History 10; Leiden: Nederlands Instituut voor het Nabije Oosten, 1996). Also significant here are M. A. Dandamaev and V. G. Lukonin, *The Culture and Social Institutions of Ancient Iran*, (trans. P. L. Kohl; Cambridge and New York: Cambridge University Press, 1988) and M. A. Dandamaev, *A Political History of the Achaemenid Empire*, (trans. W. J. Vogelsang; Leiden and New York: E. J. Brill, 1989).

[147] Cf., for example (with bibliography): W. D. Davies and J. Finkelstein, eds., *The Cambridge History of Judaism*, Vol. 1, Persian Period (Cambridge: Cambridge University Press, 1984), henceforth *CHJ*; P. R. Davies, ed., *Second Temple Studies 1: Persian Period*, (JSOTSup 117; Sheffield: Sheffield Academic Press, 1991); E.-M. Laperrousaz and A. Lemaire, *La Palestine à l'époque perse*, (Paris: Cerf, 1994); T. Eskenazi and K. Richards, eds., *Second Temple Studies 2: Temple and Community in the Persian Period*, (JSOTSup 175; Sheffield: Sheffield Academic Press, 1996); J. Elayi and J. Sapin, *Beyond the River: New Perspectives on Transeuphratène*, (JSOTSup 250; trans. J. E. Crowley, Sheffield: Sheffield Academic Press, 1998=Eng. tr. of *Nouveaux regards sur la Transeuphratène*, [Paris: Brépols, 1991]); Carter, *Emergence*; J. Elayi and J. Sapin, *Quinze ans de recherche (1985–2000) sur la Transeuphratène à l'époque perse*, (Suppléments à *Trans* 8; Paris: Gabalda, 2000).

[148] *Trans* 1 (1989): 131–64; *Trans* 4 (1991): 83–195; *Trans* 10 (1995): 87–211; *Trans* 17 (1999): 47–169. A full listing of the specific review articles and their authors may be found at www.perso.infonie.fr.

[149] P. Briant, "Bulletin d'histoire achéménide", in *Recherches récentes sur l'empire achéménide*, (Supplément à *Topoi* 1; Lyon and Paris: Maison de l'Orient Méditerranéen, 1997), pp. 5–127; idem, *Bulletin d'histoire achéménide II*, 1998–2000, (Persica 1; Paris: Thotm, 2001).

[150] www.achemenet.com; cf. also www.transeuphratene.com & www.perso.infonie.fr.

the beneficiaries of a large body of critical literature related to our period.

We have observed the quasi-unanimous verdict that the book of Haggai represents a rich resource for the historical reconstruction of early Persian Yehud. However, as the deficiencies of certain approaches to Haggai demonstrate, unless a comprehensive, interdisciplinary and integrative approach is used, results may be less than satisfactory. In the chapters which follow, therefore, I will present an analysis of Haggai which includes: (1) a careful philological, syntactical, and literary-rhetorical analysis of the text, including its use of theological and religious traditions found elsewhere in biblical literature; (2) an analysis of the text's redactional history; and (3) an understanding of the broader political, religious, and sociological context (involving here the resources available through archaeology as well as the judicious use of the social sciences) contemporaneous with the production of the oracles and framework of the book.

However as one examines these aforementioned elements, one must determine *how* a document such as the book of Haggai can most profitably be used, or, more particularly, what *kind of data* it is liable to yield. Especially significant here is the understanding that Haggai is a text with specific ideological goals and theological preoccupations. Stated in the simplest of terms, the book of Haggai contains dates, prophetic oracles, and brief narrative sequences relating to prophetic activity in the context of early Persian Yehud, all of which are woven into a literary whole. As such, the book has much to tell us about prophecy and society *as it was understood by the framer(s) of that literary whole, as revealed through the book's portrait of Haggai the prophet.*[151] Thus my interest is not in the naïve use of the book as a springboard from which to access the hard facts of "what really happened" but rather to examine the data in the book, in order to understand the specific perspective or perspectives contained in it vis-à-vis the issues to which the book speaks.[152]

At this point it may help to illustrate how such a reading functions, and its ultimate usefulness. It is frequently asserted that the people's

---

[151] The question of the relationship between this redactional portrait and the "historical Haggai" will be explored in ch. 2.

[152] Cf. my arguments in "The Second Year of Darius and the Prophet Haggai", *Trans* 5 (1992): 63–84. This approach is elaborated and defended in M. H. Floyd, "The Nature of the Narrative and the Evidence of Redaction in Haggai", *VT* 45 (1995): 470–90, esp. pp. 473, 489–90.

refusal to come and build the temple (Hag 1:2) was rooted in theological
and eschatological convictions regarding the appropriate time for its
reconstruction. It is affirmed that, in the eyes of the people, the divinely
appointed time for such a project had not yet arrived, whereas Haggai
advocated immediate rebuilding.[153] However, as I have endeavoured to
demonstrate elsewhere,[154] and as will be discussed in the exegesis below,
whatever the historical realities may have been, both the syntactical
formulation of Hag 1:2 and the context of Hag 1 as a whole make it
clear that the editor of Haggai does not want the reader of the text
to perceive the debate as theological, nor its resolution to be the result
of Haggai's theological expertise and sophisticated scholarly handling
of the relevant texts and traditions. Quite to the contrary, the reader
is meant to view the people as self-centred and obstinate, and Haggai
as a profoundly effective prophet whose words cut through hardened
hearts and achieved the desired result. The question to be asked, then,
is not so much, "what *really* happened?" (although that question is not
an invalid one) but rather "why was it important for the redactor to set
Haggai in this *particular* light and for the reader/hearer to perceive the
situation in such a way?" The same can be said regarding the various
social, political, and theological issues touched upon in the book. It is
my conviction that, if the book of Haggai is read this way, a significant
piece of the mosaic of perceptions current in early Persian Yehud may
be brought to light.

Viewed from this perspective, the book of Haggai may be analyzed
as an expression of the culture or sub-culture that produced it.[155] Put

---

[153] For a survey of the development of this position, cf. ch. 5, pp. 123–25, *infra*.
For a statement of it, cf. P. R. Bedford, "Discerning the Time: Haggai, Zechariah
and the 'Delay' in the Rebuilding of the Jerusalem Temple", in *The Pitcher is Broken:
Memorial Essays for G. W. Ahlström*, (JSOTSup 190; ed. S. W. Holloway and L. K. Handy;
Sheffield: JSOT, 1995), pp. 71–94 and H. Tadmor, "'The Appointed Time Has Not
Yet Arrived': The Historical Background of Haggai 1:2", in *Ki Baruch Hu: Ancient
Near Eastern, Biblical and Judaic Studies in Honor of Baruch A. Levine*, (ed. W. W. Hallo,
L. H. Schiffman, and R. Chazon; Winona Lake: Eisenbrauns, 1999), pp. 401–8. Cf.,
more recently, P. R. Bedford, *Temple Restoration in Early Achaemenid Judah*, (JSJSup 63,
Leiden: Brill, 2001), esp. pp. 168–80 and 273–90. As noted in the introduction, I
am not able to incorporate my response to Bedford's recent work in the present
study.

[154] J. Kessler, "'t (le temps) en Aggée i, 2–4: conflit théologique ou 'sagesse mondaine'?" *VT* 48 (1998): 555–59.

[155] Cf. from a different perspective, E. T. Mullen, *Narrative History and Ethnic Boundaries:
The Deuteronomistic Historian and the Creation of Israelite National Identity*, (SemeiaSt; Atlanta:
Scholars Press, 1993), and idem, *Ethnic Myths and Pentateuchal Foundations*, (SemeiaSt;

another way, the book of Haggai can serve not so much as a lens through which history may be reconstructed (although, with due critical caution certain elements of it can be used in such a fashion), but as an unselfconscious testimony to the vision of prophecy and society which was nurtured and promulgated by those who configured and disseminated the book of Haggai.[156] Smith, similarly, invites modern readers to view Haggai, Ezra, and Nehemiah from the perspective of an "exilic consciousness" which has significantly shaped the perception of the social and religious experience reflected in them."[157] This approach to the reading of Haggai is also consistent with the general orientation of "contextual archaeology"[158] which treats texts, material remains, social structure, and ideological and theological convictions as valid means of reconstructing the larger whole.

I return to my point of departure. My goal in this study is to pursue an understanding of the distinctive portrait of Yehudite society in general, and the prophetic role in particular, which is encountered in the book of Haggai. In order to do this, my study will proceed as follows. Chapter 2 will discuss the book's redactional history and set that process within a chronological framework. In this connection the question of the relationship between Haggai and Zechariah 1–8 will also be discussed. Chapter 3 will examine a number of specific historical issues, critical to an understanding of the text, which are contemporaneous with the text's creation. Yet in order not to prejudice the reading of the text, these historical questions will be resolved either apart from the data in Haggai, or with minimal appeal to it. This redactional and historical analysis will provide a "platform" from which a reading of the text will then be undertaken in chapters 4–8. In these chapters, each pericope of the book will be examined in four sections: (1) translation and textual criticism; (2) structural and literary consider-

---

Atlanta: Scholars Press, 1997). Mullen (*Ethnic Myths*, p. 2) asserts that quite frequently national identity is developed via traditions created from whole cloth. This position has been vigorously challenged by F. Deist, as it relates to Yehud, on the analogy of the South African experience (F. E. Deist, "The Yehud Bible: A Belated Divine Miracle?", *JNSL* 23 [1997]: 117–42). On the broader issues involved in the discussion of ethnicity cf. S. Jones, *The Archaeology of Ethnicity: Constructing Identities in the Past and Present*, (London and New York: Routledge, 1997).

[156] Cf. ch. 10, *infra*.

[157] Smith, *Landless*, p. 197. Despite my serious disagreements with Smith regarding the exegesis of Hag 2:10–19, this methodological approach to reading Haggai is highly appropriate.

[158] Cf. n. 122 and 123, *supra*.

ations; (3) exegesis; and (4) rhetorical and hermeneutical use of religious traditions. Chapter 9 will present a literary analysis of Haggai, with special attention to its structure, form, and purpose. Chapter 10 will summarize the distinctive perspectives of the book which were identified in the course of this study, and subsequently set forth a proposal regarding the social location and purposes of the framers of the book.

# CHAPTER TWO

# THE LITERARY HISTORY OF THE BOOK OF HAGGAI

## 2.1. INTRODUCTION

The purpose of this chapter is to trace the redactional history of the book of Haggai and to delimit, in so far as it is possible, the chronological parameters of that redaction. Due to its brevity and relative simplicity, Haggai may be one of the few biblical texts where such an enterprise can generate a sustainable critical consensus.

## 2.2. THE LITERARY DEVELOPMENT OF THE BOOK OF HAGGAI

The book of Haggai is composed of date formulae (1:1, 15; 2:1, 10, 20) generally attached to a formula introducing the advent of the prophetic word (*Wortereignisformel*), prophetic oracles (1:2–11, 13b; 2:2–9, 15–19, 21–23), a brief prose narration (1:12–14), and a prose narration introducing a prophetic oracle (2:11–14). The more traditional approach to the literary development of the book has been to see the originally oral, oracular material as having circulated in an earlier written form, which was subsequently reinterpreted and set in its present form by the author of the redactional framework. The following survey reflects several variations on this basic approach.

P. R. Ackroyd elaborated his understanding of the redactional history of Haggai in a series of articles published from 1951 to 1954.[1] According to Ackroyd, the oracles of Haggai were delivered by the prophet in a quasi-poetic form.[2] For a relatively brief period, these oracles were transmitted orally.[3] Quite quickly, however, an early col-

---

[1] P. R. Ackroyd, "Studies in the Book of Haggai", *JJS* 2 (1951): 163–76; "Studies in the Book of Haggai", *JJS* 3 (1952): 1–13; "The Book of Haggai and Zechariah 1–8", *JJS* 3 (1952): 151–56; "Some Interpretative Glosses in the Book of Haggai", *JJS* 7 (1956): 163–67; "Two Problems" (1958). His later publications, such as *Exile and Restoration* (1968), and "Problems in the Handling of Biblical and Related Sources in the Achaemenid Period", in *Achaemenid History III: Method and Theory*, (ed. A. Kuhrt and H. Sancisi-Weerdenburg; Leiden: Nederlands Instituut voor het Nabije Oosten, 1988), pp. 33–54, reflect his ongoing thinking regarding the book of Haggai.

[2] Ackroyd, "Studies", p. 165–66.

[3] Ibid., p. 174.

lection was produced, with two redactional features: the addition of
1:12–14 and the re-editing of 2:3–5 and 11–14a.[4] Anywhere from one
to two centuries later, this collection was completely reworked.[5] This
later redactor's activity consisted of the following changes: the expansion of the poems, the reinterpretation of the oracles, the addition of
the dates,[6] and some brief commentaries. At certain points this redactor completely modified the order and structure of the oracles (for
example 1:2, 4–8, 9–11; 2:3–5).[7] For Ackroyd, the goal of this final
edition was to counter the claims of the Samaritan community, especially concerning the worship and ordinances of the Second Temple.[8] The last stage of the literary growth of the book occurred when
some interpretive glosses (2:5a, 9b, 14b, 17b) were added.[9] For Ackroyd, the foundational distinction to be made is between the oracles (to
be dated early) and the full redactional framework (to be dated much
later).

W. A. M. Beuken, a Dutch scholar whose doctoral dissertation was
published in 1967,[10] followed Ackroyd in accepting the identification
of the final form of Haggai with the theological perspectives of the
Chronicler. Like Ackroyd, Beuken maintained that an early version of
the oracles of Haggai was produced and disseminated in the form of
a *Sammlung* (collection) reasonably close to the time of their proclamation.[11] However, in contrast to Ackroyd, Beuken affirmed that dates
were attached to the oracles as soon as the latter were written down.
Subsequently, a first reworking of the *Sammlung* was undertaken, comprising 1:3–11, 12b and 2:15–19. This reworking transformed the oracles
into sketch scenes (*Auftrittsskizzen*).[12] Later, at the time of the Chronicler, one or several redactors re-edited the *Auftrittsskizzen* into a series of
episodes (*Episoden*), reminiscent of the structure of 1 and 2 Chronicles.[13]

---

[4] Ibid.
[5] Ibid., p. 173. This material includes 1:1, 3, 15; 2:1–2, 10, 18 and 20–21a.
[6] Ackroyd, "Two Problems", p. 22.
[7] Ackroyd, "Studies", p. 3.
[8] Ibid.
[9] P. R. Ackroyd, "Interpretive Glosses", p. 163–167, *passim*.
[10] W. A. M. Beuken, *Haggai - Sacharja 1–8: Studien zur Überlieferungsgeschichte der frühnachexilischen Prophetie*, (SSN 10; Assen: Van Gorcum, 1967).
[11] Ibid., pp. 3–8. Beuken's position concerning this stage of the book's development
is somewhat vague.
[12] Ibid., pp. 184–216.
[13] Ibid., p. 331.

Later, certain modifications were made.[14] Beuken puts the main division between the earlier material, (the oracles and *Auftrittsskizzen*) and the later *Episoden*.

According to Beuken, in the first restructuring (the *Auftrittsskizzen*), Haggai was a representative of the non-exiled Judaean landowners.[15] Condemning syncretism and having his theological roots in the Yahwistic traditions of the pre-exilic agricultural population, our prophet favoured a return to the *status quo* that existed before the catastrophe of 587. According to Haggai, the people would find blessing and prosperity through the temple and their Davidic leader.[16] The final redaction (the *Episoden*), by contrast, had a threefold purpose. First, it sought to refute Samaritan claims concerning the temple. In order to achieve this, it underlined the continuity (*Übereinstimmung*) which existed between the earlier edifice and its successor.[17] Zerubbabel, like David, was a divinely authorized chief-builder. Yahweh had promised to fill the Second Temple with his presence. Thus the Jerusalem Temple was the only legitimate successor of its earlier counterpart. The second redactional theme was that of repentance.[18] Having violated the covenant, the people were called to return to Yahweh and renew their commitment to him. The third redactional element of importance was the efficacy of postexilic prophecy.[19] It had the power to shape human history because through it Yahweh intervened and manifested himself to his people.

Close to the time Beuken's work appeared, K. Koch and O. H. Steck published form-critical analyses of Haggai which had significant implications regarding the book's redactional history. K. Koch posited the existence of three units within the text, each bearing a similar structure.[20] He identified three common formal elements in 1:3–9; 2:2–9 and 2:10–19, namely: (1) an allusion to the contemporary situation (*Hinweis auf die Lage*), 1:2–4; 2:3, 11–13; (2) the present moment as decisive (*gegenwärtige Zeitpunkt als Wendepunkt*), 1:5–6; 2:4–5, 14; and (3) a promise for the future (*Ankündigung*), 1:7–8; 2:6–7, 15–19. Further, he noted the key role played by ועתה (and now) within these literary units,[21] as well as

---

[14] Ibid., pp. 335–36.
[15] Ibid., pp. 228–29, 334.
[16] Ibid., p. 334.
[17] Ibid., p. 56.
[18] Ibid., p. 334.
[19] Ibid., p. 332.
[20] K. Koch, "Haggais unreines Volk", *ZAW* 79 (1967): 52–66.
[21] Ibid., pp. 59–60.

the repeated use of the dates, address formulae, and the formula of the reception of the word (*Wortempfangsnotiz*).[22] Most significant is that fact that, according to Koch, this structure had its origins in the prophet's use of a specific rhetorical form (*Heilsweissagung*) and predated the book in its final form.[23] A similar approach was taken by O. H. Steck who attempted to delimit and interpret the redactional activity in 1:2–11 before it was integrated into its present context (1:1–15) by a later redactor.[24] Steck concluded that two originally independent speeches of Haggai, given to two different audiences, were united by a redactor prior to the incorporation of the larger unit into the present work. Like Koch, Steck attributed the content of 1:3–11 to Haggai, who proclaimed these oracles roughly on the dates attached to them in the present form of the book.

R. A. Mason's 1977 reconstruction of the literary history of Haggai challenged Ackroyd and Beuken's hypothesis that the book's final redaction was significantly later than the oracles and to be situated in a "chronistic milieu."[25] Mason began by delineating the redactional framework of Haggai as comprising the following verses: 1:1, 3, 12, 13a, 14, 15; 2:1, 2, 10, 20, and perhaps 2:5. Mason did not discuss the theological approach or the vocabulary of the oracles. His goal was to determine the milieu in which the framework was produced. Mason maintained that none of the thematic evidence adduced by Beuken[26] conclusively demonstrated that the book's framework derived from a chronistic milieu. He concluded that the terminology and the vocabulary of the framework were more Deuteronomistic than chronistic. For Mason the use of expressions such as ביד (through), שמע בקול יהוה (to obey the voice of Yahweh), ירא יהוה (to fear Yahweh), the proclamation of the message of Yahweh to the leaders of the community, and the use of the roots חזק (to strengthen) and עשה (to do) in the context of an oracle of salvation constituted evidence of a Deuteronomistic milieu (cf. Deut 31; Josh 1; 10:25; 2 Sam 11). Further, he identified certain priestly expressions and preoccupations in the book: ביד (through Hag 1:1) etc.

---

[22] Wolff and Beuken employ the term *Wortereignisformel* for this.
[23] Koch, "Haggais", p. 56.
[24] O. H. Steck, "Zu Haggai 1:2–11", *ZAW* 83 (1971): 355–79.
[25] Mason, "Editorial Framework", pp. 413–21.
[26] These themes include concern for the temple and its rites, the maintaining of the Davidic line, the prophet as messenger, the Lord who revives the spirit of individuals, the prophet as intermediary, the proclamation of the message to the leaders of the community, as well as certain specific linguistic formulations.

used in connection with Moses in Exod 9:35; 35:29 etc.; the temple as the abode of Yahweh (Hag 1:9; cf. Ezek 37:27); the term מלאכה (work Hag 1:14; cf. Exod 35:29). Mason viewed this priestly-Deuteronomistic redaction as having occurred quite rapidly following the proclamation of the oracles.[27] According to him, the goal of the framework was to attenuate the eschatological hope found in the oracles, thereby integrating such notions into a more theocratic context. Mason concluded that despite the fact that many of the promises announced by the prophet were not yet fulfilled, for the author of the redactional framework, the firstfruits were already present in the community: the existence of a people sensitive to the divine word, and a rebuilt temple. In such a context the role of the leaders was not to advocate a political messianism, but to be models of piety. The faithful were also called to follow their example until the complete fulfillment of Haggai's promises came to pass.[28]

In his 1986 commentary, H. W. Wolff elaborated his own approach to the literary criticism of the book.[29] For Wolff the main distinction was not between oracles and framework (Ackroyd and Mason) or between two *Auftrittsskizzen* and four *Episoden* (Beuken), but between a series of five appearances by the prophet set in the form of *Auftrittsskizzen*, and the work of the final redactor, Haggai's Chronicler, who reconfigured the book into four scenes. Wolff suggested that the literary development of the book progressed as follows. First, an early prophetic school produced a booklet structured in the form of five "sketch scenes" or *Auftrittsskizzen*. These scenes comprised the oracles of Haggai (1:4–11; 2:15–19; 2:3–9; 2:14; 2:21b–23) as well as brief descriptions of the results of his preaching (1:12b–13), or other circumstances surrounding the oracles (1:2; 2:11–13). Subsequently, Haggai's Chronicler added introductions describing the "confronting event of the word" (*Wortereignisein-führungen*) that are found in 1:1–3, 15a, 15b-2:2; 2:10, 21a. This editor also added the precise dates, the names and titles of the recipients, and several supplementary details.[30] Haggai's Chronicler also modified the text, detaching 2:15–19 from 1:15a, adding the name of Joshua in 2:4, and the word "now" in 2:15 and the date in 2:18. According to Wolff,

---

[27] Ibid., p. 421.

[28] Ibid.

[29] Wolff, pp. 3–6.

[30] This is in contrast to Beuken who places the date formulae at the earliest point in the literacy history of the text.

the work of Haggai's Chronicler may have been carried out in two
stages.[31] The first redaction, made before the twenty-fourth day of the
ninth month, uses the order year-month-day, the expression ביד חגי,
and the title הנביא for the prophet. The second redaction, made after
the twenty-fourth of the ninth month, uses the order day-month-year,
and אל חגי (to Haggai) in 2:10, 20.[32] Finally, other minor additions were
made by an unknown glossator: 2:5a,17; the last two words of 2:18; the
four first words of 2:19 and the additions to the text that are found in
LXX in verses 2:9, 14, 21, 22.[33]

Wolff distinguishes the *Auftrittsskizzen* from the work of Haggai's
Chronicler according to philological and stylistic criteria. Haggai's
Chronicler portrays the prophet as addressing Zerubbabel, Joshua, and
"the remnant of the people" (1:12a, 14a), whereas in the *Auftrittsskizzen*
only "the people" are addressed (1: 12b, 13a). Haggai's Chronicler designates Haggai as "the prophet" (1:1, 3, 12a; 2:1, 10) in contrast to the
*Auftrittsskizzen* where he is called "Yahweh's messenger" (1: 13a), or no
title is attached to his name (2:13, 14). In the work of Haggai's Chronicler the word of Yahweh comes through (ביד) the intermediary of the
prophet. In the *Auftrittsskizzen* divine speech proceeds from Yahweh via
the "Messenger Formula" (*Botenformel*) כה אמר יהוה (eight times) or the
"Divine Oracle Formula" (*Gottesspruchformel*) [צבאות] נאם יהוה (twelve
times). In contrast to Ackroyd and Beuken, and in agreement with
Mason, Wolff maintains that the redaction of the oracles occurred
at a date relatively close to their proclamation. For Wolff, the socio-
political difference between these two main sections is as follows. The
*Auftrittsskizzen* display a spirit of openness. Everyone was invited to participate in the rebuilding, both Judaeans and Samaritans. However,
it was Zerubbabel's rejection of foreign aid (described in Ezra 4:1–
5) which brought about the revision of the sketch scenes by Haggai's
Chronicler. Since Zerubbabel had rejected foreign aid, the book had to
be reconfigured to reflect his importance.[34]

In contrast to Mason and Wolff, R. J. Coggins proposed a later date
for the final version of Haggai and Zech 1–8. He viewed the production of these texts as being contemporaneous with the redaction of the

---

[31] Wolff, pp. 18–20, 35, 98–99. Verses 2:5a; 2:17 and some elements of 2:18 and 19
belong to this second redaction, according to Wolff.

[32] Wolff, p. 35; cf. my discussion of the date formulae in ch. 3.

[33] Wolff, p. 18.

[34] Wolff, pp. 19–20, 35–36.

book of Ezra.[35] He suggested that the redactional framework of Haggai-Zechariah 1–8 added the notion of a "new beginning after the exile" to the oracular material—a notion absent in Haggai's words.[36] This would place the final redaction a century after the oracles. A similar dating is proposed by A. Sérandour. He posits a single and unifying redaction of Haggai-Zechariah-Malachi which is distinguishable from earlier material through its approach to the form of the community's leadership. Sérandour concurs with Tollington's division of the text into oracles and framework, and with the latter's insistence upon the importance of Joshua and Zerubbabel.[37] However he sees the oracles and framework as reflecting two completely different perspectives. For him, the prophet Haggai spoke exclusively to "the people" and did not know either Joshua or Zerubbabel.[38] The editorial framework, by contrast, which extends through the books of Haggai, Zechariah and Malachi, retroprojected a later dyarchic ideology, which assigned equal authority to civil and religious leadership, on to the book of Haggai.[39] Thus, according to Sérandour, in contrast to our prophet himself, the redactional framework views the temple builders, Joshua and Zerubbabel, as the founders of dynasties whose perpetuity is guaranteed by covenant.[40] Sérandour sees the redactional framework as being sufficiently extensive so as to have reworked the content of the oracles.[41] Nevertheless he situates that redaction around 450 BCE, a significant chronological distance from the oracles.[42]

In contrast to these approaches, several recent studies have tended to minimize or abandon the search for an earlier literary form of the book. Petersen endorses Beuken's delimitation of two *Auftrittsskizzen* at 1:3–11, 12b and 2:15–19, and Koch's argument for three units structured in a similar fashion, but suggests that reconstructing any earlier setting "yields unconvincing, even artificial results."[43] Redditt takes a

---

[35] R. J. Coggins, *Haggai, Zechariah, Malachi*, (OTG; Sheffield: JSOT Press, 1987), pp. 30–31.

[36] Ibid.

[37] A. Sérandour, "Réflexions à propos d'un livre récent sur *Aggée-Zacharie* 1–8", *Trans* 10 (1995): 75–84, esp. p. 76.

[38] Ibid., pp. 76, 80.

[39] Ibid., p. 77.

[40] Ibid., p. 76; cf. also idem, "Zacharie et les autorités de son temps", in *Prophètes et rois: Bible et Proche Orient*, (LD; ed. A. Lemaire, Paris: Cerf, 2001), p. 259–98.

[41] Ibid., p. 80.

[42] Sérandour, "Récits", pp. 16–18.

[43] Petersen, pp. 38–39.

similar view.[44] Meyers and Meyers seem to accept the hypothesis that an "editorial framework has been superimposed on a core of original material."[45] However, noting the "literary continuity between the oracles and the so-called narrative portions of Haggai" the authors see "little hope or purpose in separating out all of the individual units."[46] In her monograph Tollington delimits the extent of the editorial framework.[47] However she mentions no earlier written form of the oracular material and dates the composition of the framework to a period closely following the proclamation of the oracles.[48] This leads her, in large measure, to treat the text as a literary whole. In her thematic analysis of the book's content, she makes no major distinctions between the perspective of the prophet and that of the redactional framework, despite the fact that she suggests that the framework places special emphasis on the community's leaders.[49] In a 1995 article, M. Floyd argued at length that "the kind of analysis that seeks to distinguish redactional material from source material ... should be abandoned, along with the historical speculation that has often been based on this practice."[50]

The quest for earlier forms of the book, and the setting of these forms within a specific theological and sociological context has not generated a critical consensus. As a result, as we have seen, the tendency has been simply to posit the existence of two elements (oracles and redactional framework) and to view the two as reflecting some points of discontinuity within a general framework of continuity. This continuity is the result of the extensive redactional activity undergone by the

---

[44] P. L. Redditt, *Haggai, Zechariah, Malachi*, (NCBC; Grand Rapids: Eerdmans, 1994), pp. 11–12.

[45] Meyers and Meyers, p. lxviii.

[46] Ibid., p lxx.

[47] Tollington, *Tradition*, pp. 19–23, esp. p. 23.

[48] Ibid., p. 23.

[49] Ibid., pp. 22–23. In a later piece ("Readings in Haggai: From the Prophet to the Complete Book, a Changing Message in Changing Times", in *The Crisis of Israelite Religion. Transformation of Religious Tradition in Exilic and Post-Exilic Times*, [OS 42; ed. B. Becking and M. C. A. Korpel ; Leiden: E. J. Brill, 1999], pp. 194–208) Tollington appears to have taken a different approach and argues for a subsequent thoroughgoing reordering of the text and its date formulae in 164 BCE. Tollington's suggestions are difficult to evaluate, in that they are largely hypothetical. It remains to be seen whether such a radical reordering of a biblical text would have been undertaken at such a late date.

[50] M. H. Floyd, "The Nature of the Narrative and the Evidence of Redaction in Haggai", *VT* 45 (1995): 473.

oracles,[51] or the genuine similarity of the perspectives of all involved in the book's production.[52] Such an approach, in my view, is a valid methodological step for at least two reasons. First, there has been no final agreement on the precise extent of the redactional activity.[53] Second, the framework clearly seeks to use the oracles to promote a particular redactional perspective, and it is therefore questionable whether any significant discontinuity ought to be posited between the two.[54] This line of argument will be elaborated below.

## 2.3. The Dating of the Redactional Framework

The dating of the redactional framework of Haggai is a question of critical importance. An early date for the book's final form would tend to minimize the differences between prophet and redactor and set the two in a relatively similar socio-political context. A much later redaction lends itself more readily to the hypothesis of a more thorough reworking and "actualization" (Beuken) of the prophet's words and thoughts.

### 2.3.1. *Evaluation of the Evidence for a Fifth- or Fourth-Century Redaction*

The arguments advanced in favour of a fifth or fourth-century date for the final redaction of Haggai are open to serious criticism at a variety of key points. Beuken attributed the book's final form to the fourth century principally because of its alleged theological affinities with the Chronicler's work. As we have seen, Mason has justly questioned whether the data presented by Beuken supports this connection.[55] Beuken explained the cases where the vocabulary of Haggai-Zechariah 1–8 differs from that of the Chronicler[56] through the hypo-

---

[51] So Sérandour, "Récits", pp. 16–18, Petersen, p. 39, and Floyd, "Narrative", *passim*, esp. p. 479.

[52] So Meyers and Meyers, p. lxx and Verhoef, p. 13.

[53] Sérandour, "Récits", pp. 16–18 sees 2:1–9 and 20–23 as being an integral part of the redactional framework of the book. Wolff (pp. 18–20 and 34) and Beuken (pp. 184, 214ff.) see the non-oracular material as reflecting differing perspectives.

[54] In addition to his earlier article, Floyd also develops this point in his commentary: M. H. Floyd, *Minor Prophets, Part 2*, (FOTL 22; Grand Rapids: Eerdmans, 2000), pp. 259–60.

[55] Mason, "Editorial Framework", *passim*.

[56] The expression Yahweh Sebaoth, found frequently in Haggai and Zechariah 1–8, is relatively rare in 1 and 2 Chronicles; cf. H. G. M. Williamson, *1 and 2 Chronicles*,

thesis of several chronistic circles at work.[57] However this explanation
rests on an entirely hypothetical literary and historical basis. Ackroy-
d's principal arguments in favour of a final redaction contemporary
with the Chronicler are: (1) the form of the dates;[58] (2) the fact that
in Ezra 5:1, as in the books of Haggai and Zechariah 1–8, the initiative for the resumption of the reconstruction of the temple comes
from our two prophets;[59] and (3) the polemical anti-Samaritan goal that
is manifested throughout the book, but especially in 2:11–14.[60] These
arguments are, however, inconclusive. First, (as I will demonstrate later
in this chapter), the form of the dates in no way establishes a fourth
century context, and does not demonstrate a common source with
Chronicles.[61] Beuken himself admits this point.[62] Second, the naming
of Haggai and Zechariah in Ezra 5 is in no way conclusive since (1) it
is not universally admitted that the author of the book of Ezra should
be identified with the Chronicler,[63] and (2) the fact that the rebuilding of the temple was seen as the fruit of the exhortations of Haggai
and Zechariah could have been accepted by the redactors of the two
books without their belonging to the same circle and writing at the
same period. Third, there are many considerations, both exegetical[64]
and historical[65] which call into question a "Samaritan" interpretation
of 2:11–14. The identification of Haggai-Zechariah 1–8 with the work
of the Chronicler and the question of the Samaritan schism is therefore tenuous and represents an inadequate basis for the *terminus* of the
redaction of Haggai.[66]

---

(NCB; Grand Rapids/ London: Eerdmans/Marshall, Morgan and Scott, 1982), p. 101.
Stuhlmueller, (p. 17) notes that Haggai shows little interest in matters of liturgy or details
of cultic practice.

[57] Beuken, p. 35.

[58] Ackroyd, "Studies", p. 174.

[59] Ibid., p. 1.

[60] Ibid., pp. 2–9.

[61] Cf. *supra*, pp. 41–44.

[62] Beuken, p. 25.

[63] Cf. H. G. M. Williamson, *Ezra, Nehemiah*, (WBC; Waco: Word, 1985), pp. xxi–xxiii;
S. Japhet, "The Supposed Common Authorship of Chronicles and Ezra-Nehemiah
Investigated Anew", *VT* 18 (1968): 330–71.

[64] See the exegesis, *infra*, and Petersen, and Meyers and Meyers, *in loco*.

[65] See Coggins, *Haggai*, p. 28.

[66] It would only be possible, it appears to me, to identify the work of the Chronicler
with the author of the redactional framework of Haggai if one dated the work of the
former to the middle of the sixth century, as does D. N. Freedman, "The Chronicler's
Purpose", *CBQ* 23 (1961): 236–42. However this appears unlikely.

Coggins' assertion that the editorial framework adds the notion of a "new start" to the oracles (which do not include such a concept) lacks exegetical support.[67] Haggai's call to rebuild the temple must imply some new beginning. Sérandour's position is far more complex. He argues that Haggai-Zechariah-Malachi is a triptych promoting the concept of dyarchic rule based on a perpetual covenant made with the two founders of the Second Temple, Joshua and Zerubbabel.[68] However it would appear that the text of Haggai does not fully corroborate Sérandour's thesis. His argument rests essentially upon the framework's emphasis on Joshua and Zerubbabel's leadership in the reconstruction of the temple.[69] However clear evidence of this participation constituting an eternal dynastic covenant is hard to come by in Haggai. Especially difficult is 2:20–23 where Zerubbabel alone is singled out for special attention. Sérandour responds by seeing that passage as being of one redactional piece with Zech 6:12–13 and Mal 2:1–3; 3:1–5 where the priestly covenant is established.[70] It is however debatable whether such evidence from Malachi (and Zechariah) can adequately determine the date of the final redaction of Haggai. Could it not be equally argued that themes already present in Haggai were expanded and debated in later texts?[71] In sum, the redactional insistence on Joshua and Zerubbabel does not constitute adequate proof of a late date for Haggai. Such an emphasis may be accounted for in other ways, as we shall see.

## 2.3.2. *Evidence for a Late Sixth-Century Redaction*

### 2.3.2.1. *The Date Formulae*

In contrast to the hypothesis of a later redaction, several significant indices suggest that the book's redaction took place at an earlier period. The first and most significant of these is the evidence of the date formulae. I am here presupposing that the dating of the oracles constitutes one element of the larger redactional activity manifested in Haggai, and that the date formulae ought not to be viewed in abstraction from the other redactional aspects of the book. In my opinion, there is

---

[67] Coggins, *Haggai*, p. 31.
[68] Sérandour, "Récits", pp. 12–13, 18–19; "Réflexions", p. 83.
[69] Sérandour, "Réflexions", pp. 76, 80.
[70] Sérandour, "Récits", pp. 10, 18.
[71] Indeed, Sérandour notes ("Récits", p. 18–19) that Bosshard, Krantz and Steck see Malachi as a redactional appendix to Haggai and Zech 1–8.

nothing inherently improbable or implausible about the supposition
that the dates were attached to the oracles at an early stage. In point of
fact, when one places the date formula in Haggai in the broader context of the use and form of dating formulae in both biblical and extra-
biblical sources from the late seventh to third centuries BCE, this conclusion appears quite probable. This is apparent especially as it relates
to (1) the degree of precision in the dating formula, (2) the number and
order of the elements of the date, and (3) the specific form used to designate the month. Let us examine these three issues.

### 2.3.2.1.1. *Precision in the Date Formulae*

An analysis of the relevant data reveals a progressive movement toward
precision in dating from the late seventh century BCE. Both biblical and
extra-biblical materials prior to the seventh century demonstrate dating
only to the year.[72] However, dating to the month and day becomes quite
common by the beginning of the sixth century. This may be seen in the
paleo-Hebrew ostraca found at Arad, sometimes called the "Archive of
Eliashib," dating to the late seventh, and early sixth centuries. These
texts record various commercial transactions between the fortress at
Arad and the Kittim, commonly assumed to be a colony of Greek
mercenaries.[73] Several of these texts note the day of the month, using
the order day-month. Lemaire notes that both the Arad ostraca (1.4)
and Ezekiel (24:2) contain the specific order to "write down the name
of the day."[74] Exact dating had become so commonplace that one text
evidences the practice of falsifying the date for practical purposes.[75]
Thus the recipient of the ostracon is instructed to date the delivery
notice to the second, rather than to the first of the month, to hide
the fact that delivery was made on the new moon, a designated day
of rest.[76] Similarly, the Egyptian Aramaic papyri of the late sixth and
early fifth centuries manifest the regular practice of dating to the precise

---

[72] For an excellent survey see A. Lemaire, "Les formules de datation en Palestine au
premier millénaire avant J.-C.", in *Proche-Orient Ancien: Temps vécu, temps pensé*, (Antiquités
sémitiques 3; ed. F Briquel-Chatonnet and H. Lozachmeur; Paris: J. Maisonneuve,
1998), pp. 58–62. Lemaire cites a series of examples from the Samarian ostraca, 1–2
Kings, Isaiah and Amos.

[73] A. Lemaire, "Les formules de datation dans Ezéchiel à la lumière de données
épigraphiques récentes", in *Ezekiel and his Book: Textual and Literary Criticism and their
Interrelation*, (ed. J. Lust; Leuven: Leuven University Press, 1986), p. 361.

[74] Lemaire, "Datation en Palestine", p. 66 and "Formules de datation", p. 361.

[75] Lemaire, "Formules de datation", pp. 362–63.

[76] Ibid.

day.[77] This precision in dating is also in evidence in the fourth century Wadi Dâliyeh papyri[78] and Beer-Sheba ostraca.[79] The Aramaic ostraca of Idumea, which number in excess of 800, of which over 400 have been published,[80] reveal the systematic practice of dating to the specific day.[81]

The relevant biblical materials reveal the same progression. Sources earlier than the late seventh century date to the year alone (1 Kgs 15:9; 16:10 etc.; Isa 14:28; Amos 1:1).[82] By the early to mid-sixth century, as evidenced in 2 Kings 25, Ezekiel and Jeremiah, dating formulae manifest greater precision. 2 Kings 25 includes several indications of year, month and day (25:1, 3, 8, 27).[83] Texts in Jeremiah frequently include year and month (28:1, 17; 36:9, 22; 39:1), month and day (52:12)[84] or year, month and day (39:2; 52:4; 52:5–6). The extensive chronological notices in Ezekiel almost uniformly date to the year, month and day (Ezek 1–2; 20:1, etc.).[85] Persian period works such as Haggai, Zechariah, Chronicles, Ezra, Nehemiah, and Esther similarly follow the general

---

[77] Cf. the survey in R. Yaron, "The Schema of the Aramaic Legal Documents", *JJS* 2 (1957): 33–61, esp. pp. 33–35, 60–61. Yaron summarizes the material in A. Cowley, *Aramaic Papyri of the Fifth Century B. C.*, (Oxford: Clarendon Press, 1923); cf. also, more recently, B. Porten, "The Calendar of Aramaic Texts from Achaemenid and Ptolemaic Egypt", in *Irano-Judaica II: Studies Relating to Jewish Contacts with Persian Culture Throughout the Ages*, (ed. A. Netzer and S. Shaked; Jerusalem: Ben-Zvi Institute, 1990), p. 13–32.

[78] F. M. Cross, "Samaria Papyrus I: An Aramaic Slave Conveyance of 335 BCE found in the Wadi ed-Dâliyeh", in *N. Avigad Volume*, (ErIsr 18; ed. B. Mazar and Y. Yadin; Jerusalem: Israel Exploration Society, 1985), pp. 7*-17*; Lemaire, "Datation en Palestine", pp. 71–72.

[79] Lemaire, "Datation en Palestine", pp. 72–73.

[80] A. Lemaire, *Nouvelles inscriptions araméennes d'Idumée au Musée d'Israël*, (vol. 3; Paris: Gabalda, 1996); I. Eph'al and J. Naveh, *Aramaic Ostraca of the Fourth Century BC from Idumea*, (Jerusalem: Magnes/Hebrew University/Israel Exploration Society, 1996).

[81] Lemaire, "Datation en Palestine", pp. 72–73; idem, "Der Beitrag idumäischer Ostraka zur Geschichte Palästinas im Übergang von der persischen zur hellenistischen Zeit", *ZDPV* 115 (1999): 12–23.

[82] The dating of biblical materials is always controversial. Thus while the dating of biblical texts in this section to the seventh century has been contested, there still exists a significant body of critical scholars who accept these dates. Should one or another of these dates prove to be later, however, my overall point still stands.

[83] The year in 25:1 is to be inferred for the rest of the dates.

[84] However the year is to be inferred from 52:5.

[85] On the dates in Ezekiel, especially their early exilic dating and authenticity, see Lemaire, "Formules de datation", pp. 364–66; K. S. Freedy and R. B. Redford, "The Dates in Ezekiel in Relation to Biblical, Babylonian and Egyptian Sources", *JAOS* 90 (1976): 462–85; L. Boadt, *Ezekiel's Oracles against Egypt*, (BiOr 37; Rome: Biblical Institute Press, 1980), pp. 11, 17; E. Kutsch, *Die chronologische Daten des Ezechielbuches*, (OBO 39; Freiburg/Göttingen: Universitätsverlag/Vandenhoeck & Ruprecht, 1985).

pattern of dating to the specific day.[86] One can therefore affirm that the
dating of the oracles of Haggai precisely to the day conforms readily to
sixth-century scribal practice and is in no way exceptional or surprising.

### 2.3.2.1.2. *Form of the Date Formulae*

An analysis of the form of the date formulae in Haggai, specifically as it
relates to the order of the elements, is also significant with reference to
the time when they were composed. The texts of Haggai and Zechariah
1–8[87] do not reveal any consistent pattern concerning the elements
of the dates. The following configurations emerge: In Hag 1:15; 2:10,
and Zech 1:7 the order day-month-year is followed. The reverse order,
year-month-day appears in Hag 1:1. Zech 7:1 is configured year-day-
month, inverting the order of these last two elements.[88] When only two
elements are mentioned, the order is once month-day (Hag 2:1), and
once day-month (Hag 2:18).

In his 1957 analysis of the form of Aramaic legal documents, R.
Yaron suggested that "The Bible, as a rule, has the sequence year-
month-day. But the late, definitely postexilic books, Ezra, Nehemiah,
1 and 2 Chronicles, Haggai, Zechariah, and Esther disclose a trend
to a new sequence day-month-year, or where the year is omitted, to
day-month instead of month-day." He goes on to note that this is the
prevalent form in later Jewish documents.[89] In 1968, B. Porten affirmed
Yaron's conclusion.[90] Ackroyd, by contrast, suggested that this "new"
sequence was potential evidence that the dates in Haggai were inserted
at a later date, but he withheld judgment, awaiting a more detailed
analysis of the biblical dates.[91]

A fresh examination of the evidence is warranted in order to evaluate Yaron's hypothesis in general, and more specifically, to analyze the

---

[86] For example, Hag 1:1, 15; 2:1, 10, 20; Zech 1:7; 7:1; 2 Chr 3:2. This material, as
well as the dates in Ezra, Nehemiah, and Chronicles will be discussed at greater length
below.

[87] I include the data from Zechariah here as both texts contain dates from the early
years of Darius' reign.

[88] Meyers and Meyers (p. 6), suggest that this is an intentional rhetorical device,
placing an inclusio around Haggai and Zechariah 1–8. The suggestion is difficult to
evaluate, and would be slightly more compelling if the form of the two dates were
identical. I am suggesting a less "intentional" reading of the date formulae.

[89] R. Yaron, " Schema", p. 60.

[90] B. Porten, *Archives from Elephantine: The Life of an Ancient Jewish Military Colony*,
(Berkeley: University of California Press, 1968), p. 197.

[91] Ackroyd, "Two Problems", p. 22, n. 62.

form of the dates in Haggai. Furthermore, new extra-biblical data has appeared since 1957. I will therefore survey the relevant material with a view to situating the dates in Haggai in the broader context of the form of the dating formulae in the Hebrew and Aramaic texts of the sixth to fourth centuries. As noted above, both biblical and extra-biblical texts from the seventh century provide evidence of dating to the regnal year alone and are thus not immediately relevant to my discussion here.[92] However the latter part of 2 Kings, as well as Jeremiah and Ezekiel evidence bipartite and tripartite dating formulae.[93] In Jeremiah, the formula year-month-day (Yaron's "older" order) appears in 39:2 and in 52:4, 31. Moreover the notices in Jer 52:6, 12 presuppose the year mentioned in 52:4 and can be taken as representing the complete formula in the year-month-day sequence. Jeremiah 28:1 and 39:1 contain only two elements and follow the year-month sequence. The situation in Ezekiel is one of a predominantly year-month-day sequence (1:1; 8:1; 24:1; 29:1; 30:20; 31:1; 32:1; 40:1). Ezekiel 26:1 and 32:17 follow the same model, but the second element (month) is lacking.[94] Ostracon 7, from the paleo-Hebrew Arad ostraca, mentioned above, and datable to the early sixth century, uses a month-day order, corresponding to the general pattern in the biblical sources noted above. Similarly, a late seventh-century fiscal bulla appears to evidence the order year-month.[95] It is worth noting at this point that the dates in the Behistun inscription (521 BCE) were configured in the day-month order.[96]

---

[92] Cf. Lemaire, "Datation en Palestine", pp. 62–63.

[93] For a discussion of these texts, see *supra*, pp. 43–44.

[94] On Ezek 26:1; 32:1, 17, and the specific problems they pose see Lemaire, "Formules de datation", p. 365, and Kutsch, *Chronologische Daten*, pp. 65–67.

[95] On this bulla see Lemaire, "Datation en Palestine", p. 66. Cf. more recently R. Deutsch, *Messages from the Past: Hebrew Bullae from the Time of Isaiah through the Destruction of the First Temple, Shlomo Moussaieff Collection and an Up to Date Corpus*, (Tel Aviv: Archaeological Centre, 1999), pp. 166–72, and R. Deutsch and M. Heltzer, *West Semitic Epigraphic News of the First Millennium BCE*, (Tel Aviv: Archaeological Center, 1999), pp. 64–68.

[96] See J. C. Greenfield and B. Porten, *The Bisitun Inscription of Darius the Great: Aramaic Version*, (Corpus Inscriptionum Iranicarum; London: Lund Humphries, 1982). The inscription was engraved in Elamite (2 versions), Old Persian and Akkadian. From the presence of copies found in Babylon and at Elephantine (on which see B. Porten and A. Yardeni, *Textbook of Aramaic Documents from Ancient Egypt. Vol. 3. Literature. Accounts. Lists*, [Winona Lake: Hebrew University/Eisenbrauns, 1993], p. 58ff.) it would appear that copies and translations were made and sent throughout the empire. The extant Aramaic copy is badly damaged. However, as it closely follows the Akkadian, date formulae have been restored in various places (cf. Porten and Yardeni, *Textbook*, 3:59). Date formulae in the Akkadian using the day-month order occur in, for example, §12, 23, 26, 28, 29, 31. As F. Malbran-Labat notes (*La version akkadienne de l'inscription trilingue de Darius*

Turning to the Aramaic data from the fifth and fourth centuries, we have evidence from the Egyptian papyri, the Wadi Dâliyeh papyri, and the Beer-Sheba and Idumean ostraca. In the Egyptian contracts,[97] where tripartite dates appear, the order is day-month-year, or month-year in bipartite dates. Papyrus Meissner constitutes an important exception to this pattern, and uses year-month-day.[98] It is noteworthy that Meissner, datable to 515 BCE, is the earliest text of the corpus, while the rest of the documents, where dated, belong to the fifth century.[99] Turning to the fourth century Samarian or Wadi Dâliyeh papyri,[100] the order month-year is in evidence, for example, in SP 1. 1[101] and 2. 12.[102] In the Beer-Sheba ostraca, several tripartite dates appear, exclusively with the order day-month-year.[103] Finally, in the highly numerous Idumean Aramaic ostraca,[104] the date formulae regularly manifest the

---

à *Behistun*, [Documenta Asiana; Rome: Gruppo Editoriale Internazionale, 1994], p. 64) the date formulae in the Akkadian all follow the same configuration: numbered day followed by named month. She further notes that whereas the Elamite and Old Persian versions use Persian month names, the Akkadian text uses the Babylonian calendar and month names (idem, "La trilingue de Behistun et les singularités de la version babylonienne", *Sem* 48 [1998]: 61–75, esp. p. 66). Her article provides excellent insights into the language and redactional shaping of the Akkadian text. Her monograph also provides a fresh translation of the text, as reconstituted by E. N. von Voigtlander, (*The Bisitun Inscription of Darius the Great, Babylonian Version*, [Corpus Inscriptionum Iranicarum, I: Inscriptions of Ancient Iran, Texts I; London: Lund Humphries, 1978]) and gives corresponding references to the paragraphs in the Old Persian text, where the two versions differ. Cf. also, recently, J. Tavernier, "An Achaemenid Royal Inscription: The Text of Paragraph 13 of the Aramaic Version of the Bisitun Inscription", *JNES* 60 (2001):161–76.

[97] B. Porten and A. Yardeni, *Textbook of Aramaic Documents from Ancient Egypt. Vol. 2. Contracts*, (Winona Lake: Hebrew University/Eisenbrauns, 1989).

[98] As noted in 1957 by Yaron ("Schema", p. 34).

[99] Porten, and Yardeni, *Textbook* 2:12.

[100] On which see Lemaire, "Datation en Palestine", pp. 71–72. F. M. Cross, "Samaria Papyrus I"; idem, "Papyri of the 4th Century B.C. from Dâliyeh", in *New Directions in Biblical Archaeology*, (ed. D. N. Freedman and J. Greenfield; Garden City: Doubleday, 1969), pp. 45–69.

[101] 335 BCE cf. Cross, "Papyri of the 4th Century B.C.", p. 48.

[102] The examples are Lemaire's ("Datation en Palestine", p. 72) and he dates these to 335 and 352/51 respectively. On Papyrus 2 see F. M. Cross, "A Report on the Samaria Papyri", in *Congress Volume, Jerusalem 1986*, (SVT 40; ed. J. A. Emerton; Leiden: E. J. Brill, 1986), pp. 17–26.

[103] Cf. Lemaire, "Datation en Palestine", p. 73, for a summary. For the texts in full see J. Naveh, "The Aramaic Ostraca", in *Beer-Sheba I*, (ed. Y. Aharoni; Tel Aviv: Tel Aviv University Institute of Archaeology, 1973), pp. 79–82; idem, "The Aramaic Ostraca from Tel Beer-Sheba", *Tel Aviv* 6 (1979): 182–98.

[104] See *supra*, n. 80–81.

order day-month-year.[105] Lemaire comments, regarding the great regularity of form observed in these dates, "These examples clearly illustrate that the various scribes at work on these ostraca were trained and accustomed to recording the precise date, down to the day, in accordance with a precise system of accounting …"[106]

Turning to the later biblical materials,[107] the following patterns emerge. In Ezra we find a tripartite formula in Aramaic at 6:15 using the order day-month-year. Elsewhere, in Ezra and Nehemiah the preponderant sequence is again the later day-month (Ezra 3:6; 6:19;[108] 7:9 [twice]; 8:31; 10:16, 17; Neh 8:2; 9:1). We find the formula month-day once (Ezra 10:9). The year-month sequence is found in Ezra 3:8 and the reverse in Ezra 7:8. In Chronicles the three elements appear only once (2 Chr 3:2 [MT]), and there, the order is somewhat anomalous, month-day-year.[109] Month-year is followed in 2 Chr 15:10. When only the month and day are noted, the day-month order is followed (2 Chr 7:10; 29:17; 35:1). In 2 Chr 29:3 the order is year-month. The book of Esther follows the day-month configuration in 3:13; 8:12 and 9:15, whereas the order month-day is found in 3:12 and 9:1.

It appears from the above data that the customary order of the elements in the older Judaean date formulae was year-month-day, or, where the year was omitted or inferred, month-day, or where the day was omitted, year-month. By contrast, the clearly Persian period texts use an overwhelmingly day-month-year, day-month, or month-year order.[110] Thus Yaron's intuition appears to have been largely borne out by the evidence.

What then can be said regarding the date formulae in Haggai? Haggai uses the older Judaean order (year-month-day) in 1:1 (three elements) and 2:1 (month-day). The more typical Persian period order is followed in 1:15; 2:10 (three elements), and 2:18 (day-month). Thus the system used is far from self-consistent. What explanation can be

---

[105] See, for example, ostraca 1–11, 13–15, 48–58 in Eph'al and Naveh, *Aramaic Ostraca*.

[106] Lemaire, "Datation en Palestine", p. 75.

[107] All the date formulae in this section are in Hebrew, with the exception of the Aramaic Ezra 6:15.

[108] The year here, however, is probably to be inferred from 6:15. Similarly, the year may be determined from the immediate context in many of the verses which follow. However since the three elements are not included in the formula we shall consider them as bipartite.

[109] On the text critical problem in this verse, see Williamson (*Chronicles*, p. 205) who rejects the indication of the day as dittography.

[110] P. Meissner is the only clear exception among the non-biblical materials.

given for this asymmetry? I have suggested elsewhere that this lack of consistency may be explained as reflecting a period of transition in the early Persian period, during which earlier formulations were progressively displaced by later ones.[111] A second and by no means mutually exclusive possibility is that the older formulation, especially in its single tripartite use at the opening of the book, is used for effect. The opening of the book thus "sounds like" the superscriptions attached to the oracles of the "pre-exilic" prophets, dated according to the ruling king of Israel or Judah.[112] It is therefore also possible that the book of Haggai begins with the older formulation for rhetorical effect, but subsequently shifts to the more customary Persian order. In sum, I conclude that nothing in the form of the dates in Haggai is incompatible with redactional activity close to the time designated by the dates.

### 2.3.2.1.3. *The Designation of the Month*

The conclusions reached in the two preceding sections are reinforced by the specific way in which months are designated in Haggai. Lemaire has noted that Jeremiah and the latter part of 2 Kings preface the numerical month reference with חדשׁ (month), a term which, apart from two anomalous references (Ezek 24:1; 32:1), is absent in the date formulae in Ezekiel.[113] He suggests that these references in Ezekiel, with their use of חדשׁ reflect later material, added in light of 2 Kgs 25:1.[114] Indeed, further investigation bears out the preference for the inclusion of חדשׁ in later periods. The books of Ezra, Nehemiah, Chronicles, and Esther show the consistent use of חדשׁ before the name or number of the month (Ezra 3:1, 6, 8; 6:19; 7:8, 9 [twice]; 8:31; 10:9 [twice], 16, 17; Neh 1:1[Q]; 2:1; 8:2 [Eng. 7:73]; Esth 2:16; 3:7 [three times], 12, 13 [twice]; 8:9 [twice], 12 [twice]; 9:1 [twice], 15, 17, 19, 21). No simple numerical month designation (without חדשׁ) occurs in these later books. The designation by simple numerical reference is clearly attested in Arad ostracon 7 (ca. 600 BCE) and perhaps as early

---

[111] J. Kessler, "The Second Year of Darius and the Prophet Haggai", *Trans* 5 (1992): 63–84, esp. p. 69.

[112] On the question of the date of the redaction of these prophetic works, cf. *infra*, pp. 50–51. On the distinctions between Hag 1:1 and other prophetic superscriptions, cf. Floyd, "Narrative", pp. 473–77.

[113] Lemaire, "Datation en Palestine", pp. 65–66.

[114] Ibid., p. 66; idem, "Formules de datation", p. 365.

as 626 on one fiscal bulla,[115] in addition to the numerous references in Ezekiel (1:1; 8:1; 20:1; 29:1, 17; 30:20; 31:1; 45:18, 21, 25).[116] Thus while both systems of notation appear in earlier material, later texts prefer the systematic inclusion of חדש. This accords well with an earlier date for the formulae in Haggai, where חדש appears with the month in 1:1 but is absent in 1:15; 2:1, 10.[117] To this may be added the observation that the later books progressively abandon the simple numerical system of notation in favour of either a double notation, using Babylonian month names and numerical notices, or simply the Babylonian names (Ezra 6:15; Neh 1:1; 6:15; Zech 1:7; 7:1; Esth 2:16; 3:7, 13; 8:9, 12; 9:1, 15, 17, 21). An additional evidence of the priority of the date formulae in Haggai to those in Zechariah, Ezra, Nehemiah and Esther may be the total absence of such Babylonian months in Haggai.[118]

### 2.3.2.1.4. *The Date Formulae: Evaluation and Conclusions*

In light of the foregoing evidence, the most probable assumption is that the dates in Haggai were formulated at a point close to the time indicated by the dates themselves. By contrast, to assume, with Ackroyd and Coggins, that a redactor, about one hundred years after the fact, added a series of well-organized, but formally asymmetrical dates to a collection of oracles already in existence for some time leaves several questions unresolved. First, what would influence the choice of such dates by the redactor, and why would he date the oracles with such precision? If, as Ackroyd concedes,[119] they may come from traditional elements, why not assume that they were attached to the oracles at a previous stage?[120] Second, if, following Ackroyd's suggestion, the dates fulfill the specific function of demonstrating that the prophet's words came

---

[115] Lemaire, "Datation en Palestine", p. 66.

[116] Lemaire, "Formules de datation", p. 365.

[117] While it may be true that the term *yom* in Ezek 45:21, 25 may represent a later addition (cf. ibid., p. 365) the presence or absence of *yom* cannot assist us regarding the choice between an early or later dating of the formulae in Haggai. This is so because the use of *yom* is inconsistent in Haggai as well as in Ezra and Esther, as the following tabulation demonstrates: Haggai, present in 1:1, 15 and 2:18 but omitted in 2:1, 10 and 20; Ezra, present in 3:6; 10:16, 17 but absent in 10:9; Esther, present in 3:12; 9:1, 15, 17, 19, 21, but absent in 3:13; 8:9, 12.

[118] Lemaire, "Datation en Palestine", pp. 75–77; cf. J. Finegan, *Handbook of Biblical Chronology*, (Princeton: Princeton University Press, 1964), pp. 38–39.

[119] Ackroyd, "Two Problems", p. 22.

[120] As do Beuken, Petersen, and Meyers and Meyers.

from God, and as a result would prove true, why is the main fulfillment, that is, the completion of the temple's reconstruction and its subsequent rededication, not mentioned in the text of Haggai-Zechariah 1–8?[121]

Furthermore, the question of the time at which the date formulae were attached to the oracles must be considered in relation to more general issues related to the writing down and dating of prophecy, and the religious and theological context of the late sixth century. Even earlier than the Persian period, prophecy, both inside and outside Israel, was written down[122] and frequently dated, sometimes at a moment close to its utterance.[123] Millard evaluates a variety of ancient Near Eastern evidence and suggests that the writing down of a prophecy close to its proclamation served two primary functions. First a transcript of a prophecy could serve as a test of the authenticity of the prophet.[124] Second, prophecies could be incorporated into larger collections and serve as examples which could be consulted in other circumstances.[125] If the scribes of the period typically dated, even to the day, the most mundane of documents, it is probable that such a practice would be extended to the proclamation of a word from Yahweh. Such an event was considered, even in earlier periods, to be of supreme importance.[126] Accordingly divine statements were dated, albeit with less precision than in Haggai and Zechariah 1–8, in relation to significant political and social events (Amos 1:1; Isa 6:1; 7:1; Jer 1:2, 3; 28:1; 34:1–2). It would therefore seem unlikely that Haggai's oracles remained in an oral, undated, or

---

[121] Cf. Meyers and Meyers, xliii–xlv.

[122] On prophecy in the Mari and Neo-Assyrian texts, with an excellent bibliography, see A. Lemaire, "Traditions amorrites et Bible: le prophétisme", *RA* 93 (1999): 49–56, and more recently D. Charpin, "Prophètes et rois dans le Proche-Orient amorrite", in *Prophètes et rois: Bible et Proche Orient*", (LD; ed. A. Lemaire; Paris: Cerf, 2001), p. 21–53. Cf. also A. R. Millard, "La prophétie et l'écriture: Israël, Aram, Assyrie", *RHR* 202 (1985):125–44; H. M. Barstad, "No Prophets? Recent Developments in Biblical Prophetic Research and Ancient Near Eastern Prophecy", *JSOT* 57 (1993): 39–60; idem, "Lachish Ostracon III and Ancient Israelite Prophecy", in *A. Malamat Volume*, (ErIsr 24; ed. S. Aḥituv and B. A. Levine; Jerusalem: Israel Exploration Society, 1993), pp. 8*–12*, and A. Lemarie, "Prophètes et rois dans les inscriptions ouest-sémitiques (IXe–VIe siècle av. J.-C.)", in A. Lemaire, ed., *Prophètes et rois*, pp. 85–115.

[123] See especially Millard, "Prophétie et écriture", pp. 136–45.

[124] Ibid., pp. 126, 140–1.

[125] Ibid., p. 141. Millard concludes, "On the one hand, prophecies were written down and preserved until their fulfillment was clearly out of the question, or they were incorporated into other compilations, whether they had been fulfilled or not. On the other hand, prophecies were written down, preserved and disseminated through scribal tradition in such a way that their content lost its precise and specific historical rooting."

[126] Cf. Wolff, p. 20.

unedited state for a hundred years, especially in view of the generally recognized movement toward codification, consolidation and preservation of traditions which occurred during the postexilic period.[127] Rather when the oracles were written down, dates were attached to them to mark the highly significant event of the reception of a word from Yahweh as the community stood on the threshold of a new political and religious situation.[128]

We may conclude our discussion of dating formulae by affirming that the dates were in all likelihood formulated at a time close to the proclamation of the oracles. It therefore follows that these dates may provide us with significant chronological data relative to both the preaching of Haggai and the duration of the redactional process.

### 2.3.2.2. *Other Evidence for a Sixth-Century Redaction*

Two possibilities present themselves at this point. One could affirm that the dates and oracles are early, but that the redactional framework, which incorporated the existing dates, was added much later. If this is the case, we still have, in the oracles, a significant body of material in Haggai which relates to the late sixth century. However, if one can find further evidence for an early redaction of the book, these data, in addition to the date formulae, would enable the bulk of the text to be read in a late sixth-century context.

Five indices suggest that the redaction of the book took place toward the end of the sixth century. These have been widely noted in the critical literature and can be dealt with briefly.[129] First, the promise of Zerubbabel's future elevation in 2:20–23 is not attenuated. The

---

[127] Mason, "Prophets of the Restoration", p. 142.

[128] Wolff, (p. 20), notes, "The actual event which the Haggai-Chronicler has to report, and which dominates everything that follows is the *going forth of a word or oracle from Yahweh*. For a messenger of God to be seized by the word was a confronting event that again and again determined Israel's history." It would appear that Ackroyd has attenuated his position. He states ("Problems in the Handling", p. 42), "If [the dates] were obviously schematic, it would be natural to suppose them invented to provide a specific emphasis. But there are no clear indications of such deliberation; the dates themselves are sufficiently haphazard for a majority of scholars to accept them without question."

[129] The argument regarding the dyarchy present in the framework can be used for both an early and late date, and is therefore inconclusive. Mason ("Editorial Framework", p. 417) sees dyarchy as early, and the pre-eminence of the high priest as later. Sérandour sees full dyarchy as a later development, and dates the framework accordingly (Sérandour, "Réflexions", pp. 76–77).

oracle is transmitted without hesitation. This most probably indicates that, at the time of the book's redaction, the governor still held his office and that the redactor of Haggai considered the fulfillment of the promise to be still possible.[130] Second, there is no mention of the temple rededication ceremony in 515. As Meyers and Meyers under-line,[131] if the redaction had occurred after this very important event, it is likely that some allusion would be made to it.[132] Third, the redac-tor most probably knew only Darius I. His name suffices without any other detail.[133] Fourth, the theological themes of Haggai show affini-ties with the two main traditions of the exilic period: Deuteronomism and the priestly tradition.[134] Fifth, and perhaps most importantly, the dates constitute an integral element of the framework as a whole. They serve as the foundational structuring device for the book. They move the reader forward from the stalemate with which the book opens to the future hope with which it ends. If the dates were mere addenda to the oracles which the framework integrated, one would expect them to be more like appendices randomly scattered in the text. This how-ever is far from the case. It is more likely that they are of a piece with the redactional transformation of the words of Haggai into a prophetic *livret*.[135] The sum of these considerations appear sufficient to place the *terminus ad quem* of the main redaction of the book in 515 BCE.[136]

It is of course possible that certain additions to the text were made subsequent to this main redaction. Ackroyd sees the additional material in the LXX as evidence of this process.[137] Wolff considers 2:5aα, 2:17, the two last words of 2:18 ("consider your ways" and the mention of "the vine, the fig tree and the pomegranate" in 2:19aβ) to be later

---

[130] Mason, "Editorial Framework", p. 417; Chary, p. 12; Verhoef, p. 10. But cf. my comments on the assumed "transferability" of this promise to Zerubbabel's descen-dants, *infra*, p. 239.

[131] Meyers and Meyers, p. xliii–xlv.

[132] M. Prokurat calls into question the historical evidence advanced for this event, ("Haggai and Zechariah 1–8: A Form Critical Analysis", [Ph. D Thesis; Graduate Theological Union, Berkeley, California, 1988], p. 12, n. 25).

[133] Verhoef, p. 10.

[134] Cf. M. Weinfeld, *Deuteronomy and the Deuteronomic School*, (Oxford: Oxford University Press, 1972), Stuhlmueller, p. 17, and Mason, "Editorial Framework", pp. 416, 421.

[135] This issue will be taken up on the discussion of the form of the book in ch. 9, below. On this cf. also Floyd, "Narrative", p. 479.

[136] This position is also taken by Meyers and Meyers, Verhoef, Marti, Mitchell, Sellin and Deissler.

[137] Ackroyd, "Interpretive Glosses", pp. 164–66.

additions, but is hesitant to assign a particular redactional origin to them.[138] The possible presence of such small later additions, however, does not preclude the reading of Haggai as a late sixth century text.

I therefore conclude that both the "oracles" and the "redactional material" in Haggai most likely have their origins in a similar setting. If one were to assume that the oracles in the book represent a "verbatim" account of Haggai's preaching, then it would be methodologically appropriate to attempt to distinguish the voice of the prophet, speaking in the second year of Darius, from that of the redactor, writing some time afterwards. The difficulty with this approach is that, aside from the emphasis upon the community's leadership, there are few, if any, linguistic, syntactical, theological or ideological indications of discontinuity between the oracles and the framework as the two are defined by most scholars.[139] On the other hand, there are several indications that both framework and oracles move in the same theological and ideological world, and are tightly woven together. Several indices of *linguistic continuity* exist between the two sections. The epithet צבאות יהוה (Yahweh Sebaoth) is found in the oracles in 1:2, 5, 7; 2:7, 8, 9a, 9b, and 23 and in the framework in 1:14. The voice of Yahweh is heard in the framework (1:13b),[140] as well as in the oracles (1:2, 8; 2:7, 11). The temple is the house of Yahweh in both parts; oracles: 1:9; 2:3, 9; framework: 1:14. Dates occur in both sections; framework: 1:1, 15a; 2:1, 10, 20; and in the oracles in 2:18.[141] Further, the order of elements of the date in 2:18 (day-month) is identical to 1:15a and 2:10. Both sections refer to Haggai in the third person: oracles, 2:13;[142] framework, 1:1, 3, 12, 13.

---

[138] Wolff, p. 18.

[139] Indeed, the differences in vocabulary between the two sections are largely due to the fact that the framework primarily consists of dates, names, and formulae concerning the reception of the prophetic word, whereas the oracles contain many of the more traditional forms of prophetic speech, such as the oracles of judgment, salvation and reproach. Sérandour, ("Récits", pp. 13–19) by contrast, working from his assumptions regarding the theological perspective of the redactor, assigns *all* of 2:1–9 and 20–23 to the framework.

[140] Tollington (*Tradition* p. 23) excludes this verse from the framework. Wolff (p. 18) assigns it to the earlier redaction of Haggai's speech into *Auftrittsskizzen*. Similarly, Ackroyd ("Studies", pp. 166–68) regards all of v. 13 as part of an earlier redaction, and integral to the oracles. In my opinion Ackroyd and Wolff are clearly right. To excise v. 13b from the framework simply because it is first person speech is to accept *a priori* that no such speech could appear in the framework.

[141] Tollington (*Tradition*, p. 23) sees the date as secondary. I discuss its integrity in my textual criticism *infra*.

[142] Tollington (*Tradition*, p. 20, n. 4) accepts the third person reference here as part of

Even more striking, however, are the *theological similarities* between
the two sections. Both oracles and framework display Deuteronomistic
and priestly affinities. In the framework, we note the presence of the
following expressions, commonly recognized as Deuteronomistic:[143] שמע
בקול יהוה (to obey Yahweh),[144] Hag 1:12a; ירא יהוה (to fear Yahweh),[145]
Hag 1:12b; היה דבר יהוה ביד[146] (the word of Yahweh came through
PN) Hag 1:1, 3. Regarding the declaration of the word of Yahweh to
the leaders of the community (Hag 1:1; 2:1, 20 etc.), Mason observes
that in the book of Kings, every time the expression ביד is found, a
king is addressed.[147] Deuteronomistic vocabulary characterizes also the
oracles. The maledictions of Deut 28:38 are echoed in Hag 1:6a. The
vocabulary and thought of Deut 28:23 are paralleled in Hag 1:11. Hag
1:11 and Deut 28:51 contain similar descriptions of the devastation of
the land. The barrenness in Hag 1:11 echoes Deut 28:18. "The work
of your hands" (Hag 1:11) parallels Deut 28:20. Other Deuteronomistic
themes concern the election of Jerusalem and its temple (Hag 2:6–9),[148]
the exhortation to strength and courage (Hag 2:4),[149] the verb בחר[150]
(Hag 2: 23, to choose, elect; especially concerning the election of the
house of David) and the exhortation not to fear (Hag 2:5b).[151]

The presence of priestly traditions is also manifested in the two parts.
In the framework these include: (1) ביד as a term that indicates the
intermediary by which the word of Yahweh is transmitted (Hag 1:1,
cf. Exod 9:35; Lev 8:36; Num 4:37; 9:23; 10:13). The intermediary *par
excellence* in the priestly tradition is Moses. (2) The notion of the stirring up of the spirit of certain individuals that is found in Hag 1:12 and
Ezek 36:27. (3) The term מלאכה in Hag 1:14 that refers to the reconstruction of the temple is used in a similar fashion in Exod 35:29 and

the oracles.
    [143] For our general purposes here cf. the lists provided by Weinfeld, *Deuteronomy*,
appendix AA and S. R. Driver, *Deuteronomy*, (ICC; New York: Charles Scribners' Sons,
1916), pp. lxxxii–lxxxiv.
    [144] Weinfeld, *Deuteronomy*, p. 337.
    [145] Ibid., p. 365. On the distinctive formulation of this expression in Hag 1: 12b, cf.
the exegesis *infra*.
    [146] Mason, "Editorial Framework", p. 415–16.
    [147] Ibid., p. 417.
    [148] Weinfeld, *Deuteronomy*, p. 324–25.
    [149] Ibid., p. 343. Tollington (*Tradition*, pp. 22–23) assigns the reference to Joshua to the
framework, but the rest of the verse to the oracles.
    [150] Weinfeld, *Deuteronomy*, pp. 327, 354.
    [151] Ibid., p. 344.

36:2.[152] (4) The notion of the temple as the place where Yahweh dwells in his glory is identifiable both in Hag 1:8, and Ezek 37:27.[153] Priestly traditions can also be seen in the oracles. Haggai 2:10–14 manifests a concern regarding questions of purity.[154] Furthermore, Haggai's preoccupation with the rebuilding of the temple (1:2–11) cannot be abstracted from the cult which that building housed.

Floyd convincingly argues that in addition to these areas of continuity *syntactical and literary* considerations favour the unity of oracles and redaction. He notes that, in contrast to other prophetic superscriptions, the introductory formulae in Haggai are integrated into the material which follows, and form complete sentences.[155] Second, he observes that from a form-critical and literary perspective, the book's portrayal of Haggai oscillates between "the conventions of narrative report and prophetic speech" and blends the outlook of prophet and narrator.[156] He concludes that the result is "a particular kind of story in which the prophetic revelation of messages constitutes the main narrative action."[157]

In conclusion, then, the oracles and framework share a good deal of common ground. It may be appropriate to say that the insistence on the importance of the community's leaders may constitute one area in the present text that was especially significant to the narrator.[158] However, given the broader areas of continuity between oracles and framework, it is more judicious to presuppose that, whatever the original focus of the oracles may have been, they have now been redactionally integrated into the final form of the text in such a way that they are full participants in the overall redactional form, structure and purpose of the book. Thus the book ought to be read as "an integral whole"[159] which

---

[152] Mason, "Editorial Framework", p. 419.

[153] Ibid.

[154] Meyers and Meyers, p. 71.

[155] Floyd, "Narrative", pp. 474–77.

[156] Ibid., pp. 478–79.

[157] Ibid., p. 479.

[158] I am unconvinced by Mason's assertion that the oracles were proclaimed by a "thorough-going eschatological prophet" (Mason, "Editorial Framework", p. 420), whose words the framework sought to theocratize. As the exegesis will show, not all the oracular material is eschatological. What is more, eschatological thought cannot be excluded from the framework, as Mason himself notes (ibid., p. 421).

[159] Floyd, p. 259. He also maintains that there is a constant fluctuation between the perspective of the prophet and that of the narrator (p. 260). He attributes this blurring to the narrator's close identification with the prophet, and the notion that the narrator sought to apply the insights gained from the study of the prophet, to

presents a reasonably coherent perspective upon the issues it discusses. In stating this, however, I do not wish to imply that the narrator had no source material at hand, nor that the form and content of the oracles in the book are redactional creations and bear little or no resemblance to the preaching of Haggai. I also do not wish to imply that it is entirely improper to discuss potential indications of particular emphases in the words attributed to Haggai in the text, versus the perspectives found in those not attributed to him. I am affirming that the evidences of over-all continuity in the present text render it an unstable platform from which to launch a "quest for the historical Haggai." The most viable working hypothesis, I would maintain, is one which views the book as a holistic redactional presentation of Haggai's words and their effects which stands in general continuity with the words of the prophet himself, notwithstanding potential differences in emphasis, scope of application, and the presence of redactional reshaping.[160]

These conclusions regarding the redactional history of Haggai stand in some tension with one recent trend in biblical scholarship which treats Haggai as if it were of a piece with Zechariah 1–8.[161] Meyers and Meyers declare Haggai-Zechariah 1–8 to be a "composite work" or a "single compendious work."[162] This assertion, however, ignores the very real differences between the two books. Of special note are features such as the absence of Babylonian month names in the date formulae in Haggai and their presence in Zechariah 1–8, the insistence on the specific date of the "foundation ceremony" in Haggai and the lack of such emphasis in Zechariah 1–8,[163] the use of the term פחה (governor) in Haggai and its absence in Zechariah, as well as the absence of any reference to visionary experience or angelic interpretation in Haggai.[164] Furthermore, all of the indices proposed by Meyers and Meyers to prove that Haggai-Zechariah 1–8 constitute a single unified piece

---

the narrator's own day. Floyd's perspective here closes mirrors my own approach, developed independently, and applied in the exegesis below.

[160] Cf. Floyd's similar conclusions, "Narrative", pp. 483–87.

[161] In a recent paper presented at the annual meeting of the Society of Biblical Literature in Nashville, TN, one presenter compared Ezekiel to "Haggai-Zechariah" (S. S. Tuell, "Haggai-Zechariah: Prophecy after the Manner of Ezekiel", [paper presented at the annual meeting of AAR/SBL, Nashville, TN, 19 November 2000]. The hyphen is quite telling.

[162] Meyers and Meyers, p. xliv.

[163] Observed by Sérandour, "Réflexions", p. 79.

[164] The use of מלאך in Hag 1:13 is quite different from the *angelus interpres* in Zechariah. See the exegesis *infra*.

could equally be cited to demonstrate that Zechariah 1–8 was written to complement the text of Haggai which was *already in existence*. To be sure, both books contain date formulae, but, as we have seen, this is not surprising in light of the scribal practices of the period. Furthermore, since Zech 1:1 contains a date earlier than the last date in Haggai, it is not surprising that the two books share certain similarities. However there are no substantial reasons for reading them as a single, continuous composition, and several factors which would favour the reading of Haggai as a discrete unit.[165] None of the arguments presented by Meyers and Meyers convincingly demonstrate that the form and substance of Haggai ought to be read as a work whose configuration extends to Zechariah 1–8, and which, without the inclusion the latter text, would form an incomplete work.[166]

In sum, the preceding argument has sought to demonstrate that the book of Haggai may be read as a document produced between 520 and 515 BCE, which may legitimately be read as an literary unit, reflecting a generally unified perspective.

---

[165] Not the least of these is Haggai's transmission as a separate book. Haggai's literary independence will become evident as the content and structure of the book is analyzed.

[166] For example, Meyers and Meyers assert that the date formulae at Hag 1:1 and Zech 7:1 form a chiastic structure, however the fact that the latter date uses year-day-month whereas the former has year-month-day weakens this assertion. Furthermore not all of the illustrations of the 7+1 pattern they cite need necessarily indicate literary volition (for example, seven dates in the second year of Darius and one in the fourth). The fact that the two references to II Dar 24/9 are found at the centre of the date formulae in the two books could equally indicate that the editor of Zech 1–8 organized the dates in that book to create a redactional unity between it and the earlier book of Haggai.

# CHAPTER THREE

# PERSIAN RULE AND YEHUD, 539–515:
## CRITICAL ISSUES

### 3.1. INTRODUCTION

We have thus far argued that the content and redactional composition of the book of Haggai may be situated against the backdrop of the early years of Darius I, prior to the rededication of the temple in 515.[1] In this section I will seek to address several preliminary historical problems relating to this period. However, to avoid reasoning in a circle, I have chosen to deal only with those problems whose solution is not primarily dependent upon the analysis of the text of Haggai, but which add significant data to the reading of the book. Recent publications on the history of the Persian Empire, and Palestine and Yehud in the Persian period, provide great assistance in the resolution of many of these debated questions. Many of these issues are discussed in the commentaries and surveys of Persian-period Palestine and it is not my purpose to restate widely held positions here. However at times on the basis of an abbreviated discussion, certain questions are too hastily declared resolved or irresolvable, and insufficient attention is paid to the richness of the analysis in the scholarly literature.[2] As a result I shall attempt to provide a survey of the historical issues most germane to the reading of Haggai, and, where applicable, interact with literature which is sometimes passed over.

---

[1] Cf. L. Dequecker ("Darius the Persian and the Reconstruction of the Jewish Temple in Jerusalem [Ezra 4, 24]", in *Ritual and Sacrifice in the Ancient Near East*, [OLA 55; ed. J. Quaegebur; Leuven: Uitgeverij Peeters en Departement Oriëntalistiek, 1993], p. 67–92) who situates the rebuilding of the temple in the reign of Darius II. Dequecker's position has few adherents in modern scholarship, and an analysis of his position is beyond the scope of this study.

[2] See for example, B. Schram (*Opponents of Third Isaiah*, p. 69) who, on the basis of a very brief discussion, declares that the demographic situation in Yehud during the Babylonian period cannot be determined, nor can the status of Yehud prior to Nehemiah be resolved.

## 3.2. THE "DECREE OF CYRUS" AND
## THE NATURE OF THE EARLY RESTORATION

The most common starting point taken for the study of the Persian Period in Yehud is the so-called "Decree of Cyrus," found in Hebrew in Ezra 1:2–4 and 2 Chr 36:22–23, and in Aramaic in Ezra 6:3–5. Generally speaking, the Aramaic version has been considered as more historically reliable, whereas the Hebrew texts are viewed as being primarily a literary production reflecting theological concerns.[3] A significant body of literature, however, affirms that both versions have independent goals and are both authentic to a certain degree. According to Bickerman,[4] an oral proclamation was written down by a Hebrew scribe. Schultz,[5] Clines,[6] Ackroyd,[7] and de Vaux,[8] among others, consider both versions as having independent origins and goals. Williamson suggests that the Hebrew version reflects an independent literary source used by the author of Ezra 1–6.[9]

The general consensus regarding the goals of the two passages is that the Hebrew text is a call to return,[10] or an authorization to return,[11] whereas the Aramaic text is primarily an economic document.[12] The critical question for our purposes here regards the historical use which can be made of these texts. Briend and Williamson have well demon-

---

[3] See, recently, J. Briend, "L'édit de Cyrus et sa valeur historique", *Trans* 11 (1996): 33–44. Cf. also J. Blenkinsopp, *Ezra-Nehemiah: A Commentary*, (OTL; Philadelphia: Westminster, 1988), p. 42.

[4] E. J. Bickerman, "The Edict of Cyrus in Ezra 1", *JBL* 65 (1946): 249–75.

[5] C. Schultz, "The Political Tensions Reflected in Ezra-Nehemiah", in *Scripture in Context: Essays in the Comparative Method*, (ed. W. W. Hallo; Pittsburgh: Pickwick, 1980), p. 226.

[6] D. J. A. Clines, *Ezra, Nehemiah, Esther*, (NCBC; London: Marshall, Morgan and Scott, 1984), pp. 36–38.

[7] P. R. Ackroyd, "The Jewish Community in Palestine in the Persian Period", in *CHJ*, p. 138; idem, *Israel Under Babylon and Persia*, (London: Oxford University Press, 1970), p. 203.

[8] R. de Vaux, "Les décrets de Cyrus et de Darius sur la reconstruction du temple", *RB* 46 (1937): 29–57.

[9] Williamson, *Ezra*, pp. 6–19. Williamson suggests (pp. 6–7) that the typically Jewish elements in the decree could reflect the fact that a localized announcement for the leaders of the Jewish community was expanded into a more universal proclamation. Alternatively, the decree has been subjected to a theological reworking.

[10] Schultz, "Political Tensions", pp. 226–27; Ackroyd, "Community in Palestine", p. 138; Weinberg, "Demographische Notizen", p. 51.

[11] Williamson, *Ezra*, p. 14.

[12] Clines, *Ezra-Nehemiah*, p. 36.

strated the literary and theological shaping at work in Ezra 1:1–6.[13]
Williamson rightly points out that the notion of a call or permission
to return is unique to 1:1–6 and absent from 6:3–5.[14] Furthermore,
as Kuhrt has argued, the analogy of the "Cyrus Cylinder" cannot be
unduly pressed, and does not in itself provide independent testimony
of widespread repatriation of exiles under Cyrus.[15] Williamson appropriately concludes, "we must primarily rely on the biblical evidence for
any historical reconstruction and admit only that the Cyrus Cylinder
is compatible with a positive evaluation of this evidence."[16] Analogical
evidence, specifically the case of the Neirab community, is frequently
cited as an example of an ethnic minority which returned to its place of
origin in the early Persian period.[17] The cuneiform tablet recently published by Joannès and Lemaire demonstrates the existence of a community of Judaeans in Babylon in 498 BCE.[18]

If, as seems probable, Ezra 6:3–5 records an authentic authorization
for the rebuilding of the temple, including its financial details, it would
be altogether natural for the Judahite community in the heartland of
the empire to be permitted to participate in the project. This would be
especially so if this community included some of the former ruling élite
and religious leaders.[19] Thus a decree containing permission to return,

---

[13] Briend, "L'édit", *passim*; Williamson, *Ezra*, pp. 6–16; idem, *Ezra and Nehemiah*, (OTG; Sheffield: JSOT Press, 1987), pp. 33–34.

[14] Williamson, *Ezra*, pp. 13–14. As Williamson notes, the passage in the Cyrus Cylinder which reads "I (also) gathered all their (former) inhabitants and returned (them) to their habitations" refers to towns near Babylon, not a more generalized policy.

[15] A. Kuhrt, "The Cyrus Cylinder and Achaemenid Imperial Policy", *JSOT* 25 (1983): 83–97, esp. pp. 93–95.

[16] Williamson, *Ezra*, p. 14.

[17] K. G. Hoglund, *Achaemenid Imperial Administration in Syria-Palestine and the Missions of Ezra and Nehemiah*, (SBLDS 125; Atlanta: Scholars, 1992), p. 27; I. Eph'al, "The Western Minorities in Babylonia in the 6th-5th Centuries B. C.", *Orientalia* 47 (1978): 74–80. Briant (*Histoire*, 1:913), however, urges caution, and alludes to significant historical and chronological problems posed by these texts.

[18] F. Joannès and A. Lemaire, "Trois tablettes cunéiformes à onomastique ouest-sémitique (collection Sh. Moussaïeff)", *Trans* 17 (1999): 17–34. Cf. Eph'al, "Minorities" and B. Oded, "Observations on the Israelite/Judaean Exiles in Mesopotamia during the Eight-Sixth Centuries BCE", in *Immigration and Emigration within the Ancient Near East: Festschrift E. Lipiński*, (ed. K. van Lerberghe and A. Schoors; Leuven: Uitgeverij Peeters en Department Oriëntalistiek, 1995), pp. 205–12; E. J. Bickerman, "The Diaspora: The Babylonian Captivity", in *CHJ*, pp. 342–57.

[19] On the composition of the exilic community see, for example, Oded, "Judaean Exiles", *passim*.

if such was even required,[20] may have been implicit in the declaration in Ezra 6.[21] If such an official, general declaration of permission was given, despite its clear differences from official Persian documents, Ezra 1:1–6 may preserve some echoes of it.[22] Furthermore, Ezra 1–3 need not imply a single mass return possible only with a special authorization, similar to the journeys of Ezra (Ezra 8) and Nehemiah (Neh 2). Thus groups of returnees moving over a longer period of time may be envisaged. The period between Cyrus' accession and the beginning of Cambyses' Egyptian campaign could have seen some progressive installation.[23]

The issue of the size of the population in Yehud in 538–520 and the number of returnees will be taken up in the demographic analysis later in this chapter. The sources that describe the early return provide few specific details. The list in Ezra 2 is most likely composite, reflecting

---

[20] J. Liver ("The Return from Babylon, its Time and Scope", *B. Mazar Volume*, [ErIsr 5; ed. M. Avi-Yonah et. al.; Jerusalem: Israel Exploration Society, 1958], p. 90*) maintains that no special authorization was required. W. S. McCullough, (*The History and Literature of the Palestinian Jews from Cyrus to Herod 550 B.C. to 4 B.C.*, [Toronto: University of Toronto Press, 1975], pp. 24–25) posits travel with few restrictions. On the broader issues involved, cf. P. Garelli, "Les déplacements de personnes dans l'empire assyrien", in *Immigration and Emigration within the Ancient Near East*, (cf. prev. note) pp. 79–82 and H. Limet, "L'émigré dans la société mésopotamienne", in *Immigration and Emigration in the Ancient Near East*, pp. 165–79. It is important to distinguish (1) an official imperial decree from specific official travel documents and (2) the documents required by official travelers, and the more general movement of individuals for personal reasons. On these last points see D. F. Graf, "The Persian Royal Road System in Syria-Palestine", *Trans* 6 (1993): 149–67, esp. p. 150. Briant (*Histoire*, 1:377) discusses the documents required of official travelers, and the provisions allotted to them. He entertains the possibility, however, of an ongoing parallel commercial use of the road system between Babylon and Syria-Palestine (*Histoire*, 1:390–91; 395–96). It is significant to note that such commercial relations were in existence prior to Cyrus' conquest (ibid., 1:396). It would appear to be most likely that in many cases those desirous of returning to Yehud would have had to make use of their own resources as did commercial travelers. It is also highly important to take into account the fact that the actual application of Persian rule in the west came about progressively (on this see F. Bianchi, *I superstiti della deportazione sono là nella provincia (Neemia 1,3). Ricerche storico-bibliche sulla Giudea in età neobabilonese e achemenide (586 a.C.–442 a. C.)*, [AIONSup 82, 55/1; Napoli: Instituto Universitario Orientale, 1995], p. 17, with bibliography). Future references to this work will use the short form "*I superstiti-2*" to differentiate it from Bianchi's 1993 monograph. Cf. also Ackroyd, *Exile and Restoration*, p. 141, and Briant, *Histoire*, 1:59. It is, therefore, uncertain whether later travel restrictions were in force in the earliest period of Persian rule.

[21] Ackroyd (*Exile and Restoration*, p. 143, n. 21) comments perceptively, "the permission to restore must imply some measure of permission to return."

[22] Williamson, *Ezra*, p. 14; Liver, "The Return", p. 90*.

[23] Williamson, *Ezra*, p. 31.

immigration to Palestine over a longer period.[24] This being the case, it is most judicious to follow those scholars who see the earliest return as being quite limited in scope.[25]

Significant questions and problems arise when one seeks to sort out the personalities involved in the return and their relative chronology. The problem is made more complex by the fact that Ezra 1–3 appears to situate the activities of both Sheshbazzar and Zerubbabel in the reign of Cyrus, while Ezra 5 places the activity of Sheshbazzar during the reign of Cyrus, and that of Zerubbabel in the reign of Darius, some eighteen years later. Haggai and Zechariah also place the activity of Zerubbabel in the latter period. It is to these issues that we now turn.

## 3.3. SHESHBAZZAR

Several questions are raised concerning this individual, whose name is mentioned in Ezra 1:8, 11; and 5:14, 16. The question of Sheshbazzar's ethnic origin can be resolved with certain degree of reliability. H. W. Kosters[26] and A. C. Welch[27] saw him as a non-Jew. However this position has few adherents in modern criticism. The fact that biblical tradition unanimously assigns him a role in the return of the sacred temple vessels speaks in favour of his Jewish origins.[28] A second question concerns his identification with Shenazzar, who is mentioned in 1 Chr 3:18. This possibility, suggested by E. Meyer in 1896[29] is followed by several modern authors, including Albright,[30] Bickerman,[31] Bright,[32] Clines,[33] and Cross.[34] The main argument in favour of such an identification is the designation of Sheshbazzar as "prince of Judah" in Ezra

---

[24] See *infra*, p. 95, n. 246.

[25] So, for example, Beyse, *Serubbabel*, pp. 19, 23, and Williamson, *Ezra*, p. 14.

[26] H. W. Kosters, *Die Wiederstellung Israels in der persischen Period*, (Heidelberg: Hurning, 1885), pp. 28–29.

[27] A. C. Welch, *Post-Exilic Judaism*, (Edinburgh and London: Blackwood, 1935), p. 98.

[28] S. Japhet, "Sheshbazzar and Zerubbabel: Against the Background of the Historical and Religious Tendencies of Ezra-Nehemiah", *ZAW* 94 (1982): 96.

[29] E. Meyer, *Die Entstehung des Judentums: Eine historische Untersuchung*, (Halle: Niemeyer, 1896), pp. 41–46.

[30] W. F. Albright, "The Date and Personality of the Chronicler", *JBL* 40 (1921): 104–24; idem, *The Biblical Period from Abraham to Ezra*, (New York and Evanston: Harper and Row, 1963), p. 86.

[31] Bickerman, "The Diaspora", p. 356.

[32] Bright, *History of Israel*, p. 362.

[33] Clines, *Ezra-Nehemiah*, p. 41.

[34] F. M. Cross, "Reconstruction of the Judean Restoration", *JBL* 94 (1975): 12, n. 43.

1:8. Given that Shenazzar is member of the Judaean royal family (1 Chr 3:18), should the two names not be seen as referring to the same individual? It is also noted that the Persians customarily appointed to the position of governor members of the former royal family.[35] Japhet adds a third argument, maintaining that the books of Ezra and Nehemiah tend to minimize eschatological expectations (a tendency manifested in the work's concealment of Zerubbabel's Davidic origins). Thus, the absence of Sheshbazzar's genealogy argues in favour of his Davidic lineage.[36] In spite of the widespread acceptance of this position, the identification of the two has been strongly contested for two reasons.[37] First, it is unlikely that a Jew would bear two different Babylonian names.[38] Second, it has been convincingly argued that the two names could not be variations of the same original.[39] Thus the best approach is to view these two figures as separate individuals.[40]

A third consideration relative to Sheshbazzar concerns the hypothesis that he is one and the same person as Zerubbabel. This possibility appears in 1 Esd 6:18.[41] More recent exegetes who adopt this position include H. Ewald, H. E. Ryle, J. Gabriel, M. B. Pelaia,[42] and A. Bartal.[43] Two main objections have been raised against this identification. First, it would be unlikely for a Jew have two Babylonian names when there is no mention of his Hebrew name.[44] Second, it would appear that in Ezra 5:14–16 Sheshbazzar is differentiated from Zerubbabel.

---

[35] Dandamaev, *Institutions*, p. 97.

[36] Japhet, "Sheshbazzar and Zerubbabel", p. 95.

[37] Ackroyd, "Community in Palestine", p. 138.

[38] Williamson, *Ezra*, p. 17; A. Demsky, "Double Names in the Exile and the Identity of Sheshbazzar", in *These are the Names*, (Studies in Jewish Onomastics 2; ed. A. Demsky; Ramat Gan: Bar Ilan University Press, 1999), pp. 23–39.

[39] Demsky, "Double Names", pp. 36–37; P. R. Berger, "Zu den Namen ששבצר und שנאאצר", *ZAW* 83 (1971): 98–100; P.-E. Dion, "ששבצר and סמנורי", *ZAW* 95 (1983): 111–12.

[40] So, for example, Ackroyd, "Community in Palestine", p. 138, and Williamson, *Ezra*, p. 17.

[41] The data in Josephus *Ant.* 11. 1. 5 is disputed.

[42] Cited by Clines, *Ezra-Nehemiah*, p. 41. M. Saebø ("The Relation of Sheshbazzar and Zerubbabel—Reconsidered", *SEA* 54 (1989): 173, n. 17) calls this harmonization the "traditional position."

[43] A Bartal, "Once Again—Who Was Sheshbazzar?" *Beit Miqra* 79 (1979): 357–69, cited in Demsky, "Double Names", p. 36, n. 28.

[44] However, it is possible to assume that Zerubbabel is composed of the Hebrew roots זרע and בבל. For an evaluation of this possibility see Demsky, "Double Names", p. 29.

Two recent studies have sought to deal with these objections. J. Lust,[45] following A. van Hoonacker, maintains that some Jews did indeed have two Babylonian names. He furthermore suggests that Zerubbabel may in fact be a Hebrew name. More importantly, he proposes the hypothesis that Zerubbabel may have been a popular name while Sheshbazzar was a more formal or legal name.[46] M. Saebø carries Lust's argument one step further by seeking to provide an explanation for why the name Zerubbabel, rather than Sheshbazzar, became predominant. He asserts that this was due to the similarity between the meaning of Zerubbabel (offspring of Babylon)[47] and the messianic associations attached to the term "branch" or "offspring" in Jer 23:5; 33:15; Zech 8:2 and 6:12.[48]

Despite these two recent rebuttals, certain problems still persist with the identification of Zerubbabel and Sheshbazzar. Ezra 5:14 does appear to distinguish them.[49] Moreover, a double Babylonian name is indeed exceptional given the function of double names used by Jews in "bicultural" contexts.[50] What is more, if, as seems possible in the light of onomastic data from Arad, Zemah is to be read as a Hebrew name (as opposed to a symbolic designation),[51] then Zemah/Zerubbabel (rather than Zerubbabel/Sheshbazzar)[52] would constitute the pair of names for

---

[45] J. Lust, "The Identification of Zerubbabel with Sheshbassar", *ETL* 63 (1987): 90–95.

[46] Ibid., pp. 90–91.

[47] Saebø, "Sheshbazzar", pp. 176.

[48] Ibid., pp. 175–77. Saebø, however, rejects the hypothesis of a Hebrew origin for the name in question.

[49] This despite Lust, "Identification", p. 91. The text does appear to create some distance between the original decree and subsequent activities. Petit notes the difference in the nature of the financing of the activities of the two figures. Sheshbazzar is given assistance through personal gifts and direct imperial support. Zerubbabel's financial needs were met through the provincial taxation system, a system which was not functional in the earlier period (T. Petit, *Satrapes et satrapies dans l'empire achéménide de Cyrus le Grand à Xerxes Ier*, [Bibliothèque de la Faculté de Philosophie et Lettres de l'Université de Liège 254; Paris: Les Belles Lettres, 1990], p. 65).

[50] So Demsky, "Double Names", p. 36. The function of double name is to permit the individual in question to balance his or her identity as a member of an ethnic minority, with a desire to integrate into the broader society (cf. Demsky, "Double Names", pp. 26–28 and Lemaire, "Zorobabel", p. 51). Furthermore the analogy of Esther/Hadassah to Zerubbabel/Sheshbazzar cited by Lust is not without problems, notably regarding the origin of the name Hadassah (Demsky, "Double Names", p. 28, cf. Lust, "Identification", p. 90).

[51] Lemaire, "Zorobabel", pp. 49–52.

[52] Lemaire, "Zorobabel", pp. 49–52. One of the strengths of Lemaire's argument is that it takes into account the basis on which name pairs are chosen (pp. 51–52; cf. Demsky, "Double Names", pp. 33–34). Demsky (ibid., p. 29) seems to support Lemaire's

that individual. Saebø argues that Zerubbabel become more popular than Sheshbazzar because of its messianic overtones.[53] However it is far more likely that this function would have been fulfilled by the name Zemah, if indeed Zerubbabel/Zemah formed the double name. From a different perspective, Demsky has suggested that if Sheshbazzar had a second name, it was likely Shealtiel, the father (or uncle) of Zerubbabel.[54]

A further problem for the hypothesis of Sheshbazzar/Zerubbabel as a double name is the absence of any explanatory gloss in Ezra indicating that the two names refer to the same person. Such an absence is surprising in the light of such explanations elsewhere (cf. Esth 2:7 and Dan 1:7). What is more, if the composition of Ezra 1–6 took place at period significantly later than the events it recounts,[55] such an explicit identification would be a most natural way of relieving the tension created by the text in its present form. Furthermore, Saebø does not explain (1) what made Sheshbazzar a "formal" name as opposed to Zerubbabel, and (2) why the name Sheshbazzar is completely absent in all other sources. In the light of these considerations, it seems difficult to resolve the Sheshbazzar/Zerubbabel question on the basis of a double name.

In reality, the identification of the two leaders is sometimes a way of reconciling the fact that the laying of the temple's foundations is attributed to both Zerubbabel and to Sheshbazzar, and that in Ezra 2–3 both individuals appear to have been active in the early return. The reference to both individuals having laid the foundations of the temple is open to other explanations.[56] Furthermore, literary concerns in Ezra 1–6 may have contributed to the close identification between the two.[57] Williamson's suggestion that the compiler of Ezra 1–6 would

---

position, but he does not make reference to the article in question. This identification is vigourously challenged by W. H. Rose, *Zemah and Zerubbabel: Messianic Expectations in the Early Postexilic Period*, (JSOTSup 304; Sheffield: Sheffield Academic Press, 2000).

[53] Cf. Saebø, "Sheshbazzar", p. 176.

[54] Demsky, "Double Names", pp. 37–39. Demsky's suggestion seems to me to have significant merit, despite the fact that, as he admits, its strongest arguments are the similarity of the two names and the explanation which it provides for the question of the lineage of Zerubbabel.

[55] H. G. M. Williamson, "The Composition of Ezra i–vi", *JTS* ns 34 (1983): 1–30.

[56] Cf. F. I. Andersen, "Who Built the Second Temple?", *ABR* 6 (1958): 1–35. and A. Gelston, "The Foundations of the Second Temple", *VT* 16 (1966): 232–35.

[57] Williamson, *Ezra*, pp. 44–45 and Japhet, "Sheshbazzar and Zerubbabel", p. 94. Given that the only source which identifies both Zerubbabel and Sheshbazzar as being

have assumed Zerubbabel to have been present along side Sheshbazzar, on the basis of the list from Neh 7 which he used for his composition, may provide some explanation for both the close proximity as well as the differentiation of the two characters.[58] What is clear is that the bulk of the biblical traditions regarding Zerubbabel place his primary activities in the early part of Darius' reign, while Sheshbazzar's activity is limited to the reign of Cyrus.

There is significant debate as to whether or not Sheshbazzar was a member of the Judaean royal family, or simply a high official. Williamson dismisses the possibility that Sheshbazzar was of royal lineage by citing the absence of his name in the royal genealogy of 1 Chr 3 and the unlikelihood of the identification between Sheshbazzar and Shenazzar (1 Chr 3:18).[59] Japhet considers Sheshbazzar's Davidic lineage to be quite probable, but calls the evidence indecisive. Perhaps the strongest argument for Sheshbazzar's Davidic lineage is the Persian "dynastic model" whereby members of earlier ruling houses were appointed to or maintained in positions of leadership in the petty kingdoms and states which were subject to them.[60] There is significant evidence from Sogdiana, Bactriana, Phoenicia, Cyprus, Cilicia, and Egypt[61] to demonstrate the extent to which the Persians employed this dynastic model. This being the case it is likely that Sheshbazzar was a Davidide, and that the term "prince of Judah" implies royal descent and local political authority.[62] Demsky argues, on the basis of Ezek 37:22–25, that the term designates the Davidic scion.[63] He counters Williamson's appeal to the absence of Sheshbazzar's name in the royal list of 1 Chr 3 by maintaining that Sheshbazzar and Shealtiel were one and the same.[64]

---

active in the reign of Cyrus is Ezra 1–6, it is perhaps equally possible that the author of Ezra 1–6 was in possession of traditions which revered the role of Sheshbazzar in the early restoration.

[58] Williamson, *Ezra*, p. 45.

[59] Ibid., p. 17.

[60] P. Briant, "Contrainte militaire, dépendance rurale et exploitation des térritoires en Asie achéménide", in P. Briant, *Rois, tributs et paysans. Etudes sur les formations tributaires du Moyen-Orient ancien*, (Centre de Recherche d'Histoire Ancienne 43; Paris: Les Belles Lettres, 1982), pp. 199–225, and F. Bianchi, "Le rôle de Zorobabel et la dynastie davidique en Judée du VIe siècle au IIe siècle av. J.-C." *Trans* 7 (1994): 153–65.

[61] For bibliography see Lemaire, "Zorobabel", pp. 53–54 and F. Bianchi, "Rôle de Zorobabel", pp. 156–57.

[62] This understanding of the phrase is compatible with both the understanding of Judah as designating the territory (so Japhet) as well as the tribe (so Williamson).

[63] Demsky, "Double Names", p. 35.

[64] Ibid., pp. 37–39.

Ezra 5:14 designates Sheshbazzar as the "governor" (Aramaic, פחה) of Yehud. The sense of this term with reference to Sheshbazzar has been taken to mean either (1) political subordinate to the governor of Samaria,[65] (2) descendent of Jehoiachin, and therefore the legitimate "king" of Judaea which still continued to exist as a vassal-kingdom within the Babylonian Empire (and did not come effectively under Persian rule until Cambyses),[66] or (3) the Persian appointed governor of the province of Yehud.[67] Arguments for the third position, which appears to me to be most likely, will be presented *infra*. As noted above, Ezra 1:8 calls Sheshbazzar the "prince of Judah" (הנשיא ליהודה). The political import of the term "prince of Judah" is difficult to determine. Japhet sees it as a unique Hebrew equivalent for the Aramaic פחה.[68] She suggests that the point of departure for the discussion of the phrase must be the term "Judah" and not "prince,"[69] and that, generally in the post-exilic period, "Judah" designates the Persian province of that name.[70] Thus the phrase would simply mean "governor of Yehud." A second series of approaches views the term נשיא as implying more than simple governorship. L. Rost has maintained that the intent is to identify Sheshbazzar with the prince (נשיא) of Ezek 40–46.[71] Apart from literary critical questions,[72] it is difficult to see in what manner Sheshbazzar, as he is presented in Ezra, would correspond to the "prince" in Ezekiel. Whereas in the text of Ezekiel the title appears to designate a Davidide (especially in 46:16–18) with various responsibilities, this theme is not found in Ezra, where Sheshbazzar is only presented as the one

---

[65] Petersen, p. 27.

[66] So Bianchi, *I superstiti-2*, pp. 15–18, with bibliography, following Liver and Sacchi.

[67] Williamson, *Ezra*, p. 18; Petit, "Satrapes" pp. 59–61. On the meaning of the term פחה and the status of Yehud, see *infra*, pp. 72–80.

[68] Japhet, "Sheshbazzar and Zerubbabel-I", p. 98. This position was also maintained by Y. Kaufmann (*History of the Israelite Religion*, 4:166–67) as cited by Demsky, "Double Names", p. 35.

[69] Japhet, "Sheshbazzar and Zerubbabel-I", p. 98.

[70] This conclusion seems judicious. If this is so, then Williamson's argument that the expression refers to the tribe of Judah is somewhat weakened, cf. Williamson, *Ezra*, pp. 17–18.

[71] L. Rost, "Erwägungen zum Kyroserlass", in *Verbannung and Heimkehr: Beiträge zur Geschichte und Theologie Israels im 6. und 5. Jahrh. v. Chr: Festschrift W. Rudolph*, (ed. A. Kuschke; Tübingen: J. C. B. Mohr, 1961), pp. 301–7. For a recent examination on the question cf. D. Bodi, "Le prophète critique la monarchie: le terme *nasi'* chez Ezéchiel", in *Prophètes et rois: Bible et Proche Orient"*, (LD; ed. A. Lemaire; Paris: Cerf, 2001), pp. 249–57.

[72] Rost's position presupposes that the author of Ezra knew the final form of Ezekiel and deliberately sought to identify Sheshbazzar with the figure of "the prince" in that work.

to whom the temple vessels have been entrusted.[73] If our author has Ezek 40–46 in mind, the significance would have simply been that the position of Persian governor corresponds to that of נשיא in that text.[74] Williamson suggests that for the purpose of establishing a redactional parallelism between the Exodus and the return in 538, the author of Ezra may have designated Sheshbazzar as "prince" to identify him with the princes that carried silver and gold vessels for the altar dedication (cf. Num 7:84–86).[75] Perhaps the most that can be said is that while the term can clearly designate a member of the Davidic line, it should be seen as "politically imprecise."[76]

Little can be stated regarding Sheshbazzar's activities. The text of Ezra 1 credits him with the safe return of the temple vessels to Jerusalem. While it is impossible to verify this statement, the sending of the temple vessels to Jerusalem early in the reign of Cyrus poses no inherent improbability.[77] Far more important, however, is the issue of the literary and theological significance of the return of these vessels. Ackroyd has persuasively demonstrated the degree to which these objects constituted a concrete manifestation of the continuity of Yahweh's relationship with his people, despite the desecration of the nation's holy place and the tumultuous events of the exile and return.[78] The Aramaic text of Ezra 5:16 portrays Sheshbazzar as responsible for laying the temple foundations. Some scholars have posited two somewhat similar acts of temple refoundation, one by Sheshbazzar and the second by Zerubbabel.[79] This is sometimes taken to mean that the work begun by Sheshbazzar was soon abandoned, and Zerubbabel had to undertake similar procedures.[80] However, such a view is by no means necessary, and it is better to see the activities of the two as distinct. First, the issue

---

[73] Williamson, *Ezra*, p. 18–19; Japhet, "Sheshbazzar and Zerubbabel-I", pp. 96–97.

[74] For other objections to Rost's theory, see Williamson, *Ezra*, pp. 17–18.

[75] Ibid., p. 18.

[76] Lemaire, "Zorobabel", p. 54, n. 50.

[77] On Persian treatment of the religions of conquered peoples, especially with reference to images, religious objects, and shrines, cf. the detailed treatment in P. R. Bedford, "Early Achaemenid Monarchs and Indigenous Cults: Towards the Definition of Imperial Policy", in *Religion in the Ancient World: New Themes and Approaches*, (ed. M. Dillon; Amsterdam: A. M. Hakkert, 1996), pp. 17–39, esp. pp. 22–33. The temple need not have been completed before the vessels were sent; cf. Williamson, *Ezra*, p. 79.

[78] P. R. Ackroyd, "The Temple Vessels—A Continuity Theme", in *Studies in the Religion of Ancient Israel*, (SVT 23; ed. H. Ringgren et. al.; [Leiden: Brill, 1972]), pp. 166–81.

[79] So, for example, Baldwin, pp. 52–53.

[80] Baldwin (p. 53) appears to imply this.

at stake in Ezra 5 is not the precise architectural step taken by Sheshbazzar, but the fact that some movement was made toward the imple-
mentation of Cyrus' decree in the earliest phase of the return.[81] Indeed
for the author of Ezra 5–6 to admit that nothing at all was done in the
earlier period could potentially call into question the ongoing validity
of the permission to rebuild. Second, as we shall see, the precise state of
the temple and the extent of the needed repairs in 538 or 520 is difficult
to determine. It is unlikely that Haggai's call to the people envisages
a temple in such poor condition that wholesale removal of the existing
debris and complete re-laying of the foundations and reconstruction
of the temple's walls was necessary.[82] Third, as I will argue, the reference in Haggai 2:18 is not to an architectural step *per se*, but to a
re-foundation ceremony.[83] Fourth, the semantic range of יסד is broad
enough to include the specific action of laying foundations, as well as
the restoration of a building, or the act of building in general.[84] Thus
Sheshbazzar was likely responsible for some initial activity of a ritual or
material nature, but its precise details remains largely inaccessible to us.

### 3.4. ZERUBBABEL

The historical questions surrounding Zerubbabel are less numerous
and complex than those concerning the years following 539. It is generally admitted that Zerubbabel was a Davidide,[85] that he was involved
in the temple rebuilding in the first years of Darius' reign, and that
he disappeared from the scene before the rededication of the temple
in 515.[86] Questions persist regarding the date of his arrival in Yehud.
Ezra 5, along with Haggai and Zechariah place his activity during the
reign of Darius, while Ezra 2–3 also situate his activity in the earlier
period under Cyrus. Three major positions have emerged. First, it is
maintained that, since Ezra 2–3 places the beginning of Zerubbabel's

---

[81] Williamson, *Ezra*, p. 79.

[82] See provisionally Meyers and Meyers, pp. 63–64. Clines (*Ezra*, pp. 88–89, with
bibliography) following G. T. Tuland and M. Dunan, sees the foundation here as
involving the reconstruction of the platform or podium upon which the temple was
constructed. Petersen (pp. 88–89) takes a similar position.

[83] See *infra*, p. 208–9.

[84] See Gelston, "Foundations", *passim*, Baldwin, pp. 52–53, Wolff p. 66, and Meyers
and Meyers, pp. 63–64.

[85] See the exegesis at 1:1 for a discussion of his genealogy.

[86] For a survey of the critical and historical options here, cf. K. Beyse, *Serubbabel*,
p. 28–49, and Rose, *Zemah*, pp. 33–36.

activity in the period immediately following the decree of Cyrus, this must have been the initial time of his arrival.[87] This option is axiomatic for those who identify Zerubbabel and Sheshbazzar as one. It is also followed by those who see Sheshbazzar as the senior leader with Zerubbabel, who actually laid the foundation of the altar, acting under his aegis.[88] A second approach sees the narrative of Ezra 3 as a parallel to Ezra 5–6, and describing the events in the reign of Cambyses and early years of the reign of Darius.[89] Thus, whatever earlier attempts were made at restoration of the temple and altar, they have left no record.[90] A third position sees Ezra 3–4 as indeed referring to the period early in the reign of Cyrus. However the introduction of Zerubbabel into the narrative is seen as a literary and theological device whose aim is to involve Zerubbabel, the prominent Davidide and temple builder, and Joshua, the celebrated high priest, in the earliest attempts at temple restoration.[91] Given that Zerubbabel's activity is clearly situated in the reign of Darius in Haggai, Zechariah, and Ezra 5, and the significant chronological difficulties in Ezra 3–4,[92] the focus of Zerubbabel's activity should be situated after Cyrus' rule.[93]

On these latter two views, Zerubbabel could have arrived either during the reign of Cambyses, or immediately following Darius' accession. Williamson,[94] Beyse,[95] and Ackroyd[96] among others, suggest a date in the middle of Cambyses' reign that would be connected with his Egyp-

---

[87] Bright (*History*, p. 367) appears to favour this possibility. Williamson (*Ezra*, p. 45) argues that the author of Ezra 1–6 includes Zerubbabel here under the constraint of a source, but adds the qualification that this material may not be suitable for historical reconstruction.

[88] For a survey of the proposed harmonizations regarding Zerubbabel and Sheshbazzar, see Japhet, "Sheshbazzar and Zerubbabel-I", p. 91–94, and Williamson, *Ezra*, pp. 43–45.

[89] So Ackroyd, *Exile and Restoration*, pp. 147–48; Beyse, *Serubbabel*, p. 20.

[90] Beyse, *Serubbabel*, p. 27.

[91] So Japhet, "Sheshbazzar and Zerubbabel", p. 94; Blenkinsopp, *Ezra*, pp. 96–97.

[92] The most serious of these is the reference to the "seventh month" in Ezra 3:1 which appears to have been carried into the text from Neh 7:73b, when the list in Neh 7 was incorporated into Ezra 2. On this see Williamson, *Ezra*, pp. 28–32.

[93] Thus the balance of probability would indicate that the references to the activity of Zerubbabel in the early period are literary and theological in nature. If, however, some sources available to the author of Ezra 1–6 placed Zerubbabel in that period, allowance should be made for the albeit unlikely possibility that such may have been the case.

[94] Williamson, *Ezra*, p. 45.

[95] Beyse, *Serubbabel*, p. 32.

[96] Ackroyd, *Exile and Restoration*, p. 147.

tian campaign. Galling proposes a time immediately after the suppression of the last Babylonian revolt during Darius' second year.[97] Meyers
and Meyers seem to follow Galling.[98] Against this position, it is argued
that in the year immediately following Darius' accession all travel would
have been restricted, leaving only the clandestine flight of refugees (cf.
Zech 2).[99] This is countered by the claim that despite the uprisings further east, the situation in the West was relatively calm, and travel was
altogether possible.[100] The earlier date may be somewhat more probable for the reasons put forth by Beyse. The instability of the years
522–520 could have made that time ill-suited for the sending and installation of Zerubbabel. Be that as it may, Haggai includes him with the
other members of his audience, all of whom appear to have been in
Jerusalem for some time.[101] Nothing in the text implies that he is a new-
comer.[102]

We conclude therefore these introductory observations by suggesting, mainly according to literary evidence, the hypothesis of a gradual
and progressive return to Palestine from 538 of a segment of the Jewish
Babylonian population. Governors of Jewish Babylonian origin, related
to the Judaean royal family, were appointed by the Achaemenids.

### 3.5. THE POLITICAL STATUS OF YEHUD, THE NATURE OF ITS LEADERSHIP, AND THE ROLE OF THE DAVIDIC DYNASTY

The Davidic origins of both Sheshbazzar and Zerubbabel naturally
raise the question of the political status of Yehud and of its leader.
These questions have been extensively examined over the past thirty
years. Put briefly, there are four major positions. First, Alt, Galling,
Petersen and McEvenue[103] and with some qualifications also

---

[97] K. Galling, *Studien zur Geschichte Israels im persichen Zeitalter*, (Tübingen: J. C. Mohr, 1964), p. 59.
[98] Meyers and Meyers, p. xxxviii.
[99] Beyse, *Serubbabel*, p. 22.
[100] Ibid.
[101] Beyse notes that Haggai's appeal to agricultural failures make sense only if his addressees had been in the land long enough to be frustrated by them (Beyse, *Serubbabel*, p. 18). Despite the validity of Beyse's argument as it relates to the addressees, it still provides no conclusive data regarding the time of Zerubbabel's arrival.
[102] Japhet ("Sheshbazzar and Zerubbabel", p. 90) states, "The general impression from the prophecies of Haggai … is that Zerubbabel's star has just now risen." However this need not imply that he is new to the situation.
[103] Alt, "Die Rolle Samarias", pp. 313–37; K. Galling, *Geschichte Israels*; Petersen,

Smith[104] and Weinberg,[105] maintain that Judah was annexed to the province of Samaria by the Babylonians in 587, and that it remained under the rule of the Samaritan authorities until the arrival of Nehemiah in 445. Weinberg and Smith view this as the result of a longer process wherein pre-existing ethnic units were ultimately recognized and given legitimacy by the Persian authorities. Thus for Smith, Zerubbabel was appointed as head over the community of returnees.[106] Second, Stern posits a short period of independence at the time of Zerubbabel, whom the Persians appointed governor, followed by reversion to Samaritan domination.[107] Third, Williamson, Lemaire, Avigad, and Meyers postulate the existence of a Persian province under the rule of an uninterrupted line of Jewish governors from Sheshbazzar to Nehemiah and beyond.[108] Fourth, Liver, Kochman, Sacchi, Bianchi and Niehr suggest that Judah/Yehud continued to be a vassal-kingdom ruled by a member of the Davidic line during the Babylonian and early Persian periods.[109]

---

pp. 26–27; S. McEvenue, "The Political Structure in Judah from Cyrus to Nehemiah", *CBQ* 43 (1981): 353–64. For a good summary of these arguments, see Grabbe, *Judaism*, 1:81–82.

[104] Smith, *Landless*, p. 114.

[105] Weinberg, "Zentral-und Partikulargewalt", pp. 25–43.

[106] Smith, *Landless*, pp. 106–14, esp. pp. 112–13. A critique of Smith's assessment of the role of Zerubbabel will be presented *infra*.

[107] E. Stern, "The Persian Empire and the Political and Social History of Palestine in the Persian Period", in *CHJ*, p. 213.

[108] H. G. M. Williamson, "The Governors of Judah Under the Persians", *TynBul* 39 (1988): 59–82; A. Lemaire, "Histoire et administration de la Palestine à l'époque perse", in *La Palestine à l'époque perse*, ed. E.-M. Laperrousaz and A. Lemaire. Paris: Cerf, 1994, pp. 11–53. esp. pp. 16–19; N. Avigad, *Bullae and Seals from a Post-Exilic Judean Archive*, (Qedem 4, Monographs of the Institute of Archaeology; Jerusalem: Hebrew University, 1976), p. 34; E. M. Meyers, "The Shelomith Seal and the Judaean Restoration, Some Additional Considerations", in *N. Avigad Volume*, (ErIsr 18; ed. B. Mazar and Y. Yadin; Jerusalem: Israel Exploration Society, 1985), pp. 31*-38*. See also E.-M. Laperrousaz, "Jérusalem à l'époque perse (étendue et statut)", *Trans* 1 (1989): 55–66, esp. pp. 61–63.

[109] Liver, "The Return", *passim*; M. Kochman, "The Status and Extent of Judah in the Persian Period" (Ph. D dissertation, Hebrew University of Jerusalem, 1980), cited in Carter, *Emergence*, p. 51; P. Sacchi, "L'esilio e la fine della monarchia davidica", *Henoch* 11 (1989): 131–48; Bianchi, "Rôle de Zorobabel", pp. 153–65; idem, *I superstiti-2*, pp. 21–29, 95–97; H. Niehr, "Religio-Historical Aspects of the 'Early Post-Exilic' Period", in *The Crisis of Israelite Religion: Transformation of Religious Tradition in Exilic and Post-Exilic Times*, (OS 62; ed. B. Becking and M. C. A. Korpel; Leiden: E. J. Brill, 1999), pp. 228–44. Liver, ("The Return", pp. 114–16, cited in Bianchi, "Rôle de Zorobabel", p. 157) sees the Davidic dynasty as ending with Zerubbabel.

The seals and bullae published by Avigad in 1976,[110] are frequently cited as definitive evidence in favour of the view that Yehud constituted an independent entity in the late sixth century.[111] What is not so often stated, however, is the fact that significant debate still exists regarding the legitimacy of such a conclusion.[112] The primary areas of discussion include: (1) the actual reading of the seals, especially the question of whether one ought to read *phw'* or *phr'*; (2) the reason for the unusual spelling of *phw'*; (3) the meaning of *phw'*; and (4) the dating of the bullae.

The general consensus prefers the reading *phw'* frequently rendered "governor" to the suggestion that it be read *phr'* "the potter."[113] Based on a small sample of inscriptions which he dated to the fifth or fourth centuries, Cross[114] argued that the "sharp" or "peaked" right shoulder on the letter in question made it impossible for that letter to be a *waw* since *waw* at that period never displayed such a form. The letter was rather a *resh*.[115] Thus Cross proposed the reading "the potter" for the inscriptions under discussion, affirming that it was highly probable that the potter's name would be placed upon his work. This reading, argued Cross, resolved the difficulty of the unusual spelling for governor on the seals (*phw'* whereas the normal Aramaic singular, emphatic form, was spelled *pht'*).[116] This unusual spelling had been labeled a "back formation" by E. Y. Kutscher, based on the normal plural form, *phwt'*.[117] Cross felt that his reading rendered Kutscher's hypothesis superfluous. In 1976, however, Avigad's new lot of inscriptions added significant

---

[110] See *supra*, n. 108. Cf., for a survey of the inscriptional evidence for Palestine in the Persian period, A. Lemaire, "Les inscriptions palestiniennes d'époque perse: un bilan provisoire." *Trans* 1 (1989): 87–104, esp. pp. 93–96, for Yehud.

[111] So, for example, Meyers, "Shelomith Seal", *passim*.

[112] A number of these debated issues are taken up by F. Bianchi, *I superstiti della deportazione sono là nella provincia (Neemia 1,3). Ricerche epigrafiche sulla storia della Giudea in età neobabilonese e achemenide (586 a.C.-442 a.C.)*, (AIONSup 76, 53/3; Napoli: Instituto Universitario Orientale, 1993), henceforth, *I superstiti-1*.

[113] J. C. Greenfield and J. Naveh, "Hebrew and Aramaic in the Persian Period", in *CHJ*, pp. 115–29.

[114] F. M. Cross, "Judean Stamps", in *W. F. Albright Volume*, (ErIsr 9; ed. A. Malamat; Jerusalem: Israel Exploration Society, 1969), pp. 20–27.

[115] Ibid., p. 24.

[116] Ibid., p. 24; Grintz had already indicated in 1961 that this regular form was used in the Aramaic version of the Behistun inscription, Bianchi, (*I superstiti-1*, p. 17) citing Y. Grintz, "Yeho'ezer, the Unknown High Priest", *JQR* 50 (1960–61): 338–45.

[117] E. Y. Kutscher, "*Phw'* and its Cognates", *Tarbiz* 30 (1960–61): 112–19 (Heb.), cited in Cross, "Stamps", p. 24.

data to the debate, most notably the name Elnathan, in association with the debated Aramaic term, and the territorial designation Yehud (*yhd* and *yhwd*).[118] Most significant was seal no. 14, which included the name Shelomith, and set her in relation to Elnathan.[119] This data led Avigad and a significant number of commentators to conclude that the disputed term could not refer simply to the potter who made the vessel, but to an individual of some political importance.[120] It should be noted, however, that the reading "potter" has not been totally abandoned.[121]

Some scholars who accept the reading *phw'* have nevertheless expressed doubts regarding the sixth century dating proposed for the seals.[122] F. Bianchi, summarizing a variety of epigraphic evidence, concludes that nothing prevents the dating of bulla no. 5 (*l'lntn phw'*) to the fourth or third centuries.[123] Similarly he concludes that since it cannot be proved that all the bullae come from the same source and period, they could date from any time in the sixth to third centuries, and thus cannot be used to determine the status of Yehud.[124] It must be admitted that absolute certainty here is not possible.[125] However, various considerations make a late sixth century date a viable working hypothesis. First, the fact that a cache of various inscriptions may not represent a single source does not preclude all attempts at dating the individual texts. Second, and consequently, the fact that women's names were relatively rare both on seals and in genealogical tables, and as such would indicate that the owner of the seal was a person of some importance, makes it reasonable to connect the Shelomith of seal no. 14 with the

---

[118] N. Avigad, *Bullae and Seals, passim*. For a brief discussion of each seal, with bibliography, see Bianchi, *I superstiti-1*, pp. 9–31.

[119] The text reads *lšlmyt//'mt 'ln//tn ph[w']*. As Lemaire notes ("Zorobabel", p. 56, n. 62), *'mt* (lit. 'maidservant') in this context, is a formula of politeness, underlining the faithfulness and devotion of the woman in question to her husband (*b'lh*).

[120] Avigad, *Bullae and Seals*, pp. 6, 11, 22. The validity of this claim has been challenged by McEvenue, "Political Structure", p. 361, n. 22. McEvenue's approach has been criticized by Williamson, "Governors", pp. 59–82, esp. p. 71, n. 40.

[121] It appears, for example, as a possibility in G. I. Davies, *Ancient Hebrew Inscriptions. Corpus and Concordance*, (Cambridge: Cambridge University Press, 1991), pp. 252–53.

[122] For the sixth century dating, cf. Avigad, *Bullae and Seals*, p. 35f.

[123] Bianchi, *I superstiti-1*, p. 19.

[124] Ibid., p. 50.

[125] It would seem that the main thrust of Bianchi's analysis is to demonstrate the existence of reasonable doubt regarding the dating of the materials and the meaning of *phw'*. However, it remains to be seen whether such doubt is sufficient to render the material inadmissible as evidence with reference to the late sixth century.

Davidide mentioned in 1 Chr 3:19.[126] Third, seal inscriptions frequently use archaizing writing styles.[127] Thus the similarity between the orthography of the *waw* in the seals and the seventh century inscriptional evidence from Neirab[128] does not preclude a late sixth century date. It is important to note that paleographic data alone is seldom able to determine precise dating.[129] Thus, on balance, the approach which sees the seals as late sixth to early fifth century remains a better option than the outright rejection of the use of the seals for historical reconstruction, notwithstanding the validity of the questions raised with reference to such use.

Finally, among those who accept the reading *phw'* there exists a divergence of opinion regarding the meaning of the term. Lipiński sees it as referring to one who was responsible for the management of royal cellars,[130] while Naveh, Greenfield and Eph'al see it as referring to a lower governmental official.[131] Williamson however, has countered these contentions by asserting that: (1) if *phw'* is a back-formation, it is formed from a plural (*phwt'*) which is quite frequently used for governors; (2) it would be highly unusual for the wife of a petty official to own a seal found in an official archive; (3) the fourth century Yehud coins,[132] which bear the analogous Hebrew inscription *yhzqyh hphh* (Hezekiah the governor) clearly refer to the provincial governor; and (4) the clay seal found at Wadi Dâliyeh, in Paleo-Hebrew, *[sn']blt pht šmr[n]* clearly uses

---

[126] These points were suggested by Lemaire in 1977, ("Review of N. Avigad, *Bullae and Seals from a Post-Exilic Archive*" in *Syria 54* [1977]: 129–31). Similar arguments have been advanced by E. M. Meyers, "Shelomith Seal", pp. 31*-38*.

[127] Lemaire, "Review of Avigad", p. 130; Williamson, "Governors", esp. p. 75.

[128] On which see the argument and bibliography in Bianchi, *I superstiti-1*, p. 19.

[129] A. Lemaire, "Populations et territoires de la Palestine à l'époque perse", *Trans 3* (1990): 34; Williamson, "Governors", p. 75.

[130] E. Lipiński, "'Cellériers' de la province de Juda", *Trans 1* (1989): 107–9.

[131] Greenfield and Naveh, "Hebrew and Aramaic", p. 123; I. Eph'al, "Syria-Palestine under Achaemenid Rule", in *Cambridge Ancient History. Vol. IV, Persia Greece and the Western Mediterranean c. 525–479 B. C.*, (Cambridge: Cambridge University Press, 1988), pp. 158, 161, cited in Bianchi, *I superstiti-1*, p. 18. Bianchi (ibid., p. 18), cites personal correspondence from Naveh maintaining that the term refers to an official whose authority would have been no greater than the local military commander of an Italian city.

[132] Cf. J. W. Betlyon, "The Provincial Government of Persian Period Judea and the Yehud Coins." *JBL* 105 (1986): 633–42; P. Machinist, "The First Coins of Judah and Samaria: Numismatics and History in the Achaemenid and early Hellenistic Periods", in *Achaemenid History VIII, Continuity and Change*, (ed. H. Sancisi-Weerdenburg et al.; Leiden: Nederlands Instituut voor het Nabije Oosten, 1994), pp. 365–80; A. Lemaire, "Epigraphie et numismatique palestiniennes", in *La Palestine à l'époque perse*, (ed. E.-M. Laperrousaz and A. Lemaire. Paris: Cerf, 1994), pp. 261–87.

the corresponding Hebrew term (*phh*) with reference to the governor of Samaria.[133] Bianchi has countered by arguing that it is unlikely that seal no. 14 comes from an official archive, and therefore the argument from Shelomith's name carries little weight and furthermore her status and the nature of the archive cannot be inferred from her name since we do not know enough about the status of women in ancient Israel to really say whether it would be unusual for a woman to own an archive.[134]

Smith, following the earlier arguments of Weinberg,[135] sees the term "governor" as referring to an "administrator of a population, that is, an 'ethnarch'" or a "Persian official under the Satrap who was a semi-military officer in charge of a specific area or a particular population."[136] His subsequent comments make it clear that for him the focus ought to be on the ethnic and social dimensions of Zerubbabel's authority.[137] Smith concludes that the transfer of communal leadership from governor to high priest is "only logically possible if we do not consider the governor as an administrator of a geographic unit."[138] Smith's position, however, is doubtful. In addition to the data mentioned above, two points speak against it. First, given the flexibility in the Persian administrative system,[139] it is hard to see why governance could not be shifted from the former royal family to a priestly one.[140] Second, the linguistic data regarding the relevant terms clearly points in the direction of the administrator of a geographically defined circumscription.[141] I am unaware of any instance where the terms in question refer to a ruler whose authority is over an ethnically defined community living within the borders of a province ruled over by another governor. This is especially unlikely given the Persian practice of collecting tribute in

---

[133] Williamson, "Governors", pp. 73–74.

[134] Bianchi, *I superstiti-1*, p. 29.

[135] Weinberg, "Zentral-und Partikulargewalt", p. 33. Weinberg saw Zerubbabel as simply a local leader of the community and the temple reconstruction.

[136] Smith, *Landless*, p. 112.

[137] Ibid., pp. 106–14, esp. pp. 112–13.

[138] Ibid.

[139] Cf. Lemaire, "Zorobabel", pp. 53–54.

[140] Lemaire, (ibid. pp. 56–57) observes that this transition from Davidic to priestly rule probably occurred "*en douceur*" i.e. quietly and discretely.

[141] Cf. T. Petit, "L'évolution sémantique des termes hébreux et araméens *phh* et *sgn* et accadiens *pāḥātu* et *šaknu*", *JBL* 107 (1988): 53–67, esp. p. 56 where he concludes, "It is evident that *peḥâ* carries the specific sense of the 'governor' of a specific territory or district." Cf. also Lemaire, "Populations et territoires", pp. 33–38, esp. p. 37, n. 34.

terms of geographical regions.[142] Third, as Bianchi notes, it is dubious whether a region as small as Yehud would have a double bureaucratic structure.[143]

While the precise status of the archive remains a matter for discussion, in view of the lack of any indisputable evidence that the term *pḥwʾ* clearly carries some other meaning[144] and was meant to be explicitly distinct from *pḥtʾ*, it would not appear injudicious to take it to mean "governor." If this is accepted, the data published by Avigad can be seen as indicating that in the relevant passages in Haggai and Zechariah, as well as in Ezra and Nehemiah, Yehud should be viewed as a province within the Persian Empire under the leadership of a Persian appointed governor.

This conclusion, however, stands in opposition both to the view that Yehud was dependent on Samaria, as well as the position that it was effectively a vassal-kingdom. While it is beyond doubt that the Persians generally followed a "dynastic model" and therefore put or left in power the former ruling elites,[145] this does not in itself determine the political status of the territory. This is the weakness of the positions of Bianchi and Niehr, who appear to assume that dynastic continuity implies kingdom.[146] Lemaire underlines the telling fact that *mlk* is never used in the biblical or extra-biblical material with reference to Zerubbabel or any other governor during our period.[147] He furthermore observes that Hag 2:20–23 appears to foresee a change in the status

---

[142] Briant, (*Histoire*, 1:423–24), speaks of the process by which the empire was 'territorialized' i.e. divided into administrative units for taxation purposes. This attention extended to the precise delimitation of individual holdings. He states, "The determination of the level of tribute payable necessitated the establishment of a registry of land holdings and their relative values, or at very least, some way of indicating the boundaries of the various land parcels."

[143] Bianchi, *I superstiti-2*, pp. 50–51. Cf. H. Kreissig, "Eine beachtenswerte Theorie zur Organization der vorderorientalischen Tempel Gemeinde in Juda", *Klio* 66 [1984]: 35–39.

[144] The one place where *pḥwt* (pl.) appears to designate a ruler of quite limited authority is the so-called "migdol" papyrus. However this evidence from a private letter, using the plural form, may be of limited value relative to the seals and impressions, cf. T. Petit, "Evolution sémantique", p. 57, n. 19.

[145] Briant, "Contrainte militaire", 199–225; Lemaire, "Zorobabel", p. 44; Bianchi, "Rôle de Zorobabel", pp. 156–57.

[146] Briant ("Bulletin-1", p. 47) views Bianchi's argument as unconvincing.

[147] Lemaire, "Zorobabel", pp. 53–55. This may be contrasted to the Phoenician evidence, cf. J. Elayi, "Pouvoirs locaux et organisation du territoire des cités phéniciennes sous l'Empire perse achéméide", in *Espacio, Tiempo y Forma, Serie II-Historia Antigua* 10 (1997): 63–77, esp. 67–76.

of Zerubbabel and of Yehud, moving in the direction of greater autonomy. The most sober conclusion is that Zerubbabel was not referred
to as a king by those whom he governed. It is clear that the Persians
tolerated such appellation elsewhere.[148] It is furthermore unlikely that
the ruling Davidides would have eschewed such language should its use
have been permitted to them.[149] The most logical explanation is therefore that the Persian crown viewed Yehud as a province, not a vassal-
kingdom. Thus, despite the presence of a series of Davidic governors,
and the fact that the Persians permitted vassal-kingdoms to exist elsewhere,[150] the evidence does not allow us to conclude that Yehud was
functioning as a vassal-kingdom at the time of Zerubbabel's governorship.[151]

In conclusion, the supposition that Sheshbazzar and Zerubbabel
were governors of a province which was separate and distinct from
Samaria remains the most viable working hypothesis for the understanding of early Persian Yehud. It is important to underline the fact
that the Achaemenid Empire should not be conceived as a modern
centralized bureaucracy.[152] Furthermore, as noted above, Persian control in the West was imposed progressively. It is, therefore, not improbable that, as such control increased, questions and conflicts may have
developed in the relations between the various regional authorities. Furthermore local autonomy was encouraged as long as it did not affect
imperial prerogatives. A certain measure of flux and movement, therefore, was undoubtedly inevitable with regard to the governor's role.

---

[148] Lemaire, "Zorobabel", pp. 53–54.

[149] I would not go so far as to affirm that the use of such terminology would have
been acceptable to all members of the community. However, I have no reason to believe
that the editor of Haggai would not have employed it, should this have been possible.

[150] Cf. E. A. Knauf, "The Persian Administration in Arabia", *Trans* 2 (1990): 201–18,
esp. p. 204; J. Elayi, "Pouvoirs locaux", pp. 67–76; Briant, *Histoire*, 1:503–6, 513–16.

[151] It seems to me that Niehr's statement ("Religio-Historical Aspects", p. 231), "So
the status of Judah/Yehud as a province and a vassal kingdom were [*sic*] not mutually
exclusive" is unsustainable. Cf. Lemaire, ("L'exploitation des sources ouest-sémitiques
[araméennes, phéniciennes, hébraïques et minéennes]", in *Recherches récentes sur l'empire
achéménide*, [Topoi Sup 1, Lyon/Paris: Maison de l'Orient Méditerranéen], p. 305–32)
who clearly notes the difference between the two. He states (p. 308), "At the beginning of the Persian period, the Judaeans could have hoped that, under Zerubbabel's
authority, their province could have become a kingdom once again. Apparently Darius
refused to permit such a transformation."

[152] P. Briant, "Pouvoir central et polycentrisme culturel dans l'empire achéménide.
Quelques réflexions et suggestions", in *Achaemenid History I: Sources, Structures and Synthesis*,
(ed. H. Sancisi-Weerdenburg; Leiden: Nederlands Instituut voor het Nabije Oosten,
1987), p. 2.

Consequently, at this period the role and prerogatives of the *peḥâ* of Yehud were in a state of transition and may have been open to modification and clarification (cf. Ezra 5–6).[153]

Despite some uncertainty at certain points, one thing seems assured: Zerubbabel was named to his post by the Persian throne and owed his whole jurisdiction to it. This implies that in 520, the Jewish community in Yehud enjoyed its autonomy based on the imperial policy of the Persian crown, and that official relations with the Persian administration would have appeared as a means *toward* the community's aspirations, and not as an obstacle to them.

### 3.6. The Second Year of Darius

I now turn to the question regarding the exact referent, in terms of the Gregorian calendar, of the expression "the second year of Darius" found in Haggai. The reference is taken by the majority of scholars to designate the year 520–519. This date is arrived at via the assumption that Haggai, in conformity with the normal Babylonian system of regnal calculation, reckons the reign of Darius by means of the accession year, or postdating system.[154] However this assumption has been called into question by L. Waterman and E. J. Bickerman. Waterman argues that the dates in Haggai used a non-accession year system, or antedating.[155] This would place Haggai's oracles in 521–520, a year characterized by violent uprisings following the accession of Darius I. Bickerman also maintains that Darius' rule was antedated, but for different reasons.[156]

It would seem most natural to interpret the regnal year designations in Haggai according to the practice of postdating. This was the sys-

---

[153] Petersen (p. 27) suggests that at this period, there was a progressive movement towards local autonomy in the Persian governance of the West. Ackroyd judiciously comments, "The title *peḥah*, governor, is used very broadly, for different levels of officials. ... Perhaps we are making unreal distinctions if we talk of 'special commissioners' and 'governors' as if they were quite different." ("Archaeology, Politics and Religion", p. 11, cited in Carter, *Emergence*, p. 52 n. 75).

[154] On which see, R. A. Parker and W. H. Dubberstein, *Babylonian Chronology 626 BC-45 AD*, (Chicago: University of Chicago Press, 1946); M. Cogan, s. v. "Chronology, Hebrew Bible", *ABD* 1: 1006.

[155] Waterman, "Messianic Conspirators", pp. 73–78; cf. Bright, *History of Israel*, pp. 369–70.

[156] Bickerman, "En marge", pp. 23–28; Bickerman's position is accepted as possible by Tadmor, "Appointed Time", pp. 407–8.

tem used by the Babylonians,[157] and it was employed by the Persian administration in the western part of the empire.[158] Thus it would be most natural, when referring to an Achaemenid monarch, to use the system of dating commonly in use in the empire. While antedating was the older Judahite system of regnal calculation,[159] postdating may have been used in some of the date notices of the late seventh and early sixth centuries.[160] It would appear that it was employed, at the very least, in some of the designations of the regnal years of Nebuchadnezzar in Jeremiah.[161] Furthermore, given the fact that the spring New Year, used

---

[157] Parker and Dubberstein, *Babylonian Chronology*, pp. 10–24.

[158] See L. Depuydt, "Evidence for Accession Dating under the Achaemenids", *JAOS* 115 (1995): 193; Tadmor, "Appointed Time", p. 407, and E. J. Bickerman, "Calendars and Chronology", in *CHJ* , pp. 60–69. On the Old Persian calendar see W. Hartner, "Old Iranian Calendars", in *The Cambridge History of Iran. Vol. 2, The Median and Achaemenian Periods*, (ed. I. Gershevitch; Cambridge: Cambridge University Press, 1985), pp. 714–92. Depuydt ("Accession Dating", pp. 193–94), and Hartner ("Old Iranian Calendars", pp. 741–48) note that the months of the Babylonian and Old Persian calendars likely coincided, despite possible differences in the placement of intercalary months. Depuydt examines the possibility that an alternative system of calculation was used in the East, and finds it to be a possibility (see *infra*).

[159] Cogan, "Chronology", p. 1006.

[160] Indeed, this is the "majority" position. The bibliography on this point, (and on related issues such as the date of the fall of Jerusalem, and the starting point for regnal calculation) is extensive. On the presence of postdating in some seventh or sixth-century sources see, for example, D. J. A. Clines, "Regnal Year Reckoning in the Last Years of the Kingdom of Judah", *AJBA* 2 (1972): 9–34; H. Tadmor, "The Chronology of the First Temple Period", in *The World History of the Jewish People. Vol. 4/1, The Age of the Monarchies*, (ed. A. Malamat; Jerusalem: Massada, 1978), pp. 44–55; G. Galil, "The Babylonian Calendar and the Chronology of the Last Kings of Judah", *Bib* 72 (1991): 367–78, with bibliography; Cogan, "Chronology", p. 1006. Clines, ("Regnal Year Reckoning", p 23–25) adopts an interesting approach to the question, which differs from many of the other discussions which focus on the harmonization of dates, or the question of the time of the new year. He argues that a postdated reckoning better fits the historical context of certain passages in Jeremiah than antedating.

By contrast, it should be noted that arguments have been made to the effect that antedating, being the traditional Judahite system of reckoning, is used with reference to all pre-exilic Judahite kings. For the view that all postdating is the result of a postexilic redaction see H. Cazelles, "587 ou 586?", in *The Word of the Lord Shall Go Forth: Essays in Honor of David Noel Freedman in Celebration of his Sixtieth Birthday*, (ed. C. L. Meyers and M. O'Connor; Winona Lake: Eisenbraun's/American School of Oriental Research, 1983), pp. 427–35. Such an approach dates the fall of Jerusalem in 587 and presupposes a shift to a spring new year in approximately 605.

As this point is not critical to my argument, I shall not develop it further. Should postdating be ruled out with reference to all Judahite kings (a point upon which I have yet to be convinced), the assertion that postdating is generally used in the Persian period is not weakened.

[161] Cf., for example, Jer 52:28–29, where the biblical text and the Babylonian Chron-

by the Babylonians, was in use in Judah by at least 600, if not before,[162] it is possible that the Babylonian practice of postdating in regnal calculations would also be known in Judah and employed in certain contexts.

Be that as it may, postdating, as the official Babylonian system of regnal calculation, would have been commonly practiced in Judah under Neo-Babylonian rule. It is also in evidence in various Aramaic texts of the Persian period. Clear references to the accession year itself are found in an Egyptian Aramaic text of the fifth century,[163] and a fourth century Aramaic text from Wadi Dâliyeh.[164] In an earlier article,[165] I presented detailed argumentation for the use of postdating and thus a 520–519 date. Those arguments, refined and updated, will be presented in their essence here.[166]

Waterman suggests that Haggai antedates.[167] This appears unlikely in light of the fact that since the Babylonian conquest, postdating was the normative scribal practice. Furthermore none of the evidence cited by Waterman[168] sufficiently demonstrates that antedating was used in Persian Yehud. While it might be argued that the redactor of Haggai-Zechariah antedates for archaizing or nationalistic effect,[169] it would

---

icle are in full accord. Bickerman ("Calendars", p. 61) maintains that the term *resh mamleket* and its close equivalents testify to postdating in Jeremiah. This is challenged by Cazelles who sees these references as redactional and inconclusive (Cazelles, "587", p. 426). Similar observations are expressed in E. H. Merrill, "The 'Accession Year' and Davidic Chronology", *JANES* 19 (1990): 101–12, esp. pp. 105–6.

[162] Lemaire, "Formules de datation", pp. 363–64; cf. idem, "Datation en Palestine", p. 68 on the date of the origin of the use of numbered months in Judah.

[163] Porten and Yardeni, *Textbook*, 2:20, (cf. Cowley No. 6=Grelot No. 33). The text reads ראש מלוכתא כזי ארתחששש "the beginning of the reign of Artaxerxes".

[164] F. M. Cross, "Papyri", pp. 45–69; idem, "Samaria Papyrus I", pp. 7\*-17\*. The text reads ראש מלכות [ד]רי[הוש "the beginning of the reign of Darius".

[165] Kessler, "Darius and Haggai", pp. 63–84.

[166] I have made a number of modifications and corrections here vis-à-vis my earlier article, esp. the transliterations.

[167] Waterman, "Messianic Conspirators", pp. 76–77; Bright, *History of Israel*, pp. 369–70, suggests that antedating may be present in Haggai, but admits that "it is impossible to be certain."

[168] Waterman, (ibid., p. 77), appeals to E. R. Theile (*The Mysterious Numbers of the Hebrew Kings*, [Chicago: University of Chicago Press, 1951], p. 30) to the effect that both accession and non-accession systems of dating were in use at various periods. He also argues that the call to flee Babylon in Zech 2:7 and Haggai's declaration of Zerubbabel's imminent messiahship only make sense if the oracles were proclaimed in 521. Neither of these arguments sufficiently demonstrates antedating in Haggai.

[169] Waterman, (ibid., pp. 76–77), appears to see this as the reason for the use of antedating in Haggai. He similarly cites Neh 1:1 and 2:1 as a proof of a postexilic dating

seem incongruous to use this system with reference to a foreign, non-Jewish ruler, and difficult to see how this would emphasize Judaean nationalism. This of course assumes that the redactor of Haggai was so eager to promote Jewish nationalism that even the form of the dates was used to this end. However, as will be argued in the exegesis *infra*, this assumption is not borne out by the text. Furthermore, even if antedating was practiced in the Persian period (and there appears to be no conclusive evidence of it), the use of a date formula different from the standard scribal practice seems odd in a notice whose basic purpose would appear to be chronological precision. Antedating, without any redactional comment, would certainly lend itself to confusion.[170]

E. J. Bickerman proposes a second approach to the question of the dates in Haggai. He appears to argue for the existence of two concurrent yet different systems of regnal computation within the Persian Empire. One was postdating, the standard administrative and economic system, inherited from the Babylonians. The second, in use on the Persian Royal Court was a system of absolute calculation, based upon the actual date of the monarch's accession.[171] However, in the case of Darius I, Bickerman posits antedating. He suggests that Darius, having assassinated Gaumata, would have antedated the beginning of his reign so that it would coincide with the death of Cambyses, thus denying any legitimacy to Gaumata.[172] Bickerman cites several historical examples of this phenomenon, including the calculation of Camby-

---

system which emphasized Jewish nationalism. Cf. the diametrically opposed position of Bickerman, "En marge", pp. 19–23, Depuydt, "Accession Dating", p. 193–96, and Williamson, *Ezra*, p. 169. These authors argue that the dates in Nehemiah may be evidence of a distinctly Persian system of dating, calculated from the specific day of the ruler's accession.

[170] As Williamson notes, *Ezra*, p. 169.

[171] Bickerman, ("En marge", p. 20), gives several historical examples of concurrent but differing calendars. He cites Neh 1:1 and 2:1 as examples of this. Williamson, *Ezra*, p. 170, considers Bickerman's hypothesis favourably. For a full examination of the accession dating hypothesis see Depuydt, "Accession Dating", *passim*, who concludes (p. 199), "this paper has scoured sources from all over the Achaemenid Empire in an attempt to detect signs of accession dating in Persia. In particular the statements in Thucydides and Nehemiah raise a challenge as to how else to explain the sources. But the paper reveals how woefully scant the evidence is." Depuydt's (and by extension Bickerman's) claim that Cambyses dates his reign in Egypt from 529 BCE has been challenged by D. Devauchelle, "Un problème de chronologie sous Cambyse", *Trans* 15 (1998): 9–17.

[172] Bickerman, "En marge", p. 25–27.

ses' reign in Egypt. Thus for Bickerman, Darius' court and the territories other than Babylon reckon the time of Gaumata's rule as belonging to Darius, and the civil year that began March 27, 522 beginning his first year of reign.[173] For Haggai and Yehud, following this calculation, the second year of Darius would have begun in April 14, 521, when the Persian Empire was in a revolutionary chaos.

However Bickerman's hypothesis has several weaknesses. First, the use of antedating, beside being an irregular practice at that time, creates a significant problem. As Wolff notes, such a step was unnecessary, and impossible, because Gaumata's accession and reign took place in Cambyses' eighth year and did not last into the following year.[174] Thus to date the first year of his reign from March 522 would deny to Cambyses the final year of his reign.[175] Second, in DB, Darius boasts of the fact that he became king *after* he killed Gaumata.[176] He is thus quite concerned that the usurper's illegitimate reign not be lost from view. Third, as Ackroyd clearly demonstrated in 1958, even if (for the sake of argument) Darius' first year is calculated from March 522, given the efficient system of communication which existed in the Persian Empire,

---

[173] Ibid., p. 25. It seems to me that Bickerman could have explored another option in his article. He argues for absolute (or factual) dating in the first section, with reference to Neh 1:1 and 2:1. Then, in his section on the second year of Darius, he argues for antedating, for the purposes of legitimization. In line with section 1, he could have argued that Darius and his court counted his rule from the date of Cambyses death, which DB §11 appears to put as July 1, 522 (Parker and Dubberstein, *Babylonian Chronology*, p. 14). However, even if this possibility is granted, it would be highly irregular for the editor of Haggai to use such a calculation. Even if one admits, with Bickerman and Williamson, the possibility that Nehemiah, as an intimate of the Persian Court, would have used a specifically Persian system, what possible reason would the redactor of Haggai have for doing so?

[174] Wolff, pp. 75–76.

[175] Unless one is meant to assume a retroactive co-regency!

[176] In DB §13 Darius specifically asserts that the kingship was in Gaumata's hands, and that he alone was able to wrest it from him. He specifically dates Gaumata's assassination and counts it as the beginning of his reign. In §10 and §15 Darius appears to place the death of Gaumata after his accession, but this may be an unwarranted conclusion. Given the very specific dating in §13, and Darius' explicit statement that it was only after killing Gaumata that he received the kingship, we should read §10 and 15 in the light of §13, and see Gaumata's assassination as the starting point of Darius' reign. For the view that Darius' kingship precedes Gaumata's death, see P. Lecoq, *Les inscriptions de la Perse achéménide. Traduit du vieux-perse, de l'élamite, du babylonien, et annoté*, (L'aube des Peuples; Paris: Gallimard, 1997), p. 190 (re: DB §10, n. 1). For the opposite, and in my opinion more likely view, see Depuydt, "Accession Dating", p. 196, and J. Wiesehöfer, (*Der Aufstand Gaumatas und die Anfänge Dareios' I*, [Bonn: Rudolph Habelt, 1978]) who asserts (p. 218), "Before the death of the Magian, Darius was not yet king."

by the time he proclaimed his final oracles (2:10–23), Haggai would have been aware of the victories of Darius and the pacification of the rebellion in Babylon.[177]

One final reason stands against Bickerman's and Waterman's hypothesis. Both scholars admit that the majority of exegetes believe that the "second year of Darius" in Haggai designates the year April 4, 520-March 3, 519 BCE. For Bickerman and Waterman, the primary reason for pushing back the date is the supposition that Haggai had announced the imminent fall of the Persian Empire, or was inciting Zerubbabel to rebellion, and that such statements would have been possible in the fall of 521 but absurd in the fall of 520.[178] But such an assumption, as the exegesis below will show, is entirely unwarranted. Haggai does not incite Zerubbabel to active rebellion. The oracles in 2:6–9 and 21–23 have an eschatological tone and setting, and primarily relate to divine intervention in favour of Zerubbabel. Thus their plausibility in the context in which they were delivered is really a secondary issue. Besides, if plausibility is deemed important, one could maintain that Haggai and his hearers could easily have believed that the recently acquired peace in the Empire would be short lived, and that rebellions would soon break forth.[179] Indeed, as Wolff notes, even though Darius' hold on power was secure by 520, ongoing military engagements were necessary.[180]

In conclusion, I would assert that understanding the dates in Haggai in terms of the customary Babylonian and Persian practice of postdating is the most likely hypothesis. Haggai's oracles should thus be dated between September and December 520.

---

[177] Ackroyd, "Two Problems", pp. 13–27, esp. pp. 17–18.

[178] Bickerman states, "A fanatic who, in October-December 520, announced the crumbling of the empire 'in a very little while' would have been thrown in the dungeon by Zerubbabel and Joshua" ("En marge", p. 24). To me, this overstates the case.

[179] Furthermore, the difference between war and peace in the empire as a whole, and the actual experience of the citizenry of Yehud, may not have been so clearly demarcated. Thus the broader question of the relative stability of Darius' hold on power may have been only loosely related to local day-to-day experience and to popular perceptions regarding the stability of the empire. I am indebted to Prof. Ursula Franklin (Massey College, University of Toronto) for this line of reflection.

[180] Wolff, p. 76.

## 3.7. The Impact of Persian Rule on Yehud from 538–515

To what extent did Persian rule impact life in Yehud? Certain reconstructions view Persian policy as having a highly formative influence
on the daily life and literature of early Persian Yehud. Berquist reads
the construction of the temple and the message of the book of Haggai as a very immediate response to Persian imperial concerns, specifically Darius' expedition to Egypt in 519.[181] Person has argued at length
that Persian prerogatives favoured the growth of the Deuteronomistic
movement in Yehud, specifically under Darius.[182] The evidence at our
disposal indicates that Persian influence in Yehud was relatively limited, especially before the completion of the temple. As noted above, it
was probably not until Cambyses' expedition to Egypt that Persian rule
was effectively imposed upon the West.[183] Certainly the inhabitants of
Yehud would have been aware of the military movements accompany-
ing Cambyses' conquest of Egypt. Cambyses' troops (supported by the
naval forces assembled at Acco), passed to the West of Yehud and followed the coastal road past Gaza across the desert[184] to Egypt.[185] However it is difficult to see how the presence of the Persian troops would
have impacted life in Jerusalem and rural Yehud in any material way
at this early period. Bianchi notes that in the late sixth century military
installations were limited to the coastal regions, and thus Yehud was
in a marginal position.[186] Once Egypt was conquered, Yehud's strategic

---

[181] Berquist, *Judaism*, pp. 63–70. For example, he states (p. 63), "The immediate
motivation for the temple construction is the threat of force. This links the temple
construction more closely to Persian imperial policies than to Yehudite internal debates.
As a center for the Persian administration the temple would assure tranquillity and
supplies for the Persian army as it passed nearby on the way to Egypt." He then
exegetes the text of Haggai in such a way as to make the book a polemic in favour
of Persian policy. I find this approach to be difficult both exegetically and historically.

[182] R. Person, "The Deuteronomic History in its Postexilic Context", in *Second Temple
Studies 3* (forthcoming).

[183] Bianchi, *I superstiti-2*, p. 17, Ackroyd, *Exile and Restoration*, p. 141 and Briant, *Histoire*,
1:59.

[184] Cf. Graf ("Royal Road System", *passim*) for a discussion of the Persian period
sites and roads. Cf. also E. Stern, "La *Via Maris*", in *Les routes du Proche Orient*, (ed.
A. Lemaire, Paris: Desclée de Brouwer, 2000), pp. 59–65.

[185] Katzenstein, "Gaza", pp. 68–82; J. M. Cook, "The Rise of the Achaemenids and
the Establishment of their Empire", in *The Cambridge History of Iran. Vol. 2. The Median
and Achaemenian Periods*, (ed. I. Gershevitch; Cambridge: Cambridge University Press,
1985), pp. 214–21, esp. p. 214. Berquist appears to suggest that the entire Persian army
traveled by ship (*Judaism*, pp. 45–46), but this seems unfounded.

[186] Bianchi, *I superstiti-2*, p. 45.

importance increased. This importance, however, should not be over-estimated.[187] Yehud was one province among many in Syria-Palestine. The Phoenician coastal cities, the provinces of Samaria and Dor, and the Idumean territory had far greater economic and military signifi-cance than Yehud, whose geography posed significant challenges for both agriculture and transportation.

In general, Persian policy encouraged local autonomy in so far as it did not conflict with imperial interests.[188] The loyalty of the vari-ous regions was frequently sought by means of support for the exist-ing ruling dynasties,[189] and an attitude of non-interference in matters of a legal[190] and religious nature.[191] Yehud would have been viewed as a source of income for the support of imperial interests.[192] Such inter-ests would have been significantly furthered by the reconstruction of the temple, the renewal of the economic infrastructure of the region and the repopulating of devastated regions.[193] There is no evidence that Darius had any concerns regarding the loyalty and submission of either the population of Yehud or its governor, Zerubbabel. Thus, the most significant area in which Persian interests would impact life in Yehud would be the former's desire to maximize taxation revenues in the province. The demographic and economic development of the province, as well as the reconstruction of the temple[194] would have well

---

[187] Cf. P. Briant, ("Histoire impériale et histoire régionale. A propos de l'histoire de Juda dans l'Empire achéménide", in *Congress Volume Oslo 1998*, [SVT 80; ed. A. Lemaire and M. Saebø; Leiden: E. J. Brill, 2000], pp. 235–45) who states, "I am highly reticent (to say the least) when faced with lines of argumentation which attribute a decisive strategic position to Judah in the Achaemenid configuration, simply because I cannot see why or in what way Judah and Jerusalem ought to be considered to be strategic positions vis-à-vis Egypt. As far as I know Judah is not situated on the Egyptian frontier, and Jerusalem is located at a significant distance from the main routes leading to the Nile valley" (p. 238).

[188] Briant, "Pouvoir central", pp. 5–6.

[189] Ibid., p. 13

[190] Briant, *Histoire*, 1:528

[191] Cf. S. E. Ballentine, "The Politics of Religion in the Persian Period", in *After the Exile: Essays in Honour of Rex Mason*, (ed. J. Barton and D. J . Reimer; Macon, GA: Mercer University Press, 1996), pp. 129–146, and Briant, "Pouvoir central", p. 4ff.

[192] For an extensive discussion of the economy of the empire under Darius, cf. Briant, *Histoire*, 1:399–487. For a survey of various approaches to the question, with evaluations, and special attention to Yehud, see Bianchi, *I superstiti-2*, pp. 35–56. Bianchi evalu-ates the approaches of Briant, Dandamaev, Wittfogel, Hoglund, Kreissig, Kippenberg, M. Smith, and Weinberg, among others.

[193] On the Persian desire to repopulate devastated regions, see Kuhrt, "Achaemenid Imperial Policy", pp. 83–97, esp. p. 90, and Bianchi, *I superstiti-2*, p. 56.

[194] Temples were a key factor in the Achaemenid taxation structure, cf. J. Schaper,

served these aims. E. Kuhrt suggests that the Achaemenids could have
followed the Assyrian practice "whereby cities occupying a key position in troubled regions, or in regions susceptible to conflicts, saw their
privilege and/or exoneration status guaranteed by the central government."[195] This being the case, it will be readily observable that the
interests of the Persian crown and those of the nascent community
were, to a great degree, in harmony with one another. It remains to
be seen however, whether the "Deuteronomistic School" can be viewed
as having been promoted by Darius in a manner similar to the role
he assigned to Udrahorresset in Egypt.[196] Nevertheless, general Persian
support for the temple reconstruction would have certainly been con-
ducive of internal religious developments and the consolidation of traditions.

### 3.8. The State of the Jerusalem Temple

The condition of the temple building in 520 is a much discussed and
vexing question, and one to which only an approximate response may
be given.[197] The biblical descriptions speak of the burning of the building, the smashing of bronze, and the pillaging of the temple vessels
(2 Kgs 25:9–15). It is unclear, however, to what degree the fundamental structure of the building was undermined. Some scholars intimate
quite extensive and systematic destruction,[198] while others posit significant damage to the ramparts, but less extensive destruction within the
city, and less damage to the temple.[199] Wolff suggests that the initial
burning and later weathering would have resulted in the collapse of the

---

"The Jerusalem Temple as an Instrument of Achaemenid Fiscal Administration", *VT*
45 (1995): 528–39. Cf. also Lemaire, "Histoire et administration", pp. 21–22.
    [195] Kuhrt, "Achaemenid Imperial Policy", p. 93; cf. Bedford, "Achaemenid Mo-
narchs", pp. 22–33.
    [196] Cf. Person, "Deuteronomistic History", *passim*.
    [197] Ackroyd's survey of the data, although dated, still remains valuable (*Exile and
Restoration*, pp. 25–31).
    [198] Wolff, pp. 42–43, with bibliography; cf. also O. Lipschits ( "Nebuchadnezzar's
Policy in 'Hattu-Land' and the Fate of the Kingdom of Judah", *UF* 30 [1998]: 477)
speaks of the systematic destruction of the city. Cf. L. G. Herr, "The Iron Age Period",
*BA* 60 (1997): 154 and A. Mazar, *Archaeology of the Land of the Bible, 10,000- 586 B.C.E.*,
(ABRL; New York: Doubleday, 1990), p. 458.
    [199] Cf. H. Barstad (*The Myth of the Empty Land: A Study in the History and Archaeology
of Judah During the 'Exilic' Period*, [SOSup 28; Oslo: Scandinavian University Press,
1996], pp. 51–54), who states, "It is more than unlikely that he [Nebuchadnezzar] went

walls and virtual destruction of the building.[200] While the severity of the assault on Jerusalem cannot be minimized, any estimation of the extent of damage to the temple building must remain conjectural. Jeremiah 41 implies ongoing worship at Jerusalem[201] in the Babylonian period, but the exact nature of the worship is elusive.[202] Furthermore, we do not know what, if any, restorative steps were taken during the Babylonian period. The same may be said of the activity of Sheshbazzar and the community present in the early part of the return. What is more, we do not know what unused materials may have been stocked at Jerusalem.[203] Haggai's description of the site as חרב (abandoned, desolate; 1:4, 9) reveals more about the degree to which the temple was frequented, than its actual state.[204] What is clear is that in 520 the local population is called upon to put forth the effort required to restore the temple site to a more appropriate and acceptable state. In Haggai, no mention is made of any appeal to the local community for financial support. Thus the traditions regarding Persian provision for the rebuilding of the temple can be seen as corresponding quite well to imperial fiscal interests.[205]

---

about demolishing all of the 600 dunams of the fortified city" (p. 53). See also Meyers and Meyers (pp. 63–64), who maintain the temple's foundations were not destroyed. For a survey of the Jerusalem excavations, see, Y. Shiloh et al., s. v. "Jerusalem", in *New Encyclopedia of Excavations in the Holy Land*, (ed. E. Stern, New York: Simon and Schuster, 1993), 2:698–804, esp. p. 709; idem, "Judah and Jerusalem in the Eighth-Sixth Centuries B.C.E.", in *Recent Excavations in Israel: Studies in Iron Age Archaeology*, (ed. S. Gitin and W. G. Dever, Winona Lake: ASOR/Eisenbrauns, 1989), pp. 97–105; M. Steiner, "The Archaeology of Ancient Jerusalem", *CR:BS* 6 (1998): 143–68. For a survey of the Persian material in Jerusalem see Carter, *Emergence*, pp. 134–48.

[200] Wolff, pp. 42–43.

[201] Cf., however, the view of Blenkinsopp ("The Judaean Priesthood during the Neo-Babylonian and Achaemenid Periods: A Hypothetical Reconstruction." *CBQ* 60 [1998]: 25–43, esp. p. 27) who feels that a sanctuary in or near Mizpah is being alluded to.

[202] Ackroyd (*Exile and Restoration*, p. 28–29) sees the site as in use to some degree. M. Noth, ("La catastrophe de Jérusalem en l'an 587 avant Jésus-Christ et sa signification pour Israël", *RHPR* 33 [1953]: 81–102, esp. pp. 85–86) suggests that the offerings mentioned in Jer 41:5 may have been made as tokens of respect and grief at the ruined site.

[203] Meyers and Meyers (pp. 27–28) posit, on the basis of Hag 1:8, that the wood mentioned in that verse is for the construction of building paraphernalia rather than as an actual building material. They assume that such materials may have been provided by the Persians at an earlier date, and laid in store. Cf. my alternative proposal in the exegesis *infra*.

[204] Cf. Kessler, "Haggai's Jerusalem" pp. 149–50 and Amsler, p. 22.

[205] Schaper, "Jerusalem Temple", p. 534.

Perhaps this support, combined with the fact that the temple's condition did not require complete reconstruction, coalesced to enable the community to complete the project in a relatively brief period.

### 3.9. THE POPULATION OF YEHUD

Significant attention has been devoted to the question of the population of Persian Yehud in recent years. As I have argued elsewhere, well founded demographic estimates provide a highly useful point of reference for the evaluation of competing sociological reconstructions.[206] Methodologically, the utility of such estimates is maximized when they are introduced *before* or at very least *at the same time* as the application of sociological analogies, the reading of texts, or the reconstruction of social, political and economic circumstances. Demographic assessment thus provides the backdrop against which other factors may be considered. This can be illustrated, for example, in the way P. Hanson describes the role of Haggai in his social environment. A sampling of quotes from Hanson demonstrates the extent to which his demographic portrayal of Yehud is essential for his view of Haggai. He mentions the desire of the "hierocratic group" to win the confidence "of the masses ... captivated by the vision of a rival group"[207] and of the movement of "many people" from one camp to the other.[208] He sees Haggai and Zechariah as having made the hierocratic program "attractive for the masses"[209] by "rallying popular support."[210] Hanson himself posits the population of Yehud in 520 to have been in excess of 42,000.[211] Clearly such language, and the social dynamics which it implies would require some modification should the population have been significantly lower.

The question of the size of the population of Persian Yehud is contingent upon issues such as the population of pre-exilic Judah and Jerusalem, the absolute number and percentage of the population which was deported, the extent of the Babylonian destruction, the

---

[206] Kessler, "Haggai's Jerusalem", pp. 146–47.
[207] Hanson, *Dawn of Apocalyptic*, p. 244.
[208] Ibid., p. 245.
[209] Ibid., p. 246.
[210] Ibid., p. 256.
[211] Hanson (ibid., pp. 266–67) states that the list in Ezra 2 "is a genuine list of those returning from exile in the period after Cyrus' decree." It is difficult to know, however, whether this means immediately following, or over an extended period. It would seem, in the context of his discussion of the religious and political dynamics of 520, that he assumes this population to be already in place.

archaeological evidence of the Babylonian and early Persian periods and its interpretation, as well as the literary evidence, most specifically the value of the list in Ezra 2. A detailed study of all of these factors is beyond the scope of the present study, and therefore only those questions most directly germane to the situation in 520 will be discussed in detail.[212] Leaving to one side the excessively high estimate of J. P. Weinberg, who sees the population of Yehud in the Persian period as having been in excess of 200,000,[213] two major positions emerge. The first posits a relative stability in the population before and after 587, and a moderately high density of population in Babylonian and Persian Yehud. The second asserts that a significant decline in population took place following 587, leaving a low population density well into the Persian period.

The principal proponent of the first view is Hans Barstad,[214] whose argumentation frequently resembles that of E. Janssen, H. Kreissig and R. Carroll[215] and to a lesser extent E.-M. Laperrousaz.[216] This approach emphasizes that the population of Judah was relatively stable and homogeneous before and after 587.[217] Furthermore, the depar-

---

[212] On the number of exiles and their relative percentage of the population see, Kessler, "Le livre d'Aggée", pp. 77–78, with bibliography; cf. Bianchi, *I superstiti-2*, pp. 4–5.

[213] J. P. Weinberg, *Der Chronist in seiner Mitwelt*, (BZAW 239; Berlin: Walter de Gruyter, 1996), p. 37, and "Demographische Notizen", pp. 44–47. Weinberg's estimate is closely linked to his "Burger-Tempel-Gemeinde" theory and his assumption that Yehud was not a contiguous, self contained unit but pockets of population enclaves (Weinberg, "Demographische Notizen", *passim*) which existed within a Yehud already densely populated by the non-exiled population. Cf. Carter's discussion of Weinberg, (*Emergence*, pp. 297–98). H. Kreissig sees the number of deportees and sees this as representing about 15% of the population (*Situation*, pp. 22–23). Such high population figures have few adherents today.

[214] Barstad, *Myth*, pp. 47–55.

[215] E. Janssen, *Juda in der Exilszeit: Ein Beitrag zur Frage der Entstehung des Judentums* (FRLANT 69; Göttingen: Vandenhoeck & Ruprecht, 1956); Kreissig, *Situation*, pp. 20–34. R. P. Carroll, "The Myth of the Empty Land", *Semeia* 59 (1992): 79–93; idem, "Exile! What Exile? Deportation and the Discourses of Diaspora", in *Leading Captivity Captive*, (JSOTSup 278; ed. L. L. Grabbe; Sheffield: Sheffield Academic Press, 1998), pp. 62–79. Kreissig implies a level of social conflict not discernible in Barstad's work.

[216] E.-M. Laperrousaz, "Jérusalem", pp. 55–65. Cf. Laperrousaz's writings on the size of Jerusalem, "Quelques remarques sur le rempart de Jérusalem à l'époque de Néhémie", *FO* 21 (1980): 179–185; "L'étendue de Jérusalem à l'époque perse", in *La Palestine à l'époque perse*, ed. E.-M. Laperrousaz and A. Lemaire; Paris: Cerf, 1994, pp. 123–153, with bibliography.

[217] Barstad, *Myth*, pp. 53–55. Kreissig, (*Situation*, p. 22) nuances this somewhat, and incorporates the effects of the population loss following Gedeliah's assassination into his

ture and return of a small number of elite citizens is said not to have radically affected the religious and economic life of the community.[218] This conclusion is based upon the following related assumptions: (1) Notions of quasi-total deportation, and its concomitant, the "Myth of the Empty Land" are not primarily intended to be statements of historical detail, but rather essential components of ancient story-telling.[219] For Barstad, such notions are thus rhetorical and descriptive devices which stress the importance of the Babylonian conquest (in Kings)[220] or the importance of the returnees (in Chronicles).[221] (2) The Babylonian destruction in Jerusalem was limited to breaches in the wall, the removal of the city gates, and damage to the central shrine. The residential sections of the city (which extended to the Western Hill) were left largely untouched.[222] (3) Babylonian and early Persian Judah was the source of several major literary works such as Lamentations, Isa 21, the Deuteronomistic History, Obadiah, Pss 44, 74, 79, 89, 102, Jeremiah, Ezekiel, and Deutero- and Trito-Isaiah.[223] (4) The notion of a "shift of gravity"[224] from Palestine to Babylon is pure mythology. The community which remained in Judah was vital and creative.[225] While Barstad does not explicitly state his estimate of the population of Jerusalem or Yehud, he clearly assumes it to be rather substantial.[226]

In contrast to the preceding view, proponents of the second position, including C. E. Carter and E. Ben Zvi, and to a lesser extent, Magen Broshi,[227] envisage a Yehud and Jerusalem which are rather

---

reconstruction.

[218] Barstad, *Myth*, pp. 67–71; Kreissig, *Situation*, pp. 22, 26. Kreissig is more hesitant that Barstad regarding the extent of economic activity during the exile.

[219] Barstad, *Myth*, pp. 31–32, 53; Kreissig, *Situation*, pp. 21–22; 30f.

[220] Barstad, *Myth*, pp. 31, 34.

[221] Ibid., pp. 41–42.

[222] Here Barstad substantially follows the arguments of Janssen, *Exilszeit*, pp. 42–45 which were also taken up by Ackroyd, *Exile and Restoration*, pp. 20f. Cf. Kreissig, *Situation*, p. 22, and the contrasting view in Shiloh, "Jerusalem", p. 109.

[223] Barstad, *Myth*, pp. 19–23. See also his *The Babylonian Captivity of the Book of Isaiah: 'Exilic' Judah and the Provenance of Isaiah 40–55* (Oslo: Novus instituttet for sammenlignende kulturforskning, 1997), pp. 86–87 and idem, "On the History and Archaeology of Judah during the Exilic Period. A Reminder", *OLP* 19 (1988): 22–25.

[224] It would appear that this *tournure* which has found its way into the warp and woof of scholarly discussion of the period originated with J. Bright (*History of Israel*, p. 345). It has become a somewhat customary way of describing the theological landscape (to mix metaphors) of the period.

[225] Barstad, *Myth*, pp. 80–82.

[226] Ibid., pp. 53–54.

[227] I include Broshi here due to the relative comparison between his population

sparsely populated during the Babylonian and early Persian periods.[228] The studies of O. Lipschits and I. Milevski, (which do not use the ethnoarchaeological demographic methodology employed by the three previous authors),[229] based largely on archaeological survey material, see a significant diminution of the population in the period following 587.[230] Aharoni similarly posited a "population vacuum" during this period.[231] Carter maintains that, while some increase in the population did occur in the late sixth century and early fifth century,[232] no significant growth occurred until the mid fifth century. This increase may have been related to broader Persian political initiatives in the Levant as a whole. Broshi originally estimated the population of mid fifth-century Jerusalem as approximately 4,800.[233] This figure was later revised downward by Carter, primarily due to his conclusions regarding the size of the residential area of the city and its population

---

estimates and those of Laperrousaz, for example. Next to the latter's estimate of the population of Jerusalem as 12,000 in the mid fifth century, Broshi's 4,800 is quite restrained (see *infra*).

[228] E. Ben Zvi, "The Urban Center of Jerusalem and the Development of the Literature of the Hebrew Bible", in *Urbanism in Antiquity* (ed. W. E. Aufrecht, N. A. Mirau and S. W. Gauley. JSOTSup 244; Sheffield: JSOT Press, 1997), pp. 194–209; Broshi, "Population of Ancient Jerusalem", pp. 10–15; idem, "Population de Jérusalem", pp. 5–14; Carter, *Emergence*; ch. 4–6; idem, "The Province of Yehud in the Post-Exilic Period: Soundings in Site Distribution and Demography", in T. C. Eskenazi and K. H. Richards (eds.), *Second Temple Studies 2: Temple and Community in the Persian Period* (JSOTSup 175; Sheffield: JSOT Press, 1994), pp. 106–145.

[229] On the development and use of the demographic methodology employed by Carter, Broshi, Finkelstein, Gophna and Shiloh see Carter, *Emergence*, pp. 195–99, with bibliography. Cf. also the brief but extremely useful discussion of demographic methodology, with attention to population growth and longevity in J. Pastor, *Land and Economy in Ancient Palestine*, (London: Routledge, 1997), pp. 6–8.

[230] Lipschits, "Nebuchadnezzar's Policy" pp. 467–87; idem, "The History of the Benjamin Region under Babylonian Rule", *Tel Aviv* 26 (1999): 155–90; I. Milevski, "Settlement Patterns in Northern Judah during the Achaemenid Period, According to the Hill Country of Benjamin and Jerusalem Surveys", *BAIAS* 15 (1996–7): 7–29.

[231] Y. Aharoni, *The Land of the Bible: A Historical Geography* (London: Burns and Oates, 1979), p. 409.

[232] Carter, "Province of Yehud", pp. 134–35. The same may be said for Galilee, cf. J. Briend, "L'occupation de la Galilée occidentale à l'époque perse", *Trans* 2 (1990): 121, and Lemaire, "Populations et territoires", p. 43. A similar phenomenon may be seen in Samaria, cf. A. Zertal, "The Pahwah of Samaria (Northern Israel) during the Persian Period. Types of Settlement, Economy, History and New Discoveries", *Trans* 3 (1990): 12.

[233] Broshi, "Population" p. 9. I arrive at this figure by multiplying Broshi's estimates of size (120 dunams) and his population coefficient (40).

density.[234] He estimates the population of Yehud as follows: Persian I
(539–450): 13,350; Persian II (450–333): 20,650.[235] He views the population of Jerusalem as approximately 1,500 in Persian II and suggests
that the city's size may have been fifty percent smaller in Persian I.[236]
On the basis of Carter's estimates Ben Zvi concludes that the bodies
of literature which Barstad would assign to the exilic period (with one
or two minor exceptions) could not have been written either during the
exile or in Persian I. The reason for this, according to Ben Zvi, is that
until 450 the demographic and economic conditions in Yehud would
not have been sufficiently developed to sustain any significant literary
activity.

The position which maintains a high degree of continuity and stability is open to criticism at several key points.[237] First, the degree
to which population density can be successfully inferred from literary
production is an ongoing discussion.[238] Second, the destruction and
depopulation of Jerusalem and its environs appears to have been far
more extensive than Barstad or Janssen assume.[239] Third, Samaria and
Galilee experienced similar population declines in the late Babylonian
and early Persian periods and had population levels corresponding to
the lower range of the estimates for Yehud.[240] Fourth, according to
Milevski, recent survey material reveals a diminution of about seventy-
five percent following the Babylonian invasions.[241] Therefore, even if the
more precise "areal" methodology discussed above is not employed,[242]
a significant diminution in the population appears to have occurred.
Due attention should be paid to the repeated allusions to destruction

---

[234] Carter, *Emergence*, pp. 147–48; 196–201 and esp. p. 201, n. 89.

[235] Ibid., pp. 201–2. For his earlier figures for Yehud (10,850 and 17,000) see Carter,
"Province of Yehud", p. 135.

[236] Carter, *Emergence*, pp. 200–201, and "Province of Yehud", p. 129.

[237] For a fuller discussion of these see Kessler, "Haggai's Jerusalem", pp 146–48.

[238] On this see Carter, *Emergence*, pp. 286–88 and Ben Zvi, "Urban Center", *passim*.

[239] On this see Lipschits, "Benjamin Region", p. 158, esp. n. 6, 7, and idem, "Nebuchadnezzar's Policy", pp. 473–74, with bibliography.

[240] On Galilee cf. Briend, "L'occupation", p. 121, and Z. Gal, "Israel in Exile", *BAR*
24 (1998): 48–53, esp. p. 53. On Samaria cf. Zertal "The Pahwah", p. 11. Zertal appears
to posit a population of approximately 20,000 for Samaria in the early Persian Period.

[241] Thus, Milevski ("Settlement Patterns", p. 18–20) citing the evidence and conclusions of Finkelstein. Similar data is cited by Lipschits, "Benjamin Region", p. 182.

[242] Milevski, (ibid., p. 18) believes that due to our present inability to construct an
accurate chronology of the surveyed sites, and the lack of precision regarding their
size, "it is better to leave the question (of population figures) untouched until new
information becomes available."

through famine, sword, plague and disease present in the biblical texts (for example Jer 5:12; 14:15–16; 21:7–9; 27:8 etc.), and to the biblical traditions which reflect a sufficient loss of population so as to permit some redistribution of land to members of the more disadvantaged members of society (2 Kgs 25:12; Jer 52:16; cf. Ezek 11:2–11, 14–18; 33:23–28).[243] Furthermore, Lipschits suggests that, despite the existence of Mizpah as an administrative centre in the Babylonian period, there was a progressive movement away from Yehud to other neighbouring regions,[244] likely as a result of the severe damage done to its infrastructure by the Babylonians.[245] Fifth, in my view, the list in Ezra 2 may well reflect an ongoing tabulation subject to several redactional updatings, and therefore reflect population and genealogical data up to the mid fifth century.[246]

It is therefore best to view early Persian Yehud and the city of Jerusalem as relatively sparsely populated. Should Carter's estimates be accepted, it is most judicious to see them as reflecting the lower end of a broader spectrum, since it is more likely that Persian I occupation will be posited in new sites than such occupation will be rejected for sites where it is currently assumed. Carter clearly states that his estimates are "provisional at best."[247] Thus a reasonable range for the population of early Persian Yehud might be somewhere between Carter's estimate of 13,350[248] and the figure of about 20,000 proposed by Albright and Verhoef.[249] Allowing for a similar margin for Jerusalem, that city would have a population of somewhere between 750 and 2,000 inhabitants.

---

[243] See, on this J. N. Graham, "Vinedressers and Ploughmen: 2 Kings 25:12 and Jeremiah 52:16", *BA* 47 (1984): 55–58. Cf. also, Smith, *Landless*, pp. 184–97; Pastor, *Land*, pp. 13–14; Kreissig, *Situation*, pp. 25–34.

[244] On the loss of population in Judaea, and the contrasting situation in the Transjordan cf. J. A. Sauer, "Transjordan in the Bronze and Iron Ages: A Critique of Glueck's Synthesis", *BASOR* 263 (1986): 1–26. On the presence of Judaean refugees in Ammonite territory, including an evaluation of the paleo-Hebrew seals of Ammonite provenance, cf. A. Lemaire, "Les transformations politiques et culturelles de la Transjordanie au VIe siècle av. J.-C." *Trans* 8 (1994): 9–27, esp. p. 19.

[245] Lipschits, "Benjamin Region", pp. 181–82. I had proposed a similar reconstruction in "Le livre Aggée", p. 82.

[246] For similar views cf. Albright, *Biblical Period*, p. 87, n. 180; Blenkinsopp, *Ezra*, p. 85; Bright, *History of Israel*, p. 384; Lemaire, "Populations et territoires", pp. 37–38; S. Mowinckel, *Studien zu dem Buche Ezra-Nehemia*, (2 vols.; Oslo: Universitetsforlaget, 1964), 1:98.

[247] Carter, *Emergence*, p. 202.

[248] Ibid., p. 201.

[249] Albright, *Biblical Period*, p. 87; Verhoef, p. 29.

Such a margin also leaves room for the potential inclusion of any extra-mural population, should such have existed.[250]

The implications of the foregoing for the reading of Haggai are significant. It is most likely that the text was produced by and for a numerically insignificant population, struggling to contend with economic hardship, the payment of taxes, and diversity of socio-economic status amongst its members.

Thus, in conclusion I propose the following framework for the understanding of Persian rule in Yehud. During the earliest period (538–525) Yehud was relatively untouched by Persian imperial activities. Authorization was given for the temple's reconstruction and a small number of the exiles returned to their homeland. Taxation was instituted. Cambyses' conquest of Egypt increased the significance of Yehud in two ways. First, additional revenue was needed to sustain the Empire's control over its vast territory.[251] Second, stability in Yehud, as a part of the broader stability in Syria-Palestine as a whole, became significant for Persian rule and aspirations in the West. The small and economically impoverished population had neither the means nor any pressing reason to resist Persian rule. The restoration of the temple and its worship, as well as continuity with the past through the restoration of the former ruling house, were permitted to the community in Yehud by their Persian overlords. The more likely loci of conflict would have been between members of the community over theological or economic issues, with other Yahwists of different geographical roots or political affiliations, or with competing economic and political interests in neighbouring provinces.[252] The biblical traditions clearly attest to these types of conflict. Overt conflict with the Persian crown is absent.

---

[250] Cf., Carter, *Emergence*, pp. 145–47.

[251] Briant, *Histoire*, 1:399–433.

[252] On this see the extensive discussion in E. Ben Zvi, "Inclusion in and Exclusion from 'Israel' in Post-Monarchic Biblical Texts", in *The Pitcher is Broken, Memorial Essays for G. W. Ahlström*. (JSOTSup 190; ed. S. W. Holloway and L. K. Handy; Sheffield: JSOT Press, 1995), pp. 95–149.

# CHAPTER FOUR

# INTRODUCTION TO THE EXEGESIS OF HAGGAI

## 4.1. ORGANIZATION AND APPROACH

Given that my purpose in this study is not an exhaustive exegesis of Haggai but rather a reading of the text with reference to the prophetic role and the social context of early Persian Yehud, I have chosen a specific approach in the following chapters. Rather than writing a full commentary on Haggai, what will follow is *focused* exegesis directed particularly to the issues within the text which are most germane to my study. When questions which are less directly connected to this central concern arise, I will not attempt to deal with them in detail, but will refer the reader to the discussions in relevant specialized literature.

Each pericope of the book will be analyzed in four sections: (1) Translation and Textual Criticism; (2) Structural and Literary Considerations; (3) Exegesis; and (4) Use of Theological Traditions.

## 4.2. THEOLOGICAL TRADITIONS IN HAGGAI

My methodology for analyzing the theological traditions in Haggai is central to my investigation, and as such, requires some elaboration at this point. In addition to biblical studies, various branches of the social sciences, specifically the discipline of religious anthropology, have devoted significant attention to the study of religious traditions.[1] As noted above, a crucial distinction must be made between the transmission process[2] (*traditio*) and that which is transmitted (*traditum*).[3] Furthermore, in this process, neutrality is precluded by the fact that

---

[1] Cf., for example M. Meslin, *Pour une science des religions*, (Paris: Seuil, 1973) and idem, *Expérience humaine*. An earlier and programmatic series of essays on this theme as it relates to biblical studies was D. A. Knight, ed., *Tradition and Theology in the Old Testament*, (Philadelphia: Fortress, 1977). For a recent series of essays devoted particularly to religious traditions during and after the exile cf. B. Becking, and M. C. A. Korpel, eds., *The Crisis of Israelite Religion: Transformation of Religious Tradition in Exilic and Post-Exilic Times*, (OS 62, Leiden: E. J. Brill, 1999).

[2] See, for example, J. Audinet, "Du transmettre", pp. 109–15; idem, "Dispositifs", pp. 166–205.

[3] D. A. Knight, "Tradition History", p. 633.

existing traditions are taken up and transmitted by specific individuals, with their own perspectives and approaches, and communicated
within a particular cultural and ideological context.[4] Thus far from a
mechanical and lifeless process, the use of theological traditions, especially where earlier or existing traditions are applied to new or changed
contexts, is a dynamic and creative one.

Closely linked to the reshaping of religious traditions in the process of their transmission is the question of the relationship between
the prophet and his or her environment. Even a cursory reading of
the Hebrew prophets reveals that they were in constant dialogue with
the "intellectual world" or the *geistige Welt*[5] in which they lived. This
involves the totality of the prophet's sociological, linguistic, historical,
political, and literary context,[6] but most especially the *Vorstellungen*, or
the contemporaneous "conceptions and notions" which surrounded
them.[7] A critically important place within these *Vorstellungen* is occupied
by the then current religious and theological traditions. As Blenkinsopp
has observed, "This appeal to tradition, mediated or filtered through
intense personal experience and brought to bear on the interpretation
of contemporary events, is of course a crucial aspect of the complex
phenomenon of prophecy."[8] The prophet is involved in a dialogical
and dynamic process[9] with this intellectual world and religious tradition. In this process the prophet enjoys a significant degree of freedom in the use of tradition and consequently may exhibit creativity,
using existing tradition in unexpected and novel ways.[10] We may, there-

---

[4] For a development of the ideological aspects of the use of religious tradition cf.
D. J. A. Clines, *Interested Parties: The Ideology of Writers and Readers of the Hebrew Bible*,
(JSOTSup 205; Sheffield: JSOT Press, 1995).

[5] Steck's expression, ("Streams of Tradition", p. 186).

[6] Ibid., pp. 186–87, Knight "Tradition History", p. 637.

[7] Steck, "Streams of Tradition", p. 187. Steck uses the following expressions to
describe this intellectual environment: "antecedent intellectual world", (p. 187), "antecedent material", (p. 190), "intellectual ingredients", (p. 190), "accepted prior notions
and thought patterns", (p. 192). Knight, ("Tradition History", p. 637), calls them
"themes and motifs." A similar perspective is found in W. Kaiser who speaks of a
text's "antecedent or informing theology" (W. Kaiser, *Toward an Old Testament Theology*,
[Grand Rapids: Zondervan, 1978], p. 19). Kaiser draws upon the term "informing theology," coined by J. Bright, (*The Authority of the Old Testament*, [1967, repr. Grand Rapids:
Baker, 1978], pp. 143, 170).

[8] Blenkinsopp, *History*, p. 156.

[9] Cf. Meslin, *Expérience humaine*, p. 381.

[10] Zimmerli, "Prophetic Proclamation", p. 76–93, G. Fohrer, "Remarks on the Modern Interpretation of the Prophets", *JBL* 80 (1961): 309–19 and the brief but insightful
observations of von Rad in "City", pp. 232–42, esp. p. 232.

fore, speak of the prophet as one who "interprets and actualizes" the traditions to which he or she is heir[11] or of a "process of tradition"[12] within the prophetic corpus. We can also conceive of the prophet as the one who is active in the "independent fashioning"[13] of the religious traditions of the day. In sum, the innovative activity of a given prophet can be appreciated by means of that prophet's use of religious traditions. An analysis of such use needs to be undertaken with great attentiveness to the contours of the prophetic text. At times the prophet's use of existing tradition is stark, bold, and easily identifiable. At other times allusions may be quite subtle. Such subtlety is possible since both prophet and readers or hearers were participants in the same religious and cultural environment, and sometimes the mere mention of one significant term or concept would be sufficient to evoke in the minds of the intended audience other related concepts, assumptions, and theological systems.[14] Steck observes that religious traditions frequently consist of smaller elements organized around major themes and ideas.[15] Thus an allusion to one element which is customarily a part of a larger complex or configuration frequently calls to mind the other ideologically related components of that tradition.[16] One might think, for example, of the motif of the pilgrimage of the nations as one element in the broader tradition of Zion theology.[17]

The issue at stake in my analysis of the use of religious traditions in Haggai is thus the quest for any distinctive utilization of religious tradition, either in terms of the content which was transmitted, the hermeneutical assumptions underlying the way in which tradition is re-utilized, or the rhetorical and literary structures used as vehicles for the communication of that tradition. In this context two further points of clarification need to be made. First, I make no assumptions regarding

---

[11] Knight, "Tradition History", p. 634.

[12] Zimmerli, "Prophetic Proclamation", p. 76.

[13] Steck, "Streams of Tradition", p. 188.

[14] Ibid., p. 193.

[15] Steck (ibid., p. 193) suggests the following hierarchical ordering: elements of a notion < notion < tradition < conceptual design (*Konzeption*).

[16] Ibid., p. 193.

[17] This configuration of smaller traditional elements into larger traditional wholes can at times create difficulties in nomenclature. Thus in the following discussion the plural *religious* or *theological traditions*, will frequently designate the totality of the religious traditions used in Haggai. By contrast I will attempt to use the singular *tradition*, or *traditional element etc.* for the constituent parts of a broader traditions.

any "texts" which Haggai or his redactors may have had at their disposal.[18] I am concerned primarily with traditions, that is to say with the religious or theological conceptions which may underlie various texts. In my own opinion a good case can be made for the writing down of certain narrative and prophetic traditions by the end of the exile. Proof of the existence of such a collection, however, is not essential to my discussion. What is more, given that redactional smoothing and shaping of the earlier materials may have occurred during the Persian period, the mere existence of earlier written materials does not, in and of itself, preclude the simultaneous redaction of several texts.[19] The approach taken here is therefore neither dependent upon evidence of textual citation, a phenomenon which involves a great number of methodological and historical complexities,[20] nor linked to any detailed chronology regarding the various biblical materials. Sufficient for my argumentation is the assertion that the framers of the book of Haggai and their intended audience would have viewed the traditions used and alluded to in the book as a part of their own traditio-religious framework. Texts may have existed, but my primary interest lies in the particularities and distinctive configuration of the traditions present in Haggai.[21]

A second and related clarification concerns the designations which may be used appropriately of the major traditions or configurations of traditions in the early Persian period.[22] It seems appropriate to speak

---

[18] Cf. Tollington (*Tradition*, pp. 12–19, esp. p. 19) who suggests that Haggai and Zechariah may have had access to some earlier texts. She is critiqued for assuming this without demonstrating it by Sérandour, "Réflexions", p. 75. She does, however, clearly state "the availability of such texts implies nothing about the use to which these prophets may have put such material" (p. 19). Thus it would appear that the existence of such texts is not essential to her argument.

[19] See, for example the discussion in E. Ben Zvi, "Looking at the Primary (Hi)story and the Prophetic Books as Literary/Theological Units within the Frame of the Early Second Temple: Some Considerations", *SJOT* 12 (1998): 26–43, and Sérandour, "Réflexions", p. 75.

[20] On the difficulties involved in the notion of citation, see R. R. Schultz, *The Search for Quotation: Verbal Parallels in the Prophets*, (JSOTSup 180; Sheffield: Sheffield Academic Press, 1999), esp. p. 110. Interestingly, Schultz's work contains no references to Haggai.

[21] Despite the fact that she maintains that textual sources may have been in existence at the time of Haggai, Tollington generally argues from tradition rather than text, in line with my own approach. For example, she states (*Tradition*, p. 76), "in order to gain prophetic credibility [Haggai and Zechariah] drew on the long-established religious traditions of the people, as did their pre-exilic predecessors, to reinforce their authenticity."

[22] Steck ("Streams of Tradition") devotes a significant section of his article to the

of the following commonly identified themes, motifs and theological foci as representing some major constituents of the theological landscape of early Persian Yehud: (1) Zion theology, and its close relative, Jerusalem royal theology;[23] (2) Deuteronomism,[24] which, at this point, would include the traditions of the Exodus and conquest,[25] and be in evidence in the Deuteronomistic History, and certain prophetic compilations including Amos, Hosea, and Jeremiah;[26] (3) wisdom traditions;[27] and (4) priestly theology, as manifested in portions of Exodus, Numbers, and most especially in Leviticus and Ezekiel.[28] In addition to these major configurations one finds evidence for various independent and disparate prophetic traditions.[29] Significant theological developments

---

delimitation and historical progression of theological streams within the history of Israel. It is not my purpose to dialogue with the particular details of his analysis, however I must hasten to underline the fact that Steck's analysis of whether or not a given motif or tendency can be called a "theological stream" is not germane to my own analysis. I am interested in the use of tradition, not the relative importance or systemic complexity of the tradition.

[23] Cf. N. W. Porteous, "Jerusalem-Zion: The Growth of a Symbol", in *Verbannung und Heimkehr: Beiträge zur Geschichte und Theologie Israels im 6. und 5. Jahrh. v. Chr., Festschrift W. Rudolph*, (ed. A. Kuschke; Tübingen: J. C. B. Mohr, 1961), pp. 235–51; R. E. Clements, "Deuteronomy and the Jerusalem Cult Tradition", *VT* 15 (1965): 300–12; J. J. M. Roberts, "The Davidic Origin of the Zion Tradition", *JBL* 92 (1973): 329–44; M. Weinfeld, "Zion and Jerusalem as Religious and Political Capital: Ideology and Utopia", in *The Poet and the Historian*, (HSS 26; ed. R. E. Friedman; Chico, CA: Scholars Press, 1983), pp. 75–113.

[24] For a survey of recent literature on Deuteronomism and the Deuteronomistic school see, with bibliography, R. Person, "Deuteronomic History". Cf. also E. W. Nicholson. *Deuteronomy and Tradition*, (Philadelphia: Fortress, 1967); idem., *Preaching to the Exiles: A Study of the Prose Tradition in the Book of Jeremiah*, (Oxford: Basil Blackwell, 1970); L. Derousseaux, *La crainte de Dieu dans l'Ancien Testament*, (LD 63; Paris: Cerf, 1970), pp. 205–57; Weinfeld, *Deuteronomy*.

[25] Nicholson, *Deuteronomy and Tradition*, p. 49; Steck, "Streams of Tradition", pp. 202–4.

[26] Cf. R. Person (*Second Zechariah and the Deuteronomic School*, [JSOTSup 167; Sheffield: Sheffield Academic Press, 1993], pp. 171–72) who posits a postexilic Deuteronomic canon. Blenkinsopp, (*History*, pp. 161–65) envisages an exilic canon including the Deuteronomistic History and various prophetic texts. Person views this canon as a precursor to a postexilic Deuteronomistic canon.

[27] Cf. J. Blenkinsopp, *Wisdom and Law in the Old Testament: The Ordering of Life in Israel and Early Judaism*, (Oxford: Oxford University Press, 1995) and L. G. Perdue, *Wisdom and Creation: The Theology of Wisdom Literature*, (Nashville: Abingdon, 1994).

[28] P. P. Jenson, *Graded Holiness: A Key to the Priestly Conception of the World*, (JSOTSup 106; Sheffield: Sheffield Academic Press, 1992); J. G. Gammie, *Holiness in Israel*, (OBT; Minneapolis: Fortress, 1989).

[29] Cf. Blenkinsopp, *History*, pp. 163–93.

subsequent to our period would include the work of the Chronicler,[30] the Ezra and Nehemiah corpus[31] and the literature relative to the worship at the Second Temple.[32]

Early Persian Yehud was a highly distinctive and novel context. In such conditions how could the older traditions still be meaningful—particularly those involving royal hopes, national pre-eminence, and the eschatological rule of Yahweh over the nations?[33] At the conclusion of each of Chapters 5–8, I will present an analysis of the rhetorical and hermeneutical strategies in Haggai which address these questions.

---

[30] Cf. P. Abadie, "Une 'histoire corrective': le modèle du chroniste", *Théophilyon* 2 (1997): 65–90; P. R. Ackroyd, "The Theology of the Chronicler", *LTQ* 8 (1973): 101–16.

[31] Cf. Williamson, *Ezra*.

[32] On which cf. G. Wanke, "Prophecy and Psalms in the Persian Period", in *CHJ*, pp. 162–87.

[33] Cf. P. R. Ackroyd, "Faith and Its Reformulation in the Post-Exilic Period: Sources", *TD* 27 (1979): 323–34; idem, "Faith and Its Reformulation in the Post-Exilic Period: Prophetic Material", *TD* 27 (1979): 335–46; Tollington, "Readings in Haggai", pp. 194–208.

CHAPTER FIVE

# HAGGAI 1:1–15

## 5.1. TRANSLATION AND TEXTUAL CRITICISM

[1] In the second year of Darius the King, in the sixth month, on the first day of the month, the word of Yahweh came through Haggai the prophet[1] to Zerubbabel, son of Shealtiel, governor[2] of Yehud, and to Joshua, son of Jehozadak, the high priest, as follows:[3]

[2] This is what Yahweh Sebaoth says,[4] "This people says,[5] 'This is not[6] the time to come,[7] the time for the house of Yahweh to be rebuilt.'"

---

[1] The LXX adds λέγων εἰπὸν here (saying: say ... ), and in some MSS δὴ (surely, indeed). The Tg, Syr, and Vulg follow the MT. In 1:1 the prepositions ביד and אל introduce, respectively, the intermediary through whom the word comes, and its addressees, while לאמר introduces what is contained in that word (Wolff, p. 13). The LXX reading disrupts this pattern (Amsler, p. 19). When the prophet's role as one who receives the word of Yahweh is underlined, אל is employed (2:10, 20) followed by a command to speak. This schema is not followed in 2:1, 2 (MT), on which see below. It is therefore likely that the LXX represents an addition, modeled upon 2:1 and 10.

[2] On the meaning of פחה cf. the discussion of the political status of Yehud in ch. 3. The LXX renders פחה here and in 1:12, 14; 2:21, 22 by ἐκ φυλῆς Ιουδα (of the tribe of Judah). Bianchi ("Rôle de Zorobabel", pp. 158–59), following Sacchi ("L'esilio", p. 142, n. 17) sees the LXX as reflecting an original Hebrew reading such as "*mimmišpāḥat yehûdâ.*" Alternatively, Wolff (p. 29) suggests that the Greek translators assumed פחה to be synonymous with משפחה. Amsler (p. 19 n. 2) opines that the LXX messianizes here. The Targum reads *zerubbabel rabba' debêt yehûdâ* ("Zerubbabel the great one [cf. Ezra 4:10] of the house of Judah" a rendering which Bianchi ("Zorobabel", p. 158, n. 42) calls "mid-way" between the LXX and the MT. The Peshitta reads *zrbbl rb' dyhwdh*. Bianchi (ibid., p. 158) further notes that the Vetus Latina, I Esdr 5:2 and Josephus (*Ant.* 12.73) follow the LXX and see a reference here to Zerubbabel's Davidic origins. The book of Haggai is the only place where the LXX renders פחה in this way.

[3] On לאמר as a complementizer introducing direct speech cf. C. L. Miller, *The Representation of Speech in Biblical Hebrew Narrative: A Linguistic Analysis*, (HSM 55; Atlanta: Scholars, 1996).

[4] Translating the Messenger Formula כה אמר יהוה with Chary and the JB, by the present rather than the past, thus reflecting the lively and polemical character of the debate.

[5] On this translation of the perfect, see the exegesis.

[6] Wolff (p. 29) suggests a restrictive sense for לא i.e. "not yet" cf. Gen 2:5; 29:7; Ps 139:16; Job 22:16. Such a translation would imply that the debate was centred around theological issues relative to the divinely appointed moment for the undertaking of the project. On this cf. the exegesis. The usual sense of negation of לא is more appropriate here.

[7] The principal problem here concerns the repetition of עת in the MT, a repe-

[3] Then the word of Yahweh came through Haggai the prophet,
[4] "Is it time for you yourselves,[8] to live in your[9] paneled houses while this house is desolate?"

---

tition which is not reflected in the versions. The LXX reads Οὐχ ἥκει ὁ καιρὸς τοῦ οἰκοδομῆσαι τὸν οἶκον κυρίου, a reading which is also reflected in the Vulg and Syr. The Tg adds כען (now). There are four major solutions to the textual problem. (1) One may emend עֶת־בֹּא to בָּא [עַתָּה] (it is not now ... ). The second עת would be a masculine noun and the subject of בא, in the qal pf. 3 m. sg. (van Hoonacker, Sellin, Elliger, Horst, Deissler, JB, NEB), cf. D. Barthélemy, ed., *Critique textuelle de l'Ancien Testament. Tome 3: Ezéchiel, Daniel et les 12 prophètes*, (OBO 50/3; Fribourg/Göttingen: Editions Universitaires/Vandenhoeck & Ruprecht, 1992), p. 923. (2) One may delete עֶת־בֹּא (Wolff) or עֶת־בֵּית יהוה להבנות (North) as glosses. (3) One may retain the MT and consider עת as a masculine noun and subject of בא construed as a perf. or an inf. abs., thus reading "the time has not come, the time to rebuild the house of Yahweh" cf. Reventlow, Meyers and Meyers, Verhoef, Petersen, and the TOB. (4) One may retain the MT with its twofold use of עת and reading the verbal form בא as an inf. cs. used genitivally (GKC §114b, cf. Tadmor, "Appointed Time", p. 403), thus "it is not a time for coming." Taken this way, the subject of בא is not עת, but rather, by implication, the people, as is explicitly the case in v. 14. The second עת supplies a further explanation of the specific time under discussion (thus Barthélemy, *Critique textuelle*, 3:924 citing also Van der Woude. This yields the translation, "It is not the time [for us] to come, the time for the house of Yahweh to be rebuilt." Cf. the proposal of L. Bauer *Zeit des Zweiten Tempels-Zeit der Gerechtigkeit: Zur sozio-ökonomischen Konzeption in Haggai-Sacharja-Maleachi-Korpus*, [BEATAJ 31, Frankfurt-am-Main: Peter Lang, 1992], p.150–53. Bauer views the people's words in 1: 2 as a verbless clause of identification, with את־בא as the subject.

In spite of the MT's isolation I reject the first two options for the following reasons. First the MT carries the *lectio difficilior* and the absence of the second עת in the versions is easily explained by the desire to simplify the text. Furthermore the conjectural emendation to עַתָּה] בָּא] is not necessary to explain the LXX reading. As well, emending to the apocopated form of עתה is rather dubious in a book where the full form appears frequently (1:5; 2:3, 4, 15, cf. Wolff p. 29). The threefold repetition of עת (v. 2, 2x, v. 4, 1x) fits well with the passage's rhetorical emphasis on the critical question of the opposing opinions of the appropriate use of time held by Yahweh and the people (see exegesis, and cf. Meyers and Meyers, p. 20, Amsler, p. 19, n. 3 and Steck, "Zu Haggai", pp. 361–62, n. 21. Retaining the MT, option (4) appears more satisfactory than (3) for the following reasons: (1) the subject of בוא in v. 14 is the people. This is highly significant in that v. 14 describes the people as doing that which they formerly rejected, and as such forms a counterpoint to v. 2. (2) The question at issue is the use of time not its calculation (see exegesis). (3) The demographic data would indicate that Jerusalem was sparsely populated at the time, and that it would be necessary to journey to the site from elsewhere, cf. Barthélemy, *Critique textuelle*, 3:924, *supra* ch. 3 and the exegesis).

[8] The pronouns לכם and אתם as well as the possessive בבתיכם underline the contrast between the people's neglect of Yahweh and his house and their preoccupation with their own interests, cf. Joüon §146d; GKC §135d.

[9] The *BHS*, following a few MSS of the LXX, the Tg, and Vulg, proposes the omission of the pronominal suffix. The MT nevertheless makes good sense. The versions most likely omitted the possessive due to its proximity to the personal pronoun אתם, ὑμῖν, *vobis*. The inclusion of the possessive reinforces the polemical tone of the

[5] Now then, this is what Yahweh Sebaoth says, "Ponder your conduct and its results.[10]

[6] "You have sown much, but you have harvested little.[11] You eat,[12] but you are not satisfied. You drink, but not to your fill.[13] You clothe yourselves, but you are never warm enough. The wage earner earns income[14] [only to put it] in a pierced money pouch."

[7] Therefore this is what Yahweh Sebaoth says,[15] "Ponder your conduct and its results.

[8] "Go up[16] to the mountain and bring back[17] wood and build the temple. I will take pleasure in it,[18] and I will receive the glory it brings me.[19]

---

passage, cf. Amsler p. 19, n. 4; Wolff p. 30.

[10] The sense of דרך here is more comprehensive than simply "conduct" or "the way you have chosen." It refers to the choices the people have made and the outcome of those choices.

[11] Inf. abs. (hi) of בוא. The subject and temporal value of the verbal form here are to be implied from the context, Joüon §123y. The movement from conjugated verb to inf. is stylistic, cf. Joüon §123x; *IBHS* §35.5.2.

[12] Inf. abs. to be translated by the present, since it describes an ongoing reality. The absence of *waw* here indicates a series of questions and assertions whose temporal value is to be presupposed from the context, cf. *IBHS* §35.5.2.a.

[13] Inf. cs. fem., Joüon §49d; BL §43d.

[14] MT מִשְׂתַּכֵּר. Two Hebrew MSS read יִשְׂתַּכֵּר (hi impf. 3 m. sg.). The ptc. in the MT presupposes the durative nuance of the verb here (Joüon §121c).

[15] The *BHS* suggests dittography here. Consequently the Messenger Formula could be either omitted (Wellhausen, p. 173) or moved to the beginning of v. 9 (Amsler, van Hoonacker, Horst, Chary). However no MS omits the phrase and its repetition sets in bold relief the gap between the results of the people's choices and the way Yahweh would have them choose, cf. Meyers and Meyers, p. 27. I therefore retain the phrase.

[16] The verbal structure of the first part of the v. is thus: impv. עלו + wcs+ perf., והבאתם indicating succession (Joüon §119i, l) + impv. ובנו.

[17] LXX κόψατε. Wolff (p. 30) notes that Budde and van der Woude suggest reading וּבְרֵאתֶם (בְרא, meaning to "clear the ground" cf. Josh 17:18) but rejects the suggestion.

[18] The verbal form here could be impf. or coh. If coh., the verb expresses Yahweh's purpose or intention (GKC §108d). If it is an impf. it could carry either a final sense as in the coh. (GKC §107n), thus "so that I might delight in it" or a sense of simple futurity, "and I will delight in it." See following note.

[19] Q coh.; K impf. It is possible that an archaic subj. ending was taken to be a coh. (Meyers and Meyers p. 28). In this case a final sense is to be implied, "so that I might be glorified." One may also follow the K, and read a ni impf. of כבד (the verb here carrying a passive or reflexive nuance), conveying the idea of permission or acceptance, thus, "and I will [let myself] be honoured" (Wolff p. 14). The second option seems more likely. If this option is taken, it would seem most appropriate to see the preceding verb as an impf. as well.

[9] "You expected[20] much, but alas, [it turned] to[21] so little. And when you brought it home, I blew it away. Why? —oracle of Yahweh Sebaoth—because of my house which itself[22] stands desolate, while all of you run to your own houses.

[10] "For this reason, the skies[23] above you[24] have withheld [their] dew,[25] and the earth has withheld[26] its produce.

[11] "I called for[27] a drought upon the land, the mountains, the grain, the fresh oil,[28] and that which[29] the earth brings forth; upon people and beasts and upon all human endeavour."

[12] Then Zerubbabel, son of Shealtiel,[30] and Joshua, son of Jehoza-dak, the high priest, and all the remnant of the people responded in obedience[31] to the voice of Yahweh their God, that is to[32] the words of

---

[20] Inf. abs. whose temporal value is to be inferred from the context, as above, n. 12.

[21] MT והנה, LXX καὶ ἐγένετο suggesting the emendation of והנה to וְהָיָה or וְהִיא (cf. BHS). The correction is unnecessary. The Vulg supports the MT, cf. Wolff p. 30.

[22] The masc. pers. pron. הוא underlines the importance of the description of Yah-weh's house in the following relative clause, and the contrast introduced by the 2 m. pl. pers. pron. אתם which follows (Wolff, p. 30).

[23] MT שָׁמַיִם. One Hebrew MS adds the def. art. Wolff, (p. 30) notes the frequent omission of the def. art. in lists. Furthermore, there is no def. art. in Deut 28:23 which contains a similar formulation. See following note.

[24] MT על־כן עליכם. The words על־כן are lacking in the LXX and Syr. Dittography is suggested by Chary, Wolff, and Wellhausen. Nevertheless the presence of the phrase in the Vulg and Mur would argue in favour of its retention. Meyers and Meyers retain the MT and translate "because of you" or "against you." Alternatively the MT עַל־כֵּן שָׁמֶיךָ אֲשֶׁר עַל־רֹאשְׁךָ עֲלֵיכֶם can be considered a Deuteronomism inspired by Deut 28:23, and translated "for this reason the skies above you." Therefore with the RSV, TOB, Meyers and Meyers, and Amsler I retain the MT, and with Barthélemy, (Critique textuelle, 3:925) accept the last translational option above.

[25] The MT has מטל (from dew), a reading supported by the LXX, Vulg, and Syr. The Tg reads מטרא (from rain). Wolff (p. 15) proposes emending to טלם (their dew), however such a correction lacks any textual support, cf. Barthélemy, Critique textuelle, 3:925. The pron. suf. on יבולה however can be seen as doing double duty, and is likely to be implied here.

[26] The מן preceding טל and governed by כלא does "double duty" and has been elided before יבולה, cf. Meyers and Meyers, p. 31.

[27] Wcs. + impf. continuing the temporal sequence of v. 10.

[28] The BHS, based on no textual evidence, suggests that this item may be a sec-ondary addition.

[29] Over 20 Hebrew MSS, as well as some MSS of the Vulg and Syr, add כל (all) before תוציא. Barthélemy (Critique textuelle, 3:926), notes that here כל is a facilitating reading. The MT has the support of the older MSS of the LXX, and is the lectio difficilior (Wolff. p. 31). It therefore should be omitted.

[30] Apocopated form, cf. Wolff p. 31.

[31] Singular verb and compound subject, cf. Joüon §150q and exegesis.

[32] The translation of ועל and the phrase which follows it is highly significant. For

Haggai the prophet because[33] Yahweh their God[34] had sent him.[35] And the people were[36] gripped with fear before Yahweh.

[13] Then Haggai, the messenger of Yahweh through Yahweh's mandate,[37] said to the people, "I am with you, oracle of Yahweh."

[14] Thus[38] Yahweh stirred up the spirit of Zerubbabel, son of Sheal-

---

Wolff, (p. 31), ועל consists of a *waw-explicativum* plus על, (cf. GKC §146f). In that case the translation would be, "The voice of Yahweh their God, that is to say, the words of Haggai the prophet." Meyers and Meyers (pp. 24–35) implicitly follow this rendering. For Amsler, על means "based on" (p. 24). Petersen translates "because of" citing Williams §291. However the *waw* attached to the preposition על proves difficult to translate if a causal sense is attributed to על. The JB, Verhoef, and Chary translate ועל as if it were the equivalent of ב in שמע בקול יהוה, thus "They obeyed the voice of Yahweh their God and the words of Haggai." This however does not do justice to the Hebrew which is expressing something about the relationship between Yahweh's voice and Haggai's words. Wolff's translation is to be followed.

[33] כאשר has three primary acceptations: (1) similarity, "like, as, just as" (cf. GKC §161, comparative sense); (2) a causal sense, "for, because;" and (3) a temporal sense, "when." The third option, which is taken by Meyers and Meyers is rather redundant. The first acceptation would introduce the concept of the idea of a "mission" (so JB, Chary) but such a notion is absent here. The causal sense is preferable: Haggai's words were Yahweh's words because the former was sent by the latter (this despite Verhoef [pp. 82–83] who follows van der Woude, and affirms that the pron. suf. refers to the message not the prophet).

[34] The LXX reads πρός αὐτούς (= אֲלֵיהֶם). Several MSS of the LXX as well as the Syr, Vulg, and Tg reflect אליהם as well as אלהיהם. Wolff considers the MT's reading (אלהיהם) a dittography caused by the same expression a few words earlier. I retain the MT for the following reasons: (1) the absence of any variants in the Hebrew MSS; (2) the frequent use of repetitions in Haggai (for example שים לבב and נאם יהוה); (3) the rhetorical purpose of the repetition, (cf. Meyers and Meyers, pp. 34–35; 45–46); and (4) the importance of the expression in the Deuteronomistic tradition.

[35] Verb to be translated as a pluperfect, Joüon §112c.

[36] Verb in the plural with collective subject, as frequently in postexilic Hebrew, cf. U. Schattner-Rieser, "L'hébreu post-exilique", in *La Palestine à l'époque perse*, (ed. E.-M. Laperrousaz and A. Lemaire; Paris: Cerf, 1994), pp. 189–224, esp. p. 217.

[37] The words במלאכות יהוה are not found in most MSS of the LXX (cf. Wolff, p. 31, for the relevant readings). Given that מלאכות is a *hapax*, its omission is understandable. The present translation gives ב a causal sense (Williams §247), and attributes to מלאכות the idea of charge, mandate or commission (thus with Wolff, "at Yahweh's charge [*Auftrag*]", Rudolph, "by virtue of Yahweh's commission [*Sendungsauftrag*]" and *pace* Verhoef, "according to the mission of the Lord"). Amsler seems inconsistent in his interpretation of the phrase. In his translation he renders it "according to the message of Yahweh" (p. 20) whereas in the commentary he uses "through Yahweh's sending" (p. 25). On the meaning "to send" of the root לאך cf. Wolff, p. 51.

[38] The translation, "Then Yahweh stirred up ..." adopted by Verhoef, Petersen, Chary, and Wolff is incongruous in that the obedience mentioned in 1:12 consisted of the willingness to undertake the rebuilding of the temple which is carried out in v. 14. Rudolph (p. 28) presents a better option in his recapitulative translation, "In this manner, Yahweh stirred up (*So erweckte* ... ), cf. exegesis.

tiel, governor of Judah, and the spirit of Joshua, son of Jehozadak the high priest, and the spirit of all the remnant of the people, and they came and they set to work on[39] the house of Yahweh Sebaoth their God.

[15] This was[40] on the twenty-fourth day of the sixth[41] month of the second year of Darius.[42]

## 5.2. STRUCTURAL AND LITERARY CONSIDERATIONS

From a purely formal point of view Hag 1:1–15[43] may be divided into three sections, 1:1–3; 4–11, and 12–15, corresponding to the more poetic language of the central section and the prose of the introduction and conclusion.[44] However from a thematic and rhetorical point of view vv. 2–3 cannot be abstracted from vv. 4–11 and thus vv. 2–11 must be considered as a unit. The scene begins with an introductory formula which draws the reader/hearer into the world of the drama that will follow, and introduces the main characters (1:1). The introductory formula begins with a date formula (v. 1a) which situates Haggai's words in a very precise historical context.[45] This date formula is followed by the *Wortereignisformel* or Word-Event Formula,[46] ויהי דבר־יהוה ביד ("the

---

[39] Meyers and Meyers and Petersen rightly translate, "on the House of Yahweh." The implication is that the builders addressed whatever needed to be done.

[40] A significant number of exegetes place 2:15–19 after 1:15a (Amsler, Wolff, Sellin, Rothstein, Mitchell). Notwithstanding the arguments advanced in favour of this transposition, three considerations speak strongly against it. (1) The date formula which closes the first scene is not inappropriate, but may be explained as an inclusio whose rhetorical function is to underline the rapidity with which the work was begun. The lapse of time (*pace* Amsler, p. 27) is rather brief, given that it includes the time when the decision was made, the work organized and the material procured. (2) The transposition lacks any MS evidence. (3) The separation of 2:15–19 from 2:10–14 is artificial as the text appears to be a unified composition, cf. K. Koch, "Haggais", p. 60.

[41] Wolff, (p. 39) considers בששי to be a gloss, the *beth* preceding the month being unusual in the context of the book (cf. 1:1a, השּׁשּׁי; 2:1a, לשּׁשּׁי; 2:10, 18 לתשׁיעי). But why would a glossator add an aberrant form? The MT's *lectio difficilior* should be retained.

[42] This regnal year notice is frequently considered to be the first element of the date formula at 2:1 (Amsler, Wolff). Indeed, if a choice needs to be made, it would seem judicious to place the regnal year with the date in 2:1 and deem the year in the date in 1:15a to be implied from the context. It is however possible that the year designation does double duty and serves both formulae (cf. Meyers and Meyers, pp. 34–36).

[43] On the inclusion of the full date formula in 1:15, see previous note.

[44] This following the *BHS*, as opposed to the BHK³.

[45] On the form of the date formula, cf. ch. 2, *supra*, on the specific dates cf. ch. 3, and exegesis.

[46] The Eng. tr. (p. 32) renders the term as the "confronting event of God's word."

word of Yahweh came to" v. 1bα) which has a dual function. First, it introduces and identifies the one event which is foundational to all else in the book, the reception and proclamation of a word from Yahweh.[47] Second, it prepares the readers/hearers for the content of the divine word that will follow in v. 2, in the form of direct discourse. Following the Word-Event Formula the reader encounters three central characters in the dramatic movement of the book: Haggai, Zerubbabel, and Joshua (v. 1 bβ). As Floyd has noted, in contrast to many "prophetic superscriptions" the introductory formula in Hag 1:1 contains syntactically complete clauses and is integrated into that which follows.[48]

Verse 2 is frequently alluded to in discussions of the earlier stages in the book's formation.[49] The verse is thought to be awkward here[50] because of the quotation of the people's words introduced by the Messenger Formula (*Botenformel*, כה אמר יהוה צבאות [thus says Yahweh of Hosts]).[51] However, from a literary and dramatic point of view, v. 2 plays a critical role: a new *dramatis persona*, the people (העם), is introduced as well as the dramatic conflict which moves the pericope forward. This conflict is presented to the reader by means of a citation of the thoughts of the people, introduced by לאמר.[52] This citation contains the *Leitworten* of 1:1–15: אמר (to say); עת (the moment); בוא (to come); בנה (to build); בית יהוה (the house of Yahweh).[53] As we will see, a very clear and sharp triangular opposition is created between Yahweh and Haggai on one hand, and Zerubbabel, Joshua, and the people, on the other.

Having introduced the dramatic conflict in v. 2, the next verse repeats the Word-Event Formula of v. 1, in order to introduce the prophetic response contained in vv. 4–11. This response consists primarily

---

This, however is too cumbersome to use as a regular designation, hence my choice of Word-Event Formula. To facilitate the reading of the text, following the first reference to the relevant German terms, I will use capitalized English equivalents.

[47] Wolff, p. 37.

[48] Floyd, "Narrative", p. 476.

[49] Cf. Wolff, pp. 32–33, and W. S. Prinsloo, "The Cohesion of Haggai 1:4–11", in *"Wünschet Jerusalem Frieden": Collected Communications to the XIIth Congress of the International Organization for the Study of the Old Testament, Jerusalem 1986*, (BEATAJ 13; ed. M. Augustin and K.-D. Schunck; Frankfurt am Main: Peter Lang, 1988), pp. 337–43.

[50] Cf. Wolff, pp. 32–33, Beuken, p. 30, and Rudolph, p. 32.

[51] Floyd, ("Narrative", p. 478f) notes the difficulty in knowing who is speaking here. In contrast to his position, I maintain that it is neither the narrator not the prophet, but Yahweh who repeats to the leaders what the people have been saying.

[52] On the use of לאמר as a complementizer introducing direct discourse, cf. n. 3, *supra*.

[53] Cf. Verhoef p. 21.

of questions and exhortations which employ various forms of prophetic reproach and disputation, as well as a promise of salvation (v. 8).[54] Koch and Steck maintain that the unity of vv. 3–8 on the one hand, and vv. 9–11 on the other is redactional, the two parts each having had an earlier, independent existence. Steck maintains that vv. 9–11 is a second speech on the same theme as vv. 3–8, but delivered to a different audience. He opines that vv. 3–8 are addressed to the non-exiled Judaeans, whereas the content of vv. 9–11, was originally directed to the *golah*. The two oracles were later redactionally united, and in the present text, are directed to the repatriated population.[55] For Koch, vv. 9–11 are a second discourse redactionally added to reinforce the message of the first.[56]

While the hypothesis of the fusion of two originally separate prophetic discourses is certainly possible, several elements within the text indicate that vv. 3–11 in its present form is undergirded by a consistent rhetorical structure. Two major approaches have been taken to the structure of this section. Whedbee has maintained that vv. 3–11 constitute a chiasm: v. 8 forms the centre, while vv. 3–7 and vv. 9–11, which contain several corresponding elements, surround it.[57] This conclusion has been contested by Prinsloo, who sees the passage as having a "climactic" structure that builds up to v. 11.[58] Prinsloo's argument, however, is unconvincing. It is difficult to see in what way v. 11 is the climax of the pericope, when v. 8 represents both the *logical* terminus of the pericope (Haggai's whole point is to encourage the rebuilding of the temple and the restoration of Yahweh's relationship with his people) as well as its furthest *chronological* extension (Yahweh's future acceptance of the people's labour).[59] Prinsloo may be correct in seeing vv. 7–8 as a

---

[54] Beuken, (*Haggai*, p. 19) sees the section as containing: v. 4, *Scheltwort*; vv. 5–6 *Mahnwort*; vv. 7–8 *Auftrag* and *Heilswort*; v. 9 *Disputationswort*; v. 10 *Spruch/Entfaltung*; v. 11 *Eingreifen Gottes*. Steck ("Zu Haggai", p. 367) sees it as a *Diskussionswort* followed by a promise of salvation.

[55] Steck, "Zu Haggai", pp. 372–73. Steck's arguments for two distinct audiences are convincingly challenged by J. W. Whedbee, "A Question-Answer Schema in Haggai 1: The Form and Function of Haggai 1:9–11", in *Biblical and Near Eastern Studies. Essays in Honour of* William Sanford LaSor, (ed. G. A. Tuttle; Grand Rapids: Eerdmans, 1978), pp. 184–94, esp. p. 187, and by Floyd, "Narrative", p. 489.

[56] Koch, "Haggais", p. 58.

[57] Whedbee, "Question-Answer", pp. 188–89.

[58] Prinsloo, "Cohesion", p. 339.

[59] On the issue of time in narrative cf. C. H. J. vander Merwe, "'Reference Time' in Some Biblical Temporal Constructions", *Bib* 78 (1997): 503–24.

unit. However v. 7 is clearly transitional, facilitating the passage from
past/present to present/future. Nevertheless, the point remains that
Haggai's argument reaches its apex in v. 8, and vv. 9–11 return both
logically and chronologically to the same standpoint as vv. 4–6. Thus,
when one views vv. 7–8 as central to the passage, the following structure emerges. The Word-Event Formula of v. 3 introduces the prophetic
response to the popular sentiments expressed in 1:2. As in v. 1, the title
"prophet" is applied to Haggai. In v. 4, a polar rhetorical question[60]
calls into doubt the legitimacy of the people's opinion, expressed in v. 2.
The very clear opposition between the perspectives of Yahweh and his
people is emphasized by the exaggerated use of personal pronouns.[61]
The key terms עת and בית יהוה, found first in the peoples' attitude (v.
2), are taken up in the prophetic response. The question of v. 4 is followed by a call to reflection, introduced by ועתה (and now).[62] Verse
6 specifies which aspect of the people's behaviour is in view in v. 5.
Here the prophet uses vocabulary and motifs frequently employed in
"futility curses."[63] Verse 7 repeats v. 5, verbatim, with the exception of
ועתה and serves as a point of transition between the present and future.
The structure of the first half of the chiasm is therefore: question (v.
4); exhortation to reflection (v. 5), followed by the truth to be reflected
upon (v. 6); renewed call to reflection as an impetus to move from the
present to the future (v. 7), a future which is described in v. 8. Messenger Formulae are found in the beginning (v. 2), in the middle (v. 5), and
toward the end (v. 7) of the first half of the chiasm. The apex is found
in v. 8 where the solution to the dilemma is proposed.

Verse 8, an oracle of promise and assurance, is itself in chiastic form.
It employs five verbal forms with בנה הבית (build the house) in central
position. This central requirement is followed by a Messenger Formula
that ties it to the preceding section. The two volitives which precede the
central injunction specify preliminary steps required before the building
can take place "go … bring wood" (עלו … והבאתם); the two first person
forms which follow the central exhortation describe the divine response
to the people's activity (ארצה, אכבד).[64]

---

[60] Cf. *IBHS* §18.

[61] Cf. exegesis, *infra*.

[62] On the role of ועתה as a transitional indicator cf. Koch, "Haggais", pp. 56–60.

[63] D. R. Hillers, *Treaty Curses and the Old Testament Prophets*, (BibOr 16, Rome: Pontifical
Biblical Institute, 1964), pp. 28–29. Tollington (*Tradition*, pp. 189–98) is reticent to see
futility curses here. See my discussion, *infra*, in the exegesis.

[64] These forms are more fully discussed in the textual criticism and exegesis.

The second half of the chiasm (vv. 9–11) strengthens, deepens and concludes the argument begun in vv. 3–7. Verse 9a reopens the dispute with the people and, as is the case in v. 6, takes up the theme of disappointment and futility. However, here for the first time a verb in first person singular is employed with reference to Yahweh's role in the community's misfortunes, underlining the fact that it is Yahweh himself who is the author of these experiences.[65] By means of a rhetorical question, v. 9b further clarifies the activity of Yahweh by specifying the cause of the divine displeasure. There are at least three echoes of v. 4 in v. 9: (1) the interrogative form, (2) the terms חרב (desolate) and בית (house), and (3) the contrast between the community's preoccupation with its own interests and its neglect for the house of Yahweh. The verbs ישב (v. 4) and רוץ (v. 9) may form a sort of merism: whether they are at home or elsewhere, the people are preoccupied with their own interests, and show no concern for the house of Yahweh.[66]

Verses 10–11 are a fuller explanation of the preceding themes.[67] They make explicit that which is intimated in v. 6 and v. 9. First, the failure of sky and earth to yield their normal issue was due to the community's neglect of the temple (v. 10). Second, the drought[68] which was decimating the economic life of the community was called by Yahweh himself. In conclusion, vv. 4–11 is best characterized as a "prophetic disputation."[69] The rhetorical goal of the section is thus quite clear. The hearers/readers are called to a decision: "Are we going to remain under Yahweh's displeasure, or will we choose to obey him and live in his favour?" The unity of vv. 4–11 is thus far from superficial.

A dramatic epilogue in the form of a prose narration[70] is appended to the oracular material and completes the scene.[71] The text passes

---

[65] Prinsloo ("Cohesion", p. 338) claims Whedbee to have been in error in stating that the 1 c. sg. appears for the first time in v. 9. It would seem evident that Whedbee's meaning was that the 1 c. sg. appears for the first time in relation to the adversities mentioned in the passage.

[66] Meyers and Meyers, p. 30.

[67] Whedbee ("Question-Answer", p. 188) qualifies them as expressions of divine judgment.

[68] חרב occurs here for the third time, clearly indicating the link between neglect of the temple (vv. 4, 9) and the community's misfortunes.

[69] Floyd, p. 273.

[70] The wcs. in v. 12 indicates the resumption of the narration begun in v. 1 and continued in v. 3. Thus the events described in vv. 12–14 are linked to the narrative framework introduced by the formula היה דבר־יהוה ביד־חגי הנביא in v. 1.

[71] Several scholars maintain that vv. 12–14 consist of two earlier redactional conclusions to 1:2–11, which have been conflated in the present text (cf. Ackroyd, "Studies",

from divine speech in the first person, to a third person[72] description of the response of the community to the prophet's words. The quasi-omniscient perspective of the narrator[73] permits the audience to penetrate into the hidden world of human motivation and divine activity.

Verse 12 signals an important transition. The reader awaits the outcome of the conflict described in 1:11.[74] What will the popular response be? The return to narration indicates that this outcome will be presented in the form of a dramatic denouement without which the logical and thematic movement of the text cannot proceed.[75] The obstacles and the challenges described in the subsequent three scenes presuppose the response described here.

The narration progresses by means of two identifiable units found in vv. 12–13, followed by a conclusion (v. 14). Each unit includes a description of the reaction of the principal *dramatis personae* to Yahweh, followed by a definition of the role and the identity of Haggai. In the first unit, Zerubbabel, Joshua, and the people obey Yahweh (v. 12aα). This is followed by a statement concerning the relationship between Haggai's words and Yahweh's voice (v. 12aβ). The second unit similarly begins by the people's response to Yahweh, this time one of fear (v. 12b). Again the role, status, and authority of Haggai are specified (v. 13a). This is followed by a declaration of the divine assistance and assurance, or Formula of Assistance (*Beistandformel*, אני אתכם, "I am with you"), followed by a Divine-Saying Formula (*Gottesspruchformel*, נאם יהוה, "oracle of Yahweh") that responds to the fear of the people (v. 13b). Verse 14 should be understood as a summary or a conclusion to vv. 12–13. The *waw* that begins it is to be translated "thus, so."[76] Verses 12 and 14 frame the

---

p. 167; Wolff, pp. 33–34; 49–53). This may indeed be the case, however it is equally viable to see the conclusion as a unified composition or an intentional reworking of an earlier conclusion into this present form, (Beuken, p. 30).

[72] With the exception of 1:13b, which should, nevertheless, be seen as an integral part of the narrative of the people's response, cf. Wolff, p. 18.

[73] Cf. House, *Zephaniah*, pp. 82–84.

[74] There are numerous stylistic, theological and thematic correspondences between 1:1–11 and 12–15, such as: the framing of the pericope by date formulae in 1:1 and 1:15a; the "house of Yahweh" in 1:2 and 14; the epithet יהוה צבאות in 1:2 and 1:14; the transformation of "this people" (העם הזה) in 1:2 to a "remnant" (וכל שארית העם) in v. 12; the contrast between the inactivity of vv. 2 and 8 and the activity of the people and their leaders in 1:14; the "words of Haggai" mentioned in 1:12 and the content of those words in 1:4–11.

[75] Cf. Floyd, p. 277.

[76] Cf. my discussion in the textual criticism and exegesis, cf. Williamson, *Ezra*, pp. 43–44.

narrative epilogue. Both verses include the names of the primary actors as well as the phrase "Yahweh their God."[77] However in v. 12, the subject is tripartite and the object singular (the voice of Yahweh), whereas in v. 14 the subject is singular and the object tripartite. The description of the people as a "remnant" (v. 14, שארית), which stands in contrast to the contempt expressed in v. 2, is highly important.[78] A major change has occurred. The editorial epithets attached to Haggai's name are also significant. The paronomasia of v. 13 (מלאך / מלאכות) links the prophet with the work undertaken by the people. The dating formula in v. 15, while unexpected, fulfills two important functions. First, it frames the scene,[79] and second, it underlines the fact that the resumption of the work occurred quickly.[80]

## 5.3. EXEGESIS

**[1]** The "second year of Darius, the sixth month, the first day of the month," refers to August 28, 520 BCE.[81] Darius I Hystaspes had quelled the series of revolts which broke out subsequent to his accession. The stability of his rule was known in Judah, and peace reigned in the western empire. The sixth month refers to the month of Elul.[82] It is possible that at this period the new moon was celebrated by an assembly (cf. Amos 8:5; 2 Kgs 4:23; cf. Ezek 45:17).[83] If so, this oracle, like the others in the book (2:1, 10, 18, 20), is to be associated with a festival. The link between the prophet's name (which is derived from

---

[77] On the threefold repetition of "Yahweh their God", cf. Meyers and Meyers, pp. 44–45.

[78] See R. Alter, *The Art of Biblical Narrative*, (New York: Basic Books, 1981), p. 975, on the significance of slight variations in narrative repetitions.

[79] Meyers and Meyers, p. 36.

[80] Cf. the exegesis and ibid., p. 46.

[81] Cf. ch. 3, *supra*. Petersen (p. 43) suggests that this date parallels Zech 1 which he describes as a "lament against the permanence of an unsatisfactory status quo." As I will demonstrate, Haggai views the present as acceptable, albeit impermanent.

[82] The numbered months follow the Babylonian calendar, which began in the spring with the month of Nissan.

[83] Amsler, p. 21. Petersen (p. 44) suggests that the "seventh month" mentioned in Ezra 3:1 should be situated in 520. Haggai would have therefore proclaimed his first oracle one month before the reconsecration of the altar and the resumption of regular sacrifice. Haggai's oracle would have come, in that case, at a particularly auspicious moment: not during a festival but at the time when one would normally have been celebrated. However a total cessation of sacrifice is widely seen as an unlikely hypothesis, cf. Ackroyd, *Exile and Restoration*, p. 25, n. 52.

the root חגג, meaning to make a pilgrimage or observe a pilgrimage feast)[84] and his preaching on festive occasions has often been noted.[85] Dating to the precise day is consistent with current scribal practice.[86] The dating formula thus identifies the precise moment of the coming of a word from Yahweh and roots that event in a precise historical context. This enables a situationally specific word from Yahweh, as well as the people's response to it, to be used paradigmatically as a means through which other analogous situations may be understood.[87]

The year is dated according to the reign of "Darius the king." The use of the epithet המלך has several literary and rhetorical repercussions. First, by employing a dating formula similar to the form used in collections attributed to the pre-exilic prophets and in 1–2 Kings—the reader almost passes over the fact that Darius is a non-Israelite king— the redactor subtly and implicitly situates Haggai in the lineage of his earlier prophetic homologues, granting him a status and authority similar to theirs.[88] Second, the author adds no epithet or qualification to the name Darius. Consequently, his position as king over Yehud is not challenged.[89] This implies the acceptance, at a certain level, on the part of the book's framer(s), of the legitimacy of his occupation of that position.[90] The definite article is normal in the designation of an office, profession, or honourific title in apposition to a proper name.[91] This use of the article is found frequently in Haggai (1:1, 3, 12, 13, 14, etc.).

The term דבר יהוה (the word of Yahweh) designates a divine message, or an oracle emanating from Yahweh and addressed to human-

---

[84] Petersen, p.17; cf. Rudolph, p. 82 and Amsler, p. 11.

[85] Petersen, p. 44; Chary, p. 17. T. André (*Le prophète Aggée*, [Paris: Fischbacher, 1895]) suggests that the name Haggai is merely a cipher, similar to that of Malachi. This suggestion has been repeatedly rejected, cf. Verhoef, p. 4–5 and Meyers and Meyers, pp. 8–9.

[86] Cf. ch. 2 *supra*. Meyers and Meyers (p. 6) suggest that the precision in the recording of the dates was related to the expectation of the end of the exile prophesied in Jer 25:11–12. While such a motivation cannot be excluded, it is difficult to prove.

[87] Verhoef, p. 47. Floyd, "Narrative", p. 478–79. Millard, "Prophétie et écriture", p. 141. Millard discusses the ANE practice of the inclusion of prophetic texts in collections as models for the interpretation of prophecy. Cf. my discussion of the function of date formulae, in ch. 2 and the exegesis of 2:20–23, *infra*.

[88] Even if one sees the pre-exilic prophetic books to be postexilic literary creations, the point still stands: Haggai is being portrayed as one of their number. For a defense of the existence of prophets and their books, cf. Barstad, "No Prophets?", esp. p. 41.

[89] Rudolph, p. 31; Petersen, p. 43.

[90] Meyers and Meyers, p. 5; Rudolph, p. 31.

[91] Joüon §131k; Wolff, p. 37.

kind.[92] The verb היה (to be), is used quite frequently with reference to the reception of the divine word by a prophet.[93] While היה is generally used with the preposition אל (to)[94] designating the recipient of the divine word, here it is followed by ביד (by the intermediary of). The presence of this less common construction has evoked several explanations. Wolff's suggestion, that ביד has the effect of causing the prophet to "recede into the background"[95] in order to underline the importance of the word, is questionable in light of the book's frequent allusions to the prophet, his titles, and his importance.[96] Equally dubious is Petersen's suggestion that the phrase is used because of the "dialogic" nature of Haggai's preaching, a style that characterized Haggai perhaps more than any other prophet.[97] A more satisfactory approach views ביד as an intensification of the *beth instrumentalis*.[98] Thus it stresses a specific human agent as the mediator through whom the divine message is communicated. This is quite clear, for example, in Exod 9:35; Lev 8:36; 10:11; Num 4:37–45 where Moses' role as intermediary is in view. In fact, in Exodus-Numbers, where the phrase דבר יהוה אל (the word of Yahweh [came] to) occurs frequently, when the act of communication is described "as it happens," the word comes from Yahweh to (אל) the individual spoken to, and then to (אל) its final recipient (Exod 6: 10–11, 28–29; 14:1–2; 16:11–12; 25:1–2; Lev 4:1–2; 11:1–2; 12:1–2; 15:1–2; 16:2, etc.; Num 5:5–6, 11–12; 6:1–2; 15:17–18, etc.). However, when this act is summarized, or when the text emphasizes the human agent involved, ביד is used. This is clearly seen in the expressions [כ]אשׁר ... ביד and על־פי ... ביד (Lev 8:36; Num 4:45; 9:23; 10:13; 17:5 [Eng. 16:40]; 27:23; 36:13). However, it is in the texts more specifically dealing with prophets and prophecy that this distinction between the source of the message, the intermediary who passes it on (ביד), and its recipient (אל) is most evident. This can be seen in the quasi-formulaic expression "the word of Yahweh through (ביד) his servant[s] …" (1 Kgs 8:53, 56; 14:18; 15:29; 2 Kgs 9:36; 10:10; 14:25). The same distinction between intermediary (ביד) and addressee (אל) may be observed in 1 Kgs 16:7, 12 and Jer 50:1.

---

[92] Meyers and Meyers, p. 7.

[93] Wolff (p. 37) cites the following statistics: Deut, 12x; Jer, 30x; Ezek, 50x.

[94] This idiom is found frequently in Exod-Num, Jer, and Ezek, but rarely in Deut-2 Kgs and 1–2 Chr.

[95] Wolff, p. 20.

[96] This theme will be expanded below.

[97] Petersen, p. 45.

[98] Wolff, p. 20; BDB 4d.

In all these texts ביד emphasizes the importance of the prophet rather than a diminution of his importance or authority.[99] Floyd notes that the use of ביד is well suited to the narrator's "objective" focus upon and interest in Haggai, rather than the prophet's "subjective" revelatory experiences.[100]

Thus, in Haggai, when the narrator specifically indicates that an oracle is addressed to a particular individual or group the formula PN אל חגי ביד is used (1:1, 3). However when the prophet is called upon to address questions to his hearers or to communicate the word of Yahweh without any indication of its recipient the word "comes" to him (אל, vv. 2, 10, 20). The only exception to this pattern is 2:1 where ביד occurs, whereas אל would have been expected.[101] The simplest explanation is that here the redactor has not followed the general schema present in the rest of the book. The position of Haggai's name in second place, after Yahweh and before the governor and high priest, is likely an indication of his importance in the eyes of the author[102] and of his mediating position between Yahweh and those whom he addresses.

Haggai is designated as הנביא, the prophet. A detailed discussion of the phenomenon of prophecy and the nature of the prophetic office cannot be undertaken here.[103] As Wilson observes, little can be deduced from the etymology or the verbal forms of נבא. The meaning of הנביא must be rather ascertained from an analysis of the behaviour of the individuals so designated.[104] Nevertheless, as a working definition, a prophet may be described as one who is privy to the divine perspective on particular human situations and, generally by divine command, transmits that knowledge to those to whom it is relevant.[105]

---

[99] Meyers and Meyers, p. 7.

[100] Floyd, "Narrative", p. 477.

[101] Cf. the discussion of the text critical issue, *in loco*.

[102] This order (intermediary-addressee) is reversed in 1 Kgs 16:12; 17:13; Jer 50:1.

[103] Cf. the bibliography cited *supra*, ch. 1, pp. 24–25.

[104] Wilson, *Prophecy and Society*, pp. 136–37.

[105] M. J. Buss (*IDB[S]* s. v. "Prophecy in Ancient Israel", p. 694) observes, "[T]he heart of prophecy lies in divine revelation in response to actual situations." To this could be added the definition proposed by M. Weippert (cited in Barstad, "No Prophets?", p. 46), "A prophet(ess) is a person … who (1) through a cognitive vision, a dream or the like becomes the subject of the revelation of a deity or several deities, and (2) is conscious of being commissioned by the deity/deities in question to convey the revelation in speech or metalinguistic behaviour to a third party who constitutes the actual recipient of the message."

The inclusion of the epithet הנביא is significant. The definite article[106] and the structural parallelism with the titles attributed to Darius, Zerubbabel, and Joshua clearly indicate that, for the redactor of
Haggai, the prophet occupies a social role which carries with it a very
real status, authority, and dignity. Haggai the prophet therefore takes
his place among the other recognized political and religious authorities of the time. The formula "PN הנביא" is found frequently in the
Deuteronomistic History (e.g., 2 Sam 7:2; 12:25; 24:11; 1 Kgs 1:10, 22,
23, 32, 34, 38, 45; 14:18; 16:7; 2 Kgs 9:1; 14:25) and becomes almost
exaggerated in Jeremiah (Jer 20:2; 25:2; 28:5, 6, 10, 11, 12, 15; 29:1, 29;
32:2; 38:9, 10, 14, etc.). With this designation, the redactor clearly situates Haggai within the lineage of the pre-exilic prophets (cf. Zech 1:4).[107]

It is important at this point to consider the literary and traditional
rooting of the presentation of the prophet by means of the phrase
ויהי דבר־יהוה ביד. Beuken maintains that ביד reflects both a Deuteronomistic and a chronistic milieu.[108] Mason proposes a priestly and
Deuteronomistic origin.[109] At least four significant literary considerations render the attribution of the expression to the Chronicler somewhat unlikely. (1) The phrase ביד הנביא PN (Hag 1:1, 3; 2:1), found
several times in the Deuteronomistic History and Jeremiah,[110] occurs
only once in Chronicles (2 Chr 29:25). (2) The use of הנביא as an
epithet is more frequent in Deuteronomy-2 Kings and in Jeremiah
than in Chronicles.[111] (3) Mason correctly notes that the use of ביד
in the Deuteronomistic tradition differs from its use in Chronicles.[112]
While the Deuteronomistic tradition uses the expression with reference to a variety of individuals, in Chronicles the only proper names
used with ביד are Moses (2 Chr 33:8; 34:14; 35:6) and Ahijah (2 Chr
10:15). Twice ביד is used concerning some unspecified prophets (2 Chr
29:25; 36:15).[113] (4) While the formulation היה דבר יהוה ביד PN הנביא
only appears in Hag 1:1 and 2:1, the analogous expression היה דבר
יהוה אל PN הנביא is found in Jer 46:1; 47:1; 49:34, and Zech 1:1, 7, none

---

[106] Joüon § 131k.
[107] Cf. Barstad, "No Prophets?", pp. 41–42, and n. 63, *supra*.
[108] Beuken, p. 28.
[109] Mason, "Editorial Framework", pp. 414–16.
[110] 2 Sam 12:25; 1 Kgs 14:18; 16:7, 12; 2 Kgs 14:25; Jer 37:2; 50:1.
[111] For example the term נביא is found only 19 times in 1–2 Chr, against 61 times in
Deut-2 Kgs and 50 times in Jer.
[112] Mason, "Editorial Framework", p. 415.
[113] Ibid., p. 415.

of which are to be identified with the Chronicler. While the specifics of the relationship between the Deuteronomistic tradition and Jeremiah remains disputed,[114] it is beyond doubt that this formulation was current in the Babylonian and early Persian periods in both prophetic and Deuteronomistic literature. It would be more accurate to say that the description of the coming of the divine word to Haggai offers more affinities with the Deuteronomistic tradition than with any other theological or literary matrix.

Having discussed the question of the time of Zerubbabel's arrival in Yehud,[115] a few further remarks are germane here. His name is Babylonian, meaning "seed of Babylon".[116] First Chronicles 3:19 lists Pedaiah, son of Jekoniah, as the father of Zerubbabel, whereas in Haggai (1:1, 12, 14; 2:2), Ezra (3:2, 8; 5:2), Nehemiah (12:1), and the NT (Matt 1:12; Luke 3:27), his father's name is given as Shealtiel. Various explanations have been proposed: he was the fruit of a levirate marriage,[117] or an adoption;[118] the redactor of Ezra, for political and ideological reasons sought to conceal his Davidic descent;[119] the question is one of textual criticism;[120] the same individual bore two names (Pedaiah and Shealtiel).[121] Certainty here appears to be impossible.

It is, however, highly likely that the redactional placement of his name at the head of the list of addressees grants him preeminent status[122] or at least the equality with Joshua as a communal leader.[123] As noted above, Zerubbabel is not to be equated with Sheshbazzar.[124]

---

[114] See, provisionally, Nicholson, *Deuteronomy and Tradition*, and idem, *Preaching to the Exiles, passim*; cf. also Person, "Deuteronomic History", p. 1, n. 1 (with bibliography) and idem, *Second Zechariah*, pp. 173–75.

[115] Ch. 3, above.

[116] Demsky, "Double Names", p. 29, n. 15; Lemaire, "Zorobabel", p. 49.

[117] Rudolph, p. 31; Beyse, *Serubbabel*, p. 30.

[118] Demsky, "Double Names", p. 38.

[119] Japhet, "Sheshbazzar and Zerubbabel", p. 71.

[120] Mitchell, p. 43.

[121] Meyers and Meyers, p. 11. However, cf. Demsky ("Double Names", p. 38) who maintains that Sheshbazzar and Shealtiel are two names for the same individual.

[122] J. Becker, *Messianic Expectations in the Old Testament*, (trans. D. E. Green; Philadelphia: Fortress, 1980), p. 66, cited in Tollington, *Tradition*, p. 134.

[123] D. W. Rooke, *Zadok's Heirs: The Role and Development of the High Priesthood in Ancient Israel*, (Oxford Theological Monographs; Oxford and New York: Oxford University Press, 2000), pp. 129–30; Petersen, p. 45; Chary, p. 18.

[124] Ch. 3, pp. 64–66.

His title "governor" indicates that he was the chief political authority of the Persian province of Yehud.[125]

Zerubbabel's name is followed by that of Joshua, son of Jehozadak, the high priest. Likely born in exile,[126] he was of Zadokite stock (2 Kgs 25:18; 1 Chr 5:40–41 [Eng. 6:14–15]), in conformity with the requirement of Ezek 44:15.[127] The designation "high priest" has called forth much discussion due to its relative infrequency in biblical sources.[128] Several explanations have been given for the meaning of the term and its presence here. De Vaux[129] and, to a certain extent, Amsler[130] and Beyse[131] consider it to be a postexilic term that replaced the earlier הכהן (priest) and הכהן הראש (head or chief priest).[132] Furthermore, Beuken and Amsler believe that in spite of its absence in the Chronistic tradition, the term was used by circles who supported Joshua to designate his position as the head of the Jerusalemite clergy.[133] This usage prevailed and ultimately displaced other designations.[134] In both of these reconstructions, the high priest is simply a neologism replacing other earlier titles, and designates the head or chief priest. Meyers and Meyers, by contrast, maintain that the expression "high priest" differs from הכהן הראש (head or chief priest) or הכהן (the priest) in terms of the functions and responsibilities fulfilled by the individual in question.[135] They affirm that even in pre-exilic times the "high priest" would be the one responsible for the collection and management of funds[136] and certain

---

[125] Cf. ch. 3 for a detailed discussion of this term.

[126] His grandfather, Seriah, was put to death in 587. His father, Jehozadak, was taken into exile, where Joshua was likely born, cf. Meyers and Meyers, p. 16. These authors suggest that he was about 50 in 520 BCE, and possibly older than Zerubbabel.

[127] Chary, p. 18.

[128] For a fuller discussion cf. Rooke, *Zadok's Heirs*, ch. 3 and Tollington, *Tradition*, pp. 126–31. See also the analysis in R. de Vaux, *Ancient Israel*, (trans. J. McHugh; London: Longman, Darton & Todd, 1961), 2:397–403.

[129] Ibid., 2:241.

[130] Amsler, pp. 79–80.

[131] Beyse, *Serubbabel*, p. 33, n. 1. Beyse and Galling see the title as anachronistic in Hag and Zech 1–8. They maintain that it only became current after the completion of the Second Temple. De Vaux sees it as authentic in Hag.

[132] 2 Kgs 12:8, 10; 22:12, 14 in this sense would be later redactional additions.

[133] Beuken, pp. 309–16.

[134] Amsler, p. 80.

[135] Meyers and Meyers, pp. 180–81; cf. also Rooke (*Zadok's Heirs*) p. 130 who views the term as designating a "new office."

[136] For example, Hilkiah, 2 Kgs 22:4, 8 and Jehoiada, 2 Kgs 12:11 [Eng. 10].

governmental activities,[137] in contrast with the "priest" or "head priest" whose field of activity was more cultic. Tollington takes an intermediate position, seeing the term as a continuation of its pre-exilic use with reference to "any senior priest who had special duties connected with the fabric of the temple and its upkeep."[138] Redactionally speaking, there is no insuperable objection to its use by a sixth-century editor, as evidenced by its presence in Lev 21:10; Num 35:25, 28; 2 Kgs 12:11 [Eng. 10]; 22:4, 8. The term could, therefore, refer to Joshua's managerial functions in the rebuilt temple (so Meyers and Meyers and Tollington), seen as analogous to the "high priest's" role at an earlier period. However, given its uneven presence in the sources, it is more judicious to see the term as simply a rough equivalent of the term הכהן הראש which evolved out of the realities of the life in the Babylonian period, without any special reference to managerial functions.[139]

At first glance Haggai's words of reproach to the leaders of the community appear misplaced. Why does the prophet confront them regarding the attitude of the people? Beuken views this as a stylistic predilection of the Chronicler.[140] However the reason is literary and dramatic in nature. Addressing the leaders serves both to introduce the book's foundational dramatic conflict and to open the curtain progressively on its principal characters. The reader encounters first Yahweh and his spokesman, then the local authorities, then finally the people. Furthermore, this progressive presentation also reveals the redactor's conception of the relationship between the community and its leaders. Wolff suggests that the prophet is calling the leaders to choose between allegiance to the people or Yahweh.[141] However, nothing else in the text would indicate that leaders were torn between the two. It is more likely that the address to the leaders indicates in some way their responsibility for promoting the temple's reconstruction, a role which they had thus

---

[137] Num 35:25, 28; Josh 20:6. Meyers and Meyers consider these three texts to be archaic.

[138] Tollington, *Tradition*, p. 131.

[139] If the term is seen to have evolved out of the high priest's managerial role in the (completed and well-established) Second Temple, its presence in Haggai would be best explained as a later gloss, or as evidence that the book was redacted much later than 515. However in light of the arguments in ch. 2 and the fact that the term does not necessarily imply a managerial role, I do not feel it to be a determinative factor in assessing the text's redactional history.

[140] Beuken, p. 32.

[141] Wolff, p. 23.

far neglected.[142] The text thus portrays a fragmented community: the prophet reproves the governor and the high priest about the people. Yahweh thus confronts a stalemate. Neither the civil authority, nor the religious leadership, nor the population in general will take any initiative. The solution must come from another quarter.

**[2]** Like his pre-exilic counterparts, Haggai speaks for Yahweh in first person direct discourse. Here the divine speech is introduced by the classical Messenger Formula.[143] The use of this formula encapsulates the book's view of the relationship between the oracles of Haggai and the words of Yahweh. When Haggai speaks, God speaks. Westermann notes, "In the words of the prophets, we deal with the word of God ... the prophetic discourse does not allow a division into two categories—(a) the word of God, and (b) the word of the prophet; a literary separation ... is not possible."[144] The epithet Yahweh Sebaoth has been the object of extensive critical investigation, the details of which cannot be discussed here.[145] It is important to note, however, the great frequency with which the epithet is used in Haggai (14 times) and Zechariah (53 times). One explanation attributes this frequent use to the desire to affirm the sovereignty and omnipotence of Yahweh, in spite of the defeat of his people, the sack of Jerusalem, the profanation of the temple, and Yehud's subjection to Persian rule.[146] However the term also had strong cultic connections. It is used in connection with Shiloh (1 Sam 1:3, 11), the ark (and especially the enthronement of Yahweh between the cherubim, 1 Sam 4:4; cf. 2 Sam 16:18), and the Jerusalem temple as Yahweh's dwelling place (Ps 48:9 [Eng. 8]; Isa 6:3, 5). It is therefore entirely apposite that it should become a widely used term in Haggai, Zechariah, and Malachi, texts that evidence special concern for the temple as the divine dwelling.[147]

---

[142] Cf. Petersen, p. 47.

[143] C. Westermann, *Basic Forms of Prophetic Speech*, (trans. H. C. White; Louisville: John Knox, 1991), pp. 93–95.

[144] Ibid., p. 95. Cf. also Meyers and Meyers, p. 18.

[145] See, provisionally, C. Dogniez, "Le Dieu des armées dans le Dodekapropheton: quelques remarques sur une initiative de traduction", in *IX Congress of the International Organization for Septuagint and Cognate Studies Cambridge 1995*, (SBLSCS 45; ed. B. A. Taylor), Atlanta: Scholars, 1997), p. 19–36; T. N. D. Mettinger, *The Dethronement of Sabaoth: Studies in the Shem and Kabod Theologies*, (ConBOT 18, Lund: Gleerup, 1982); B. N. Wambaq, *L'épithète divine Jahvé Seba'ôt. Etude philologique, historique et exégétique*, (Bruges: de Brouer, 1947), and Baldwin, pp. 44–45.

[146] Verhoef, p. 52.

[147] Meyers and Meyers, pp. 18–19. Much of this discussion is drawn from the excel-

The prophet questions the leadership concerning העם הזה (this people). This term is frequently one of reproach (cf. Hag 2:14; Zech 8:11;
Isa 6:9–10; 8:6, 12; Jer 4:11).[148] It is employed extensively in Isaiah (Isa
6:10; 8:6, 11–12; 9:15 Eng. 16]) and is also found in the Deuteronomistic
tradition (Deut 5:28; 9:13, 27; 31:16; Josh 7:7) and in Jeremiah (Jer 5:14;
6:19, 21; 7:16, 33; etc.). It has been suggested that in Hag 1:2 the term
is used to designate only a portion of the population.[149] However in the
present form of the book, by addressing this word to the leaders, the
term "the people" would most naturally imply the totality of the community over which they presided.[150] Joshua and Zerubbabel are told,
"this people says (and it is an established and ongoing conviction)[151]
that it is not time to come[152] [to Jerusalem][153] to restore[154] the house of
Yahweh."[155]

What was the basis of this popular conviction? Central to the issue
is the sense of the word עת (time, moment).[156] One line of interpretation asserts that theological or eschatological considerations are at
issue. The refusal of the people to begin the restoration of the temple is based upon the conviction that the time designated by Yahweh
for such an undertaking had not yet arrived. It is interesting to trace
the development of this hypothesis. In 1889, Wellhausen suggested that
two opposing theological conceptions were present in Hag 1. On one

---

lent survey in Baldwin, pp. 44–45.

[148] Wolff, pp. 23–23, despite A. Cody, "Chosen People", pp. 1–7.

[149] Rudolph, pp. 32–33; Steck, "Haggai", pp. 372–78.

[150] Meyers and Meyers, p. 19; Petersen, p. 47.

[151] The perfect aspect carries here a nuance similar to that of the gnomic aorist in
Greek and designates a frequent, customary or regular occurrence, GKC §106k.

[152] Cf. the textual criticism.

[153] As noted above, Barthélemy (*Critique textuelle*, 3:924) suggests that most of the
population lived at a distance from Jerusalem. If as Lipschits suggests ("Benjamin
Region", pp. 184–85) the reconstruction of Jerusalem coincided with the diminution
of the population of Mizpah, the people's statement may reflect this demographic
situation.

[154] On the state of the temple building, cf. the discussion in ch 3, above. The book of
Haggai presupposes situation in which human effort is required in order to make the
structure a suitable dwelling place for Yahweh. This basic premise is sufficient to move
the drama of the pericope forward. Cf. Ackroyd, *Exile and Restoration*, p. 25; Gelston,
"Foundations", pp. 232–35; S. Talmon, s. v. "Ezra and Nehemiah", *IDB[S]*, p. 319;
Petersen, pp. 88–89; and Meyers and Meyers, p. 39.

[155] This is a commonly used term with reference to the Jerusalem temple, cf. Meyers
and Meyers, p. 21.

[156] I have examined this question in an earlier article (Kessler, "ʿt [le temps]",
pp. 555–59), but will summarize and expand its argumentation here.

hand, there were those who saw the rebuilding of the temple as an essential and preliminary step to the coming of the messianic era. Others, however, viewed the temple's restoration as occurring subsequent to the arrival of the hoped-for age.[157] In his study of the exilic period, Janssen followed this approach.[158] However, neither scholar sought to identify these divergent viewpoints with any specific portions of the population. In 1971, Steck attributed the desire to postpone the restoration of the temple to the non-exiled population.[159] A year earlier, however, R. G. Hamerton-Kelly had attempted to identify the two opposing positions, not with various demographic communities, but with specific theological and sociological factions.[160] Following the pioneering work of Plöger,[161] Hamerton-Kelly identified the proponents of immediate rebuilding with the priestly group, who based its convictions upon the theological perspectives of Deuteronomy.[162] That group's opponents, by contrast, followed the eschatological views of Ezekiel.[163] Hanson took a similar approach, situating the theological opposition (in contrast to Hamerton-Kelly) between the priestly-Ezekielian coalition, on one hand, and an amalgam of the disciples of Deutero-Isaiah and disenfranchised Levites, on the other.[164] According to Hamerton-Kelly, Haggai proposed a theological compromise between the two camps, suggesting that the reconstruction of the temple would bring in the hoped-for days of blessing.[165] For Hanson, Haggai became a puppet of the ruling Zadokite group.[166] Both believe that Haggai linked the temple's rebuilding to the eschatological era. P. R. Bedford argues in a similar vein. He maintains that the cessation of divine displeasure, manifested by concrete signs, was seen to be a necessary prerequisite to temple (re)building both in Israel and in the ancient Near East.[167] The

---

[157] Wellhausen, (p. 173) speaks explicitly of a *messianic* age. Other commentators who follow Wellhausen's approach prefer to speak in more general eschatological terms.

[158] Janssen, *Exilszeit*, p. 78.

[159] Steck, "Haggai", pp. 375–76. Steck maintained that only the non-exiled population had houses. Here Steck follows Galling's view (*Studien*, p. 56) that Zerubbabel and the returnees only arrived in 521–520. Steck's argument lacks sufficient historical and exegetical support, cf. Whedbee, "Question-Answer", p. 187.

[160] Hamerton-Kelly, "Temple and Origins" pp. 1–15.

[161] O. Plöger, *Theokratie und Eschatologie*, cf. ch. 1. n. 65.

[162] Hamerton-Kelly, "Temple and Origins", pp. 4–11.

[163] Ibid.

[164] Hanson, *Dawn of Apocalyptic*, p. 225.

[165] Hamerton-Kelly, "Temple and Origins", p. 13.

[166] Hanson, *Dawn of Apocalyptic*, p. 244ff.

[167] Bedford, "Discerning the Time", pp. 71–94.

end of the time of the deity's abandonment of the site could be discerned by means of "dreams, extispicy and planetary omens."[168] The Judaean community, according to Bedford, would have known it was time to rebuild the temple by means of "tangible signs, such as the repatriation of all the exiles, the blessing of Yahweh's people and land, the destruction of enemies, the acknowledgement by the nations of Yahweh's sovereignty, the re-establishment of the kingship of David, and the reunification of Judah and Israel."[169] In the absence of such tangible signs, the Jerusalemite community staunchly refused to rebuild the temple. A slight variation on this approach sees the refusal of the people as deriving from convictions based upon calculations regarding the seventy year desolation of Jerusalem as found in the book of Jeremiah.[170] Tadmor considers the phrase לא עת בא in Hag 1:2 as a "popular slogan" that reflected the "orthodox interpretation" which originally saw the seventy year period as referring to the Babylonian domination, but was later re-applied to the duration of the exile.[171] Thus the termination of the building project was timed to coincide with the seventieth anniversary of the fall of Jerusalem.

All these hypotheses founder in light of the text of Haggai. Put simply, such interpretations sit uneasily with the grammatical configuration of v. 2 and the context of 1:1–15. It is perfectly true that in certain contexts עת may refer to an epoch or a moment designated by Yahweh for a particular purpose (Ps 102:14 [Eng. 13]; Jer 46:21; 50:27, 31).[172] However the inappropriateness of such a nuance here is demonstrated by the fact that Haggai's response to the people's conviction does not consist of any theological or exegetical arguments.[173] This is evident in v. 4 where Haggai reformulates the people's affirmation, repeating the word עת. There the term cannot mean a divinely designated moment. The nuance is rather the well attested notion of "an appropriate or suitable time" for a given activity.[174]

---

[168] Ibid., p. 78.

[169] Ibid., p. 84, cf. also p. 94.

[170] Thus Meyers and Meyers, p. 10, and Tadmor, "Appointed Time". Tadmor cites Jer 25:12–13; 29:10.

[171] Tadmor, "Appointed Time", *passim*, p. 405, cf. also Meyers and Meyers, p. 10.

[172] BDB, עת 1 and 2c.

[173] Wolff, p. 24.

[174] Job 22:16; Prov 15:23; Eccl 3:2–11; 7:17; 8:5–6. Cf. *THAT*, s. v. " עת ", p. 377. Cf. J. R. Wilch, *Time and Event*, (Leiden: E. J. Brill, 1969), Amsler, p. 22, and Bauer, *Zweiten Tempels*, pp. 150–53.

The idea of an "appropriate" or "suitable" time is well rooted in sapiential literature (Eccl 8:5–6).[175] Frequently the noun עת is followed by an infinitive construct indicating the activity which is appropriate or inappropriate in the time under consideration.[176] What is more, the translation which makes "the time" the subject of the verb "to come" further obscures the sapiential orientation of the phrase. As noted in the textual criticism above, the implied subject is the people who say, "It is not the appropriate time to come …"[177] This sapiential orientation is evident in several passages which contain the same construction. In Eccl 3:2–8, for example, עת is followed by several infinitive constructs describing activities appropriate to certain periods of life. Thus there is a time to be born (עת ללדת), to die (עת למות), to plant (עת לטעת), and to pluck up (עת לעקור נטוע). Genesis 29:7 provides an excellent parallel. There it is stated, "It is still day, it is not the time to gather in the flocks" (לא עת האסף). The intent is clearly that given the external circumstances, gathering in the flocks constitutes an inappropriate activity. In each of these instances the construction refers not to a *divine judgment* regarding whether or not an activity should be undertaken, but rather to a *human evaluation* in response to the question, "Would the activity under consideration be wise, prudent, appropriate or well situated in the existing circumstances?" What is more, such an evaluation can be called into question, by the prefixing of an interrogative *he* to עת as in Hag 1:4. Thus 2 Kgs 5:26 contains a virtually identical interrogative structure. There Elisha asks Gehezai, "Is it the time to receive (העת לקחת) silver, to receive (לקחת) garments, olive trees, vineyards, sheep and cattle, manservants and maidservants?"[178] Haggai, like Elisha, calls into question a course of action chosen by the people based on their view of the appropriateness of the circumstances, presumably the adversities mentioned in 1:4–6; 9–11. In other words, the people have said, "It is clear, given the external circumstances, that wisdom dictates that the rebuilding of the temple be put off until a more appropriate time."

---

[175] G. von Rad, *Wisdom in Israel*, (trans. J. D. Martin; London: SPCK, 1972), pp. 138–43.

[176] Joüon §124d; GKC §114b; *IBHS* §36.2.1.c.

[177] So Barthélemy, *Critique textuelle*, 3:923–24.

[178] Cf. the discussion of this text in D. P. O'Brien, "Is This The Time to Accept? (2 Kings v 26b): Simply Moralizing (LXX) or an Ominous Foreboding of Yahweh's Rejection of Israel (MT)?", *VT* 46 (1996): 448–57.

It is only when the people's attitude is understood in this way that Haggai's response, and more importantly the redactor's purpose may be understood. Haggai's words show no sign of being directed to a pious community, fearful of offending their deity by reconstructing his dwelling place at an inappropriate moment. Had this been the case the prophetic response would have been one of comfort and divine assurance that the time had indeed come. Haggai's confrontational response,[179] however, presupposes a people who had used sapiential reasoning as a justification for neglect of that which *they should have understood* to be a legitimate, even necessary activity.[180] This perspective is reinforced by the use of futility curse language in vv. 4–11, and terminology evocative of the renewal of Yahweh's relationship with his people.[181] Such language sets 1: 1–15 within the broader motif of alienation and restoration found elsewhere in the Deuteronomistic tradition.

Historiographically speaking, it is critical to note that, quite apart from the question of the degree to which this portrait corresponds to the actual historical situation,[182] it is indeed the social and religious portrait that the book's redactor seeks to depict to the reader. The reason for this is the narrator's desire to portray Haggai not as a scribe or an interpreter of earlier prophetic words, but as a prophet who confronts an unwilling and resistant community. Thus, like Jeremiah, Haggai confronts a people who may use pious language (cf. Jer 7) but whose ways need mending.

[3] Verse 3, which repeats 1b, serves to introduce the prophetic response to the words of the people cited in v. 2. The repetition is neither problematic nor redundant. It marks the transition from the popular attitude that has generated the conflict which has called forth

---

[179] From a form-critical perspective, the response is best categorized as a prophetic disputation, or a variety of forms (*Scheltwort, Mahnwort* etc. cf. n. 54, *supra*).

[180] Chary (p. 19) is adamant that they understood the necessity of that which they were refusing to do. He states, "By repeatedly objecting 'it is not the right time to rebuild the temple' the people were admitting that they understood its necessity, but were paralyzed by a luke-warm attitude."

[181] On these points cf. the exegesis, *infra*.

[182] Cf. for some of the issues involved, P. de Robert, "Pour ou contre le second temple", in *"Dort ziehen Schiffe dahin …": Collected Communications to the XIVth Congress of the International Organization for the Study of the Old Testament, Paris, 1992,* (BEATAJ 28; ed. M. Augustin and K.-D. Schunck; Frankfurt am Main: Peter Lang, 1996), pp. 179–182 and S. Amsler, J. Asurmendi, J. Auneau, and R. Martin-Achard, *Les prophètes et les livres prophétiques.* (Petite Bibliothèque des Sciences Bibliques; Paris: Desclée, 1985), pp. 292–97.

prophetic intervention, to the reproaches and promises that follow. It also serves to stress both the divine origin of the words and the human agency through whom they have come. The fact that vv. 1–2 address the leaders and vv. 3–11 the people has led some to conclude that the two divine words were given in two different settings,[183] or alternatively, that an original oracle has been redactionally edited to include the leaders.[184] However it is essential to note that no addressee is specified in v. 3 for the words of vv. 4–11 (which logically provide a response to the opinion expressed in v. 2). The literary and rhetorical effect of the presentation of a word to the leaders followed by a response to an unspecified audience is to present that response as a word to the community as a whole. Thus the leaders and the people are in some sense seen as one.

[4] As noted above, the interrogative structure of the verse functions as a challenge to the attitude of the populace. By means of a rhetorical question העת ("Is it time for you ... ?"),[185] Haggai challenges his hearers' conclusion that the time was inappropriate for undertaking the rebuilding of the temple. The verse draws a strong contrast between the house of Yahweh and the houses of the people. The former is described as חָרֵב. This root can have three general meanings: "to be dry", "to be devastated", or "to be abandoned". The people's houses, by contrast, are said to be סְפוּנִים, which can be translated either "paneled" indicating relatively luxurious homes[186] or "covered" indicating that adequate roofing had been constructed.[187] Given the lack of any other reference to luxury in the book, and the excessive amount of detail given to the description of economic hardships, the latter interpretation is most probable.

The use of חרב here is intentional. If the contrast were simply one regarding the relative material states of the two structures in question, one would anticipate a more concrete term describing the temple's physical state of disrepair. Indeed, several such terms were available. Four examples are as follows: (1) נתץ which is used passively to describe broken down cities (Jer 4:26) or houses (Jer 33:4; Ezek 16:39). It may also be used actively to describe the tearing down of altars (Exod

---

[183] Verhoef, p, 57.

[184] Tollington, *Tradition*, p. 21; Sérandour, "Réflexions", pp. 75–77.

[185] Cf. the discussion of 2 Kgs 5:26, *supra*.

[186] Cf. 1 Kgs 6:9; 7:7; Jer 22:14. So Ackroyd, *Exile and Restoration*, p. 155; Petersen, p. 48.

[187] Thus Mitchell, p. 45; Meyers and Meyers, p. 24.

34:13; Deut 7:5), towers (Judg 8:9), houses (Isa 22:10; Ezek 26:9) or, significantly, the temple of Baal (2 Kgs 10:27; 11:18; 2 Chr 23:17). (2) הלם which is used with reference to the damaging of the wood in the temple during the Babylonian invasion (Ps 74:6). (3) פרץ which is used passively with reference to the tearing down of the walls of Jerusalem (Neh 1:3; 2:13; 4:1 [Eng. 7]; cf. Ps 80:13 [Eng. 12]; 89:41 [Eng. 40]; Isa 5:5; 2 Chr 25:23. (4) הרס which is used passively of the breaking down of cities (Ezek 36:35), walls (Jer 50:15), and foundations (Ezek 30:4).

The verbal root חרב (Isa 34:10; Jer 26:9; Ezek 29:19), the adjective חָרֵב (Jer 33:10, 12; Ezek 36:35, 38), and the noun חָרְבָּה (Ezra 9:9; Jer 7:34; 27:17; 44:2, 6, 22; Ezek 36:10) by contrast, frequently refer not to the physical dismantling of structures, but to the results of such destructive activity, that is a state of abandonment and depopulation which comes to a region as a result of invasion and devastation by enemies. As Carroll notes, the term implies the cessation of normal and expected activities.[188] Amsler is certainly correct in his observation that חרב "is not to be taken as a description of the ruined state of the temple building, but designates more precisely a lonely deserted place, forgotten by all, and left for dead."[189] Thus the term in 1:4 does not refer primarily to the unrepaired state of the building (this, of course, is taken for granted as it is the entire premise of Haggai's call to action), but more generally to neglect of any construction activity at the site—activity which had been undertaken with regard to private homes.

Furthermore the root חרב may have been chosen here due to a particular nuance it carried in connection with the events of 587, as evidenced especially in Jeremiah and Ezekiel (Jer 22:5; 25:9, 11, 18; 27:17; 33:12; 44:2, 6, 22; Ezek 5:14; 33:24, 28; 36:4, 10, 33, 35, 38).[190] The devastation of the Judaean towns and Jerusalem temple had a symbolic significance: that of the distancing of Yahweh from his people. A temple in ruins was a public witness of shame and disgrace (cf. Lev 26:30–33). For Haggai, the fact that the community lived in covered houses while the temple was in ruins constituted an intolerable situation. Accepting

---

[188] R. P. Carroll, *Jeremiah: A Commentary* (OTL; Philadelphia: Westminster, 1986), pp. 635–36.

[189] Amsler, p. 22. So also Andersen, "Second Temple", cited in Verhoef, p, 59, n. 55.

[190] Cf. Meyers and Meyers (p. 24) who also underline the abandonment of the site. Even if some cultic activity was regularly practiced, this was insufficient for Haggai, who sought a duly restored and consecrated cult site.

the *status quo* on this issue (as opposed, for example, to the subaltern political status of Yehud) amounted, in the eyes of the prophet, to a profound dereliction of duty vis-à-vis Yahweh.

The question Haggai raises is one of priorities: what statement is being made by a community whose members construct adequate dwelling places for themselves but who neglect their deity's dwelling place? This neglect was *a fortiori* more culpable since the Persian crown was in support of such an undertaking. This incongruity is set in stark relief by the three-fold repetition of the second person plural pronoun (לכם, אתם,בביתכם)[191] set in contrast to הבית הזה (this house), a structure which was central to the community both in a geographical[192] and a socio-religious sense. Beyond these priorities, an even deeper question is posed: one concerning wisdom.[193] The people had made a judgment (v. 2) concerning the wisdom of reconstruction in the light of their economic circumstances. The heart of Haggai's reproach relates to the use and abuse of wisdom. Haggai's question implies (1) the possibility that external circumstances can prevent carrying out one's religious duties, but that (2) the presence of covered houses clearly indicates that such was not the case. Thus for Haggai the use of sapiential reflection to justify a clearly illegitimate choice is tantamount to making "wisdom" prevail over piety.[194] Therefore, Haggai's question is fundamentally, "Is the time propitious to neglect the rightful honouring of Yahweh?" The argument that follows is designed to prove that such a perspective is in no way wise.

**[5]** Verse 5 marks a transition, signaled by the repetition of the Messenger Formula with the name Yahweh Sebaoth (cf. v. 2), and the use of ועתה. The latter term is not common in the Deuteronomistic literature.[195] As Koch notes, here it indicates a call to reflection on present circumstances.[196] The prophet continues to reason sapientially. His premise is that, given the people's desire to act in their own self interest (as evidenced by their choices vis-à-vis their own homes and

---

[191] Joüon §161a; *IBHS* §16.3.4.a.

[192] It is worth noting that this expression, like "the mountain" (1:8) gives the ambiance of an oracle proclaimed at or near the temple site.

[193] On the use of questions in wisdom traditions, cf. H. W. Wolff, *L'enracinement spirituel d'Amos*, (Genève: Labor et Fides, 1974), p. 21.

[194] As manifested, for example, by the woman in Gen 3:1–6. The opposite attitude is enjoined in Prov 1:7.

[195] Cf. 1:5; 2:4, 15; Deut 6:55.

[196] Koch, "Haggais", pp. 59–60.

the temple), they should consider whether they were being well served by their decisions. He calls them to consider their ways. The expression שִׂים לֵב (lit. set your heart) occurs in Deut 32:46; Isa 41:22; Ezek 40:4; 44:5, and Hag 1:5, 7; 2:18. It is similar to שִׁית לֵב in Prov 24:32; 27:23; Ps 48:14 [Eng. 13]; 62:11 [Eng. 10], where its sapiential nuance is evident. An analogous expression is נָטָה לֵב (Prov 2:2) which carries a similar meaning. The people must therefore reflect upon the consequences[197] of their chosen way. The phrase "your ways" here indicates not so much what the people are actually doing but the results that have accrued from their choices.[198] The prophet will go on to use the Deuteronomistic motif of divine displeasure manifested through temporal adversity to demonstrate that the people are acting against their own self interest,[199] given the negative divine response to their choices.

[6–7] As evidence that its decisions have not achieved the desired results, the prophet describes the community's situation using a variety of current life experiences. The verses contains nine[200] assorted[201] verbal forms. Since grammatically the temporal referent of these forms is to be inferred from the context, it would seem best to see them as realties of life both past and present.[202] The variety of forms is stylistic. The frequent use of the infinitive absolute as equivalent to a preceding form is characteristic of late biblical Hebrew.[203] The prophet makes his point by means of five examples of frustrated expectations. Each example is characterized by the motif of an activity in which the desired result is

---

[197] דֶּרֶךְ here includes not only the people's way of life and priorities, but also the results of these choices, the latter being clearly under divine control, cf. 1:6–7, 9–11; 2:15–17.

[198] Chary, p. 19; Verhoef (p. 60) citing Driver, Koole and G. A. Smith.

[199] Meyers and Meyers (pp. 24–25) suggest that the term "welfare" conveys the idea of Haggai's words. This is quite correct at the level of the logic of the prophet's argument. However I do not feel that it is an appropriate translation for דֶּרֶךְ here. See the conclusion of this chapter on the eudaemonistic nature of the reasoning here.

[200] I have not included the inf. abs. הַרְבֵּה which functions adverbially, and the participles מִשְׁתַּכֵּר and נָקוּב which function substantivally and adjectivally.

[201] Perf.; inf. abs.; inf. abs.; inf. cs.; inf. abs.; inf. cs.; inf. abs.; inf. cs.; ptc., cf. Beuken, p. 196. Verhoef (p. 61) notes that the verbal structure here creates an "excited style" cf. Meyers and Meyers, p. 23.

[202] See textual criticism, *supra*. The participle here implies that the community was still suffering these experiences. Cf. Schattner-Rieser, ("L'hébreu", p. 199) who notes that in late biblical Hebrew the participle is the normal means of speaking of the present. Schattner-Rieser also notes the movement away from the temporal orientation of the various conjugations, toward a more aspectual one, under the influence of Aramaic.

[203] Joüon §123x.

not attained for various reasons (poor crop yield, scarcity of commodities, crippling wage-price ratios).[204] The first example concerns the sowing of much seed, and the reaping of little harvest. The phrase זרעתם הרבה והבא מעט (you have sown but harvested little) in 1:6 is close to זרע רב תוציא השׂדה ומעט תאסף (you will bring much seed to the field, you will harvest little) in Deut 28:38. As Amsler notes, the three examples chosen (eating, drinking, being clothed, cf. Exod 21:10; Hos 2:11) reflect traditional formulaic language regarding the basic necessities of life.[205] The second concerns having something to eat, but not enough to be filled. The phrase אכול ואין־לשׂבעה (you will eat but not be satisfied, 1:6) recalls ואכלתם ולא תשׂבעו (you will eat without being satisfied, Lev 26:26). The third involves having something to drink, but not enough to be satisfied.[206] If a chiasm is to be seen, drinking is at its apex. The fourth instance concerns the experience of putting on garments, yet being unable to feel warm. The noun חם (heat) is not used elsewhere of the warmth derived from clothing, and the source of the heat is generally to be inferred from the context (Gen 18:1; 1 Sam 21:7 [Eng. 6]). It has been suggested that this experience may have been the result of the poor quality of the garments, the fact that finances did not permit the purchase of enough garments, or the poor nutritional state of the individual.[207] Lack of clothing is found in the traditional vocabulary of curse (Deut 28:48) and disgrace (Amos 2:16; Isa 20:4; Ezek 16:39), making it the most likely allusion.[208] The final example concerns the day labourer or wage earner.[209] It is difficult to determine the precise status, identity, and economic activity of these individuals in the context

---

[204] Tollington (*Tradition*, pp. 188–98) examines the question of whether, following Hillers, (*Treaty Curses*, pp. 28–29), Hag 1:6 can be said to contain the *Gattung* of the "futility curse". She decides it reflects only a "general awareness of futility curses and the use of them in law codes and prophetic proclamations" (p. 192). I will examine Haggai's particular use of the "futility curse motif" below.

[205] Amsler, p. 22.

[206] The verb שׂכר can mean simply "to be quenched, satisfied" or it may refer to the effects of alcohol. Petersen (p. 50, n. 16) suggests the former, Meyers and Meyers (p. 26) the latter. The latter is the more common usage, (cf. Gen 9:21; 43:34), and corresponds well to the related noun שׂכר which is generally translated "strong drink", cf. Lev 10:9, Deut 14:26; Isa 28:7.

[207] Verhoef, pp. 61–62.

[208] Verhoef (p. 61) adds that ל functions here as an individualizing singular indicating that the lack of clothing was experienced widely in the community, cf. Joüon §152d.

[209] Verhoef (p. 62), citing Mal 3:5, Lev 19:13 and 25:6, suggests that this was seen as a humiliating status. These texts portray such individuals as living in a state of relative poverty.

of early Persian Yehud.[210] Here the text implicitly portrays them as full participants in society, rather than marginal individuals. The reference may therefore be to those members of society whose means of livelihood involved the reception and spending of silver (or copper) pieces.[211] The image of the bag with holes refers to the seemingly inexplicable and immediate disappearance of that which is earned, presumably due to the individual's burden of debt and the high cost of living.

Having adduced evidence in v. 6 that the community's choices had brought it woe instead of weal, the prophet once again calls the people to reflection. Verse 7 repeats v. 5 with the exception of ועתה. The movement is therefore: call to reflection (v. 5), object of reflection (v. 6), then in v. 7, a transitional, second call to reflection which looks both back to the frustrations of the recent past, as well as forward toward something better. The way to this better future is presented in v. 8.

**[8]** Verse 8 is the culmination of the prophet's argument thus far. It also bears a chiastic structure. It contains a central focal requirement (the imperative בנו), preceded by two preliminary injunctions (עלו imperative, and והבאתם waw-consecutive plus perfect). This injunction is followed by two volitives whose form and sense will be discussed below.

The prophet calls the people to move from their inactivity by going up to "the mountain"[212] and bringing wood. Various suggestions have been made regarding the mention of wood here. It has been seen as a call to undertake measures similar to those of the construction of the first temple,[213] or understood as the preparation of scaffolding for the needed stonework.[214] Others have suggested that woodwork was all

---

[210] Cf. Kreissig, *Situation*, pp. 27–28 and 91–98; Smith, *Landless*, ch. 8; Kippenberg, *Religion und Klassenbildung*, ch. 3.

[211] On the issue of coinage and currency, see P. Machinist, "First Coins of Judah", pp. 365–80; Lemaire, "Epigraphie et numismatique", pp. 261–87; and idem, "La circulation monétaire phénicienne en Palestine à l'époque perse", *Actes du IIIe congrès international des études phéniciennes et puniques, Tunis, 11–16 novembre, 1991, vol. 2;* (ed. M. H. Fantar and M. Ghaki; Tunis, 1995), pp. 192–202. It would seem more likely that in 520, silver shekels were in use, cf. Zech 11:12 (Verhoef, p. 62; Baldwin, p. 41). On payment in silver pieces in the Persian Empire, see Briant, *Histoire*, 1:417–19.

[212] The vividness of the scene is heightened by the definite article (cf. Joüon [§137n] who indicates that the article here designates a local object) and the singular הר, presupposing that speaker and hearer both know which mountain is meant, and perhaps that it is even within sight. One could even imagine the prophet indicating the place as he spoke.

[213] Peckham (*History*, p. 743) suggests the call is to seek wood from Lebanon.

[214] Meyers and Meyers (pp. 27–28) suggest that the wood was for scaffolding and

that was required to complete the construction of the temple.[215] All
of these suggestions, however, are problematic in that it hardly seems
possible that the sum of the needed work could be resolved by the
bringing of wood.[216] It is therefore better to see the wood here as a form
of metonymy, specifically a synecdoche. Thus the bringing of wood,
perhaps a first step, represents the totality of work still needing to be
done. This literary device is also used in 1:9 where "running to one's
house" stands for all that is involved in being preoccupied with one's
interests, in 2:8 where silver and gold stand for the totality of the world's
wealth, and in 2:22 where the throne stands for all power, and chariots,
horses and riders stand for all weaponry. Thus the two volitives serve
to call the hearers to begin the multi-faceted process of rebuilding. In a
similar, non-descript way, the central command, "build my house" gives
no details regarding what is required and how it ought to be done. The
implication is that the various members of the community and their
religious and political leaders would be able to supply or to access the
required skills and information.

The relation of the two verbs which follow is difficult to ascertain due
to the ambiguity of the form of the first one (ארצה can be either cohortative or imperfect) and the presence of a *qere/ketib* (כבד Q, imperfect;
K, cohortative) for the second verb. If one reads וְאֶכָּבֵד in the imperfect, (according to *ketib*), it would be most logical to do the same for
ארצה. If the forms are read as imperfects, the nuance would be one of
simple temporal succession, indicating the response promised by Yahweh: "And I will take pleasure in it (or I will accept it) and I will be
glorified."[217] Similar promissory expressions may be found in Zech 1:3
and Num 21:16. In the cohortative, וְאֶכָּבְדָה (according to *qere*) the implication would, by contrast, be one of a final or consecutive clause:[218]
"so that I may take pleasure in it, so that I may be glorified."[219] Meyers and Meyers maintain that here the significance of the imperfect

---

ramps, and that the other required materials may have been stockpiled in Jerusalem.

[215] Chary, p. 19.

[216] As Meyers and Meyers observe, p. 28.

[217] This is the position taken by Petersen, Verhoef, Amsler, Ackroyd, Wolff, Chary
and Rudolph. Cf. GKC §110a on the co-ordinated imperative with ו.

[218] On this construction see Joüon §169; GKC §108d, 166a.

[219] With Meyers and Meyers, p. 3, "'Go up to the hills so that you may bring in
wood/ And build the house so that I may be pleased with it/ That I may be glorified',
said Yahweh."

would not be different from the cohortative.[220] Rudolph, on the contrary, affirms that the cohortative here conveys the same meaning as the imperfect.[221] The resolution of these grammatical and textual questions requires attention to the meaning and usage of the verbs in question.

The use of the root רצה coupled with the syntax of בו which follows it, favours the imperfect (*ketib*) of כבד and therefore the expression of a promise concerning the future. רצה can have the more general, quasi-affective sense of "to take pleasure in" or "to be happy with" (Ps 102:15 [Eng. 14]; 1 Chr 29:17; Isa 42:1; Ps 44:4 [Eng. 3]; Job 33:26; Ps 149:4). But in cult-related contexts[222] this root connotes "delighting in" with reference to the reception or acceptance of a sacrifice, a cultic act, or a person.[223] Especially significant here are Amos 5:22; Hos 8:13, and Mal 1:8–10, 13, where Yahweh signals his refusal to accept the sacrifices offered by Israel. A similar kind of acceptance, that is of a people and their acts of worship, is promised in Ezek 20:40, 41. Those faithful to Yahweh request such acceptance in Ps 119:108. The vocabulary in these cases is similar to that of Hag 1:8–11. Therefore it seems most likely that here Yahweh promises to "delight in" (that is, to accept or receive) that which is done for him.[224] This conclusion is reinforced when one asks whether the antecedent of בו is the building itself, or the act of building. The preposition ב is dependent upon רצה in Mic 6:7; Ps 149:4; 147:10, 1 Chr 28:4. In each case, a person or an object is the object of Yahweh's delight, but never an action. Similarly, in Hag 1:8, בו most likely refers to the temple. This being the case, a consecutive sense seems scarcely possible. It would be illogical to require the rebuilding of the temple so that one might accept it.[225] The sense of simple succession, that is the expression of a promise of acceptance, seems far more apposite here. Thus the sense would be, "Build my house, and I will take pleasure in it" (receive it gladly).[226]

---

[220] Meyers and Meyers, p. 28.

[221] Rudolph, (p. 29) renders it "then I will take pleasure in it, and I will be glorified through it."

[222] Verhoef, p. 67; Beuken, p. 187.

[223] Cf. Wolff, p. 45.

[224] Ibid.

[225] The nuance of the impv. followed by the coh. is that the first action is indispensable to the second cf. GKC §108d (e.g. bring so that I might eat). Such an idea is difficult here.

[226] Here Haggai's thought is indeed similar to that of the Chronicler. Both agree that repentance and restoration are possible at any time, cf. Williamson, *1 and 2 Chronicles*, pp. 31–33.

Since the preceding verb is best read as an imperfect expressing a future promise, it is likely that אכבד should be read in the same way. However the translational value of the niphal ואכבד requires careful analysis. The following translations have been proposed: (1) an active translation "I will appear in glory" or "I will show my glory";[227] (2) a passive translation "I will be glorified"; or (3) a middle or permissive translation "I will get glory for myself" or "I will let myself be glorified."[228] The use of the niphal of כבד with Yahweh as subject is quite limited.[229] In each case Yahweh shows himself worthy of adoration because of his deeds.[230] Leviticus 10:3 is particularly close to our text. There, after cultic actions unacceptable to him, Yahweh announces: בקרבי אקדש ועל־פני כל־העם אכבד. (By those who draw near to me, I will insist on being treated as holy; and before all the people I will see that I am honoured). This means that he will insist on ritual practices that are according to his will and only thus will he let himself be glorified. Consequently Ackroyd is correct in translating Hag 1:8, "then I will accept it and I will let myself be glorified ... I will accept the worship due to my honour."[231] Furthermore, the use of כבד with Yahweh as subject implicitly conveys the promise of Yahweh's presence in the sanctuary built in his honour. In this sense the third option presupposes the second. Here, then, God promises in advance to accept the work of the people. An abbreviated Messenger Formula closes the verse.

The message of the prophet is clear: for too long you have neglected your duties towards me. I have hampered your economic initiatives and personal projects. But it is not too late. Go up to the mountain, look for timber, build the house. I will accept it and I will receive your worship.

**[9]** As noted above, whatever the oral history of this oracle may have been, verses 9–11 take up and reinforce the ideas expressed in 4–7.[232] The experience of disappointing results is reintroduced in v. 9. The idea of 9aα (פנה אל־הרבה והנה למעט) is once again that of the discrepancy between expectation (this is the sense of פנה here)[233] and

---

[227] Wolff, p. 46; Verhoef, pp. 67–68;. R. E. Clements, *God and Temple*, (Philadelphia: Fortress, 1965), p. 124.

[228] Ackroyd, *Exile and Restoration*, p. 160.

[229] Non-participial forms: Ezek 28:22; 39:13; Exod 14:4, 17, 18; Lev 10:3; Hag 1:8. In Isa 26:15 Yahweh is referred to by the speaker in the passage.

[230] Petersen (p. 31) notes that in these contexts divine vengeance is frequently in view.

[231] Ackroyd, *Exile and Restoration*, p. 160.

[232] Whedbee, "Question-Answer", pp. 188–89; Steck, "Zu Haggai", pp. 368–72; Chary, p. 21.

[233] Wolff, p. 46, *pace* Elliger.

reality,[234] cf. 1:6a; 2:16, 17. That which is specifically related to the sowing of seed in v. 6 is stated in the most general of terms here:[235] where much would normally be expected, little is received. Verse 9aβ has been interpreted in two primary ways: (1) as referring to Yahweh's rejection of the offerings brought to his house (הבית being understood as a reference to the temple, and נפח as metaphorical for Yahweh's rejection);[236] or (2) as alluding to the subsequent diminution of that which was produced once it was brought home, in addition to the already disappointing results described in 9aα.[237] The latter is most probable in that the argument of vv. 4–7 and vv. 9–11 hinges on the community's subjective experience of disappointment in their personal pursuits. The idea of divine displeasure over what is offered appears at 2:15, but seems absent here. Furthermore, while the use of נפח to describe rejection or displeasure is present in Mal 1:13, it is not used there with Yahweh as subject. Where Yahweh is the subject of this verb, the idea is one of divine force or power (Gen 2:7; Ezek 22:21; 37:9). Most likely, then, the metaphor here, similar to the image of blowing the coals of a fire (cf. Ezek 22:20; Isa 54:16), is that of Yahweh's mighty breath blowing away that which was gained and brought home.[238] The idea mirrors that of 1:6b where wages disappear the moment they are earned. As in Amos 5:19, Yahweh's judgment is operative in several successive steps. It is important to note that in v. 9aβ that which was implicit in vv. 4–7 is stated plainly: Yahweh declares himself to be the author of the community's misfortunes.

In v. 9bα, Yahweh poses a rhetorical question to his people, asking them to reflect upon the possible reasons why he would act in such a way. The question presupposes, first that such activity is contrary to Yahweh's desires for and general approach to his people, and second, that the community would be able to understand that such behaviour on Yahweh's part must have a cause. Thus the Deuteronomistic notion of covenant blessings and misfortunes must be presupposed. The ques-

---

[234] The ל on למען here may be emphatic (Verhoef, p. 70), or, more likely, an indication of an ellipsis, thus "it [turned into] so little." Cf. Williams §598.

[235] As Petersen (pp. 51–52) rightly notes.

[236] Thus Steck, " Zu Haggai", p. 370, n. 46; Ackroyd, *Exile and Restoration*, p. 158; F. Peter, "Zu Haggai 1, 9", *TZ* 2 (1951): 150–51.

[237] So Petersen, p. 52, and Whedbee, "Question-Answer", p. 187.

[238] Given the generalized description of expectation and failure, it is probably unnecessary to speculate on precisely how that which is brought home is blown away. Cf. Verhoef, who lists several possibilities.

tion concludes with a Messenger Formula. In v. 9bβ Yahweh answers his own question. In contrast to 1:2 where the rhetorical question is polar[239] and implies a negative answer, here the rhetorical question requires a detailed answer or explanation.[240] Even though the resolution to that which has caused the divine displeasure has been given in v. 8, the prophet repeats it: "It is because of my[241] house which[242] remains desolate,[243] whereas each[244] of you is preoccupied[245] with his own house." Similar to v. 4, v. 9bβ uses a series of oppositions to stress the people's self interest on one hand, and neglect of Yahweh, on the other: my house and your houses; your abandonment of my house, and your feverish and constant[246] activity entirely[247] dedicated to your own interests. The term "house"[248] is best taken as a synecdoche[249] for all that is related to one's personal or familial interests.[250]

Wolff, following Whedbee, makes an important point concerning the formal similarity between the question and answer schema here, and a similar phenomenon found elsewhere in Deuteronomistic literature.[251] In those passages a question is raised regarding why a specific act of divine judgment has occurred. The answer is then given that this is a result of covenant violation, usually the worship of other gods (Deut 29:22–28; Jer 22:8–9). As noted above, for the book's redactor, Haggai

---

[239] *IBHS* §18.1.a.

[240] The expression יען מה is only found at Hag 1:9, however its meaning, "why", is clear, cf. BDB, יען. It is of interest to note (cf. Beuken, Wolff) that יען occurs frequently in Deut-2 Kgs (about 63 times), but is rare in 1 and 2 Chr (6 times).

[241] Here the pronominal suffix is used with בית in contrast to its absence in 1:4, 8.

[242] Here the personal pronoun functions as the copula of the nominal sentence, cf. GKC §141g,h; RGBA §30.

[243] On the meaning of חרב, cf. v. 4, above.

[244] איש לביתו expresses a distributive sense, cf. Williams §131.

[245] For רוץ (to run) as meaning "to be busy or preoccupied with", cf. Wolff, pp. 47–48.

[246] רצים implies effort and energy. The participial construction reinforces the regular and habitual nature of the activity (Williams §220) and the fact that attention to one's own house, and neglect of the house of Yahweh were simultaneous.

[247] Meyers and Meyers (p. 30) may be correct in proposing that רוץ (v. 9) and ישב (v. 4) constitute a kind of merism: whether at home or elsewhere the people are focused upon their own concerns.

[248] Attempts have been made to identify the group being addressed here on the basis of their need to build homes for themselves (so Steck, "Haggai", pp. 370–72, but cf. Verhoef, p. 72).

[249] Cf. the wood in v. 8.

[250] Meyers and Meyers, p. 30.

[251] Wolff, p. 47; Whedbee, "Question-Answer", pp. 190ff.

and his hearers are able to understand and reason on the basis of such a notion. A discussion of the particular use of these motifs in Haggai will be presented *infra*.

[**10–11**] The progression of thought in vv. 10 and 11 is analogous to that of vv. 9aα and 9aβ. A more general description of the failure of sky or earth to yield that which they usually provide (v. 10) is followed by a divine declaration, in the first person, regarding the role of Yahweh in these events (v. 11). The verse begins with the assertion that it is for this reason (עַל־כֵּן), alluding to the community's neglect of the temple mentioned in v. 10, that the sky above[252] has not yielded its dew,[253] nor the land its produce, evoking the Deuteronomistic judgment themes of drought and famine (cf. Deut 28:23; Lev 26:19–20). Sérandour rightly notes the presence here of the notion of the earth's mirroring the equilibrium in the heavenly realm, an equilibrium which is clearly seen as disrupted in 1:4–11.[254]

Verse 11 moves from effect to ultimate cause. Yahweh has called forth these events. The *waw* consecutive that begins the verse does not indicate a chronological progression (to say that the drought was called after the lack of rain would be a *non sequitur*). Thus the עַל־כֵּן (therefore) found at the beginning of v. 10 is to be implied in v. 11. The statement that Yahweh has called for a drought (וָאֶקְרָא חֹרֶב) contains two rhetorically important allusions. The first is the word play on the terms desolate (חָרֵב vv. 4, 9) and drought (חֹרֶב v. 11). It is the abandonment of the temple that has brought forth the drought. Yahweh, who personally gives water to the land (Deut 11:10–12), will withdraw his favour because of the disobedience of his people (Deut 11:17; 28:22). Second, the verb קרא (to call) is found in prophetic oracles of judgment (Isa 13:3; 46:11; Jer 25:29; Ezek 38:21; Amos 7:4, cf. the analogous notion in Isa 7:20).[255] Rhetorically this evokes the theme of Yahweh calling forth natural or human agents to accomplish his will in acting against his people. Haggai places this divine action in the past, and as v. 8 indicates, portrays Yahweh as willing to reverse it,

---

[252] Retaining the MT עֲלֵיכֶם and reading it as "above you" (cf. Deut 28:23), as argued in the textual criticism, *supra*.

[253] Cf. Meyers and Meyers (p. 31) and Verhoef (p. 74) on the agricultural significance of dew.

[254] Sérandour, "Récits", pp. 14–16. Sérandour notes this theme in connection with heavenly and earthly harmony in ch. 2, but does not comment on its opposite here. Cf. Petersen, p. 52.

[255] Wolff, p. 48, with bibliography.

should appropriate attention be paid to the temple. The drought and its effects[256] touch nine areas, each introduced by וְעַל. The land and mountains may refer to arable lands and mountainous regions where most rain fell.[257] The three commodities of grain, new wine, and fresh olive oil occur together frequently in the Deuteronomistic tradition (Deut 7:13; 11:14; 12:17; 14:23; 18:4; 28:51; Jer 31:12; Hos 2:10, 8:24 [Eng. 22]) and elsewhere,[258] and often designate the primary economic products of the land, especially seen as Yahweh's gifts, as in Deut 11:14 and Hos 2:10, 24. The three terms may refer to the products in their unprocessed state, emphasizing fertility[259] or simply be a stock phrase or "cliché."[260] Furthermore this situation will affect the fecundity and productivity of the soil, human beings and animals. The inclusion of animals echoes the various passages in the Hebrew Bible where the animals are seen as objects of God's concern, yet subject to suffering as a result of human evil.[261] The series concludes with the more general reference to the fruit of all human activity.

It is significant to note the rhetorical effect of returning to and concluding with the theme of desolation with which the prophetic reproach began. This strategy brings the reader back to the oracle's rather gloomy point of departure, a situation in which no forward movement had previously transpired. All of this stands in great contrast to that which will follow in 1:12–15.

**[12]** The dramatic tension created at the end of the foregoing oracle is resolved in the narrative epilogue which follows it.[262] The first unit of the epilogue begins with the affirmation that the individuals addressed and referred to in vv. 1–2 responded positively to the message of Haggai. As in v. 1, Zerubbabel is mentioned first, however this time without his official Persian title, whereas Joshua's name, which follows in the list, includes his. Wolff sees the absence of Zerubbabel's title as a redactional means of attenuating the fact that he was a Persian delegate.[263]

---

[256] חרב should be understood broadly here, since it refers both to the drought itself and its effects on various agricultural and economic activities.

[257] Verhoef, p. 75.

[258] Examples in ibid., p. 76, and Wolff, pp. 48–49.

[259] Cf. Tollington, *Tradition*, p. 197. Meyers and Meyers (p. 33) note that this suits the context of Haggai well.

[260] Beuken, pp. 201–02.

[261] Joel 1:19–20; 2:22; Jonah 3:11; Zeph 1:3; Jer 36:29; Ezek 14:13 etc. Cf. Verhoef, p. 77, n. 88.

[262] Cf. my discussion of the structure of 1:1–15 *supra*.

[263] Wolff, p. 51.

Meyers and Meyers suggest that this is a potential indication of the incipient ascendancy of the high priest.[264] Floyd suggests the reverse, that this prepares the reader for the preeminence of Zerubbabel in 2:20–23.[265] Wolff's suggestion seems unlikely given the presence of the title in v. 14, and elsewhere in this short book, and the general ancient Near Eastern tendency to stress the royal authority under whose aegis temple construction takes place.[266] The hypothesis of Meyers and Meyers is unlikely given the role of Zerubbabel in the oracle which closes the book (2:20–23). It is also difficult to demonstrate that the variations in designating Zerubbabel are intentional, and serve a rhetorical end. Thus, like the inclusion of Zerubbabel's title in 2:4, which seems somewhat irregular, its absence here may be of no discernible import. By contrast, the designation "the remnant of the people" (שארית העם cf. 1:2) is highly significant. A full discussion of the term שארית cannot be undertaken here.[267] It is nevertheless critical to ascertain whom it designates here and why it is employed. Dumbrell, North, Mitchell, and especially Wolff suggest that the term makes reference to the *golah*, as opposed to the non-exiled Judaeans.[268] This however is unlikely, since the redactor of vv. 12–14 allowed the phrase "remnant of the people" (v. 12, 14) to stand alongside the shorter designation "the people", (cf. 1: 2) referring to those who fear Yahweh and to whom Yahweh speaks in vv. 12b and 13.[269] Thus the redactor saw the two designations as coextensive, and inclusive of the entire community.[270] If such is the referent

---

[264] Meyers and Meyers, p. 50.

[265] Floyd, "Narration", p. 482.

[266] Sérandour, "Réflexions", pp. 76–77; idem, "Récits", pp. 11–13.

[267] See, provisionally, R. de Vaux, "Le 'reste d'Israël' d'après les prophètes", *RB* 42 (1933): 526–539; G. Hasel, *The Remnant: The Theology and History of the Remnant Idea from Genesis to Isaiah*, (Berrien Springs: Andrews University Press, 1974), and idem, s. v. "Remnant" IDB[S], pp. 735–36. Cf. also L. V. Meyer, s. v. "Remnant", *ABD* 5:669–71.

[268] W. J. Dumbrell, "Kingship and Temple in the Post Exilic Period", *RTR* 37 (1978): 39; North, p. 14; Mitchell, p. 54; Wolff, pp. 51–52.

[269] Wolff (p. 52) appears to assume that the redactor of Haggai could not have used the term in a different way, and have had a differing perspective, from the hand responsible for Ezra 3:8; 4:1 and 6:16 where the sons of the *golah* undertake the temple building. Furthermore, how does Wolff know that the *golah* group was "mentally more alert and economically more vigorous" (p. 52) than the non-exiled population?

[270] Floyd (pp. 275–77) sees the "remnant" as those who responded to Haggai's words and "the people" as the population as a whole, who became paralyzed with fear. It seems to me that this kind of distinction is too subtle, and the difference between the two groups overdrawn. Furthermore the use of כל before שארית would be illogical if the שארית constituted the portion of the community in Yehud who responded in faith. If however the Judaean community as a whole is portrayed as a שארית (vis-à-vis the

of שארית, what is its significance here? The term can simply designate
the survivors or escapees of a catastrophe, who flee to other territories
or return to the land.[271] However, since the community is viewed as a
single entity (in both oracles and framework), and the use of term follows the people's obedience, a more theological nuance is to be implied
here. Minor variations may be highly significant in narrative.[272] Thus
"this people" (העם הזה) show themselves to be worthy of the designation
"remnant" (שארית) after their obedience.[273] This return to Yahweh on
the part of the remnant occurs in prophetic texts such as Zeph 3:12–
13; Isa 10:20; 28:5; Jer 31:7–9; Mic 7:18.[274] As Herntrich observes, the
"conversion" or "return" of the "remnant" occurs subsequent to and
because of the deliverance that is granted to it.[275] It is therefore best
to conclude that the use of the term here reflects the narrator's desire
to underline the fact that the community as a whole has responded
appropriately to Yahweh.[276] Such a return is in full harmony with the
Deuteronomistic concept of hardship and misfortune (cf. Hag 1:4–11)
promoting a return to Yahweh, and a re-acceptance by him (Deut
4:28–32).

The leaders and people are said to have "obeyed the voice (שמע בקול)
of Yahweh their God."[277] The *waw* consecutive here situates this activity
in the flow of events which began in v. 1 and was continued in v. 3. The
expression שמע בקול is part of the standard Deuteronomistic vocabulary
with reference to a faithful response to Yahweh.[278] Using the analysis of

---

broader Diaspora), then כל insists on the fact that *all* of them were involved. In sum, I
argue here that the redactor seeks to present the community as a whole as responding
in concert to the preaching of Haggai. Whatever the historical realities may have been,
this is how the reader is meant to perceive the situation. As regards the historical reality
one can only venture a guess, cf. Chary's suggestion (p. 24) that those who responded
consisted primarily, but not exclusively, of returnees.

[271] Cf. Wolff, pp. 51–52 for examples of this use, eg. Isa 46:3, Jer 23:3, Mic 2:12; 4:7,
and its use with reference to the exiles of 597, 587, and the later returnees (e.g., 2 Kgs
19:31; Ezra 9:14; Neh 7:71), as well as those in nearby territories who returned with
Gedaliah (Jer 42–44) or those who went into exile in Egypt (Jer 43:5).

[272] Alter, *Biblical Narrative*, p. 97ff.

[273] Cf. Mason, "Editorial Framework", p. 418 and idem, *Preaching the Tradition: Homily
and Hermeneutic after the Exile*, (Cambridge: Cambridge University Press, 1990), p. 192.

[274] The Isaiah texts use שאר as opposed to שארית. On the related term נשאר cf. the
discussion at 2:3.

[275] V. Herntrich, s. v. "λειμμα", *TDNT* 4:206–7.

[276] So Verhoef, p. 81.

[277] On the singular verb with a plural subject cf. Joüon §150q.

[278] Driver, *Deuteronomy*, p. lxxxiii; Weinfeld, *Deuteronomy*, p. 336.

A. K. Fenz,[279] Beuken states that the phrase שמע בקול יהוה is found 71 times in a form similar to Hag 1:12, with 18 in Deuteronomy and the Deuteronomistic source of Jeremiah. Further illustrations of the same Deuteronomistic usage are found with the shorter phrase שמע בקול.

The expression usually refers to a response to the revealed commandments of Yahweh, as Verhoef notes.[280] It is frequently found in conjunction with the quasi-fixed Deuteronomistic expression "to be careful to obey [all] his commandments [and ordinances]" (Deut 15:5; 28:1, 15; 30:10). In certain contexts, to "obey the voice of Yahweh" is to respond appropriately to a message delivered in his name, as is the case in Hag 1:12. Thus in Exod 5:2, Pharaoh's refusal to "obey the voice of Yahweh" is a refusal to heed the words of Moses. In Exod 23:21–22[281] obedience to the voice of Yahweh is linked to obedience to the "angel/messenger of Yahweh" (מלאך יהוה), a phrase used with reference to Haggai in Hag 1:13. It would be difficult to see any deliberate allusion here. However it can be asserted without hesitation that the same motif of obedience to Yahweh through obedience to a mediator is at work in both texts. A similar theme is found in Isa 50:10 where the motifs of obedience to Yahweh via obedience to his servant, and fearing Yahweh are found together, as in Hag 1:12–13 (of interest also is the expression "who among you" found both in Isa 50:10 and Hag 2:2). In conclusion then, while the term frequently designates obedience to the commandments of Yahweh given through Moses, in Hag 1:12 and elsewhere, it may be used to describe a positive response to the words of Yahweh delivered in specific situations by his messengers. The fact that the expression is Deuteronomistic, and is used in conjunction with the "futility curse" form in 1:4–11, as well as the designation of the people as a "remnant" (v. 12) indicates that, for the author of this section, the reconstruction of the temple was a covenantal duty, and by hearkening to the voice of Yahweh the people and their leaders have begun to fulfill that which Yahweh required of them. This understanding is reinforced by the inclusion of יהוה אלהיהם (Yahweh their God) a quintessentially Deuteronomistic expression of the covenantal relationship between Yahweh and his people.[282] The sense of the phrase שמע

---

[279] A. K. Fenz, *Auf Yahwes Stimme hören. Eine biblische Begriffsuntersuchung*, 1964, pp. 38, 44–50, 65., cited by Beuken, p. 32.

[280] Verhoef, p. 80.

[281] On the literary critical issues in this text see B. S. Childs, *The Book of Exodus*, (OTL, Philadelphia: Westminster, 1974), pp. 486–87.

[282] So Beuken, pp. 33–34.

בקול as used in 1:12 is "to be obedient to; to act in accordance with the will of"[283] and signifies, on the part of the people, a commitment to do as the prophet commanded them.[284]

Beuken's hypothesis of the redaction of Haggai in a "Chronistic milieu" is somewhat weakened by the fact that the expression שמע בקול is rarely found in 1 and 2 Chronicles.[285] By contrast, several interesting points emerge when one compares the use of the phrase in Jeremiah to Hag 1:12. As Beuken notes, in Jeremiah the expression frequently enjoins or describes faithfulness to the Sinai covenant, often with reference to the deliverance from Egypt (7:23 and 11:4, 7; cf. Hag 2:5a). Furthermore, as noted above, "to obey the voice of Yahweh" may mean explicitly or implicitly, "to respond to the message communicated by the prophet". The use of שלח in Jer 42:6 (cf. Hag 1:12) and the parallelism between prophet and divine voice in Jer 38:20 (cf. Hag 1:12–13) are noteworthy. Especially significant with reference to Hag 1:12 is the almost exaggerated usage of the phrase לא שמע בקול יהוה אלהי/הם/ו/נו/כם/ך in Jeremiah. The phrase is found in 3:25; 7:28; 9:12 [Eng. 13]; 18:10; 22:21; 32:23; 42:13, 21; 43:4, 7; 44:23. Jeremiah 43:4 is very interesting in this regard. Whereas, in most instances בקול directly follows לא שמע, in Jer 43:4, as in Hag 1:12, a tripartite subject occurs between לא שמע and בקול.

Jer 43:4

ולא־שמע יוחנן בן־קרח וכל־שרי החילים וכל־העם
בקול יהוה לשבת בארץ יהודה:

Hag 1:12

וישמע זרבבל בן־שלתיאל ויהושע בן־יהוצדק הכהן הגדול וכל שארית
בקול יהוה אלהיהם

The syntactical resemblance here is obvious. The relationship between the redaction of Haggai and that of Jeremiah has been analyzed in a

---

[283] The other two primary nuances are (1) to hear (audible sounds or noise), Isa 21:36 [Eng. 35], and (2) to hear with agreement or acceptance, or to receive (as in, for example, the prayer or entreaty of someone), Gen 30:6; cf. BDB.

[284] Floyd, p. 266. Floyd, however, makes a distinction between "heeding" and "obeying" which is unnecessary if one reads v. 14 as a concluding summary, cf. textual criticism and exegesis below.

[285] Beuken (p. 35) opines that there were two chronistic schools at work, one responsible for Haggai and Zech 1–8, and another which produced 1–2 Chr.

number of recent studies, and it is a subject to which we shall return.[286] Here it suffices to note that the text uses a style and vocabulary similar to that of the prose sections of Jeremiah. From a rhetorical perspective, this sets the success of Haggai in stark opposition to the repeated and total failure the people and their leaders to heed the equally divine words of his pre-exilic counterpart.[287]

In conclusion, the presence here of שמע בקול is not fortuitous. Rooted in the traditions of the Sinai covenant, and the Deuteronomistic tradition, it expresses the obedience required by Yahweh from his people as a fundamental response to the covenant. It is frequently used to designate the negative response to Jeremiah's preaching. Hag 1:12 seems to underline the success of Haggai and the people's faithful response in typical Deuteronomistic language.

Within the context of this broadly based spiritual response, the redactor then underlines and explains the means through which this change occurred. This is clearly seen in the supplementary explanations that follow. The narrator adds first ועל־דברי חגי הנביא. The *waw* that begins the phrase is a *waw explicativum*[288] which designates an explanation of that which precedes. Thus the voice of Yahweh consists of the words spoken by Haggai. Beuken aptly states, "'To obey the voice of Yahweh' is parallel to 'the word of the prophet Haggai'. ... To obey him is to obey the voice of Yahweh."[289] No distinction of substance should be made of the use of על rather than ב to introduce Haggai's words, since a variety of prepositions are used with שמע.[290] Then, to underline Haggai's role, the redactor repeats his title "the prophet"

---

[286] Peckham, *History*, p. 741, Y. Goldman, *Prophétie et royauté au retour de l'exil*, (OBO 118; Freiburg/Göttingen: Universitätsverlag/Vandenhoeck & Ruprecht, 1992), p. 229; C. Seitz, "The Crisis of Interpretation over the Meaning and Purpose of the Exile: A Redactional Study of Jeremiah xxi–xliii", *VT* 35 (1985): 78–97. Cf. also B. Gosse, "Nabuchodonosor et les évolutions de la rédaction du livre de Jérémie", *ScEs* 47 (1995): 177–87.
[287] Cf. my discussion on this point in ch. 10. If Haggai is read as a *Flugblatt des Freundskreis* vaunting the merits of Haggai in contrast to another prophet (Zechariah, as Rudolph suggests, [p. 22], but the suggestion is dubious, cf. the discussion in Verhoef, pp. 10–11), the more likely candidate would be Jeremiah than Zechariah, given the contrast described here, as well as the reversal of the imagery of Jer 22:24 in Hag 2:23. Furthermore, Petersen (pp. 34–36) notes the formal similarities between Haggai and Jer 37–41.
[288] Williams §343.
[289] Beuken, pp. 32–33. See also Verhoef, who, citing GKC §154, n. 1(b) takes the same position.
[290] Verhoef, p. 82

(חגי הנביא). Subsequently, a further clarifying note is inserted with reference to Haggai, his words and their authority, by means of the phrase כאשר שלחו יהוה אלהיהם.[291] Two of the three primary senses of כאשר,[292] that is, "according to" and "when" are not appropriate here. It is rather the causal sense which best suits this context. Thus the phrase explains how it was that Haggai could proclaim the words of Yahweh: it was Yahweh himself who had sent him.[293] Yahweh's sending (שלח) of the prophets is a theme that is found frequently in Judges to 2 Kings and Jeremiah but rarely elsewhere.[294] Furthermore, שלח is seldom used with Yahweh as subject and נביא as object.[295] In texts where Yahweh sends prophets, three main themes emerge. First, the sending of the prophet occurs because Yahweh wants to deal with a situation of need or distress (Judg 6:8; 2 Kgs 17:13; Jer 44:4; Mal 3:23 [Eng. 4:5]). Second, to be sent by Yahweh guarantees the veracity of the message (Jer 28:9, 15; Zech 7:12). Third, to be sent by Yahweh confirms the credibility of the one sent (Jer 28:9, 15). These themes are clearly present in Hag 1:12. Thus the redactional framework underlines the importance of the role of Haggai in the response of the people: he conveyed the words of Yahweh and his intervention occurred because Yahweh sent him. The Deuteronomistic and covenantal atmosphere of the passage is reinforced by the repetition of the phrase יהוה אלהיהם (Yahweh their God).[296]

The redactor's description of the obedience of the people[297] continues by noting their fear.[298] The fear of Yahweh is a vast subject, and a detailed discussion of it cannot be undertaken here.[299] It is customary to distinguish three main senses of the notion of the fear of God

---

[291] Ibid., p. 32.

[292] BDB "כאשר". Verhoef (p.83) opts for "according to"—a sense which seems strained here.

[293] Cf. the textual criticism for an evaluation of Verhoef's suggestion (pp. 82–83) that the antecedent of the pron. suf. is the message.

[294] The only instances outside Judg-2 Kgs and Jer are Hag 1:12; Zech 7:12; Mal 3:23; 2 Chr 25:15.

[295] Judg 6:8; 2 Kgs 17:13; Jer 28:9, 15; 44:4; Hag 1:12; Zech 7:12; Mal 3:23; 2 Chr 25:15.

[296] Cf. textual criticism, *supra*, for a fuller analysis and the retention of יהוה אלהיהם.

[297] Although not explicitly mentioned, the leaders are to be implied here.

[298] Plural verb with collective noun (cf. Schattner-Rieser, "L'hébreu", p. 217), the reverse of 1:12a.

[299] See the full study of L. Derousseaux, *La crainte de Dieu dans l'Ancien Testament*, (LD 63; Paris: Cerf, 1970).

or Yahweh: (1) a sacral fear that occurs when the creature comes into direct contact with the divinity;[300] (2) a moral fear, which may be found both within and outside of Israel, which indicates a knowledge of and respect for basic standards of morality, usually indicated by a form of ירא with אלהים;[301] and (3) a covenantal fear which denotes a disposition of fidelity to the God of the covenant, usually using a form of ירא followed by את יהוה.[302] This usage is prevalent in Deuteronomy and the Deuteronomistic literature.[303] Derousseaux views the expression as frequently meaning "to adhere loyally to Yahweh as the God of the covenant"[304] or "to observe the commandments."[305]

The form in Hag 1:12 is, however, ירא followed by מפני יהוה. As Derousseaux notes, ירא followed by מן with יהוה or אלהים as complement is rare in the Hebrew Bible, occurring only at Exod 9:30; Hag 1:12; Eccl 3:14, and Ps 33:8.[306] He concludes that its meaning here is similar to the instances where ירא is followed by מן or מפני and a personal name.[307] Such instances generally indicate subjective feelings of fear with reference to someone. Thus, having set about to obey Yahweh, the people were afraid.[308] A similar response, using different vocabulary, may be seen in the Deuteronomistic description of Josiah's response to the finding of the book of the law (2 Kgs 22:8–20) and the similar motif in Neh 8:9 and 9:1–5. Haggai's word of assurance in v. 13 comes as a response to this experience of fear. The covenantal flavouring of these words should not be missed. Despite the fact that "fearing Yahweh" has a fundamentally different sense in the Deuteronomistic literature,[309] the presence of subjective fear on the people's part should be seen as indicating, for the book's redactor, a response to Haggai's words in line with faithful obedience to Yahweh's covenant.

---

[300] Ibid., pp. 82–27.

[301] Ibid., pp. 169–73.

[302] Ibid., pp. 209f, esp. pp. 221, 255–56.

[303] See Driver (*Deuteronomy*, p. lxxxii) who cites Deut 4:10; 5:26 [Eng. 29]; 6:2, 13, 24; 8:6; 10:12; 13:5 [Eng. 4]; 14:23; 17:19; 28:58; 31:12, 13).

[304] Derousseaux, *La crainte*, p. 221.

[305] Ibid., p. 256. Derousseaux, in contrast to Becker, sees a theological development in the concept from its origins in the northern Elohistic traditions, to Deuteronomy, to the Deuteronomistic redaction of Deuteronomy, to the Deuteronomistic History.

[306] Ibid., p. 296.

[307] Cf. for example 1 Sam 7:7 (with מפני) which parallels Hag 1:12 closely. Cf. also Josh 10:8; 1 Sam 18:12; 21:13 [Eng. 12]; Isa 10:24; Jer 10:5; 42:11 (with מפני); Ezek 2:6.

[308] So Wolff, p. 49; Verhoef, p. 83 with bibliography.

[309] Derousseaux, *La crainte*, pp. 205–57.

Prophetic preaching brought about a radical transformation. The community was previously subject to the displeasure of Yahweh and experienced the consequences of covenant disobedience. But now the people fulfill a cardinal condition of the covenant in that they obey the voice of Yahweh. Beuken sees the verse as indicating covenant renewal.[310] This terminology may, however, imply too much. Chary aptly surmises, "It is a re-awakening of faith. Prophetic preaching has been effective, an event very rarely attested in the history of the people."[311]

**[13]** Verse 13 presents a response to the fear of the people, as well as a further definition of the role of Haggai.[312] Before relating Haggai's words of assurance, the redactor adds two further qualifying statements regarding Haggai himself. He is first of all מלאך יהוה (the messenger of Yahweh). The reader is immediately struck by the fact that מלאך[313] stands in apposition to חגי, who has just been designated a הנביא in 1:1, 12. Some of the meanings of the term מלאך יהוה are clearly excluded here. Our text does not involve the motifs of a theophany or an exceptional manifestation of the presence of Yahweh (cf. Gen 19:1, 15; 28:12; 32:2; etc.). Equally foreign is the *angelus interpres* of Zechariah.[314] In Zechariah the distinction between prophet and messenger is quite clear. The meaning of מלאך in Hag 1:13 is therefore "'messenger' sent by a man, or … God."[315] Prophets are so described in Isa 42:19; 44:26 and 2 Chr 36:15, 16.[316] Chary's suggestion that the use of מלאך יהוה with reference to Haggai serves as evidence "of an evolution of the conception of the prophetic role that is more executive than creative,"[317] is dubious. The most judicious conclusion is that the use of מלאך here serves to underline the authority of Haggai as an agent of Yahweh as well the authority of the message he conveys.[318]

---

[310] Beuken, pp. 33–34, cf. *infra* n. 327.

[311] Chary, p. 21, as noted above. It is not necessary to assume (cf. Floyd, p. 269) that this fear paralyzed a portion of the people and required prophetic and divine intervention to overcome, cf. n. 269, *supra*.

[312] Cf. Wolff, pp. 31–35, and Verhoef, pp. 83–84, for various approaches to the literary history and authenticity of this verse.

[313] The word occurs approximately 119x in the Hebrew Bible.

[314] On which cf. von Rad, s. v. "ἄγγελος", *TDNT* 1:79. My position here stands in contrast to that of Sérandour, "Réflexions", p. 81.

[315] Von Rad, "ἄγγελος", pp. 77.

[316] Verhoef, p. 84, cf. also Meyers and Meyers, p. 35; Hanson, *Dawn of Apocalyptic*, p. 125.

[317] Chary, p. 23.

[318] Petersen, p. 56.

A second clarification follows the first. The author adds that Haggai is the messenger of Yahweh "according to the commission of Yahweh" (במלאכות יהוה). The noun מלאכות is an Old Testament *hapax* from the root לאך.[319] Several translations of it have been suggested, including "message,"[320] "mission,"[321] or "commission."[322] The first option links the meaning of the noun to מלאך, and the second to מלאכה. I suggest that the third translation is preferable. The link with מלאך appears weak, and the acceptation "message" is almost redundant. מלאכות should rather be identified with the Yahweh's mandate, charge or commission. The preposition ב here carries a causal sense.[323] The redactor thus specifies how it was that Haggai came to be the "messenger of Yahweh": he was commissioned to that post by Yahweh himself.[324] Rudolph aptly summarizes the thought here, "So that no one will think he claims an authority that is not his own with this sudden positive encouragement, or that he lays claim to a position that is not rightly his, it is again explicitly affirmed that Haggai speaks as the messenger of Yahweh according to the commission (*Sendungsauftrag*) of Yahweh."[325] Haggai, consequently, is Yahweh's appointee. While the book contains no mention of Haggai's call, such an event (cf. Jer 1; Isa 6; Amos 7) is presupposed by this expression.

By means of a declaration in the form of a Formula of Assistance (אני אתכם)[326] frequently found in priestly oracles of salvation, Haggai

---

[319] BDB, "לאך". The sense of the root is "to send", cf. Wolff, p. 33. On the frequent use of nouns ending in -ut in late Hebrew, cf. Schattner-Rieser, "L'hébreu", p. 202.

[320] Meyers and Meyers, p. 35.

[321] Verhoef, p. 84.

[322] Wolff, p. 34; Rudolph, pp. 37–38.

[323] Williams §247.

[324] Driver translates the phrase במלאכות יהוה "in virtue of his being commissioned as his prophet", as cited in E. Cashdan, "Haggai: An Introduction and Commentary", in *The Soncino Books of the Bible: The Twelve Prophets*, (ed. A. Choen; London: Soncino, 1948), p. 258.

[325] Rudolph, pp. 37–38. Verhoef (p. 84) opts for the translation "mission" here. Yet he fails to explain why "commission" would be unacceptable.

[326] On the *Beistandformel*, see Wolff, p. 33 and Beuken, pp. 37–42. This formula may be found in several variant forms: (1) the preposition employed may be עם (Gen 28:15; 31:38; Ps 39:13) or את (Jer 42:11; 46:28); (2) the pronominal suffix may be 2 m. sg. or 2 m. pl. (It is more frequently found with the 2 m. sg. pron. suf. [Gen 26:24; Isa 43:2, 5; Jer 1:8, 19; 15:20; 30:11; 46:28]; (3) the word order is variable. Hag 1:13; 2: 4 and Jer 42:11 are the only three instances where this specific form is found (את plus 2 m. pl. pronominal suffix, and even at that the word order is not identical in each case). Wolff (p. 50) and Beuken (p. 39) link its form to that of the "priestly oracle of salvation"; cf. J. Begrich, "Die priesterliche Tora", *ZAW* 66 (1936): 63–88. Beuken, (pp. 41–42),

declares to the members of the community that Yahweh is present among them. Here Haggai's first person speech for Yahweh is not introduced by a Word-Event Formula or any specific order to speak. The omission of such a formula should be seen as a redactional variation, rather than an indication that Haggai was speaking for Yahweh on his own initiative. The presence of the Messenger Formula attests to the fact that these are indeed Yahweh's words.

The import of the brief oracle is to assure the hearers that the rupture which previously existed between Yahweh and his people has now been overcome. The declaration of the presence of Yahweh thus certifies that, even though the temple has not been completed, or the actual work even begun, the primary obstacle, the community's resistance, is now no longer a factor.[327] Yahweh will be actively present with his people to make their work efficacious.[328]

[14] The relationship of v. 14 to vv. 2–11 and 12–13 can potentially be understood in two ways. On one hand it could be seen as an action subsequent to that which has previously transpired.[329] However as Petersen admits, this creates an incongruity. "There is, consequently, a tension produced in 12–15a. On the one hand, the words of Haggai were effective; but on the other hand, Yahweh had to intervene in order for the work to resume."[330] Such a two-tiered approach to the inauguration of the reconstruction seems foreign to vv. 12–15 as a whole. Indeed the description of the people obeying and fearing in vv. 12–13 leaves no suggestion that any further obstacle remained requiring divine intervention. However Petersen's tension disappears if an alternative approach is taken, that of viewing v. 14 as a summary of the scene. This reading is entirely consistent with the use of *waw* consecutive with imperfect

---

however notes that the fact that it is not followed by אל תרא indicates that it has become detached from its formal matrix and has taken on an independent existence. Both agree that there is no substantial difference between אני את at and אני עם.

[327] Beuken (p. 42) sees the inauguration of temple's reconstruction and the declaration of the divine presence as a renewal of the covenant. He views this as intimately connected with the Chronicler's preoccupation with the Jerusalem cult. Petersen (p. 60), however, argues vigorously that the covenant cannot be seen to have been totally ruptured, since the imposition of its punishments in vv. 4–11 implies its ongoing validity. In a sense the text here is patient of both interpretations. On this, see *infra*, on the use of religious traditions, and S. D. Sperling, "Rethinking Covenant in the Late Biblical Books", *Bib* 70 (1989): 50–73.

[328] Cf. Exod 4:15–16, where an analogous formulation of Yahweh's presence is used.

[329] Thus Verhoef, Petersen and Wolff. Cf. my preliminary observations in the textual criticism *supra*.

[330] Petersen, p. 58.

elsewhere where such verbs occur at the conclusion of a pericope. Such a phenomenon is found, for example, in Gen 25:45. In this text, the phrase ויבז עשו את־הבכרה (and thus Esau despised his birthright) does not speak of an action subsequent to the main action of the narrative, but constitutes a summary of the narrative as a whole. The same structure is seen in Gen 24:67b and 26:6, and in 2 Sam 15:6b. Williamson observes it in Ezra 4:4–5.[331] It is therefore preferable to understand ויער (and he stirred up) as a recapitulating summary of all the preceding actions. This interpretation is implicit in Chary[332] and Amsler,[333] and explicit in Meyers and Meyers[334] and Rudolph.[335] Rudolph observes that v. 14 represents a conclusion of the narrative that balances all its elements. He states, "It is Yahweh, the *primus movens* who fulfills his plan. He uses human agents, notably the people and their leaders, but in order for them to assume their own responsibilities, there must be the divine word through the prophet, a word that shakes and rebukes, so that the work might be accomplished."[336]

The hiphil of עור (to stir up) describes Yahweh's hidden activity which touches the inner workings of human decision and volition such that his purposes may be attained.[337] Chary postulates the existence of an underlying messianic theme in vv. 12–15 from the use of the term here.[338] However such an inference appears unwarranted in that 1:1–15 as a whole contains no promise that the reconstruction of the temple will inaugurate a new "messianic" age or that a messianic figure will appear. The implicit understanding of the passage is rather that, now that the community's alienation from Yahweh has been successfully dealt with, the disruption of normal agricultural and economic pursuits will cease, and the regularly expected yields and productivity will be attained. This is an important observation given the often repeated assertion that Haggai viewed the reconstruction of the temple as the

---

[331] Williamson, *Ezra*, pp. 43–44. J. L. Ska ("Sommaires proleptiques en Gn 27 et dans l'histoire de Joseph", *Bib* 73 [1992]: 518–27) illustrates a similar phenomenon at the beginning of narratives.

[332] Chary (p. 21) states, "v. 14 gives a fuller description of the awakening narrated in v. 12 and 13."

[333] Amsler, p. 25.

[334] Meyers and Meyers (p. 4) translate, "Thus Yahweh stirred up the spirit".

[335] Rudolph, p. 38.

[336] Ibid., p. 30.

[337] Chary, p. 21, and Wolff, pp. 52–53; cf. Isa 41:2, 21; 45:13; Ezra 1:15; Jer 50:9; 51:1, 11.

[338] Ibid., p. 21.

guarantee of the arrival of "the age to come." Equally unlikely is the suggestion made by Meyers and Meyers that the rousing of the spirit of the populace and leaders carries political significance, the reconstruction of the temple being "an act intimately associated with the control and administration of a political unit."[339] While such an act doubtlessly carried this kind of significance, the point in 1:14 relates primarily, if not entirely, to the fact that it was by means of Haggai's prophetic intervention that the inertia with which the book began was overcome. This is underscored in final part of v. 14. The community and its leaders come (בוא, in contrast with the refusal to come expressed by the same verb in v. 2) to begin[340] work[341] (ויעשׂו מלאכה) on[342] the house of Yahweh. The inertia of vv. 2–9 disappears following Haggai's intervention. Thus Haggai's declarations became the basis and the primary means through which Yahweh stirred up the spirits of his people.

The repetition of רוח before Zerubbabel, Joshua, and "all the remnant of the people"[343] underlines the comprehensive scope both of the divine work and the human response. Everyone is involved.[344] Wolff asserts that only the leaders and returnees are designated here as having participated in the temple's reconstruction.[345] However, as noted above, the redactor's purpose here is to portray the efficacy of Haggai's words as inclusively and extensively as possible.[346] Thus the book begins by presenting the reader/hearer with the image of a community which *en masse* decided that work on the temple could be put off until better times prevailed. Similarly the redactional purpose at the conclusion of the pericope is to demonstrate that as a result of Haggai's preaching

---

[339] Meyers and Meyers, p. 35.

[340] On the inceptive nuance in these two verbs cf. Verhoef, p. 87 and Wolff, p. 53.

[341] Chary (p. 32) deduces from the use of מלאכה here, without the article, that the work involved did not constitute the first attempts at reconstruction. While such a conclusion need not necessarily be the case, the expression here is certainly quite vague and general. The term is frequently used for work on the tabernacle (Exod 31:3, 5; 35:29, 31; 36:3, 4) or the temple (1 Chr 9:13, 19, and especially 23:4 which is quite similar to Hag 1:14) cf. Wolff, p. 53. The paronomasia between מלאך v. 13, מלאכות v. 13, and מלאכה is noteworthy, cf. Prokurat, "Haggai", p. 113. The same can be said of the triple repetition of יהוה אלהיהם in vv. 12a, 12b and 15 (cf. Meyers and Meyers, pp. 35–36).

[342] Cf. textual criticism, *supra*.

[343] On this term see *supra*, v. 12.

[344] Williams §15–16; *IBHS* §7.2.3.

[345] Wolff, pp. 51–53.

[346] Cf. ch. 10, *infra*.

and Yahweh's activity the same community comes *en masse* to do that
which was previously eschewed. The dating formula in 15a serves to
indicate the rapidity with which the resumption of the work was undertaken.[347]

In sum then, vv. 12–15a constitute a tightly packed unit, narrative
in form, revealing the over-arching redactional themes into which the
oracles of Haggai are being integrated. The section stresses the authority and role of the prophet, and the efficacy of his words. The content
of this section is utterly essential to the rest of the book, since all of
what follows presupposes a restored relationship between Yahweh and
his people, and a building whose reconstruction is in process.[348]

## 5.4. Rhetorical and Hermeneutical Use of Religious Traditions

The preceding exegesis has revealed the presence of various religious
traditions in 1:1–15. At this point I wish to point out two particularly
distinctive uses of this tradition. It is important to view these as *rhetorical
and hermeneutical strategies* employed, at least in part, to deal with the
tension created by the radically changed circumstances of the Persian
period vis-à-vis earlier periods in which many of these traditions were
current.

### 5.4.1. *Tradition as a Basis for Understanding the Present*

As we have seen, in 1:4–11 the prophet understands the community's
lack of economic and agricultural success to be the result of its neglect
of the temple. Broadly speaking, the vocabulary and ideology employed
situate the line of reasoning here in the context of the Deuteronomistic
concept of divine corrective activity designed to bring Israel to repentance. Two classical loci of this motif are Deut 4:25–32 and Amos 4:6–
13. The latter text especially demonstrates the use of the kinds of sufferings described in Deut 28 and Lev 26 in a remedial or corrective sense,
rather than as retributive, quasi-mechanical "curses." Micah 6:13–16
uses many of the same motifs as Hag 1, but in a future oriented sense.[349]

---

[347] Meyers and Meyers, p. 46. Verhoef (p. 89) observes that the redactor here insists
on the fact that "something actually happened".
[348] Floyd, p. 273.
[349] Cf. Tollington, *Tradition*, pp. 190–97.

Tollington notes that in Haggai the implicit assumption is that the current situation will continue until the people do what is required.[350] In my opinion she does not adequately stress the restorative nature of the curse material in Haggai, versus its more punitive use in Deut 28, Lev 26, Mic 6 and elsewhere. Thus the prophet, in a fashion similar to Amos, sees in the community's experiences a warning or reproach.

As noted above, the language of Hag 1:6, 9–11 closely resembles Lev 26 and Deut 28 at several points.[351] The phrase זרעתם הרבה והבא מעט (you have sown but harvested little, Hag 1:6) is close to זרע רב תוציא השדה ומעט תאסף (you will bring much seed to the field, you will harvest little, Deut 28:38). The statement אכול ואין־לשׂבעה (you eat but are not satisfied, Hag 1:6) recalls ואכלתם ולא תשׂבעו (you will eat without being satisfied, Lev 26:26). The themes of drought and barrenness are found elsewhere in Deut 28:23 and Lev 26:19 where the skies and the land become as נחשׁתand ב רזל (bronze and iron). The drought of Hag 1:11 is echoed in Deut 28:51. Both texts mention the same three agricultural products. The barrenness of the land, flocks, and humans (Hag 1:11) is also found in Deut 28:18. The futility of כל־יגיע כפים (all the work of your hands, Hag 1:11b) is parallel to the frustration experienced בכל־משׁלח ידך (in every endeavour of your hands, Deut 28:20). The exhortation "consider your ways" (שׂימו לבבכם על־דרכיכם, Hag 1:5 and 7) moves in a similar realm to Deut 28:29, ולא תצליח את־דרכיך (and you will not succeed in your ways). Haggai 1:6 and 9a in particular use these motifs in a way that closely resembles a "futility curse."[352] Such curses frequently consist of a protasis describing an activity directed at a precise result (undertaken by the one guilty of covenant violation), followed by an apodosis where the reverse occurs (as a consequence of the violation).[353] Both dramatic irony and futility curse formulations often serve to describe the ultimate futility of all human endeavours which seek to attain their own goals through opposition to or neglect of Yahweh and his purposes.[354]

---

[350] Ibid., p. 198.

[351] The form and traditional history of the "curse" material in the Hebrew Bible cannot be discussed here. See Nicholson, *Deuteronomy and Tradition*, p. 445; Hillers, *Treaty Curses*, p. 11–89, and Beuken, p. 190f.

[352] Hillers, *Treaty Curses*, p. 28–29.

[353] Petersen, p. 50; Wolff, p. 27.

[354] Cf. T. Jemielity, "Divine Derision and Scorn: Satire and Irony in the Prophets", in T. Jemielity, *Satire and the Hebrew Prophets*, (Louisville: Westminster/John Knox, 1992), pp. 84–118.

Both in content and form, the "futility curse" material appears in distinctive ways in Haggai. First, the community's misfortunes are not viewed as possibilities (and hence warnings to repent) but as tangible evidence both of its failure and of Yahweh's response to it.[355] The population is, therefore, invited to consider their situation in light of these evidences of divine displeasure. The prophet becomes an *interpreter* of historical circumstance, and as such invites his audience to draw the appropriate conclusions.[356] In Amos 4:6–13 similar misfortunes are sent to bring the people back to Yahweh, but are imposed without prophetic explanation, perhaps due to the earlier rejection of prophetic speech mentioned in Amos 2:11–12. In Haggai (as in Amos, and to a lesser extent Deut 4), and in contrast to Micah, Deut 28, and Lev 26, the prophet declares the community's misfortunes to be the evidence of Yahweh's displeasure. The situation, however, may be reversed by appropriate action on the people's part. There is no hint in Haggai that a point of no return has been risked or reached (in contrast, for example, to Amos 4:12; Mic 6:16b). Thus, in Haggai 1:1–11, the consequences of covenant violation are viewed as disciplinary and restorative in nature, and less temporally focused on a major crisis (such as exile).

### 5.4.2. *Fusion of Independent Traditions and Extended Sphere of Application*

A second innovative step in Hag 1:3–11 is the linking of two independent traditions: covenant violation and the neglect of the temple.[357] The prophet finds a new "sphere of application" for an existing body of traditional material, that is the curses of the Deuteronomistic tradition. Such "curses" are normally imposed for cases of flagrant disobedience to the law, especially idolatry (cf. Deut 28:14–15, 46–48, 58–59;[358] Lev 26:3, 14, 15.[359]) In 1:3–11, Haggai applies the curse vocabulary to a question not dealt with in that tradition.[360] The prophet reasons from a

---

[355] Petersen, p. 50; Wolff, p. 27.

[356] Tollington, *Tradition*, p. 192, and myself, independently, "Le livre d'Aggée", pp. 292f.

[357] Beuken, p. 197. Whedbee, "Question-Answer", p. 192.

[358] On the literary history of Deut 28, see Nicholson, *Deuteronomy and Tradition*, p. 445.

[359] On the literary history of Lev 26 and the relation between it and Deut 28, cf. Weinfeld, *Deuteronomy*, pp. 124–26 and J. E. Hartley, *Leviticus*, (WBC, Dallas: Word, 1992), p. 459.

[360] Petersen, p. 50.

broader notion, found elsewhere in the Deuteronomistic tradition, that of due respect for the divine name. For example Deut 28:58–59a[361] associates lack of respect or reverence for Yahweh's glorious and fearsome name with a curse:

אם־לא תשמר לעשות את־כל־דברי התורה הזאת הכתובים בספר הזה
ליראה את־השם הנכבד והנורא הזה את יהוה אלהיך:
והפלא יהוה את־מכתך ואת מכות זרעך מכות גדלות

While neglecting to rebuild the temple does not constitute idolatry or flagrant disobedience to the commandments, our prophet sees in it a gesture of contempt.[362] The text portrays Haggai as deploying a hermeneutical strategy whereby his specific situation is viewed on the basis of a tradition that never specifically envisaged such a state of affairs.[363] The broader notion of the fear of Yahweh is thus interpreted and applied with reference to a specific historical situation.

Haggai also rhetorically undergirds his theological interpretation of the community's covenantal obligation to rebuild the temple through the language and forms of wisdom traditions. For Haggai, to neglect the temple manifests both faithlessness to the covenant and a lack of wisdom.[364] The use of sapiential themes is not unusual in postexilic prophecy.[365] Haggai's question in v. 4 revolves around the common wisdom motif of appropriate choices at specific moments. He does not attempt to call into question the validity of such reasoning, but objects to its selective, selfish, and hypocritical application.[366] To this he adds a eudaemonistic dimension, common in wisdom, in which the basis of his appeal is, in part, choosing that which will bring the greatest ultimate personal happiness. To move his hearers to a point of decision, Haggai calls for two well-known sapiential responses: (1) observation, and (2) reflection upon that which has been observed (Hag 1:6b, 9a, 11).

---

[361] Von Rad, *Deuteronomy*, pp. 29–30, who maintains that this section is part of the latest redactional level of the book. Even if this is so, the same theme appears in the earlier sections.

[362] Ackroyd, *Exile and Restoration*, p. 160. In my view, Tollington (p. 190) overstates the case when she suggests that it is a "bold suggestion" to equate temple reconstruction with covenantal obedience in Haggai.

[363] Even if one considers Deut 28:58 to be exilic, it is unlikely that an exilic redactor would have envisaged such an application.

[364] On wisdom as obedience to the law in Deuteronomistic literature (e.g., Deut 4:6); cf. M. Weinfeld, *Deuteronomy*, p. 625.

[365] Meyers, "*tôrâ* in Haggai 2", p. 75, n. 5.

[366] Kessler, "'*t* (le temps)", pp. 555–57.

Thus the use of religious traditions in Hag 1:1–15a manifests a creative reformulation, mixing, and re-application of a variety of traditions and genres.[367]

---

[367] Mason ("The Prophets of the Restoration", pp. 141–42) describes this phenomenon well: "[T]he undeniable process of reinterpretation and re-application of earlier prophecy to later situations ... can be viewed as illustrative of the power and vitality of the divine word ... [P]ostexilic prophecy becomes increasingly derivative, and takes on more of the nature of exegesis, the reinterpretation and re-application of the earlier 'authoritative' word. To say this, however, does not mean it shows no originality or inventiveness. The three prophets of the restoration (to say nothing of Isa 56–66) show considerable creativity in their selection and use of earlier material and traditions."

CHAPTER SIX

# HAGGAI 2:1–9

## 6.1. TRANSLATION AND TEXTUAL CRITICISM

[1] In the seventh month, on the twenty-first of the month, the word of Yahweh came through[1] Haggai as follows:

[2] "Say to Zerubbabel, son of Shealtiel, governor of Judah, and to Joshua, son of Jehozadak, the high priest, and to the remnant of the people,[2]

[3] "'Is there still anyone[3] left[4] among you who saw this house in its former splendour?[5] And how does it look to you now? Does it not seem to be[6] nothing at all in your eyes?'

[4] "But now be strong Zerubbabel—oracle of Yahweh;[7] and be strong, Joshua, son of Jehozadak, the high priest, and be strong, all you people of the land—oracle of Yahweh, and work, for I am with you—oracle of Yahweh Sebaoth.

---

[1] MT ביד; Mur אל. In spite of the fact that Mur maintains the distinction cited above (ch. 5, n. 1) between the intermediary and addressees of the word of Yahweh, the *lectio difficilior* of the MT, which is followed by the LXX, Syr, Vulg, and Tg is to be retained. Verhoef (pp. 94–95) plausibly suggests an ellipsis of אל followed by the addressees here.

[2] The LXX adds πάντας (=Heb כל), and is followed by the Syr and Vet Lat. The Tg and Vulg support the MT. The LXX made the addition perhaps through the influence of 1:12, 14a. Chary and Meyers and Meyers, correct the MT, *pace* Wolff, Petersen and Amsler.

[3] On the partitive use of מי cf. *IBHS* §18.2b

[4] On this translation of the ni ptc. of שאר see the exegesis.

[5] הראשון modifies כבוד and not בית.

[6] On the repetition of כ see Joüon §141i.

[7] The *BHS* proposes the omission of the first נאם יהוה, of the words between יהושע and ועשו, and the last word of the verse צבאות. No MS evidence supports this suggestion.

[5] "This is[8] the word[9] that I sealed by covenant with you when you came out of Egypt, my Spirit remains in your midst, do not fear.

[6] For this is what Yahweh Sebaoth says, "One more[10] time, and it will happen very soon,[11] I will shake[12] the heavens and the earth, the sea[13] and the dry land.

---

[8] Two significant problems appear in this verse: (1) The words את ... מצרים are lacking in the LXX, Syr, and Vet Lat, but appear in the Tg and Vulg, and probably in Mur, (cf. Petersen, p. 61). Should it be deemed a gloss? (2) If the words are retained, what do they mean, and what is their relationship to that which follows and precedes them? Closely linked to this is the question of the meaning of את here.

(1) From a text-critical point of view, the disputed phrase is solidly attested in the proto-massoretic tradition (Barthélemy, *Critique textuelle*, 3:928). The introduction of the phrase into that tradition is more difficult to explain than its omission in the LXX. Barthélemy (ibid., 3:928) appropriately concludes, "Whether or not the phrase is secondary, its omission would have to be made on literary critical rather that text-critical grounds."

(2) The words at issue may be linked with that which precedes or follows. They may be seen as the object of עשה in v. 4b, "do [obey] the word which I covenanted with you …" (Meyers and Meyers, and the rabbinical tradition, cf. Wolff, p. 51). Alternatively they may be considered to be an explanation of אני אתכם (v. 4b, cf. Barthélemy, *Critique textuelle*, 3:928) or an introduction to the presence of the spirit of Yahweh in 2:5b. In either case את would carry the well-attested meaning "concerning, regarding" cf. Ezek 43:7; 44:3, or "this is" cf. Ezek 47:17, 18, 19; Zech 7:7; 8:17; Num 35:6, (ibid., p. 928). My preference is for the latter option, cf. exegesis.

[9] The *BHS* and Chary suggest reading זאת הברית but no textual support exists for the suggestion.

[10] For the implicit sense of finality, cf. the exegesis, *infra*.

[11] Two problems are encountered here, one of textual criticism, the other of translation. Textually, the LXX reads ἔτι ἅπαξ which would appear to reflect only עוד אחת. Wellhausen, Mitchell, and with some reservations Ackroyd (*Exile and Restoration*, p. 153), suggest the MT contains two alternative readings. However it is difficult to conceive of מעט היא standing alone as an alternative to עוד אחת. The absence of מעט היא in the LXX is more easily explicable (possibly due to the prophecy's delay in fulfillment)—a suggestion made by Sellin and endorsed by Rudolph [p. 41]) than the insertion of one or another variant in the massoretic tradition, Tg and Vulg. Consequently, with Wolff, Amsler, Chary, Petersen, Verhoef, and Meyers and Meyers, I opt for the retention of the complete phrase. Meyers and Meyers, (p. 52) appropriately conclude, "The uniqueness and strangeness of the term argue in favour of its originality."
The syntactical and philological decisions which lie behind the translation presented here will be defended in the exegesis below.

[12] The verbal structure of vv. 6–7 is as follows: the ptc. מרעיש, (v. 6), constitutes a *futurum instans* (GKC §116p) indicating an imminent event (Joüon §119n). It is followed by a series of verbs in wcs.+ perf. in v. 7, ומלאתי ... ובאו ... והרעשתי. Joüon (§119n) notes that this construction frequently indicates successive actions, cf. n. 117 *infra*. For this reason Amsler's telic translation (p. 30), "so that the treasures of the nations might come" is untenable.

[13] MT ואת. The *waw* is lacking in a fragment of the Cairo Geniza, which Wolff (p. 71) considers to be the original reading.

[7] "And I will make all the nations tremble, and the treasures[14] of all the nations will come in, and I will fill this house with glory—oracle of Yahweh Sebaoth.

[8] "Mine is the silver! And mine is the gold!—oracle of Yahweh Sebaoth.

[9] "The future splendour[15] of this house will far exceed its former state, —oracle of Yahweh Sebaoth. And in this place, I will give peace[16]—oracle of Yahweh Sebaoth."[17]

## 6.2. STRUCTURAL AND LITERARY CONSIDERATIONS

This second section is structured in four stages similar to those in 1:1–11. It begins with an introductory formula in 2:1–2 with the following structure: (1) the date, in the order year-month-day (the year notice of 1:15b is perhaps doing double duty here);[18] (2) the Word-Event Formula, identical to the one in 1:1, 3[19] (in spite of the difference in structure in the divine speech); (3) the names of the addressees (including "the people," as in 1:12 and 14 and in contrast to 1:2).

Following this introductory formula, the pericope's dramatic conflict is introduced in vv. 2–3. As in 1:2, this conflict is expressed by means of the people's opinions and thoughts. However in contrast to 1:2, where the conflict is introduced by citing the people's words, here the prophet, at Yahweh's request, addresses a series of three rhetorical questions

---

[14] MT חֶמְדַּת, LXX τὰ ἐκλεκτά. Two main options exist: pointing חֶמְדַּת (sg.), with the MT, Syr, Tg, and Vulg, or (2) following the LXX, reconstituting the Hebrew pl. חֲמֻדֹת, which agrees with the following pl. verb וּבָאוּ. The Vulg gives the sg. a messianic translation *et venit desideratus cunctis gentibus*. The textual isolation of the LXX, and the fact that the sg. may carry a collective sense (GKC §145e) which would have led to the choice of the pl. verb (a frequent phenomenon in later Hebrew, [Joüon §150e]) indicates that the text is best read as a collective, non-messianic sg. Cf. Petersen, (p. 67), who proposes an ellipsis of כלי before חֶמְדַּת. Wolff, (p. 71), GKC (§145e), and Meyers and Meyers, (p. 47) emend to the pl.

[15] Because of the parallel with v. 3, הָאַחֲרוֹן (latter) should be read as modifying כבוד (glory) not הזה הבית (this house). So the LXX, Vulg, Wolff and Amsler, *pace* Meyers and Meyers, and Petersen.

[16] Syr reads "My peace."

[17] The LXX adds: καὶ εἰρήνην ψυχῆς εἰς περιποίησιν παντὶ τῷ κτίζοντι τοῦ ἀναστῆσαι τὸν ναὸν τοῦτον; "and peace of soul as a possession for all who build to erect this temple" (Peterson's translation, p. 70). Petersen plausibly suggests that a scribe has "spiritualized" a more material promise. Cf. also Ackroyd, "Interpretative Glosses", pp. 164–65.

[18] Meyers and Meyers, p. xlvi.

[19] Cf. textual criticism *supra*.

to the people (2:2–3). The first deals with the past: "Who has seen?"
The second and third relate to the present: "how does it appear to you
now?" and "is it nothing in your eyes?" Although no response is given,
the questions are clearly meant to reveal widespread discouragement
regarding the appearance of the temple. This discouragement becomes
the principal dramatic conflict in this scene. The prophet responds to
this problem in the two subsequent sections: the first response, in 2:4–
5, consists of an encouragement to persevere in the reconstruction.
The second, in vv. 6–9, is a promise regarding the temple's glorious
future.

   The structure of the third part of the scene (2:4–5), which consists
of a series of oracles of encouragement and assurance, is somewhat
complex. The section is introduced by ועתה, which has a slightly adver-
sative sense here.[20] What follows is essentially a thrice-repeated Encouragement Formula (*Ermutigungsformel*),[21] addressed to the leaders and the
community, followed by a command to continue to work (2:4aγ). This
command is then followed by an oracle of salvation, consisting of a Formula of Assistance, identical to the one found in 1:13, here introduced
by a causal כי. This is then followed (as in 1:13) by a Divine-Saying Formula.[22] Verse 5aα contains an explanatory comment situating the postexilic community in relationship to the Sinai covenant.[23] This explanatory comment is then followed by a second declaration of the divine
presence which is epexegetical of the Formula of Assistance in v. 4. The
presence of Yahweh with his people is said to be manifested in terms
of his Spirit's presence among them. This assertion is then followed by
the classical and stereotypical exhortation not to fear (אל־תיראו), that
is found both in priestly oracles of salvation as well as "holy war" contexts.[24] Verses 4–5 have been formally viewed as either an "installation
to office" or a "royal war oracle." These suggestions, however, fail to do

---

[20] H. A. Brongers, "Bemerkungen zur Gebrauch des adverbialen *we ʿattah* im Alten
Testament. Eine lexikogischer Beitrag." *VT* 15 (1965): 289–99, esp. p. 295, and Wolff,
p. 78.

[21] Petersen, p. 65, and Beuken, pp. 52–53.

[22] In 2:4b the divine name is יהוה צבאות whereas 1:13b has only יהוה.

[23] See the discussion in the textual criticism, *supra*.

[24] Derousseaux, *La crainte*, p. 93, n. 59. On the origin and development of the exhortation, cf. his full discussion, pp. 90–97, with bibliography. Unlike Begrich, who sees the
priestly oracle of salvation as the original form, Derousseaux plausibly maintains that
the priestly oracle is a later configuration of a formula that had its origins in the holy
war traditions (pp. 93–97). Petersen (p. 65) and Beuken (pp. 52–53), following Lohfink,
see vv. 4–5 as constituting an investiture formula attested elsewhere in Chronicles.

justice to the text in certain regards, and the passage is better viewed as an "encouragement for a task."[25]

After the encouragement to perseverance in the present, the prophet pronounces a promise for the future (2:6–9), that constitutes a second reason to continue working. It begins with כי[26] followed by a Messenger Formula (2:6aα), followed by a chronological clarification (2:6aβ), and then presents a series of four successive steps with the glory of the temple forming the culminating point. The four steps with their corresponding verbal forms are: (1) the shaking of the cosmos (*futurum instans*), v. 6b; (2) the terror of the nations (*waw* consecutive + the perfect), v. 7aα; (3) the arrival of the treasures of the nations in the temple (*waw* consecutive + perfect), v. 7aβ; (4) the glorification of the temple (*waw* consecutive + perfect), v. 7bα, a recapitulating clause, as in 1:14. Verses 8–9 reinforce and expand the promise of the temple's future glory, v. 8a providing the basis for the promise (all the treasures of the earth belong to Yahweh), followed by a Divine-Saying Formula in v. 8b. Verse 9a supplies a fuller description of the כבוד mentioned in v. 7b, using vocabulary that alludes back to 2:3aβ, where the present and the past are contrasted. Finally, an additional element, peace, is promised, and a Divine-Saying Formula closes the oracle. 2:1–9 may quite appropriately categorized as a prophetic exhortation.[27]

### 6.3. EXEGESIS

**[1]** In this second scene the redactor continues the "story" begun in 1:1–15. The date formula that opens the scene situates Haggai's next prophetic intervention some six weeks after his initial one, and four weeks after the work on the temple had begun. The scene is dated on the twenty-first of the seventh month, the seventh day of the feast of booths.[28] The date is also associated with the dedication of the first temple in 1 Kgs 8:2, 65; 2 Chr 7:8–10.[29] While the text makes no explicit mention of the significance of the date, it is quite likely that such associations would have been made by both redactor and

---

[25] Thus Mason *Preaching the Tradition*, pp. 24–25. See Floyd's resumé (p. 29) of Mason's arguments.

[26] The second כי [v. 6] stands in the same relationship to v. 4a as the first one, which provides the basis upon which the work can and should continue.

[27] Floyd, p. 285.

[28] North, p. 15. Amsler, p. 31. On the form of the date, see ch. 2.

[29] Wolff, p. 73; North, p. 15, and Deissler, 2:491.

readers. Certainly, if the date here is accurate, and Haggai delivered his oracles at the temple site,[30] tremendous attention would be focused on the building. Setting the delivery of this oracle on this date serves to highlight the tension created by the past, remembered as a time of great prosperity, and the present with its disappointing results both in terms of economic success and temple reconstruction. Verhoef suggests an ellipsis of אל plus the addressees following ביד (cf. 1:1). Thus ביד here stresses Haggai's intermediary function. Haggai receives the command to speak to the leaders and ask them the questions found in v. 3.[31]

**[2]** Here, as in 1:1; 2:11 and 21, the prophet is commanded to address specific individuals. In this instance it is those who resumed the work of the temple in 1:12, 14. It is difficult to see the presence of -נא here as having any attenuating force, given its absence in 2:11 and 21.[32] As in 1:1 and 1:12 Zerubbabel heads the list, and his official title is stated (it is omitted in 1:12). Subsequently, as in 1:1 and 12, Joshua's name and title are given. Finally the prophet is to address the "remnant of the people."[33] The phrase "the remnant of the people" (שארית העם) carries the same meaning as in 1:12 and 14.[34] In 2:1–9 the fragmentation of the community, evidenced in 1:1–3, has disappeared.

**[3]** Haggai now proceeds to address the issue at the heart of the dramatic conflict of this section. He does so by means of three rhetorical questions. The first seeks to identify the members of the community who would be especially sensitive to the comparison between the earlier temple and the building under renovation. He thus asks, "is there anyone[35] still here among you who has seen this house in its former splendour?" The participle הנשאר requires some attention. This term can be used in the more theological sense of those who turn to Yahweh after a time of purificatory suffering (cf. 2 Kgs 19:30; Isa 37:31; Isa 4:3; Ezek 17:21). While such a sense appears to be implied in the use of שארית in 1:12 and 14, it seems unlikely here. A second acceptation designates the

---

[30] Verhoef, p. 94; Wolff, p. 73.

[31] Verhoef, pp. 94–95. As Floyd notes ("Narrative", p. 477f.) ב ביד here produces a tension between the perspective of the prophet and that of the narrator.

[32] Cf. S. A. Kaufman, "An Emphatic Plea for Please", *Maarav* 7 (1991): 195–98; Joüon §105c.

[33] Cf. 1:12 and 14 where the text adds *all* the remnant of the people. No appreciable difference should be inferred from the absence of כל here.

[34] It is the community as a whole that is portrayed as being faithful to Yahweh, cf. Mason, p. 17; Ackroyd, *Exile and Restoration*, pp. 162–63.

[35] The interrogative pronoun functions as the subject of the clause in the indefinite sense of "anyone" cf. *IBHS* §18.2.e. It is followed by a singular participle, as in Judg 7:3.

survivors of military actions directed against Israel, often as divine chas-
tenings. It is important to note in this connection that the term may be
used both for those who went into exile (2 Kgs 25:11; Jer 8:3; 52:15;
Ezra 1:4), as well as for those who remained in the land (Jer 24:8; 40:6;
41:10). It is likely that the niphal participle became a quasi-technical
term for those who survived the ravages of war, especially wars sent as
divine judgments (Lev 26:36, 39; Deut 7:20; 19:20). נשאר can also have
the more general sense of "those who remain or are left over" out of a
larger group which for some reason has been subject to diminution (cf.
Gen 14:10; 1 Sam 11:11; 2 Kgs 10:21). Thus the prophet is quite simply
designating a portion of the community, individuals more than seventy
years of age who had seen the pre-exilic temple, (regardless of whether
they had left the land or not).[36] Given the relatively small population
in Jerusalem at the time and the data on life expectancy in the ancient
Near East,[37] it is unlikely that such individuals would have been very
numerous. However it is not the number of such people, but their function as a *dramatis persona* which is important here. The rhetorical effect
of calling to mind the existence, or even potential existence, of such
people in some sense causes the rest of the community and the read-
ers/hearers to view the situation "through their eyes." This heightens
the affective impact both of the miserable state of the building under
construction (v. 3) but more importantly its magnificence which will follow (2:6–9).

The prophet describes this group as having seen this house "in
its former splendour." Here כבוד refers to the striking appearance of
the building. However the presence of viable alternatives such as הדר
(adornment, splendour; Lam 1:6; Ps 145:12), יפי (beauty; Lam 2:15; Ezek
27:3–4), צבי (beauty; Isa 13:19; Ezek 25:9) suggests that its use here (and
in 6–9) is intentional. Its associations with the manifold aspects of the
temple, including the divine presence made it a rhetorically powerful
term.[38] The same could be said of תפארה (beauty, glory; cf., Isa 60:7;
64:10 [Eng. 11]). It is important to note that the subject of comparison
here is not two different houses, but rather the past and present state
of the same house. In Haggai the temple, in spite of its destruction

---

[36] On the question of whether any such individuals would have been present, cf.
Verhoef, pp. 95–96.

[37] J. Blenkinsopp, "Life Expectancy in Ancient Palestine", *SJOT* 11 (1997): 44–55,
and Pastor, *Land*, p. 7.

[38] Meyers and Meyers, p. 50.

and desecration, is one single house (הבית הזה) whose former state was far more impressive than its present one. Continuity with the past is thus affirmed.[39] This parallels the use of vocabulary related to covenant violation in 1:1–11 that equates the postexilic community with its earlier counterpart, and the form of the book's superscription which sets Haggai in continuity with his earlier prophetic homologues.

The second question concerns the perceptions of the individuals designated in 3aγ, as well as, presumably, those of the population in general. The prophet asks how the building appears to them now (lit.: "how are you seeing it now"). Once again, the text employs the verb to see ראה, already used in 2:3a. In 2:4 the participle is used to underline the durative aspect[40] of the feelings expressed. Haggai's question is clearly rhetorical, for it is immediately followed by another one, which anticipates a positive response.[41] The people are asked whether or not the prophet's description of their perceptions is indeed accurate. The prophet asks, "[This building], is it not like nothing at all[42] in your eyes?" This polar question calls the people to admit their true sentiments. Wolff opines that the discouragement of the older members of the population had infected the others,[43] however the text does not necessarily imply this.

The text divulges nothing vis-à-vis the actual state of the renovated temple, or in precisely what ways it appeared to be inferior to its predecessors. This absence of detail suggests that the purpose of the comparison is as much rhetorical as real.[44] In this light it is important to

---

[39] Continuity between past, present, and future is a highly important motif in Haggai, and one that is expressed in a variety of ways throughout the text. On continuity between destroyed and reconstructed buildings see D. Petersen, "Zerubbabel and Jerusalem Temple Reconstruction", *CBQ* 36 (1974): 366–72, and Petersen, pp. 89–91. For a more general approach, cf. P. Ackroyd, "Temple Vessels", *passim*.

[40] Joüon §121c, d.

[41] Verhoef, p. 97.

[42] Joüon (§174i) notes that when כ is used comparatively with two nouns, it denotes a fully identical or equivalent relationship between them (cf. Gen 44:18). Thus the temple under construction was not seen as less valuable by the builders, but of no worth at all (כאין). Deissler, (2:491), appropriately translates the text, "Is it not like completely nothing in comparison with former times?" Wolff (p. 77) cites Targum Rashi as translating: "'It' (the temple) and 'nothing' are alike." Chary (p. 26) notes that in Isa 40:17 כאין stands parallel to תהו (formlessness, emptiness).

[43] Wolff, p. 57.

[44] On the reference to the pre-exilic temple in Ezra 6:3 see Williamson, *Ezra*, p. 71–72. On the rabbinical tradition regarding that which was lacking in the second temple, see Wolff, p. 43. Meyers and Meyers (p. 72) underline the fact that very few citizens of Judah, at the end of the pre-exilic period, had seen the inside of the temple.

note the role that the appearance of the temple fulfills in this passage. This theme functions at two different reading levels. At the level of the drama "within" the text, the prophet is addressing builders and citizens who are discouraged with the disappointing results of their efforts, and indeed this may have been the case. However the depth of the sentiments in the text would seem to extend beyond the dejection of the population after only four weeks of work. After all, how much could reasonably have been expected in so little time? Verhoef senses this inconsistency and relates the discouragement to the community's view of what the building could be expected to be when it was completed.[45] This seems an inadequate response, especially in light of the prophet's statement, "how does it appear to you *now*?" A far more satisfactory solution would be to view these sentiments as part of a rhetorical/literary strategy relating to the second reading level, that of the redactor's concern to address popular sentiment at the time of the book's production.[46] Hence the discouragement is portrayed in such a way as to be applicable to the state of the building around the time of its dedication, when, despite the passage of several years, the building was still somewhat inglorious. It is likely that in the eyes of the postexilic community the external appearance of the temple symbolized the favour Israel enjoyed before Yahweh,[47] as well as its status and political importance.[48] In this light, the commands to continue working (v. 5) and the promises of the temple's future splendour (vv. 6–9) would have held an ongoing significance for the hearers and readers of the text.

[4] Two problems troubled the immediate and more distant hearers of Haggai's questions. Objectively, the building under construction was disappointing. Subjectively, this disparity provoked fatigue and discour-

---

Furthermore, at that time the temple had in fact been stripped, in large part, of its former treasures. The details of the ongoing stripping of the temple's goods are chronicled in Verhoef, p. 96. Meyers and Meyers (p. 50) appropriately conclude that the appeal to the earlier state of the temple is primarily rhetorical. This is in line with my argument in this section.

[45] Verhoef, p. 97. Petersen (p. 64) senses the same problem, saying, "the overall perception was that the splendour of this second temple *would* not match that of the Solomonic structure" (emphasis mine).

[46] Tollington ("Readings", p. 199) also uses this methodological approach, but directs it to other issues, cf. 2:23.

[47] R. Mason ("The Relation of Zechariah 9–14 to Proto-Zechariah", *ZAW* 88 [1976]: 227–39) accurately observes, "The beauty of the restored temple … carries with it the overtone that it is so particularly because its restoration is the mark of God's favour on the community which has thus been enabled to complete its task" (p. 232).

[48] Meyers and Meyers, p. 72.

agement. As we have noted, Hag 2:4–9 responds to this situation in vv.
4–5 by exhortations and assurances regarding the present, and in vv. 6–
9 by promises for the future. Verses 4–5 use language typical of oracles
of salvation. The first such feature is the exhortation to "stand fast" or
"be strong"[49] introduced by ועתה. The encouragement to be strong, חזק,
repeated three times, is quite frequent in Deuteronomistic literature
(Deut 31:6, 7, 23; Josh 1:6, 7, 9, 23; 10:25; 2 Sam 10:12; 13:28), as well as
in the Chronicler (1 Chr 19:13; 22:13; 28:10, 20; 2 Chr 19:11; 25:8; 32:7).
The imperative of חזק is frequently attached to the formula אל־תיראו
(do not fear) in oracles of salvation (cf. Isa 35:4; 41:6). The verb חזק in
the imperative calls for perseverance in the task to which one is called,
in spite of any reasons for fear and discouragement. It is associated with
עשׂה in 1 Chr 28:10, 20; 2 Chr 19:11, and Ezra 10:4.[50] This exhortation
to strength is first addressed to Zerubbabel, whose name appears here
without title or patronymic, then to Joshua, to whose name both are
attached, and finally to the "people of the land."

Here, in contrast to 1:2, 12, 14 and 2:2, the people are addressed as
כל־עם הארץ (all the people of the land).[51] In the pre-exilic period, the
term frequently referred to landowners and the political elite.[52] In postexilic times it appears to have had a variety of referents. In Ezra 4:4,
it refers to Yahwistic inhabitants of Samaria, possibly of foreign stock,
who offered their assistance in the rebuilding of the temple but were
rebuffed by the returnees.[53] Such a designation appears unlikely here.
North[54] suggests that the term refers to the non-exiled population. This
group, according to Coggins, were descendants of nationalistic extrem-
ists of the earlier period.[55] Andersen views them as postexilic landowners.[56] The difficulty in Haggai is that, on a rhetorical level, nothing in
the text appears to differentiate them from the *dramatis persona* of the
people introduced in 1:2, who experience a change of heart in 1:12 and
14, and who are addressed in 2:2.[57] I therefore conclude that the term

---

[49] Wolff, p. 79.

[50] Ibid.

[51] For an earlier survey of the term, cf. E. W. Nicholson, "The Meaning of the
Expression עם הארץ in the Old Testament", *JJS* 10 (1965): 59–66.

[52] Wolff, p. 78.

[53] Ibid., p. 78.

[54] North, p. 15.

[55] R. J. Coggins, "The Interpretation of Ezra 4:4" *JTS* 16 (1965): 124–27.

[56] Andersen, " Second Temple", pp. 30–31.

[57] Floyd (pp. 280–81) affirms that this is indeed the same sub-group within the
population (mostly returnees), but that the appellation in 2:4 indicates that these people

in Haggai simply refers to the whole community, returnees and non-exiled alike.[58] Thus Haggai adopts an inclusive stance, and the totality of the community is called to work (עשׂו).

The relationship between the imperative עשׂו (work) and vv. 4–5 as a whole has been the object of significant discussion. Meyers and Meyers, following the rabbinical tradition, view ועשׂו (and work) to have as its direct object את־הדבר אשר־כרתי אתכם בצאתכם ממצרים (the word which I covenanted with you when you came out of Egypt).[59] In support of this position, they note that דבר is found as the object of עשׂה in Gen 22:16; 2 Sam 17:6; Ps 33:6; 103:20; 148:8; and Joel 2:11. They could have also indicated the fact that the phrase לעשׂות את דברי ברית occurs in 2 Chr 34:31. While this solution resolves some of the syntactical difficulties of the sentence, it is problematic for the following reasons: (1) the unusually great distance between the imperative and its direct object; (2) the infrequent pairing of עשׂה and ברית, and (3) the contextual difficulty of placing an exhortation to obey the law here. Therefore עשׂו is better seen as an independent exhortation to continue the work,[60] followed by a motivation in the form of a Formula of Assistance. The repetition of this formula (cf. 1:12) constitutes further evidence of literary continuity between this pericope and the narration that precedes it (1:12–15). Petersen calls attention to the assonance between אין in v. 3 and אני in v. 4.[61] The work can and must continue because, in spite of appearances to the contrary, Yahweh is in the midst of his people. We note also the emphasis placed upon the exhortation by the Divine-Saying Formula which is repeated three times (4aα, 4aγ, 5bβ).

**[5]** Having opted for the retention of v. 5a, it is essential to consider its meaning and function, and to explain its presence. It is most likely an explanatory phrase inserted between the two formulations of the divine presence with the community (the Formula of Assistance of v. 4bβ and the mention of the Spirit in v. 5bα). Motyer's suggestion[62]

---

have undergone a change of status and are now the dominant group. This seems to me to be overly subtle. Once again the presence of כל preceding the term argues for it as an alternative inclusive name for the population of Yehud, all of whom are portrayed as being supportive of the reconstruction project.

[58] See Ackroyd, *Exile and Restoration*, pp. 150 n. 50, 162, 167; Baldwin, p. 47, and Wolff, p. 59.

[59] Meyers and Meyers, p. 51.

[60] Joüon § 114c notes that the Hebrew impv. may be used to express various volitional nuances, and thus to encourage the continuation of an activity.

[61] Petersen, pp. 64–65.

[62] Motyer, pp. 988–99. The *Gottesspruchformel* would not appear to be the equivalent

that vv. 4aγ-5b constitute a unified chiastic structure seems strained. This explanatory phrase sets the presence of Yahweh in the postexilic community in some relationship to the "word" which Yahweh "cut" with the community as it came out of Egypt. Various explanations for the origin of the phrase have been proposed, including a scribal gloss,[63] or the work of a prophetic traditionist.[64] The first suggestion does not deal with the question of how a gloss came to contain the first person speech of Yahweh.[65] If the phrase is viewed as redactional, the most satisfactory solution is to view it as an elaboration of the implicit connotations of Haggai's words.[66]

Much turns on the meaning attributed to "word" and its relationship to the surrounding phrases. If, as suggested above, דבר should not be construed as the direct object of עשׂו, the phrase can be viewed as affirming that the presence of Yahweh with the community testifies to the ongoing validity of the covenant. Furthermore this also equates word and Spirit in a way similar to Isa 48:16 and 59:21.[67] Read this way, דבר carries the sense of promise (so Verhoef) or perhaps covenant in a broader sense. The particle את could mean either "with" (Sellin, Rudolph), "according to" (Verhoef), or preferably "regarding, concerning."[68] The phrase would therefore be rendered "regarding the promise [or covenant] I made with you when you came out of Egypt, my Spirit is abiding in your midst."[69]

The purpose of the explanatory comment here is to bring out the implications of the Spirit's "standing in the midst" of the postexilic community, set against the backdrop of the historical relationship between Yahweh and his people. It is important to note that an appeal to covenantal, and especially Sinaiatic traditions, is not out of place here.[70] Sinai-exodus traditions are not foreign to the oracles or the framework

---

of the phrase "the word which I covenanted with you when you came out of Egypt" either functionally or semantically, as he suggests.

[63] Baldwin, p. 47, and many others.

[64] Petersen, p. 66.

[65] Clearly the words are meant to be read as forming a part of the divine speech.

[66] As noted in ch. 2, I view the book as a whole to be an interpretation of the significance of the prophet's words and their effect.

[67] So Verhoef, pp. 99–100; Wolff, p. 71; Sellin, p. 410; Rudolph, pp. 40–41.

[68] Barthélemy, *Critique textuelle*, 3:928 and textual criticism *supra*.

[69] As Wolff notes (p. 71), although the explanatory comment may be taken with either the first or second statements of the divine presence, it appears to fit best with the latter one.

[70] *Pace* Amsler, p. 32, and Petersen, p. 61, n. b.

of Haggai. In Hag 2:21–23 language that is rooted in the traditions of the Sea of Reeds is employed. Similarly, Hag 1:4–11 employs vocabulary and theological perspectives rooted in Deuteronomistic covenantal concepts, which included exodus and Sinai traditions.[71] Similar concepts are to be found in 1:12–14. As such, a clarification regarding the status of the covenant is not alien to the outlook of the book.

It is also noteworthy that the phrase stresses the continuity between the original recipients of the covenant and the postexilic community by the repetition of the second plural pronominal suffix in v. 5a, "with *you* when *you* came out of Egypt." Thus, the ones told not to fear (v. 5b) are implicitly seen as standing in continuity with those who came out of Egypt and with whom Yahweh has entered into covenant. This is analogous to the conception of one, not two temples, in 2:4. This continuity has already been implied in the assurance of the divine presence in 1:13 and 2:4. The comment thus explicitly affirms that (1) the Sinai covenant is still applicable to Yahweh's relationship to the community, and (2) the small collection of Yahwists gathered around the Jerusalem temple does indeed stand in historical continuity with the Israelite population of earlier times. Thus the phrase takes up the continuity theme seen elsewhere in the book.

This explanatory comment expresses the implications of the presence of the Spirit in v. 5b. The expression "my Spirit," רוחי is somewhat innovative. The term רוח is used sparingly in Genesis-Numbers with the name Yahweh.[72] Such language occurs much more frequently in the Deuteronomistic History (Judg 3:10; 1 Sam 10:6; 1 Kgs 18:12) and in the Prophets (cf. Isa 11:2; 40:7, 13; 61:1; Ezek 37:1; Mic 2:7, and especially Zech 4:6). The participle עמדת is especially noteworthy and somewhat enigmatic. The noun רוח is frequently coupled with שכן and sometimes with ישב but nowhere else with עמד. For Wolff,[73] and Chary,[74] who follow Beuken,[75] the allusion here is to the presence of Yahweh manifested within the community through the prophets. A more traditional approach affirms that עמדת constitutes a paronomasia alluding indi-

---

[71] Weinfeld, *Deuteronomy*, p. 326f; Nicholson, *Deuteronomy and Tradition*, pp. 41ff., esp. p. 49.

[72] As opposed to אלהים which is more common, Gen 6:3; Num 11:29; cf. Exod 31:3; 35:31.

[73] Wolff, pp. 59–60.

[74] Chary, p; 27.

[75] Beuken, pp. 57–58.

rectly to עמוד the theophanic pillar of cloud of Exod 13:21, etc.[76] Meyers and Meyers see it as a powerful expression of the presence of Yahweh,[77] while Amsler views it as an image of an officiating minister.[78]

Despite Beuken's arguments, an allusion to prophecy appears unlikely here. Beuken affirms that the Chronicler links Yahweh's Spirit and prophecy.[79] However, this association is also evident in non-Chronistic contexts (Isa 42:1; 48:16; 59:21; Ezek 11:5).[80] It is also true that the Targum sees a reference to prophecy here.[81] In Haggai 2:5, by contrast, רוח designates the active presence of God with his people. In v. 5, ורוחי עמדת בתוכ כם stands parallel to the first Formula of Assistance of v. 4b, and just before אל־תיראו the traditional formula of divine reassurance in oracles of salvation. Furthermore, the participle עמדת underlines the durative aspect of the activity of Yahweh's Spirit,[82] and corresponds well to Yahweh's ongoing presence with his people in v. 4b. By contrast, in Haggai prophetic intervention is more intermittent in nature. Spirit (רוח) denotes the efficacious power of Yahweh's self.[83] It is this active and ongoing presence that carries with it the needed resources to bring the temple building to completion, and that provides the reason why the community may be strong and not fear. Despite the high view of prophecy in Haggai, it is the Spirit of Yahweh which makes the prophetic word efficacious. It is therefore preferable to see the phrase as an affirmation of the presence of Yahweh attesting to the abiding validity of the Sinai covenant. Yahweh's Spirit, in a way analogous to the pillar of cloud at the exodus, stands in the midst of the people, (cf. Exod 13:21; 14:19, 24; 25:8; 29:45).[84] It is for this reason that the community is exhorted not to fear (v. 5b). Derousseaux points out that this formula is intended to enable those so addressed to banish fear, "before humans and the dangers with which they are faced; Yahweh (or his representative) calls [his people] to a rejection of this fear because of his saving presence."[85] This formula, quite widespread

---

[76] See Verhoef, p. 100, Amsler, pp. 31–32.
[77] Meyers and Meyers, p. 52.
[78] Amsler, pp. 31–32.
[79] Beuken, pp. 57–58.
[80] As Wolff (p. 80) notes.
[81] It reads ונביי מלפין ביניכון לא תדלון.
[82] Joüon §121c.
[83] Wolff, p. 80.
[84] Cited by Beuken, p. 57.
[85] Derousseaux, *La crainte*, p. 91. See p. 90 n. 50 for bibliography.

in the Deuteronomistic tradition (Deut 20:3; 31:6; Josh 10:25; 1 Sam 12:20; 2 Kgs 25:24; Jer 10:5; 40:9), is found frequently in Haggai.

[6] This verse moves to the second reason given to the builders for persevering in their work. Having reassured them of the presence of Yahweh, the prophet now considers the future. He describes the ultimate destiny of the building, with all the cosmic implications that were connected to it. The conjunction כי is causal, linked directly to אל־תיראו. In the larger context of the pericope, this conjunction, in parallel with כי of v. 4b, introduces a second reason to continue working.

I have opted to retain the phrase עוד אחת מעט היא as a whole,[86] but its translation and meaning must be examined in greater detail. In my opinion the most fruitful way of ascertaining the meaning of the phrase is to begin with the more common expression עוד מעט which would appear to have some connection to the wording here. It is found in Exod 17:4; Ps 37:10; Isa 10:25; 29:17; Jer 51:33 and Hos 1:4 and simply means "soon" or "in a little while." Scribal error aside, there are two main ways in which our phrase could be related to its more common counterpart. The first is to view אחת (one) as having been introduced into the phrase עוד מעט to emphasize the imminence of the events.[87] Subsequently היא was added (feminine, by attraction to אחת) to provide the copula. The result would be "it is only a very short time" or "it will be in a very little while." The chief difficulty with this approach is grammatical. It has been observed that אחת (one) cannot modify מעט (a little) because of the word order (אחת should normally follow מעט) and absence of accord.[88] In such a translation עוד is seen as simply a part of the fixed phrase עוד מעט and carries no repetitive force (i.e. "once again"). The primary difficulty with this view is that אחת seems quite awkward in the middle of a fixed phrase. Thus the translation "it is still one small one,"[89] would appear to be somewhat difficult grammatically.

A second possibility is to view the fixed phrase עוד מעט as having been broken up, and thus עוד אחת and מעט היא would constitute two complementary phrases. This yields the translation, "Once again, and it shall be soon."[90] Here too, grammatical difficulties arise. As has been

---

[86] Cf. textual criticism, *supra*.

[87] So Wolff, p. 51, and Meyers and Meyers, p. 52.

[88] Rudolph, p. 41.

[89] As proposed by Ackroyd, "Exile and Restoration", pp. 153–54, or Baldwin "wait one little while" (p. 47) and Wolff (p. 70) "it is only a little while."

[90] Chary, p. 27.

pointed out that היא (feminine) cannot be considered as copula of מעט (masculine).[91] This difficulty, however, can be dealt with in one of four ways: (1) by assuming that somehow a confusion has arisen between מעט and פעם (feminine);[92] (2) by seeing היא as feminine either by reason of an accord with אחת or to express a general sense, and governing the sentence as a whole.[93] On this proposal מעט could still be retained (cf. [1] above) and considered a masculine noun, whose accord was somehow overridden; (3) by assuming מעט to have an adverbial force here, as in its original idiom,[94] thus rendering agreement unnecessary, or (4) by assuming an adverbial sense for מעט as in (3) but presupposing that היא does "double duty" and supplies the predicate both for עוד אחת and for מעט. In all of these suggestions עוד is construed with אחת and retains its repetitive sense. The sense of the phrase would be "once again, it will be very soon." I view 2–4 as equally viable solutions.

In a sense, the choice between these two major translational alternatives (that is, "it will be a very little while," or "once again, in a little while") turns on whether עוד ought to be given any sense of repetition in Hag 2:6. It is clear that עוד can connote either the continuing of an action in progress (Gen 18:22) or the repetition of an action now ceased (Gen 4:25). The question at issue in v. 6 is the following: does עוד refer to a waiting period that will still continue for a short while, or to an act of shaking that will occur once again (presumably *a fortiori*) in the not too distant future? It is hard to see in what sense אחת can add emphasis.[95] Here it more likely has an adverbial function ("once") as in Exod 30:10; Lev 16:34 and 2 Kgs 6:10.[96] If we attribute a repetitive sense to עוד, as in Zech 1:17; 2:16b [Eng. 12] and 8:4, then the first two words (עוד אחת) can be easily translated "once again." Chary suggests that the phrase connotes "once again and for the *last* time."[97] Petersen argues against any sense of repetition because he sees no historical or theological precedent for the shaking of the heavens and earth and the adorning of the temple by wealth of the nations.[98] But significant prece-

---

[91] Keil, 2:190.

[92] Mitchell, p. 65.

[93] On the use of the feminine in this way, cf. GKC §141b; Joüon §154 i, j.

[94] BDB, "מעט" 1.d, p. 590.

[95] Cf. Meyers and Meyers, p. 52.

[96] Rudolph's examples, p. 41.

[97] Chary, p. 27.

[98] Petersen, pp. 61–62.

dents can be proposed.[99] Furthermore, Hos 12:10 [Eng. 9]; Jer 31:4, 5, 23; 32:15; and especially 33:12–13 provide interesting parallel usages of the repetitive sense of עוד. In each case, in an eschatological context, Yahweh acts in favour of his people and עוד is placed at the head of the phrase. In each case the sense of עוד is repetitive. Therefore, instead of understanding אחת as an insertion in the expression עוד מעט, it is better to consider עוד אחת (once again) and מעט (a little [while]) as two adverbial clarifications indicating that what will happen in a short time will be both a definitive act, as well as one that is in some ways a climax of several events already experienced.[100] I therefore follow Chary's translation, "Once again, and it will be soon"[101] and propose "One more time, and it will be soon."

With this introduction, clearly eschatological in scope (cf. the similar expression ביום ההוא, in 2:23), and intended to underline the imminence of the coming intervention,[102] the prophet describes the future events that will crown the builders' efforts with stunning success.[103] The future events occur in four stages, and are identifiable through the verbal forms employed in the passage. The first stage occurs in 2:6b in the form of a participial phrase or *futurum instans*[104] whose usual function is to announce an event as imminent or near.[105] The three following stages are indicated by three perfect verbs preceded by *waw* consecutive, which stand in a relationship of succession to the participle.[106]

First of all Yahweh will shake the heavens and the earth, the sea and the dry land. The *waw* preceding אני is not unexpected, since *waw* usu-

---

[99] Keil, (2:191) suggests the shaking at Sinai. W. J. Dumbrell, ("Some Observations of the Political Origins of Israel's Eschatology", *RTR* 37, [1978]: 38) sees the coming of non-Israelites to the temple (for example the Queen of Sheba, 1 Kgs 10) as a precedent. Rudolph, (p. 43) sees an allusion here to the political turmoil from the emergence of Nebuchadnezzar II to the accession of Darius I.

[100] Cf. the *Urzeit/Endzeit*, formula in eschatological descriptions, as described by Dumbrell, "Political Origins", p. 38.

[101] Chary, p. 27. Cf. also Rudolph, "Yet once, soon" (p. 40). Rudolph (p. 43) follows Chary in seeing the future action as ultimate and definitive.

[102] Von Rad, *Theology*, 2:245. Carroll's suggestion, (*When Prophecy Failed*, p. 157ff.), that the phrase עוד אחת מעט היא was inserted to make this prophecy refer to a more distant future, given its failure to materialize, is dubious. It is not in any way clear that the phrase attenuates the *futurum instans* which follows it.

[103] On the eschatological orientation of the oracle, cf. J. Kessler, "The Shaking of the Nations: An Eschatological View", *JETS* 30 (1987): 159–66.

[104] GKC §116p.

[105] Joüon §119n.

[106] Ibid., and GKC §112p.

ally follows the temporal expression עוֹד מְעַט. The object of Yahweh's shaking constitutes a double merism denoting the totality of the cosmos, heavenly and earthly.[107] The shaking in v. 6 is expressed using hiphil participial form of רעשׁ, a critically important verb here and in 2:20–23. It may be used transitively (Isa 14:16) or intransitively (Judg 5:4), with either personal (Ezek 31:16) or impersonal (Ps 77:19 [Eng. 18]) subjects or objects. This verb and its corresponding noun may be used in a literal sense of earthquakes (Amos 1:1; Zech 14:5; Ezek 38:19) or of the shaking of buildings (Amos 9:1; Ezek 26:10). The hiphil is found in only seven of the thirty occurrences of the verb, three of which are found in Haggai (Job 39:2; Ps 60:4 [Eng. 2] ; Isa 14:16; Ezek 31:16; Hag 2:6, 7, 21). Sometimes the shaking or the quaking described is the result of natural phenomena. However, in most contexts, it is the deeds or presence of Yahweh that caused the shaking. This stereotypical language frequently belongs to the vocabulary of the fear of God, and conveys fear before "the numinous" (R. Otto).[108] Bornkamm notes that shaking motifs with Yahweh as subject are found in three primary contexts: (1) theophanies (Exod 19:18; 1 Kgs 19:11); (2) Yahweh as divine warrior (Judg 5:2–31), and (3) eschatological scenarios.[109] F. M. Cross and P. D. Miller have observed the presence of this "vocabulary of shaking" in divine warrior contexts, both in the Old Testament or elsewhere in the ancient Near East.[110] When the "divine warrior" arrives, both humans and nature tremble.

A distinction of critical importance appears when this verb is used with a personal versus an impersonal subject or object. When that which trembles or is caused to tremble is *impersonal*, the verb forms part of an hyperbole, metaphor and/or personification. Thus, that which is usually considered to be steadfast or immovable, such as mountains or stars, is said to shake or to be shaken. The point of the hyperbole is to stress *the infinite and awesome power of the one who causes the shaking*. This use is common in the prophetic books. In Nah 1:5, for example, the mountains and hills quake and dissolve at Yahweh's presence. In Joel 4:16 [Eng. 3:16] when Yahweh roars, the heavens and the earth shake. Other references include Isa 13:13; Jer 10:10;

---

[107] Cf. Sérandour, "Récits", p. 14.

[108] Cf. Derousseaux, *La crainte*, pp. 73–90.

[109] G. Bornkamm, s. v. "σειω", *TDNT* 7:197–98 and B. S. Childs, "The Enemy from the North and the Chaos Tradition", *JBL* 78 (1959): 187–98.

[110] Cross, *Canaanite Myth*, pp. 79–111, 148–94; P. D. Miller, *Divine Warrior*, pp. 36, 74–171.

50:46; Ezek 26:10; 27:28; 38:20, (cf. Ps 18:8 [Eng. 7:8]; 77:19 [Eng. 18]). It is this nuance that is in view in Hag 2:6. The intervention of Yahweh the warrior and divine judge will send the whole cosmos (את־השׁמים ואת־הארץ ואת־הים ואת־החרבה) into convulsions.

In v. 7 we move to the second stage of the prophetic description, and the second nuance of רעשׁ.[111] In contrast to its use with impersonal subjects or objects, when this verb is used with a *personal* subject or *personal* object (or a personification), the connotation is that of literally "trembling with fear." Here the emphasis is not so much upon the awesomeness of that which causes the shaking, but rather upon the *total powerlessness of the one who trembles.* Flight or resistance are impossible. Trembling in abject terror signifies complete submission. Such trembling frequently appears in prophetic literature to describe the response of the nations to Yahweh's acts of judgment. In Ezek 31:15–16 Yahweh will cause the nations to tremble with fear as they behold the fall of Egypt.[112] Similarly, in Ezek 38:19–20, following an earthquake, all the inhabitants of the earth tremble with fear before Yahweh. In Jer 8:16 and 49:21, the earth (a metonymy or personification, referring to its inhabitants) trembles with fear before the terrifying perturbations of nature.[113]

Isaiah 14:16 is a significant passage here. It is one of the seven instances of רעשׁ in the hiphil and involves a personal object (or personification). The kings in Sheol are addressing the fallen King of Tyre. They ask הזה האישׁ מרגיז הארץ מרעישׁ ממלכות. The sense of רעשׁ here could be either "is this the man who overthrew nations?" or "is this the man who caused the nations to tremble with fear?" The parallel verb (רגז) overwhelmingly refers to a state of rage or fear.[114] As noted above, Verhoef objects to seeing two nuances of the verb in such close proximity.[115] Yet this appears to be the case in Ezek 26, a passage describing the siege of Tyre. In v. 10 the walls shake, either literally or metaphorically, to express the overwhelming might of the invading cavalry (often

---

[111] Verhoef, (p. 102) objects that it is improbable that one verb would be used in two senses in such close proximity. Cf. my response *infra*.

[112] Cf. Deissler (2:492) aptly comments, "In Ezek 31:16 Yahweh causes the nations to tremble at the fall of Pharaoh's empire. In other words the tremble with fear at the thought of suffering the same lot."

[113] Cf. Jer 8:16; Joel 2:10, cf. Kessler "Shaking of the Nations" pp. 161–62 for a fuller discussion.

[114] Cf. BDB "רגז".

[115] Verhoef, p. 102.

an hyperbole, cf. first nuance, *supra*). However in v. 15 the coastlands shake (ירעשו האיים). This shaking is then described in v. 16. There, the princes of the sea will step down, remove their robes and clothe themselves with trembling (חרד),[116] sit on the ground and tremble (חרד), and be appalled (שמם). This is the second nuance noted above, that of trembling with fear indicating powerless and submission. A general pattern thus emerges in these descriptions of divine judgment. Yahweh moves forth, and the inhabitants of the earth are terrified and fall into disarray.

Thus, integrating these two nuances of רעש (vv. 6–7), we see the following chain of events. First, Yahweh's presence and power are brought into proximity to the created order, and as a result that which is considered to be immovable is suddenly shaken, resulting in terrifying perturbations in the cosmos (v. 6). Then, in reaction to the natural disasters, the nations will tremble with fear in abject submission (cf. Nah 1:5).

The fact that the fear of the nations *follows* the upheavals within creation, is confirmed by two additional considerations. First, we note the *futurum instans* followed by *waw* consecutive, plus the perfect (והרעשתי). In this grammatical construction the perfect normally refers to an action which follows the one described by the preceding participle.[117] It is significant to note that both the LXX and Vulgate distinguish the two verbal forms (מרעיש and והרעשתי). The participle מרעיש in 2:6 and 20 is translated by σειω and *moueo*. By contrast, in v. 7, (for והרעשתי) συσ-σειω and *commoueo* are used. The reason for the variation in translation could be either syntactical or lexical. It is possible the prefixes συν-[118] and *com-* are added to denote intensification. Alternatively, according to the usual meaning of συν-, "with or together," the idea of the nations trembling as one may be in view. On a more lexical level, I note in passing that *moueo* can mean "to provoke political or social disorder in a country or nation" but not specifically "to cause to fear."[119] *Commoueo*,

---

[116] Always "dread, fear" cf. Exod 19:16; Isa 19:16; 41:5; Ezek 32:10.

[117] Joüon (§119n) states: "As in most instances one participle does not follow another, a participle which denotes the future is normally followed by a *waw* consecutive plus the perfect, similarly with a future sense. Normally the construction contains an idea of succession; GKC (§112p) notes that the *futurum instans* plus perfect is used "to express future actions as the temporal or logical consequence of tenses or their equivalents which announce or require such future actions or events."

[118] Cf. C. F. D. Moule, *An Idiom Book of New Testament Greek*, (Cambridge: Cambridge University Press, 1968), pp. 87–88.

[119] *Oxford Latin Dictionary*, "*moueo*".

in contrast, can take the specific meaning "to make anxious, to trouble, to terrify," but not "to cause political instability."[120] Whatever the case may be, it seems that the activity designated by רעש with respect to the nations was seen to be more appropriately translated by intensive verbal forms.

Secondly, the resulting order of events belongs to a traditional scenario whose elements unfold in a quasi-fixed progression. In this scenario, discernible in various biblical texts including Joel 3:4 [Eng. 3], Zech 12–14, and Ezek 38–39, the upheavals within creation precede the fear of the peoples. Allen, alluding to Joel 3, states, "The prophet takes up the terrifying traditional motif of the disfigurement of the sun and moon, which would cause men to 'faint from fear' in anticipation of what is to befall the world."[121] In Hag 2:6–9, the scope of the divine action is universal, a fact reinforced by the words "all the nations" (את־כל־הגוים). In this context it is clear that a manifestation of divine power such as the disfigurement of the fundamental elements of the universe is intended, since only such an extreme manifestation would be able to reduce the totality of the foreign nations to trembling.[122] Such a concept would appear to be an expansion of the analogous tradition of the shaking of the earth in conjunction with a powerful thunderstorm.[123]

In 2:7aβ, with the second *waw* consecutive plus the perfect (ובאו), the text progresses to the third stage, namely the coming of the treasures of the nations to Jerusalem. The plural verb conjugated with a singular subject[124] precludes a personalizing and messianizing interpretation.[125] The classical position, expressed by Keil,[126] that חֶמְדַּת is a collective singular and agrees *ad sensum* with the plural verb[127] remains the simplest

---

[120] Ibid., "*commoueo*".

[121] L. C. Allen, *The Books of Joel, Obadiah, Jonah and Micah*, (NICOT; Grand Rapids: Eerdmans, 1976), p. 101.

[122] On the broadly inclusive sense of כל see GKC §135 l, m.

[123] Ps 68:9 [Eng. 8]; 77:19 [Eng. 18]; Judg 5:4; Nah 1:5; Isa 24:18–20; Ezek 38:19–23.

[124] MT חֶמְדַּת. It is frequently suggested that this noun be repointed to the pl. חֲמֻדֹת, cf. Ackroyd, *Exile and Restoration*, p. 161, n. 38; Meyers and Meyers, p. 53.

[125] Amsler, p. 33 with most commentators. North (p. 16) comments, succinctly, "*Hemda*, or 'desire' could signify either a person eagerly desired or 'desirable things, precious stones' such as the gold and silver of v. 8. Nothing in the text appears to prepare the reader for the appearance of an extraordinary individual in relationship to the temple." Cf. textual criticism.

[126] Cf. Keil, 2:193.

[127] On this see Schattner-Rieser, "L'hébreu", p. 217.

and most adequate explanation. Moreover, the suggestion of Meyers and Meyers that the subject of ובאו is not the treasures, but the nations, is unnecessary.[128]

Haggai's words speak directly to the dramatic conflict of the pericope. Once the temple is rebuilt, Yahweh will be glorified and will manifest his favour toward the community (cf. 1:8) through the coming of the wealth of the nations. This evokes the broader prophetic theme of divine judgment and national wealth. When a nation becomes the object of Yahweh's judgment, it is stripped of its treasures (cf. Num 31:9; Isa 8:4; Jer 15:13; 17:3; Ezek 26:12; Dan 11:8; Hos 13:15; Nah 2:9; 2 Chr 36:10). This process can be reversed, and the booty taken can be restored (Zech 14:1). Various suggestions have been made regarding the way in which the treasures of the nations will come back to Jerusalem. Will they (1) be taken as war booty,[129] (2) sent as tribute to a suzerain from a vassal,[130] (3) offered as thanksgiving gifts,[131] or does the phrase in question merely refer to (4) the return of the cultic vessels taken away in 587?[132] Regarding (1) it is certainly accurate to affirm that the root חמד is often used for booty (cf. Dan 11:8; Hos 13:15; Nah 2:10 [Eng. 9]; 2 Chr 32:27; 36:10), and that the notion of the conflict between Yahweh and the nations is present in 2:20–23 and is to be implied in 2:6–9.[133] Nevertheless the extent of the glorification of the temple envisaged by the prophet (especially in light of Yahweh's ownership of the world's riches, v. 8) would appear to be on a magnitude far beyond the mere acquisition of goods plundered from routed armies (although not precluding all reference to such goods). For similar reasons, it seems improbable to limit the enrichment in 2:7 to (4), the mere return of the temple vessels, since this does not seem to be at issue in 2:1–9. An examination of the use of the qal of בוא conjugated with an inanimate object reveals that, in such cases, the means through which the inanimate object is moved may be inferred from the context. For example in 1 Sam 4:5–6 when the ark "came" to the camp, the context clearly indicates by whom it was carried. Similarly, in Isa 60:5, often mentioned as

---

[128] Meyers and Meyers, p. 53.

[129] Verhoef, p. 103; cf. Mic 4:13; Zech 14:1.

[130] Meyers and Meyers, p. 53; Ackroyd, *Exile and Restoration*, p. 161, n. 40.

[131] Mitchell, p. 11; Siebeneck, "Messianism of Aggeus", p. 314, n. 5; May, "This People", p. 196.

[132] Petersen, p. 68.

[133] An eschatological battle does not preclude an eschatological pilgrimage, cf. the discussion *infra*.

parallel to our text, the qal of בוא describes the coming of the treasures (חיל) of the nations to Jerusalem,[134] in conjunction with a pilgrimage to Jerusalem for worship. Other examples of the phrase are found in Gen 32:14; 43:23. It would therefore appear that in Hag 2 the treasures of the nations are brought by the latter to the Jerusalem temple. But what is the significance of this act? Among the possibilities cited above, is it (2) a payment of tribute, or (3) an offering presented by the nations for the worship of Yahweh? This question will be considered at greater length in the context of the rhetorical use of theological traditions in 2:1–9, at the conclusion of this section.

In 2:7b the text reaches the fourth stage of its progression with the third *waw* consecutive plus the perfect, ומלאתי. This phrase ("I will fill this house with splendour") continues Yahweh's response to the problem of the temple's appearance. The use of מלא (to fill or fill up) stresses the magnitude of that which will be added. Despite the fact that the expression מלא כבוד is used for the divine presence in his dwelling in Exod 40:34–35; 1 Kgs 8:10–11; Isa 6:3, and Ezek 43:5; 44:4, it appears that Haggai's meaning is more reserved. The syntagmatic relationships operative in the phrase and pericope require that כבוד be understood in its sense of "honour, splendour" rather than as a reference to a theophanic phenomenon. Thus, in Hag 2:7, כבוד is more specifically the splendour or honour that is the result of the presence of the nations' riches offered to Yahweh,[135] rather than the riches themselves (cf. Gen 45:13; Job 29:20; Isa 4:2; Hos 9:11; 10:5). It does, however, appear likely that this vocabulary, related to the theme of the divine presence filling the temple, was chosen for its rhetorical effect and was evocative of the presence of Yahweh filling the temple in other contexts.[136] A Divine-Saying Formula concludes the progression.

[8–9] These verses contain two supplementary affirmations which reinforce vv. 6–7. First, in v. 8, Yahweh declares that the treasures of the nations will come to him because all the world's silver and gold (here a merism or a synecdoche for all the world's wealth)[137] belongs to him. The position of לי (to me) is not necessarily emphatic, for the subject frequently follows the predicate when the predicate consists of a

---

[134] J. Muilenberg underlines the almost excessive use of בוא in Isa 60 (at least 7 times). s. v. "Isaiah—Introduction", *IB* 5:69.

[135] Keil, 2:194 and most commentators.

[136] Cf. above, on 2:3.

[137] Cf. Verhoef, p. 105.

preposition with a noun or pronoun.[138] The affirmation can be taken in two ways. It is possible that Yahweh is simply declaring his sovereignty over all his creation, as in Exod 19:5 and Ps 24:1.[139] However the mention of silver and gold (כסף וזהב), appears to have a more specific connotation.[140] In several contexts this fixed expression refers to the fruits of Yahweh's victory over the nations, sometimes in relationship to the restitution of the treasures taken by them. Before leaving Egypt, the Israelites were ordered to request gold and silver objects from the Egyptians. Exod 12:36b concludes "thus they plundered the Egyptians." Later, such silver and gold was consecrated to the worship of Yahweh (Exod 25:3–8). In the conquest narrative, Israel devotes the gold and silver of Jericho to the service of Yahweh (Josh 6:19, 24). In Joel 4:5 [Eng. 3:5] an adaptation of the same theme appears. The silver and gold taken by Tyre and placed in the service of its gods will be returned. In fact these two precious metals are often taken as war booty or offered to a suzerain.[141] In general, where כסף וזהב or חיל, המדה are used with reference to the worship of a deity, greater emphasis is placed upon the one who receives such worship, than upon the manner in which such worship is presented. Haggai therefore expresses the fact that Yahweh has a right over everything the nations possess, since he is creator and victor.[142]

Verse 9 consists of Yahweh's affirmation regarding the temple's future, based upon the statement of his universal sovereignty made in v. 8. As in v. 3 and 7, the expression כבוד הבית הזה (the glory of this house)

---

[138] Joüon § 154f.

[139] See Deissler, 2:492 and Amsler, p. 32.

[140] The word order here which places silver before gold is more typical of pre-exilic Hebrew, as well as Akkadian, Egyptian, Ugaritic, Old Aramaic, and Phoenician (cf. Schattner-Rieser, "L'hébreu", p. 218). The reverse order is found frequently in postexilic texts and reflects a more wide-spread tendency in that period to invert the elements of certain fixed phrases (ibid., pp. 218–19). Meyers and Meyers (pp. 53, 348) attempt to relate the various orders to relative availability and value of the two precious metals. Given the eschatological nature of the text here, current economic conditions would appear less relevant than literary and theological concerns.

[141] Cf. the seizure of wealth in Gen 34:29; Num 31:9; Isa 8:4; 10:13–14; 30:6; Jer 15:13; 17:3; Mic 11:3.

[142] Von Rad (Theology, 2:296) observes, "Haggai really only took one feature from the whole range of concepts [in the motif of the pilgrimage of the nations to Zion], that of the solemn conveyance of the treasures of all the nations to Yahweh. Yahweh alone has a rightful claim to all the valuables which now lie scattered among the nations; only at the eschaton, once the temple has been prepared will the treasures which are his by right, and which have meanwhile been apportioned among the nations, revert to Yahweh's possession."

designates external splendour. The adjective האחרון refers to כבוד and
not בית. The meaning is clear. In the future the appearance of the
house will be far more splendid than at the time of Solomon. The
oracle concludes with the affirmation ובמקום הזה אתן שלום (I will give
peace in this place). The phrase נתן שלום is found in divine speech in
Lev 26:6 and Jer 14:13. In the first of these texts, responding to the
obedience of the people to the covenant, Yahweh promises peace in
the land. In the second text, in contrast to the false prophets who had
announced peace for Jerusalem, Yahweh declares שלום אמת אתן לכם
במקום הזה (truly I will give peace in this place). The parallel with Hag
2:9 is striking. In contrast to the situation reflected in Jeremiah where
the temple was popularly considered to be a kind of talisman capable of
guaranteeing peace, Yahweh now declares that the temple will become
a true centre of world peace.[143] In the words ובמקום הזה there is a sense
of movement from the temple to the whole land. Blessings emanate
from the former and spread throughout the latter. Similar symbolism
exists in Ezek 47:1–12. For its part, Zech 14:8 is certainly not far from
this text. In the LXX, a glossator has given this eschatological promise
a more contemporary application, including a promise of "peace of
soul as a possession for all who build, to erect this temple."[144]

The absence of a dramatic epilogue leaves the reader with no explicit
description of the result of this prophetic intervention. However the
final form of the book implies that the work was resumed, and that
once again Haggai's words were highly effective.

## 6.4. RHETORICAL AND HERMENEUTICAL USE OF THEOLOGICAL TRADITIONS

In this section, the text uses a variety of widely known theological
traditions for specific rhetorical purposes. Four aspects are especially
noteworthy in this regard.

### 6.4.1. *Tradition as Basis for Continuity with the Past*

In 2:1–5 the prophet conveys divine approval for the work in progress.
This is achieved in a striking manner. Using language which was highly
evocative of older traditions, the prophet affirms the ongoing valid-

---

[143] Verhoef, p. 106.
[144] Petersen's translation, p. 70; cf. Ackroyd, "Interpretative Glosses".

ity of pre-exilic institutions and conceptions.[145] In contrast to Amos or Jeremiah, Haggai perceives the events which transpired earlier that century as having constituted no irretrievable break with Israel's earlier institutions. This is seen in several ways. First, the prophet does not conceive of two different temples. In spite of the destruction and desecration of the pre-exilic structure, for Haggai the cult site under repair stood in perfect continuity with its earlier counterpart. He speaks, rather, of the past, present, and future glory of the same house (2:3, 9). Second, in his words to the builders, the prophet uses the classical Encouragement Formula. The imperative of the root חזק (be strong), directed to the leaders and the community as a whole, places these individuals in the long line of the people thus addressed in the Deuteronomistic tradition.[146] The same can be said of the injunction not to fear (אל־תיראו), traces of which may be seen in the Patriarchal cycles (Gen 15:1; 26:24; 35:17), in the Sinai traditions (Exod 14:13; 20:20; Num 14:9; 21:34), as well as in the Deuteronomistic tradition (Deut 1:21, 29; 3:2, 22; 20:3; 31:6; Josh 10:8, 25). This places Haggai's addressees in a long line of venerable individuals and groups including Abraham, Moses, Joshua, and the generation which left Egypt and entered Canaan. The Formula of Assistance that stands with it evokes a wide variety of earlier traditions (cf. Gen 26:24; 28:15; Josh 3:7). Third, the pericope contains a pastiche of diverse images drawn from details of the Sinai traditions. The exodus and the Sinai covenant are explicitly mentioned in 2:5, where the perpetuity of that covenantal relationship is affirmed. The Spirit of Yahweh, in a fashion similar to the cloud in the desert, serves as a witness to the presence of Yahweh among the community at Jerusalem. In an innovative and unique fashion, the prophet configures a variety of traditional elements in order to assure his audience that the postexilic community stands in continuity with the Yahwistic community of the past, and that the postexilic community was the legitimate heir of the institutions (covenant, temple) and beneficial acts (deliverance, presence of Yahweh) of the past.

---

[145] Petersen (p. 66) remarks, regarding Hag 2:4–5, "[T]he dynamics of Haggai's situation required him to use traditional language in order to address successfully the distresses created by the reconstruction of the second temple."

[146] Similar exhortations are given to the people as they enter the land: Deut 31:6; Josh 10:25 as well as to Joshua in Deut 31:7; Josh 1:6–9.

Analogous to his insistence upon continuity between past and present, Haggai also re-affirms traditional motifs regarding the future. In so
doing, he engages a broader subject, one which appears to have preoccupied the postexilic community (cf. the complaint of the angel of Yahweh in Zech 1:11). That issue was the perceived imbalance[147] created
by the supremacy of foreign nations over Israel. Thus Haggai underlines the continuity, not only of the pre-exilic *institutions* (and the deeply
rooted traditions associated with them), but of the traditional *eschatological notions*, especially those standing within the framework of Zion
theology, dealing with the future of Israel, Jerusalem, and the nations.
Put another way, the continuity that Haggai presupposed would have
been incomplete without the re-affirmation of these earlier traditions.
Chary qualifies 2:6–9 as being of "great messianic density."[148] The
term "eschatological" is probably more appropriate since no explicitly
messianic reference is in view in 2:6–9. The leading themes of 2:6–
9 and 20–23 (theophany, the shaking of the cosmos, the assault and
defeat of the nations, the pilgrimage of the nations to Jerusalem, the
enriching of the temple, and eschatological peace) are stock components of a common eschatological scenario deeply rooted in Israelite
traditions, especially those of Zion theology.[149] A more nuanced analysis of the use of these themes in Haggai will be presented in the
following sections. Here it suffices simply to note that in his historical context, Haggai holds out to his audience an expression of hope
whose origin is found in the eschatological notions already deeply
rooted in the community's theological framework. Von Rad underlines the significance of this hermeneutical and theological step. He
states,

> [The post-exilic prophets] shared a common certainty that the new thing
> which they expected was already prefigured in the old, and that the old
> would be present in the new in perfect form. Thus ... they were certain
> that Yahweh was not going to nullify what he himself had begun and
> established. ... Projecting the old traditions into the future was the only
> possible way open to the prophets of making material statements about a
> future which involved God.[150]

---

[147] Petersen, p. 68.

[148] Chary, *Prophètes and culte*, p. 132.

[149] Cf. von Rad, *Theology*, 2:292–97; Hanson, "Zechariah 9", pp. 37–59; Roberts,
"Davidic Origin", pp. 329–44; Weinfeld, "Zion", pp. 75–113.

[150] Von Rad, *Theology*, 2:299.

### 6.4.2. *Harmonization and Systematization of Traditional Elements*

Von Rad's understanding of the eschatological traditions relating to Jerusalem in the postexilic period provides a useful starting point for an analysis of Hag 2:6–9. He maintained that there were two eschatological cycles closely linked to Jerusalem, both dealing with the future renewal and glorification of that city.[151] He furthermore affirmed that prophetic eschatology was frequently expressed in images and concepts derived from one or another of these cycles. For von Rad, the first cycle concerned the announcement of the failure of a hostile attack against the city[152] and included the following elements: the gathering of the nations against Zion, the coming of Yahweh with earthquakes and darkness, a great battle, and the deliverance and preservation of Zion.[153] Variations on this theme may be found in Ezek 38–39, Joel 2–4, and Zech 9 and 12–14.[154]

Von Rad's second cycle centres on the pilgrimage of the nations to Zion.[155] The fundamental distinction between the two cycles is the pacific character of the latter, which concerns the salvation of the nations rather than their judgment. This second cycle begins with a miraculous geographical change. Mount Zion is elevated above all other mountains and becomes visible in all the earth. Subsequently the nations will come to Zion to present their worship and offerings. Diverse aspects of this pilgrimage are highlighted by various texts. Isa 2:2–4 and Mic 4:1–4 describe the nations as coming to receive divine arbitration in instances of international conflict. In Isa 49:8–21, the Jews of the Diaspora arrive at Jerusalem, carried on the shoulders of the *goyim*. In Isa 45:14–15, in a similar context, a monotheistic confession par excellence is placed on the lips of the non-Jews.[156] Isaiah 60 describes in detail the coming of the nations, and their presentation of their wealth and offerings, for the service of Yahweh.[157]

---

[151] Ibid., *Theology*, 2:292–97.

[152] Ibid. Von Rad sees the origins of this cycle as emanating from pre-Davidic Jerusalem. For an opposing view, cf. Roberts, "Davidic Origin" *passim*.

[153] Cf. von Rad, *Theology*, 2:293–91; cf. Hanson, "Zechariah 9"; Petersen, *Late Israelite Prophecy*, pp. 17ff.

[154] For a fuller discussion of these texts, cf. Kessler, "Shaking of the Nations", pp. 163–65.

[155] See also the detailed analysis in A. Causse, "Le mythe de la nouvelle Jerusalem du Deutéro-Esaie à la IIIe Sibylle", *RHPR* 18 (1938): 377–414.

[156] Von Rad, *Theology*, 2:295.

[157] Cf. ibid., 2:294–97.

More recently M. Weinfeld has re-examined these motifs.[158] In light of Near Eastern parallels, he proposes the existence of two streams of tradition different from those suggested by von Rad. These are: (1) the ideology of the royal capital, and (2) the ideology of the royal temple.[159] For Weinfeld the constitutive elements of the first theme include taxes and tribute for the city and its king, the subjugation of foreign nations, and a universal reign characterized by justice and peace. The second stream, by contrast, stresses the elevation of the royal city and its sanctuary as well as its position at the centre of the world, the gathering of the nations and their kings with offerings for the building of the sanctuary, and the nations' submission to any legal decision made there.[160] It is beyond the scope of the present study to evaluate the relative merits of the two preceding reconstructions. Sufficient for our purposes here is their recognition that diverse traditional elements were organized around differing central themes relating to a single broader subject area.[161] The existence of such configurations of traditional elements provides a useful starting point from which to discuss Hag 2:1–9.

A survey of the scholarly literature reveals that, in general, Hag 2:6–9 is seen as reflecting one or another of von Rad's cycles, but not both. For example Dumbrell,[162] von Rad,[163] Chary,[164] Weinfeld,[165] and Amsler[166] opt for the "peaceful" cycle. Cross,[167] Petersen,[168] Verhoef,[169] and Meyers and Meyers[170] see in Haggai's words an allusion to the eschatological battle, holy war, or the theophany of the divine warrior. However, the lack of any clear data in Hag 2:1–9 permitting a definitive identification of the text with either cycle should caution against any overly hasty conclusions in this regard. It is more judicious to

---

[158] Weinfeld, "Zion", pp. 75–113.

[159] Ibid., pp. 93–94.

[160] Ibid., pp. 95–115.

[161] Weinfeld ("Zion", p. 94) concludes that these two configurations do not constitute two distinct visions of the future, but rather two types of literary compositions. Such a conclusion appears quite judicious.

[162] Dumbrell, "Political Origins", p. 38.

[163] Von Rad, "City ", p. 232.

[164] Chary, p. 27.

[165] Weinfeld, "Zion", p. 111.

[166] Amsler, p. 32.

[167] Cross, *Canaanite Myth*, p. 170.

[168] Petersen, p. 68.

[169] So Verhoef, (pp. 102–3), citing also Koole and van der Woude.

[170] The position of Meyers and Meyers (p. 53) is more nuanced. They see the silver and gold as a form of tribute brought to a conquering king.

affirm that Haggai is moving more freely within the context of various
common traditions.[171] The creativity of our prophet is thus discernible
through a careful analysis of his particular use of these broader traditions.

Such creativity is evident in Haggai's reconfiguration and harmonization of traditions concerning the future of the foreign nations. In
the two cycles mentioned above, the role of the nations is distinct: they
are either defeated as enemies (bellicose cycle), or they recognize the
supremacy of Yahweh and worship him (pacific cycle). In contrast to
the opinions cited above which seek to identify 2:6–9 and 20–23 with
one or another of the cycles, allusions and echoes of both are discernible in 2:6–9. The following elements of the bellicose scenario[172]
are in evidence in Hag 2:6–9: (1) the shaking of the cosmos with catas-
trophes and plagues in 2:6 (cf. Isa 24:17–20; Ezek 38:19–20; 48:3–4, 7;
Joel 4:16 [Eng. 3:16]; Nah 1:5; Ps 46:3, 7 [Eng. 2, 6]); (2) terror and panic
among the nations in 2:7 (cf. Isa 19:16; Ezek 38:19–20; Joel 4:15–16 [Eng.
3:15–16]; Zech 14:13; Ps 46:7 [Eng. 6]); (3) the ingathering of the wealth
of the nations in 2:7–8 (cf. Isa 60:5; Ezek 39:9–10; Joel 4:5–7 [Eng. 3:5–
7]; Mic 4:13; Zech 14:1); (4) the annihilation of the power of the nations
in 2:22 (cf. Ezek 38:22–23; Joel 4:9–14 [3:9–14]; Mic 7:15–17; Zech 14:3,
12–13); (5) the slaughter of foreign armies, each at the hand of his com-
patriot in 2:22 (cf. Isa 19:2; Ezek 38:21; Zech 14:13); (6) the eschatological reign of Yahweh in 2:9, 23 (cf. Isa 60:12; Mic 5:9; Zech 14:17). The
language of Haggai is thus filled with echoes of militaristic images.

Haggai's use of the pilgrimage motif is far more subtle. The text
lacks explicit allusions to the geographical changes described in other
prophetic texts (cf. Isa 2:2–4), or to the resolution of conflicts between
nations (cf. Isa 2:2–4; Mic 4:1–4), or the return of the exiles (cf. Isa
49:14–21). However the text does explicitly mention the presence of
nations' treasures (cf. Isa 60) and culminates with a vision of universal
peace emanating from Jerusalem (cf. Isa 2:1–4, Mic 4:1–4; Zec 14:16–
20).

What then can be said with reference to Haggai's use of these two
traditional motifs? First, it seems evident that the prophet *interweaves*

---

[171] G. Fohrer, ("Remarks", pp. 309–19, esp. p. 313) criticizes J. Bright, who (according
to Fohrer) maintains that while prophets did adapt traditions to a certain extent, they
did not engage in innovation.

[172] The elements often associated with this theme are discussed, for example, by
Petersen (*Late Israelite Prophecy*, pp. 16–19) and Hanson ("Zechariah 9", p. 53).

and *mixes* various elements found in the two cycles.[173] At times the result of this fusion and intermingling is that the precise significance of a given element within the text is difficult to identify. This may explain the wide divergence of scholarly opinion regarding the goal and purpose of the nations' treasures.[174] Furthermore, this fusion of themes is not unique to Haggai.[175] A similar conflation of these same motifs is observable in Isa 19; 60; Mic 4:5–6,[176] and in some of the "Royal Psalms" such as 47, 68, 76, 96, 97, and 99.[177] Causse alludes to a similar transformation of motifs within the prophetic literature. He notes that, in the prophets, the image of Yahweh undergoes a transformation from the commander-in-chief of the armies of Israel, the *gibbor* of the holy war, and hero of the eschatological judgment, into "the arbitrator of the nations, the peace making king."[178] According to Roberts,[179] the addition of the theme of the pilgrimage of the nations to the traditions of the victory of Yahweh does not represent a radical change. He discerns this thematic conflation in Isa 2:1–5; Mic 4:1–7; Zech 14:16–19; Ps 2:10–11, and Ps 76:11–13. Allen[180] and Kapelrud[181] have

---

[173] P. R. Ackroyd, "The Chronicler as Exegete", *JSOT* 2 (1977): 21, mentions T. Willi's observation that the same exegetical tendency may be found in the Chroncler's work. Ackroyd (p. 24) appears to agree with Willi.

[174] Weinfeld's evidence demonstrates that the theme of the enrichment of the capital by the treasures of the nations was one that was widespread in the ancient Near East ("Zion", p. 94). At times such wealth was tribute, and at other times war booty or offerings for the temple (cf. ibid., p. 109 for some highly illuminating parallels). It is therefore not surprising that this same ambiguity is to be found in Hag 2:6–9 and that attempts to fit this text into other existing patterns prove frustrating.

[175] Von Rad, (*Theology*, 2:296), sees the first evidence of the fusion of these cycles in Zech 9–14. But, as argued here, it is already in evidence in Hag 2.

[176] D. Schibler, *Le livre de Michée*, (CEB; Vaux-sur-Seine: Edifac, 1989), p. 91, excludes the theme of the inviolability of Zion from Mic 4:1–4. He is, however, willing to see traces of it in Mic 4:9–10 (p. 101, n. 3). Weinfeld ("Zion", pp. 103–4) and Allen (*Joel*, p. 243) see both as present in 4:1–4.

[177] A demonstration of the presence of both themes in these texts cannot be attempted here.

[178] A. Causse, *Israël and la vision de l'humanité*, (Strasbourg: Istra, 1924), p. 17, cf. also pp. 46, 64–65.

[179] Roberts, "Davidic Origin" p. 329. Roberts, following E. Rohland, affirms that the four basic motifs in the Zion tradition are as follows: Zion is the highest mountain, it is the source of the River of Paradise; there God repulsed the assault of the waters of chaos; there God overcame the revolt of the kings and peoples of the earth. Added to these (according to H. Wildberger), is the pilgrimage of the nations.

[180] Allen, *Joel*, p. 323.

[181] A. S. Kapelrud, "Eschatology in the Book of Micah", *VT* 11 (1961): 392–405, esp. p. 396.

observed this phenomenon in certain prophetic texts. Wilson affirms, "The theological views of the prophets at this period [the postexilic period] are an amalgam of positions that had been distinct in the preexilic period."[182] There is, therefore, little basis upon which to call into question the notion that Haggai could have reconfigured the traditions to which he and the Judaean community at Jerusalem were heirs, and readapted them in new and creative ways in line with his own rhetorical goals.

In addition to the conflation of traditional motifs, a careful reading of Haggai yields indications of a clear structuring and chronological progression. The shaking of the cosmos spreads panic among the Gentile powers (2:6–7). In the resulting confusion, foreign armies annihilate one another (2:21–22). Yahweh enthrones his royal representative in Jerusalem (2:23). The nations, realizing the sovereignty and omnipotence of Yahweh, present their treasures at the Jerusalem temple (2:8–9). Meyers and Meyers note the structuring of these elements.[183] The eschatological scenario described by Haggai is both general and coherent.

### 6.4.3. *Adaptation of Tradition for the Needs of the Present*

A striking hermeneutical tendency in Haggai is the prophet's ability to reformulate tradition to suit the needs of his audience. In 2:6–9 the prophet finds himself confronted with the discouragement of a small group of Yahwists in the midst of reconstructing their devastated cult site. To respond to this situation he uses two hermeneutical techniques, which I describe as generalization and focalization.

### 6.4.3.1. *Generalization*

The term "generalization" refers to the attenuation or deliberate obscuring of certain details of a theme, so as to render it applicable to a specific situation, one which may be different from its original setting. Haggai 2:6–9 manifests this technique in its use of the "battle cycle." This is seen in a variety of ways. First, the text generalizes the location

---

[182] Wilson, *Prophecy and Society*, p. 306.
[183] Meyers and Meyers (p. 53) comment, "Presumably the downfall of the nations of verse 21 would then lead to their acknowledgment, as in this passage, of Yahweh's universal rule." Cf. Wolff, p. 60.

of the eschatological battle. In spite of the many similarities between Hag 2 and Ezek 38–39, 40–48, Joel 4 [Eng. 3] and Zech 14, a question nevertheless remains. Is Haggai describing a battle around Jerusalem, as is found in the traditional "assault on Zion" motif? Nothing in the context would specifically seem to indicate that this is the case. In Zech 14 the battle occurs in Jerusalem, in Joel 4 [Eng. 3] it takes place in the valley of Jehoshaphat, and in Ezek 38–39, on the "mountains of Israel." Only Ezek 39:6 seems to portray a larger conflagration. Haggai, on the other hand, sketches a conflict that is both more extensive and less detailed than the one described the texts cited above. The nations and the kingdoms of 2:7 and 22 are neither named nor described. Haggai speaks of Gentile power in general. While our prophet may on some level be alluding to the Persian Empire, this does not exhaust his perspective. Second, the details of the battle are vague. The slaughter of the nations' armies is described in highly general terms. This contrasts with the much greater detail found in Ezek 38–39 and Zech 14. Third, the scope of the conflict is very broad. In Ezek 38:21 and Zech 14:13 the siege of Yehud and Jerusalem is in view and it is the besieging troops who kill one another. Hag 2:22 uses the same language, without any explicit mention of a siege. It is the armies of all the nations of the earth[184] who annihilate themselves in the panic of that catastrophic day. Similarly, in contrast to Zech 14:5–6, where an earthquake provides a way of escape for the inhabitants of Jerusalem, or Ezek 38:17–23, where the earthquakes and other plagues frustrate and terrorize the conquering armies, the cosmic perturbations of nature in 2:6–9, 20–23 have a universal character.[185] Thus when Haggai employs elements of the "battle cycle," he universalizes and generalizes the tradition he uses.[186]

---

[184] As Deissler (2:497) comments, "*mamlakot* designates, in a very general way, the various powers other than Israel."

[185] Petersen (p. 67) observes, "Haggai has used this traditional language in a distinctive way. In Haggai the shaking of the earth is not a reaction to Yahweh's appearance *per se* but rather is linked to new activity of Yahweh on behalf of his people. Further distinguishing this language from typical theophanic descriptions is the scope of such violent agitation. It is no longer just the mountains which quake. The entire cosmos vibrates, as indicated by the two polar sets: earth-heavens, sea-dry land."

[186] This phenomenon has also been noted by Amsler (p. 32), "The universal shaking which is announced has no precedent. The prophets had often described Yahweh's intervention in catastrophic terms, but never as is the case here, in terms of a shaking which was cosmic and universal in scope." Cf. Meyers and Meyers, p. 53.

6.4.3.2. *Focalization*

By "focalization" I refer to the highlighting of certain details of a theme or tradition. In Haggai such focalization stands out strikingly against the generalization noted in the previous section.[187] Haggai uses this technique in his adaptation of the "pilgrimage cycle." What strikes the reader here is the suppression of several key details of the cycle, in order to highlight one central idea—the future adornment of the temple. As noted above, geographical changes, the influx of the treasures of the nations to the temple, the declaration and reception of Yahweh's instruction, and universal peace were common elements in this motif. As noted, Weinfeld has shown that, from the second millennium BCE, such themes were frequently found both in the imperialist ideology of the ancient Near East, and in various prophetic texts.[188] Moreover Weinfeld demonstrates that the theme of the "temple as world centre" existed in a variety of forms both in Israelite and non-Israelite literature.[189] Thus, the traditional wellspring from which Haggai draws his vocabulary and through which he transmits his message is widespread in the ancient Near East.[190]

The use of "focalization" in Haggai is evident when the book's use of the "enrichment of the temple" and "pilgrimage" motifs is juxtaposed with similar prophetic texts, such as Zech 14, Isa 2, Mic 4, and Isa 60.[191] Zech 14 comprises several elements of the cycle. Radical geographical

---

[187] In essence, generalization and focalization can be said to form part of the same hermeneutical manoeuvre, since the former accentuates the latter. It is, however, conceivable that the two techniques could be used independently.

[188] Weinfeld, "Zion", pp. 94–100. As noted above, these themes included taxes and tribute for the royal city as well as for its king; subjugation of foreign nations; universal reign; the establishment of justice and peace. Weinfeld (ibid., pp. 101–5) sees these themes as present in certain prophetic texts relative to Jerusalem, such as Mic 4–6; Zech 9:9–10, and Isa 11:1–10. He correctly points out that, in the prophets, such political and nationalistic motifs were frequently "spiritualized" (Weinfeld's term, ibid., p. 112). It follows that, given the political basis of the images used, it is not surprising to find motifs of political domination, including the collection of booty and the presentation of tribute, mixed together with notions of gifts offered freely. Thus it is at times quite erroneous to see a specific meaning in a given element in a text on the basis of the presence of that meaning in another, similar text, cf. Schibler's criticism (*Michée*, p. 93) of Wolff.

[189] Weinfeld, "Zion", p. 110.

[190] For examples see ibid., pp. 111–12.

[191] Due to the limits of this study, texts such as the "Royal Psalms," Tob 13 and 14, and Isa 25:6, which manifest similar themes, cannot be analyzed here.

changes elevate Jerusalem above all other mountains (vv. 4, 8, 10). A decisive battle (vv. 2, 12–15) precedes eschatological peace (v, 9, 12, 18). The only riches to arrive in Jerusalem are the gold, silver and garments picked up as war booty (v. 14). The pilgrimage is undertaken during the feast of booths (vv. 16, 19) by all the nations of the world (vv. 16–17). The resulting peace is in no way "spontaneous or voluntary." Stability is maintained through the threat of plagues and divine chastisements (vv. 17–19).

Isa 60 presents a different configuration of the elements of the cycle. If geological upheavals are to be implied here, as von Rad affirms,[192] the nuance is subtle. If present, such an inference is discernible in the light upon Zion and the darkness that dominates the nations. There is no evidence of an eschatological battle or an attack against Jerusalem. Those who bring their gifts are foreign nations (vv. 3–9). Various categories of offerings are presented. Sacrifices for the worship of Yahweh are mentioned in v. 7. In v. 5, 10–17 gifts and manpower intended for the rebuilding of the temple are in view. Most surprising is the image of the Jews of the Diaspora being carried home upon the arms of the *goyim*. Here the prophet introduces the issue of the demographic imbalance (small Yehud in contrast to the extensive Diaspora), which was a major preoccupation of the Jewish literature of the period.[193] The text thus portrays the Diaspora community being brought home on the shoulders of Gentiles, and presented as gifts to the community in Yehud (v. 4).[194] The text portrays the Gentiles as subservient to the Jewish community. The nations and even their kings will become simple workmen (v. 10), porters in the service of Yahweh, of his temple, and of his people (v. 11). They become the "nurse" who feeds the people of Yahweh (v. 16). The object of the service of the nations (שרת, a term of cultic connotation) is not only Yahweh, but also Israel.[195] The oppressor will be humbled and will bow down before Israel (v. 14). The worship offered to Yahweh seems sometimes spontaneous and free, as in vv. 6, 9 and

---

[192] Von Rad, "City", p. 237.

[193] Cf. Tob 13:10–11; 14:5–7, and D. A. Gowan, *Eschatology in the Old Testament*, (Edinburgh: T. & T. Clark, 1986), pp. 24–32. Gowan cites the following texts as evidence of the importance of this question: Isa 45:14–17; 49:22–23; 43:5–7; 51:11; Zech 8:7–8.

[194] Weinfeld ("Zion", p. 110, n. 75) notes that in the Egyptian royal inscriptions both children and tribute are presented as offerings.

[195] Von Rad, "City", p. 238, n. 12.

sometimes constrained, as in v. 12.[196] Peace will reign (vv. 17–18), but it appears to be an "imposed" peace (v. 12).[197]

Isaiah 2:2–4 is much less complex than the preceding texts.[198] Geographical changes are found in v. 2, but no explicit mention is made of a battle. The same may be said of the influx of treasures or of formal worship of Yahweh at the temple by the nations. The peace established is entirely due to the will of the nations to come to Jerusalem to learn from Yahweh how to settle their disputes (vv. 3b-4). What is underlined, therefore, is the promulgation and the fulfillment of the eschatological law.[199] In spite of some differences,[200] Mic 4 uses the same traditional elements in a similar way.

Hag 2:6–9 presents several significant contrasts to the preceding texts, particularly the first two. In Haggai, we find no explicit mention of physical changes in the Jerusalem topography. A battle may be implied from 2:21b-22. The traditional elements which are present in the text, that is the influx of treasures and world peace, are mentioned without detailed explanations. Even the fact that it is the nations that will bring their riches is not explicitly stated. No details are given regarding the presence of the nations' wealth, nor whether the nations act under threat of divine retaliation. The same may be said of the concept of peace in the text. It is unclear whether our prophet envisages a universal peace imposed by Yahweh or a voluntary forsaking of war and its instruments. The question of the Diaspora is not even broached, a highly surprising omission. Thus in Haggai several themes found in analogous texts are minimized and one is highlighted: the future glory of the temple.

---

[196] This ambiguity led J. Morgenstern, "Two Prophecies", pp. 365–431 to conclude that Isa 60:1–3, 5–7 contained a universalistic vision, in which the nations would eagerly and voluntarily come to worship Yahweh without the slightest constraint or intimidation. The rest of the chapter, by contrast, was starkly nationalistic. The nations were to be exploited for Israel's benefit (pp. 396–98). It must be said that the two perspectives are not necessarily mutually exclusive. In essence, given the political origin of the imagery (cf. Weinfeld, "Zion", p. 112), it is possible to follow May ("This people", pp. 195–96) and speak of a "nationalism whose eschatology is more explicitly universalistic." Cf. Dumbrell, "Political Origins", passim.

[197] Weinfeld, "Zion" pp. 101–2.

[198] On the origins, redactional history and function of this text cf. H. Cazelles, "Qui aurait visé, à l'origine, Isaïe II 2–5?", VT 30 (1980): 409–20.

[199] Von Rad, "City" p. 235.

[200] Cf. Allen, Joel, p. 243, Schibler, Michée, pp. 89–93, and Kapelrud, "Eschatology", p. 396.

The best explanation of this "minimalist" presentation in Hag 2 is to be found in the prophet's particular adaptation of the traditions upon which he draws. In addition to being a response to the community's discouragement Haggai's presentation seems particularly suited to the context of the Jerusalem community in early Persian Yehud. Haggai offers only very vague and general images of the more militaristic aspects of his tradition. Such themes as the presence of non-Jews in the temple and their worship of Yahweh, the subjugation of non-Jews, the return of the exiles are omitted entirely. Worldwide political stability is mentioned in the vaguest of terms. The role of the Gentile nations vis-à-vis Israel and Yahweh is left undefined, despite the reference to the treasures of these nations. Dogmatism is impossible here, but the most likely explanation for this highly generalized and strikingly non-detailed presentation appears to me to stem from the rhetorical concerns of the prophet and/or the theological concerns of his redactor. Both view temple reconstruction as *the* problem to be dealt with and both seem to adopt a broad and inclusive stance to the community at Yehud.[201] Such a stance would mean seeking to involve the population as a whole, and to minimize or obfuscate those issues that could be troubling or divisive. This may explain why the themes mentioned above receive little or no attention. They were either divisive, troubling or not immediately relevant. Thus for the prophet who encouraged the reconstruction, and the redactor who viewed both temple and prophecy as central aspects of the community's life, lesser matters could be passed over in favour of those of primary importance. Thus, prophet and redactor call the populace to unite around Yahweh's word through his servant, and around his "house."

In conclusion then, three interpretive and hermeneutical strategies are in evidence in Hag 2:1–9. First, religious traditions are used to affirm the continuity between the present and the past, and to affirm hope for the future. Second, various traditions, sometimes of disparate origins[202] are mixed together, harmonized, and systematized. Third, traditions are selectively reformulated, highlighting certain aspects and minimizing others, in light of broader rhetorical and redactional goals.

---

[201] I disagree with Wolff who, based on his exegesis of 2:10–15, sees Haggai's Chronicler as exclusivistic, cf. the exegesis of that section, *infra*.

[202] Ackroyd ("Chronicler as Exegete", p. 24) maintains that the Chronicler is the first OT theologian, since he harmonizes and unifies traditions of diverse origin (Deuteronomistic, priestly, etc.). It seems evident, however, that this process is already at work in Haggai. Cf. Wilson, *Prophecy and Society*, p. 306.

CHAPTER SEVEN

# HAGGAI 2:10–19

## 7.1. TRANSLATION AND TEXTUAL CRITICISM

[10] On the twenty-fourth day of the ninth month, in the second year of Darius, the word of Yahweh came to Haggai the prophet, as follows:

[11] This is what Yahweh Sebaoth says, "Ask the priests for a ruling.[1]

[12] "If[2] someone carries consecrated meat in the fold of a garment, and with this fold touches bread, vegetables,[3] wine, oil, or any kind of food, will it become consecrated?" The priests responded and said, "No."

[13] Then Haggai said, "If someone who has been made unclean by contact with a corpse touches any of these things, will it become unclean?" And the priests responded and said, "It will become unclean."

[14] Then Haggai responded and said, "So is this people and so is this nation before me—oracle of Yahweh—and so is all the work of their hands; and what they offer there is unclean."[4]

---

[1] Heb. תורה cf. exegesis.

[2] הן is an Aramaism equivalent to אם (Wolff p. 88).

[3] The translation "vegetables" is accepted by Amsler, Chary and Wolff. נזיד is only found elsewhere in Gen 25:29, and 2 Kgs 4:38, 39, 40. Petersen (p. 71) suggests that some kind of vegetable stew is in view, cf. Verhoef and Meyers and Meyers.

[4] The LXX adds: ἕνεκεν τῶν λημμάτων αὐτῶν τῶν ὀρθρινῶν, ὀδυνηθήσονται ἀπὸ προσώπου πόνων αὐτῶν· καὶ ἐμισεῖτε ἐν πύλαις ἐλέγχοντας ("Because of their early profits, they shall be pained because of their toil, and you have hated those who reprove in the gates" (Petersen's translation, p. 71, n. c). Here again, the LXX moralizes and spiritualizes, borrowing the language of Amos 5:10. Ackroyd ("Interpretative Glosses", p. 165) suggests that an early Hebrew exegetical interpolation was integrated into the text by the LXX. He notes that the point of the gloss is to assert the necessity of righteous behaviour, without which the act of restoring the temple is useless.

[15] "And now[5] reflect carefully,[6] from this day forward:[7] Before[8] you[9] set stone upon stone in the temple[10] of Yahweh,

[16] "how did you fare?[11] When one came[12] to a heap[13] of twenty measures,[14] there were only ten. When one came to the wine vat to

---

[5] Those who transpose 2:15–19 after 1:15a delete ועתה as a secondary redactional insertion whose purpose is to strengthen the connection between 2:15–19 and the date in 2:10, cf. Wolff p. 40. Horst (p. 198) inserts the formula of address in 1:1b here. Rothstein, (*Juden und Samaritaner*, p. 64 ) adds the Messenger Formula. However as Petersen (p. 87) and Koch, ("Haggais", pp. 59–60) have demonstrated ועתה is not normally found at the head of a new section, but rather continues a discussion already begun. I have expressed my objections to the transposition *supra* p. 108, n. 40; cf. *infra*, p. 248. If the transposition is rejected, the discussion of the authenticity of ועתה becomes superfluous.

[6] I have chosen to translate שים לבב in this pericope as "reflect carefully" or "consider" (cf. "ponder" in 1:1–11). The future orientation of this passage (see *infra*) makes this translation more appropriate.

[7] An earlier exegetical tradition (Mitchell, pp. 73–74) saw מעלה as referring to the past. Such an acceptation has been recently proposed by Meyers and Meyers, p. 59. However a future sense is far more probable (cf. exegesis). Mitchell sees the phrase as a gloss. However the chronological difficulties posed by a future sense of מעלה are resolved if 2:15b-17 is read as a rhetorical parenthesis describing the situation before the date in 2:18.

[8] The מן before טרם is pleonastic and thus ought not to be translated (so Petersen, p. 59; Meyers and Meyers, p. 58; Wolff, p. 39, and Amsler, p. 26). טרם retains its basic sense of "before" (despite Verhoef who gives it the meaning "beginning" for which there exists little solid evidence. What is more, whereas he rejects the notion of anteriority in v. 15, he appears to subtly reintroduce the idea in v. 16). The preposition מן indicates that the chronological qualifications in the phrase (that is מן־יום and מטרם) are parallel (although antithetically so).

[9] Inf. abs., subject to be supplied from the context.

[10] היכל here is synonymous with בית in 1: 4, 8, cf. Rudolph, p. 45.

[11] MT מהיותם "before they were" (*min*+qal inf. cs.+ 3 m. pl. pron. suf.); LXX τίνες ἦτε "how were you?" (= Heb מה־הייתם or מי־). Three options emerge: (1) Retain the MT, thus yielding, "before they were there, one came" cf. the TOB. (2) Correct to מה־ הייתם (cf. JB, Deissler, Wolff) "how did you fare?" or "what condition were you in?" (3) correct to מי־הייתם, (Barthélemy, *Critique textuelle*, 3:930), מי having the sense of "in what state" or "in what capacity" cf. Isa 51:19; Amos 7:2, 5. The MT is isolated. The Vulg, Syr, and Tg seem to have read מהיותכם and the LXX מי־הייתם, (ibid., 3:930). In light of the isolation of the MT and the difficulty of rendering it in an acceptable way, solutions (2) or (3) are preferable. מי occurs less frequently than מה, nevertheless (3) מי before the verb and carrying the meaning "in what state, situation or capacity" makes the best sense here. This emendation is accepted by Wolff, and Meyers and Meyers.

[12] Vocalizing בֹא. The MT reads בָא, however the inf. cs. is far more frequent in Haggai and fits well here.

[13] Cf. Meyers and Meyers (pp. 60–61) who emend עֲרֵמַת, sg. (MT) to עֲרֵמֹת pl. cf. 2 Chr 31:6–9.

[14] No units of measure are stated here. The prophet presumably assumes that this will be clear to his hearers. What is at issue is the difference between expectation and

draw[15] fifty measures from the vat,[16] there were only twenty.

[17][17] I struck you[18] with blight and mildew;[19] with hail [I struck] all the work of your hands; but you did not return to me[20]—oracle of Yahweh.

---

reality. Units of measurement are supplied by the versions (cf. Amsler, p. 26, n. 4).

[15] The *BHS* suggests that לחשׂף (to draw) is a secondary addition, likely corresponding to the lack of a second verb in 2:16a, cf. Meyers and Meyers, p. 60. No textual witnesses support this hypothesis.

[16] The translation of פורה, (only here and in Isa 63:3) is disputed. It cannot be simply an explanatory gloss for יקב as the latter is more common and better known (Wolff, p. 58). Mitchell (p. 74) sees it a unit of measurement. The most likely suggestion is that it refers to either wine vats, or the location where the crushed fruit was stored (Amsler, p. 26).

[17] The *BHS* suggests that the verse as a whole is a gloss inspired by Amos 4:9 and ought to be omitted, cf. also Wolff (p. 58–59). For lack of any other MS evidence, the MT should be retained.

[18] The double accusative here is difficult. אתכם is lacking in Kennicott 29, but that fifteenth century MS has "no particular authority" (Barthélemy, *Critique textuelle*, 3:931). Four solutions appear possible: (1) a double accusative, cf. Joüon §125w, and a translation giving both objects the same syntactical value. Thus the RSV, "I smote you and all the products of your toil …" cf. the NEB "I blasted you and all your harvest"; (2) viewing אתכם as the direct object and את כל מעשׂה ידיכם as an accusative of limitation, Joüon §125e. This translation is followed by the TOB, "Je vous ai frappés dans tout le travail de vos mains …" (I smote you in all the work of your hands …)" However את is quite rare in such a construction, Joüon §126g. Cf. also the rabbinical tradition which sees the second object as standing in apposition to the first (Barthélemy, Critique textuelle, 3:931; (3) omitting the first accusative, as the JB, and translating, "I smote by …"; (4) viewing הכיתי as doing double duty (so Meyers and Meyers, p. 62), and dividing the verse after ובירקון. This option is followed in my translation.

[19] On the specific nature of this grain fungus cf. Verhoef, p. 127, who, following Clark, sees it as produced by a combination of heat and humidity.

[20] Those who correct MT וְאֵין־אֶתְכֶם אֵלַי generally follow one of three approaches: (1) presupposing שׁוב after ואין and vocalizing אֶתְּכֶם. The Vulg appears to have read the text this way, "*et non fuit in vobis qui reverteretur ad me*", (but there was no one among you who returned to me, Wolff's translation, p. 59); (2) substituting שַׁבְּתֶּם for אתכם cf. LXX, καὶ οὐκ ἐπεστρέψατε πρός με (but you did not return to me) cf. Mitchell, Chary; (3) vocalizing אֶתְּכֶם and correcting אֵלַי (to me) to אֲנִי (I), thus yielding, "And I was not with you …" (Sellin, Rudolph). Barthélemy, (*Critique textuelle*, 3:931–2), lists other conjectures.

These emendations assume the "impossibility" of the MT (Mitchell) or its "barbaric" character (Petersen) and prefer the versions, which frequently followed Amos 4:9. However the MT is not necessarily "impossible." Amsler, Petersen, Meyers and Meyers, van der Woude, and Barthélemy, despite their differing approaches to the translation of אתכם, retain it. The critical question is whether אתכם ought to be construed as a subject or object.

(1) אתכם as subject: Barthélemy considers את, (here as in 2:5) as a kind of introductory particle of reference (*particule de présentation*) meaning, "concerning, about, with reference to" and translates "But there was no [movement toward] a return to me [on] your part." Verhoef follows P. Saydon, ("Meanings and Uses of the Particle את", *VT* 14 [1964]: 192–210, esp. pp. 193, 207) who maintains that in the form אתכם the

[18] So consider from this day forward, from the twenty-fourth day of the ninth month,[21] that is[22] from the day when the temple of Yahweh was refounded,[23] and reflect carefully.[24]

[19] Is there still[25] grain[26] in the granary; and have even[27] the vine,

---

particle את designates the subject, (Verhoef, p. 128), and translates "But you did not return to me." Other arguments advanced in favour of this approach include (a) אל without a verb carries the nuance "to be on the side of, or in favour of" in Hos 3:3; 2 Kgs 6:11; Jer. 15:1, and Ezek 36:9; (b) אין in Jer 15:1 and יש in Gen 23:8; 2 Kgs 10:15, without any verbal forms, are followed by an independent form plus a pronominal suffix. Thus אין אלי "is not as surprising as it seems at first glance" (Barthélemy, *Critique textuelle*, 3:932); (c) In Exod 32:26 אל has a dynamic sense, the verb "to come" being implied.

(2) אתכם as object: Amsler, (p. 26, n. 6) and Meyers and Meyers (p. 62), without any detailed explanation treat אתכם as the object and presuppose either בוא or שוב in the hiphil (thus Amsler, "Without bringing you back to me"; Meyers and Meyers, "But [nothing] brought you back to me." In my opinion, the arguments in favour of (1) אתכם as subject are persuasive.

Given that the MT can yield a satisfactory sense, and that it carries the *lectio difficilior*, I have retained it here. את designates the subject, and אל carries a dynamic sense indicating movement toward someone. D. J. Clark, ("Problems in Haggai 2:15–19", *BT* 34 [1983]: 432–39) is doubtlessly correct in observing that with or without the correction the sense is clear: the people did not return to God.

[21] Certain commentators see this date as a gloss inserted to link vv. 15–19 to vv. 10–14. The suggestion is questionable for three reasons: (1) the lack of any written evidence; (2) the proposed gloss loses its *raison d'être* if 2:10–19 is seen as a unified composition, cf. ch. 1 p. 33 and ch. 7 n. 5, 63, 67. (3) As Meyers and Meyers (p. 63) point out, the triple repetition of this date in Haggai serves to underline the importance of the date.

[22] Here ל introduces a "more precise explanation" (Wolff, p. 59).

[23] On this translation cf. exegesis.

[24] The *BHS* proposes the omission of מן ... לבבכם as secondary. However these words are not absent in any MS or version. Furthermore, the threefold repetition of שים לבב (2:15, 18a, 18b) mirrors its repetition in 1:5, 7 (Meyers and Meyers, p. 58).

[25] The translation of this verse is difficult and much debated, cf. Verhoef, pp. 131–35 and Clark "Problems." Is it (1) two questions, (2) one question and one affirmation, or (3) two affirmations? Following Clark, I view the text as two questions which imply negative responses; cf. exegesis.

[26] MT הזרע. The LXX reads εἰ ἔτι ἐπιγνωσθήσεται reading הודע for הזרע. The *BHS* suggests reading מגרע (a diminution) in place of הזרע or inserting גרע (cf. Sellin, Elliger, Horst (ni perf. 3 m. sg. of גרע "to be diminished."). Verhoef and Clark rightly reject this emendation as unnecessary.

[27] The versions and a majority of commentators correct עד (while, until) to עד (still, once again). Such a correction is certainly possible. Barthélemy (*Critique textuelle*, 3:933) proposes the retention of the MT, noting that עד ... לא is found with the meaning "still not" or "not even yet" in Job 25:5 and 2 Sam 17:22. Given that עוד is found elsewhere in Haggai in *plene scriptum* (2:6), that the MT bears the harder reading, and that the versions likely read עוד (which occurs a few lines above) for עד, I retain the MT.

the fig tree and the pomegranate and the olive tree still not yet yielded[28] fruit? From this day on, I will bless."

## 7.2. Structural and Literary Considerations

The third scene follows a structural progression similar to that of the first two. It begins with a formula of introduction (2:10) consisting of a dating formula following the order: month-year-day, followed by a Word-Event Formula (2:10b) as in 1:1 and 2:1. The absence of an epithet after the name of the king has no particular significance.[29] The dramatic conflict is presented in vv. 11–14. Similar to 1:2 a Messenger Formula opens the discussion of the conflict. Here, as in 2:2, the divine word is addressed to (אל) Haggai.[30] The prophet is explicitly commanded by Yahweh[31] to seek priestly opinion on a specific matter. By means of two polar questions,[32] and two priestly answers,[33] an analogy is drawn that serves as the basis for the oracle of judgment in v. 14.[34] At this juncture, the text moves from a narrative of the dialogue between Haggai and the priests, to the first person singular divine speech which continues until the end of the oracle (with the exception of the third person references to 'the house of Yahweh' in 2:15 and 18). The judgment concludes with a Divine-Saying Formula (v. 14 aβ).

---

[28] Singular verb with compound subject, cf. Joüon § 150q. The omission of the three trees mentioned before the olive tree is not necessary, *pace* Wolff, p. 59. Verhoef, Petersen, Wolff, Amsler, and Chary render נשא by the present, while Meyers and Meyers opt for the past. Both are grammatically and contextually possible (Joüon § 111c, GKC § 106g). A present translation fits best with my understanding of the meaning of the verse, cf. Verhoef, pp. 130–35.

[29] Wolff, p. 68.

[30] Cf. 2:2 where the prophet is commanded to speak (אמר), whereas he must ask שאל. There is no *Botenformel* in 2:1–2.

[31] The second question presupposes the repetition of the divine order of v. 11, cf. Amsler, p. 34, and *pace* Meyers and Meyers, pp. 56–57. Cf. 1:13 where the prophet speaks without any explicit command to do so.

[32] On the use of "polar" questions in priestly judgments, see Meyers and Meyers, p. 55.

[33] Floyd (p. 290) and Amsler (p. 34) observe the presence of a prophetic-symbolic act (*symbolische Handlung*) in this passage. On the form itself, cf. G. Fohrer, "Die Gattung der Berichte über symbolische Handlungen der Propheten", *ZAW* 64 (1952): 101–20; and idem, *Die symbolische Handlungen der Propheten*, (ATANT 25, 2nd. edtn., Zürich: Zwingli, 1968). *Pace* Amsler, the presence of such a form here does not undermine the literary unity of 2:10–19.

[34] This section of vv. 10–19 can therefore be classified as a report of a prophetic symbolic action, cf. Floyd, p. 294, with bibliography.

In this verse, כֵן is repeated three times (cf. the other threefold repetitions noted later on in this passage). In v. 15 the text moves to its next stage, consisting of exhortations[35] introduced again by וְעַתָּה. What follows is structured around three similar exhortations (שִׂים לֵב, vv. 15, 18, and 19). These exhortations call the community to reflect upon the marked difference between the past and the future. In vv. 15aβ-17 the prophet describes the period prior to the day when the oracle was pronounced, a date repeated three times in the passage, (vv. 15, 18, 19). At that time the effects of Yahweh's displeasure, (similar to the descriptions in 1:6, 9–11) were operative (vv. 16–17). This description reaches its climax in the statement that the misfortunes sent by Yahweh failed to have the desired effect of returning his people to him (v. 17b). A striking contrast is presented in vv. 18–19, where the future, characterized by divine blessing, is described in the form of a promise. The dividing line between past and future is the twenty-fourth day of the ninth month.[36] Everything has changed.

The third scene represents a logical development in the dramatic progression of the book. It presupposes that the problem encountered in 2:1–9 has been resolved. Construction is moving ahead, yet an obstacle still remains that the pericope in 2:10–19 will address and resolve. For this reason, 2:10–19 retains the same ambiance and polemical tone as 1:1–15. Several structural and linguistic resemblances exist between the two: the Messenger Formula immediately preceding the statement of the dramatic conflict; the phrase הָעָם־הַזֶּה with its polemical connotations, and the theme of futility and failure in 1:4, 6–9 and 2:15–17. The tone of this pericope, with its reproaches and condemnation, is somewhat surprising after the positive response of the people in 1:12–14 and the divine approbation in 2:6–9. This return to a more sober tone, however, reveals something of the thematic and literary structure of the book. Haggai alternates between oracles of reproach and comfort.[37] Consequently, on a structural level, 2:10–19 corresponds to 1:3–11, just as 2:1–9 corresponds to 2:20–23.[38]

---

[35] Floyd, (p. 295) classifies 15–19 as a prophetic exhortation.
[36] Meyers and Meyers, p. 65.
[37] Childs, *Introduction*, pp. 469–70; cf. Chary, pp. 12–13 and Stuhlmueller, p. 33.
[38] This will be taken up further in ch. 9.

## 7.3. EXEGESIS

**[10–14]** Verse 10, like 1:1 and 2:1, begins with a dating formula. The date in question in the twenty-fourth day of the ninth month, (Kislev), or Dec. 18, 520,[39] a date with no particular religious significance.[40] In the Word-Event Formula following the date, the word of Yahweh comes אל (to) Haggai instead of ביד (by the intermediary of, or through) Haggai, as in 1:1, 3; 2:1. Petersen sees the use of אל as evidence that the prophet speaks to a restricted audience.[41] It is difficult to see in what way the use of אל implies this and, what is more, in 2:14 and 15–19 the whole community is addressed. Thus, if there is a paradigmatic implication to the choice of the term,[42] it is there to underline that the prophet receives an order to speak to a third party, and that the action of the prophet and its results will serve as platform for the divine intervention that will follow.[43] Haggai is commanded to inquire of the priests who, according to Lev 10:10–11,[44] were required, under threat of divine censure, to provide a response (cf. Ezek 22:26). The response which Yahweh solicits from the priests is described as a תורה, a term which means a priestly judgment[45] on a question relative to cultic practices. The question is essentially one requiring a technical decision regarding the transmissibility of purity and impurity (cf. Lev 7:17–21). Petersen notes that normally the binary semantic oppositions are קדש and חל or טהור and טמא. Thus the juxtaposition of קדש (v. 11) and טמא (v. 12) is somewhat unusual. The four terms, however, can be understood as constituting the following continuum: טמא־חל־טהור־קדש (cf. Deut 14:2–3, 21).[46] Thus the two terms at the extreme ends of the continuum, קדש and טמא designate the most powerful forces and the only ones which are truly contagious, whereas the middle terms חל and טהור represent more neutral stages, which in themselves are not communicable.[47]

---

[39] Meyers and Meyers, p. 55.

[40] Amsler, p. 35. Amsler notes that the date is three months after the beginning of the work in 1:15.

[41] Petersen, p. 72.

[42] Ackroyd ("Studies", p. 69) sees none, cf. Beuken, pp. 65–66.

[43] Thus Wolff (pp. 68–69) and Amsler (p. 34) who both see a prophetic-symbolic act here.

[44] Petersen, p. 73, cf. Deut 33:10; Mic 3:11; Jer 18:18; and Ezek 7:26.

[45] Petersen, p. 73; Meyers and Meyers, p. 55.

[46] Petersen, p. 74.

[47] Ibid., pp. 74–76. On the subject in general cf. Jenson, *Graded Holiness*.

Haggai's first question concerns an instance when sacred meat, that is the flesh of an animal offered on the altar, is transported outside the sacred enclosure, carried within the fold of a garment.[48] The consumption of consecrated foodstuffs outside the temple was somewhat unusual, but was permissible in the case of peace offerings (שלמים cf. Lev 7:15–16).[49] The fundamental question put to the priests concerns involuntary and indirect contact[50] between the consecrated meat and other common foods. The question does not relate to the effect upon the foodstuff which is transported in the garment[51] but upon the foods with which the garment comes in contact: הלחם ואל־הנזיד ואל־היין ואל־ שמן (bread, vegetables, wine or oil) or כל־מאכל (any food) indicating the generality of his question. Will these things become consecrated or not? The priestly answer is negative, in conformity with the ruling of Lev 6:20 [Eng. 27] according to which contact must be direct to transmit holiness.[52]

The second question (v. 13) concerns the transmission of impurity.[53] The situation involves contact between a person made ritually impure by contact with a corpse,[54] and the same foodstuffs referred to in v. 12. The prophet asks whether they become unclean. The answer this time is affirmative.[55]

In v. 14 the priestly judgment serves as an analogical basis for an oracle of judgment. Here Yahweh himself declares:

---

[48] Did the garment become holy? According to Petersen (p. 78, n. 17) it remains neutral. J. Milgrom (*Leviticus 1–16*, [AB; New York: Doubleday, 1991], pp. 450–51) maintains that Lev 6:20 affirms that sacred foods can only transmit their sacred status to other foods.

[49] Meyers and Meyers, p. 55. Verhoef, p. 117.

[50] Amsler, p. 35.

[51] *Pace* Amsler, p. 35. Contact between the pure and the impure (cf. Lev 7:19) does indeed contaminate the former, but this is not at issue here.

[52] According to Milgrom (*Leviticus*, p. 450), objects, rather than people, are in view. Verhoef (p. 118) notes that the priests' response raises something of a problem, in that Ezek 44:19 appears to imply that the consecrated state is transmissible via the priestly garments. The priests' response in this case could indicate (1) the existence of a diversity of priestly opinion on the subject; (2) that the priestly response was primarily redactional, dramatic, and literary, and inserted simply to 'set up' the analogy of v. 14, or (3) that Ezek 44:19 was either unknown to these priests or regarded as a future and eschatological legislation.

[53] On this vast area cf. Milgrom, *Leviticus*, p. 641ff.

[54] Such is the meaning of טמא־נפש cf. Lev 21:6; Num 19:22.

[55] As Meyers and Meyers note, (p. 57) one way of indicating an affirmative answer is the simple repetition of the question. On contact with a corpse, cf. Milgrom, *Leviticus*, pp. 270–78.

כן העם־הזה וכן־הגוי הזה לפני נאם־יהוה וכן כל־מעשה
ידיהם ואשר יקריבו שם טמא הוא:

Several problems of interpretation are raised by this statement. At
this juncture I will examine the various elements of the verse, reserving
my broader conclusions for the end of this section. The adverb כן
which begins the oracle normally indicates a similarity with that which
precedes.[56] At significant issue here is whether the analogy introduced
by כן refers primarily to the existing state of impurity[57] or to the larger
motif, whereby one impure element contaminates others. A decision
on this point must be related to the broader meaning of the section
as a whole, and thus it will be discussed below. In either case it can
be affirmed that the centre of the comparison is ritual impurity, and its
implications for the people, the work of their hands and everything they
offer.

At this point it is essential to define these elements more closely. In
the phrase כן העם־הזה וכן־הגוי הזה (so is this people, and ... this nation)
the terms עם and גוי should be seen as designating the same community and reflecting the use of parallelism in this quasi-poetic oracle of
judgment.[58] Similar language has been used earlier (1:2) to designate
the community in Yehud. The most natural referent in 2:14 is therefore
the same group.[59] The people are said to be unclean לפני (before me, in
my sight). This term underlines the fact that the foundational problem
in the pericope is the state of affairs as it appears to and affects Yahweh. This is followed by the phrase כל־מעשה ידיהם (all the work of their
hands). While certain commentators have attempted to see an allusion
to the temple here, the most obvious contextual referent of the expression is its meaning in 2:18 where it designates the agricultural activities
of the community.[60] The phrase is used in the same way in Deut 14:29;
16:15; 24:19; 28:12, and 30:9.[61] The fruit of their labour is therefore
unclean. The third unclean element ואשר יקריבו שם טמא הוא (that which

[56] BDB, "כן".
[57] So Beuken (pp. 74–75) who affirms that the essential point of the analogy is the
impurity of the people, rather than process of the transmission of impurity described in
the two questions. Beuken's observations here are underlined by Verhoef, p. 119, n. 26.
[58] May, "This People", pp. 193–95.
[59] So Verhoef, pp. 119–20, Blenkinsopp, *History*, p. 201, and numerous other interpreters, see *infra*.
[60] Meyers and Meyers, pp. 57–58; Petersen, p. 83 *pace* Blenkinsopp, (*History*, p. 201)
who thinks an altar such as the one at Bethel may be meant.
[61] Once again the Deuteronomistic tone of the book is clearly evident.

they offer there) concerns that which is offered at a specific location. The verb קרב in the hiphil is frequently used for the presenting of sacrifices at the altar (Lev 1:5; 3:3–9 etc.). It is quite unnecessary, despite the arguments of those who see an allusion to Samaria in the adverb שָׁם (there), to assume that the prophet had any other site in mind than the altar in Jerusalem where such sacrifices were offered.[62] Here, as earlier in Haggai, the book seeks to project its readers/hearers into the actual physical circumstances in which the oracles were proclaimed.[63] The Jerusalem altar was presumably visible (or redactionally formulated so as to appear visible) to the hearers of the oracle. Furthermore, the expression לִפְנֵי often refers to the cultic context where Yahweh is present (Exod 16:9, 33, 34; Lev 1, 5, 11).[64] In sum, v. 14 describes the nature of the obstacle standing between Yahweh and his people. The people, the fruit of their economic undertakings, as well as that which they offer are all impure, and consequently, unacceptable to Yahweh. Since Yahweh is unable to receive the people's sacrifices, their intended function is not achieved. According to priestly understanding, such sacrifices make it possible for Yahweh to dwell with his people. As such, this impurity posed a very real threat to the presence of Yahweh with his people and, most especially, to his presence in the temple.

**[15–19]** The adverb וְעַתָּה, as in 1:5 and 2:4, introduces a new stage in the pericope,[65] that of the divine response to the dramatic conflict of vv. 10–14. Yahweh calls the community to consider their earlier situation (cf. 1:5b, 7b). However, in contrast to the two preceding exhortations, here the object of reflection is no longer the people's actions and their results. Rather, the community is called to reflect upon the *marked difference* between the situation which existed before the date of the proclamation of the oracle and the one which will obtain in the future. The oracle, in this sense, is essentially and primarily a promise of blessing. In this regard, Haggai's discourse is similar to those instances where signs are given whose significance is only recognizable subsequent to their fulfillment (cf. Exod 3:12; Isa 7:14; Ezek 7:4). Thus a full appreciation of what the prophet says will only be possible from a future vantage point. The phrase מִן־הַיּוֹם הַזֶּה וָמָעְלָה means "from

---

[62] Ackroyd, *Exile and Restoration*, pp. 25–31.

[63] Cf. 1:8, הָהָר (the [i.e., a specific] mountain), 2:3, עַתָּה אֹתוֹ רֹאִים אַתֶּם וּמַה (how do you see it now?), 2:3, 9; הַזֶּה הַבַּיִת (this house), 2:9 הַזֶּה וּבַמָּקוֹם (and in this place).

[64] Petersen, p. 83.

[65] וְעַתָּה here, as Verhoef notes, (p. 113) makes it unlikely that vv. 15–19 constitute a separate pericope.

this day on and in the future," notwithstanding the comments of Meyers and Meyers and the earlier exegetical tradition which, troubled by the negative descriptions that follow, attributed a retrospective meaning to מעלה. Its usual meaning of "above" or "moving onward" in space or time (1 Sam 16:13; 30:25), as well as its significance in v. 18, make such an approach difficult. The phrase that follows poses a rhetorical question concerning the community's situation prior to the day of the proclamation of the oracle (היום הזה, v. 15aβ). The prophet asks, " in what state were you (מי־הייתם) before stone was laid upon stone in the temple of Yahweh (מטרם שום־אבן אל־אבן בהיכל יהוה?)." The preposition מטרם (before) thus introduces a retrospective parenthesis into the prophet's exhortation to the community to consider its present and future experience (2: 15–19).[66] The allusion to "stone upon stone" (2: 15b) refers to some decisive step in the temple's reconstruction.[67] Various suggestions have been made regarding the nature of this step. Meyers and Meyers suggest that it was related to a stage of the construction undertaken subsequent to the laying of the foundations.[68] I view שום־אבן אל־אבן as parallel to the phrase היום אשר־יסד היכל־יהוה in v. 18,[69] and see both phrases as referring to a step of a more ritual and ceremonial nature that enabled the community to enter into a new phase in its relationship with the deity. The nature of that ritual undertaking will be discussed below.

Having asked how the people fared before the day in question, Haggai provides the response in the form of several descriptions, similar to those of 1:5–7, 9–11. Verse 16 presents two instances of disappointing results: the wheat harvest and wine production.[70] Verse 17 moves from the perspective of the average citizen to that of Yahweh, the

---

[66] Cf. the textual criticism, *supra*.

[67] Cf. Amsler, p. 27. Amsler accurately perceives that a decisive step is being referred to here. Nevertheless he sees the reference here as being to the beginning of the reconstruction alluded to in 1:12–15. Sensing the incongruity of a prophetic invective on the subject three months after the work had begun, he separates 2:15–19 from 2:10–14 and places it after 1:15b. If, however, 2:10–19 is about something other than the beginning of the reconstruction activity, the transposition loses its rationale.

[68] Meyers and Meyers (p. 59) suggest masonry work.

[69] Floyd (p. 289) sees the former phrase as referring to the resumption of work on the temple, and the latter to the refoundation ceremony. The suggestion is possible, however as Petersen argues (p. 88), it is likely that both phrases refer to the refoundation ceremony.

[70] For specific details regarding harvesting and wine production, cf. Clark, "Problems" pp. 433–34.

one who caused such infelicitous results. A similar shift of perspective
has already appeared in 1:11. In 2:17 Yahweh strikes[71] his people with
plagues (blight, mildew and hail) in the area of their principal economic
activities (את כל־מעשׂה ידיכם, cf. v. 14).[72] Once again the text moves
in the same Deuteronomistic atmosphere as in 1:3–11 (cf. Deut 28:22;
Amos 4:9).[73] As was the case in Amos 4:9, which this text appears to
echo, Yahweh's attempts to bring back the community to himself were
unfruitful. The divine verdict is an acknowledgment of failure:[74] ואין־
אתכם אלי (you did not come back to me).[75] Thus, the parenthesis of vv.
15b–17 describes the state of alienation which existed prior to the day
upon which the oracle was proclaimed.

In v. 18 the repetition שׂימו־נא לבבכם (which frames vv. 15–18) brings
the hearers back to the point of departure, and once again calls them
to reflect upon what they have experienced in the past and what the
future will hold for them. This call to reflection is immediately followed
by several further clarifications regarding the critical importance of the
day in question. The date and the formula מן־היום הזה ומעלה (cf. v. 15)
are repeated. The prophet then describes the crucial event which transpired on that day by means of the qualification אשׁר־יסד היכל־יהוה.[76]
What is the meaning of this phrase which stands parallel to מטרם שׂום־
אבן אל־אבן בהיכל יהוה (v. 15)? The translation of the pual of יסד in 2:18
is critical. The verb frequently means "to lay a foundation." However
in 2 Chr 24:27[77] and 31:7 the reference is to the restoration or rededication of a damaged building.[78] Given the relative chronological position
of the oracle as following the resumption of the work in 1:12–15 and its
continuation in 2:1–9, this sense of rededication or reconsecration fits

---

[71] נכה with Yahweh as subject and Israel as object occurs in the Deuteronomistic
tradition, cf. 1 Kgs 14:15; Jer 2:30; 21:6.

[72] Here, I follow the suggestion of Meyers and Meyers (p. 62) that the verse is chiastic
in structure, with the second occurrence of the verb נכה being elided for the purposes
of stressing the first and second person personal pronouns and the marked contrast
between the second stich and 1:13b, אני אתכם נאם־יהוה; cf. Prokurat, *Haggai*, p. 154.

[73] Meyers and Meyers, p. 61.

[74] This prophetic declaration of failure will serve to highlight the striking success of
the Haggai later in the pericope.

[75] On the various translational and text critical issues here, cf. the textual criticism,
*supra*.

[76] אשׁר having here a temporal sense, BDB 1, 4, b.

[77] Here the form is the noun יסוד.

[78] Hence my translation "refounded"; cf. Baldwin, pp. 52–53; Meyers and Meyers,
p. 63; Andersen, "Second Temple", pp. 1–35, esp. pp. 21–27; Gelston, "Foundations",
pp. 232–35.

well in Hag 2:17. Thus, the most likely understanding of the phrase is that of a ritual of rededication, similar to those found in certain Babylonian and Seleucid sources[79] known as a *kalu* ceremony. This ritual consisted of the removal of a brick or stone from a destroyed temple or building and its placement in the foundations of a new structure. The primary goal of such a ceremony in the Mesopotamian texts appears to have been to establish continuity between the old and new temples.[80] Given the mention of the impurity in v. 14, one would assume that the rite also had a purificatory function.[81] Allusions to the same ceremony may also be discernible in Zech 4:6–7, 8–10, and 8:9.[82] Because of its clearly cultic (rather than architectural) nature, a certain degree of flexibility was possible regarding the timing of this ritual activity. It is entirely likely that, if what is in view is the ritual laying of a brick or stone,[83] it was necessary for the reconstruction to have reached a certain stage before such a ceremony could be performed. Furthermore, a reference to a procedure associated with the building of the temple after a pericope that presupposes the ongoing process of reconstruction (2:1–9) does not appear to trouble the compiler of the book. Thus in light of philological, literary, and historical evidence, it is best to view the event of the twenty-fourth day of the ninth month, not as the laying of the temple's foundations, but as a ritual act establishing continuity and purification. The prophet's exhortation to take special note of this highly significant day demonstrates its unique status in the progress of the Judaean community.[84]

The prophet then moves to a promise concerning the future. This turning point is marked by a change of tone and tense in v. 19. The

---

[79] Meyers and Meyers, pp. 63–64; B. Halpern, "The Ritual Background of Zechariah's Temple Song", *CBQ* 40 (1978): 171–72; Petersen, p. 320 as well as his earlier article, "Jerusalem Temple", pp. 366–72, esp. p. 368; cf. R. Ellis, *Foundation Deposits in Ancient Mesopotamia*, (Yale Near Eastern Researches 2; New Haven: Yale University Press, 1968).

[80] So Petersen, "Jerusalem Temple", pp. 368–69, drawing extensively on Ellis, *Foundation Deposits*, esp. p. 29.

[81] Petersen (p. 93) states, "It was a day on which the site was ritually purified and thus became once again functional holy space."

[82] Cf. A. Petitjean, *Les oracles du proto-Zacharie. Un programme de restauration pour la communauté juive après l'exil*, (EtB Paris/Louvain: Gabalda/Imprimerie Orientaliste, 1969), pp. 241–51. Meyers and Meyers (p. 64) note the clear similarities which exist between Hag 2:18 and Zech 8:9. They note especially that only in the latter text are יסד and בנה (ni) brought together.

[83] Ibid., pp. 368–69; cf. E. Lipiński, "Recherches sur le livre de Zacharie", *VT* 20 (1970): 30–53, esp. pp. 30–33.

[84] As Amsler (p. 27) has noted.

verse begins with a series of two questions whose precise meaning is
bound up with the ecological conditions and agricultural practices of
the time. As Clark points out, the first half of the verse should be
interpreted in light of the clear and unambiguous affirmation of its
latter part. There, the prophet declares that from that day onward the
community will experience the renewed blessing of Yahweh.[85] The two
questions most likely relate to the fertility of the land.[86] According to
Clark, these questions call for a negative response. Thus the absence
of seed from the barns (presumably because it has been sown), and
the fact that neither vine, fig tree, pomegranate, nor olive tree[87] have
yet yielded fruit (since mid-December would be far too early even for
blossoms)[88] serve as indications that there is nothing in the present state
of affairs which precludes the imminent arrival of Yahweh's promised
blessings. Seeds may soon sprout and trees may soon bear fruit. It is
important to note that the linking of a *kalu* or refoundation ceremony
and the fertility of the land is a theme found widely in the ancient Near
East.[89] J. Bewer pointed out the similarities between Hag 2 and the
temple hymns of Gudea. The latter texts associate temple refoundation
with abundance of agricultural produce, water, oil, and wool.[90]

The thrust of 2:10–19 is that, prior to the date of the oracle's proclamation, the people, the work of their hands, and their offerings were
contaminated. This created a state of alienation, and consequently,
Yahweh's blessings were withheld. However, from that day onward, as
a result of the decisive step which had been taken, all would change
and blessing would ensue.

The contextual significance of this pericope is bound up with a variety of hermeneutical issues, with an understanding of the relationship
of the priestly instruction to the historical situation, and with the meaning attributed to the impurity in the passage. In Rothstein's view, the
various details of Haggai's question and the priests' response had to
do with the inclusion of the Samaritans in the temple's reconstruction

---

[85] Clark, "Problems", p. 436.

[86] Ibid., p. 439; Petersen, "Jerusalem Temple", p. 369.

[87] Petersen (p. 94) notes that these plants were economically significant as well as
symbolizing the abundance of the land.

[88] This is the understanding of v. 19 proposed by Verhoef (pp. 134–35) at the end of
his careful analysis of the issues in the passage. Even if the meaning and responses are
understood differently, the outcome remains clear: from now on Yahweh will bless.

[89] Petersen, "Jerusalem Temple", p. 369.

[90] J. A. Bewer, "Ancient Babylonian Parallels to the Prophecies of Haggai", *AJSLL*
35 (1919): 128–33.

and worship.[91] Both literary and historical considerations render such
an approach highly unlikely.[92] If such was the intent of the analogy, it is
difficult to explain why it is not explicitly stated.[93] Similarly, the hypothesis proposed by Meyers and Meyers that the prophet responds to a
practical question posed by the people regarding cultic purity,[94] seems
ill suited to the context. It is certainly true that in 520 an altar existed,
that sacrifices were offered there, and that such a question would not
have been impossible. However, in this pericope the initiative for the
questions comes from Yahweh (as in 1:9–10 and 2:1–3) and serves as
a basis for an application broader than specific details regarding the
transportation of consecrated foods. The alleged parallel in Zech 7,
though frequently mentioned, differs significantly from Hag 2:10–19 at
this key point.

An exegesis of the passage that views ritual purity as a metaphor for
ethical integrity has been proposed by commentators both ancient and
modern.[95] Thus the impurity of the people is due to their moral las-
situde, manifested either in neglect of the temple[96] or an attitude that
stressed ritual and neglected obedience.[97] The uncleanness in view in
2:14 would be due to ethical breaches of covenant such as those enu-
merated in Ps 15 and 24. Ackroyd sees the LXX gloss, which may well
represent the most primitive interpretation of the passage, as proof.[98]
Chary seems to have changed his position. Advocating a rather cultic position in 1956,[99] he later affirmed that indifference and lack of

---

[91] Cf. Rothstein, *Juden und Samaritaner*, passim.

[92] Chary (p. 31) notes, "The comparison falls flat. … Furthermore Rothstein himself
senses this difficulty and insists that one should not press the comparison too tightly, lest
one fall into 'inextricable difficulties' (*Juden*, p. 36, n. 1). This admission undermines his
entire position."

[93] Verhoef, p. 114, Baldwin, p. 51.

[94] Meyers and Meyers, p. 56. Stuhlmueller (p. 35) takes a similar approach. He
maintains that Haggai is here demonstrating a new prophetic approach by referring
a question on ritual purity to the priests, something quite unusual for a prophet to do.
But this assumes that Haggai is asking the question because he or someone else requires
an answer to a practical problem, a notion which is absent from the text.

[95] Amsler (p. 36) includes the following: Calvin, van Hoonacker, Mitchell, Chary,
Ackroyd, May, and Townsend. Cf. more recently D. R. Hildebrand, "Temple Ritual: A
Paradigm for Moral Holiness in Haggai II 10–19", *VT* 18 (1989): 154–68.

[96] Verhoef, p. 120; Chary, p. 32.

[97] Amsler, p. 37; Ackroyd, *Exile and Restoration*, pp. 166–69, idem, "Studies", pp. 5–6;
idem, "Interpretative Glosses", pp. 166–67.

[98] Ackroyd, "Interpretative Glosses", p. 169.

[99] Chary, *Prophètes et Culte*, pp. 137–38.

faith had seized the people.[100] May holds a similar position, maintaining that the people were unclean, in a metaphorical way, because
of their neglect and *laissez-faire* regarding the rebuilding project then
underway.[101] The phrase ואין־אתכם אלי could also be marshalled in
support of this position due to its use with reference to non-cultic
covenant violations in Amos 4:9. The chief obstacle to this approach
is that the root problem in the pericope appears to be the ritual impurity, and there is no indication that such impurity is to be taken as a
metaphor for something else. There is no textual data, apart from the
later gloss, that wrong doing of an ethical order is the cause of the
uncleanness. Neglect of the reconstruction should be ruled out since
that problem was resolved in 1:12–14 and there is no evidence of its
reappearance. Most importantly, if the fault were essentially ethical,
how could the prophet have declared that from that specific date blessing would certainly follow, since this would imply a knowledge that the
moral life of the people had been sufficiently transformed? It is therefore quite difficult to exclude the whole cultic referent from the pericope.[102]

Mason adds an eschatological element to the ethical interpretation of
the passage.[103] He suggests that the expression "the work of their hands"
in 2:14 refers to the temple, and that the goal of the discourse is to
underline that only the eschatological presence of Yahweh in his temple
will fill the edifice with glory. "The people have no capability for self-
regeneration, certainly not by the frenzy of their activity. It is God alone
who can renew them, and who, by His presence in the Temple, will do
so."[104] However this position is problematic. First, an allusion to the
temple as the "work of their hands" is difficult to maintain.[105] Second,
while the oracles of 2:6–9 and 20–23 are deeply eschatological, in 2:10–
19 (as in 1:3–11) eschatological blessings are not primarily in view. Just
as the community experienced failure in its daily economic activities
as a result of its alienation from Yahweh, it will now experience the

---

[100] Chary, pp. 32–33.
[101] May, "This People", pp. 194–95.
[102] Chary comments, (*Prophètes et culte*, p. 137), "In all the numerous occurrences of
*teme'* [sic] either in a verbal or an adjectival form (more than 200x) not once is the word
to be taken in anything other than a cultic or ritual sense."
[103] Mason, "Prophets of the Restoration", p. 144.
[104] Ibid., p. 144.
[105] Petersen, pp. 82–83.

reverse.[106] The seed sown, the vine, the olive tree and the pomegranate will yield a favourable harvest (v. 19). The prophet clearly differentiates the near future from the eschatological era. Third, Mason's approach does not seem to square with certain aspects of the text. It seems unlikely that the contaminating ritual impurity of the passage refers to frenetic human activity. What is more, it is hard to see any frenzy in the activities of the community as portrayed in the text.

A more promising approach begins by understanding Haggai's questions to the priests as a "prophetic-symbolic action."[107] The prophet conveys his message through an act whose goal is to baffle the hearers and thereby stimulate their curiosity. This technique occurs frequently in Jeremiah[108] and Ezekiel.[109] The questions of vv. 12–13 serve primarily as a platform from which to launch the prophetic denunciation of v. 14. This is the conclusion of the majority of commentators, whatever their methodological approach to the passage.[110]

If then the point of the prophetic-symbolic act is related to ritual defilement, it remains to be seen who is described as defiled, and why. With May, Meyers and Meyers, Petersen, Mason, Amsler, van Hoonacker, Chary, and Mitchell, I reject the hypothesis that the impurity of the people is caused by their inclusion of non-Judaean Yahwists in the construction and worship of the Jerusalem temple. Hag 2:14–17 describes the state of alienation which has existed between Yahweh and the community in Yehud. The phrase העם־הזה וכן־הגוי הזה (this people and this nation), despite the objections of Amsler, Petersen, Cody, and Koch,[111] does carry a negative nuance in this context. Arguments to the effect that Haggai frequently uses the demonstrative pronoun, and that the term גוי is not necessarily pejorative when it refers to Israel, are

---

[106] As A. Caquot, ("Le judaïsme depuis la captivité de Babylone jusqu' à la révolte de Bar-Kokheba", in *Encyclopédie de la Pléiade: Histoire des Religions, vol. 2*, [ed. H.-C. Puech, Paris: Gallimard, 1972], p. 130) notes. Few commentators note this important distinction in Haggai.

[107] Floyd p. 290; Amsler, p. 34; Wolff, p. 68; cf. G. Fohrer, *Symbolischen Handlungen*; and idem, "Berichte über symbolische Handlungen", *passim*. Cf. also K. G. Friebel, *Jeremiah's and Ezekiel's Sign Acts*, (JSOTSup 283; Sheffield: Sheffield Academic Press, 1999).

[108] For example Jer 13:1–4; 19:1–13; 27:1–15.

[109] For example Ezek 5:1–17; 24:15–24.

[110] Floyd, (p. 290) comments, "The symbolic nature of the request is evident from the way in which the prophet does not pursue the priestly ruling as an end in itself, but rather uses it as the basis for an analogy." Cf. Meyers and Meyers, p. 79.

[111] Amsler, p. 37; Petersen, pp. 80–81; Cody, "Chosen People", pp. 1–7; Koch "Haggais", p. 65.

unpersuasive. On the contrary, הזה־העם constitutes a term of reproach in 1:2 and is so used elsewhere in the prophetic tradition (cf. Isa 6:9–10; 8:6; Jer 6:19, 21; 7:16; 13:10; 14:10–11).[112] As for Haggai's frequent use of the demonstrative, it is essential to note that the nuance of the demonstrative pronoun can vary enormously according to its antecedent, and thus may have both pejorative and non-pejorative connotations in the book. In this passage Yahweh cannot accept the sacrifices offered to him, due to their uncleanness. A similar theme is found in the prophetic denunciations of hypocritical cult practices such as Hos 8:13; Amos 4:4–6; Zech 7:4–7; Mal 1:6–14. In these texts the expectation of the one who offers the sacrifice is juxtaposed with Yahweh's refusal to accept that which is offered. As in 1:4–11, in 2:17, it is clear that the community's misfortunes, which in the context of 2:10–20 must be linked to the question of defilement, were intended by Yahweh to cause his people to return to him.

Seeing 2:10–19 as reflecting a state of alienation, however, leads to a further question: how can the prophet announce that the people have been under judgment, but have moved inexorably from an era of misfortune to one of blessing? The resolution of this difficulty lies in the determination of the nature of the community's fault and the grounds of the prophet's reproach. This is especially important in light of Yahweh's promise to accept the community's work on the temple in 1:8, the narrative approbation of the people's response to Yahweh's stirring in 1:12–15, the assurances of Yahweh's presence in 2:4–5, and the hope of the glorious future of the temple in 2:6–9. Those who see the problem as essentially cultic or ritual in nature follow several lines of approach. For Mowinckel, Hammershaimb, and Welch the problem was that Haggai deemed the altar which was being used to be unacceptable.[113] In 1956 Chary maintained that the oracle concerned the non-exiled population, who had used a temporary altar during the exile and who, later on, did not want to abandon their practices in favour of the approved altar of the temple.[114] Blenkinsopp sees a reference to the Bethel altar, and by extension, to syncretistic worship.[115] For Amsler, the issue is the antagonism or indifference of certain priests

---

[112] May, "This People", p. 193.
[113] Opinions cited in Ackroyd, *Exile and Restoration*, p. 168, n. 73.
[114] Chary, *Prophètes et culte*, p. 137.
[115] Blenkinsopp, *History*, p. 201.

who took an unfavourable view of the construction project.[116] However,
to speak of an illegitimate altar or a priestly rejection of the new temple
seems ill suited to v. 14, which deems three things to be unclean: the
people, the fruit of their economic activities, and that which they offer
at a specific location (most likely the official altar of Jerusalem). What
is at issue, therefore, is the ritual impurity of the whole community in
every aspect of its experience, not one unacceptable altar. Furthermore,
v. 14 betrays no movement of impurity from the altar to the community,
as one would expect if a single element were in view. Petersen, who
has well perceived the necessity of the cultic position,[117] affirms that the
main problem is the source of the ritual impurity, namely the temple
enclosure and altar. The people and their offerings, since they were
not impure in themselves, were contaminated by contact.[118] However
this again seems inadequate because of its *a priori* assumption that only
the altar and the temple were unclean. This stands in contrast to v.
14 which makes no distinction between the people, their agricultural
activities and their offerings. Everything is unclean!

It is noteworthy that a similar view of the pervasiveness of impurity
is also found in Ezekiel. Such traditions were assembled and preserved
by the *golah* during the exile,[119] and as such possessed, at least for a
portion of the community of early Persian Yehud, an important value.
In these traditions, the people themselves were unclean (Ezek 22:3–4,
23:7). This impurity was the result of a variety of practices including
idolatry (Ezek 20:43; 22:4; 23:7, 13, 20), proscribed political alliances
(Ezek 23:7, 13, 17, 20), the shedding of blood (Ezek 9:7–9; 20:26) as well
as murder, oppression, incest, rape, and adultery (Ezek 22:6–16; 23:36–
39; 33:23–26). As well, the temple was unclean (Ezek 6:4–5; 9:7) because
of blood and injustice.[120] The sanctuary was profaned by the idolatry of
the people (Ezek 5:11). The altar, by implication, is also unclean (Ezek
43:13–26). Even the land was unclean because of blood and idolatry
(Ezek 36:17–18). Thus both Hag 2:14 and Ezekiel see the question of

---

[116] Amsler, p. 37.

[117] Petersen, pp. 82–85.

[118] Ibid., pp. 84–85.

[119] On this vast area cf. the survey in J. F. Fager, *Land Tenure and the Biblical Jubilee:
Uncovering Hebrew Ethics through the Sociology of Knowledge*, (JSOTSup 155, Sheffield: JSOT
Press, 1993), pp. 64–81, with bibliography.

[120] Whatever the origin of this material (cf. W. Zimmerli, *Ezekiel: A Commentary on the
Book of Ezekiel*, vol. 1, [trans. R. Clements; Hermeneia, Philadelphia: Fortress, 1979],
pp. 248–49) it still is evidence of an exilic interpretation of the issue.

impurity as a far-reaching problem that jeopardized Yahweh's dwelling in the land. It is difficult to determine, however, whether Haggai sees this impurity as a result of the earlier defilement mentioned in Ezekiel. The text does not describe its source.[121]

What is certain, however, is that Hag 2:15–19 views the actions taken on the day of the oracle as providing the solution for the impurity of v. 14. Thus, in a way that the text does not precisely define, the impurity affecting the totality of the community is remedied by the ceremonial purification of the temple and the restoration of the continuity between the destroyed temple and the rebuilt one. As noted above, v. 18 most likely refers to an Israelite version of a *kalu* or refoundation ceremony.[122] Viewed in this light, 2:10–19 can be seen as a *thematic and parallel restatement* of 1:2–11,[123] but one that focuses on a different resolution. In 1:2–11 the essential problem was the community's willful refusal to rebuild the temple, even though circumstances permitted them to construct adequate housing for themselves. The problem is resolved when, by means of prophetic speech, Yahweh stirs them to action. In 2:10–19, the essential problem is that Yahweh cannot dwell among his people since no requisite purification had been made to permit such dwelling, nor has continuity been established with the earlier structure. This is remedied when the temple is ceremonially purified and "reconnected" with its earlier counterpart. From this moment, says the prophet, things will be very different.

It may be possible to explain the text's insistence on this transformation from two perspectives. First, from the point of view of the community in 520, it probably seemed as if very little had changed in the few months since the work had begun. Certainly not enough time had passed for any great agricultural successes to have been achieved. Perhaps commercial activities fared no better. Thus the prophet once again depicts the past as dark. This darkness, he announces, will finally give

---

[121] In my earlier work ("Le livre d'Aggée", pp. 353–55) I argued that the primary purpose of the pericope and the refoundation ceremony was to deal with the lingering impurity of the past. While this may be true, it is not an idea which is explicitly developed in the text, although it may be implied. In a sense, similar to the techniques of generalization and focalization noted in 2:1–9, the nature and source of the defilement may have been deliberately downplayed, and the fact of its removal highlighted.

[122] So Petersen (pp. 89–93) following the work of Halpern and Ellis.

[123] This explains, at least in part, 2:17 where Yahweh seeks to cause the people to return to him. 2:17 should be viewed as referring both to the time before reconstruction is begun, as well as to the time prior to the temple's refoundation. Such reconstruction was necessary prior to the refoundation ceremony here.

way because of the refoundation ceremony, which would open the way for further blessing.

The fact that 2:10–19 is set on the day of the refoundation ceremony raises the question of the relationship between the events narrated in the text and the ceremony itself. If Haggai's words were declared publicly at the time of the event, their import would have been clear and straightforward. As such 2:15–19, and especially v. 19, would have had a *declarative* value. Yahweh would thus declare that the ceremony had fulfilled its purpose and that blessing would soon follow. Within the context of the ceremony, the questions to the priests should therefore be understood as a form of dramatic dialogue enacted before those present.[124] Thus before the assembled people, the prophet evokes the need for purification (2:10–14). He continues by describing the consequences of this situation, of which they were aware and which they were gathered to correct (2:15–17). The point of the oracle then, is not so much to *convict* the nation of its need for purification, but to *affirm*, as the prophet does in vv. 18–19, that the ceremony then in progress will accomplish the purpose for which it is being enacted. Put another way, the text is not stressing the community's refusal to undertake the refoundation ceremony, but rather the benefits which will now accrue. Thus our prophet can assert without hesitation or doubt that, as a result of the temple's purification, Yahweh will usher in a period of blessing and abundance (2:18–19).

From a second perspective, it may be that for the redactor and his community, living some few years later, things were not that much better. If the redaction of Haggai is to be associated with the temple's rededication in 515, then perhaps this pericope sought to link the rededication with the earlier refoundation ceremony and to hold before the readers and hearers of the text the hope that the promised blessings would soon arrive.

---

[124] Thus the *symbolische Handlung* could be seen as a dramatic presentation in the context of the refoundation ceremony, stressing its critical importance. Certain commentators have come close to this suggestion, but without seeing 2:10–14 as a part of the ceremony. Meyers and Meyers (p. 77) sensing the dramatic ambiance in 2:11–14, state, "The situation portrayed in this dialogue may be staged, in the way that prophetic actions in general are contrived for symbolic purposes. ... Yet any artificiality that may adhere to a staged scene is offset by the dialogic mode. The direct speech of the human characters creates for the audience a sense of the reality of the issues that are being examined." Floyd has sensed this dramatic component as well. He speaks of Haggai's "dramatic interaction with the priests" (p. 258) and calls prophetic-symbolic acts "guerrilla theater" (p. 295).

Finally, it is important to consider the broader significance of the refoundation ceremony and the blessing pronounced. Given the prophet's (and the redactor's) attachment to Deuteronomistic traditions already in evidence in the book, it is licit to assume that the refoundation ceremony here is not to be viewed in abstraction from the broader values and demands of that tradition. Thus, like the commitment of 1:12–14, this ceremony implies a desire to be purified from the past and to renew a relationship to Yahweh. It is at this point that the more "ethical" aspect of Haggai's words may be legitimately introduced.

## 7.4. RHETORICAL AND HERMENEUTICAL USE OF RELIGIOUS TRADITIONS

In this pericope, Haggai draws his phrases and concepts from several traditions: priestly theology (vv. 12–14), Deuteronomism (vv. 14, 16–18) and wisdom (vv. 16, 17). Furthermore, the priestly traditions as used in Haggai appear to hold a significant level of authority.[125] These diverse traditions are interwoven in the text. In contrast to 1:2–11 and 2:6–9, the prophet does not use these traditions in a highly novel way in this pericope. Nevertheless, the use of priestly traditions here is noteworthy. The judgment of v. 14 is not a simple application of priestly requirements. Rather, the reasoning is analogical. What is true concerning the sacred foodstuffs is applied *a fortiori* to the people of Yahweh and their undertakings. It is significant that a cultic code of priestly norms is presupposed. Haggai first approaches these traditions in a "literal" way, then subsequently draws an analogous secondary axiom from them. In this sense, it may be legitimate to view the hermeneutical approach in this pericope as a precursor of certain later hermeneutical techniques, such as *qal wahomer* and *gezerah shawah*.[126]

---

[125] Ibid., pp. 78–79.
[126] R. N. Longenecker, *Biblical Exegesis in the Apostolic Period*, (Grand Rapids: Eerdmans, 1975), p. 34.

# CHAPTER EIGHT

# HAGGAI 2:20–23

## 8.1. Translation and Textual Criticism

[20] The word of Yahweh came a second time to Haggai on the twenty-fourth day of the month, as follows:

[21] "Say to Zerubbabel,[1] governor of Judah, 'I am about to shake[2] the heavens and the earth.[3]

[22] "'I will overthrow the throne[s] of the kingdoms.[4] I will destroy the strength of the kingdoms[5] of the nations. I will overthrow chariots and charioteers.[6] Horses and their riders will fall, every man by the sword of his fellow.[7]

[23] "'On that day—oracle of Yahweh Sebaoth[8]—I will take you Zerubbabel, son of Shealtiel, my servant,[9]—oracle of Yahweh Sebaoth—and I will make you like a signet ring, for I have chosen you—oracle of Yahweh Sebaoth.'"

---

[1] The LXX adds τὸν τοῦ Σαλαθιηλ (son of Shealtiel).

[2] Again, as in 2:6 a *futurum instans* is employed, GKC § 116p.

[3] The LXX adds καὶ τὴν θάλασσαν καὶ τὴν ξηράν cf. 2:6.

[4] The sg. כסא (throne) should be translated as a pl. (GKC § 124r) and thus ought not to be taken as a specific reference to the Persian rule. The LXX βασιλέων (kings) reflects no known Hebrew MS. It is possible that the *iota* in βασιλείων (kingdoms) has been lost or that the Greek translator put βασιλεύς for βασιλεία by metonymy or synecdoche. It is therefore unnecessary to correct the MT, as does the NEB.

[5] The *BHS* suggests the omission of the second ממלכות as a gloss, cf. Mitchell, Elliger, Chary, and Wolff. Budde, Duhm and Sellin emend ממלכות to המלכים (Barthélemy, *Critique textuelle*, 3:933). Nevertheless the word is present in Mur. Even though the omission of the word *metri causa*, gives a more symmetrical reading, there is no MS evidence to support it.

[6] The LXX^A adds καὶ καταστρέψω πᾶσαν τὴν δύναμιν αὐτῶν καὶ καταβαλῶ τὰ ὅρια αὐτῶν καὶ ἐνισχύσω τοὺς ἐκλεκτούς μου ("I will overthrow all their power, I will bring down their borders, and I will strengthen my chosen ones"; Petersen's translation, p. 97).

[7] The *BHS* suggests that these words are a gloss, inspired by Ezek 38:21. Nevertheless the MT is to be retained.

[8] The *BHS* considers the occurrence of the Messenger Formula as secondary. However repetitions are frequent in Haggai.

[9] Still a vocative, in apposition to Zerubbabel; cf. Wolff, p. 98.

## 8.2. STRUCTURAL AND LITERARY CONSIDERATIONS

The structure of the fourth scene is quite simple. It opens with an introductory formula (vv. 20–21a), which, as in the third scene, begins with a Word-Event Formula followed by אל (2:20a), in contrast to the first two scenes where ביד occurs. The use of אל here reflects the fact that the word is addressed first to Haggai and will later be conveyed to Zerubbabel (cf. 2:1).[10] Here, in contrast to the preceding pericopae, the dating formula follows the Word-Event Formula. If this inversion reflects a redactional theological concern, it would be to link the two oracles pronounced on the same day.[11] However a simple stylistic variation may provide a sufficient explanation. The presence of the adverb שנית (a second time) may have influenced the placement of the Word-Event Formula at the head of the phrase. The absence of a title for Haggai, as in the preceding scene, does not carry any significant redactional nuance.[12] This is followed by a date formula including only the day (the month and year being supplied in 2:10, as indicated by שנית). The introductory formula concludes with a divine command to Haggai to speak to Zerubbabel, who is mentioned here without patronymic (as contrasted with 1:1, 12; 2:2 and 23 but as in 2:4) but with his official title (2:21a, as in 1:1, 14; 2:2, but in contrast to 1:12 and 2:4 and 23). The oracle to Zerubbabel contains an implied dramatic conflict, relating to the disparity between the reality of Yehud's subjection to Persian rule, and the grandiose promises found in Israelite traditions regarding its place in the world of nations, the role of the Davidic dynasty, and the universal recognition of Israel's deity.[13] This theme of disequilibrium was already introduced in 2:6–9 where the treasures of the world, scattered among the nations, were seen as returning to the house of Yahweh. A similar notion is reintroduced in v. 22 where the Gentile powers will be reduced, and v. 23 where the Davidide Zerubbabel is exalted. This dramatic conflict is addressed in 2:21b-23 through the oracle to Zerubbabel which, from a rhetorical perspective, is both a call to encouragement in

---

[10] Westermann, *Basic Forms*, pp. 98f.

[11] Beuken, pp. 78–79.

[12] Even Wolff (p. 77) deems these minor variations to be insignificant with reference to the book's redactional history.

[13] *Pace* Rothstein who sees this oracle as having been engendered by the opposition Zerubbabel experienced due to his exclusion of the Samaritans (so Verhoef, p. 142, n. 8).

the present (as in 2:4) as well as a promise for the future (as in 2:6–9). The oracle has a poetic and rhythmic structure.[14] We note in it a tripartite progression toward the centre of interest: (1) the upheaval of nature (v. 21b), (2) the humbling of the nations (v. 22), and (3) the future exaltation of Zerubbabel, Yahweh's chosen servant.[15] The verbal structure of vv. 21b-23 is as follows: *futurum instans* (participle) followed by four verbs with *waw* consecutive plus the perfect. As in v. 7, the action of the perfect verbs is to be understood as subsequent to the action expressed by the participle in v. 21b. However in contrast to 2:7, these verbs express four simultaneous actions rather than successive ones. The meaning of the verbs and the repetition of הפך makes this clear. The four ideas thus described occupy two parallel stichoi. The first describes the *effect* of the divine intervention, namely the global reduction of the power of the nations (v. 22a). The second stich views *the means* by which this result is obtained: a conflagration whose outcome is the destruction of all foreign armies (v. 22b). But in the final analysis, v. 22 simply sets the stage for the oracle's centre of interest: the elevation of the Davidide Zerubbabel (v. 23).[16] The verse begins with the adverbial temporal phrase ביום ההוא (v. 23aα) and a Divine-Saying Formula. A principal clause follows, made up of an imperfect followed by a *waw* consecutive with perfect. Zerubbabel is directly addressed. His patronymic[17] is included but in place of his official title he is called Yahweh's servant. Another Divine-Saying Formula follows. A causal clause introduced by כי gives the reason for the Zerubbabel's future exaltation. Another Divine-Saying Formula concludes the oracle. Such a high frequency of this formula is matched only in 2:4.[18]

---

[14] Wolff, p. 99.

[15] Sauer, "Serubbabel", p. 200.

[16] Petersen, p. 104. The nature of this change has been the subject of much debate and will be discussed *infra*.

[17] Meyers and Meyers (p. 68) maintain that the governor's name is found seven times in Haggai and that here, as in Hag 1:1, the spelling is *plene scriptum*, thus forming an inclusio around the book of Haggai. As with the inclusion or exclusion of Zerubbabel's patronymic and title, this phenomenon may be seen as a simple variation without any specific function.

[18] See Wolff (pp. 78–79) for a discussion of this formula in the redactional history of the book.

## 8.3. Exegesis

**[20–21a]** For the fourth and final time the word of Yahweh is addressed to Haggai.[19] The fact that this oracle was proclaimed the same day as the preceding one underlines the importance of this date in the experience of the postexilic community.[20] Various explanations have been advanced for the separation of these oracles into two distinct scenes. Wolff maintains that the oracle was proclaimed to Zerubbabel before a limited audience rather than the general public,[21] while Beyse suggests that it was proclaimed in his absence.[22] Neither hypothesis, however, has any textual evidence to support it. In any case, the redactor who set this oracle in its present structure makes it "public knowledge" and gives it a very significant rhetorical and literary role. This fourth scene constitutes the climax of the book's chronological, literary, and thematic movement. The text begins with a situation of stagnation and inactivity, but it ends with great hope for the future. In the third scene, the prophet assures the people that very soon Yahweh will bless their agricultural and economic endeavours. In this fourth scene, the prophet broaches the larger question of the ultimate destiny of the community in Yehud and of its leadership in the broader context of the world of nations and their rulers. The placement of this oracle in a separate "scene" marks this change of topic and focus.[23] The prophetic discourse, though addressed primarily to Zerubbabel, has as its goal the reassurance of the community concerning its future. This would have been especially apposite in view of the questions which would have naturally arisen regarding the earlier traditions of Zion's preeminence as well as the perpetuity of the Davidic line. The temple's refoundation (2:18–19) would have naturally evoked the question of the future of other pre-exilic institutions and traditions. The oracle to Zerubbabel supplies a brief response to these questions, however the import and meaning of this response proves to be somewhat enigmatic, as we shall see.

Haggai, for the second time on the twenty-fourth day of the ninth month, receives the order to convey a message to (אל) Zerubbabel,

---

[19] On אל here see the discussion of the scene's structure *supra*.
[20] Meyers and Meyers, p. 66.
[21] Wolff, p. 80.
[22] Beyse, *Köningserwartungen*, p. 53.
[23] Meyers and Meyers, p. 82.

governor of Judah. The inclusion of Zerubbabel's official title of governor, here as in 2:1, implies that Yahweh addresses the word to Zerubbabel in the context of the official mandate he holds from the Persian
throne. This fact proves highly significant in the oracle that follows.

**[21b-22]** The divine discourse begins in v. 21b with the same words
as are found in 2:7 (אני מרעיש את־השמים ואת־הארץ). This places the
oracle in the same thematic and traditio-theological context as 2:6–
9. As such, the oracle announces the future intervention of Yahweh
on behalf of his people. Haggai's language is saturated with typical
prophetic eschatological vocabulary.[24] The verb רעש conjugated with an
impersonal direct object implies the perturbation of the stable elements
of the natural world producing terrifying portents (cf. 2:7). The mention
of the heavens and the earth (את־השמים ואת־הארץ) constitutes a merism:
the totality of the universe will be in upheaval.

In vv. 21b-22 the prophet moves, as in vv. 6–7, from the terrifying upheavals in the natural world to their effects upon humankind.[25]
These effects are described in two rhythmically structured stichoi.[26]
The first stich describes the result of Yahweh's intervention: any power
not submitted to him will be reduced and humbled. The verb הפך in
the first hemistich (2:22aα) is frequently found with Yahweh as subject
in descriptions of divine overthrowing or overturning.[27] The "parade
paradigm" of such divine activity is the overthrowing of Sodom and
Gomorrah (Gen 19: 21, 25, 29; Deut 29:22 [Eng. 23]; Jer 49:18; 50:40).
However Petersen accurately observes that the presence of the verb
הפך (overturn) in Jer 20:16 (where the names of these two cities are not
mentioned) attests to a tendency toward generalization of this theme
to include the abasement of all nations which oppose the divine will.
This theme is also evident in Hag 2:22.[28] The expression "throne of
the nations" is placed here as a metonymy for political and military
power.[29] The plural ממלכות (kingdoms) indicates that כסא (throne) is
collective, rendering the sense of the phrase, "every throne of every

---

[24] Chary, p. 33.
[25] Hag 2:7 manifests a similar progression, cf. the structure in 1:3–9 and 2:15–19
where the misfortunes experienced are described, then followed by the affirmation that
Yahweh was their author.
[26] Chary, p. 33.
[27] Cf. Amos 4:11. Elsewhere it may mean "to transform," i.e., to change x into y, cf.
Exod 7:17; Deut 23:6 [Eng. 5]; Amos 8:10.
[28] Petersen, p. 99.
[29] BDB "כסא"; Mitchell, p. 77.

nation."[30] The question of the degree to which this phrase can be viewed as referring to the Persian Empire will be examined below.

The second hemistich (2:22aβ) takes up the thought of the first. The strength of the nations will be annihilated. The noun חֹזֶק (strength), like its synonym כֹּסַא, refers here to the nations' military power or ability to use force to attain their objectives (cf. Exod 13:2; 14:16; Amos 6:13).[31] The verb שׁמד (to destroy, abolish, annihilate) is well attested and frequently used in contexts of sacred or legal judgment.[32] Perhaps more significant is the fact that in Deuteronomy this verb is used with reference to the punishment of Israel due to covenant violations (Deut 28:20, 24, 45, 61).[33] Hag 2:22 thus echoes the broader postexilic theme of divine wrath which, although first directed against Israel, is subsequently turned toward the nations (cf. Zech 1:14–16).[34] The term שׁמד is found frequently in oracles against the nations (Isa 14:23, Babylon; Isa 23:11, Phoenicia; Jer 48:8, 42, Moab).

The second stich (2:22b) describes the means by which this destruction of the nations' power is accomplished. As in 2:6–9, the image of a decisive military conflagration is employed. Chariots and riders are overthrown (והפכתי מרכבה ורכביה),[35] horses and riders will die, foreign armies will kill one another in panic (וירדו סוסים ורכביהם איש בחרב אחיו). The fall of horse and rider (ירד) is a quasi-fixed expression deriving from the traditions of the deliverance at the Sea of Reeds (Exod 14:9, 23; 15:1, 19, 21). Panic and the ensuing mutual annihilation on the part of the adversaries' armies (on which see below) occurs in Judg 7:22; 2 Chr 20:20–25, as well as in the oracles against the nations in Isa 19:2 (Egypt), Jer 46:16 (Egypt), and Ezek 38:19–21 (Gog and Magog). The text may also implicitly allude to the presence of this theme in Darius' Behistun Inscription,[36] and foresee its re-enactment on a universal scale.

---

[30] GKC § 124r.

[31] Cf. Deissler (2:213) who also notes the similarity between Hag 2:22 and Ezek 34:16.

[32] Wolff, pp. 81–81; Deissler, 2:497 (cf. Amos 2:9; 9:8).

[33] Amos 9:8 uses it with reference to the Northern Kingdom.

[34] Cf. Petitjean, *Oracles*, pp. 80–81.

[35] Wolff (p. 103) notes that the reference here is probably to the team which rode in the chariot. Such a team would have been composed of the driver, and a bowman, and possibly a shield-bearer.

[36] For example, in §10 (Akkadian Version) Cambyses kills his brother, Bardiya. Gaumata, knowing this and pretending to be Bardiya, rises in rebellion. Wolff (pp. 103–4) states, "Fratricide is one of the main themes of the Behistun Inscriptions." In §21 (Akkadian Version) the Elamites kill their own commander.

As Chary, Petersen, and Rudolph have noted, v. 22 fuses and reconfigures several traditions.[37] The reader is struck immediately by the
obvious use of vocabulary drawn from the tradition of the conflict
between Yahweh and the nations. Yahweh's conflict with foreign kingdoms (ממלכות Hag 2:22) is also found in Jer 28:8 and Isa 23:11.[38] The
nouns ממלכה and גוי are united in Isa 13:4 (an oracle against Babylon). The throne of Yahweh is juxtaposed with the power of Elam in
Jer 49:34–39. In that pericope, Yahweh will break the bow of Elam,
and will scatter and destroy its people. Then he will establish (שׁים cf.
Hag 2:23) his throne (כסא cf. Hag 2:22) in Elam (Jer 49:38). Jeremiah
perceives a time when Jerusalem will become the throne of Yahweh
and where the people will gather in the holy city (Jer 3:17–18). Ezekiel
calls the temple the throne of Yahweh (Ezek 43:7). The image of the
horse and rider occurs frequently in the oracles against the nations (Isa
43:17, Babylon; Jer 46:9, Egypt; Jer 50:37, Babylon; Ezek 26:10, Tyre;
Ezek 38:15, 20, Gog and Magog). The text also draws upon Israel's
epic traditions. Haggai's language evokes the destruction of Sodom
and Gomorrah (הפך cf. Hag 2:22), and the Sea of Reeds (ירד cf. Hag
2:22). Sauer,[39] followed by Petersen,[40] sees the submission of the nations
in Hag 2:22–23 as analogous to such submission encountered in texts
involving royal enthronement in Jerusalem (Ps 2; 110). In addition, Hag
2:22 draws upon traditions of the divine warrior and the day of Yahweh.[41] Several features reflect this theme. The shaking of the cosmos
(Hag 2:22; cf. Isa 13:13; Jer 10:10; 50:46; Ezek 26:10; 27:28; Joel 2:10;
4:16 [Eng. 3:16]) is frequently found in eschatological descriptions. As
well, the mutual destruction of armies in panic is a common element.
The origin of this motif is likely to be sought in a variety of historical
traditions. For example in Judg 7:22 when Yahweh routs the enemies
of Gideon, the sword of each warrior is turned against his neighbour.
Similar scenarios may be found in 1 Sam 14:20 and 2 Chr 20:20–25
and 32:20–23. There the armies are routed by Yahweh without Israel's
intervention.[42] This is similar to certain eschatological passages in which

---

[37] Chary, p. 34; Petersen, p. 101; Rudolph, pp. 53f. Chary states that our text is made
up of "commonly used traditional images" (*clichés traditionnels*).
[38] Petersen, p. 99.
[39] Sauer, "Serubbabel", p. 202.
[40] Petersen, p. 100.
[41] Sauer, "Serubbabel", pp. 202–203. Cf. *supra*, pp. 186–95.
[42] Chary, pp. 33–34.

Yahweh wages war against nations.[43] In Isa 19:2, Jer 46:16, Ezek 38:19–21 and Zech 14:13, Yahweh intervenes and the armies of the nations kill one another, while Israel takes no active role. In conclusion then, the text employs a multiplicity of echoes drawn from diverse traditions. Even if the prophet's words contain some veiled allusions to the political situation of the time (and such allusions would not be foreign to his central premise),[44] the principal thrust of his words concerns the destiny of Zion, rather than cryptic allusions to events in recent Persian history.[45] The prophet affirms above all else that any power that stands in opposition to the reign of Yahweh will be destroyed.

**[23]** This verse constitutes the climax of the oracle, and contains allusions to two or possibly three quite distinct chronological moments.[46] The prophet states: (1) that which Yahweh will do in a future time (introduced by the formula ביום ההוא [on that day] followed by the imperfect of לקח and the *waw* consecutive with the perfect of שׂים); (2) the state of affairs in the present (vocative עבדי, addressed to Zerubbabel), and (3) that which stands as an accomplished fact, expressed in the perfective (perfect of בחר).[47] The verse contains a multiplicity of theologically loaded terms,[48] and bears a special relationship to Jer 22:24–30, where the rejection of Jehoiachin is pronounced. It is important to state at the outset that this text cannot be understood accurately

---

[43] G. von Rad, "The Origin of the Concept of the Day of Yahweh", *JSS* 4 (1959): 97–108.

[44] Cf. my discussion of Yehud and Persian domination in ch. 10.

[45] Verhoef, p. 142. Beyse (*Königserwartungen*, pp. 55–56) maintains that these two interpretative approaches are not mutually exclusive.

[46] I.e., present and future, or past, present, and future.

[47] Theoretically this verb could be translated in the future, as a so called "prophetic perfect" (cf. Joüon §112g). It would seem more contextually coherent, however, to view it as a statement of Yahweh's choice which obtains in the present (Joüon §112e) even before Zerubbabel is given the role he will hold in the future. Furthermore, even if the verb is translated in the future, the use of the perfective aspect identifies it as an action already completed in the counsel of Yahweh. Against a present translation (Joüon §112f) implying that the election of Zerubbabel occurs at the time of the oracle, it is clear that most cases where a present translation is to be followed constitute "speech events" and concern juridical acts which are deemed to be done when spoken. בחר in the perfect, by contrast, when referring to Yahweh's election, most generally refers to past decisions (Deut 6:7; 1 Sam 10:24; 1 Kgs 11:13; 2 Chr 12:13; Ps 132:13; Isa 44:1; Jer 33:24. Even 2 Chr 7 relates Yahweh's attentiveness to the temple in the present (v. 15) to his previous choice of it (v. 16). Cf. p. 233, *infra*.

[48] Sauer ("Serubbabel", p. 203) comments, "Haggai almost randomly selects from the extensive treasures of tradition. לקח, עבד, חותם, and בחר are stacked up one after the other, in such a way that their specific, individual content cannot be fully drawn out."

unless all of its vocabulary, its relationship to the passage in Jeremiah
22, the broader hermeneutical techniques used in Haggai, as well as
the socio-political context into which the oracle was spoken are brought
to bear on its interpretation. For this reason, "atomistic" approaches,
which attempt to delimit the precise meaning of each component of the
verse in isolation[49] and then to attempt a synthesis, fail to do justice to
the text. Here, consequently, I will begin with a brief discussion of the
verse's key terms as a prelude to the discussion of the text as a whole.
In order to best reflect the rhetorical structure of the verse, my analysis
of its terms will follow the order in which they are encountered in the
text.

Haggai's words are introduced by the quasi-classical prophetic expression ביום ההוא (on that day).[50] The phrase is commonly associated
with the "day of Yahweh"[51] and is frequently used in oracles of salvation.[52] Westermann suggests that in later texts, the phrase implies that
the action thus introduced will transpire at a time somewhat removed
from the present.[53] This distinction would appear to be justified in Haggai. The near, "historical" future is described by מן־היום הזה (from this
day) in 2:17, 18. The eschatological future, by contrast, is introduced by
ביום ההוא (v. 23).[54] Verses 21b-22 return to the eschatological intervention already referred to in 2:6–9. A Divine-Saying Formula follows the
temporal indicator, and stresses the divine origin of Haggai's words.

In v. 23 Haggai affirms that Yahweh will carry out two specific
actions. First, he will "take" Zerubbabel (אקחך). The verb לקח when
used with Yahweh as subject, frequently designates the setting apart
of groups or individuals. It is employed in this sense regarding Israel
as a nation (Exod 6:7; Deut 4:20), the Levites (Num 3:12; 8:16; Ps 68:19
[Eng. 18]), Aaron (Lev 8:2) Joshua (Num 27:18, 22), David (2 Sam 7:8; Ps

---

[49] J. Barr's cautions regarding "illegitimate totality transfer" (*The Semantics of Biblical Language*, [London: SCM, 1961], pp. 218, 222) are especially appropriate here. Great mischief would come if every nuance associated with heavily loaded terms such as "servant" or "choose" were to be implied in our text.

[50] On ביום ההוא see C. Westermann, *Prophetic Oracles of Salvation in the Old Testament*, (trans. K. Crim; Louisville: Westminster, 1991), pp. 255f. As Tollington notes (*Tradition*, p. 136, citing Beuken, p. 79) this phrase introduces the key point of the oracle as a whole (i. e., v. 23).

[51] Petersen, p. 102.

[52] Westermann, *Oracles of Salvation*, pp. 255–57.

[53] Ibid., p. 257.

[54] Cf. Caquot, "Le judaïsme", p. 130.

78:70), and Amos (Amos 7:15).[55] As Rose points out, in many instances the individual or group thus designated is "taken" and appointed to a new position or responsibility. However in certain passages, such as Num 3:12, Deut 4:20, 2 Sam 22:17=Ps 18:17 [Eng. 16], and Hos 11:3, while role and responsibilities may be implied, the accent is on a special relationship to Yahweh.[56] Here, with respect to Zerubbabel, the imperfect verb clearly designates a future transition. On that day Zerubbabel, as the object of Yahweh's action, will experience a significant change in his role and status.[57] The nature of that change will be discussed below.

Yahweh's declaration of what he will do (I will take you) is broken by a vocative parenthesis (O Zerubbabel, son of Shealtiel, my servant, 2:23). Yahweh calls Zerubbabel by his name and patronymic. The motif of Yahweh calling individuals by name and speaking to them of their future is well rooted in various traditions (Gen 12:1–3; 17:4–8; Exod 3:4–10; 1 Sam 3:6–14; cf. Judg 6:12b where Gideon's name is not mentioned but where he is addressed as "mighty warrior"). This gives the present text a certain similarity in flavour to other biblical "calls."

Thus before telling him what he will become, Yahweh affirms to Zerubbabel that he already is עבדי (my servant). This term is associated with several important individuals and groups in Israelite traditions:[58] Abraham (Gen 26:24), Isaac and Jacob (Exod 32:13), Moses (Num 12:7–8, Deut 34:5 and many times in the Deuteronomistic History), Joshua (Judg 2:8; Josh 1:1, 7; 14:17 etc.), Job (Job 1:8; 2:3), and especially David (2 Sam 7:5, 8; 1 Kgs 11:13; 14:8; 2 Kgs 19:34). The term is also used with reference to Nebuchadnezzar (Jer 25:9; 27:6; 43:10) as well as the nation of Israel (Isa 41:8–9), and the nation under the name Jacob (Isa 44:1; 48:20; Jer 30:10, 46:27–28; Ezek 28:25; 37:25).[59] Rose points out

---

[55] Cf. the fuller discussion in Rose, *Zemah*, pp. 216–18 and Tollington, *Tradition*, p. 137.

[56] Rose, *Zemah*, p. 217.

[57] Wolff, p. 86. Petersen as well seems to be imprecise in his evaluation of this change. On p. 104 he states that the sense of Haggai's words is, "I designate you as my earthly representative, equivalent in significance," whereas on p. 104 he maintains that "Haggai ... addressed the Davidide Zerubbabel as if he were to have royal status at some future time." The first statement goes far beyond the second.

[58] Cf., the excellent chart in Rose, *Zemah*, pp. 210–11. The limitation of Rose's data, however, is that it does not include texts where names stand in apposition to עבד without any personal pronoun, (as in Exod 32:13). Cf. also the survey in Tollington, *Tradition*, pp. 139–41.

[59] On these last references, cf. Tollington, *Tradition*, p. 139. The literature on the Servant of Yahweh in Isa 40–55 is immense. See, most recently, B. S. Childs, *Isaiah*, (OTL; Louisville: Westminster/John Knox, 2001), pp. 409–23, with brief bibliography.

that while the noun is frequently used of David, it occurs only once vis-à-vis another Davidic monarch (Hezekiah in 2 Chr 32:16).[60] In Ezek 34:23; 37:24–25 the epithet is used of a future unnamed Davidic ruler.[61] Two nuances of the term can be excluded from Hag 2:23. First, the theme of intercession, often associated with this designation[62] has no relevance here. Second, the suggestion of Meyers and Meyers that the term refers to the future role of the Israelite ruler,[63] moves in the opposite direction of the chronological structure of the text. Zerubbabel is *already* the servant of Yahweh, his subaltern status notwithstanding. The logical implication of this designation is therefore that Zerubbabel, as political head of the community and active participant in the temple's reconstruction, was acting as one who stood in continuity with those who had chosen to ally themselves with Yahweh and his purposes in the past.[64] The veracity and authenticity of the prophet's words are once again underlined by the repetition of the Divine-Saying Formula.

The text then moves to the further description of that for which Zerubbabel will be "taken." Zerubbabel's future role is described by the phrase ושמתיך כחותם (and I will make you like a signet ring). The verb שׂים, whose semantic field is quite broad, frequently carries a meaning similar to לקח, namely the installation of an individual as a chief, official, or authority (Exod 1:11; 18:21; Deut 1:13 etc.). The term חותם appears only thirteen times in the Hebrew Bible (Gen 38:18; Exod 28:11, 21, 36; 39:6, 14, 30; 1 Kgs 21:8; Job 38:14; 41:7 [Eng. 15]; Cant 8:6; Jer 22:24; Hag 2:23). A signet-ring is a ring holding an inscribed seal. Such seals were closely guarded, since each was distinct and could be used as a validating signature by its owner.[65] Clearly then, the use of the term in Hag 2:23 is figurative. This is evident

---

See also the earlier comprehensive study of C. R. North, *The Suffering Servant in Deutero-Isaiah: An Historical and Critical Study*, (London: Oxford University Press, 1956).

[60] Rose, *Zemah*, pp. 211–12.

[61] Petersen, p. 103, and Rose, *Zemah*, p. 211.

[62] For a discussion of this nuance see J. Lévêque, *Job et son Dieu*, (EtB; 2 vols.; Paris: Gabalda, 1970), 1:140–43.

[63] Meyers and Meyers, p. 68.

[64] Tollington (*Tradition*, pp. 139–41) appropriately notes that the motifs of obedience, faithfulness, and intimacy are to be found in the use of the term in the Isaianic, Deuteronomistic, wisdom and diverse historical traditions.

[65] On seal and sealings, and the use of signet rings cf. Rose, *Zemah*, pp. 218–30, with bibliography. Cf. also, M. Gibson and R. D. Biggs, eds., *Seals and Sealings in the Ancient Near East*, (Bibliotheca Mesopotamica 6, Malibu, CA: Udena, 1977).

from the presence of כ (as) preceding it.[66] Generally speaking, most exegetes attempt to understand this text in terms of the symbolism of the signet ring. Commentators consequently try to identify which nuance of חותם forms the basis of the simile. Is it: (1) the highly personal and intimate nature of the relationship between the seal and its owner, and its value in the latter's eyes (cf. Cant 8:6);[67] (2) the seal as a symbol of authority;[68] or (3) the giving of seals by a superior to a subordinate to indicate the latter's authority either to represent the former[69] or to reflect his or her subordination to the superior?[70] All these nuances may be associated with seals,[71] but the specifics of Jer 22:24 and Hag 2:23 preclude several of them. Rose, following a long standing exegetical tradition, accurately sees the metaphor in Jer 22:24 as one of preciousness or great value.[72] There Yahweh says that even if Jehoiachin were as precious in his eyes as a signet (and the form of the condition may well indicate that such was the case),[73] he would still reject him. In neither Jeremiah nor Haggai can the seal be said to be a symbol of royal authority, or delegated authority, since it is removed from or placed back on the hand of Yahweh.[74] The historical referent of the metaphor in Jer 22 would appear to be the exile of Jehoiachin and his family, their death in exile, and the exclusion of his progeny from future royal tenure.[75] Hag 2:23, with its use of the image of the

---

[66] As Rose (*Zemah*, p. 238) accurately notes; cf. Joüon §133g for an excellent discussion of the range of similarity implied by כ.

[67] Meyers and Meyers, p. 70. Rose, *Zemah*, pp. 233–38, esp. pp. 233–34, with extensive bibliography.

[68] Verhoef, p. 147.

[69] Petersen, p. 104.

[70] Wolff, pp. 83–84; Chary, *Prophètes et culte*, p. 135.

[71] See Amsler (pp. 39–40) for other, less likely suggestions, such as a guarantee to Zerubbabel regarding the success of his mission.

[72] Rose, *Zemah*, p. 224, n. 26, with bibliography. This tradition includes Kimchi, André, Duhm, Hallo, and Holladay, among others.

[73] Cf. Rose, *Zemah*, pp. 244–45. If the text is taken as a real condition, it serves to highlight the divine pathos involved in the rejection of Jehoiachin and the judgment of the nation. The situation is so grave that, in spite the preciousness of king and nation to Yahweh, he will still execute his judgment (cf. the contrasting result in Hos 11:6, if this verse is understood to be a renunciation or attenuation of judgment). If the condition is hypothetical and contrary to fact (i.e., Jehoiachin is not as precious as a signet) the certainty of Yahweh's judgment is in view. Taken this way the meaning of the phrase is, "even if you were as precious as my signet (and you are not) I would still throw you away, therefore your doom is assured."

[74] Rose, *Zemah*, pp. 223–24, and esp. pp. 237–38.

[75] Sauer, "Serubbabel", p. 204.

signet in relation to a Davidide, clearly constitutes an addendum to the prophetic judgment conveyed in Jer 22:24. Thus the reference to the signet stems not so much from its particular appropriateness with respect to Zerubbabel and his situation, but from a desire to take up and extend the issue raised in Jer 22:24.[76] It is important to take the full context of the passage in Jeremiah into account. Chapter 21 begins a denunciation of Judah's last kings.[77] Jeremiah 21:11 contains a generalized warning to the Davidic rulers: they must administer justice or be destroyed. The sins of Shallum are not listed (22:10–11) but his fate situates him as falling under condemnation. Jehoiakim's evils are explicitly mentioned in 22:13–19. Jehoiachin's sins are only referred to in passing (22:22) but he would appear to be no better that his predecessors. The rejection, symbolized through the use of the signet in v. 24, is thus a result of the unworthiness of the individual. Hag 2:23 reverses this picture. Zerubbabel is Yahweh's obedient servant and, as a result of this faithfulness, Yahweh responds to him in a way which stands in contrast to his response to Jehoiachin.[78] It follows from this that what is at issue in both texts is not as much the *particular symbolic meaning of the signet ring*, but rather *the significance of the broader metaphor in which that simile is embedded.*[79] That broader metaphor is the image of Yahweh discarding his signet and subsequently restoring it to himself. A fuller discussion of the implications of Haggai's use of this image will be presented below. It is sufficient at this point to affirm that the metaphor of the taking off and the putting on of the signet functions in both Haggai and Jeremiah as *an image of Yahweh's favour withdrawn or bestowed, and the manifestation of that favour in the experience of the individual addressed.*

Haggai roots the future activity of Yahweh on behalf of Zerubbabel in Yahweh's choice of him (כִּי־בְךָ בָחַרְתִּי).[80] Like the other terms in the passage, the verb בחר is found extensively in various traditions. It may be used with reference to Yahweh's choice of Israel as nation (Deut 7:6;

---

[76] Cf. Goldman, *Prophétie*, pp. 231–35.

[77] On the structure of Jer 21:1–24:10 and the redactional theme of the responsibility of the royal house for the nation's fall cf. Carroll, *Jeremiah*, p. 404.

[78] Amsler (p. 39) comments, "Clearly Haggai takes up the imagery found in Jeremiah and transforms it into a promise."

[79] It is precisely for this reason, in my opinion, that attempts to understand Hag 2:23 which *begin* with the question of the sense of the simile yield such disparate and unsatisfactory results.

[80] Petersen, p. 104.

14:2; 1 Kgs 3:8; Ezek 20:5) or the selection of specific tribes (1 Chr 15:2; 28:4; Ps 78:67). In Deuteronomy and the Deuteronomistic History, it particularly designates the divine choice of David and Jerusalem (Deut 7:6; 12:5, 11, 14 etc.; 14:23; 18:6). The same can be said of Chronicles (2 Chr 6:5–6, 34, 38; 7:12). In these texts בחר generally refers to the divine election of an individual for a specific task, status or position.[81]

Most significant for our passage, however, is a nuance of the verb which appears in texts describing the gracious activity of Yahweh after a period of judgment. In Isa 14:1 the verb בחר stands parallel to רחם and refers to Yahweh's acts of mercy and compassion towards Israel subsequent to her devastation and destruction. Israel returns to her own land, and her former captors yield themselves in submission.[82] In a strikingly similar fashion, Zech 1:17 pairs בחר with נחם and associates this divine election with the rebuilding of the temple and the repopulating of the land. Zechariah 2:16 [Eng. 2:12] uses בחר in a similar way and identifies Yahweh's choice with a dense population in the land. In Zech 3:2 the verb occurs once again, this time in conjunction with the reconstruction and purification of the temple. Petitjean has noted the link between the jealousy of Yahweh and his choice of Zion. He states, "In 1:14b-17 Zechariah announces that Yahweh will now show, on Israel's behalf, the ardent love implied in election. This electing love explains and causes events whose goal is the deliverance of Israel: the return of Yahweh … and new election (*ûbahar 'od*)."[83] I therefore maintain that the starting point for an understanding of Yahweh's "choosing" Zerubbabel must be the highly specific postexilic concept of the renewal of divine favour subsequent to former rejection or judgment. This sense fits perfectly with the dialogue between Hag 2:23 and Jer 22:24, and the contrast between Jehoiachin and Zerubbabel noted above. Like the image of the signet that will be put on once again, בחר here indicates the restoration of something that was formerly disrupted or withdrawn.

---

[81] Cf. H. Seebass, s. v. "בחר", *TDOT* 2:87. In Deut 7:7 the election of Israel is rooted in the loving choice of Yahweh, in spite of the insignificance of the people. A similar notion is found in relationship to the election of Jerusalem (1 Kgs 11:13) and the Davidic dynasty (2 Sam 7) in the Deuteronomistic tradition as well as in Chronicles (1 Chr 17; 2 Chr 7:12). These texts underline the fact that Yahweh's choice is not based upon the merits of the chosen, and thus excludes human pride. Furthermore, this election can be withdrawn should Yahweh so choose, cf. Zech 1:17; 2:16 [2:12]. Cf. also the surveys in Tollington, *Tradition*, pp. 137–39, and Rose, *Zemah*, pp. 212–15, with chart.

[82] Childs, *Isaiah*, p. 125.

[83] Petitjean, *Oracles*, p. 81.

In light of the clearly future referent of the perfect of בחר in Zech 1:17 and 2:16 [Eng. 2:12], it could be suggested that Hag 2:23 ought to be given the future translation, "I will choose [or show renewed compassion to] you" as a so called "prophetic perfect."[84] In point of fact, in v. 23, בחר could be viewed as relating to the past (I will set you … because I have chosen you), the present (I will set you … because I choose you), the future (I will set you … because I will choose you), or the future perfect (I will set you … because I will have chosen you).[85] It should be noted, however, that the futurity of the choice in Zech 1:17 and 2:16 [Eng. 12] is underscored by the presence of עוד (again), a term absent from Hag 2:23. It would seem more contextually coherent, therefore, to view it as a statement of Yahweh's established (here the perfective) choice, which obtains in the present[86] (hence the epithet "my servant" for Zerubbabel) even before Zerubbabel is given the role he will hold in the future. The precise moment of Yahweh's choice, and its basis, are not explicitly stated.[87] In a very similar way, 2 Chr 7 relates Yahweh's attentiveness to the temple in the present (v. 15) to his previous choice of it in the past (v. 16). Whatever translational value is accepted, Yahweh's election of Zerubbabel is the ground of the former's action toward the latter.

In conclusion, then, Haggai addresses Zerubbabel the governor and deems him to be the servant of Yahweh. However the future holds even better things in store. In contrast to Jehoiachin, who suffered Yahweh's rejection, Zerubbabel will experience Yahweh's favour. All this is grounded in Yahweh's renewed compassion for his people subsequent to their judgment and suffering. But what precise form will this manifestation of Yahweh's favour take? It has been frequently suggested that the implication of Haggai's words is that upon Yahweh's eschatological intervention, Zerubbabel will rule as a king in a reconstituted nation.[88] Similar notions are implicit in the view that Zerubbabel will become

---

[84] Joüon §112g.

[85] On the future perfect cf. Joüon §112i.

[86] Cf. also n. 47, *supra*.

[87] As we have seen, Zerubbabel's faithfulness in the temple's reconstruction may be linked to his being called Yahweh's servant. Furthermore, this faithfulness may be, at some level, related to Yahweh's "choice" of him. Be that as it may, the text is quite discreet regarding these matters, and dogmatism is ill-advised.

[88] Mason, p. 25; Japhet, "Sheshbazzar and Zerubbabel-I", pp. 77–78. Petersen (p. 104) sees the verse as highlighting the "royal prerogatives" of Zerubbabel. Meyers and Meyers (p. 69) speak of Zerubbabel at the head of an "independent Davidic state" as an "eschatological ruler" (pp. 69–70).

Yahweh's vice-regent.[89] In this connection, it has been argued that Hag
2:23 utilises the form of an appointment or designation, drawn from
court traditions,[90] and that 2:22 resonates with motifs drawn from Ps
2 and 110 and thus has political overtones.[91] In a variation on this
approach, which views the promised transition as far more modest in
nature, Lemaire suggests that Haggai is expressing the hope of a change
in status of the province of Yehud, and of Zerubbabel's emergence as
king of a vassal state within the Persian Empire.[92] In quite a different line of argumentation, some scholars see the royal and messianic
themes here as faint or absent. The oracle is therefore thought merely
to constitute a guarantee that Zerubbabel will complete his task.[93] Rose
argues that the language of 2:23, which may in other instances have
royal overtones, need not be read in such a way here.[94] He maintains
that the oracle is proclaimed to reassure Zerubbabel that he will be
protected in the coming world upheaval.[95]

At this point I will argue for an approach to Zerubbabel's future role
that I feel is more fruitful, in that it lies closer to the hermeneutical
stance of the book of Haggai in its political and sociological context.
As noted in my exegesis, the extended metaphor of Yahweh's setting
Zerubbabel upon his finger like a signet ring[96] serves several purposes
and makes several points. The image provides a further comment on
Jer 22:24 and juxtaposes Zerubbabel's faithfulness to Jehoiachin's lack
thereof. Most significantly, it contrasts Yahweh's rejection of Jehoiachin,
manifested by the latter's experience of exile and death in a foreign
land, with Yahweh's approbation of Zerubbabel. What is lacking, however, in the text in Haggai (as opposed to the explicit descriptions of

---

[89] Amsler (p. 40) and Beyse (*Köningserwartunen*, pp. 56–57, with bibliography) call
Zerubbabel the "vizier" of Yahweh over the world. In this they follow Sellin and
Winton-Thomas. Verhoef (pp. 147–49) takes a similar view. See Rose, *Zemah*, pp. 230–33
for an excellent survey (with bibliography) of the variations on this theme.

[90] Wolff, p. 99

[91] Petersen, p. 100.

[92] Lemaire, "Zorobabel", p. 55 and "Exploitation des sources", p. 308. As noted in
the discussion of the status of Yehud (ch. 3, *supra*) such vassal-kingdoms did exist, and
the Persians frequently followed a "dynastic model" in appointing their leadership.

[93] Thus Wolff, p. 106.

[94] Rose, *Zemah*, pp. 241–43.

[95] Ibid.

[96] If Haggai is indeed continuing the metaphor of the finger ring in Jer 22:24. Rose
(*Zemah*, p. 237) notes that this is not explicitly stated in Haggai, but I believe it can
be assumed. Even if the signet in view is some other kind of seal, the meaning is not
changed.

Jehoiachin's misfortunes) is any indication of the precise nature of the *correspondingly positive future experience* of Zerubbabel. Two comments are in order here. First, in the context of the book of Haggai, the experience of Zerubbabel in 2:23 may be viewed as parallel to that of the temple in 2:6–9. In both cases the existing state of affairs is acceptable (the building is "Yahweh's house" [2:4, 9] and Zerubbabel is Yahweh's servant [2:23]). Yet in both cases the present will be dramatically and drastically surpassed in the future. The temple will be glorified by the nations' treasures, and Zerubbabel will be the object of a future manifestation of Yahweh's favour. Second, the use of highly evocative language in a generalized fashion, with the result that a precise referent is difficult to determine, corresponds to the way religious traditions are handled in elsewhere in Haggai. We have observed this in relationship to several motifs in 2:6–9 and vv. 21b-22, such as the incoming of the treasures of the nations, the assault of the nations upon Zion, and the status of Israel among the nations. Several scholars have noticed this vagueness and generality in v. 23. Japhet thus suggests that Haggai only "hints" at Zerubbabel's future role.[97] For Lagrange it is deliberately veiled.[98] The most probable explanation of this phenomenon is that, as was the case in 2:6–9, the prophet (or redactor[s]) sought to blur and homogenize those aspects of the tradition that were secondary to the rhetorical point under consideration, so that the latter might stand in stark relief. In the context of Haggai 2, I would maintain that the themes being underlined are: (1) that the rejection of the Davidic line expressed in Jer 22:24 is not final; (2) that Zerubbabel is a faithful servant of Yahweh and as such (3) he will be greatly honoured and blessed in the future. By extension the text very deliberately does not reveal how and in what way that future exaltation will be experienced, since ultimately that issue lay beyond the rhetorical purview of the pericope. The rhetorical focus, from the perspective of both the prophet and his redactors, was the stimulation of hope in the future despite the apparent incongruity of the present with earlier hopes and aspirations (e.g. unimpressive temple, subjection to Persian rule). The prophet therefore proclaims that both governor and temple will see "better days" and the community can therefore continue its daily life in confident expectation.

---

[97] Japhet, "Sheshbazzar and Zerubbabel-I", p. 78.
[98] M.-J. Lagrange, "Notes sur les prophéties messianiques des dernires prophètes", *RB* 3 (1906): 67–83, esp. p. 69, cited in Rose, "Zemah", p. 234, n. 54.

This approach to Haggai's view of the future of the Davidic line stands in contrast to two positions in the literature. First, in distinction to Rose, whose arguments against an inflated and "messianic" reading of Hag 2:23 are quite sound, I do not believe that the Davidic component can be completely excised from 2:20–23. It is not merely the presence of several evocative terms associated with the Davidic line, but supremely the dialogue with Jer 22:24 which makes this so. The fate of the house of David and the theological traditions associated with it was clearly an open-ended question after the exile of Jehoiachin, and one to which various traditions offered responses. This is especially true of the Deuteronomistic History and Jeremiah.[99] Carroll and Goldman have suggested that Jer 22:24 reflects a postexilic debate concerning the authority of Zerubbabel and the Davidic line, however they reach opposite conclusions. Carroll affirms that in Jer 22:30 a redactional extension is appended to the judgment upon Jehoiachin in 22:24, so as to exclude his descendants (i.e. Zerubbabel) from any future political leadership. This extension, he argues, originated from an anti-Zerubbabel faction.[100] Goldman by contrast sees Jer 22:26–30 as containing several slight redactional modifications to the original words of Jeremiah. These retouches served to *limit* the judgment on Jehoiachin and his family to those born in Judah. This would consequently allow those who venerated the words of Jeremiah to accept the leadership of the Davidide Zerubbabel, who thus would not have fallen under Jeremiah's condemnation. From this perspective, the outlook of Hag 2:23 and the redactor of Jer 22:24–30 are of a piece.[101] However one understands Jer 22, the two texts do seem to bear witness to questions relating to the future of the Davidic house. The allusion to Jer 22:24–30 in Hag 2:23 cannot be understood apart from this issue. Pomykala's suggestion that Haggai's language would have still been appropriate even if Zerubbabel had not been of Davidic stock may be true, but it misses the point.[102] The metaphor of the donning of the signet in

[99] The literature on these issues is vast, cf. recently, D. F. Murray, "Of all the Years the Hopes—or Fears? Jehoiachin in Babylon (2 Kings 25:27–30)", *JBL* 120 (2001): 245–65. Cf. Ackroyd, *Exile and Restoration*, pp. 58–61, 78–83; J. G. McConville, *Judgment and Promise*, (Winona Lake: Eisenbrauns, 1993), pp. 54–60; Nicholson, *Preaching*; Goldman, *Prophétie, passim*.

[100] Carroll, *Jeremiah*, pp. 441–43.

[101] Goldman, *Prophétie*, pp. 231–35.

[102] K. E. Pomykala, *The Davidic Dynasty Tradition in Early Judaism: Its History and Significance for Messianism*, (SBLEJL 7; Atlanta: Scholars Press, 1995), p. 49, cited in Rose, *Zemah*, p. 239.

2:23 was chosen precisely because it served as a vehicle to contrast the diverse fates of two different Davidides.[103] The implication is that Hag 2:23 views the promises to David as having ongoing validity. Furthermore, since this hope is reflected in other exilic and postexilic traditions (Jer 23:5–6; 33:14–16; Ezek 34:23; 37:24–25)[104] it is not unwarranted to see its presence here.

This being said, however, I equally reject the opposite suggestion that Haggai is designating Zerubbabel as king or messiah. Haggai studiously avoids any explicitly royal language.[105] While such an absence could be accounted for in terms of political discretion,[106] such caution seems somewhat unnecessary, given the Persians' knowledge of Zerubbabel's Davidic origins and the fact that vassal kingdoms ruled by local dynasties existed elsewhere in the Empire.[107] I would see the avoidance of such language as a *deliberate reticence* to portray the future as an exact replica of the past.[108] The general, yet evocative, vocabulary of v. 23 is entirely congruent with the tendency, already noted in Haggai, to obfuscate specific details where such were deemed to be secondary to the primary rhetorical goal of the text. This makes it difficult, if not impossible, to affirm that Haggai viewed Zerubbabel as "the messiah."[109] The passage's generalizing language, motif of future exaltation,

---

[103] Cf. R. Mason who judiciously observes ("The Messiah in the Postexilic Old Testament Literature", in *King and Messiah in Israel and the Ancient Near East: Proceedings of the Oxford Old Testament Seminar*, [ed. J. Day; JSOTSup 270; Sheffield: Sheffield Academic Press, 1998], p. 342), " The balance of probability (it is no more) seems to me to tilt toward a belief that Haggai thought, [*sic*, punctuation] that when Yahweh began his universal reign in the completed temple, Zerubbabel would succeed to royal status. His Davidic descendant [*sic* descent?], and especially the fact that Jehoiachin was the last Davidic king, the reversal of whose banishment is here suggested by the use of the rare word 'signet ring', seem more than coincidence."

[104] On the Jeremiah passages, especially with regard to issues of textual criticism and redactional history, (specifically a redaction of Jeremiah in the early postexilic period), cf. Goldman, *Prophétie, in loco*.

[105] Rose, *Zemah*, p. 241, citing Van der Woude, p. 74. Cf. also Lemaire, "Zorobabel", pp. 54–55, who notes that such an absence is striking.

[106] So Coggins, *Haggai*, p. 36, and others.

[107] Bianchi, "Rôle de Zorobabel", pp. 156–57.

[108] My conclusions at this point are similar to those of Sérandour, who states, regarding 2:20–23, ("Récits", p. 17), "The atmosphere of a royal theophany leaves no room for doubt: the prophet affirms the eternal validity of the Davidic covenant, including its messianic component, without, however calling Zerubbabel 'king'. He is rather the 'minister' [Hebrew *'bd*] of Yahweh the king." On a similar transformed royal role in Ezekiel, cf. Bodi, "Critique", pp. 256–57.

[109] Thus explicitly Chary (p. 34) and Amsler (p. 40). Such a notion appears implicit in the designation of Zerubbabel as Yahweh's "vizier" (Sellin) or the "universal world

and the book's broader hermeneutical structure, do not warrant such a conclusion.[110] Deissler aptly comments, "It would be difficult to explain why the prophet used such equivocal language if he wished to make a directly messianic promise to Zerubbabel."[111] It is preferable to interpret Zerubbabel's destiny in 2:20–23 in a way that parallels the temple's in 2:1–9. The prophet sees and employs both temple and governor as realities in the present which provide a link with the past and hope for the future. As such, Zerubbabel is a *persönlicher Hoffnungsträger*[112] in that he in his very person embodies hope for the future. Thus the emphasis is not placed on Zerubbabel's future status and role, but rather on his presence in the community, which serves both as a link with the past and as evidence of the firstfruits of good things to come, for both the nation and its royal house.[113]

---

ruler" (Winton-Thomas, Verhoef, Baldwin, Beyse, among others). Deissler, van Hoonacker, Siebeneck, Rose, and Tollington all reject a messianic designation.

[110] Petersen (pp. 104–106) well appreciates this deliberately general phraseology. However he relates it primarily to Haggai's political savvy rather than to theological or rhetorical concerns.

[111] Deissler, 2:498.

[112] Wolff, (German ed., p. 86). The English translation renders the term as "personal bearer of hope" (p. 108) which is less forceful, in that it could also be taken to mean "one who has hope." Wolff seems to mean that Zerubbabel himself is one who is a tangible embodiment of hope, due to the promise of Yahweh made to him. In a similar vein Deissler (2:499) calls him a "type" or "substitute."

[113] Tollington (*Tradition*, pp. 142–43) reaches conclusions similar to my own, yet which differ at certain key points. She affirms, as do I, that Hag 2:23 is meant to serve as an addendum to Jer 22:24. She states that Hag 2:23 is intended "to contrast Zerubbabel, a Davidic descendant who is again being chosen by Yahweh, with the rejected king, the Davidic Jehoiachin. Haggai 2:23 is then seen ... as the refocusing of the Davidic traditions on Zerubbabel." Tollington, however, appears to adopt the "authority" view of the signet in Hag 2:23 (which, as Rose has convincingly demonstrated, is inappropriate) and speaks of Zerubbabel as "representative of Yahweh and his authority in the coming eschatological era" (p. 143). This is surprising given her far more sober comments a few lines later. There she states, "Haggai's use of these motifs has messianic connotations but this is far removed from suggesting that he understood Zerubbabel to be the messiah, a concept which belongs to a later age. It appears probable that Haggai envisaged imminent eschatological activity by Yahweh which would result in political independence for the community in Jerusalem and necessitate there being a political leader, and that Zerubbabel would be that leader appointed by Yahweh. Haggai ... was anticipating some form of restored monarchy ... distinctive from the pre-exilic monarchy but still heir to the Davidic covenant and promises ..."(pp. 143–44). These latter positions are quite similar to my own, although I would be somewhat hesitant to affirm that, apart from some elevation of Zerubbabel, Haggai envisaged (or chose to reveal) any detailed conception of Yehud's future. Tollington has nuanced her position further by affirming that although Haggai envisaged Zerubbabel as head of a "restored Davidic monarchy" ("Readings", p. 198), the redactor later attenuated these hopes,

In this connection it is critically important to note that the fact that Zerubbabel is mentioned by name need not preclude the possibility that the promises made to him could be passed on to his descendants, should they not be fulfilled in his lifetime. Millard points to a prophecy made to Asharhaddon which was seemingly only fulfilled during the reign of his successor. Yet the prophecy was retained in scribal collections.[114] Von Rad, in a similar vein, posits an analogous perspective in Israelite prophetic traditions whereby seemingly unfulfilled prophecies were "absorbed in the great complex of tradition … [and] applied to a future act of God."[115]

## 8.4. RHETORICAL AND HERMENEUTICAL USE OF RELIGIOUS TRADITIONS

The rhetorical and hermeneutical use of religious tradition in this pericope contains elements similar to those in the preceding sections, with certain peculiarities and innovations. Four areas are especially noteworthy.

### 8.4.1. *Generalization*

As we have already seen in 2:6–9, Haggai attenuates and blurs certain details of the traditions he uses. The image of the horse and rider (2:22), drawn from the traditions of the Sea of Reeds, stands as a synecdoche or metonymy for Gentile power in general.[116] Similarly, the overturning designated by הפך is no longer linked with Sodom and Gomorrah but applied more broadly and generally. As well, in contrast to certain other prophetic eschatological traditions, the precise location of the coming eschatological conflict is not specified. Even the future role of Zerubbabel, the central point of the oracle, is vague and difficult to determine with precision.[117] Nothing in our prophet's words belies the

---

most notably by the placement of the כ on כחותם, and believed that "The community was not to be an independent nation, but would remain under Persian rule" (ibid., p. 200). Such a redactional addition or attenuation is a hypothetical suggestion, and difficult to substantiate.

[114] Millard, "Prophétie et écriture", p. 140.
[115] Von Rad, *Theology*, 2:285.
[116] Sauer, "Serubbabel", p. 202.
[117] Meyers and Meyers, p. 83.

notion of a bellicose role for Zerubbabel[118] as is sometimes affirmed.[119] As Dumbrell observes, the model of the Davidic empire is frequently used in prophetic texts as basis for the description of the eschatological reign of Yahweh, without necessarily implying that the empire would be reconstituted.[120] If this is the case here, (and I believe it to be), it is to be expected that Zerubbabel's role remain unspecified and vague. Despite the announcement of the defeat of the nations, no mention is made of either an active role for Zerubbabel in this defeat (in contrast to the traditions of David's military exploits) or of Zerubbabel's supremacy over the nations (in contrast to the themes of David's imperial rule and that of the royal figure in Pss 2 and 110). In 2:20–23, the details of the relationship between Zerubbabel and the vanquished nations remain completely unspecified. Thus here, as elsewhere, the prophet employs a hermeneutic of generalization and attenuation in his use of traditional materials. This proclivity for general and non-specific descriptions constitutes an integral part of the rhetorical artistry and strategy of the book.[121]

## 8.4.2. *The Conflation and Harmonization of Divergent Traditions*

Hag 2:6–9 and 2:20–22 contain several elements, often of variegated origins, which are organized to form a more coherent unity.[122] The following scenario emerges from this re-organization: (1) terrifying signs and wonders appear in the heavens and upon earth (2:21b); (2) as a result, the nations are terrified and their armies annihilate one another (2:22); (3) Yahweh's favour is restored to Israel. This favour is manifested by (4) the presentation of the treasures of the nations at the Jerusalem temple, (5) the glorification of the temple, and (6) universal peace (2:6–9).[123] In this context (7) Zerubbabel will experience exaltation and honour as a symbol of Yahweh's renewed favour to him and his house (2:23). This configuration, as we have seen, is made up of elements drawn from several theological streams, found elsewhere in the use of

---

[118] Ibid.

[119] Petersen, p. 105; Sauer, "Serubbabel" pp. 202–203.

[120] Dumbrell, "Political Origins", pp. 36ff.

[121] Petersen has rightly noticed that Haggai's language reflects a "generalizing trend" (p. 99) and could be called "hopelessly general" (p. 101). Such language is, however, extremely effective at a rhetorical level if the goal is the fostering of future hope.

[122] Beyse, *Königserwartungen*, p. 65.

[123] These last three can be inferred from 2:6–9.

tradition in Haggai.[124] The book, therefore, presents a more logical, internally consistent, and harmonized version of the eschaton than is sometimes the case in other prophetic descriptions.

### 8.4.3. *Tradition as a Basis for Continuity with the Past*

In this pericope the reader is struck by the numerous echoes of diverse religious traditions (holy war, exodus, conquest, oracles against the nations, election of Israel, Zion, etc.). By means of these allusions the prophet establishes a continuity between the community at Jerusalem and its cherished traditions regarding the past. He reiterates and reaffirms older eschatological traditions in order to authenticate the abiding validity of those hopes which remained unfulfilled at the time of his speaking. Petersen observes, "Haggai shows himself capable of presenting himself as a prophet advocating the religion of an older period. The image thus created is highly conservative."[125] The use of such language casts Haggai in the likeness of an authentic Israelite prophet.[126] Like the covenant of Sinai alluded to in 2:5, Haggai here proclaims that pre-exilic hopes, including those attached to the house of David, were not defunct.

### 8.4.4. *Actualization of Religious Traditions*

The realities of Persian rule necessitated the reformulation of certain facets of earlier traditions. In 2:20–23 such an adaptation may be seen in the way Haggai formulates his message so that, despite the clear stability of Darius' rule, Israel could in some sense conceive of herself as a nation under Davidic leadership.[127] By designating Zerubbabel as Yahweh's servant (עבד), by describing this status as the result of Yahweh's choice (בחר), and by projecting great hopes concerning him into the future, Haggai creates what can be described as a "theological compromise." In 520, Israel was not an independent nation, and Zerubbabel was not a king. However by his use of tradition, the prophet assures his

---

[124] Sauer, "Serubbabel", p. 203.

[125] Petersen, p. 101.

[126] Petersen, ibid., comments, "What has appeared to most commentators as hopelessly general language is, in fact, highly affective and effective discourse, serving to link Haggai to normative Israelite traditions and to define him as an authentic prophet in his own time."

[127] Petersen, p. 106.

hearers that the postexilic community, with its temple, priesthood, and governor constituted a *provisional yet valid equivalent* which is acceptable in the eyes of Yahweh.[128] Furthermore, in the future, Yahweh would transform this modest provisional equivalent into a complete fulfillment of his promise.[129] This being so, the community could gather around the defining structure provided by the temple, the high priest, and the Davidic governor in complete assurance that these institutions, which were linked to the past and held hope for the future, were fully acceptable to Yahweh in the present.

Viewed this way, the eschatological scenario sketched by Haggai corresponds well to the realities of his time and to the needs of his hearers. Yehud was sparsely populated, without any military strength, ruled by a foreign king, and under the authority of a governor. Nevertheless, Haggai's eschatological scenario would have been perceived by his hearers as capable of fulfillment in the context of early post-exilic Yehud. His words call for no military activity on Israel's part. Yahweh would deal with the nations. The eschatological battle would not consist of an assault on the gates of Jerusalem (cf. Zech 14). The Jerusalem of Haggai's day would hardly have been seen as a prize to be conquered! The form of the future government envisaged by Haggai was neither a pure hierocracy, nor absolute monarchy.[130] The vision of the future he sets before his hearers could therefore be realized at any moment. What is more, the highly general nature of that vision enabled the community to accommodate itself to the realities of Persian rule, while maintaining hope in a future whose contours would ultimately be determined by God.

---

[128] Meyers and Meyers (p. xliii) accurately note that Haggai and Zechariah "succeeded in an unprecedented way in helping to reconcile the present circumstances with sacred traditions."

[129] Beyse, *Königserwartungen*, pp. 65–66.

[130] Beyse (ibid., p. 65) says, "In designating Zerubbabel as Yahweh's royal representative Haggai finds a third way for his people and his time, one that is somewhere between pure hierocracy and absolute monarchy." Cf. also Meyers and Meyers, p. 83.

# CHAPTER NINE

# THE BOOK OF HAGGAI: LITERARY SYNTHESIS

## 9.1. INTRODUCTION

I have argued thus far that the book of Haggai reflects a distinct perspective on prophecy and society, formulated early in the reign of Darius I. The preceding exegesis has elucidated the meaning of the text, and, in so doing, touched on the book's perspective regarding various significant issues of the day. This chapter will present a literary synthesis of the book, including its form, structure, and rhetorical emphases. I have chosen to address these issues at this point rather than before the exegesis (as is traditionally done in commentaries) for two reasons. First, statements regarding such matters are better made on the basis of a detailed analysis of the text. Second, form and structure quite frequently serve as vehicles for the leading themes of a document, and hence may be best perceived once the text has been closely read.

## 9.2. THE FORM OF HAGGAI

As we have seen, the book of Haggai has been traditionally understood as being the result of a series of redactional additions to the oracles proclaimed by the prophet (Ackroyd, Beuken, Mason, Koch, Steck, Wolff). This being the case, evidence of the redactional activity is seen as diminishing the closer one comes to the original prophetic core.[1] These redactional additions are generally said to consist primarily of introductory formulae and conclusions. Accordingly it is deemed possible to distinguish earlier from later redactions on the basis of vocabulary, political ideology, or theological affiliation (so Wolff and Beuken), or to differentiate the oracles from the framework on the basis of the degree of each's eschatological orientation (so Mason). This being the case, attempts are made to determine the various forms which may have been present in the original oracles. The literary outcome of the redactional activity is frequently described as a series of episodes or

---

[1] For detailed illustrations of this approach, cf. ch 2, above.

sketch scenes set in a chronicle-like format. Given this approach, *a priori*, one would not expect to find any deeply-rooted and consistent form and structure either in the book as a whole, or in its constituent parts.

This "oracles versus redaction" approach has been called into question from a variety of angles.[2] First, there is significant evidence of continuity between the "oracles" and "framework" both on a linguistic and traditio-theological level.[3] Second, and conversely, there is no clear evidence of radical discontinuity between the two.[4] Third, in contrast to other prophetic books where redactional activity can be easily distinguished from earlier oracular material, in Haggai the oracles are thematically and grammatically integrated into the material which surrounds them.[5] Fourth, a variety of means are used to move the action of the book forward. These include not only the dates, but also such elements as citations of popular sayings, the content of the words of the prophet, and brief narrative descriptions. The result is a work which has a beginning and an end point, reflects dramatic movement, and develops its characters, plot, and theme.[6] In sum, in contrast to most of the other prophets in the Book of the Twelve (apart from Jonah), as well as to Isaiah or Jeremiah,[7] Haggai, while not a traditional narrative *per se*, reads in a way that closely resembles one.[8] By this I mean that no complex methodology must be deployed in order to read the text as a narrative of a series of situations which the prophet Haggai addressed, rather than a simple collection of his oracles.[9] Put simply, the book reads somewhat like a story.

---

[2] Cf. *supra*, ch. 2, pp. 37–39.

[3] Ch. 2, pp. 53–56

[4] Ch. 2, p. 53.

[5] Floyd, "Narrative", pp. 477–79 and Petersen, pp. 32–33.

[6] These points will be developed *infra* in this ch.

[7] As Petersen well notes, pp. 32–33.

[8] Floyd (p. 259) aptly comments, "The book of Haggai is a continuous series of episodes in which a prophetic speaker plays the central role, not a collection of prophetic speeches to which narrative notations have been added." This may slightly overstate the case, in that the production of the book may have indeed involved redactional additions to existing oracles. Nevertheless I believe Floyd's general thrust to be sound.

[9] Cf., for example, P. R. House (*Zephaniah: A Prophetic Drama*, [JSOTSup 69; Sheffield: Almond, 1989]) who argues for a dramatic structure in Zephaniah. Whether or not one may justly describe Zephaniah as a "prophetic drama," my point is that if it is one, its essential dramatic structure and form are far less evident than those of Haggai. House's approach is dismissed by Floyd, p. 167. It seems to me that House's methodology has a significant weakness. He delimits certain characteristics of a drama,

It is not possible, however, to view Haggai as a narrative in the traditional sense of the word. Without entering into a technical discussion of narrative here, suffice it to say that, in contrast to the more typical biblical narratives, the bulk of the material in the book consists of words attributed to Haggai. This being the case, it seems more judicious to see the book as a hybrid form of prophecy and narrative. This approach was taken by D. Petersen in his 1984 commentary.[10] Petersen analyzed Haggai in terms of the genre designation *historische Kurzgeschichte*, formulated by N. Lohfink.[11] In a 1978 article Lohfink argued for the existence of a late pre-exilic prose narrative genre with an apologetic focus, featuring short scenes of unequal length bounded by date formulae, focusing on important characters, and set in a chronological-historical framework.[12] He found this genre to be in evidence in such sixth-century texts as Jer 26, 36, 37–41 and 2 Kgs 22–23. Petersen saw Haggai as belonging to Lohfink's genre, but suggested his own label for it: a "brief apologetic historical narrative."[13] In 1995 I critiqued the assignation of either of these two descriptive labels to Haggai.[14] I argued that these designations failed to do justice to the strongly *prophetic orientation* of the text. When one compares Haggai with the texts adduced by Lohfink and Petersen, the narrative form of the texts in Jeremiah and 2 Kings stands in distinct contrast to the very focused interest in the person, and, most especially, the words of one prophet seen in Haggai. More recently Floyd has also contested the application of Petersen's category to Haggai. He argues that (1) Haggai is more intentionally "historical" than the other works deemed as belonging to the genre (i.e., Jonah and Ruth), and (2) the designation does not give enough weight to the "prophetic nature" or "mantic" focus of the apologetic presented in Haggai.[15] Floyd maintains that the narrator mixes the words and perspectives of Haggai the prophet with

---

then finds evidence of them in Zephaniah. However this may merely prove that Zephaniah shares certain characteristics with the dramatic form, without necessarily being a drama. Even if House is correct in seeing such elements in Zephaniah, the book hardly reads like a story. Haggai, though certainly quite different from a traditional narrative, can be read as a story about Haggai's words and deeds.

[10] Petersen, pp. 32–36.

[11] N. Lohfink, "Die Gattung der 'Historischen Kurzgeschichte' in den letzten Jahren von Juda und in der Zeit des Babylonischen Exils", *ZAW* 90 (1978): 319–47.

[12] Petersen's summary, pp. 34–35.

[13] Ibid., p. 35.

[14] Kessler, "Le livre d'Aggée", pp. 233–34.

[15] Floyd, p. 261.

his own reflections. This results in a dual perspective in the book: Haggai's prophetic insights are presented as well as those "that the author has derived from studying Haggai, which extend Haggai's perceptions of Yahweh's involvement in earlier events to show how he might also be involved in new situations." Floyd calls this highly specific type of narrative "prophetic history."[16]

While I concur with Floyd's critique of Petersen, I do feel his own designation may be improved upon in three significant areas. First, the book of Haggai uses its date formulae not only for the *narrative and dramatic* purpose of moving the story forward and marking its divisions, but also *rhetorically* as a means of making the book of Haggai resemble *other prophetic collections*. Thus its formal and literary links with other prophetic compilations should not be minimized. Second, the first three scenes in Haggai (1:1–15; 2:1–9; 2:10–19), if not all four, evoke and resolve a dramatic conflict or *agon*.[17] Thus the work, in addition to its prophetic and narrative quality, has a highly intentional *dramatic* focus.[18] Third, despite my strong sympathies with Floyd's work in general, I am not convinced that he adequately demonstrates that Haggai's narrator has gained his own prophetic insight through the study of Haggai's words. Based on the foregoing exegesis, I maintain that, rather than being a *student* of Haggai, the narrator is one who reveres Haggai and his contribution, and seeks to assure that the prophet's historical significance, as well as the ongoing relevance of his words will not be forgotten. This being the case, the descriptive label which I propose is that of a *dramatized prophetic compilation*, with an apologetic focus.[19] In truth, all of the above cited designations are valuable in their ability to describe this text, somewhere between prophecy and narrative, with its focus on the significance of Haggai, both in his own historical moment and for future generations.

---

[16] Ibid., pp. 261–62.

[17] On *agon* cf. House, *Zephaniah*, p. 61, with bibliography. On this structure in Haggai, cf. *infra*.

[18] This focus has been well observed by Peckham (*History*, p. 741) who calls attention to the dramatic ebb and flow within the pericopae.

[19] Kessler, "Le livre d'Aggée", p. 234, where I used the phrase *receuil prophétique dramatisé*.

## 9.3. THE STRUCTURE OF HAGGAI

If such is the form of the book, what of its structure? As noted above, scholars who view the book's production as a series of revisions and reworkings tend to minimize any search for a coherent macro-structure, and focus instead on the structure of the individual units in their present and earlier forms (Amsler, Wolff, Beuken). Those who view the final form of the book as reflecting a greater degree of intentionality have made various suggestions as to its organization. These suggestions fall into two groups. The first group includes those who divide the text into its major segments and then analyze the constituent parts and structure of each unit (so Verhoef, Meyers and Meyers). A second group, however, proceeds further and seeks to discover any structural or literary correspondences between the various pericopae at the level of their internal structure, as well as the broader configuration of the pericopae as units within the structure of the book as a whole. My own proposal falls within this second group.

Three authors serve as illustrations of this second approach. Baldwin divides the book into two cycles of three elements: (1) Accusation, 1:1–11 and 2:10–17; (2) Response, 1:12–14 and 2:18–19; (3) Assurance of success, 2:1–9 and 2:20–23.[20] Chary proposes two cycles of four corresponding elements: (1) Criticism addressed to the people, 1:1–5 and 2:10–14; (2) Reminder of material poverty, 1:6–9 and 2:15–17; (3) Return to grace, 1:12–14 and 2:18–19; (4) Messianic oracle 2:2–9 and 2:20–23.[21] Peckham posits three units: (1) 1:1–15a; (2) 1:15b-2:9; (3) 2:10–23. He maintains that each unit "rises to a crescendo and then ends as it begins" reflecting a pattern of denouement and inclusion. The first two sections consist of pairs of matching paragraphs, while the third, a later addition, does not.[22]

In my view, an adequate structural analysis of Haggai must proceed from an understanding of the text as being comprised of four rather than three or five units. Thus, I view 1:12–15 as a narrative conclusion to 1:1–11 which, while distinct from it (as signaled by the movement from direct discourse to narration),[23] must be considered as of a piece

---

[20] Baldwin, p. 31.
[21] Chary, pp. 12–13. Stuhlmueller follows Chary's structural analysis.
[22] Peckham, *History*, p. 741.
[23] *Pace* Floyd (p. 270) who includes 1:12 with 1:1–11. Floyd (ibid.) does, however refer to vv. 12–15 as a "narration."

with it. Key terms link the two sections. These include בוא (1:2, 14), בית (1:2, 4, 9, 14), the divine name יהוה צבאות (1:2, 5, 7, 14), the names and titles of prophet, governor, and high priest (1:1, 12), the people (1:2, 12, 14) as well as a variety of thematic issues. Conversely, 2:20–23 must be distinguished from 2:10–19 and seen as a distinct pericope. The redactor inserts a date formula in v. 20, with the specific notation that this was a second and separate oracle (שנית). Furthermore, the oracle stands in sharp contrast to that which precedes it by its distinctive focus on Zerubbabel, its eschatological frame of reference, and its traditio-theological rootings (Davidic dynasty, Zion theology, Israel and the nations). As a result it is essential to see 1:1–15; 2:1–9; 2:10–19 and 2:20–23 as the constituent components of the text.

If these are the text's basic elements, what correspondence, if any, exists between them? K. Koch, identified three common formal elements in 1:3–9; 2:2–9, and 2:10–19.[24] These were: (1) an allusion to the contemporary situation (*Hinweis auf die Lage*), 1:2–4; 2:3, 11–13; (2) the present moment as decisive (*gegenwärtige Zeitpunkt als Wendepunkt*), 1:5–6; 2:4–5, 14, and (3) promise for the future (*Ankündigung*), 1:7–8; 2:6–7, 15–19. Furthermore, he highlighted the key role played by ועתה within the individual oracles,[25] as well as the repeated use of the dates, address formulae and the Word-Reception Formula (*Wortempfangsnotiz*).[26] Given the limits of his study, Koch did not discuss 2:20–23 or the book's overall structure and thematic development. However, his analysis did bring to light clear evidence of a repeated pattern in the pericopae he examined.

Using Koch's three elements as a point of departure, I find evidence of an internal structural similarity in all four scenes in Haggai. However, I find this structural undergirding to be a loose and flexible one that is adapted to the particulars of each pericope. The fact that it is not slavishly followed at every point should not be seen as an obstacle to its presence as a structuring device. I suggest therefore that the pericopae are built around the following elements:

1. Introductory Formula. This normally consists of a date, an indication of recipients of the message and a Word-Event Formula[27] which includes the name and title of Haggai (1:1; 2:1, 10, 20).[28]

---

[24] Koch, "Haggais", pp. 52–66.
[25] Ibid., pp. 59–60.
[26] Wolff and Beuken use the term *Wortereignisformel*.
[27] I.e., ויהי דבר־יהוה ביד־חגי הנביא לאמר.
[28] Haggai's title is absent in 2:20.

2. Dramatic Conflict. These dramatic conflicts are diverse in nature and revealed by various means, such as citations of the people's words (1:2), questions (2:2–3), or a prophetic symbolic act (2:11–13). Such conflicts may consist of the attitude and choices of the people that have set them in opposition to Yahweh (1:2), or it may concern their perception and resultant sentiments (2:3). It may also relate to situations of imbalance or disequilibrium. In 2:14 such a state of affairs consists of the problem of ritual impurity and its effect on Yahweh's dwelling place. Despite the fact that in 2:20–21 no dramatic conflict is explicitly stated, the question of the subaltern status of Israel and of her governor may be implied as the dramatic tension which drives the pericope.

3. Divine Response. This response to the dramatic conflict takes the form of questions, dialogue or debate (1:4–7, 9–11; 2:4–5, 14–17), often including challenges and exhortations, frequently introduced by ועתה[29] and associated with a form of the verb עשׂה.[30] The sense of exhortation or encouragement may be seen as implicit in 2:20–23 in that 2:1–9 (which uses similar eschatological motifs) contains an explicit oracle of encouragement (2:4).

4. Declaration of Promise. These promises may be either eschatological in scope (2:6–9 and 21b-23) or relate more directly to the resumption of normal or even abundant results in the community's economic and agricultural endeavours (2:18–19, and implied in 1:4–11) or to Yahweh's acceptance of the community's efforts (1:8).

The narrative in 1:12–15 is unique in the book. It serves as *post-scriptum* to 1:1–11 and fulfills two functions: (1) it shows that Haggai's words were, with Yahweh's help, effective, and they received an immediate response, and (2) it advances the dramatic movement of the book and prepares the reader for the conflict to be encountered in 2:1–3. Its presence is virtually indispensable in this regard. No narrative conclusion is attached elsewhere in the book, however 2:1–9 and 2:10–19 are prefaced by quasi-narrative introductions (2:2–3; 11–13).

The four scenes in Haggai thus follow a similar progression.[31] Following an introductory formula, a dramatic conflict is presented or implied. Yahweh responds with a challenge to his people to respond decisively and appropriately in the present, and offers them hope for

---

[29] 1:5; 2:4, 15.
[30] 1:14; 2:4, 17.
[31] Cf. Peckham, *History*, pp. 741f.

the future. In this way the conflicts or threats posed in each pericope are overcome, one by one.

In the first scene (1:1–15) the dramatic conflict is relational in nature. The community has lost its sense of priorities and become alienated from Yahweh's blessing. Yahweh answers with both rebuke and promise. The people must set to work immediately. If they do, he promises to accept the work of their hands and, implicitly, to restore that which has been withdrawn from them. A short narrative (1:12–15) relates the results of the prophet's intervention. Its conclusion (v. 14) asserts that by means of Haggai's words, Yahweh acted upon the hearts of the leaders and people, the work was resumed, and the relation between Yahweh and Israel was renewed.

In the second scene (2:1–9) the dramatic conflict involves a problem of perception. Having set to work, the people are overcome by strong feelings of disappointment at the physical appearance of the reconstructed temple (2:2–3). Here the solution is not (as in 1:1–11) to be found in renewed obedience or a restored relationship with Yahweh. Rather, since the essential problem is one of disappointment, Yahweh provides assurances both for the present and the future. He states that he will bless the community with his presence and assistance in the present (2:4–5) and promises that, in the context of a great and dramatic eschatological intervention, he will bring such an influx of wealth to the temple that its future splendour will far outstrip anything the site had previously known. These assurances provide the ground for perseverance in the task at hand (2:4–5).

In the third scene (2:10–19) the dramatic conflict centres around the question of ritual purification. Both people and temple require purification (2:14). The conflict is resolved by the ceremonial refoundation of the temple, which both secures its purification and establishes continuity with its pre-exilic counterpart (2:18). The necessary measures having been taken, Yahweh promises to bless the agricultural and economic pursuits of the community (2:15–19).

The fourth scene (2:20–23) once again takes up the question of the future (cf. 2:6–9). Here the dramatic conflict is to be implied from the oracles in vv. 21b-23 which, as in 2:6–9, evoke Yahweh's promises for the future as a basis for hope and perseverance in the present. The implied conflict centres around the seeming failure of the traditional promises regarding Israel's preeminence among the nations and the exalted status of her Davidic ruler. Haggai's response, which is intentionally imprecise, promises Zerubbabel that in the context of a spectacular divine intervention (cf. 2:6–9), he will be exalted far beyond his present status. Like the temple in 2:6–9, Zerubbabel's apparent insignificance in the present will be transformed into great glory through Yahweh's activity.

When these successive conflicts and resolutions are viewed in their thematic development, the following progression emerges. There is an alternating A/B/A/B structure, between, on the one hand, two problems whose effect is to produce a rift in the relationship between Yahweh and his people (1:2–11; 2:10–19) and, on the other, two problems that concern the disappointment of the people in light of the realities of the day (2:1–9; 20–23).[32] This larger structure functions in tandem with the internal dramatic structure of the individual pericopae and serves as the vehicle for the thematic and dramatic progression of the book. The text moves from the past, a period of futility and curse, to the present, a critical moment that provides an opportunity for action to be taken which can radically change the experience of the community, then finally, to the future, which holds forth the promise of divine blessing both for daily life and for the great day of Yahweh. In the course of the book we move from failure (1:4–11; 2:15–18) to blessing (2:18–19), from humiliation (1:4–11; 2:15–17) to exaltation (2:6–9, 20–23), and from alienation and rejection (1:2) to acceptance and restoration (1:13–14; 2:5, 18, 23).

## 9.4. LEITWÖRTER AND LEITMOTIVEN IN HAGGAI

The identification of the text's *Leitwörter* and *Leitmotiven*[33] provides additional evidence of the book's structure and its main themes. Six areas are especially significant here. The first concerns the preponderance of proper names in such a short book. The name Yahweh occurs 35 times, Haggai, 9 times, the people, 8 times, Zerubbabel, 7 times, and Joshua, 5 times, yielding a total of 64. Titles and genealogies (or epithets in the case of Yahweh) are frequently attached to these names. The narrator therefore insists upon the importance of the designations of main characters of the drama, as well as their authority, social status and filiation.

The second area concerns the various terms used in relationship to the reception and proclamation of the prophetic word, and the role and status of the prophet. In addition to the Word-Event Formula (1:1, 3;

---

[32] Cf. Childs, *Introduction*, pp. 469–70.
[33] On this aspect of literary analysis cf. Alter, *Biblical Narrative*, ch. 5.

2:1, 10, 20), the relevant terms include: ביד (1:1, 3; 2:1), אל (2:10, 20), נביא (1:1, 3, 12; 2:1, 10), מלאך יהוה (1:13), שלח (1:13), as well as the parallelism between the words of Yahweh and those of Haggai (1:12).

The third major theme is the notion of time. The importance of this issue can be seen in the multiple chronological points of reference in the text. The book includes five date formulae (1:1, 15; 2:1, 10, 20). The adverb ועתה (and now) is repeated four times (1:5; 2:3, 4, 15). In 1:1–11 the dispute between Yahweh and his people revolves around their respective evaluations of whether or not the community is in a position to undertake the temple's reconstruction. In this debate עת (time; 1:2, 4) plays a central role. The present-future antithesis is expressed by ראשון־אחרון (former-latter) in 2:3. The same terms contrast the present and future in 2:9. Similarly in 2:15, the past (introduced by מטרם, before), is to be distinguished from the future. That future has a precise starting point (מן־היום הזה, from this day; 2:18–19), and will continue without interruption (מעלה, forward; 2:18). Haggai's vision of the resplendent eschatological future is designated by the two temporal expressions עוד אחת מעט היא (one more time, in a little while; 2:6) and ביום ההוא (on that day; 2:23). Yet despite these distinctions, for Haggai the past, present, and future are linked at a deeper level through the community's relationship to Yahweh. Thus, continuity becomes a key factor in the book's understanding of time. Neither the catastrophic events of the Babylonian invasion, nor the people's negligence of the temple have caused a definitive rupture. This is seen in the language of continuity used with reference to Yahweh's house (2:3, 9) and the identification of the postexilic community with the people who left Egypt (2:5).

Fourth, the text allocates significant attention to the theme of speech. Vocabulary related to speech and verbal communication is disproportionate in this small book. The verb אמר is found 15 times (apart from the complementizer לאמר). On ten occasions the subject is Yahweh (1:2, 5, 7, 8; 2:6, 7, 9, 11, 21), three times it is Haggai, (1:13; 2:13, 14), twice the priests (2:12, 13) and once the people (1:2). Other terms related to communication include דבר (to say, speak; 1:1, 3; 2:1, 10, 20), ענה (to answer; 2:12, 13), and שאל (to ask; 2:11). Direct discourse is most frequently employed, לאמר[34] being found 10 times (1:1, 2, 3, 13; 2:1, 2, 10, 11, 20, 21). As Floyd has noted, the limits of the direct speech and the

---

[34] Cf. Miller, *Representation, passim.*

identity of the specific speakers are at times extremely difficult to determine.[35] Second person pronouns or pronominal suffixes are employed approximately 24 times, and those of the first person 11 times. Volitives appear approximately 10 times. Further, 10 questions are found (1:4; 2:3 [3x], 12, 13, 15–16, 19 [3x]). Very frequently, the first person singular and the second person (singular or plural) are juxtaposed (1:9, 13; 2:4, 5a, 5b, 17a, 17b, 23aα, 23aβ, 23b). Thus this book strongly emphasizes verbal communication.

The fifth *Leitmotiv*, and the one most often referred to, is the temple, its reconstruction and consecration. The term בית (house), referring to the temple is found 10 times (1:2, 4, 8, 9a, 9b, 14; 2:3, 7, 9)[36] and היכל (temple) is found twice (2:15, 18). Building materials are also mentioned: עץ (wood) 1:8 and אבן (stone) 2:15. Verbs related to activities undertaken upon the building include: בנה (to build) 1:2, 8; עשה (to carry out, perform) 1:14; שׂים (to place) 2:15; and יסד (here, to consecrate, re-found), 2:18.

The sixth central theme is that of reversal. Similar to dramatic irony in tone, this theme encompasses both the disappointment caused by the failure of expectations, as well as the hope that the seemingly impossible will indeed occur. This motif is discernible in the descriptions of the community's disappointing experience in its economic and agricultural activities. The reversal of expectations may be expressed by the antithesis רבה / מעט (few, many, 1:4–11; 2:15–18) or by the pairing of greater and lesser numbers עשרים / עשרה or חמשים / עשרים (twenty/ten; fifty/twenty; 2:16). It is also evidenced by the disparity between expectation and reality expressed by the verbs פנה (to expect, 1:9), ראה (to see, 2:3) and בוא (to come, 1:9; 2:15a and 15b). This theme is also present in Haggai's eschatological descriptions of the total overthrow of the present order as a prelude to the inauguration of a new and blessed age. The verbs רעש (to shake, 2:6, 7, 21) and הפך (to overturn, 2:22a, 22b) figure prominently in this regard.

The significance of these six motifs and their relevance to the central theme of Haggai will be discussed below.

---

[35] Floyd, "Narrative", pp. 478ff.
[36] The term is also used with reference to the people's houses in 2:4 and v. 9b.

## 9.5. CHARACTERS AND ACTION

There are seven characters or *dramatis personae* in Haggai: Yahweh, Haggai, Zerubbabel, Joshua, the people,[37] the priests, and the nations and their armies. It is not necessary to rehearse the activities and attitudes of each character here. Two points, however, deserve special notice. The first concerns the book's perspective on the power of Yahweh. The second involves the relationship between Yahweh and Haggai.

The book of Haggai portrays Yahweh as active and powerful in a variety of ways. Nature is under his control. He can diminish the productivity of the land, bring natural calamities such as drought and hail, or cause grain to rot with diseases (1:11; 2:16–17). Conversely, he can bring about fruitfulness and prosperity (2:18). He is capable of destabilizing the entire cosmos and can cause terrifying signs and wonders visible throughout the whole world (2:6–9, 20–23). He can throw the nations of the earth into panic, destroy their power, move their armies to mutual annihilation and ensure their ultimate submission. He is able to bring the treasures of the nations to Jerusalem (2:6–9). He has delivered his people from bondage in Egypt (2:5). He manifests his presence in the midst of his people (1:13; 2:4). He chooses particular individuals for specific tasks (2:23).

What is surprising, however, is not what Yahweh does, nor the scope of his power or dominion, but rather what such power *cannot* achieve. Hag 1:4–11 (and the comment in 2:17) are critical in this regard. Yahweh inflicted a variety of hardships and sufferings upon his people, the purpose of which was to bring them back to himself. Nevertheless his purposes went unfulfilled as the community went about its daily affairs and the religious and civil authorities took no initiative. Thus, for the book's framer(s), despite Yahweh's great power elsewhere in the universe, only his intervention through prophetic speech, mediated by Haggai, sufficed to bring about change. Prophetic intervention is thus portrayed as *the critical agency through which Yahweh is able to effect change within the community*.

The second point of note concerns the relationship between Yahweh and Haggai. The personality of the prophet appears to be deliberately veiled in the book. No biographical details are given.[38] The text con-

---

[37] *Pace* Floyd and others who view the remnant of the people (1:12, 14) as a group distinct from the people mentioned in 1:2, cf. exegesis.

[38] Genealogical notices are given for Zerubbabel and Joshua in Haggai (1:1, 12, 14

tains no indication of Haggai's personal reaction to the profound effects his oracles produced. No words are exchanged between Yahweh and his spokesman. Apart from the reference to the temple of Yahweh in 2:18, Haggai never speaks of Yahweh in the third person,[39] but always on his behalf in the first person. In the only place where the prophet speaks without an explicit order from Yahweh (1:13), he speaks in the first person. The narrator insists on the fact that the voice of Yahweh can be heard in the words of Haggai (1:12). In contrast to this minimalist representation of the prophet's personal identity and individuality, the narrator has much to say about Haggai's role and function, as we have seen. The best explanation of this "impersonal" portrait of our prophet is a redactional desire to stress Haggai's role and status as well as the institution he represents, rather than his individual identity and personality.

Thus, in Haggai, in spite of his power and his control over nature, the world, and its nations, Yahweh's purpose may be frustrated by his recalcitrant people. Such opposition, however, can be overcome by the prophetic word.

## 9.6. Plot or Thematic Centre?

At this point it is appropriate to ask whether Haggai can be said to have a plot or, failing that, a thematic centre. In identifying the book as a dramatized prophetic collection, I have sought to underline its formal similarity with collections of prophetic oracles, on one hand, and with biblical narrative, especially in its more clearly "dramatic" forms (Jonah, Ruth, Esther, the Joseph narrative), on the other. E. M. Forster defines plot as "a narrative of events, the emphasis falling on causality."[40] A plot generally involves a primary conflict (or *agon*) and a denouement or resolution.[41] Indeed, as we have seen, in Haggai the reader follows the movement of the protagonists, Yahweh and Haggai,

---

etc.) but never for the prophet himself, in contrast to the great majority of the canonical prophets in prophetic superscriptions (Isa 1:1; Jer 1:1; Zeph 1:1); cf. G. M. Tucker, "Prophetic Superscriptions and the Growth of a Canon, in *Canon and Authority: Essays in Old Testament Religion and Theology*, (ed. G. W. Coats and B. O. Long; Philadelphia: Fortress, 1977), pp. 56–70.

[39] Cf. Isa 40–55 where the prophet frequently uses the third person.

[40] E. M. Forster, *Aspects of the Novel*, (New York: Harcourt, Brace, Jovanovich, 1955), p. 86, cited in House, *Zephaniah*, p. 61.

[41] Ibid.

on one hand, and Zerubbabel, Joshua, and the people, on the other,
through a series of dramatic conflicts and resolutions. In its broadest
sense, the book tells the story of the initiation of the temple's reconstruction, of the builders' discouragement regarding their labour, of
the building's reconsecration, of the great promises attached to it, of
the ongoing perseverance of the community, and of the promises made
regarding the future of Yehud's governor. However in terms of the presence of a plot, Haggai differs quite clearly from most biblical narratives.
This is evident in the fact that each pericope raises and resolves its own
dramatic conflict in a somewhat independent fashion. Put another way,
the book does not sustain a single story line from start to finish. Rather,
it presents the same characters involved in *successive episodes*, each with
its own centre of interest, yet presupposing the events of the earlier
episodes, and moving toward some ultimate resolution.[42] This being the
case, I feel it is more apposite to examine the book for a central theme
or themes in evidence in the various episodes, rather than for a plot
running through them.

### 9.7. The Central Theme of Haggai

In light of the foregoing evidence, I believe that the thematic core
around which the book of Haggai is constructed is the effectiveness
of the "word from Yahweh" as it was mediated by the prophet Haggai.
Various scholars have noticed this theme. Wolff states, "The prophetic
word of only a few months had far-reaching results."[43] Meyers and
Meyers note, "Second Temple Judaism was to survive largely because
of the success of the careers of Haggai and Zechariah; and Haggai,
despite the fact that he was on the scene for so short a time, must be
credited with steering Israel over the most delicate stage in this critical
transition period."[44] Beuken states, "At each critical moment of the
restoration God's prophets bring change for good."[45] Chary comments,
"Prophetic preaching has been effective, an event rarely attested in the

---

[42] On this level Haggai is more than just a series of stories involving the same
characters, who remain constant and display a knowledge of their earlier shared
experiences. The individual episodes are somewhat autonomous, but relate to a larger
goal and purpose.

[43] Wolff, p. 16.

[44] Meyers and Meyers, p. xlii.

[45] Beuken, p. 332.

history of the people."[46] The "prophetic-dramatic" form of the book thus stresses its interest in prophecy and its desire to communicate that importance to succeeding generations in a dramatic form. In each episode the dramatic conflict is resolved by means of a word from Yahweh via Haggai. The *Leitwörter* and *Leitmotiven* stress the fact that in a precise historical situation, involving specific personalities, the voice of Yahweh through the words of Haggai had a transforming effect. The results of that intervention could be plainly seen in a reconstructed and duly reconsecrated temple. Through prophetic intervention, Yahweh's purpose, which was for a time frustrated by the negligence of the people, had finally been accomplished. Once the relationship between Yahweh and his people had been restored, Haggai foresaw a day when Yahweh would overturn the present world order and act in favour of his people. For the book's redactor, given Haggai's great success in the present, who could doubt the reliability of his promises for the future?

Having then undertaken a literary and exegetical analysis of Haggai, we are now in a position to present a synthesis of the book's distinctive perspectives, and to integrate those perspectives into the context of early Persian Yehud. It is to these issues that we turn in the concluding chapter.

---

[46] Chary, p. 21.

CHAPTER TEN

# CONCLUSIONS: PROPHECY AND SOCIETY
## IN THE BOOK OF HAGGAI

This concluding chapter will consist of two parts. First, based on the preceding historical, exegetical, and literary investigation, I will summarize the distinctive perspectives in evidence in Haggai regarding Yehudite society, with special attention to prophecy and the prophetic role.[1] Second, I will situate these perspectives in the broader social context of early Persian Yehud.

## 10.1. The Distinctive Perspectives of the Book of Haggai

### 10.1.1. *Yehud and Persian Domination*

I have argued that in the early years of Darius' reign, Yehud constituted an independent province within the Achaemenid Empire under Zerubbabel, the Persian appointed Davidic governor.[2] This subaltern status of both the community and its leader is candidly acknowledged (Hag 1:1). Nothing in Haggai can be read as inciting resistance to Persian rule (for example, insurrection or withholding taxes). The allusion to the future submission of the nations to Yahweh and the destruction of their armies (2:6–9; 21b–22) is drawn from traditional elements of Zion theology and focuses upon the ultimate victory of Yahweh and the glorification of Zion. Its purpose is to provide hope and encouragement in the present. The same may be said of Zerubbabel's future elevation (2:23). Thus while the Persian Empire may have provided the *model* used in Haggai to describe Gentile power in 2:6–9 and 21–23, such language should not be construed as a veiled attempt to undermine Persian rule. It is

---

[1] Detailed support for these conclusions may be found in the relevant chapters *supra*.

[2] Cf. ch. 3, *supra*. Even if one follows Liver, Sacchi, Bianchi and others in viewing Zerubbabel as a king, he is only a *vassal* king of a small and remote territory, and could have hardly pursued any policy which would have run counter to the interests of the Persian throne.

rather designed to indicate that the *status quo* was only provisional, and that Israel's hopes for the future were not to be abandoned.

This irenic attitude is fully comprehensible given imperial policy in the West. The Persians favoured the development of geographically circumscribed, semi-autonomous ethnic and political units.[3] The loyalty of such units was regularly secured by the installation of elites composed of members of the traditional ruling families. The crown sought to promote the repopulating and economic redevelopment of devastated areas, as these brought increased stability and potential for taxation. The various groupings enjoyed internal religious and legal freedom. Since temples were commonly employed as instruments of fiscal administration, the construction of such sites was supported. It appears evident that, in the context of the early Persian period, there was a large measure of congruency between the goals of the community at Yehud (both exiles and returnees) and those of the crown. Thus the community's most natural reaction would be to view the *pax Persica* as a means *toward* its own aspirations, rather than an impediment to them.

This being said, however, subjection to Persia would not have been seen as ultimately satisfactory for at least two reasons. First, on the economic level, the burden of taxation was heavy. A significant portion of the province's revenue would have been drained away in support of imperial needs. Second, national grandeur was a significant component of various Israelite religious traditions, most especially Deuteronomism (cf. Deut 28:12–13, 25, 33, 36, 43–44, 63) and Zion theology (Ps 46; 48; Zech 14; Isa 55:5; 60:1–22). Ultimate acceptance of the *status quo* would imply the abandonment of hope for the exaltation of Zion and freedom from foreign domination. In Haggai, Persian rule is viewed as a useful means for the attainment of certain goals in the present, but from a more long term perspective, irreconcilable with the aspirations held forth in the community's religious traditions. As such, Persian rule is *provisionally accepted* as a means through which Yahweh's purposes were being fulfilled. In sum, the political perspective of the book of Haggai is one of accommodation to foreign rule, in light of the hope that one day Yahweh would bring such a situation to an end, and completely reverse it.[4]

---

[3] Cf. ch. 3, *supra.*

[4] Cf. Kessler, "Darius and Haggai", p. 84. Ballentine ("Politics of Religion", p. 143) aptly states, "The biblical vision of a community centered on torah and temple, for all

This dual perspective may help to explain the somewhat ambiguous view of communal leadership discernible in the text. On one hand the community is portrayed as being co-led by the governor and high priest (1:1, 12, 14). Yet Zerubbabel is singled out for special attention (2:20–23). Rather than positing this as evidence of a difference in perspective between oracles and framework, or earlier and later redactions,[5] it is more judicious to see this as a feature of the overall thematic perspective of the text. In this present age the community is under foreign domination and the existing structure is viewed as a necessary, yet provisional, concomitant feature of such domination. Furthermore, given that such a structure is a response to foreign rule, it is implicitly non-normative and potentially subject to modification when such was needed. The age to come will be one of freedom from such domination, and in that new context Zerubbabel will hold an exalted position. However this does not necessarily imply that in Haggai the new age will mean a return to monarchy. It is accordingly inaccurate to affirm that Haggai advocated monarchism, in contrast to Zechariah who preferred a dyarchic form of government.[6] In point of fact 2:20–23 says nothing at all about the relative position, roles, and authority of the royal and priestly offices.[7] As we have seen, the future is described in the most general of terms in 2:6–9 and vv. 21–23. The ultimate glorification and exaltation of temple and governor are meant to signal the rule of Yahweh and stimulate hope for the future. This being the case, the language used with reference to Zerubbabel in 2:23, or the absence of similar language regarding the high priest, should not be viewed as a carefully formulated vision of an ideal political structure. As such, the data in Haggai provide no firm basis upon which to reconstruct the book's perspectives regarding *ideal political structures* (for example, dyarchy) for either the Persian period, or the anticipated eschatological era.

---

its theological merit, was to a large extent the result of Yehud's willingness to adjust its religious ideals to the realities of life in the Persian Empire."

[5] Cf. the discussion of the problems implicit in this approach, *supra*. ch. 2.

[6] This appears to be Petersen's conclusion, p. 106.

[7] Such detail is also absent from 2:10–19, where the legitimacy and acceptability of the newly consecrated temple and its priesthood are in view. Rather it is best to see both pericopae as statements which legitimize governor and priests in their then present roles. Meyers and Meyers (p. 82) are right in affirming that 2:20–23 discusses the question of the status of Israel's royal institutions, having broached in 2:10–19 the issue of the temple and priesthood.

### 10.1.2. *The Socio-Religious Portrait of Yehud*

Despite its relatively small population, the community in Yehud appears to have been quite diverse.[8] One of its most distinctive features was that it was comprised of both returnees and non-exiled Judaeans. Some of the latter may have owed their land holdings and economic stability to the land redistribution undertaken by the Babylonians (2 Kgs 25:12; Jer 52:16).[9] Members of the former group held significant positions vis-à-vis the Persian authorities, and were viewed by the latter as the "official" representatives of the community.[10] In addition, other factors may have given them an advantageous position relative to the local population.[11] This being the case, the returnees may be viewed as an elite "charter group."[12] Put briefly, a charter group may be defined as a group which moves into a specific geographic region from without, and successfully establishes its hegemony through control of economic, social, political, and religious institutions. The members of the charter group are generally ethnically or culturally distinct from the local

---

[8] Cf. Kessler, "Haggai's Jerusalem", pp. 137–58.

[9] On these texts cf. J. N. Graham, "Vinedressers and Ploughmen: 2 Kings 25:12 and Jeremiah 52:16", *BA* 47 (1984): 55–58. On land redistribution during the Babylonian period, cf. Kreissig, *Situation*, pp. 26–33.

[10] Cf. the early but perceptive comments of R. Kittel (*Geschichte des Volkes Israel*, [Gotha: Perthes, 1909] p. 320) whose importance was stressed by Kreissig, *Situation*, p. 36; cf. also more recently M. W. Hamilton, "Who was a Jew? Jewish Ethnicity during the Achaemenid Period", *ResQ* 37 (1995): 102–117, esp. pp. 112–14. Hamilton (p. 114) states, "The exiles were claiming to be true Jews because (in part) the Persians said they were".

[11] Lemaire appropriately summarizes ("Histoire et administration", p. 22), "They were the descendants of those taken into exile by Nebuchadnezzar. They had intellectual (scribal), commercial, and technical training. ... The time spent in Babylon made it necessary for them to master imperial Aramaic. It was therefore quite natural that they should move into the role of the ruling class." Cf. also, *supra* ch 3. n. 18 for bibliography and a general discussion. On literacy (the bibliography on the subject is voluminous) cf. R. F. G. Sweet, "Writing as a Factor in the Rise of Urbanism", in *Urbanism in Antiquity*, [JSOTSup 244; ed. W. E. Aufrecht, N. A. Mirau, and S. W. Gauley; Sheffield: JSOT Press, 1997], pp. 39–45), and bilingualism, cf. n. 13 *infra*).

[12] The concept of the charter group derives from the work of the sociologist John Porter, *The Vertical Mosaic: A Study of Social Class and Power in Canada* (Toronto: University of Toronto Press, 1965). Porter's interest is the analysis of the "sociology of power" (p. 207). His primary focus is the power base of the English and French colonists in Canada. I evaluate the appropriateness of the "charter group" as a model for the sociology of early Persian Yehud in "Le livre d' Aggée", pp. 141–78, and I intend to refine and continue this analysis in a future study. Smith (*Landless*, ch. 8) takes a very similar approach to the *golah*, however, he does not refer to Porter's work.

population. The group establishes a culture and social structure which is different from both that of the local population[13] and from that of their context of origin.[14] These two primary sectors of the population in Yehud (returnees and non-exiled Judaeans) may have experienced conflict over land tenure issues, or political allegiances.[15] As well, the community may have been marked by various other economic, theological, or political points of contention.[16] However that may be, the Persian throne had little patience for any sectors of the population that opposed their official representatives and upset the stability and economic development of the region.[17] The balance of power was strongly in favour of the governor and those most clearly identified with imperial interests. Against this backdrop of diversity and real or potential conflict, the *absence of conflict* evidenced in Haggai is highly striking. Simply put, the book contains *no "other"*— that is to say, *no degenerate population distinct from the "true Israel."* At this level the book stands in stark contrast to the sentiments expressed, for example, in Mal 3:16–18, and in a great many texts attributed by scholars to our period.[18] Thus the book deliberately obscures whatever divisions may have existed and presents a stylized

---

[13] On the use of Hebrew as a means of establishing ethnic boundaries, cf. Hamilton, "Who was a Jew?", p. 114. On broader issues of bilingualism, cf. A. Lemaire and H. Lozachmeur, "Remarques sur le plurilinguisme en Asie Mineur à l'époque perse", in *Mosaïque de langues, mosaïque culturelle. Le bilinguisme dans le Proche-Orient ancien*, (ed. F. Briquel-Chatonnet, Antiquités sémitiques 1; Paris: J. Maisonneuve, 1996), pp. 91–123, and Lemaire, "Histoire et administration", pp. 22–24.

[14] Porter, *Vertical Mosaic*, pp. 60ff. On the phenomenon of immigrant ethnic groups whose culture is distinct both from their host country and country of origin cf. Smith, *Landless*, ch. 3. On the situation of the exiles in Babylon, cf. *supra* ch. 3, n. 18.

[15] Land tenure conflicts are seen as having been extensive and divisive in certain reconstructions, cf. Weinberg, "Agrarverhältnis", pp. 479–81; and idem, "Demographische Notizen", p. 50; O. Margalith, "The Political Background of Zerubbabel's Mission and the Samaritan Schism", *VT* 41 (1991): 312–23. Kreissig, (*Situation*, pp. 103–5) sees such conflict as present but limited in scope. The hypothesis of extensive conflict over land tenure has been successfully challenged by Ben Zvi, "Inclusion and Exclusion", esp. pp. 108–10; cf. my own earlier reservations, "Le livre d'Aggée", pp. 131–40. Cf. also Pastor, *Land*, pp. 14–15 and U. Rappoport, J. Pastor, and O. Rimmon, "Land, Society and Culture in Judea", *Trans* 7 (1994): 73–82.

[16] For a survey cf. Kessler, "Haggai's Jerusalem", pp. 138–45, and Grabbe, *Judaism*, 1:103–112. Cf. also Weinberg, "Transmitter and Recipient" *passim*, and Lemaire, "Histoire et administration", pp. 22–23.

[17] Briant, "Pouvoir", pp. 5–6.

[18] My conclusion here rests on the assumption that 2:14 does not relate to the exclusion of a portion of the population and that the remnant terminology in 1:12–14 designates all of the population, not merely a portion of it. The conflict theme in other early Persian period literature cannot be developed here.

and schematic portrait of the community as *acting in concert* in obedience to the word of Yahweh through the prophet Haggai. I perceive two primary reasons for this presentation. First, such an approach reflects an "inclusivist" view of the temple and its role as a central force in Persian Period Judaism. Japhet has commented on postexilic Judaism's need for self definition and identity, given its new existence as a religious phenomenon characterized by geographic and theological diversity.[19] In a similar vein Floyd insightfully speaks of Yahweh's creation of a "worldwide covenant community whose identity is focused on the restored royal sanctuary at Jerusalem."[20] Thus the book has every interest in portraying whatever differences may have existed at the time as having been overcome through an acknowledgment of the centrality of the temple. Such an inclusive stance may have been facilitated by various "strategies of inclusion," most notably genealogical identification with the *golah*,[21] which permitted other Yahwists to be included with that group and considered to be part of the "true Israel."[22] The second reason for this non-conflictual portrait of the community relates to a desire to underline the success of the prophet's words. Haggai's words were so effective that *all* of the community was touched. Unlike Jeremiah, whose words went largely unheeded, the oracles of Haggai had a stunning effect.[23]

Theologically speaking, the book views the community in Yehud as the legitimate successor of the pre-exilic Israelite community and heir

---

[19] S. Japhet, "People and Land in the Restoration Period", in *Das Land Israel in biblischer Zeit*, (ed. G. Strecker; Göttingen: Vandenhoeck & Ruprecht, 1983), p. 114; Hamilton, "Who was a Jew?", pp. 104–14. Petersen (pp. 119–20) speaks of the phenomenon of a non-territorial Yahwism which emerged in the Persian Period.

[20] Floyd, "Cosmos and History", p. 142.

[21] On this cf. Smith, *Landless*, pp. 55–56; Albright, "History of Judah", pp. 12–23; Weinberg, "Demographische Notizen", p. 53; Japhet, "People and Land" *passim*; Ackroyd, *Exile and Restoration*, p. 57, and Hamilton, "Who was a Jew?", pp. 114–17. Cf. also R. Zadok, "On the Reliability of the Genealogical and Prosopographical Lists of the Israelites in the Old Testament", *Tel Aviv* 25 (1988): 228–54; idem, *The Pre-Hellenistic Israelite Anthropology and Prosopography*, (Leuven: Uitgeverij Peeters, 1988); and idem, "Onomastic, Prosopographic, and Lexical Notes", *BN* 65 (1992): 52–53.

[22] On the theme of inclusion in Israel and its importance in the postexilic context, cf. Ben Zvi, "Inclusion and Exclusion" esp. pp. 134–49. Ben Zvi provides an excellent analysis of the issues at stake, and proposes a well-reasoned solution. On the theme of submission to Babylon and remaining in the land as an expression of submission to Yahweh. Cf. also Nicholson, *Preaching to the Exiles*, pp. 128–30 and Seitz, "Crisis of Interpretation", pp. 83–84.

[23] Cf. the various contrasts with Jeremiah, noted in the exegesis. These issues will be taken up later in this chapter.

of its traditions and institutions. This vision of unbroken continuity is a distinctive feature of the book. Some earlier institutions are seen as functioning as they always have. The restored temple is Yahweh's dwelling place among his people (1:8; 2:10–19). The priests determine matters of purity (2:11–13). Other institutions are seen as being present as *functional equivalents*. Thus Zerubbabel functions as a Davidic leader despite his status as a Persian appointee. The book's general perspective can be said to be one which is (1) inclusive and irenic in tone, (2) strongly tradition-based and rooted in the past, (3) restorationist or reconstructionist, that is, attempting to pick up the pieces of the past and replicate, in so far as was possible, that which perished, yet (4) still open to new expressions where older forms could not be replicated due to changed circumstances.

### 10.1.3. *Prophecy and Yehud*

The preceding exegesis and literary analysis has demonstrated the importance attributed to Haggai and the prophetic office in the text. At this point I shall summarize the rich and variegated portrait of the prophet as it emerges in the book.

#### 10.1.3.1. *Titles and Designations*

The frequent designation of Haggai as "the prophet" (הנביא 1:1, 3, 12; 2:1, 10), indicates the importance of that role in the eyes of the redactor. The term הנביא typically designates an intermediary who communicates a word from Yahweh relevant to a particular circumstance in the life of his people. This intermediary role is highlighted in several ways. The Messenger Formula and first person speech in the name of Yahweh are abundantly used in the book. This is especially striking in 2:15–19 where ויען חגי (and Haggai answered) is followed by Yahweh's direct discourse. Such an intermediary function is similarly expressed by the prepositions ביד (through; 1:1, 3; 2:1) and אל (to; 2:10, 20), and the position of the name of Haggai between the word of Yahweh and its recipients in 1:1, 3. The voice of Yahweh can be heard in the words of Haggai (1:12).

Several other terms are used to describe and designate Haggai. In 1:12 Haggai is said to have been sent on Yahweh's behalf (כאשר שלחו יהוה v. 12b). The sending (שלח) by Yahweh stresses the prophet's authority, the veracity of the message proclaimed, and the elevated

status of the one sent. In 1:13 Haggai is called the messenger of Yahweh
(מלאך יהוה). Like שלח this term underlines the great importance of
both message and messenger. Similarly, 1:13 states that Haggai received
his prophetic status through the commission (מלאכות) of Yahweh. His
prophetic call likely lies behind the use of this term.

### 10.1.3.2. *Social Location and Characteristic Behaviour*

The analysis of a prophet's social location (social milieu, social expectations, support groups, relationship to socio-religious authorities) has
become a significant element in contemporary discussions of prophetic
role.[24] In Haggai the issues of the prophet's relationship to social centres of power and his aspirations for change are particularly significant. Analyses of the social location of prophets frequently distinguish
between "central" and "peripheral" prophets.[25] Generally speaking,
central prophets are said to be those who manifest a high degree of
integration in their society, are close to centres of power, and promote moderate change within existing structures. Peripheral prophets
are far more marginalized and have little access to decision makers.
Such prophets may either resist change altogether, or seek change that
benefits groups within the society that have no real voice or power base.
They may sometimes envisage change involving the total destruction of
existing social and economic structures and institutions.

Viewed in these terms, Haggai's relationship to his social context is
one which involves both general continuity and a certain degree of conflict and discontinuity. On one hand, he is well integrated in his society.
One perceives no evidence of hostility between Haggai and his general
social milieu. His words to Joshua and Zerubbabel portray him as having free access to the primary centres of power. His presence among the
people (2:2–3) and his contact with the priests (2:10–13) is presented as
natural and normal. In 1:1 his title, "the prophet," precedes those of the
governor and high priest, while standing syntactically parallel to them.
This would indicate that for the redactor, Haggai is viewed as holding a
socially significant and legitimate role within Yehudite society, one that
is of equal, if not greater, importance than that of the political and religious authorities. He is presented as working within existing institutions
rather than promoting radical social upheaval.

---

[24] Blenkinsopp, *History*, pp. 30–39, with bibliography.
[25] Wilson, *Prophecy and Society*, pp. 62–88.

However while Haggai stands in *general* continuity with his society, he nevertheless at times adopts a confrontational stance and uses traditional prophetic forms of reproach and judgment (1:3–11; 2:10–17). In 1:1–11 a very clear triangular opposition is portrayed between (1) Yahweh and his prophet, (2) the civil and religious leaders, and (3) the people. A similar opposition is created in 2:10–14 where Haggai takes a decision made by "the priests" and uses it as a judgment on the status of the nation as a whole. In Haggai, consequently, a prophet working from within the politico-social system, or a "central prophet"[26] can engage in social criticism and advocate social change.[27] The prophet thus holds a social distance and a "spiritual" authority.[28]

The book depicts Haggai in a diversity of social, religious and political contexts. His proclamation is sometimes portrayed as occurring in public, close to the temple site, as evidenced by the allusions to "this house" (1:4) or "the mountain" (1:8), as well as by the question "how does it appear to you now?"(2:3) or the indictment of "that which they offer *there*" (2:14). I have argued for his presence and participation in the refoundation ceremony, as reflected in 2:10–19. He is able to directly address the governor (2:21–23) although there is no indication of the setting in which this occurred.

Haggai displays behaviour that is typical of the prophets in the Deuteronomistic History and most of the prophetic collections.[29] He receives and mediates the divine word (1:1, 3; 2:1–2, 10, 20–21a). He confronts his hearers using a variety of traditional forms of prophetic disputation, reproach, denunciation and judgment. He points to the community's lack of faithfulness to Yahweh's covenant, and to the deleterious consequences which have ensued (1:1–11, 2:14). He invites his co-religionists to return to Yahweh, and assures them of the latter's willingness to accept them and renew his relationship with them (1:8). He employs a prophetic symbolic act (2:10–13). In a fashion similar

---

[26] Ibid., p. 272.

[27] Ibid. Wilson (ibid., p. 302) notes that the presence of a prophet at the royal court and in the cult does not prevent prophetic criticism of the people, the head of government or the priesthood.

[28] The nature of religious authority is complex. M. Weber suggests three types: traditional, rational-legal, and charismatic. Haggai would certainly have possessed the first and third type.

[29] Such behaviour is found so commonly in these bodies of literature that I will not cite examples. Furthermore, I cannot discuss here the relationship between Haggai and the distinct and specific styles of prophetic activity which are found elsewhere in biblical literature.

to the traditional "oracles against the nations" Haggai proclaims the doom of Gentile power (2:6–7, 21–22).[30] He announces the exaltation of Zion (2:6–9) and her Davidic leader (2:23).[31] He offers his people words of reassurance in their fear (1:13), encouragement in their despondency (2:4–5), and hope in their uncertainty (2:6–9, 20–23). He declares the blessing of Yahweh to be upon the agricultural and economic pursuits of the people (2:18–19). He proclaims an oracle to the political leader of the Jerusalem community concerning his election, status and future (cf. 1 Sam 10; 12; 15; 16; 1 Kgs 1:38ff.).[32] The cumulative effect of these characteristic actions is to depict Haggai as a "typical prophet" in the mould of Amos, Isaiah, or Jeremiah.[33]

This portrait of Haggai stands in contrast to certain assertions made regarding his role. The first is Rothstein's judgment that Haggai is the "father of Judaism" or the one whose words (2: 14) constituted the "birthday of Judaism" because of his rejection of the Samaritan population. However this conclusion is neither exegetically nor historically probable.[34] Second, the text does not endorse Blenkinsopp's suggestion[35] that Haggai is a "cult prophet." Such a *sobriquet* is unwarranted. In 1:1–11 and 2:10–19 Haggai's principal interest is neither the simple repair of the temple, nor the mechanical practice of its rituals. What is at stake for him is proper respect for the honour of the divine name, a notion already widespread in other traditions. Haggai is not dependent upon the temple for his support nor for his place of prophetic activity.

---

[30] Petersen (p. 100) says, "The similarities between the language in Hag 2:22a and that found in Isaiah [Isa 13:19] and Jeremiah [Jer 51:20–21] is striking. Such similarity serves to confirm Haggai's role here as a typical prophet, e.g. his inveighing against foreign nations in a manner consistent with prophets before him. Thus general though it is, the language serves to authenticate Haggai in his role as a prophet."

[31] Westermann, *Basic Forms*, pp. 204–5.

[32] On the relationship between the prophecy and monarchy cf. recently, A. Lemaire, ed. *Prophètes et rois: Bible et Proche-Orient*, (LD; Paris: Cerf, 2001). Cf. also D. L. Petersen, *Late Israelite Prophecy: Studies in Deutero Prophetic Literature and in Chronicles*, (SBLMS 23; Missoula: Scholars Press, 1977), pp. 14ff.; Hanson, *Dawn of Apocalyptic*, pp. 14–16; Blenkinsopp, *History*, pp. 54–55. Wilson (*Prophecy and Society*, pp. 172–80, 185–86, 200, 222) affirms that the confronting of rulers is characteristic of Northern pre-exilic prophets, both "peripheral" (such as Ahija, Elijah, Jeremiah) and "central" (such as Samuel, Isaiah [in 2 Kgs 18:17–19:9a] and Hulda). He furthermore maintains (ibid., p. 256) that Southern prophets also functioned in this fashion, even though they were generally central prophets (Gad, Isaiah [except in the 2 Kgs passage just noted] and Nathan).

[33] Cf. Peckham's generalization (*History*, p. 741) of Haggai as "prophecy in imitation of the book of Jeremiah."

[34] Cf. the exegesis above, ch. 7.

[35] Blenkinsopp, *History*, p. 201.

Priestly terminology and concepts are used in 2:10–14 due to their relevance to the prophet's rhetorical goals and the setting in which his oracle was delivered.[36] Third, it is also inaccurate to affirm that in 2:11–14 Haggai functions as an intermediary between the priests and the people.[37] E. Meyers argues that people need a judgment regarding to cultic purity.[38] Haggai accordingly refers the issue to a priestly court.[39] Once the decision is made he communicates it and explains it to the population.[40] He consequently becomes a "mediator between the priests and the people,"[41] two social groups in tension with each other. A variety of considerations render this reading of Hag 2:10–19 unlikely. The request for a priestly judgment does not come from the people, but from Yahweh. Rather than a request for information, Haggai's questions serve to elicit a priestly judgment which becomes the basis for the declaration of the people's uncleanness in 2:14. Thus the movement in the text is not: (1) people with a practical question; (2) priestly judgment which is difficult to accept; (3) judgment conveyed with approval by the prophet who seeks to make the judgment more acceptable to the people. The structure of the scene is rather: (1) Yahweh desires to declare the end of the state of impurity and his new purposes for the community; (2) Yahweh asks Haggai to consult the priests; (3) a dialogue occurs between Haggai and the priests; (4) the oracle of Yahweh (נאם־יהוה, v. 14) which has as its basis the priestly judgment but which is applied to the temple and the community; (5) assurance is given regarding the future.

---

[36] Blenkinsopp (ibid.) calls Hag 2: 14 "*halakah* on a point of ritual purity." I am not sure in exactly what sense Blenkinsopp means this, and thus I find it difficult to evaluate his statement. In my view, an analysis of 2: 10–14 must take as its starting point the text's form as a "prophetic-symbolic action."

[37] This is the argument of E. Meyers ("*tôrâ* in Haggai 2", p. 74).

[38] Ibid., p. 72; cf. Meyers and Meyers (p. 56) who say, "How did one handle such meat. ... The people would surely have been relieved to know ..."

[39] "Haggai refers the people to a priestly court and conveys the results to the people. The prophet represents all of us; he has a question about a situation and about its meaning within the scheme of God's design", Meyers and Meyers, p. 77, cf. also p. 55.

[40] Meyers ("*tôrâ* in Haggai 2", p. 71) says, "When Haggai offers his somewhat redundant conclusion ... (2:14) he is both supporting and promulgating the priestly decision offered just before. Indeed, the force of *wy'n* in 2:14 is quite clearly to indicate, indeed to underscore the prophet's role in supporting and mediating the priestly decision to the people."

[41] Ibid., p. 74.

10.1.3.3. *Goals and Results*

In 1:1–11, Haggai has two objectives: (1) the rehabilitation of the cult site to be a fitting dwelling place for Yahweh, and (2) the restoration of the relationship between Yahweh and his people. The changes he advocates in 1:1–11 are rather limited in scope. They can be accomplished within the framework of the existing social and political structure, and do not imply major upheavals. In 1:12–14 it is clear that his preaching had the desired effect. In 2:1–9 Haggai's goal is that the builders persevere in their work. Once again no major conflict or rupture with existing structures is required for this goal to be accomplished. Haggai's words in 2:6–9 do imply a radical transformation of the political order. However this is not held forth as a goal to be accomplished, but a divine prerogative. In 2:10–19 two goals appear to be in view: (1) the ceremonial refoundation of the temple and (2) the declaration of divine blessing on the community as a result of such an act. These goals were clearly possible within the existing social and religious structures. The fact that such blessing was indeed pronounced (2:18–19) indicates that once again these goals were achieved. The oracle to Zerubbabel must therefore be understood, at least in part, as a word of assurance.[42] The Judaean governor was called to persevere in his tasks, assume his responsibilities (as the priesthood also was called to do in the new context of the restored temple) without shame or doubt. Furthermore, the community of Yehud was to treat him with all due respect as Yahweh's chosen servant, despite his political subordination to the Persian throne. No active political opposition to Persian rule is intended or implied. However Haggai did not see Zerubbabel's status as reflecting Yahweh's ultimate purposes. In the eyes of our prophet, Zerubbabel was a *persönlichen Hoffnungsträger*,[43] a person whose existence constituted a sign of hope. In Haggai the Davidide Zerubbabel is viewed as tangible evidence of the ongoing validity of the community's hope in the future reign of Yahweh, his recognition by the nations of the world, and Israel's glorious destiny. Zerubbabel is therefore the guarantee for that which has not yet been fulfilled, but which soon will be.

---

[42] Amsler, p. 40. On oracles of salvation as words of encouragement cf. Westermann, *Oracles of Salvation*, pp. 54–62.

[43] Wolff, p. 86.

10.1.3.4. *Rhetorical and Hermeneutical Use of Religious Traditions*

The preceding exegesis of Haggai has revealed evidence of a wide variety of theological traditions: Deuteronomistic and priestly vocabulary and thought, Zion theology, prophetic oracles against the nations, wisdom, and early epic traditions. The presence of these diverse traditions, configured in innovative ways, is clearly reflective of the consolidation of earlier traditions in the Persian period. Of special interest is the book's portrait of Haggai as one who adapted theological traditions to meet the needs created by the changed circumstances of the early Persian period. This is especially relevant where new political realities, specifically the loss of national independence and subjection to Persia, cast significant doubt on the ongoing validity of certain traditions. Haggai's innovative rhetorical and hermeneutical use of earlier traditions allowed the broad range of Israelite traditions to speak anew. My analysis of the book reveals the following features of the use of religious traditions in Haggai, which I will summarize briefly here.[44]

First, tradition is used as the *basis for a theological understanding of the present.* This is evident in 1:4–11 where the prophet uses the language and themes of "futility curses" in a distinctive way. In Deut 28 and Lev 26, (typical examples of this form) such curses are presented as consequences which will indeed occur if Israel is unfaithful to the covenant. In Amos 4 and Mic 6 such consequences are seen as warnings of coming judgment which went unheeded. However in Haggai these serve as evidence of divine displeasure, yet convey the hope that the situation may still be reversed. The prophet becomes, therefore, an *interpreter* of divine providence and stresses Yahweh's restorative purposes—it is still not to late to return.

Second, Haggai *harmonizes and systematizes* the traditions he uses. Diverse elements belonging to various cycles of tradition associated with the future of Zion are freely inter-woven and reconfigured in a way that presents a clear structuration and chronological progression. The shaking of the cosmos spreads panic among the nations (2:6–7). In the resulting confusion foreign armies are destroyed (2:21–22). Yahweh exalts the Davidic ruler in Jerusalem (2:23). The nations, realizing the sovereignty and the might of Yahweh, present their treasures at the temple of Jerusalem (2:8–9).

---

[44] A detailed defense of these conclusions may be found at the conclusions of chs. 5–8.

Third, Haggai frequently *generalizes* the details of the traditions he employs. In contrast to other prophetic texts that envisage a decisive battle at or near Jerusalem, Haggai is rather vague as to the location of the eschatological conflict to come. The nations and kingdoms alluded to in 2:7 and 22 are neither named nor described. The universal scope of the cosmic disasters implies a world-wide conflagration in which all Gentile power is reduced. Vocabulary often associated with the overturn of Sodom and Gomorrah, or with the defeat of the Egyptians at the Sea of Reeds (2:22), is universalized and generalized. The presence of the nations' treasures in the temple is promised (2:6–9), but no details are given. The same can be said regarding the exaltation of Zerubbabel (2:21b-23). Such generalization reflects the book's rhetorical goal of restoring hope to a community whose traditional self-understanding and future expectations stood in stark contrast to the realities of its situation. In such a context, generalized expressions of hope would have created far less dissonance and been far more rhetorically effective than detailed descriptions whose fulfillment would appear highly problematic under the existing circumstances. Similarly, the book's minimization of whatever divisions may have existed within his social context, and his stylized presentation of the community as a remnant who responded favourably to Yahweh and to Haggai, reveals a desire to present a generalized, schematic portrait which would promote the unity of the community around its temple, leadership, and prophets.

Fourth, in the context of these more generalized descriptions, Haggai simultaneously *focuses* the attention of his readers upon specific aspects of his traditional base. Thus in 2:6–9 the various aspects of Zion eschatology that are mentioned serve to set the context for the central, emphatic assertion that the nations' treasures will be so abundant that the temple's future splendour will surpass anything it has known in the past. The general language of 2:21b-23 has the same function. The descriptions of Yahweh's future intervention set up the oracle concerning Zerubbabel's future.

Fifth, Haggai uses *core values* within earlier religious traditions with reference to issues not specifically addressed or envisaged in those traditions. Thus in 1:3–11 the prophet relates the Deuteronomistic futility curses for disobedience to the covenant (specifically the worship of other deities) to the issue of the community's neglect of the temple. In this way, Haggai applies a traditional form (the "futility curse" associated with covenant violation) and a broader Deuteronomistic core value (reverence for Yahweh, and for his Name, cf. Deut 28:58–59a) to a unique and unforeseen situation. Thus, hermeneutically, temple reconstruction is viewed as an expression of the meaning of the fear of Yahweh in the context of early Persian Yehud.

Sixth, Haggai provides an example of *an analogical use of cultic and priestly laws.* Hag. 2:14 is not a simple priestly judgment relative to a practical question. It forms part of a prophetic symbolic action which serves as an analogy. Thus the state of ritual impurity which obtains with reference to food products is applied *a fortiori* to the people of Yahweh and to the temple.

Seventh, Haggai uses *a hermeneutic of equivalents.* The book employs various means by which to identify the community which Haggai addressed with the Israel of memory and tradition. This continuity is achieved by a variety of *functional equivalents* often involving *theological compromises.* These theological and literary devices create a kind of *"theological fiction"* wherein the realities of foreign domination, and to a certain degree the temple's earlier destruction, the exile, and the existence of the Diaspora are passed over in silence, and the community at Yehud is portrayed as if it were the Israelite community at *any earlier period of its existence.* This is most vividly expressed in 2:5 (whatever its origin) with reference to the covenant made "with *you* when *you* came out of Egypt." Throughout the book this continuity is communicated by a variety of means. The dating formula with its allusion to the "second year of Darius the King" (notwithstanding the fact that such a dating clearly acknowledges that Yehud is under foreign rule) closely resembles the superscriptions attached to other collections attributed to pre-exilic prophets. As a result, from its opening words, the book gives the impression that Haggai is addressing a situation largely analogous to those confronted by other prophets earlier in Israel's history. This impression is reinforced in 1:1–11 where Deuteronomistic vocabulary makes it clear that the postexilic community has violated the Sinai covenant by its neglect of the temple. When the leaders and people step back from their obstinance, the book describes their response in a form typical of covenant obedience. The people, now called a "remnant" (1:12), begin to obey (1:12), and fear Yahweh (1:13) and do what he has commanded (1:14). In 2:4–5 the prophet uses classical expressions of encouragement in his words to the builders. This places the addressees in the long line of notable individuals and groups (Abraham, Moses, Joshua, and the generation that left Egypt and entered Canaan) addressed using this formula. The exodus event and Sinai covenant are explicitly mentioned in 2:5a, and the ongoing validity of that pact is affirmed. Like the pillar of cloud in the desert, the Spirit of Yahweh is among the community in Jerusalem (2:5b). Yahweh's house, now restored (1:1–15) and reconsecrated (2:10–19), would once again know great splendour (2:6–9). Zerubbabel, like his Davidic predecessors, was Yahweh's chosen servant (2:23). Furthermore, Israel could expect that her long cherished eschatological hopes would be fulfilled (2:6–9, 20–23). These theological, rhetorical, and literary strategies reinforce the impression that, in Yahweh's sight, the postexilic community constituted a *legitimate functional equivalent of the Israelite nation of tradition and history*. The result is a kind of "theological compromise" wherein certain seeming incongruities (for instance, Zerubbabel's status) could be seen as provisional yet acceptable solutions for the present. The clear implication is that where the particulars of situations differed, Haggai's words reflected deeper points of correspondence and equivalence.

The great significance of this last strategy must not be overlooked. The events of 587 radically and permanently transformed the Yahwistic faith. Most significant among these changes were the loss of national independence, the subjugation of the former ruling dynasty, and the proliferation of Yahwistic communities outside Palestine. Fresh interpretive approaches were needed to take older forms and adapt them to new social and political realities. The discipline of religious anthropology underlines the fact that transmission of religious traditions is a creative and hermeneutical process. In order for traditions to remain living forces, a delicate balance must be sought. If, in the course of transmission, the basis of the tradition is overly compromised and completely re-read in terms of changed socio-political realities, the tradition loses its transcendent richness and becomes a mere cultural reflection. Consequently, it can no longer function as an alternative[45] and in-depth explanation of life, which reveals the "really real" behind the "real."[46] On the other hand, however, if the form of the tradition remains overly rigid, it loses any cultural influence, and becomes completely dissociated from its social and intellectual context. As a result, such religious

---

[45] G. Santayana states, "Thus every living and healthy religion has a marked idiosyncrasy. Its power consists in its special and surprising message and in the bias which that revelation gives to life. The vistas it opens and the mysteries it propounds are another world to live in; and another world to live in—whether we expect to pass wholly into it or no—is what we mean by having a religion." (cited in C. Geertz, *The Interpretation of Cultures*, [New York: Basic, 1973], p. 87).

[46] Geertz, *Interpretation of Cultures*, p. 112.

expressions tend to be viewed as relics—valuable objects of historical research, but completely impracticable as systems of faith. The book of Haggai testifies to an attempt to steer this middle course in the context of early Persian Yehud. Indeed, the hermeneutical adaptations in evidence in Haggai enabled Judaism to adapt and flourish in the Persian and Graeco-Roman world, and beyond. Furthermore, it is in part with this same hermeneutical approach that primitive Christianity was able to extract from the religious traditions of Israel the fundamental notions of its faith and spirituality.

## 10.2. THE BOOK OF HAGGAI IN THE SOCIO-RELIGIOUS CONTEXT OF EARLY PERSIAN YEHUD

As the foregoing analysis has shown, the book of Haggai presents a distinctive vision. It stresses the vital role of the prophetic institution in the reconstruction of the temple, and, by implication, for the ongoing life and faith of the Jewish community in the Persian Period. It recounts the unexpected and uncharacteristic success of the prophet Haggai, and of the responsiveness of the community. It adopts an *inclusivist* stance, seeking to rally the disparate aspects of Jewish society around the temple. It is non-polemical, in that no sub-group is targeted, critiqued or excluded. It is highly *reconstructionist* and *restorationist*. It seeks to maintain, in one form or another, the institutions and traditions that were venerated by the community as belonging to its earlier experience. The book embraces, affirms, reconfigures, and re-applies a variety of traditional elements drawn from a diversity of theological streams. In this regard the book is especially interested in affirming the divine approbation of Zerubbabel, and demonstrating that the judgment pronounced against Jehoiachin in Jer 22 ought not to be seen as applicable to him, and by implication to the postexilic Davidic leadership in general. It adopts a stance of *provisional political accommodation* to the realities of life under Persian rule, while still clinging to a future transformation through divine intervention.

How do these various perspectives and emphases relate to the socio-religious landscape of early Persian Yehud? In contrast to the often highly polarized portraits of Yehudite society found both in certain biblical texts, and in modern historical reconstructions of the period, we see here a strikingly irenic approach. Similarly, in contrast to the sometimes critical attitude toward prophets in postexilic literature, here the prophet is viewed with the greatest esteem. Furthermore, in contrast to the recalcitrance and indifference of the community in pre-exilic and some postexilic texts, here the community with one accord is obedient to Yahweh and to his prophet.

In my opinion this perspective may be integrated into the socio-political landscape of the period in the following way. It seems to me beyond question that hegemony at every level was in the hands of the returnees under the leadership of the Davidide Zerubbabel. As noted above, this elite "charter group" had official recognition before the Persian crown and was responsible for the promotion of Persian interests in the region.[47] Supreme among these interests was economic development, and hence increased taxation revenue, and regional stability. Thus, where land tenure or other conflicts did arise (and it is difficult, based on the demographic and archaeological evidence to determine exactly how widespread these would have been), this dominant group would have been in a position to promote their own interests. However at the same time, the dominant group would have been constrained to do so in a way which did not generate a level of social strife which would hinder broader Persian interests. Thus, it appears to me that at this early period, social and religious integration and unity would have been values which held a distinct appeal and advantage in the eyes of the returnees.

This being said, however, the centre of interest in the book is not social cohesion, nor even the rebuilding of the temple as an end in itself. As has been demonstrated, the book's framers underline the significance of the prophetic office through a variety of linguistic, structural, and literary means. In chapter 9 I concluded that the book's thematic centre was to underline the importance of Haggai's contribution and of the prophetic institution for the ongoing life of the community in Yehud. This raises the issue of why such a defense would have been necessary. Several factors could have called forth such an *apologia*. First, as is widely admitted, the writing down and consolidation of religious tradition which took place after 587 did promote a move to a more textually based religious experience.[48] This would have naturally raised questions about the nature, legitimacy, and function of prophecy. Second, prophecy may have been viewed by some in the ruling elite as a

---

[47] Cf. *supra*, pp. 262–65.

[48] For an interesting analysis of this phenomenon, in a Greek context cf. J. Goody and I. Watt, "The Consequences of Literacy", in *Literacy in Traditional Societies*, (ed. J. Goody; Cambridge: Cambridge University Press, 1968), pp. 37–42.

potentially disruptive force. Blenkinsopp notes that "prophetic" voices, especially ecstatic ones, are rather frequently viewed with suspicion and hostility by political and religious leaders.[49] Third, and most importantly, a significant part of the population which did not belong to the community of the returnees, and which was potentially hostile to their hegemony and specifically the leadership of Zerubbabel, may have held tenaciously to the traditions associated with Jeremiah.[50] As Seitz has demonstrated, an important sub-stratum in Jeremiah sees theological legitimacy in the community which remained in the land and was subject to Babylonian rule.[51] Furthermore, the rejection of Jehoiachin in Jer 22:24 could be held by some as casting serious doubt on the leadership of Zerubbabel. As well, in contrast to Haggai, who was a supporter of the temple, Jeremiah staunchly condemned any over confidence in the temple as a means to ensure divine blessing. The Jeremiah traditions therefore could have provided a strong basis from which to challenge the legitimacy and prerogatives of the ruling elite. As noted above, in such a situation a highly probable response on the part of the ruling elite would be to downplay or even to call into question the legitimacy of the prophetic word.[52] Consequently, if the framers of Haggai were to be found within the ranks of the ruling community or sympathetic to it, it would be essential for them to demonstrate to those who revered the Jeremianic traditions that they too stood within the same prophetic tradition.

In this context it is significant to see how intentionally the framers of Haggai interact with the Jeremiah traditions. In Jeremiah, leaders and people are marked by their refusal to obey "the word of Yahweh through the prophet Jeremiah," whereas in Haggai the reverse is the case (1:12). Jeremiah stood against prophets who falsely proclaimed "peace in this place" (Jer 14:13), whereas Yahweh declares through Haggai, "In this place I will give peace" (2:9). In Jeremiah the temple becomes a false basis of hope for divine blessing (Jer 7). In Haggai a right response to the temple brings a restored relationship with Yahweh

---

[49] Blenkinsopp, *History*, pp. 37–38.

[50] Goldman, *Prophétie*, p. 235. Goldman presents extensive arguments to the effect that a postexilic redaction of Jeremiah in favour of Zerubbabel sought to attenuate Jeremiah's words and facilitate the acceptance of Zerubbabel by his followers.

[51] Seitz, "Crisis of Interpretation", pp. 78–97, esp. pp. 79–81.

[52] Carroll (*When Prophecy Failed*, ch. 2), following L. Festinger, notes that customary responses to disturbing data which creates cognitive dissonance include distancing one's self from its source and/or calling that source into disrepute.

and, consequently, his blessing (1:8). Most strikingly, Haggai reverses
Jeremiah's metaphor of Yahweh's casting off of his signet ring (2:23).

It would be wrong, however, to read these contrasts as a desire on the
part of the framers of the book of Haggai, to set Jeremiah and Haggai
in opposition. I maintain that these contrasts serve to underline the fact
that the differences between the experiences of the two prophets are
due to a *vital change* which had taken place, *one already foreseen in the traditions reflected in Jer 30:4–31:37*. There, due to Yahweh's inward activity on
heart and mind, the community, *personally and collectively*, will respond in
faithfulness to Yahweh (Jer 31:31–34). Just such a response is described
in Hag 1:12–14. Thus the followers of Jeremiah are being invited to see
themselves as participants in *the era of restoration as prophesied by Jeremiah
himself*. Furthermore, it was the faithful response of the community as
a result of the inward activity of Yahweh and the preaching of Haggai
that gave evidence that the hoped-for era had arrived. Thus, for the
redactor, the differences between Jeremiah and Haggai were not to be
found in any divergence of theological perspective, or in the relative
merits of the two, but rather in the *changed situation of early Persian Yehud*.
The time of judgment had passed. A new era had begun. Yahweh was
at work in the hearts of his people (1:14). His Spirit dwelt among them
(2:5, cf. Ezek 36:26–32). Adherence to Haggai and his words was no
betrayal of Jeremiah, but rather in complete continuity with the latter's
vision and hope.[53]

In sum then, I suggest that the book of Haggai was produced by
an individual or circle close to the prophet himself, and who held the
prophetic institution in general, and the prophet Haggai in particular,
in great esteem. As such this individual or circle sought to promote the
importance of our prophet and his role in the context of early Persian

---

[53] Similar conclusions, but from the perspective of the book Jeremiah, are advanced
by J. Goldman (*Prophétie*, pp. 235–37). Goldman maintains that in chs. 25–33, the
postexilic redactor of Jeremiah stresses the following themes: (1) the end of the exile
marks a major turning point in Israel's history; (2) Judah is the key to Yahweh's dealings
with all nations; (3) prophets played a significant role in the life of the nation; (4)
Jeremiah's invectives against the temple and its vessels are not the last word. Yahweh
will effect the return of the latter to Jerusalem; (5) the Davidic line has a vital role to
play in the new age; and (6) Yahweh will effect the return of the exiles to Judah. For
Goldman, the central point is the importance of both prophetic and royal institutions
in the early Persian period (ibid., pp. 235–37). It is beyond the scope of this study to
evaluate Goldman's arguments. However his identification in Jeremiah of themes very
similar to those I have found in Haggai provides clear evidence of their importance in
the Babylonian and early Persian periods.

Yehud. The book may have sought to convince two divergent audiences. On one hand, the dominant group of returnees may have had some doubts regarding the value of prophecy in the emerging life of Yehud. On the other hand, certain members of the non-exiled population, especially those who held staunchly to the Jeremianic traditions, may have viewed Haggai (and those who supported him) with some suspicion, particularly due to his support of the temple, and of Zerubbabel. If such a reconstruction is accurate, the book of Haggai addresses the objections of both groups in its insistence upon the authenticity of the prophet Haggai and the efficacy of his communication of the word of Yahweh.

## 10.3. CONCLUSIONS

In conclusion then, the political, social, and religious perspectives in Haggai reflect a specific vision within the pastiche of early Persian Yehud. Its vision includes all parts of the community. It is supportive of the leadership of the ruling elite (likely largely composed of returnees) under their political leader Zerubbabel and their religious leader Joshua. It advocates the perpetuation of Israelite institutions and traditions within the context of accommodation to the realities of Persian rule. It seeks to establish the importance of Haggai and his words, and the prophetic office in general, in the context of early Persian Yehud. It seeks to affirm this perspective both to the ruling group that may have been tempted to downplay the prophetic office, as well as to those outside that group who may have viewed prophetic traditions, especially those in Jeremiah, as a basis upon which to challenge the initiatives of the leadership, and to reject the authenticity of Haggai's prophetic activity.

In sum, the book of Haggai bears witness to the high value and ongoing validity with which prophecy and the prophetic office were viewed by at least a portion of the community in Yehud. The words of Haggai and their powerful effects, set in a form of a dramatized prophetic collection, serve as the vehicle through which this perspective is communicated.

# SELECTED BIBLIOGRAPHY

Abadie, P. "Une 'histoire corrective': le modèle du chroniste." *Théophilyon* 2 (1997): 65–90.

Ackroyd, P. R. "Studies in the Book of Haggai." *JJS* 2 (1951): 163–176.

———. "The Book of Haggai and Zechariah 1–8." *JJS* 3 (1952): 151–156.

———. "Studies in the Book of Haggai." *JJS* 3 (1952): 1–13.

———. "Some Interpretive Glosses in the Book of Haggai." *JJS* 7 (1956): 163–168.

———. "Two Historical Problems of the Early Persian Period." *JNES* 17 (1958): 13–27.

———. *Exile and Restoration: A Study of Hebrew Thought of the Sixth Century B.C.* Philadelphia: Westminster, 1968.

———. "The Interpretation of the Exile and Restoration." *CJT* 14 (1968): 3–12.

———. *Israel Under Babylon and Persia.* London: Oxford University Press, 1970.

———. "The Temple Vessels—A Continuity Theme." In *Studies in the Religion of Ancient Israel.* Edited by H. Ringgren et. al. SVT 23. Leiden: E. J. Brill, 1972, pp. 166–181.

———. "The Theology of the Chronicler." *Lexington Theological Quarterly* 8 (1973): 101–116.

———. "The Chronicler as Exegete." *JSOT* 2 (1977): 2–32.

———. "Continuity and Discontinuity: Rehabilitation and Authentication." In *Tradition and Theology in the Old Testament.* Edited by D. A. Knight. London: SPCK, 1977, pp. 215–234.

———. "Faith and its Reformulation in the Post-exilic period: sources." *TD* 27 (1979): 323–334.

———. "Faith and its Reformulation in the Post-exilic Period: Prophetic Material." *TD* 27 (1979): 335–346.

———. "Archaeology, Politics and Religion: The Persian Period." *Iliff Review* 39 (1982): 5–24.

———. "The Jewish Community in Palestine in the Persian Period." In *The Cambridge History of Judaism, Vol 1. Introduction; The Persian Period.* edited by W. D. Davies and L. Finkelstein. Cambridge: Cambridge University Press, 1984, pp. 130–161.

———. "Problems in the Handling of Biblical and Related Sources in the Achaemenid Period." In *Achaemenid History III: Method and Theory.* Edited by A. Kuhrt and H. Sancisi-Weerdenburg. Leiden: Nederlands Instituut voor het Nabije Oosten, 1988, pp. 33–54.

———. "The Biblical Portrayal of Achaemenid Rulers." In *Achaemenid History V: The Roots of the European Tradition.* Edited by H. Sancisi-Weerdenburg and J. W. Drivers. Leiden: Nederlands Instituut voor het Nabije Oosten, 1990, pp. 1–16.

———. "The Written Evidence for Palestine." In *Achaemenid History IV. Centre and Periphery: Proceedings of the Groningen 1986 Achaemenid History Workshop.* Edited by H. Sancisi-Weerdenburg and A. Kuhrt. Leiden: Nederlands Instituut voor het Nabije Oosten, 1990, pp. 201–220.

Aharoni, Y. *The Land of the Bible: A Historical Geography.* London: Burns and Oates, 1979.

Aharoni, Y., J. Naveh, and A. F. Rainey. *Arad Inscriptions.* Translated by Judith Beth-Or. Jerusalem: Israel Exploration Society, 1981.

Albright, W. F. "The Date and Personality of the Chronicler." *JBL* 40 (1921): 104–124.

———. "A Brief History of Judah from the Days of Josiah to Alexander the Great." *BA* 9 (1946): 1–5.

———. *The Archaeology of Palestine.* Harmondsworth and Baltimore: Penguin, 1954.

——. *The Biblical Period from Abraham to Ezra.* New York and Evanston: Harper and Row, 1963.

Allen, L. C. *The Books of Joel, Obadiah, Jonah and Micah.* NICOT. Grand Rapids: Eerdmans, 1976.

——. *Ezekiel 20–48.* WBC. Dallas: Word, 1990.

Allen, N. "The Identity of the Jerusalem Priesthood during the Exile." *HeyJ* 13 (1982): 259–269.

Allrik, H. L. "The Lists of Zerubbabel (Nehemiah 7 and Ezra 2) and the Hebrew Numeral Notation." *BASOR* 136 (1954): 21–27.

Alt, A. "Die Rolle Samarias bei der Entstehung des Judentums." In A. Alt, *Kleine Schriften II.* Munich: Beck, 1953, pp. 313–337.

Alter, R. *The Art of Biblical Narrative.* New York: Basic, 1981.

Amsler, S., A. Lacoque, and R. Vuilleumier. *Aggée-Zacharie 1–8, Zacharie 9–14, Malachi.* CAT XI-C. Genève: Labor et Fides, 1988.

Amsler, S., J. Asurmendi, J. Auneau, and R. Martin-Achard. *Les prophètes et les livres prophétiques.* Petite Bibliothèque des Sciences Bibliques. Paris: Desclée, 1985.

Andersen, F. I. "Who Built the Second Temple?" *ABR* 6 (1958): 1–35.

André, T. *Le prophète Aggée.* Paris: Fischbacher, 1895.

Audinet, J. "Dispositifs du 'transmettre' et 'confession de la foi'." In J. Audinet et. al. *Essais de théologie pratique: l'institution et le transmettre.* Le Point Théologique. Paris: Beauchesne, 1988, pp. 166–205.

——. "Du transmettre ou la tradition comme pratique sociale." In J. Audinet et. al. *Essais de théologie pratique: l'institution et le transmettre.* Le Point Théologique. Paris: Beauchesne, 1988, pp. 109–115.

Aufrecht, W. E. "Urbanization and Northwest Semitic Inscriptions of the Late Bronze and Iron Ages." In *Urbanism in Antiquity.* Edited by W. E. Aufrecht, N. A. Mirau, and S. W. Gauley. JSOTSup 244. Sheffield: JSOT Press, 1997, pp. 116–129.

Avigad, N. "Two Hebrew Inscriptions on Wine-Jars." *IEJ* 22 (1972): 1–9.

——. *Bullae and Seals from a Post-Exilic Judean Archive.* Qedem 4. Monographs of the Institute of Archaeology. Jerusalem: Hebrew University, 1976.

——. "Hebrew Seals and Sealings and their Significance for Biblical Research." In *Congress Volume, Jerusalem 1986.* Edited by J. A. Emerton. SVT 40. Leiden: E. J. Brill, 1986, pp. 7–16.

Avigad, N., and B. Sass. *Corpus of West Semitic Stamp Seals.* Jerusalem: Israel Academy of Sciences and Humanities/Israel Exploration Society/Hebrew University Institute of Archaeology, 1997.

Baldwin, J. *Haggai, Zechariah, Malachi.* TOTC. London: InterVarsity, 1972.

Ballentine, S. E. "The Politics of Religion in the Persian Period." In *After the Exile.* Edited by J. Barton and D. J. Reimer. Macon, GA: Mercer University Press, 1996, pp. 129–146.

Barkay, G. "Excavations on the Slope of the Hinnom Valley in Jerusalem." *Qadmoniot* 17 (1984): 94–108.

——. "Jerusalem of Old Testament Times: New Discoveries and New Approaches." *BAIAS* (1985–86): 32–43.

——. *Ketef Hinnom: A Treasure Facing Jerusalem's Walls.* Jerusalem: Israel Museum, 1986.

Barkay, G., and A. G. Vaughn. "*LMLK* and the Official Seal Impressions from Tel Lachish." *Tel Aviv* 23 (1996): 61–74.

——. "New Readings of Hezekian Official Seal Impressions." *BASOR* 304 (1996): 29–54.

Barnes, W. E. *Haggai and Zechariah.* Cambridge: Cambridge University Press, 1917.

Barr, J. *The Semantics of Biblical Language.* London: SCM, 1961.

Barstad, H. M. "On the History and Archaeology of Judah during the Exilic Period. A Reminder." *OLP* 19 (1988): 25–36.

——. "Lachish Ostracon III and Ancient Israelite Prophecy." In *A. Malamat Volume.* ErIsr 24. Edited by S. Aḥituv and B. A. Levine. Jerusalem: Israel Exploration Society, 1993, pp. 8*-12*.

——. "No Prophets? Recent Developments in Biblical Prophetic Research and Ancient Near Eastern Prophecy." *JSOT* 57 (1993): 39–60.

——. *The Myth of the Empty Land: A Study in the History and Archaeology of Judah During the 'Exilic' Period.* SOSup 28. Oslo: Scandinavian University Press, 1996.

——. *The Babylonian Captivity of the Book of Isaiah: 'Exilic' Judah and the Provenance of Isaiah 40–55.* Oslo: Novus instituttet for sammenlignende kulturforskning, 1997.

Bartal, A. "Once Again-Who was Sheshbazzar?" *Beit Miqra* 79 (1979): 357–369.

Barthélemy, D., ed. *Critique textuelle de l'Ancien Testament. Tome 3 Ezéchiel, Daniel et les 12 prophètes.* OBO 50/3. Fribourg/Göttingen: Editions Universitaires/Vandenhoeck & Ruprecht, 1992.

Barton, J. *Oracles of God: Perceptions of Ancient Prophecy in Israel After the Exile.* London: Darton, Longman and Todd, 1986.

Bauckham, R. J. "The Rise of Apocalyptic." *Them* 3 (1977–78): 10–23.

Bauer, L. *Zeit des Zweiten Tempels-Zeit der Gerechtigkeit: zur sozio-ökonomischen Konzeption in Haggai-Sacharja-Maleachi-Korpus.* BEATAJ 31. Frankfurt-am-Main: Peter Lang, 1992.

Baumbach, G. "'Volk Gottes' im Frühjundentum: Eine Untersuchung der 'ekklesiologischen' Typen des Frühjudentums." *Kairós* 21 (1979): 30–47.

Baumgartel, F. "Die Formel *Ne'um jahwe.*" *ZAW* 73 (1961): 277–290.

Becker, J. *Messianic Expectations in the Old Testament.* Translated by D. E. Green. Philadelphia: Fortress, 1980.

Becking, B., and M. C. A. Korpel, eds. *The Crisis of Israelite Religion: Transformation of Religious Tradition in Exilic and Post-Exilic Times,* OS 62. Leiden: E. J. Brill, 1999.

Bedford, P. R. "On Models and Texts: A Response to Blenkinsopp and Petersen." In *Second Temple Studies 1: Persian Period.* Edited by P. R. Davies. JSOTSup 117. Sheffield: JSOT Press, 1991, pp. 154–162.

——. "Discerning the Time: Haggai, Zechariah and the 'Delay' in the Rebuilding of the Jerusalem Temple." In *The Pitcher is Broken, Memorial Essays for G. W. Ahlström.* Edited by S. W. Holloway and L. K. Handy. JSOTSup 190 Sheffield: JSOT Press, 1995, pp. 71–94.

——. "Early Achaemenid Monarchs and Indigenous Cults: Towards the Definition of Imperial Policy." In *Religion in the Ancient World: New Themes and Approaches.* Edited by M. Dillon. Amsterdam: A. M. Hakkert, 1996, pp. 17–39.

——. *Temple Restoration in Early Achaemenid Judah.* JSJSup 63. Leiden, Boston, Köln: Brill, 2001.

Begg, C. "Review of W. A. M. Beuken *Jesiah, vol. 3.*" *CBQ* 54 (1992): 514–515.

Begrich, J. "Die priesterliche Tora." *ZAW* 66 (1936): 63–88.

Beit-Arieh, I. "Edomites Advance Into Judah." *BAR* 22 (1996): 28–36.

——. "New Data on the Relationship between Judah and Edom toward the End of the Iron Age." In *Recent Excavations in Israel: Studies in Iron Age Archaeology.* Edited by S. Gitin and W. G. Dever. Winona Lake: AASOR/Eisenbrauns, 1989, pp. 125–131.

Ben Zvi, E. "Inclusion in and Exclusion from 'Israel' in Post-Monarchic Biblical Texts." In *The Pitcher is Broken, Memorial Essays for G. W. Ahlström.* Edited by S. W. Holloway and L. K. Handy. JSOTSup 190. Sheffield: JSOT Press, 1995, pp. 95–149.

——. "Studying Prophetic Texts against their Original Backgrounds: Pre-Ordained Scripts and Alternative Horizons of Research." In *Prophets and Paradigms: Essays in Honour of Gene M. Tucker.* Edited by S. B. Reid. Sheffield: JSOT Press, 1996, pp. 125–135.

——. "The Urban Centre of Jerusalem and the Development of the Literature of the

Hebrew Bible." In *Urbanism in Antiquity*. Edited by W. E. Aufrecht, N. A. Mirau, and S. W. Gauley. JSOTSup 244. Sheffield: JSOT Press, 1997, pp. 194–209.

———. "Looking at the Primary (Hi)story and the Prophetic Books as Literary/Theological Units within the Frame of the Early Second Temple: Some Considerations." *SJOT* 12 (1998): 26–43.

Bendor, S. *The Social Structure of Ancient Israel*. Jerusalem: Simor, 1996.

Bennett, R. A. "Haggai." In *New Interpreters Bible*. Nashville: Abingdon, 1994.

Bennett, W. H. *The Religion of the Post Exilic Prophets: The Literature and Religion of Israel*. Edinburgh: T. & T. Clark, 1907.

Benoit, P., J. T. Milik, and R. de Vaux. *Les grottes de Murabba'at*. DJD 2. Oxford: Clarendon, 1961.

Bentzen, A. "Quelques remarques sur le mouvement messianique parmi les Juifs aux environs de l'an 520 avant Jésus-Christ." *RHPR* 10 (1930): 493–503.

Berger, P. "Charisma and Religious Innovation: The Social Location of Israelite Prophecy." *American Sociological Review* 28 (1963): 945–950.

Berger, P. R. "Zu den Namen ששבצר und שנאצר." *ZAW* 83 (1971): 98–100.

Berquist, J. L. *Judaism in Persia's Shadow: A Social and Historical Approach*. Minneapolis: Fortress, 1995.

Betlyon, J. W. "The Provincial Government of Persian Period Judea and the Yehud Coins." *JBL* 105 (1986): 633–642.

Beuken, W. A. M. *Haggai-Sacharja 1–8: Studien zur Überlieferungsgeschichte der frühnachexilischen Prophetie*. SSN 10. Assen: Van Gorcum, 1967.

Bewer, J. A. "Ancient Babylonian Parallels to the Prophecies of Haggai." *AJSLL* 35 (1919): 128–133.

———. *The Literature of the Old Testament*. Rev. edtn. New York: Columbia University, 1933.

Beyer, B. E. s. v. "Zerubbabel." *ABD* 6:1085.

Beyse, K.-M. *Serubbabel und die Königserwartungen der Propheten Haggai und Sacharja: Eine historische und traditionsgeschichtliche Untersuchung*. Arbeiten zur Theologie 1/48. Stuttgart: Calwer, 1972.

Bianchi, F. *I superstiti della deportazione sono là nella provincia (Neemia 1,3). Ricerche epigrafiche sulla storia della Giudea in età neobabilonese e achemenide (586 a.C.–442 a.C.)*. AIONSup 76, 53/3 Napoli: Instituto Universitario Orientale, 1993.

———. "Le rôle de Zorobabel et la dynastie davidique en Judée du VIe siècle au IIe siècle av. J.-C." *Trans* 7 (1994): 153–165.

———. *I superstiti della deportazione sono là nella provincia (Neemia 1,3). Ricerche storico-bibliche sulla Giudea in età neobabilonese e achemenide (586 a.C.–442 a.C.)*. AIONSup 82, 55/1. Napoli: Instituto Universitario Orientale, 1995.

Bickerman, E. J. "The Edict of Cyrus in Ezra 1." *JBL* 65 (1946): 249–275.

———. "En marge de l'écriture." *RB* 88 (1981): 19–23.

———. "Calendars and Chronology." In *The Cambridge History of Judaism. Vol 1. Introduction; The Persian Period*. Edited by W. D. Davies and L. Finkelstein. Cambridge: Cambridge University Press, 1984, pp. 60–69.

———. "The Diaspora: The Babylonian Captivity." In *The Cambridge History of Judaism, Vol 1. Introduction; The Persian Period*. Edited by W. D. Davies and L. Finkelstein. Cambridge: Cambridge University Press, 1984, pp. 342–357.

Bienkowski, P., and C. M. Bennett, eds. *Excavations at Tawilan in Southern Jordan*. Oxford: Oxford University Press, 1995.

Biggs, R. D., and M. Gibson. *Seals and Sealings in the Ancient Near East*. Bibliotheca Mesopotamica 6. Malibu, CA: Udena, 1977.

Blenkinsopp, J. *Prophecy and Canon: A Contribution to the Study of Jewish Origins*. Notre Dame and London: University of Notre Dame, 1977.

———. *Ezra-Nehemiah: A Commentary*. OTL. Philadelphia: Westminster, 1988.

——. "Temple and Society in Achaemenid Judah." In *Second Temple Studies 1: Persian Period*. Edited by P. R. Davies. JSOTSup 117. Sheffield: JSOT Press, 1991, pp. 22–53.

——. *A History of Prophecy in Israel*. 2nd. edtn. Louisville: Westminster/John Knox, 1996.

——. "Life Expectancy in Ancient Palestine." *SJOT* 11 (1997): 44–55.

——. "The Judaean Priesthood during the Neo-Babylonian and Achaemenid Periods: A Hypothetical Reconstruction." *CBQ* 60 (1998): 25–43.

——. "The Social Roles of Prophets in Early Achaemenid Judah." *JSOT* 93 (2001): 39–58.

Bloomhardt, P. F. "The Poems of Haggai." *HUCA* 5 (1928): 153–196.

Boadt, L. *Ezekiel's Oracles against Egypt*. BiOr 37. Rome: Biblical Institute Press, 1980.

Bodi, D. "Le prophète critique la monarchie: le terme *nasiʾ* chez Ezéchiel." In *Prophètes et Rois: Bible et Proche Orient*. Edited by A. Lemaire. LD. Paris: Cerf, 2001, pp. 249–257.

Bolin, T. M. "The Temple of Yhw at Elephantine and Persian Religious Policy." In *The Triumph of Elohim: From Yahwisms to Judaisms*. Edited by D. V. Edelman. CBET. Kampen: Pharos, 1995, pp. 127–142.

——. "When the End is the Beginning. The Persian Period and the Origins of the Biblical Tradition." *SJOT* (1996): 3–15.

Bonnandière, A. M. *Les douze petits prophètes*. Paris: Bibl. Augustiana, 1963.

Bordreuil, P., F. Israel, and D. Pardee. "Deux ostraca paléo-hébreux de la collection Sh. Moussaïeff." *Semitica* 46 (1996): 49–76.

Borger, R. "An Additional Remark on P. R. Ackroyd, JNES, XVII, 23–27." *JNES* 18 (1959): 74.

——. *Die Chronologie des Darius-Denkmals am Behistun-Felsen*. NAWG 3 (1982): 103–132.

Bornkamm, G. s. v. "σειω" *TDNT* 7:196–200.

Briant, P. "Contrainte militaire, dépendance rurale et exploitation des territoires en Asie achéménide." In P. Briant, *Rois, tributs et paysans. Etudes sur les formations tributaires du Moyen-Orient ancien*. Centre de Recherche d'Histoire Ancienne 43, Annales Littéraires de l'Université de Besançon 269. Paris: Les Belles Lettres, 1982, pp. 199–225.

——. "Pouvoir central et polycentrisme culturel dans l'empire achéménide. Quelques réflexions et suggestions." In *Achaemenid History I: Sources, Structures and Synthesis*. Edited by H. Sancisi-Weerdenburg. Leiden: Nederlands Instituut voor het Nabije Oosten, 1987, pp. 1–31.

——. "Ethno-classe dominante et populations soumises dans l'empire achéménide: le cas de l'Egypte." In *Achaemenid History III: Method and Theory*. Edited by A. Kuhrt and H. Sancisi-Weerdenburg. Leiden: Nederlands Instituut voor het Nabije Oosten, 1988, pp. 137–173.

——. s. v. "Persian Empire." *ABD* 5:236–244.

——. "Bulletin d'histoire achéménide I." In *Recherches récentes sur l'empire achéménide*. Suppléments à Topoi 1. Lyon/Paris: Maison de l'Orient Méditerranéen, 1997, pp. 5–127.

——. *Histoire de l'empire perse de Cyrus à Alexandre*. 2 vols. Achaemenid History 10. Leiden: Nederlands Instituut voor het Nabije Oosten, 1996.

——. *Bulletin d'histoire achéménide II, 1997–2000*. Persica 1. Paris: Thotm, 2001.

——. "Histoire impériale et histoire régionale. A propos de l'histoire de Juda dans l'Empire achéménide." In *Congress Volume Oslo 1998*. Edited by A. Lemaire and M. Saebø. SVT 80. Leiden: E. J. Brill, 2000, pp. 235–45.

Briend, J. "L'occupation de la Galilée occidentale à l'époque perse." *Trans* 2 (1990): 109–123.

——. "L'édit de Cyrus et sa valeur historique." *Trans* 11 (1996): 33–44.

Bright, J. "Du texte au sermon: Aggée un exercise en herméneutique." *EThR* 44 (1969): 3–25.

——. *A History of Israel*. 2nd. edtn. Philadelphia: Westminster, 1972.

——. *The Authority of the Old Testament.* Grand Rapids: Baker, 1978.

——. "Haggai Among the Prophets: Reflections on Preaching From the Old Testament." In *From Faith to Faith: Essays in Honor of Donald G. Miller on his Seventieth Birthday.* Edited by D. H. Hadidian. Pittsburg: Pickwick, 1979, pp. 219–234.

Brongers, H. A. "Bemerkungen zur Gebrauch des adverbialen *we'attah* im Alten Testament. Eine lexikogischer Beitrag." *VT* 15 (1965): 289–299.

Broshi, M. "Estimating the Population of Ancient Jerusalem." *BAR* 4 (1978): 10–15.

——. "La population de l'ancienne Jérusalem." *RB* 82 (1975): 5–14.

Broshi, M., and R. Gophna. "Middle Bronze Age II Palestine: Its Settlements and Population." *BASOR* 261 (1986): 73–90.

Brunet, G. "La prise de Jérusalem sous Sédécias: les sens militaires de l'hébreu *bâqa'*." *RHR* 167 (1965): 157–176.

Buss, M. J. s. v. "Prophecy in Ancient Israel." *IDB[S]* p. 694.

Cameron, G. G. "Darius and Xerxes in Babylonia." *AJSL* 48 (1941): 316–319.

——. "Darius, Egypt and the Lands Beyond the Sea." *AJSL* 58 (1941): 307–313.

Caquot, A. "Le Judaïsme depuis la captivité de Babylone jusqu'à la révolte de Bar-Kokheba." In *Encyclopédie de la Pléiade. Histoire des Religions II.* Edited by H.-C. Puech. Paris: Gallimard, 1972, pp. 114–132.

Cardascia, G. *Les archives de Murašû. Une famille d'hommes d'affaires.* Paris: Imprimerie Nationale, 1951.

Carroll, R. P. "Cognitive Dissonance and Jeremiah 26." *TUGOS* 25 (1973–74): 12–23.

——. *When Prophecy Failed: Reactions and Responses to Failure in the Old Testament Prophets.* London: SCM, 1979.

——. "Twilight of Prophecy or Dawn of Apocalyptic?" *JSOT* 14 (1979): 3–35.

——. "Eschatological Delay in the Prophetic Tradition." *ZAW* 94 (1982): 47–58.

——. *Jeremiah: A Commentary.* OTL. Philadelphia: Westminster, 1986.

——. "Prophecy and Society." In *The World of Ancient Israel: Sociological, Anthropological and Political Perspectives.* Edited by R. E. Clements. Cambridge: Cambridge University Press, 1989, pp. 203–225.

——. "Textual Strategies and Ideology in the Second Temple." In *Second Temple Studies 1: Persian Period.* Edited by P. R. Davies. JSOTSup 117. Sheffield: JSOT Press, 1991, pp. 108–124.

——. "The Myth of the Empty Land." *Semeia* 59 (1992): 79–93.

——. "So What do We *Know* about the Temple? The Temple in the Prophets." In *Second Temple Studies 2: Temple and Community in the Persian Period.* Edited by T. C. Eskenazi and K. H. Richards. Sheffield: JSOT Press, 1994, pp. 34–51.

——. "Exile! What Exile? Deportation and the Discourses of Diaspora." In *Leading Captivity Captive.* Edited by L. L. Grabbe. JSOTSup 278. Sheffield: Sheffield Academic Press, 1998, pp. 62–79.

Carter, C. E. "A Social and Demographic Study of Post-Exilic Judah." Ph. D. diss., Duke University, 1991.

——. "The Province of Yehud in the Post-Exilic Period: Soundings in Site Distribution and Demography." In *Second Temple Studies 2: Temple and Community in the Persian Period.* Edited by T. C. Eskenazi and K. H Richards. Sheffield: JSOT Press, 1994, pp. 107–145.

——. "A Discipline in Transition: The Contributions of the Social Sciences to the Study of the Hebrew Bible." In *Community, Identity, and Ideology: Social Science Approaches to the Hebrew Bible.* Edited by C. E. Carter and C. L. Meyers. Sources for Biblical and Theological Study. Winona Lake: Eisenbrauns, 1996, pp. 3–36.

——. *The Emergence of Yehud in the Persian Period.* JSOTSup 294. Sheffield: Sheffield Academic Press, 1999.

Cary, M., and G. B. Gray. "The Reign of Darius." In *The Cambridge Ancient History. Vol.*

4. *The Persian Empire and the West*. Edited by J. E. Bury, S. A. Cook and F. E. Adcock. Cambridge: Cambridge University Press, 1974, pp. 173–227.

Cashdan, E. "Haggai: An Introduction and Commentary." In *The Soncino Books of the Bible: The Twelve Prophets. Edited* by A. Cohen. London: Soncino, 1948, pp. 253–263.

Causse, A. *Israël et la vision de l'humanité*. Paris: Istra, 1924.

———. *Les dispersés d'Israël: les origines de la diaspora et son rôle dans la formation du Judaïsme*. Paris: Alcan, 1929.

———. *Du groupe ethnique à la communauté religieuse*: le problème sociologique de la religion d'Israël. Paris: Félix Alcan, 1937.

———. "Le mythe de la nouvelle Jérusalem du Deutéro-Esaie à la IIIe Sibylle." *RHPR* 18 (1938): 377–414.

———. "From an Ethnic Group to a Religious Community: The Sociological Problem of Judaism." In *Community, Identity and Ideology: Social Science Approaches to the Hebrew Bible*. Edited by C. E. Carter and C. L. Meyers. Sources for Biblical and Theological Study. Winona Lake: Eisenbrauns, 1996, pp. 95–118.

Cazelles, H. "Qui aurait visé, à l'origine, Isaïe II 2–5?" *VT* 30 (1980): 409–420.

———. "587 ou 586?" In *The Word of the Lord Shall Go Forth. Essays in Honor of David Noel Freedman in Celebration of his Sixtieth Birthday*. Edited by C. L. Meyers and M. O'Connor. Winona Lake: Eisenbraun's/American School of Oriental Research, 1983, pp. 427–435.

———. "De la fixation du texte biblique à l'origine de son autorité." *Trans* 10 (1995): 15–27.

Charpin, D. "Prophètes et rois dans le Proche-Orient amorrite." In *Prophètes et rois: Bible et Proche Orient*. Edited by A. Lemaire. LD. Paris: Cerf, 2001, pp. 21–53.

Chary, T. *Les prophètes et le culte à partir de l'exil*. Paris: Desclée, 1955.

———. *Aggée-Zacharie, Malachie*. SB. Paris: J. Gabalda, 1969.

Childs, B. S. "The Enemy from the North and the Chaos Tradition." *JBL* 78 (1959): 187–98.

———. *The Book of Exodus*. OTL. Philadelphia: Westminster, 1974.

———. *Introduction to the Old Testament as Scripture*. OTL. Philadelphia: Fortress, 1979.

———. *Isaiah*. OTL. Louisville: Westminster/John Knox, 2001.

Christensen, D. "Impulse and Design in the Book of Haggai." *JETS* 35 (1992): 445–456.

Clark, D. J. "Problems in Haggai 2:15–19." *BT* 34 (1983): 432–439.

Clements, R. E. *God and Temple*. Philadelphia: Fortress, 1965.

———. *One Hundred Years of Old Testament Interpretation*. Philadelphia: Westminster, 1976.

———. "The Prophet and His Editors." In *The Bible in Three Dimensions*. Edited by D. J. A. Clines. JSOTSup 87. Sheffield: JSOT Press, 1990, pp. 202–220.

Clines, D. J. A. "Regnal Year Reckoning in the Last Years of the Kingdom of Judah." *AJBA* 2 (1972): 9–34.

———. *Ezra, Nehemiah, Esther*. NCBC. London: Marshall, Morgan and Scott, 1984.

———. "Haggai's Temple, Constructed, Deconstructed, and Reconstructed." *SJOT* 7 (1993): 51–77.

———. *Interested Parties: The Ideology of Writers and Readers of the Hebrew Bible*. JSOTSup 205. Sheffield: JSOT Press, 1995.

Cody, A. "When is the Chosen People called a *gôy*?" *VT* 14 (1964): 1–7.

Coggins, R. J. "The Interpretation of Ezra 4:4." *JTS* 16 (1965): 124–27.

———. *Haggai, Zechariah, Malachi*. OTG. Sheffield: JSOT Press, 1987.

———. "The Exile: History and Ideology." *ExpTim* (1998): 389–393.

Cogan, M. s. v. "Chronology, Hebrew Bible" *ABD* 1:1002–1011.

Coogan, M. D. "Life in the Diaspora." *BA* 37 (1974): 6–12.

———. *West Semitic Personal Names in the Murasu Documents*. HSM 7. Missoula: Scholars Press, 1975.

Cook, J. M. "The Rise of the Achaemenids and the Establishment of their Empire."

In *The Cambridge History of Iran*. Vol 2. The Median and Achaemenian Periods. Edited by I. Gershevitch. Cambridge: Cambridge University Press, 1985, pp. 214–221.

Coppens, J. *Les douze petits prophètes*. Paris, 1950.

Cowley, A. *Aramaic Papyri of the Fifth Century B. C.* Oxford: Oxford University Press, 1923.

Craig, Kenneth M., Jr. "Interrogatives in Haggai-Zechariah: A Literary Thread?" In *Forming Prophetic Literature: Essays on Isaiah and the Twelve in Honor of John D. W. Watts*. Edited by J. W. Watts and P. R. House. JSOTSup 235. Sheffield: Sheffield Academic Press, 1996, pp. 224–244.

Cross, F. "Judean Stamps." In *W. F. Albright Volume*. ErIsr 9. Edited by A. Malamat. Jerusalem: Israel Exploration Society, 1969, pp. 20*-27*.

——. "Papyri of the 4th Century B.C. from Dâliyeh." In *New Directions in Biblical Archaeology*. Edited by D. N. Freedman and J. Greenfield. Garden City, NY: Doubleday, 1969, pp. 45–69.

——. *Canaanite Myth and Hebrew Epic*. Cambridge: Harvard University Press, 1973.

——. "Reconstruction of the Judean Restoration." *JBL* 94 (1975): 4–18.

——. "Samaria Papyrus I: An Aramaic Slave Conveyance of 335 B. C. E. found in the Wâdi ed-Dâliyeh." In *N. Avigad Volume*, ErIsr 18. Edited by B. Mazar and Y. Yadin. Jerusalem: Israel Exploration Society, 1985, pp. 7*-17*.

——. "A Report on the Samaria Papyri." In *Congress Volume, Jerusalem 1986*. Edited by J. A. Emerton. SVT 40. Leiden: E. J. Brill, 1986, pp. 17–26.

Daiches, S. *The Jews in Babylonia in the Time of Ezra and Nehemiah according to Babylonian Inscriptions*. London: Jews College Publications no. 2, 1910.

Dandamaev, M. A. *Persien unter den ersten Achämeniden (6 Jahrhundert v. Chr)*. Beiträge zur Iranistik 7. Wiesbaden: Ludwig Reichert, 1976.

——. *Slavery in Babylonia from Nabopolassar to Alexander the Great (626–331 B. C.)*. Translated by V. A. Powell. DeKalb, IL: Northern Illinois University Press, 1984

——. "The Diaspora: Babylonia in the Persian Age." In *The Cambridge History of Judaism, Vol 1. Introduction; The Persian Period*. Edited by W. D. Davies and L. Finkelstein. Cambridge: Cambridge University Press, 1984, pp. 326–341.

——. *A Political History of the Achaemenid Empire*. Translated by W. J. Vogelsang. Leiden and New York: E. J. Brill, 1989.

——. "State Gods and Private Religion in the Near East in the First Millennium BCE." In *Religion and Politics in the Ancient Near East*. Edited by A. Berlin. Studies and texts in Jewish History and Culture. Bethesda, MD: University Press of Maryland, 1996, pp. 35–46.

Dandamaev, M. A., and V. G. Lukonin. *The Culture and Social Institutions of Ancient Iran*. Translated by P. L. Kohl. Cambridge and New York: Cambridge University Press, 1988.

Daniélou, J. "Le symbolisme eschatologique de la Fête des Tabernacles." *Irén* 31 (1958): 19–40.

Davidson, S. *The Text of the Old Testament Considered*. London: Longman, 1856.

Davies, G. I. *Ancient Hebrew Inscriptions. Corpus and Concordance*. Cambridge: Cambridge University Press, 1991.

Davies, P. R., ed. *Second Temple Studies 1: Persian Period*. JSOTSup 117. Sheffield: JSOT Press, 1991.

Davies, P. R. "Sociology and the Second Temple." In *Second Temple Studies 1: Persian Period*. Edited by P. R. Davies. JSOTSup 117. Sheffield: JSOT Press, 1991, pp. 11–19.

Deissler, A. *Les petits prophètes*. 2 vols. Paris: Letouzey et Ané, 1964.

Deist, F. E. "The Nature of Historical Understanding." *OTE* 6 (1993): 384–398.

——. "The Yehud Bible: A Belated Divine Miracle?" *JNSL* 23 (1997): 117–142.

Demsky, A. "Double Names in the Exile and the Identity of Sheshbazzar." In *These Are the Names.* Edited by A. Demsky. Studies in Jewish Onomastics 2. Ramat Gan: Bar Ilan University Press, 1999, pp. 23–39.

Depuydt, L. "Evidence for Accession Dating under the Achaemenids." *JAOS* 115 (1995): 193–204.

Dequecker, L. "Darius the Persian and the Reconstruction of the Jewish Temple in Jerusalem (Ezra 4, 24)." In *Ritual and Sacrifice in the Ancient Near East.* Edited by J. Quaegebur. OLA 55. Leuven: Uitgeverij Peeters en Departement Oriëntalistiek, 1993, pp. 67–92.

Derousseaux, L. *La crainte de Dieu dans l'Ancien Testament.* LD 63. Paris: Cerf, 1970.

Deutsch, R. *Messages from the Past: Hebrew Bullae from the Time of Isaiah through the Destruction of the First Temple, Shlomo Moussaieff Collection and an Up to Date Corpus.* Tel Aviv: Archaeological Centre, 1999.

Deutsch, R., and M. Heltzer. *West Semitic Epigraphic News of the First Millennium BCE.* Tel Aviv: Archaeological Center, 1999.

Devauchelle, D. "Un problème de chronologie sous Cambyse." *Trans* 15 (1998): 9–17.

Dever, W. "Biblical Archaeology: Death and Rebirth." In *Biblical Archaeology Today, 1990: Proceedings of the Second International Congress on Biblical Archaeology, Jerusalem, June-July, 1990.* Edited by A. Biran. Jerusalem: Israel Exploration Society/Israel Academy of Sciences and Humanities, 1993, pp. 706–22.

D'iakonov, I. M., ed. *Ancient Mesopotamia: A Socio-Economic History. A Collection of Studies edited by Soviet Scholars.* Moscow: Nauka/Central Department of Oriental Literature, 1969.

——. "The Commune in the Ancient Near East as Treated in the Work of Soviet Researchers." In *Introduction to Soviet Ethnography.* Edited by S. P. Dunn and E. Dunn. Berkeley: Highgate Road Social Science Station, 1974, pp. 519–548.

Dion, P.-E. "ששבצר and ססנורי." *ZAW* 95 (1983): 111–112.

——. "The Civic-and-Temple Community of Persian Period Judaea: Neglected Insights from Eastern Europe." *JNES* 50 (1991): 281–287.

Dogniez, C. "Le Dieu des armées dans le Dodekapropheton: quelques remarques sur une initiative de traduction." In *IX Congress of the International Organization for Septuagint and Cognate Studies Cambridge 1995.* Edited by B. A. Taylor. SBLSCS 45. Atlanta: Scholars Press, 1997, pp. 19–36.

Dombrowski, B. W. W. "Socio-religious Implications of Foreign Impact on Palestinian Jewry under Achaemenid Rule." *Trans* 13 (1997): 65–89.

Douglas, M. *Purity and Danger: An Analysis of Concepts of Pollution and Taboo.* London: Routledge & Kegan Paul, 1966.

Driver, S. R. *Deuteronomy.* ICC. New York: Charles Scribner's Sons, 1916.

——. *An Introduction to the Literature of the Old Testament.* International Theological Library. New York: Charles Scribner's Sons, 1928.

Dubberstein, W. H., and R. A. Parker. *Babylonian Chronology 626 B. C.–45 A. D.* Chicago: University of Chicago Press, 1946.

Dumbrell, W. J. "Some Observations on the Political Origins of Israel's Eschatology." *RTR* 36 (1971): 33–41.

——. "Kingship and Temple in the Post-Exilic Period." *RTR* 37 (1978): 33–42.

Eissfeldt, O. *The Old Testament: An Introduction.* Translated by P. R. Ackroyd. Oxford: Basil Blackwell, 1965.

Elayi, J. "Réflexion sur la place de l'histoire dans la recherche sur la Transeuphratène achéménide." *Trans* 8 (1994): 73–80.

——. "Pouvoirs locaux et organisation du territoire des cités phéniciennes sous l'Empire perse achéménide." *Espacio, Tiempo y Forma, Serie II. Historia Antigua* 10 (1997): 63–77.

Elayi, J., and J. Sapin. *Nouveaux regards sur la Transeuphratène.* Paris: Brépols, 1991.

——. *Beyond the River: New Perspectives on Transeuphratène*. Translated by J. E. Crowley. JSOTSup 250. Sheffield: Sheffield Academic Press, 1998.

——. *Quinze ans de recherche (1985–2000) sur la Transeuphratène à l'époque perse*. Suppléments à Transeuphratène 8. Paris: Gabalda, 2000.

Elliger, K. *Das Buch der zwölf kleinen Propheten*. Vol. 2. 7th. edtn. ATD 25/2. Göttingen: Vandenhoeck & Ruprecht, 1964.

Ellis, R. S. *Foundation Deposits in Ancient Mesopotamia*. Yale Near Eastern Researches 2. New Haven: Yale University Press, 1968.

Elmslie, W. A. L. "Prophetic Influences in the Sixth Century B. C." In *Essays and Studies Presented to S. A. Cook*. Edited by D. Winton-Thomas. Cambridge: Cambridge University Press, 1950, pp. 15–24.

Eph'al, I. "The Western Minorities in Babylonia in the 6th–5th Centuries B. C." *Orientalia* 47 (1978): 74–80.

——. "Syria-Palestine under Achaemenid Rule." In *Cambridge Ancient History. Vol. IV. Persia Greece and the Western Mediterranean c. 525–479 B. C.* 2nd. edtn. Cambridge: Cambridge University Press, 1988.

——. "Changes in Palestine during the Persian Period in Light of Epigraphic Sources." *IEJ* 48 (1998): 106–119.

Eph'al, I., and J. Naveh. *Aramaic Ostraca of the Fourth Century BC from Idumea*. Jerusalem: Magnes/Hebrew University/Israel Exploration Society, 1996.

Eshel, H. "Israelite Names from Samaria in the Persian Period." In *These Are the Names*. Edited by A. Demsky. Studies in Jewish Onomastics 2. Ramat Gan: Bar Ilan University Press, 1999, pp. 17–31.

Eskenazi, T., and K. Richards, eds. *Second Temple Studies 2: Temple and Community in the Persian Period*. JSOTSup 175. Sheffield: Sheffield Academic Press, 1996.

Finegan, J. *Handbook of Biblical Chronology*. Princeton: Princeton University Press, 1964.

Finkelstein, I. *The Archaeology of the Israelite Settlement*. Jerusalem: Israel Exploration Society, 1988.

Finkelstein, I., and Y. Magen. *Archaeological Survey in the Hill Country of Benjamin*. Jerusalem: Israel Exploration Society, 1993.

Fleishman, J. "The Investigating Commission of Tattenai: The Purpose of the Investigation and its Results." *HUCA* 66 (1995): 81–102.

Floyd, M. H. "Cosmos and History in Zechariah's View of the Restoration (Zechariah 1:7–6:15)." In *Problems in Biblical Theology: Essays in Honour of Rolf Knierim*. Edited by H. T. C. Sun. Grand Rapids: Eerdmans, 1997, pp. 125–144.

——. "The Nature of the Narrative and the Evidence of Redaction in Haggai." *VT* 45 (1995): 470–490.

——. *Minor Prophets, Part 2*, FOTL 22. Grand Rapids: Eerdmans, 2000.

Fohrer, G. "Die Gattung der Berichte über symbolische Handlungen der Propheten." *ZAW* 64 (1952): 101–120.

——. "Remarks on the Modern Interpretation of the Prophets." *JBL* 80 (1961): 309–319.

——. *Die symbolische Handlungen der Propheten*. 2nd. edtn. ATANT 25. Zürich: Zwingli, 1968.

——. *Die Propheten des ausgenhenden 6 und des 5 Jahrhunderts*. Die Propheten des Alten Testaments 5. Gütersloh: Gütersloher Verlagshaus, 1976.

——. s. v. "Σιών" *TDNT* 7:292–319.

Frame, G. "Neo-Babylonian and Achaemenid Economic Texts from the Sippar Collection of the British Museum." *JAOS* 104 (1989): 745–752.

Freedman, D. N. "The Chronicler's Purpose." *CBQ* 23 (1961): 436–442.

——. "The Earliest Bible." *MQR* 22 (1983): 167–175.

Freedy, K. S., and R. B. Redford. "The Dates in Ezekiel in Relation to Biblical, Babylonian and Egyptian Sources." *JAOS* 90 (1976): 462–485.

Friebel, K. G. *Jeremiah's and Ezekiel's Sign Acts.* JSOTSup 283. Sheffield: Sheffield Academic Press, 1999.

Friedman, R. E. *The Exile and Biblical Narrative: The Formation of the Deuteronomistic and Priestly Works.* HSM 22. Chico: Scholars Press, 1981.

Frye, R. N. *The History of Ancient Iran.* München: C. H. Beck'sche Verlagsbuchshandlung, 1984.

Gal, Z. "Israel in Exile." *BAR* 24 (1998): 48–53.

——. "The Lower Galilee in the Iron Age II: Analysis of Survey Material and its Historical Interpretation." *Tel Aviv* 15–16 (1988–89): 56–64.

Galil, G. "The Babylonian Calendar and the Chronology of the Last Kings of Judah." *Bib* 72 (1991): 367–78.

Galling, K. "The 'Gola-history' according to Ezra 2 and Nehemiah 7." *JBL* 70 (1951): 149–158.

——. "Serubbabel und der Wiederaufbau des Tempels in Jerusalem." In *Verbannung and Heimkehr: Beiträge zur Geschichte und Theologie Israels im 6. und 5. Jahrhundert v. Chr. Festschrift Wilhelm Rudolph.* Edited by A. Kuschke. Tübingen: J. C. B. Mohr, 1961, pp. 67–96.

Galling, K. *Studien zur Geschichte Israels im persichen Zeitalter.* Tübingen: J. C. B. Mohr, 1964.

Gammie, J. G. *Holiness in Israel.* OBT. Minneapolis: Fortress, 1989.

Garbini, G. *History and Ideology in Ancient Israel.* London: SCM, 1988.

Garelli, P. "Les déplacements de personnes dans l'empire assyrien." In *Immigration and Emigration in the Ancient Near East. Festschrift E. Lipiński.* Edited by K. van Lerberghe and A. Schoors. OLA 25. Leuven: Uitgeverij Peeters en Department Oriëntalistiek, 1995, pp. 79–82.

Geertz, C. *The Interpretation of Cultures.* New York: Basic, 1973.

Gelin, A. "Aggée." In *Introduction à la Bible.* Edited by A. Robert. Tournai: Desclée, 1959.

——. "Aggée, Zacharie, Malachi." In *La Bible de Jérusalem.* Paris: Cerf, 1973, pp. 1385–1401.

Gelston, A. "The Foundations of the Second Temple." *VT* 16 (1966): 232–235.

Goldman, Y. *Prophétie et royauté au retour de l'exil.* OBO 118. Freiburg/Göttingen: Universitätsverlag/Vandenhoeck & Ruprecht, 1992.

Good, E. M. *Irony in the Old Testament.* Philadelphia: Westminster, 1965.

Goody, J., and I. Watt. "The Consequences of Literacy." In *Literacy in Traditional Societies.* Edited by J. Goody. Cambridge: Cambridge University Press, 1968, pp. 37–42.

Gordon, C. H. "North Israelite Influence on Postexilic Hebrew." *IEJS* (1955): 85–88.

Gosse, B. "Nabuchodonosor et les évolutions de la rédaction du livre de Jérémie." *ScEs* 47 (1995): 177–187.

——. "L'universalisme de la Sagesse face au Sacerdoce de Jérusalem au retour de l'exil (Le don de 'mon Esprit' et de 'mes Paroles' en Is 59, 21 et Pr 1, 23)." *Trans* 13 (1997): 39–45.

Gottwald, N. K. *The Hebrew Bible: A Socio-Literary Introduction.* Philadelphia: Fortress, 1985.

Gowan, D. A. "The Beginnings of Exile Theology and the Root *glh*." *ZAW* 87 (1975): 204–207.

——. *Eschatology in the Old Testament.* Edinburgh: T. & T. Clark, 1986.

Grabbe, L. L. "Josephus and the Reconstruction of the Judean Restoration." *JBL* 106 (1987): 231–246.

——. *Judaism from Cyrus to Hadrian. Vol 1: The Greek and Persian Periods.* Minneapolis: Fortress, 1992.

——. *Priests, Prophets, Diviners, Sages: A Socio-Historical Study of Religious Specialists in Ancient Israel.* Valley Forge PA: Trinity Press International, 1995.

——, ed. *Leading Captivity Captive: 'The Exile' as History and Ideology*. JSOTSup 278.
    Sheffield: Sheffield Academic Press, 1998.
——. "'The Exile' Under the Theodolite: Historiography as Triangulation." In *Leading
    Captivity Captive*. Edited by L. L. Grabbe. JSOTSup 278. Sheffield: Sheffield Aca-
    demic Press, 1998, pp. 80–99.
Graf, D. F. "The Persian Royal Road System in Syria-Palestine." *Trans* 6 (1993): 149–
    167.
Graham, J. N. "Vinedressers and Ploughmen: 2 Kings 52:12 and Jeremiah 52:16." *BA*
    47 (1984): 55–58.
Greenfield, J. C., and J. Naveh. "Hebrew and Aramaic in the Persian Period." In
    *The Cambridge History of Judaism. Vol 1. Introduction; The Persian Period*. Edited by
    W. D. Davies and L. Finkelstein. Cambridge: Cambridge University Press, 1984,
    pp. 115–29.
Greenfield, J. C., and B. Porten. *The Bisitun Inscription of Darius the Great: Aramaic Version*.
    Corpus Inscriptionum Iranicarum. London: Lund Humphries, 1982.
Grelot, P. "La procession des peuples vers la nouvelle Jérusalem." *Assemblées du Seigneur*
    12 (1969): 6–10.
——. "Un parallèle babylonien d'Isaïe LX et du Psaume LXXII." *VT* 7 (1957): 319–321.
Gubel, E. "Cinq bulles inédites des archives de l'époque achéménide." *Semitica* 47
    (1997): 53–64.
Hallock, R. T. "Darius I, the King of the Persepolis Tablets." *JNES* 1 (1942): 230–232.
——. "The 'One Year' of Darius I." *JNES* 19 (1960): 36–39.
Halpern, B. "The Ritual Background of Zechariah's Temple Song." *CBQ* 40 (1978):
    167–190.
Hamerton-Kelly, R. G. "The Temple and the Origins of Jewish Apocalyptic." *VT* 20
    (1970): 1–15.
Hamilton, M. W. "Who was a Jew? Jewish Ethnicity during the Achaemenid Period."
    *ResQ* 37 (1995): 102–117.
Hamlin, E. J. s. v. "Nations." *IDB* 3:516.
Hanson, P. D. *The Dawn of Apocalyptic*. Philadelphia: Fortress, 1975.
——. "Zechariah 9 and the Recapitulation of an Ancient Ritual Pattern." *JBL* 92 (1973):
    37–59.
——. "Israelite Religion in the Early Postexilic Period." In *Ancient Israelite Religion.
    Essays in Honour of Frank Moore Cross*. Edited by P. D. Miller, P. D. Hanson and
    S. D. McBride. Philadelphia: Fortress, 1987, pp. 487–508.
Hartner, W. "Old Iranian Calendars." In *The Cambridge History of Iran. Vol. 2. The Median
    and Achaemenian Periods*. Edited by I. Gershevitch. Cambridge: Cambridge University
    Press, 1985, pp. 714–792.
Hasel, G. *The Remnant: The Theology and History of the Remnant Idea from Genesis to Isaiah*.
    Berrien Springs: Andrews University Press, 1974.
——. s. v. "Remnant." *IBD[S]* pp. 735–736.
Hayes, J. H., and F. C. Prussner. *Old Testament Theology: Its History and Development*.
    Atlanta: John Knox, 1985.
Heltzer, M. "A propos des banquets des rois achéménides et du retour d'exil sous
    Zorobabel." *RB* 86 (1979): 101–106.
——. "A Recently Published Babylonian Tablet and the Province of Judah after 516
    B.C.E." *Trans* 5 (1992): 57–61.
Herntrich, V. s. v. "λειμμα" *TDNT* 4:196–209.
Herr, L. G. "The Iron Age Period." *BA* 60 (1997): 114–183.
Hesse, F. "Haggai." In *Verbannung und Heimkehr: Beiträge zur Geschichte und Theologie Israels
    im 6. und 5. Jahrhundert v. Chr. Festschrift. Wilhelm Rudolph*. Edited by A. Kuschke.
    Tübingen: J. C. B. Mohr, 1961, pp. 109–134.

Hildebrand, D. R. "Temple Ritual: A Paradigm for Moral Holiness in Haggai II 10–19." *VT* 18 (1989): 154–168.

Hillers, D. R. *Treaty Curses and the Old Testament Prophets.* BibOr 16. Rome: Pontifical Biblical Institute, 1964.

Hoglund, K. G. *Achaemenid Imperial Administration in Syria-Palestine and the Missions of Ezra and Nehemiah.* SBLDS 125. Atlanta: Scholars Press, 1992.

Homès-Fredericq, D. "Influences diverses en Transjordanie à l'époque achéménide." *Trans* 11 (1996): 63–76.

Hoonacker, A. van. *Nouvelles études sur la restauration juive après l'exil de Babylone.* Paris/Louvain: Ernest Leroux/J. B. Istas, 1896.

——. *Les douze Petits Prophètes: traduits et commentés.* EtB. Paris: J. Gabalda, 1908.

Horst, F. *Die zwölf kleinen Propheten, II.* HAT 1/14. Tübingen: Mohr/Siebeck, 1964.

House, P. R. *Zephaniah: A Prophetic Drama.* JSOTSup 69. Sheffield: Almond, 1989.

Humbert, P. "La formule hébraïque en HINENI suivi d'un participe." *REJ* 17 (1934): 59–62.

James, F. "Thoughts on Haggai and Zechariah." *JBL* 3 (1934): 229–234.

Janssen, E. *Juda in der Exilszeit: Ein Beitrag zur Frage der Entstehung des Judentums.* FRLANT 69. Göttingen: Vandenhoeck & Ruprecht, 1956.

Japhet, S. "The Supposed Common Authorship of Chronicles and Ezra-Nehemiah Investigated Anew." *VT* 18 (1968): 330–371.

——. "Sheshbazzar and Zerubbabel: Against the Background of the Historical and Religious Tendencies of Ezra-Nehemiah." *ZAW* 94 (1982): 66–98.

——. "People and Land in the Restoration Period." In *Das Land Israel in biblischer Zeit.* Edited by G. Strecker. Göttingen: Vandenhoeck & Ruprecht, 1983, pp. 103–125.

——. "Sheshbazzar and Zerubbabel: Against the Background of the Historical and Religious Tendencies of Ezra-Nehemiah, Part II." *ZAW* 96 (1984): 218–229.

——. "'History' and 'Literature' in the Persian Period: The Restoration of the Temple." In *Ah, Assyria…Studies in Assyrian History and Ancient Near Eastern Historiography Presented to Hayim Tadmor.* Edited by M. Cogan and I. Eph'al. Scripta Hierosolymitana 33. Jerusalem: Magnes, 1991, pp. 174–188.

——. "The Temple in the Restoration Period: Reality and Ideology." *USQR* 44 (1991): 195–251.

Jemielity, T. *Satire and the Hebrew Prophets.* Louisville: Westminster/John Knox, 1992.

Jenson, P. P. *Graded Holiness: A Key to the Priestly Conception of the World.* JSOTSup 106. Sheffield: Sheffield Academic Press, 1992.

Joannès, F., and A. Lemaire. "Trois tablettes cunéiformes à onomastique ouest-sémitique (collection Sh. Moussaïeff)." *Trans* 17 (1999): 17–34.

Jones, D. R. *Haggai, Zechariah, Malachi.* Torch Bible Commentary. London: SCM, 1962.

——. "The Cessation of Sacrifice after the Destruction of the Temple in 586 BC." *JTS* ns 14 (1963): 12–31.

Jones, S. *The Archaeology of Ethnicity: Constructing Identities in the Past and Present.* London and New York: Routledge, 1997.

Kaiser, W. *Toward an Old Testament Theology.* Grand Rapids: Zondervan, 1978.

Kalimi, I., and J. D. Purvis. "King Jehoiachin and the Vessels of the Lord's House in Biblical Literature." *CBQ* 56 (1994): 449–457.

Kapelrud, A. S. "Eschatology in the Book of Micah." *VT* 11 (1961): 392–405.

Katzenstein, H. J. "Gaza in the Persian Period." *Trans* 1 (1989): 68–82.

Kaufman, S. A. "An Emphatic Plea for Please." *Maarav* 7 (1991): 195–198.

Keil, C. F. *The Twelve Minor Prophets.*, 2 vols. Biblical Commentary on the Old Testament. Grand Rapids: Eerdmans, 1949.

Kessler, J. "The Shaking of the Nations: An Eschatological View." *JETS* 30 (1987): 159–166.

——. "The Second Year of Darius: An Historical Investigation." Mémoire de D.S.E.B. Institut Catholique de Paris, 1990.
——. "The Second Year of Darius and the Prophet Haggai." *Trans* 5 (1992): 63–84.
——. "Le rôle du prophète dans le livre d'Aggée." Thèse de doctorat. Sorbonne-Paris IV, 1995.
——. "'t (le temps) en Aggée I 2–4: conflit théologique ou 'sagesse mondaine'?" *VT* 48 (1998): 555–559.
——. "Reconstructing Haggai's Jerusalem: Demographic and Sociological Considerations and the Quest for an Adequate Methodological Point of Departure." In *Every City Shall Be Forsaken: Urbanism and Prophecy in Ancient Israel and the Near East*. Edited by L. L. Grabbe and R. Haak. JSOTSup 330. Sheffield: Sheffield University Press, 2001, pp. 137–158.
Keunen, A. *The Prophets and Prophecy in Israel*. Amsterdam: Philo, 1969.
Kippenberg, H. G. *Religion und Klassenbildung im antiken Judäa. Eine religions-soziologische Studie zum Verhältnis von Tradition und gesellschaftlicher Entwicklung*. SUNT 14. Göttingen: Vandenhoeck & Ruprecht, 1978.
Kittel, R. *Geschichte des Volkes Israel*. Gotha: Perthes, 1909.
Kloner, A. "Rock-Cut Tombs in Jerusalem." *BAIAS* (1982–83): 37–40.
Knauf, E. A. "The Persian Administration in Arabia." *Trans* 2 (1990): 201–218.
Knight, D. A., ed. *Tradition and Theology in the Old Testament*. Philadelphia: Fortress, 1977.
——. s. v. "Tradition History." *ABD* 6:633–638.
Koch, K. "Haggais unreines Volk." *ZAW* 79 (1967): 52–66.
Koole, J. L. *Haggai*. COut. Kampen: Kok, 1967.
Kosters, H. W. *Die Wiederstellung Israels in der persischen Period*. Heidelberg: Hurning, 1885.
Kramer, C., ed. *Ethnoarchaeology: Implications of Ethnography to Archaeology*. New York: Columbia University Press, 1979.
Kreissig, H. *Die sozialökonomische Situation in Juda zur Achämenidzeit*. Schriften zur Geschichte und Kultur des Alten Orients 7. Berlin: Akademie Verlag, 1973.
——. "Eine beachtenswerte Theorie zur Organisation altvorderorientalischer Tempelgemeinden im Achameniden Reich: Zu J.P. Weinberg's 'Bürger-Tempel-Gemeinde' in Juda." *Klio* 66 (1984): 35–39.
Kuhrt, A. "The Cyrus Cylinder and Achaemenid Imperial Policy." *JSOT* 25 (1983): 83–97.
——. "Babylon From Cyrus to Xerxes." In *Cambridge Ancient History. Vol. IV. Persia Greece and the Western Mediterranean c. 525–479 B. C. 2nd edtn*. Edited by J. Boardman et. al. Cambridge: Cambridge University Press, 1988, pp. 112–138.
Kutsch, E. *Die chronologische Daten des Ezechielbuches*. OBO 39. Freiburg/Göttingen: Universitätsverlag/Vandenhoeck & Ruprecht, 1985.
Lagrange, M.-J. "Notes sur les prophéties messianiques des derniers prophètes." *RB* (1906): 67–83.
Laperrousaz, E.-M. "Quelques remarques sur le rempart de Jérusalem à l'époque de Néhémie." *FO* 21 (1980): 179–185.
——. "Le régime théocratique juif a-t-il commencé a l'époque perse ou seulement à l'époque hellénistique?" *Semitica* 32 (1982): 93–96.
——. "Jérusalem à l'époque perse (étendue et statut)." *Trans* 1 (1989): 55–66.
——. "L'étendue de Jérusalem à l'époque perse." In *La Palestine à l'époque perse*. Edited by E.-M. Laperrousaz and A. Lemaire. Paris: Cerf, 1994, pp. 123–153.
——. "Le statut de la province de Judée." In *La Palestine à l'époque perse*. Edited by E.-M. Laperrousaz and A. Lemaire. Paris: Cerf, 1994, pp. 117–122.
Laperrousaz, E.-M., and A. Lemaire, eds. *La Palestine à l'époque perse*. Paris: Cerf, 1994.
Larsson, G. "Ancient Calendars Indicated in the OT." *JSOT* 54 (1992): 61–67.
Lecoq, P. *Les inscriptions de la Perse achéménide*. L'Aube des Peuples. Paris: Gallimard, 1997.

Leith, M. J. W. *Wadi Dâliyeh I*. DJD 24. Oxford: Clarendon, 1997.

Lemaire, A. *Inscriptions hébraïques. Tome I: les ostraca*. LAPO 9. Paris: Cerf, 1977.

——. "Review of N. Avigad, *Bullae and Seals from a Post-Exilic Archive*." *Syria* 54 (1977): 129–131.

——. *Les écoles et la formation de la Bible dans l'ancien Israël*. OBO 39. Fribourg/Göttingen: Editions Universitaires/Vandenhoeck & Ruprecht, 1981.

——. "Les formules de datation dans Ezéchiel à la lumière de données épigraphiques récentes." In *Ezekiel and his Book: Textual and Literary Criticism and their Interrelation*. Edited by J. Lust. Leuven: Leuven University Press, 1986, pp. 359–366.

——. "Les inscriptions palestiniennes d'époque perse: un bilan provisoire." *Trans* 1 (1989): 87–104.

——. "Populations et territoires de la Palestine à l'époque perse." *Trans* 3 (1990): 31–74.

——. "Les transformations politiques et culturelles de la Transjordanie au VIe siècle av. J.-C." *Trans* 8 (1994): 9–27.

——. "Epigraphie et numismatique palestiniennes." In *La Palestine à l'époque perse*. Edited by E.-M. Laperrousaz and A. Lemaire. Paris: Cerf, 1994, pp. 261–287.

——. "Review of K. G. Hoglund, Achaemenid Imperial Administration." *Trans* 8 (1994): 167–69.

——. "Histoire et administration de la Palestine à l'époque perse." In *La Palestine à l'époque perse*. Edited by E.-M. Laperrousaz and A. Lemaire. Paris: Cerf, 1994, pp. 11–53.

——. "La circulation monétaire phénicienne en Palestine à l'époque perse." In *Actes du IIIe congrès des études phéniciennes et puniques. Vol. 2*. Edited by M. H. Fantar and M. Ghaki. Tunis, 1995, pp. 192–202.

——. *Nouvelles inscriptions araméennes d'Idumée au Musée d'Israël*. Trans Sup. 3. Paris: Gabalda, 1996.

——. "Zorobabel et la Judée à la lumière de l'épigraphie (fin du VIe s. av. J.-C.)." *RB* 103 (1996): 48–57.

——. "L'exploitation des sources ouest-sémitiques (araméennes, phéniciennes, hébraïques et minéennes)." In *Recherches récentes sur l'empire achéménide*. Suppléments à Topoi 1. Lyon/Paris: Maison de l'Orient Méditerranéen, 1997, pp. 305–332.

——. "Les formules de datation en Palestine au premier millénaire avant J.-C." In *Proche-Orient Ancien. Temps vécu, temps pensé*. Edited by F. Briquel-Chatonnet and H. Lozachmeur. Antiquités sémitiques 3. Paris: J. Maisonneuve, 1998, pp. 53–82.

——. "Quatre nouveaux *ostraca* araméens d'Idumée." *Trans* 18 (1999): 71–74.

——. "Nouveaux sceaux et bulles paléo-hébraïques." In *F. M. Cross Volume*, ErIsr 26. Edited by B. A. Levine et. al. Jerusalem: Israel Exploration Society, 1999, pp. 106*-115*.

——. "Traditions amorrites et Bible: le prophétisme." *RA* 93 (1999): 49–56.

——. "Der Beitrag idumäischer Ostraka zur Geschichte Palästinas im Übergang von der persischen zur hellenistischen Zeit." *ZDPV* 115 (1999): 12–23.

——, ed. *Les routes du Proche Orient*. Paris: Desclée de Brouwer, 2000.

——, ed. *Prophètes et rois: Bible et Proche Orient*. LD. Paris: Cerf, 2001.

——. "Prophètes et rois dans les inscriptions ouest-sémitiques (IXe-VIe siècle av. J.-C." In *Prophètes et rois: Bible et Proche Orient*. Edited by A. Lemaire. LD. Paris: Cerf, 2001, pp. 85–115.

Lemaire, A., and H. Lozachmeur. "Remarques sur le plurilinguisme en Asie Mineur à l'époque perse." In *Mosaïque de langues, mosaïque culturelle. Le bilinguisme dans le Proche-Orient ancien*. Edited by F. Briquel-Chatonnet. Antiquités sémitiques 1. Paris: J. Maisonneuve, 1996, pp. 91–123.

Lemche, N. P. "On the Use of 'System Theory, 'Macro Theories' and Evolutionistic

Thinking in Modern OT Research and Biblical Archaeology." *SJOT* 2 (1990): 73–88.

Lévêque, J. *Job et son Dieu*. 2 vols. EtB. Paris: Gabalda, 1970.

Levin, S. "Zerubbabel: A Riddle." *JBQ* 24 (1996): 14–17.

Limet, H. "L'émigré dans la société mésopotamienne." In *Immigration and Emigration in the Ancient Near East: Festschrift E. Lipiński*. Edited by K. van Lerberghe and A. Schoors. OLA 65. Leuven: Uitgeverij Peeters en Department Oriëntalistiek, 1995, pp. 165–179.

Lindblom, J. *Prophecy in Ancient Israel*. Oxford: Basil Blackwell, 1962.

Lipiński, E. "Recherches sur le livre de Zacharie." *VT* 20 (1970): 30–53.

——. "'Cellériers' de la province de Juda." *Trans* 1 (1989): 107–109.

——. "Géographie linguistique de la Transeuphratène à l'époque achéménide." *Trans* 3 (1990): 95–107.

Lipschits, O. "The History of the Benjamin Region under Babylonian Rule." *Tel Aviv* 26 (1999): 155–190.

——. "Nebuchadnezzar's Policy in 'Hattu-Land' and the Fate of the Kingdom of Judah." *UF* 30 (1998): 467–487.

Liver, J. "The Return from Babylon, its Time and Scope." In *B. Mazar Volume*. Edited by M. Avi-Yonah et. al. Erlsr 3. Jerusalem: Israel Exploration Society, 1958, p. 90*.

Lods, A. *The Prophets and the Rise of Judaism*. Translated by S. H. Hooke, The History of Civilization. London: Routledge & Kegan Paul, 1937.

Lohfink, N. "Die Gattung der 'Historischen Kurzgeschichte' in den letzten Jahren von Juda und in der Zeit des Babylonischen Exils." *ZAW* 90 (1978): 319–347.

Long, B. O. "Prophetic Authority as Social Reality." In *Canon and Authority: Essays in Old Testament Religion and Theology*. Edited by G. W. Coats and B. O. Long. Philadelphia: Fortress, 1977, pp. 3–20.

——. "Social Dimensions of Prophetic Conflict." *Semeia* 21 (1981): 31–53.

Longenecker, R. *Biblical Exegesis in the Apostolic Period*. Grand Rapids: Eerdmans, 1975.

Lust, J. "The Identification of Zerubbabel with Sheshbassar." *ETL* 63 (1987): 90–95.

Machinist, P. "The First Coins of Judah and Samaria: Numismatics and History in the Achaemenid and early Hellenistic Periods." In *Achaemenid History VIII, Continuity and Change*. Edited by H. Sancisi-Weerdenburg et al. Leiden: Nederlands Instituut voor het Nabije Oosten, 1994, pp. 365–380.

Malbran-Labat, F. *La version akkadienne de l'inscription trilingue de Darius à Behistun*. Documenta Asiana. Rome: Gruppo Editoriale Internazionale, 1994.

——. "La trilingue de Behistun et les singularités de la version babylonienne." *Semitica* 48 (1998): 61–75.

Margalith, O. "The Political Background of Zerubbabel's Mission and the Samaritan Schism." *VT* 41 (1991): 312–323.

Marti, K. *Das Dodekapropheton*. KHC 13. Tübingen: Mohr, 1904.

Mason, R. A. *The Books of Haggai, Zechariah, and Malachi*. Cambridge Bible Commentary. New York: Cambridge University Press, 1977.

——. "The Purpose of the 'Editorial Framework' of the Book of Haggai." *VT* 27 (1977): 413–421.

——. "The Prophets of the Restoration." In *Israel's Prophetic Tradition: Essays in Honour of Peter R. Ackroyd*. Edited by R. Coggins, A. Philipps and M. Knibb. Cambridge: Cambridge University Press, 1982, pp. 137–153.

——. "Some Echoes of the Preaching of the Second Temple: Tradition Elements in Zechariah 1–8." *ZAW* 96 (1984): 221–235.

——. *Preaching the Tradition: Homily and Hermeneutic after the Exile*. Cambridge and New York: Cambridge University Press, 1990.

——. "The Messiah in the Postexilic Old Testament Literature." In *King and Messiah in*

*Israel and the Ancient Near East: Proceedings of the Oxford Old Testament Seminar.* Edited by J. Day. JSOTSup 270. Sheffield: Sheffield Academic Press, 1998, pp. 338–364.

Mauchline, J. "Implicit Signs of a Persistent Belief in a Davidic Empire." *VT* 20 (1970): 287–303.

May, H. G. "Three Hebrew Seals and the Status of Exiled Jehoiachin." *AJSL* 56 (1939): 146–148.

——. "Theological Universalism in the Old Testament." *JBR* 16 (1948): 100–107.

——. "'This People' and 'This Nation' in Haggai." *VT* 18 (1968): 190–197.

Mays, A. D. H. "Sociology and the Old Testament." In *The World of Ancient Israel: Sociological, Anthropological and Political Perspectives.* Edited by R. E. Clements. Cambridge: Cambridge University Press, 1989, pp. 39–63.

McCullough, W. S. *The History and Literature of the Palestinian Jews from Cyrus to Herod 550 B. C. to 4 B. C.* Toronto: University of Toronto Press, 1975.

McEvenue, S. "The Political Structure in Judah from Cyrus to Nehemiah." *CBQ* 43 (1981): 353–364.

Merrill, E. H. "The 'Accession Year' and Davidic Chronology." *JANES* 19 (1990): 101–112.

——. *An Exegetical Commentary, Haggai, Zechariah and Malachi.* Chicago: Moody, 1994.

Merwe, C. H. J. vander. "'Reference Time' in Some Biblical Temporal Constructions." *Bib* 78 (1997): 503–524.

Meslin, M. *Pour une science des religions.* Paris: Seuil, 1973.

——. *L'expérience humaine du divin. Fondements d'une anthropologie religieuse.* Cogitatio Fidei 150. Paris: Cerf, 1988.

Mettinger, T. N. D. *The Dethronement of Sabaoth: Studies in the Shem and Kabod Theologies.* CB, OT Series 18. Lund: Gleerup, 1982.

Meyer, E. *Die Entstehung des Judentums: Eine historische Untersuchung.* Halle: Niemeyer, 1896.

Meyers, C. L., and E. M. Meyers. *Haggai, Zechariah 1–8.* AB. Garden City: Doubleday, 1987.

——. "Expanding the Frontiers of Biblical Archaeology." In *Y. Yadin Volume.* ErIsr 20. Edited by A. Ben Tor, J. C. Greenfield, and A. Malamat. Jerusalem: Israel Exploration Society, 1989, pp. 140\*-147\*.

——. "Jerusalem and Zion after the Exile: The Evidence of First Zechariah." In *"Sha'arei Talmon" Studies in the Bible, Qumran and the Ancient Near East. Presented to Shemaryahu Talmon.* Edited by E. Tov, W. W. Fields and M. Fishbane. Winona Lake: Eisenbrauns, 1992, pp. 121–35.

——. "Demography and Diatribes: Yehud's Population and the Prophecy of Second Zechariah." In *Scripture and Other Artifacts: Essays on the Bible and Archaeology in Honour of Philip J. King.* Edited by M. D. Coogan, J. C. Exum and L. E. Stager. Louisville: Westminster John Knox, 1994, pp. 268–285.

Meyers, E. M. "The Use of *tôrâ* in Haggai 2, and the Role of the Prophet in the Restoration." In *The Word of the Lord Shall Go Forth: Essays in Honor of David Noel Freedman in Celebration of his Sixtieth Birthday.* Edited by C. L. Meyers and M. O'Connor. Winona Lake: Eisenbraun's-American School of Oriental Research, 1973, pp. 69–76.

——. "The Shelomith Seal and the Judaean Restoration, Some Additional Considerations." In *N. Avigad Volume,* ErIsr 18. Edited by B. Mazar and Y. Yadin. Jerusalem: Israel Exploration Society, 1985, pp. 31\*-38\*.

——. "The Persian Period and the Judean Restoration: From Zerubbabel to Nehemiah." In *Ancient Israelite Religion. Essays in Honour of Frank Moore Cross.* Edited by P. D. Miller, P. D. Hanson and S. D. McBride. Philadelphia: Fortress, 1987, pp. 509–521.

——. "Second Temple Studies in the Light of Recent Archaeology. Part 1: The Persian and Hellenistic Periods." *CR:BS* 2 (1994): 25–42.

——. "The Crisis of the Mid-fifth Century B.C.E. Second Zechariah and the 'End' of Prophecy." In *Pomegranates and Golden Bells: Studies in Biblical, Jewish, and Near Eastern Ritual Law and Literature in Honor of Jacob Milgrom.* Edited by D. P. Wright, D. N. Freedman and A. Hurvitz. Winona Lake: Eisenbrauns, 1995, pp. 713–723.

Milevski, I. "Settlement Patterns in Northern Judah during the Achaemenid Period, According to the Hill Country of Benjamin and Jerusalem Surveys." *BAIAS* 15 (1996–7): 7–29.

Milgrom, J. *Leviticus 1–16.* AB. New York: Doubleday, 1991.

Millard, A. R. "La prophétie et l'écriture: Israël, Aram, Assyrie." *RHR* 202 (1985): 125–144.

Miller, C. L. *The Representation of Speech in Biblical Hebrew Narrative: A Linguistic Analysis.* HSM 55. Atlanta: Scholars Press, 1996.

Miller, P. D. J. *The Divine Warrior in Early Israel.* Cambridge: Harvard University Press, 1973.

Mitchell, H. G, et. al. *A Critical and Exegetical Commentary on Haggai, Zechariah, Malachi and Jonah.* ICC. New York: Charles Scribner's Sons, 1912.

Morgenstern, J. "Two Prophecies from 520–516 B.C." *HUCA* 22 (1949): 365–431.

Motyer, J. A. "Haggai." In *The Minor Prophets: Vol. 3.* Edited by T. E. McComiskey. Grand Rapids: Baker, 1998, pp. 963–1002.

Mowinckel, S. *Studien zu dem Buche Ezra-Nehemia, vol 1.* Oslo: Universitetsforlaget, 1964.

Muilenburg, J. s. v. "Isaiah-Introduction." *IB.*

Mullen, E. T. *Narrative History and Ethnic Boundaries: The Deuteronomistic Historian and the Creation of Israelite National Identity.* SemeiaSt. Atlanta: Scholars Press, 1993.

——. *Ethnic Myths and Pentateuchal Foundations.* SBLSS. Atlanta: Scholars Press, 1997.

Murray, D. F. "Of all the Years the Hopes—or Fears? Jehoiachin in Babylon (2 Kings 25:27–30)." *JBL* 102 (2001): 245–265.

Na'aman, N. "Hezekiah's Fortified Cities and the *LMLK* Stamps." *BASOR* 261 (1986): 5–21.

——. "Population Changes in Palestine Following the Assyrian Deportations." *Tel Aviv* 20 (1993): 104–124.

Naveh, J. "The Aramaic Ostraca." In *Beer-Sheba I.* Edited by Y. Aharoni. Tel Aviv: Tel Aviv University Institute of Archaeology, 1973, pp. 79–82.

——. "The Aramaic Ostraca from Tel Beer-Sheba (Seasons 1971–1976)." *Tel Aviv* 6 (1979): 182–95.

Neil, W. s. v. "Haggai." In *New Interpreter's Dictionary of the Bible, vol 2.* Nashville: Abingdon, 1992.

Nicholson, E. W. "The Meaning of the Expression עם הארץ in the Old Testament." *JJS* 10 (1965): 59–66.

——. *Preaching to the Exiles: A Study of the Prose Tradition in the Book of Jeremiah.* Oxford: Basil Blackwell, 1970.

Niehr, H. "Religio-Historical Aspects of the 'Early Post-Exilic' Period." In *The Crisis of Israelite Religion: Transformation of Religious Tradition in Exilic and Post-Exilic Times.* Edited by B. Becking and M. C. A. Korpel. OS 62. Leiden: Brill, 1999, pp. 228–44.

North, C. R. *The Suffering Servant in Deutero-Isaiah: An Historical and Critical Study.* London: Oxford University Press, 1956.

North, F. S. "Critical Analysis of the Book of Haggai." *ZAW* 68 (1956): 25–46.

North, R. *Exégèse pratique des petits-prophètes postexiliens: bibliographie commentée.* Rome: Biblico, 1969.

Noth, M. "La catastrophe de Jérusalem en l'an 587 avant Jésus-Christ et sa signification pour Israël." *RHPR* 33 (1953): 81–102.

——. *History of Israel.* London: A. & C. Black, 1958.

Nowack, W. *Die kleinen Propheten.* HKAT 3/4. Göttingen: Vandenhoeck & Ruprecht, 1922.

O'Brien, D. P. "Is This The Time to Accept ... ? (2 Kings v 26b): Simply Moralizing (LXX) or an Ominous Foreboding of Yahweh's Rejection of Israel (MT)?" *VT* 46 (1996): 448–457.

Ockinga, B. "The Inviolability of Zion—a Pre-Israelite Tradition." *BN* (1988): 54–66.

Oded, B. "Observations on the Israelite/Judaean Exiles in Mesopotamia during the Eight-Sixth Centuries BCE." In *Immigration and Emigration in the Ancient Near East. Festschrift E. Lipiński.* Edited by K. van Lerberghe & A. Schoors. OLA 25. Leuven: Uitgeverij Peeters en Department Oriëntalistiek, 1995, pp. 205–212.

Oesterley, W. O. E., and T. H. Robinson. *Hebrew Religion: Its Origin and Development.* London: Society for Promoting Christian Knowledge, 1930.

——. *An Introduction to the Books of the Old Testament.* London: SPCK, 1934.

Ofer, A. "The Highland of Judah During the Biblical Period 1." Ph. D. diss. University of Tel Aviv, 1993.

——. "All the Hill Country of Judah: From a Settlement Fringe to a Prosperous Monarchy." In *From Nomadism to Monarchy: Archaeological and Historical Aspects of Early Israel.* Edited by I. Finkelstein and N. Na'aman. Jerusalem: Yad Izhak Ben Zvi and Israel Exploration Society, 1990, pp. 92–121.

Olmstead, A. T. "Darius and his Behistun Inscription." *AJSL* 55 (1938): 392–416.

Orelli, C. von. *The Twelve Minor Prophets.* Translated by J. S. Banks. Edinburgh: T. &T. Clark, 1897.

Oren, E. D. "Le Nord-Sinaï à l'époque perse. Perspectives archéologiques." In *Le Sinaï durant l'Antiquité et le Moyen Age. 4,000 ans d'histoire pour un désert.* Edited by D. Valbelle and C. Bonnet. Paris, 1998, pp. 75–82.

Orlinsky, H. M. "The So-Called "Suffering Servant" of Isa 53." In P. A. H. de Boer and H. Orlinsky, *Studies on the Second Part of the Book of Isaiah.* SVT 14. Leiden: E. J. Brill, 1967.

Overholt, T. W. "Prophecy: The Problem of Cross-Cultural Comparison." In *Anthropological Approaches to the Old Testament.* Edited by B. Lang. London/Philadelphia: SPCK/Fortress, 1985, pp. 60–82.

Parker, R. A. "Darius and his Egyptian Campaign." *AJSL* 58 (1941): 373–377.

——. "Persian and Egyptian Chronology." *AJSL* 58 (1941): 285–301.

Pasto, J. "When the End is the Beginning? Or when the Biblical Past is the Political Present: Some Thoughts on Ancient Israel, 'Post-Exilic Judaism' and the Politics of Biblical Scholarship." *SJOT* 12 (1998): 157–202.

Pastor, J. *Land and Economy in Ancient Palestine.* London/New York: Routledge, 1997.

Peckham, B. *History and Prophecy: The Development of Late Judean Literary Traditions.* ABDRL. New York: Doubleday, 1993.

Person, R. F., Jr. *Second Zechariah and the Deuteronomic School.* JSOTSup 167. Sheffield: Sheffield University Press, 1993.

——. *The Kings-Isaiah and Kings-Jeremiah Recensions.* BZAW 252. Berlin and New York: de Gruyter, 1997.

——. "The Deuteronomic History in its Postexilic Context." In *Second Temple Studies. Vol. 3.* Edited by P. R. Davies. JSOTSup. Sheffield: JSOT. Forthcoming.

Peter, F. "Zu Haggai 1, 9." *TZ* 2 (1951): 150–151.

Petersen, D. L. "Zerubbabel and Jerusalem Temple Reconstruction." *CBQ* 36 (1974): 366–372.

——. *Late Israelite Prophecy: Studies in Deutero-Prophetic Literature and in Chronicles.* SBLMS 23. Missoula: Scholars Press, 1977.

——. "Rethinking the End of Prophecy." In *"Wünschet Jerusalem Frieden": Collected Communications to the XIIth Congress of the International Organization for the Study of the Old*

*Testament.* Edited by M. Augustin and K.-D. Schunck. BEATAJ 13. Frankfurt am Main: Peter Lang, 1988, pp. 65–71.

———. *The Roles of Israel's Prophets.* JSOTSup 17. Sheffield: JSOT Press, 1981.

———. *Haggai and Zechariah 1–8: A Commentary.* OTL. London: SCM, 1985.

———. "Israelite Prophecy: Change versus Continuity." In *Congress Volume: Leuven, 1989.* Edited by J. A. Emerton. SVT 43. Leiden: E. J. Brill, 1991, pp. 190–203.

———. "The Temple in the Persian Period." In *Second Temple Studies 1: Persian Period.* Edited by P. R. Davies. JSOTSup 117. Sheffield: JSOT Press, 1991, pp. 125–144.

———. "Rethinking the Nature of Prophetic Literature." In *Prophecy and Prophets: The Diversity of Contemporary Issues in Scholarship.* Edited by Y. Gitay. Atlanta: Scholars Press, 1997, pp. 23–40.

Petit, T. "L'évolution sémantique des termes hébreux et araméens *phh* et *sgn* et accadiens *pāḥātu* et *šaknu.*" *JBL* 107 (1988): 53–67.

———. *Satrapes et Satrapies dans l'empire achéménide de Cyrus le Grand à Xerxes Ier.* Bibliothèque de la Faculté de Philosophie et Lettres de l'Université de Liège 254. Paris: Les Belles Lettres, 1990.

Petitjean, A. "La mission de Zorobabel et la reconstruction du temple." *ETL* 42 (1966): 40–71.

———. *Les oracles du proto-Zacharie. Un programme de restauration pour la communauté juive après l'exil.* EtB. Paris/Louvain: Gabalda/ Editions Imprimerie Orientaliste, 1969.

Pfeiffer, R. H. *Introduction to the Old Testament.* New York: Harper and Bros., 1941.

Pfeil, R. "When is a *Gôy* a Goy?: The Interpretation of Haggai in 2:10–19." In *A Tribute to Gleason Archer.* Edited by W. C. Kaiser, Jr. and R. F. Youngblood. Chicago: Moody, 1986, pp. 261–278.

Pierce, R. W. "Literary Connectors and a Haggai/Zechariah/Malachi Corpus." *JETS* 27 (1984): 277–289; 401–411.

Plöger, O. *Theokratie und Eschatologie.* WMAT 2. Neukirchen: Neukirchener Verlag, 1959.

———. *Theocracy and Eschatology.* Translated by S. Rudman. Oxford: Basil Blackwell, 1968.

Poebel, A. "Chronology of Darius' First Year of Reign." *AJSL* 55 (1938): 142–165.

Polzin, R. *Late Biblical Hebrew. Toward an Historical Typology of Biblical Hebrew Prose.* HSM 12. Missoula: Scholars Press, 1976.

Pomykala, K. E. *The Davidic Dynasty Tradition in Early Judaism: Its History and Significance for Messianism.* SBLEJL 7. Atlanta: Scholars Press, 1995.

Porten, B. *Archives from Elephantine: The Life of an Ancient Jewish Military Colony.* Berkeley: University of California Press, 1968.

———. "The Diaspora: The Jews in Egypt." In *The Cambridge History of Judaism, Vol 1. Introduction; The Persian Period.* Edited by W. D. Davies and L. Finkelstein. Cambridge: Cambridge University Press, 1984, pp. 372–400.

———. "The Calendar of Aramaic Texts from Achaemenid and Ptolemaic Egypt." In *Irano-Judaica II: Studies relating to Jewish Contacts with Persian Culture Throughout the Ages.* Edited by A. Netzer and S. Shaked. Jerusalem: Ben-Zvi Institute, 1990, pp. 13–32.

———. *The Elephantine Papyri in English: Three Millennia of Cross Cultural Continuity and Change.* DMOA 22. Leiden: E. J. Brill, 1996.

Porten, B., and A. Yardeni. *Textbook of Aramaic Documents from Ancient Egypt. Vol. 2. Contracts.* Winona Lake: Hebrew University/ Eisenbrauns, 1989.

———. *Textbook of Aramaic Documents from Ancient Egypt. Vol. 3. Literature. Accounts. Lists.* Winona Lake: Hebrew University/ Eisenbrauns, 1993.

Porteous, N. W. "Jerusalem - Zion: The Growth of a Symbol." In *Verbannung und Heimkehr: Beiträge zur Geschichte und Theologie Israels im 6. und 5. Jahrhundert v. Chr. Festschrift Wilhelm Rudolph.* Edited by A. Kuschke. Tübingen: J. C. B. Mohr, 1961, pp. 235–251.

Porter, J. *The Vertical Mosaic: A Study of Social Class and Power in Canada.* Toronto: University of Toronto Press, 1965.

Powis-Smith, J. M. *The Prophets and their Times.* Chicago: University of Chicago Press, 1925.

Prinsloo, W. S. "The Cohesion of Haggai 1: 4–11." In *"Wünschet Jerusalem Frieden": Collected Communications to the XIIth Congress of the International Organization for the Study of the Old Testament.* Edited by M. Augustin and K.-D. Schunck. BEATAJ 13. Frankfurt am Main: Peter Lang, 1988, pp. 337–43.

Prokurat, M. "Haggai and Zechariah 1–8: A Form Critical Analysis." Ph. D. diss. Graduate Theological Union, Berkeley, California, 1988.

Pury, A. de., and T. Römer. "Terres d'exil et terres d'accueil. Quelques réflexions sur le judaïsme postexilique face à la Perse et à l'Egypte." *Trans* 9 (1995): 25–34.

Rad, G. von. "The Origin of the Concept of the Day of Yahweh." *JSS* 4 (1959): 97–108.

———. *Old Testament Theology.* Translated by D. M. G. Stalker. 2 vols. Edinburgh/London: Oliver and Boyd, 1965.

———. *Wisdom in Israel.* Translated by J. D. Martin. London: SPCK, 1972.

———. "The City on the Hill." In *The Problem of the Hexateuch and Other Essays.* Translated by E. W. T. Dicken. London: SCM, 1984, pp. 232–242.

———. "The Promised Land and Yahweh's Land in the Hexateuch." In *The Problem of the Hexateuch and Other Essays.* Translated by E. W. T. Dicken. London: SCM Press, 1984, pp. 79–93.

———. s. v. "ἄγγελος" *TDNT* 1:76–78.

Ramlot, L. "Prophétisme." *DBS* 7: cols. 811–1222.

Rappoport, U., J. Pastor, and O. Rimmon. "Land, Society and Culture in Judea." *Trans* 7 (1994): 73–82.

Redditt, P. L. *Haggai, Zechariah, Malachi.* NCBC. Grand Rapids: Eerdmans, 1995.

Reventlow, H. G. *Die Propheten Haggai, Sacharja und Maleachi.* 2. ATD. Göttingen: Vandenhoeck & Ruprecht, 1993.

Robert, P. de. "Pour ou contre le second temple." In *"Dort ziehen Schiffe dahin …": Collected Communications to the XIVth Congress of the International Organization for the Study of the Old Testament, Paris, 1992.* Edited by M. Augustin and K.-D. Schunck. BEATAJ 28. Frankfurt am Main: Peter Lang, 1996, pp. 179–182.

Roberts, J. J. M. "The Davidic Origin of the Zion Tradition." *JBL* 92 (1973): 329–344.

Robinson, G. L. *The Twelve Minor Prophets.* Grand Rapids: Baker, 1953.

Rogerson, J. W. *Anthropology and the Old Testament.* Oxford: Basil Blackwell, 1978.

———. "Anthropology and the Old Testament." In *The World of Ancient Israel: Sociological, Anthropological and Political Perspectives.* Edited by R. E. Clements. Cambridge: Cambridge University Press, 1989, pp. 17–37.

Römer, T. "Transformations et influences dans 'l'historiographie' juive de la fin du VIIe s. av. notre ère jusqu'à l'époque perse." *Trans* 13 (1997): 41–63.

Rooke, D. W. *Zadok's Heirs: The Role and Development of the High Priesthood in Ancient Israel.* Oxford Theological Monographs. Oxford and New York: Oxford University Press, 2000.

Rose, W. H. "Messianic Expectations in the Early Postexilic Period." *TynBul* 49 (1998): 373–376.

———. *Zemah and Zerubbabel: Messianic Expectations in the Early Postexilic Period.* JSOTSup 304. Sheffield: Sheffield Academic Press, 2000.

Rost, L. "Erwägungen zum Kyroserlass." In *Verbannung und Heimkehr: Beiträge zur Geschichte und Theologie Israels im 6. und 5. Jahrh. v. Chr. Festschrift Wilhelm Rudolph.* Edited by A. Kuschke. Tübingen: J. C. B. Mohr, 1961, pp. 301–307.

Rothstein, J. W. *Juden und Samaritaner: Die grundlegende Scheidung von Judentum und Heidentum. Eine kritische Studie zum Buche Haggai und zur jüdische Geschichte im ersten nachexilischen*

*Jahrhundert*. BWANT 3. Leipzig: J. C. Hinrichs, 1908.

Rudolph, W. *Haggai, Sacharja 1–8, 9–14, Malachi*. KAT XIII/4. Gütersloh: Gütersloher Verlagshaus, 1970.

Sacci, P. "L'esilio e la fine della monarchia davidica." *Henoch* 11 (1989): 131–48.

Saebø, M. "The Relation of Sheshbazzar and Zerubbabel—Reconsidered." *SEÅ* 54 (1989): 168–177.

Salles, J.-F. ""Du blé, de l'huile et du vin…" Notes sur les échanges commerciaux en Méditerraneé orientale vers le milieu du 1er millénaire avant. J.-C." In *Achaemenid History VI. Asia Minor and Egypt: Old Cultures in a New Empire. Proceedings of the 1988 Achaemenid History Workshop*. Edited by H. Sancisi-Weerdenburg and A. Kuhrt. Leiden: Nederlands Instituut voor het Nabije Oosten, 1991, pp. 207–236.

——. ""Du blé, de l'huile et du vin…" Notes sur les échanges commerciaux en Méditerraneé orientale vers le milieu du 1er millénaire av. J.-C." In *Achaemenid History VIII. Continuity and Change. Proceedings of the Last Achaemenid History Workshop*. Edited by A. Kuhrt, M. C. Root, and H. Sancisi-Weerdenburg. Leiden: Nederlands Instituut voor het Nabije Oosten, 1994, pp. 191–215.

Sancisi-Weerdenburg, H. "Darius I and the Persian Empire." In *Civilizations of the Ancient Near East*. Edited by J. M. Sasson. New York: Charles Scribner, 1995, 2:1035–1050.

Sauer, G. "Serubbabel in der Sicht Haggais und Sacharjas." In *Das ferne und nahe Wort. Festschrift Leonhard Rost*. Edited by F. Maas. BZAW 105. Berlin: Töpelmann, 1967, pp. 199–207.

Sauer, J. A. "Transjordan in the Bronze and Iron Ages: A Critique of Glueck's Synthesis." *BASOR* 263 (1986): 1–26.

Saydon, P. P. "Meanings and Uses of the Particle את." *VT* 14 (1964): 192–210.

Schams, C. *Jewish Scribes in the Second Temple Period*. JSOTSup 291. Sheffield: Sheffield Academic Press, 1998.

Schaper, J. "The Jerusalem Temple as an Instrument of Achaemenid Fiscal Administration." *VT* 45 (1995): 528–539.

——. "The Temple Treasury Committee in the Times of Nehemiah and Ezra." *VT* 47 (1997): 200–206.

Schattner-Rieser, U. "L'hébreu postexilique." In *La Palestine à l'époque perse*. Edited by E.-M. Laperrousaz and A. Lemaire. Paris: Cerf, 1994, pp. 189–224.

Schibler, D. *Le Livre de Michée*. CEB. Vaux-sur-Seine: Edifac, 1989.

Schottroff, W. "Zur Sozialgeschichte Israels in Perserzeit." *Verkundigung und Forschung* 27 (1982): 46–68.

Schram, B. *The Opponents of Third Isaiah: Reconstructing the Cultic History of the Restoration*. JSOTSup 193. Sheffield: Sheffield Academic Press, 1995.

Schultz, C. "The Political Tensions Reflected in Ezra-Nehemiah." In *Scripture in Context: Essays in the Comparative Method*. Edited by W. W. Hallo. Pittsburgh: Pickwick, 1980, pp. 221–244.

Schultz, H. *Old Testament Theology: The Religion of Revelation in its Pre-Christian Stage of Development*. Translated by J. A. Paterson. 2 vols. Edinburgh: T. & T. Clark, 1898.

Schultz, R. R. *The Search for Quotation: Verbal Parallels in the Prophets*. JSOTSup 180. Sheffield: Sheffield Academic Press, 1999.

Seebass, H. s. v. "בחר" *TDOT* 2:74–87.

Seitz, C. "The Crisis of Interpretation over the Meaning and Purpose of the Exile: A Redactional Study of Jeremiah xxi–xliii." *VT* 35 (1985): 78–97.

——. *Theology in Conflict. Reactions to the Exile in the Book of Jeremiah*. BZAW 176. Berlin: de Gruyter, 1989.

Selbie, J. A. s. v. "Gentiles." In *A Dictionary of the Bible Dealing With Its Language, Literature and Contents Including the Biblical Theology*. Edited by J. Hastings. New York: Scribners, 1898, 2:149.

Sellin, E. *Serubbabel. Eine Beitrag zur Geschichte des messianischen Erwartung und der Entstehung des Judentums.* Leipzig: A. Deichert, 1898.
——. *Das Zwölfprophetenbuch.* KAT XII/2. Leipzig: Deichert, 1922.
Sérandour, A. "Réflexions à propos d'un livre récent sur *Aggée-Zacharie* 1–8." *Trans* 10 (1995): 75–84.
——. "Les récits bibliques de la construction du second temple: leurs enjeux." *Trans* 11 (1996): 9–32.
——. "Zacharie et les autorités de son temps." In *Prophètes et rois: Bible et Proche Orient.* Edited by A. Lemaire. LD. Paris: Cerf, 2001, pp. 259–298.
Seybold, K. "Die Königserwartung bei den Propheten Haggai and Sacharja." *Judaica* 28 (1972): 69–78.
Siebeneck, R. T. "The Messianism of Aggeus and Proto-Zacharias." *CBQ* 19 (1951): 312–328.
Shiloh, Y. "Judah and Jerusalem in the Eighth-Sixth Centuries B.C.E." In *Recent Excavations in Israel: Studies in Iron Age Archaeology.* Edited by S. Gitin and W. G. Dever. Winona Lake: ASOR/Eisenbrauns, 1989, pp. 97–105.
—— et. al. s. v. "Jerusalem." In *New Encyclopedia of Excavations in the Holy Land.* Edited by E. Stern. New York: Simon and Schuster, 1993, 2:698–804.
Ska, J. L. "Sommaires proleptiques en Gn 27 et dans l'histoire de Joseph." *Bib* 73 (1992): 518–527.
Smith, D. *The Religion of the Landless.* Bloomington: Indiana University Press, 1989.
Smith, H. P. *The Religion of Israel: An Historical Study.* Edinburgh: T. & T. Clark, 1914.
Smith, M. *Palestinian Parties and Politics that Shaped the Old Testament.* New York: Columbia University Press, 1971.
——. "Jewish Religious Life in the Persian Period." In *The Cambridge History of Judaism, Vol 1. Introduction; The Persian Period.* Edited by W. D. Davies and L. Finkelstein. Cambridge: Cambridge University Press, 1984, pp. 219–278.
Smith, R. L. *Micah-Malachi.* WBC. Waco: Word, 1984.
Snyman, G. "Carnival in Jerusalem: Power and Subversiveness in the Early Second Temple Period." *OTE* 9 (1996): 88–110.
Soggin, J. A. *Introduction to the Old Testament: From its Origins to the Closing of the Alexandrian Canon.* Translated by John Bowden. 3rd. edtn. OTL. Louisville: Westminster/John Knox, 1989.
Sommer, B. D. "Did Prophecy Cease? Evaluating a Reevaluation." *JBL* 115 (1996): 31–47.
Speck, J. van der. "Did Cyrus the Great Introduce a New Policy towards Subdued Nations? Cyrus in Assyrian Perspective." *Persica* 10 (1982): 279–282.
Sperling, S. D. "Rethinking Covenant in the Late Biblical Books." *Bib* 70 (1989): 50–73.
Steck, O. H. "Zu Haggai 1, 2–11." *ZAW* (1971): 355–379.
——. "Theological Streams of Tradition." In *Tradition and Theology in the Old Testament.* Edited by D. A. Knight. Philadelphia: Fortress, 1977, pp. 183–214.
——. *Der Abschluss der Prophetie im Alten Testament.* BthSt 17. Neukirchen-Vluyn: Neukirchener Verlag, 1991.
Steiner, M. "The Archaeology of Ancient Jerusalem." *CR:BS* 6 (1998): 143–168.
Stern, E. *Material Culture of the Land of the Bible in the Persian Period 538–332 B. C.* Warminster: Israel Exploration Society, Aris & Phillips, 1982.
——. "The Archaeology of Persian Palestine." In *The Cambridge History of Judaism, Vol 1. Introduction; The Persian Period.* Edited by W. D. Davies and L. Finkelstein. Cambridge: Cambridge University Press, 1984, pp. 88–114.
——. "The Persian Empire and the Political and Social History of Palestine in the Persian Period." In *The Cambridge History of Judaism, Vol 1. Introduction; The Persian Period.*

Edited by W. D. Davies and L. Finkelstein. Cambridge: Cambridge University Press, 1984, pp. 70–87.

——. "New Evidence on The Administrative Division of Palestine in the Persian Period." In *Achaemenid History IV. Centre and Periphery: Proceedings of the Groningen 1986 Achaemenid History Workshop*. Edited by H. Sancisi-Weerdenburg and A. Kuhrt. Leiden: Nederlands Instituut voor het Nabije Oosten, 1990, pp. 221–226.

——. "La *Via Maris*." In *Les routes du Proche Orient*. Edited by A. Lemaire. Paris: Desclée de Brouwer, 2000, pp. 59–65.

Sternberg, M. *The Poetics of Biblical Narrative: Ideological Literature and the Drama of Reading*. Bloomington, IN: Indiana University Press, 1985.

Stohlman, S. "The Judaean Exile after 701 BCE." In *Scripture In Context 2: More Essays on the Comparative Method*. Edited by W. W. Hallo, J. C. Moyer, and L. G. Perdue. Winona Lake: Eisenbrauns, 1983, pp. 147–175.

Stuhlmueller, C. *Haggai and Zechariah: Rebuilding with Hope*. ITC. Grand Rapids: Eerdmans, 1988.

Sweet, R. F. G. "Writing as a Factor in the Rise of Urbanism." In *Urbanism in Antiquity*. Edited by W. E. Aufrecht, N. A. Mirau, and S. W. Gauley. JSOTSup 244. Sheffield: JSOT Press, 1997, pp. 35–49.

Sykes, S. "Time and Space in Haggai-Zechariah 1–8: A Bakhtinian Analysis of a Prophetic Chronicle." *JSOT* 76 (1997): 97–124.

Tadmor, H. ""The Appointed Time Has Not Yet Arrived": The Historical Background of Haggai 1:2." In *Ki Baruch Hu: Ancient Near Eastern, Biblical and Judaic Studies in Honor of Baruch A. Levine*. Edited by W. W. Hallo, L. H. Schiffman, and R. Chazon. Winona Lake: Eisenbrauns, 1999, pp. 401–408.

Talmon, S. "Biblical Visions of the Future Ideal Age." In S. Talmon, *King, Cult and Calendar in Ancient Israel. Collected Studies*. Jerusalem: Magnes Press, Hebrew University, 1986, pp. 140–164.

——. "The Emergence of Jewish Sectarianism in the Early Second Temple period." In S. Talmon, *King, Cult and Calendar in Ancient Israel. Collected Studies*. Jerusalem: Magnes Press, Hebrew University, 1986, pp. 165–201.

Tavernier, J. "An Achaemenid Royal Inscription: The Text of Paragraph 13 of the Aramaic Version of the Bisitun Inscription." *JNES* 60 (2001): 161–176.

Thompson, T. L. "The Exile in History and Myth: A Response to Hans Barstad." In *Leading Captivity Captive*. Edited by L. L. Grabbe; JSOTSup 278; Sheffield: Sheffield Academic Press, 1998, pp. 101–118.

Tollington, J. A. *Tradition and Innovation in Haggai and Zechariah 1–8*, JSOTSup 150. Sheffield: Sheffield Academic Press, 1993.

——. "Readings in Haggai: From the Prophet to the Complete Book, a Changing Message in Changing Times." In *The Crisis of Israelite Religion. Transformation of Religious Tradition in Exilic and Post-Exilic Times*. Edited by B. Becking and M. C. A. Korpel. OS 62. Leiden: Brill, 1999, pp. 194–208.

Torrey, C. C. *Ezra Studies*. Chicago: University of Chicago Press, 1910.

Townsend, T. N. "Additional Comments on Haggai 2: 10–19." *VT* 18 (1968): 559–560.

Toy, C. H. *Judaism and Christianity: A Sketch of the Progress of Thought from Old Testament to New Testament*. London: British and Foreign Unitarian Association, 1892.

Tucker, G. M. "Prophetic Superscriptions and the Growth of a Canon." In *Canon and Authority: Essays in Old Testament Religion and Theology*. Edited by G. W. Coats and B. O. Long. Philadelphia: Fortress, 1977, pp. 56–70.

Tuell, S. S. "Haggai-Zechariah: Prophecy After the Manner of Ezekiel." Paper presented at the AAR/SBL Annual Meeting, Nashville 2000.

VanderKam, J. C. "The Jewish High Priests of the Persian Period: Is the List Complete?" In *Priesthood and Cult in Ancient Israel*. Edited by G. A. Andersen and S. M.

Olyan. JSOTSup 125. Sheffield: Sheffield Academic Press, 1991, pp. 67–91.

———. "Joshua the High Priest and the Interpretation of Zechariah 3." In *From Revelation to Canon: Studies in the Hebrew Bible and Second Temple Literature*. Edited by J. C. VanderKam. JSJSup 62. Leiden, Boston, Köln: E. J. Brill, 2000, pp. 157–200.

Vaux, R. de. "Le 'reste d'Israël' d'après le prophètes." *RB* 42 (1933): 526–539.

———. "Les décrets de Cyrus et de Darius sur la reconstruction du temple." *RB* 46 (1937): 29–57.

———. *Ancient Israel*. 2 vols. Translated by J. McHugh. London: Longman, Darton & Todd, 1961.

———. "Le sens de l'expression 'Peuple du Pays' dans l'Ancien Testament et le rôle politique du peuple en Israël." *Revue d'Assyriologie et d'Archéologie Orientale* 58 (1964): 167–172.

Verhoef, P. A. *The Books of Haggai and Malachi*. NICOT. Grand Rapids: Eerdmans, 1987.

Vogelsang, W. J. *The Rise and Organization of the Achaemenid Empire: The Eastern Iranian Evidence*. Studies in the History of the Ancient Near East 3. Leiden, New York, Köln: Brill, 1992.

Voigtlander, E. N. von. *The Bisitun Inscription of Darius the Great, Babylonian Version*. Corpus Inscriptionum Iranicarum, I: Inscriptions of Ancient Iran, Texts I. London: Lund Humphries, 1978.

Wallinga, H. T. "The Persian Navy and its Predecessors." In *Achaemenid History I: Sources, Structures and Synthesis*. Edited by H. Sancisi-Weerdenburg. Leiden: Instituut voor het Nabije Oosten, 1987, pp. 47–77.

Wambaq, B. N. *L'épithète divine Jahvé Seba'ôt. Etude philologique, historique et exégétique.* Bruges: de Brouwer, 1947.

Wanke, G. "Prophecy and Psalms in the Persian Period." In *The Cambridge History of Judaism, Vol 1. Introduction; The Persian Period*. Edited by W. D. Davies and L. Finkelstein. Cambridge: Cambridge University Press, 1984, pp. 162–187.

Waterman, L. "The Camouflaged Purge of Three Messianic Conspirators." *JNES* 13 (1954): 73–78.

Weidner, E. F. "Jojachin, König von Juda in babylonischen Keilschrifttexten." In *Mélanges syriens offerts à M. René Dussaud*. Paris: Guenther, 1939, pp. 923–935.

Weinberg, J. P. "Demographische Notizen zur Geschichte der Nachexilischen Gemeinde in Juda." *Klio* 54 (1972): 46–50.

———. "Das *BEIT 'ABOT* im 6.-4. Jh. v.u.Z." *VT* 23 (1973): 400–414.

———. "Der *'am ha'ares* des 6.-4 Jahrhunderts v.u.Z." *Klio* 56 (1974): 325–335.

———. "Die Agrarverhältnisse in der Bürger-Tempel-Gemeinde der Achämenidenzeit." *Acta Antiqua* 22 (1974): 473–485.

———. "*Netînîm* und »Söhne der Sklaven Salomos« im 6.-4. Jh. v.u.Z." *ZAW* 87 (1975): 355–371.

———. "Zentral-und Partikulargewalt im achämenidischen Reich." *Klio* 59 (1977): 25–43.

———. "Die Mentalität der jerusalemischen Bürger-Tempel-Gemeinde des 6. -4. Jh. v.u.Z." *Trans* 5 (1992): 133–141.

———. *The Citizen-Temple Community*. Translated by D. Smith-Christopher. JSOTSup 151. Sheffield: Sheffield Academic Press, 1992.

———. *Der Chronist in seiner Mitwelt*. BZAW 239. Berlin and New York: Walter de Gruyter, 1996.

———. "The Word *ndb* in the Bible: A Study in Historical Semantics and Biblical Thought." In *Solving Riddles and Untying Knots*. Edited by Z. Zevit, S. Gitin and M. Sokoloff. Winona Lake: Eisenbrauns, 1995, pp. 365–378.

———. "Transmitter and Recipient in the Process of Acculturation: The Experience of the Judean Citizen-Temple-Community." *Trans* 13 (1997): 91–105.

Weinberg, S. S. "Post-Exilic Palestine: An Archaeological Report." *Proceedings of the Israel Academy of Sciences and Humanities* 4 (1971): 78–97.

Weinfeld, M. *Deuteronomy and the Deuteronomic School.* Oxford: Oxford University Press, 1972.

——. "Zion and Jerusalem as Religious and Political Capital: Ideology and Utopia." In *The Poet and the Historian.* Edited by R. E. Friedman. HSS 26. Chico, CA: Scholars Press, 1983, pp. 75–113.

Weippert, H. *Palästina in vorhellenisticher Zeit.* Handbuch des Archäologie. Vorderasien 2. Band 1. Munchen: C.H. Beck'sche Verlagsbuchhandlung, 1988.

Weiser, A. *The Old Testament: Its Formation and Development.* New York: Association Press, 1961.

Welch, A. C. *Post-Exilic Judaism.* Edinburgh and London: W. Blackwood, 1935.

Wellhausen, J. *Prolegomena to the History of Ancient Israel.* Translated by Black and Menzies. Gloucester, MA: Peter Smith, 1883, reprint 1973.

——. *Die kleinen Propheten übersetzt und erlärt.* Berlin: G. Reimer, 1898.

Westermann, C. *Basic Forms of Prophetic Speech.* Translated by H. C. White. Louisville: John Knox, 1991.

——. *Prophetic Oracles of Salvation in the Old Testament.* Translated by K. Crim. Louisville: Westminster, 1991.

Whedbee, J. W. "A Question-Answer Schema in Haggai 1: The Form and Function of Haggai 1: 9–11." In *Biblical and Near Eastern Studies. Essays in Honour of William Sanford LaSor.* Edited by G. A. Tuttle. Grand Rapids: Eerdmans, 1978, pp. 184–194.

Wiesehöfer, J. *Der Aufstand Gaumatas und die Afänge Dareios I.* Bonn: Rudolph Habelt, 1978.

Wilch, J. R. *Time and Event.* Leiden: E. J. Brill, 1969.

Williams, J. "The Social Location of Israelite Prophecy." *JAAR* 37 (1969): 153–165.

Williamson, H. G. M. *1 and 2 Chronicles.* NCBC. London/Grand Rapids: Marshall, Morgan and Scott/Eerdmans, 1982.

——. "The Composition of Ezra i–vi." *JTS* ns 34 (1983): 1–30.

——. *Ezra, Nehemiah.* WBC. Waco: Word, 1985.

——. *Ezra and Nehemiah.* OTG. Sheffield: JSOT Press, 1987.

——. "Post-Exilic Historiography." In *The Future of Biblical Studies: The Hebrew Scriptures.* Edited by R. E. Friedman and H. G. M. Williamson. Atlanta: Scholars Press, 1987, pp. 189–207.

——. "The Governors of Judah Under the Persians." *TB* 39 (1988): 59–82.

——. "Judah and the Jews." In *Studies in Persian History: Essays in Memory of David M. Lewis.* Edited by M. Brosius and A. Kuhrt. Achaemenid History XI. Leiden: Nederlands Instituut voor het Nabije Oosten, 1998, pp. 145–163.

——. "Exile and After: Historical Study." In *Faces of Old Testament Study.* Edited by D. W. Baker and B. T. Arnold. Grand Rapids: Baker, 1999.

Wilson, R. R. *Prophecy and Society in Ancient Israel.* Philadelphia: Fortress, 1980.

——. *Sociological Approaches to the Old Testament.* Philadelphia: Fortress, 1984.

Wolf, H., "'The Desire of All Nations' in Haggai 2:7: Messianic or Not?", *JETS* 19 (1976): 97–102.

Wolff, H. W. *Haggai: A Commentary.* Translated by M. Kohl. Minneapolis: Augsburg, 1988.

Woude, A. S. van der. *Haggai, Maleachi.* POut Nijkerk: Uitgeverij G. F. Callenbach, 1982.

Wyrick, S. V. "Haggai's Appeal to Tradition: Imagination Used as Authority." In *Religious Writings and Religious Systems, vol. 1.* Edited by J. Neusner. Atlanta: Scholars Press, 1989, pp. 117–125.

Yamauchi, E. M. *Persia and the Bible.* Grand Rapids: Baker, 1990.

——. "Cambyses in Egypt." In *Go to the Land I will Show You: Studies in Honor of Dwight*

*W. Young.* Edited by J. Coleson and V. Matthews. Winona Lake: Eisenbrauns, 1996, pp. 371–392.

Yaron, R. "The Schema of the Aramaic Legal Documents." *JJS* 2 (1957): 33–61.

Zadok, R. *The Jews in Babylonia in the Chaldean and Achaemenian Periods in the Light of Babylonian Sources.* Haifa: University of Haifa, 1979.

——. "On the Reliability of the Genealogical and Prosopographical Lists of the Israelites in the Old Testament." *Tel Aviv* 25 (1988): 228–254.

——. *The Pre-Hellenistic Israelite Anthropology and Prosopography.* Leuven: Uitgeverij Peeters, 1988.

——. "Onomastic, Prosopographic, and Lexical Notes." *BN* 65 (1992): 52–53.

Zertal, A. "The Pahwah of Samaria (Northern Israel) during the Persian Period. Types of Settlement, Economy, History and New Discoveries." *Trans* 3 (1990): 9–29.

Zimmerli, W. "Prophetic Proclamation and Reinterpretation." In *Tradition and Theology in the Old Testament.* Edited by D. A. Knight. London: SPCK, 1977, pp. 69–100.

——. *Ezekiel: A Commentary on the Book of Ezekiel, vol 1.* Translated by R. E. Clements. Hermeneia. Philadelphia: Fortress, 1979.

# INDEX OF AUTHORS

Abadie, P., 102 n. 30

Achtemeier, E., 26

Ackroyd, P. R., 5 n. 26, 31, 35, 36, 40, 40 n. 58, 44 n. 91, 49, 51 n. 128, 52, 52 n. 137, 53 n. 140, 60, 60 nn. 7, 10, 62 n. 20, 64 nn. 37, 40, 69, 69 n. 78, 71, 71 n. 89, 84, 85 n. 177, 86 n. 183, 88 n. 197, 89 n. 202, 92 n. 222, 102 nn. 30, 33, 112 n. 71, 114 n. 83, 123 n. 154, 128 n. 186, 134 n. 217, 136, 136 nn. 228, 231, 137 n. 236, 156 n. 362, 160 n. 11, 161 n. 17, 164 n. 34, 166 n. 39, 169 n. 58, 173 n. 87, 179 n. 124, 183 n. 144, 189 n. 173, 195 n. 202, 197 n. 4, 203 n. 42, 206 n. 62, 211 nn. 85, 97, 214 n. 113, 243

Aharoni, Y., 93, 93 n. 231

Albright, W. F., 63, 63 n. 30, 95, 95 n. 246, 264 n. 21

Allen, L. C., 179 n. 121, 189 nn. 176, 180, 194 n. 200

Alt, A., 22 n. 121, 72, 72 n. 103

Alter, R., 114 n. 78, 142 n. 272, 251 n. 33

Amsler, S., 25, 89 n. 204, 103 n. 1, 104 n. 7, 105 n. 9, 105 n. 15, 106 n. 24, 107 n. 32, 107 n. 37, 108 n. 40, 114 n. 83, 115 n. 84, 120, 120 n. 130, 125 n. 174, 127 n. 182, 129, 129 n. 189, 132, 134 n. 217, 151, 159 n. 2, 160 n. 11, 163 n. 28, 170 n. 70, 172, 172 nn. 76, 78, 179 n. 125, 182 n. 139, 187, 187 n. 166, 191 n. 186, 197 n. 3, 198 n. 8, 199 nn. 14, 20, 200 n. 20, 201 n. 28, 203 n. 40, 204 n. 50, 207 n. 67, 209 n. 84, 211 nn. 85, 97, 213 nn. 107, 111, 214, 215 n. 116, 230 n. 71, 231 n. 78, 234 n. 89, 237 n. 109, 247, 270 n. 42

Andersen, F. I., 66 n. 56, 129 n. 189, 168 n. 56, 208 n. 78

André, T., 115 n. 85, 230 n. 72

Asurmendi, J., 127 n. 182

Audinet, J., 21 n. 112, 97 n. 1

Auneau, J., 127 n. 182

Avigad, N., 73, 73 n. 108, 74, 75 n. 118, 78

Baldwin, J., 69 n. 79, 122 n. 145, 123 n. 147, 133 n. 211, 169 n. 58, 170 n. 63, 208 n. 78, 211 n. 93, 238 n. 109, 247, 247 n. 20

Ballentine, S. E., 87 n. 191, 260 n. 4

Barnes, W. E., 6 n. 33

Barr, J., 227 n. 49

Barstad, H. M., 50 n. 122, 88 n. 199, 91, 91 n. 214, 92 n. 218, 115 n. 88, 117 n. 105, 118 n. 107

Bartal, A., 64, 64 n. 43

Barthélemy, D., 104 n. 7, 106 n. 24, 123 n. 153, 126 n. 177, 160 n. 8, 170 n. 68, 199 n. 18, 200 n. 20, 219 n. 5

Bauer, H., 105 n. 13 (BL)

Bauer, L., 104 n. 7, 125 n. 174

Becker, J., 119 n. 122, 147 n. 305

Becking, B., 97 n. 1

Bedford, P. R., 28 n. 153, 69 n. 77, 88 n. 195, 124, 124 n. 167, 125

Begrich, J., 149 n. 326, 162 n. 24

Bennet, W. H., 5 n. 23, 10

Bentzen, A., 5 n. 26

Ben Zvi, E., 92, 93 n. 228, 94, 96 n. 252, 100 n. 19, 263 n. 15

Berger, P., 24 n. 139

Berger, P. R., 64 n. 39

Berquist, J. L., 86, 86 nn. 181, 185

Betlyon, J. W., 76 n. 132

Beuken, W. A. M., 19, 32, 32 n. 10, 33, 34, 35, 36, 39, 40, 40 n. 57, 49 n. 120, 109 n. 50, 110 n. 54, 113 n. 71, 118 n. 108, 121, 131 n. 201, 135 n. 222, 138 n. 240, 140 n. 260, 143, 143 n. 279, 144, 145 n. 289, 148 n. 310, 150 n. 327, 154 n. 351, 155 n. 357, 162 nn. 21, 24, 171 n. 75, 172 n. 79, 203 n. 42, 205 n. 57, 220 n. 11, 227 n. 50, 243, 247, 248 n. 26, 256, 256 n. 45

Bewer, J. A., 2 n. 5, 11, 210 n. 90

Beyse, K.-M., 3, 63 n. 25, 71, 71 n. 89, 72 n. 99, 119 n. 117, 120, 120 n. 131, 222, 222 n. 22, 226 n. 45, 234 n. 89, 238 n. 109, 240 n. 122, 242 n. 129

Bianchi, F., 62 n. 20, 67 n. 60, 68 n. 66, 73, 73 n. 109, 74 n. 112, 75, 75 nn. 118, 123, 76 n. 128, 77, 77 n. 134, 78, 78

n. 143, 86, 86 nn. 183, 186, 87 n. 192, 91 n. 212, 103 n. 2, 237 n. 107, 259 n. 2

Bickerman, E. J., 60, 60 n. 4, 61 n. 18, 63, 63 n. 31, 80, 81 n. 158, 82 n. 161, 83, 83 nn. 169, 171, 85

Biggs, R. D., 229 n. 65

Blenkinsopp, J., 5 n. 25, 24 n. 136, 25 n. 140, 60 n. 3, 71 n. 91, 89 n. 201, 95 n. 246, 98, 101 nn. 26, 27, 165 n. 37, 205 n. 59, 214 n. 115, 266 n. 24, 268 n. 32, 269 n. 36, 277, 277 n. 49

Boadt, L., 43 n. 85

Bodi, D., 237 n. 108

Bornkamm, G., 176, 176 n. 109

Bosshard, E., 41 n. 71

Briant, P., 26 n. 146, 61 n. 17, 62 n. 20, 67 n. 60, 78 n. 142, 79 n. 152, 86 n. 183, 87 n. 187, 96 n. 251, 133 n. 211, 263 n. 17

Briend, J., 60, 60 n. 3, 61 n. 13, 93 n. 232, 94 n. 240

Bright, J., 3 n. 14, 5 n. 25, 20, 63, 63 n. 32, 71 n. 87, 82 n. 167, 92 n. 224, 95 n. 246, 98 n. 7, 188 n. 171

Brongers, H. A., 162 n. 20

Broshi, M., 23 n. 127, 92, 92 n. 227, 93, 93 n. 228

Budde, K., 105 n. 17, 219 n. 5

Buss, M. J., 117 n. 105

Calvin, J., 211 n. 95

Caquot, A., 213 n. 106, 227 n. 54

Carroll, R. P., 5 n. 25, 15 n. 77, 16 n. 81, 17 n. 88, 91, 91 n. 215, 129, 175 n. 102, 231 n. 77, 236, 236 n. 100, 277 n. 52

Carter, C. E., 16 n. 82, 22 n. 120, 24 n. 134, 26, 73 n. 109, 89 n. 199, 91 n. 213, 92, 93, 93 n. 228, 94 n. 234, 95, 95 n. 247, 96 n. 250

Cashdan, E., 149 n. 324

Causse, A., 186 n. 155, 189 n. 178

Cazelles, H., 81 n. 160, 82 n. 161, 194 n. 198

Charpin, D., 50 n. 122

Chary, T., 6, 6 n. 30, 17 n. 87, 20, 52 n. 130, 103 n. 4, 105 n. 15, 106 n. 24, 107 n. 32, 115 n. 85, 120 n. 127, 131 n. 198, 134 n. 215, 136 n. 232, 142 n. 270, 148 nn. 311, 317, 151, 151 n. 332, 159 n. 2, 160 nn. 9, 11,

171 n. 74, 173 n. 87, 174 n. 97, 175 n. 101, 185 n. 148, 187, 187 n. 164, 197 n. 3, 199 n. 20, 201 n. 28, 202 n. 37, 211 nn. 92, 95, 96, 212 n. 100, 214 n. 114, 219 n. 5, 223 n. 24, 225, 237 n. 109, 247, 247 n. 21, 256, 257 n. 46

Childs, B. S., 22 n. 119, 143 n. 281, 176 n. 109, 202 n. 37, 228 n. 59, 232 n. 82, 251 n. 32

Clark, D. J., 200 n. 20, 207 n. 70, 210, 210 n. 85

Clements, R. E., 20 n. 102, 24 n. 136, 101 n. 23, 136 n. 227

Clines, D. J. A., 60, 60 nn. 6, 12, 63, 63 n. 33, 64 n. 42, 70 n. 82, 81 n. 160, 98 n. 4

Cody, A., 123 n. 148, 213 n. 111

Cogan, M., 80 n. 154

Coggins, R. J., 36, 37 n. 35, 40 n. 65, 41, 41 n. 67, 49, 168 n. 55, 237 n. 106

Cook, J. M., 86 n. 185

Cowley, A., 43 n. 77

Craigie, P., 26

Cross, F. M., 18 n. 94, 43 n. 78, 46 n. 100, 63, 63 n. 34, 74, 74 n. 114, 82 n. 164, 176, 176 n. 110, 187, 187 n. 167

Dandamaev, M. A., 26 n. 146, 64 n. 35, 87 n. 192

Davidson, S., 10

Davies, G. I., 75 n. 121

Davies, P. R., 23 n. 126, 26 n. 147

Davies, W. D., 26 n. 147

Deissler, A., 52 n. 136, 104 n. 7, 163 n. 29, 166 n. 42, 177 n. 112, 182 n. 139, 191 n. 184, 224 n. 31, 238, 238 n. 109

Deist, F. E., 11 n. 64, 29 n. 155

Demsky, A., 64 n. 38, 65 n. 50, 66 n. 54, 67, 67 n. 63, 119 nn. 116, 118

Depuydt, L., 81 n. 158, 83 nn. 169, 171, 84 n. 176

Dequecker, L., 59 n. 1

Derousseaux, L., 101 n. 24, 146 n. 299, 147 n. 304, 162 n. 24, 172, 172 n. 85, 176 n. 108

Deutsch, R., 45 n. 95

Devauchelle, D., 83 n. 171

Dever, W., 23 n. 125

Dion, P.-E., 64 n. 39

Dogniez, C., 122 n. 145

Driver, S. R., 10, 54 n. 143, 131 n. 198, 142 n. 278, 147 n. 303
Dubberstein, W. H., 80 n. 154, 81 n. 157, 84 n. 173
Duhm, B., 219 n. 5, 230 n. 72
Dumbrell, W. J., 141, 141 n. 268, 175 n. 99, 187, 187 n. 162, 194 n. 196, 240, 240 n. 120
Dunan, M., 70 n. 82
Durkheim, E., 22

Elayi, J., 11 n. 64, 26 n. 147, 78 n. 147, 79 n. 150
Elliger, K., 104 n. 7, 136 n. 233, 200 n. 26
Ellis, R. S., 209 n. 79, 116 n. 122
Eph'al, I., 47 n. 105, 61 nn. 17, 18, 76, 76 n. 131
Ewald, H., 64

Fenz, A. K., 143, 143 n. 279
Festinger, L., 277 n. 52
Finkelstein, J/I., 26 n. 147, 93 n. 229
Floyd, M. H., 26, 27, 38, 39 n. 51, 48 n. 112, 52 n. 135, 56 n. 160, 109, 109 n. 48, 112 n. 69, 113 n. 75, 115 n. 87, 117, 141 n. 265, 144 n. 284, 148 n. 311, 153 n. 348, 163 n. 25, 164 n. 31, 168 n. 57, 201 n. 33, 202 n. 35, 207 n. 69, 213 n. 107, 244 n. 5, 245, 245 n. 15, 247 n. 23, 252, 253 n. 35, 254 n. 37, 264, 264 n. 20
Fohrer, G., 3, 24 n. 136, 98 n. 10, 188 n. 171, 201 n. 33, 213 n. 107
Franklin, U., 85 n. 179
Freedman, D. N., 40 n. 66
Freedy, K. S., 43 n. 85
Friebel, K. G., 213 n. 107

Gabriel, J., 64
Gal, Z., 94 n. 240
Galil, G., 81 n. 160
Galling, K., 72, 72 nn. 97, 103, 120 n. 131
Gammie, J. G., 101 n. 28
Garelli, P., 62 n. 20
Geertz, C., 274 n. 45
Gelston, A., 66 n. 56, 123 n. 154, 208 n. 78
Gesenius, W., 2 n. 3, 104 n. 8 (GKC), 105 n. 18 (GKC), 107 n. 32 (GKC), 123 n. 151 (GKC), 126 n. 176 (GKC), 134 nn. 217, 218(GKC), 135 n. 225 (GKC), 138 n. 242 (GKC), 145 n. 289

(GKC), 160 n. 12 (GKC), 161 n. 14 (GKC), 175 n. 104 (GKC), 178 n. 117 (GKC), 179 n. 122 (GKC), 201 n. 28 (GKC), 219 n. 2 (GKC), 224 n. 30 (GKC)
Gibson, M., 229 n. 65
Goldman, Y., 145 n. 286, 231 n. 76, 236, 236 n. 99, 237 n. 104, 277 n. 50, 278 n. 53
Goody, J., 276 n. 48
Gophna, R., 23 n. 127, 93 n. 229
Gosse, B., 145 n. 286
Gottwald, N. K., 22 n. 121
Gowan, D. A., 193 n. 193
Grabbe, L. L., 5 n. 26, 12 n. 66, 16 n. 84, 73 n. 103, 263 n. 16
Graf, D. F., 62 n. 20, 86 n. 184
Graham, J. N., 95 n. 243, 262 n. 9
Greenfield, J. C., 45 n. 96, 74 n. 113, 76, 76 n. 131
Grintz, Y., 74 n. 116

Hallo, W. W., 230 n. 72
Halpern, B., 209 n. 79, 116 n. 122
Hamerton-Kelly, R. G., 6 n. 35, 13, 14, 124, 124 nn. 160, 162
Hamilton, M. W., 262 n. 10, 263 n. 13, 264 nn. 19, 21
Hamlin, E. J., 3 n. 12
Hammershaimb, E., 214
Hanson, P. D., 6 n. 34, 14, 15, 17, 18 n. 94, 20 n. 107, 90, 90 n. 207, 124, 124 n. 164, 148 n. 316, 185 n. 149, 186 n. 153, 188 n. 172, 268 n. 32
Hartley, J. E., 155 n. 359
Hartner, W., 81 n. 158
Hasel, G., 141 n. 267
Hayes, J. H., 7 n. 42, 8 n. 42
Heltzer, M., 45 n. 95
Herntrich, V., 142 n. 275
Herr, L. G., 88 n. 198
Hesse, F., 7, 7 n. 41
Hildebrand, D. R., 211 n. 95
Hillers, D. R., 111 n. 63, 132 n. 204, 154 nn. 351, 352
Hoglund, K. G., 61 n. 17, 87 n. 192
Holladay, W., 230 n. 72
Hoonacker, A. van, 6, 6 n. 29, 65, 104 n. 7, 105 n. 15, 211 n. 95, 238 n. 109
Horst, F., 104 n. 7, 105 n. 15, 198 n. 5, 200 n. 26
House, P. R., 113 n. 73, 246 n. 17

James, F., 4 n. 18, 5, 6 nn. 31, 36
Janssen, E., 91, 91 n. 215, 92 n. 222, 124,
   124 n. 158
Japhet, S., 11 n. 64, 40 n. 63, 63 n. 28,
   64 n. 36, 66 n. 57, 67, 68, 69 n. 73, 71
   n. 88, 72 n. 102, 119 n. 119, 233 n. 88,
   235, 235 n. 97, 264, 264 nn. 19, 21
Jemielity, T., 154 n. 354
Jenson, P. P., 101 n. 28, 203 n. 47
Joannès, F., 61 n. 18
Jones, S., 29 n. 155
Joüon, P., 104 n. 8, 105 nn. 11, 13, 106
   n. 31, 107 n. 35, 115 n. 91, 118 n. 106,
   126 n. 176, 130 n. 191, 131 n. 203,
   132 n. 208, 133 n. 212, 134 n. 218,
   142 n. 277, 159 n. 6, 160 n. 12, 161
   n. 14, 164 n. 32, 166 n. 40, 169 n. 60,
   172 n. 82, 175 n. 105, 178 n. 117, 182
   n. 138, 199 n. 18, 201 n. 28, 226 n. 47,
   230 n. 66, 233 n. 84

Kaiser, W., 98 n. 7
Kapelrud, A. S., 189 n. 181, 194 n. 200
Katzenstein, H. J., 5 n. 25, 86 n. 185
Kaufman, S. A., 164 n. 32
Keil, C. F., 174 n. 91, 175 n. 99, 179
   n. 126, 181 n. 135
Kessler, J., 7 n. 41, 16 n. 79, 28 n. 154,
   48 n. 111, 82 n. 165, 89 n. 204, 90
   n. 206, 91 n. 212, 94 n. 237, 123
   n. 156, 156 n. 366, 175 n. 103, 177
   n. 113, 186 n. 154, 245 n. 14, 246 n. 19,
   260 n. 4, 262 nn. 8, 12, 263 nn. 16,
   15
Keunen, A., 8
Kimchi, D., 230 n. 72
Kippenberg, H. G., 23 n. 129, 87 n. 192,
   133 n. 210
Kittel, R., 262 n. 10
Knauf, E. A., 79 n. 150
Knight, D. A., 18 n. 92, 21 n. 116, 97 n. 1,
   98 n. 6, 99 n. 11
Koch, K., 33, 33 n. 20, 34, 37, 108 n. 40,
   110, 111 n. 62, 130 n. 196, 198 n. 5, 213
   n. 111, 243, 248, 248 n. 24
Kochman, M., 73, 73 n. 109
Koole, J. L., 131 n. 198
Korpel, M. C. A., 97 n. 1
Kosters, H. W., 63
Kramer, C., 22 n. 123
Krantz, R. G., 41 n. 71
Kreissig, H., 23 n. 129, 78 n. 143, 87

n. 192, 91, 91 n. 213, 92 n. 218, 133
   n. 210, 262 n. 10, 263 n. 15
Kuhrt, A., 61, 61 n. 15, 88, 88 n. 195
Kutsch, E., 43 n. 85, 45 n. 94
Kutscher, E.Y., 74

Lagrange, M.-J., 235, 235 n. 98
Laperrousaz, E.-M., 26 n. 147, 73 n. 108,
   91, 91 n. 216, 93 n. 227
Leander, P., 105 n. 13 (BL)
Lecoq, P., 84 n. 176
Lemaire, A., 26 n. 147, 42 n. 72, 43 n. 78,
   45 n. 92, 46 n. 100, 47, 48, 48 n. 113,
   49 n. 115, 50 n. 122, 61 n. 18, 65 n. 50,
   67 n. 61, 69 n. 76, 73, 73 n. 108, 74
   n. 110, 75 n. 119, 76 n. 126, 77 n. 139,
   78 n. 145, 79 n. 148, 82 n. 162, 88
   n. 194, 95 nn. 244, 246, 119 n. 116, 133
   n. 211, 234, 234 n. 92, 237 n. 105, 262
   n. 11, 263 nn. 13, 16, 268 n. 32
Lemche, N. P., 23 n. 132
Lévêque, J., 229 n. 62
Limet, H., 62 n. 20
Lindblom, J., 3
Lipiński, E., 76, 76 n. 130, 209 n. 83
Lipschits, O., 88 n. 198, 93, 94 n. 239,
   95, 95 n. 245, 123 n. 153
Liver, J., 62 nn. 20, 22, 68 n. 66, 73, 73
   n. 109, 259 n. 2
Lohfink, N., 162 n. 24, 245 n. 11
Long, B. O., 24 n. 137
Lozachmeur, H., 263 n. 13
Lukonin, V. G., 26 n. 146
Lust, J., 65, 65 n. 45

Machinist, P., 76 n. 132, 133 n. 211
Malbran-Labat, F., 45 n. 96
Mannheim, K., 14, 16
Margalith, O., 263 n. 15
Marti, K., 2 n. 3, 52 n. 136
Martin-Achard, R., 127 n. 182
Mason, R. A., 5, 6 n. 27, 15 n. 77, 19,
   20 n. 107, 34, 35, 36, 39, 39 n. 55,
   51 nn. 127, 129, 52 nn. 130, 134, 54
   n. 146, 55 nn. 152, 158, 118 n. 109,
   142 n. 273, 157 n. 367, 163 n. 25, 164
   n. 34, 167 n. 47, 212, 212 n. 103, 233
   n. 88, 237 n. 103, 243
May, H. G., 180 n. 131, 194 n. 196, 205
   n. 58, 211 n. 95, 212, 214 n. 112
Mays, A. D. H., 22 n. 120
Mazar, A., 88 n. 198

McConville, J. G., 236 n. 99
McCullough, W. S., 62 n. 20
McEvenue, S., 72, 75 n. 120
Mendenhall, G. E., 22 n. 121, 24 n. 133
Merrill, E. H., 82 n. 161
Merwe, C. H. J. vander, 110 n. 59
Meslin, M., 21, 97 n. 1, 98 n. 9
Mettinger, T. N. D., 122 n. 145
Meyer, E., 63, 63 n. 29
Meyer, L. V., 141 n. 267
Meyers, C. L., 23 n. 124, 25, 38, 39 n. 52, 44 n. 88, 49 n. 120, 50 n. 121, 52, 52 nn. 131, 136, 56, 56 n. 162, 57 n. 166, 70 n. 82, 72, 72 n. 98, 89 nn. 199, 203, 104 n. 7, 105 nn. 15, 19, 106 nn. 24, 26, 107 n. 32, 108 n. 39, 112 n. 66, 114 n. 77, 115 n. 85, 117 n. 99, 119 n. 121, 120 n. 126, 122 nn. 144, 147, 123 n. 150, 125 n. 171, 128 n. 187, 129 n. 190, 131 n. 201, 132 n. 206, 133 n. 214, 134 n. 216, 135 n. 220, 139 n. 253, 140 n. 259, 141 n. 264, 148 n. 316, 149 n. 320, 151, 152, 153 n. 347, 159 n. 2, 160 nn. 8,11, 161 n. 14, 166 n. 44, 167 n. 44, 169, 172, 172 n. 77, 173 n. 87, 174 n. 95, 179 n. 124, 180 n. 128, 182 n. 140, 187 n. 170, 190 n. 183, 191 n. 186, 198 n. 7, 199 n. 15, 200 n. 20, 201 n. 28, 202 n. 36, 203 n. 39, 204 n. 49, 205 n. 60, 207 n. 68, 208 n. 78, 209 n. 79, 211 n. 94, 217 n. 124, 221 n. 17, 222 n. 20, 229 n. 63, 230 n. 67, 233 n. 88, 239 n. 117, 242 n. 128, 247, 256 n. 44, 261 n. 7, 269 n. 38
Meyers, E. M, 23 n. 124, 25, 25 n. 141, 38, 39 n. 52, 44 n. 88, 49 n. 120, 50 n. 121, 52, 52 nn. 131, 136, 56, 56 n. 162, 57 n. 166, 70 n. 82, 72, 72 n. 98, 73, 73 n. 108, 74 n. 111, 76 n. 126, 89 nn. 199, 203, 104 n. 7, 105 nn. 15, 19, 106 nn. 24, 26, 107 n. 32, 108 n. 39, 112 n. 66, 114 n. 77, 115 n. 85, 117 n. 99, 119 n. 121, 120 n. 126, 122 nn. 144, 147, 123 n. 150, 125 n. 171, 128 n. 187, 129 n. 190, 131 n. 201, 132 n. 206, 133 n. 214, 134 n. 216, 135 n. 220, 139 n. 253, 140 n. 259, 141 n. 264, 148 n. 316, 149 n. 320, 151, 152, 153 n. 347, 156 n. 365, 159 n. 2, 160 nn. 8,11, 161 n. 14, 166 n. 44, 167 n. 44, 169, 172, 172 n. 77, 173 n. 87,

174 n. 95, 179 n. 124, 180 n. 128, 182 n. 140, 187 n. 170, 190 n. 183, 191 n. 186, 198 n. 7, 199 n. 15, 200 n. 20, 201 n. 28, 202 n. 36, 203 n. 39, 204 n. 49, 205 n. 60, 207 n. 68, 208 n. 78, 209 n. 79, 211 n. 94, 217 n. 124, 221 n. 17, 222 n. 20, 229 n. 63, 230 n. 67, 233 n. 88, 239 n. 117, 242 n. 128, 247, 256 n. 44, 261 n. 7, 269, 269 nn. 37, 38
Milevski, I., 93, 94
Milgrom, J., 204 n. 48
Millard, A. R., 50 n. 122, 115 n. 87, 239, 239 n. 114
Miller, C. L., 103 n. 3
Miller, P. D. J., 18 n. 94, 176, 176 n. 110
Mitchell, H. G., 2, 5 n. 23, 10, 52 n. 136, 108 n. 40, 120, 128 n. 187, 141, 141 n. 268, 160 n. 11, 174 n. 92, 180 n. 131, 198 n. 7, 199 nn. 16, 20, 211 n. 95, 219 n. 5
Morgenstern, J., 4 n. 16, 194 n. 196
Motyer, J. A., 26, 169 n. 62
Moule, C. F. D., 178 n. 118
Mowinckel, S., 95 n. 246, 214
Muilenberg, J., 181 n. 134
Mullen, E. T., 28 n. 155
Murray, D. F., 236 n. 99

Naveh, J., 46 n. 103, 47 n. 105, 74 n. 113, 76, 76 n. 131
Nicholson, E. W., 101 n. 24, 119 n. 114, 154 n. 351, 155 n. 358, 168 n. 51, 171 n. 71, 236 n. 99
Niehr, H., 73, 73 n. 109, 78, 79 n. 151
North, F. S., 141, 141 n. 268, 163 n. 28, 168 n. 54, 179 n. 125
North, C. R., 229 n. 59
Noth, M., 22 n. 121, 89 n. 202

O'Brien, D. P., 126 n. 178
O'Connor, M., 105 n. 11 (IBHS), 111 n. 60 (IBHS), 126 n. 176 (IBHS), 130 n. 191 (IBHS), 138 n. 239 (IBHS), 152 n. 344 (IBHS), 159 n. 3 (IBHS), 164 n. 35 (IBHS)
Oded, B., 61 nn. 18, 19
Oesterley, W. O. E., 4 n. 16, 5, 11
Orlinsky, H. M., 3 n. 14
Otto, R., 176

Parker, R. A., 80 n. 154, 81 n. 157, 84 n. 173

Pastor, J., 93 n. 229, 95 n. 243, 263 n. 15
Peckham, B., 20, 133 n. 213, 145 n. 286, 246 n. 18, 247, 247 n. 22, 268 n. 33
Pelaia, M. B., 64
Perdue, L. G., 101 n. 27
Person, R. F., 86, 88 n. 196, 101 nn. 24, 26, 119 n. 114
Peter, F., 137 n. 236
Petersen, D. L., 18 n. 94, 20, 24 n. 138, 25, 25 n. 144, 37 n. 43, 39 n. 51, 49 n. 120, 68 n. 65, 70 n. 82, 72, 80 n. 153, 104 n. 7, 107 n. 32, 107 n. 38, 108 n. 39, 114 n. 81, 115 n. 84, 116, 122 n. 142, 123 n. 150, 128 n. 186, 132 n. 206, 134 n. 217, 136 n. 230, 137 n. 235, 139 n. 254, 145 n. 287, 148 n. 318, 150 nn. 327, 329, 155 n. 355, 159 n. 2, 160 nn. 8, 11, 161 n. 14, 162 n. 21, 166 n. 39, 167 n. 45, 169 n. 61, 170 n. 64, 174 n. 98, 180 n. 132, 183 n. 144, 184 n. 145, 185 n. 147, 187, 187 n. 168, 188 n. 172, 191 n. 185, 197 n. 3, 198 n. 5, 201 n. 38, 203 n. 41, 204 n. 48, 205 n. 60, 207 n. 69, 209 n. 79, 210 n. 86, 212 n. 105, 213 n. 111, 215, 116 n. 122, 221 n. 16, 223 n. 28, 225, 227 n. 51, 228 n. 57, 229 n. 61, 230 n. 69, 231 n. 80, 233 n. 88, 234 n. 91, 238 n. 110, 240 nn. 119, 121, 241, 241 n. 125, 244 n. 5, 245, 245 n. 10, 261 n. 6, 264 n. 19, 268 nn. 30, 32
Petit, T., 65 n. 49, 68 n. 67, 77 n. 141, 78 n. 144
Petitjean, A., 209 n. 82, 224 n. 34, 232, 232 n. 83
Pfeiffer, R. H., 4 n. 17, 5, 6 n. 32, 7 n. 37, 11
Plöger, O., 12, 124 n. 161
Pomykala, K. E., 236, 236 n. 102
Porten, B., 43 n. 77, 44, 44 n. 89, 45 n. 96, 46 n. 97, 82 n. 163
Porter, J., 263 n. 14
Porteous, N. W., 101 n. 23
Powis-Smith, J. M., 5 n. 23, 7, 7 n. 39
Prinsloo, W. S., 109 n. 49, 112 n. 65
Prokurat, M., 52 n. 132, 152 n. 341, 208 n. 72
Prussner, F. C., 7 n. 42, 8 n. 42

Rad, G. von, 17 n. 87, 18, 18 n. 92, 98 n. 10, 126 n. 175, 148 n. 315, 156 n. 361, 175 n. 102, 182 n. 142, 185 n. 149, 186 n. 152, 187, 187 n. 163, 189 n. 175, 193 nn. 192, 195, 194 n. 199, 226 n. 43, 239, 239 n. 115
Ramlot, L., 24 n. 136
Rappoport, U., 263 n. 15
Redditt, P. L., 25, 37, 38 n. 44
Redford, R. B., 43 n. 85
Reuss, E., 2 n. 3
Reventlow, H. G., 104 n. 7
Rimmon, O., 263 n. 15
Robert, P. de, 127 n. 182
Roberts, J. J. M., 101 n. 23, 185 n. 149, 186 n. 152, 189 n. 179
Robertson Smith, W., 22
Robinson, G. L., 2 n. 4
Robinson, T. H., 4 n. 16, 5, 11
Rohland, E., 189 n. 179
Rooke, D. W., 119 n. 123, 120 n. 128
Rose, W. H., 66 n. 52, 228 n. 56, 229 n. 65, 229, 230 n. 66, 230 n. 66, 232 n. 81, 234, 234 n. 89, 235 n. 98, 236, 237 n. 105, 238 n. 109
Rosenthal, F., 138 n. 242 (RGBA)
Rost, L., 69 n. 74
Rothstein, J. W., 5, 108 n. 40, 198 n. 5, 210, 211 n. 91, 220 n. 13, 268
Rudolph, W., 107 n. 37, 109 n. 50, 115 n. 84, 119 n. 117, 123 n. 149, 135, 135 n. 221, 149 n. 322, 151, 160 n. 11, 170, 173 n. 87, 174 n. 96, 175 n. 99, 198 n. 10, 199 n. 20, 225
Ryle, H. E., 64

Sacchi, P., 68 n. 66, 73, 73 n. 109, 103 n. 2, 259 n. 2
Saebø, M., 64 n. 42, 65, 65 n. 47, 66, 66 n. 53
Santayana, G., 274 n. 45
Sapin, J., 26 n. 147
Sasson, J. M., 24 n. 133
Sauer, G., 3, 221 n. 15, 225, 230 n. 75, 239 n. 116, 240 n. 119, 241 n. 124
Sauer, J. A., 95 n. 244
Saydon, P. P., 199 n. 20
Schaper, J., 87 n. 194, 89 n. 205
Schattner-Rieser, U., 107 n. 36, 131 n. 202, 146 n. 298, 179 n. 127, 182 n. 140
Schibler, D., 189 n. 176, 194 n. 200
Schram, B., 15 n. 77, 59 n. 2
Schultz, C., 60, 60 nn. 5, 10
Schultz, H., 7, 9 n. 47

Schultz, R. R., 100 n. 20
Seebass, H., 232 n. 81
Seitz, C., 145 n. 286, 277 n. 51
Selbie, J. A., 3 n. 12
Sellin, E., 5, 7, 7 n. 40, 52 n. 136, 104
     n. 7, 108 n. 40, 160 n. 11, 170, 199
     n. 20, 200 n. 26, 219 n. 5, 234 n. 89,
     237 n. 109
Sérandour, A., 19 n. 100, 37 n. 37, 39
     n. 51, 41, 41 nn. 68, 69, 70, 51 n. 129,
     53 n. 139, 56 n. 163, 100 n. 18, 128
     n. 184, 139, 139 n. 254, 141 n. 266, 176
     n. 107
Shiloh, Y., 89 n. 199, 92 n. 222
Siebeneck, R. T., 6, 6 n. 28, 180 n. 131,
     238 n. 109
Ska, J.-L., 151 n. 331
Smith, D. L., 23, 23 n. 131, 29, 73, 73
     n. 104, 77, 77 n. 136, 95 n. 243, 133
     n. 210, 262 n. 12, 263 n. 14, 264 n. 21
Smith, G. A., 131 n. 198
Smith, M., 12, 13, 87 n. 192
Soggin, J. A., 24 n. 136
Sommer, B. D., 3 n. 11, 25 n. 143
Sperling, S. D., 150 n. 327
Steck, O. H., 18 n. 92, 21 n. 118, 25
     n. 143, 33, 34, 41 n. 71, 98 n. 5, 99
     n. 13, 100 n. 22, 104 n. 7, 110, 110
     n. 55, 123 n. 149, 124, 124 n. 159, 136
     n. 232, 137 n. 236, 138 n. 248, 243
Steiner, M., 89 n. 199
Stern, E., 73, 73 n. 107, 86 n. 184
Stuhlmueller, C., 52 n. 134, 202 n. 37, 211
     n. 94
Sweet, R. F. G., 262 n. 11

Tadmor, H., 28 n. 153, 81 n. 158, 104
     n. 7, 125 n. 170
Talmon, S., 12 n. 66, 123 n. 154
Tavernier, J., 46 n. 96
Theile, E. R., 82 n. 168
Tollington, J. A., 20, 20 n. 110, 37, 38,
     53 nn. 140, 141, 142, 100 n. 18, 120
     n. 128, 121, 128 n. 184, 132 n. 204,
     140 n. 259, 153 n. 349, 155 n. 356, 156
     n. 362, 167 n. 46, 227 n. 50, 228 n. 55,
     229 n. 64, 232 n. 81, 238 nn. 109,
     113
Torrey, C. C., 11
Townsend, T. N., 211 n. 95
Toy, C. H., 9 n. 48
Troeltsch, E., 14, 16

Tucker, G. M., 255 n. 38
Tuland, G. T., 70 n. 82

Vaux, R. de, 60, 60 n. 8, 120, 120 n. 128,
     141 n. 267
Verhoef, P. A., 25, 39 n. 52, 52 nn. 130,
     133, 136, 95, 95 n. 249, 104 n. 7, 107
     nn. 32, 33, 37, 109 n. 53, 115 n. 85,
     122 n. 146, 128 n. 183, 129 n. 189, 131
     nn. 198, 201, 132 n. 207, 133 n. 211,
     134 n. 217, 135 n. 222, 136 n. 227,
     137 n. 234, 138 n. 248, 139 n. 253,
     140 nn. 257, 261, 142 n. 276, 143, 145
     n. 289, 146 n. 292, 147 n. 308, 148
     n. 312, 149 n. 321, 150 n. 329, 153
     n. 347, 159 n. 1, 160 n. 11, 164, 164
     n. 30, 165 n. 36, 166 n. 41, 167 n. 44,
     170 n. 67, 172 n. 76, 177 nn. 111, 115,
     180 n. 129, 181 n. 137, 183 n. 143, 187,
     187 n. 169, 198 n. 8, 200 n. 25, 201
     n. 28, 204 n. 49, 205 n. 57, 210 n. 88,
     211 nn. 93, 96, 220 n. 13, 226 n. 45,
     234 n. 89, 238 n. 109, 247
Voigtlander, E. N. von, 46 n. 96

Waltke, B., 105 n. 11 (IBHS)
Wambaq, B. N., 122 n. 145
Wanke, G., 102 n. 32
Waterman, L., 5, 80, 82, 85
Watt, I., 276 n. 48
Weber, M. 14, 16, 22, 267 n. 28
Weinberg, J. P., 23 nn. 128, 130, 60 n. 10,
     73, 73 n. 105, 77, 77 n. 135, 87 n. 192,
     91 n. 213, 263 nn. 15, 16, 264 n. 21
Weinfeld, M., 52 n. 134, 54 n. 143, 101
     nn. 23, 24, 142 n. 278, 155 n. 359, 156
     n. 364, 171 n. 71, 185 n. 149, 187, 187
     nn. 158, 165, 189 nn. 174, 176, 192
     n. 188, 193 n. 194, 194 n. 196
Weippert, M/H., 117 n. 105
Weiser, A., 2, 2 n. 6, 7 n. 38
Welch, A. C., 63, 214
Wellhausen, J., 2 n. 6, 8, 105 n. 15, 106
     n. 24, 123, 124 n. 157, 160 n. 11
Westermann, C., 122 n. 143, 220 n. 10,
     227 nn. 50, 52, 268 n. 31, 270 n. 42
Wette, W. M. de, 2 n. 3, 8
Whedbee, J. W., 110 n. 55, 112 n. 65, 124
     n. 159, 136 n. 232, 137 n. 237, 138, 155
     n. 357
Wiesehöfer, J., 84 n. 176
Wilch, J. R., 125 n. 174

Wildberger, H., 189 n. 179
Willi, T., 189 n. 173
Williams, J., 24 n. 139
Williams, R., 107 nn. 32, 37, 137 n. 234, 138 n. 244, 145 n. 288, 149 n. 323, 152 n. 344
Williamson, H. G. M., 39 n. 56, 40 n. 63, 60, 60 nn. 9, 11, 61, 61 nn. 13, 16, 62 nn. 22, 23, 63 n. 25, 64 n. 38, 66 n. 55, 67 n. 58, 68 n. 67, 69 n. 73, 70 n. 81, 71, 71 n. 87, 73, 73 n. 108, 75 n. 120, 77 n. 133, 83 nn. 169, 171, 102 n. 31, 113 n. 76, 135 n. 226, 151 n. 331, 166 n. 44
Wilson, R. R., 16 n. 82, 20 n. 107, 24 nn. 133, 138, 117 n. 104, 190 n. 182, 195 n. 202, 267 n. 27, 268 n. 32
Winton-Thomas, 234 n. 89, 238 n. 109
Wittfogel, 87 n. 192
Wolff, H. W., 10, 25, 35, 36 n. 31, 50 n. 126, 51 n. 128, 52, 53 nn. 138, 140, 84 n. 174, 85 n. 180, 88 n. 198, 103 n. 1, 104 n. 7, 105 n. 9, 105 n. 17, 106 nn. 21, 24, 107 n. 32, 108 n. 40, 109 n. 47, 113 n. 71, 116, 121, 123 n. 148, 125 n. 173, 130 n. 193, 134

n. 217, 135 n. 223, 136 n. 227, 138 n. 240, 139 n. 255, 140 n. 258, 141, 141 n. 268, 147 n. 308, 148 n. 312, 149 nn. 322, 326, 150 n. 329, 152 n. 345, 155 n. 355, 160 nn. 8, 11, 162 n. 20, 164 n. 30, 166 n. 44, 168 n. 49, 169 n. 58, 170 n. 69, 171 n. 73, 172 n. 80, 173 n. 87, 190 n. 183, 195 n. 201, 197 nn. 2, 3, 198 nn. 5, 8, 199 n. 16, 200 n. 22, 201 n. 28, 203 n. 43, 213 n. 107, 219 nn. 5, 9, 220 n. 12, 221 n. 14, 222, 222 n. 21, 224 n. 32, 228 n. 57, 230 n. 70, 234 n. 90, 238 n. 112, 243, 247, 248 n. 26, 256, 256 n. 43
Woude, A. S. van der, 104 n. 7, 105 n. 17, 107 n. 33, 199 n. 20, 237 n. 105
Wyrick, S. V., 20 n. 109

Yardeni, A., 45 n. 96, 46 n. 97, 82 n. 163
Yaron, R., 43 n. 77, 44, 44 n. 89

Zadok, R., 264 n. 21
Zertal, A., 93 n. 232, 94 n. 240
Zimmerli, W., 20 n. 107, 21 n. 117, 98 n. 10, 99 n. 12

# INDEX OF BIBLICAL REFERENCES

Old Testament

*Genesis*

| | |
|---|---|
| 2:5 | 103 |
| 2:7 | 137 |
| 3:1–6 | 130 |
| 4:25 | 174 |
| 6:3 | 171 |
| 9:21 | 132 |
| 12:1-3 | 228 |
| 14:10 | 165 |
| 15:1 | 184 |
| 17:4-8 | 228 |
| 18:1 | 132 |
| 18:22 | 174 |
| 19:21 | 223 |
| 19:25 | 223 |
| 19:29 | 223 |
| 22:16 | 169 |
| 23:8 | 200 |
| 25:29 | 197 |
| 26:24 | 184, 228 |
| 28:15 | 184 |
| 29:7 | 103, 126 |
| 30:6 | 144 |
| 32:14 | 181 |
| 34:29 | 182 |
| 35:17 | 184 |
| 43:23 | 181 |
| 43:34 | 132 |
| 44:18 | 166 |
| 45:13 | 181 |

*Exodus*

| | |
|---|---|
| 1:11 | 229 |
| 3:4-10 | 228 |
| 3:12 | 206 |
| 5:2 | 143 |
| 6:7 | 227 |
| 6:10–11 | 116 |
| 6:28–29 | 116 |
| 7:17 | 223 |
| 9:30 | 147 |
| 9:35 | 35, 54, 116 |
| 12:36b | 182 |
| 13:2 | 224 |
| 13:21 | 172 |

| | |
|---|---|
| 14:1–2 | 116 |
| 14:4 | 136 |
| 14:9 | 224 |
| 14:13 | 184 |
| 14:16 | 224 |
| 14:17 | 136 |
| 14:18 | 136 |
| 14:19 | 172 |
| 14:23 | 224 |
| 14:24 | 172 |
| 15:1 | 224 |
| 15:19 | 224 |
| 15:21 | 224 |
| 16:9 | 206 |
| 16:11–12 | 116 |
| 16:33 | 206 |
| 16:34 | 206 |
| 17:4 | 173 |
| 18:21 | 229 |
| 18:22 | 174 |
| 19:5 | 182 |
| 19:16 | 178 |
| 19:18 | 176 |
| 20:20 | 184 |
| 21:10 | 132 |
| 23:21–22 | 143 |
| 25:1–2 | 116 |
| 25:3-8 | 182 |
| 25:8 | 172 |
| 28:11 | 229 |
| 28:21 | 229 |
| 28:36 | 229 |
| 29:45 | 172 |
| 30:10 | 174 |
| 31:3 | 152, 171 |
| 31:5 | 152 |
| 32:13 | 228 |
| 32:26 | 200 |
| 34:13 | 128 |
| 35:29 | 35, 54, 152 |
| 35:31 | 152 |
| 36:2 | 55 |
| 36:3 | 152 |
| 36:4 | 152 |
| 39:6 | 229 |
| 39:14 | 229 |
| 39:30 | 229 |

| | |
|---|---|
| 40:34-35 | 181 |

*Leviticus*

| | |
|---|---|
| 1 | 206 |
| 1:5 | 206 |
| 3:3-9 | 206 |
| 4:1–2 | 116 |
| 5 | 206 |
| 6:20 [Eng. 27] | 204 |
| 7:15-16 | 204 |
| 7:17-21 | 203 |
| 7:19 | 204 |
| 8:2 | 227 |
| 8:36 | 54, 116 |
| 10:3 | 136 |
| 10:9 | 132 |
| 10:10-11 | 203 |
| 10:11 | 116 |
| 11 | 206 |
| 11:1–2 | 116 |
| 12:1–2 | 116 |
| 15:1–2 | 116 |
| 16:2 | 116 |
| 16:34 | 174 |
| 19:13 | 132 |
| 21:6 | 204 |
| 21:10 | 121 |
| 25:6 | 132 |
| 26 | 153, 154, 155 |
| 26:3 | 155 |
| 26:6 | 183 |
| 26:14 | 155 |
| 26:15 | 155 |
| 26:19 | 154 |
| 26:19–20 | 139 |
| 26:26 | 132, 154 |
| 26:30–33 | 129 |
| 26:36 | 165 |
| 26:39 | 165 |

*Numbers*

| | |
|---|---|
| 3:12 | 227, 228 |
| 4:37 | 54 |
| 4:37–45 | 116 |
| 4:45 | 116 |
| 5:5–6 | 116 |
| 5:11–12 | 116 |
| 6:1–2 | 116 |
| 7:84–86 | 69 |
| 8:16 | 227 |
| 9:23 | 54, 116 |
| 10:13 | 54, 116 |

| | |
|---|---|
| 11:29 | 171 |
| 12:7-8 | 228 |
| 14:9 | 184 |
| 15:17–18 | 116 |
| 17:5 [Eng. 16:40] | 116 |
| 19:22 | 204 |
| 21:16 | 133 |
| 21:34 | 184 |
| 27:18 | 227 |
| 27:22 | 227 |
| 27:23 | 116 |
| 31:9 | 180, 182 |
| 35:6 | 160 |
| 35:25 | 121 |
| 35:28 | 121 |
| 36:13 | 116 |

*Deuteronomy*

| | |
|---|---|
| 1:13 | 229 |
| 1:21 | 184 |
| 1:29 | 184 |
| 3:2 | 184 |
| 3:22 | 184 |
| 4:6 | 156 |
| 4:10 | 147 |
| 4:20 | 227, 228 |
| 4:25–32 | 153 |
| 4:28–32 | 142 |
| 5:26 | 147 |
| 5:28 | 123 |
| 6:2 | 147 |
| 6:13 | 147 |
| 6:24 | 147 |
| 6:55 | 130 |
| 7:5 | 129 |
| 7:6 | 231, 232 |
| 7:7 | 232 |
| 7:13 | 140 |
| 7:20 | 165 |
| 8:6 | 147 |
| 9:13 | 123 |
| 9:27 | 123 |
| 10:12 | 147 |
| 11:10–12 | 139 |
| 11:14 | 140 |
| 11:17 | 139 |
| 12:5 | 232 |
| 12:11 | 232 |
| 12:14 | 232 |
| 12:17 | 140 |
| 13:5 | 147 |
| 14:2 | 232 |

| | | | |
|---|---|---|---|
| 14:2-3 | 203 | *Joshua* | |
| 14:21 | 203 | 1 | 34 |
| 14:23 | 140, 147, 232 | 1:1 | 228 |
| 14:26 | 132 | 1:6 | 168 |
| 14:29 | 205 | 1:6-9 | 184 |
| 15:5 | 143 | 1:7 | 168, 228 |
| 16:15 | 205 | 1:9 | 168 |
| 17:19 | 147 | 1:23 | 168 |
| 18:4 | 140 | 3:7 | 184 |
| 18:6 | 232 | 6:19 | 182 |
| 19:20 | 165 | 6:24 | 182 |
| 20:3 | 173, 184 | 7:7 | 123 |
| 23:6 | 223 | 10:8 | 147, 184 |
| 24:19 | 205 | 10:25 | 34, 168, 173, 184 |
| 28 | 153, 154, 155 | 14:17 | 228 |
| 28:1 | 143 | 20:6 | 121 |
| 28:12 | 205 | | |
| 28:12-13 | 260 | *Judges* | |
| 28:14-15 | 155 | 2:8 | 228 |
| 28:15 | 143 | 3:10 | 171 |
| 28:18 | 54, 154 | 5:2-31 | 176 |
| 28:20 | 54, 224 | 5:4 | 176, 179 |
| 28:22 | 139 | 6:8 | 146 |
| 28:23 | 54, 139, 154 | 6:12b | 228 |
| 28:24 | 224 | 7:3 | 164 |
| 28:25 | 260 | 7:22 | 224, 225 |
| 28:33 | 260 | 8:9 | 129 |
| 28:36 | 260 | | |
| 28:38 | 54, 154 | *Ruth* | 245 |
| 28:43-44 | 260 | | |
| 28:45 | 224 | *1 Samuel* | |
| 28:46-48 | 155 | 1:3 | 122 |
| 28:48 | 132 | 1:11 | 122 |
| 28:51 | 54, 140, 154 | 3:6-14 | 228 |
| 28:58 | 147, 156 | 4:4 | 122 |
| 28:58-59 | 155 | 4:5-6 | 180 |
| 28:61 | 224 | 7:7 | 147 |
| 28:63 | 260 | 10:6 | 171 |
| 29:22 [Eng. 23] | 223 | 11:11 | 165 |
| 29:22-28 | 138 | 12:20 | 173 |
| 30:9 | 205 | 14:20 | 225 |
| 30:10 | 143 | 16:13 | 207 |
| 31 | 34 | 18:12 | 147 |
| 31:6 | 168, 173, 184 | 21:7 [Eng. 6] | 132 |
| 31:7 | 168, 184 | 21:13 | 147 |
| 31:12 | 147 | 30:25 | 207 |
| 31:13 | 147 | | |
| 31:16 | 123 | *2 Samuel* | |
| 31:23 | 168 | 7:2 | 118 |
| 32:46 | 131 | 7:5 | 228 |
| 33:10 | 203 | 7:8 | 227, 228 |
| 34:5 | 228 | 10:12 | 168 |

| | |
|---|---|
| 11 | 34 |
| 12:25 | 118 |
| 13:28 | 168 |
| 16:18 | 122 |
| 17:6 | 169 |
| 17:22 | 200 |
| 22:17 (= Ps 18:17) | 228 |
| 24:11 | 118 |

*1 Kings*

| | |
|---|---|
| 1:10 | 118 |
| 1:22 | 118 |
| 1:23 | 118 |
| 1:32 | 118 |
| 1:34 | 118 |
| 1:38 | 118 |
| 1:45 | 118 |
| 3:8 | 232 |
| 6:9 | 128 |
| 7:7 | 128 |
| 8:2 | 163 |
| 8:10-11 | 181 |
| 8:53 | 116 |
| 8:56 | 116 |
| 8:65 | 163 |
| 10 | 175 |
| 11:13 | 228, 232 |
| 14:8 | 228 |
| 14:15 | 208 |
| 14:18 | 116, 118 |
| 15:9 | 43 |
| 15:29 | 116 |
| 16:7 | 116, 118 |
| 16:10 | 43 |
| 16:12 | 116, 117, 118 |
| 17:13 | 117 |
| 18:12 | 171 |
| 19:11 | 176 |
| 21:8 | 229 |

*2 Kings*            45, 48

| | |
|---|---|
| 4:23 | 114 |
| 4:38 | 197 |
| 4:39 | 197 |
| 4:40 | 197 |
| 5:26 | 126, 128 |
| 6:10 | 174 |
| 6:11 | 200 |
| 9:1 | 118 |
| 9:36 | 116 |
| 10:10 | 116 |
| 10:15 | 200 |

| | |
|---|---|
| 10:21 | 165 |
| 10:27 | 129 |
| 11:18 | 129 |
| 12:8 | 120 |
| 12:10 | 120 |
| 12:11 [Eng. 10] | 120, 121 |
| 14:25 | 116, 118 |
| 17:13 | 146 |
| 19:30 | 164 |
| 19:31 | 142 |
| 19:34 | 228 |
| 22-23 | 245 |
| 22:4 | 120, 121 |
| 22:8 | 120, 121 |
| 22:8-20 | 147 |
| 22:12 | 120 |
| 22:14 | 120 |
| 25 | 43 |
| 25:1 | 43, 48 |
| 25:3 | 43 |
| 25:8 | 43 |
| 25:9-15 | 88 |
| 25:11 | 165 |
| 25:12 | 95, 262 |
| 25:18 | 120 |
| 25:24 | 173 |
| 25:27 | 43 |

*1 Chronicles*       40, 43

| | |
|---|---|
| 3 | 67 |
| 3:18 | 63, 64, 67 |
| 3:19 | 76, 119 |
| 5:40-41 | 120 |
| 9:13 | 152 |
| 9:19 | 152 |
| 15:2 | 232 |
| 17 | 232 |
| 19:13 | 168 |
| 22:13 | 168 |
| 23:4 | 152 |
| 28:4 | 135, 232 |
| 28:10 | 168 |
| 28:20 | 168 |
| 29:17 | 135 |

*2 Chronicles*       40, 43

| | |
|---|---|
| 3:2 | 44, 47 |
| 6:5-6 | 232 |
| 6:34 | 232 |
| 6:38 | 232 |
| 7:8-10 | 163 |
| 7:10 | 47 |

| | | | |
|---|---|---|---|
| 7:12 | 232 | 5:14 | 63, 65, 68 |
| 10:15 | 118 | 5:14–16 | 64 |
| 15:10 | 47 | 5:16 | 63, 69 |
| 19:11 | 168 | 6 | 62 |
| 20:20-25 | 224, 225 | 6:3–5 | 60, 61 |
| 23:17 | 129 | 6:15 | 47, 49 |
| 24:27 | 208 | 6:16 | 141 |
| 25:8 | 168 | 6:19 | 47, 48 |
| 25:15 | 146 | 7:8 | 47, 48 |
| 25:23 | 129 | 7:9 | 47, 48 |
| 29:3 | 47 | 8 | 62 |
| 29:17 | 47 | 8:31 | 47, 48 |
| 29:25 | 118 | 9:14 | 142 |
| 31:6-9 | 198 | 10:4 | 168 |
| 31:7 | 208 | 10:9 | 47, 48, 49 |
| 32:7 | 168 | 10:16 | 47, 48, 49 |
| 32:16 | 229 | 10:17 | 47, 48, 49 |
| 32:20-23 | 225 | | |
| 32:27 | 180 | *Nehemiah* | 43 |
| 33:8 | 118 | 1:1 | 48, 49, 82, 83 |
| 34:14 | 118 | 1:3 | 129 |
| 34:31 | 169 | 2 | 62 |
| 35:1 | 47 | 2:1 | 48, 82, 83 |
| 35:6 | 118 | 2:13 | ? |
| 36:10 | 180 | 4:1 [Eng. 7] | 129 |
| 36:15 | 118 | 6:15 | 49 |
| 36:22–23 | 60 | 7 | 67, 71 |
| | | 7:71 | 142 |
| *Ezra* | 37, 43 | 7:73b | 71 |
| 1 | 69 | 8:2 [Eng. 7:73] | 47, 48 |
| 1:1–6 | 61, 62 | 8:9 | 147 |
| 1:4 | 165 | 9:1 | 47 |
| 1:8 | 63, 64, 68 | 9:1–5 | 147 |
| 1:11 | 63 | 12:1 | 119 |
| 1:2–4 | 60 | | |
| 1–3 | 62 | *Esther* | 43 |
| 1–6 | 60, 66 | 2:7 | 66 |
| 2 | 62, 90, 95 | 2:16 | 48, 49 |
| 2–3 | 66, 70 | 3:7 | 48, 49 |
| 3 | 71 | 3:12 | 47, 48, 49 |
| 3–4 | 71 | 3:13 | 47, 48, 49 |
| 3:1 | 48, 71, 114 | 8:9 | 48, 49 |
| 3:2 | 119 | 8:12 | 47, 48, 49 |
| 3:6 | 47, 48, 49 | 9:1 | 47, 48, 49 |
| 3:8 | 47, 48, 119, 141 | 9:15 | 47, 48, 49 |
| 4:1 | 141 | 9:17 | 48, 49 |
| 4:1–5 | 36 | 9:19 | 48, 49 |
| 4:4 | 168 | 9:21 | 48, 49 |
| 5 | 40, 70 | | |
| 5–6 | 70, 71, 80 | *Job* | |
| 5:1 | 40 | 1:8 | 228 |
| 5:2 | 119 | 2:3 | 228 |

| | | | |
|---|---|---|---|
| 22:16 | 103, 125 | 110 | 225, 240 |
| 25:5 | 200 | 119:108 | 135 |
| 29:20 | 181 | 139:16 | 103 |
| 33:26 | 135 | 145:12 | 165 |
| 38:14 | 229 | 147:10 | 135 |
| 39:2 | 176 | 148:8 | 169 |
| 41:7 [Eng. 15] | 229 | 149:4 | 135 |

*Psalms*

| | | *Proverbs* | |
|---|---|---|---|
| 2 | 225, 240 | 1:7 | 130 |
| 2:10-11 | 189 | 2:2 | 131 |
| 15 | 211 | 15:23 | 125 |
| 18:8 [Eng. 7:8] | 177 | 24:32 | 131 |
| 18:17 [Eng. 16] | | 27:23 | 131 |
| (= Sam 22:17) | 228 | | |
| 24 | 211 | *Ecclesiastes* | |
| 24:1 | 182 | 3:2–8 | 126 |
| 33:6 | 169 | 3:2–11 | 125 |
| 33:8 | 147 | 3:14 | 147 |
| 37:10 | 173 | 7:17 | 125 |
| 44 | 92 | 8:5–6 | 125, 126 |
| 44:4 [Eng. 3] | 135 | | |
| 46 | 260 | *Canticles* | |
| 46:3 [Eng. 2] | 188 | 8:6 | 229 |
| 46:7 [Eng. 6] | 188 | | |
| 47 | 189 | *Isaiah* | |
| 48 | 260 | 1:1 | 255 |
| 48:9 [Eng. 8] | 122 | 2 | 18, 192 |
| 48:14 [Eng. 13] | 131 | 2:1-4 | 188 |
| 60:4 [Eng. 2] | 176 | 2:1-5 | 189 |
| 62:11 [Eng. 10] | 131 | 2:2-4 | 186, 188, 194 |
| 68 | 189 | 4:2 | 181 |
| 68:9 [Eng. 8] | 179 | 4:3 | 164 |
| 68:19 | 227 | 5:5 | 129 |
| 74 | 92 | 6:1 | 49 |
| 74:6 | 129 | 6:3 | 122, 181 |
| 76 | 189 | 6:5 | 122 |
| 76:11-13 | 189 | 6:9–10 | 123, 214 |
| 77:19 [Eng. 18] | 176, 177, 179 | 6:10 | 123 |
| 78:67 | 232 | 7:1 | 49 |
| 78:70 | 228 | 7:14 | 206 |
| 79 | 92 | 7:20 | 139 |
| 80:13 [Eng. 12] | 129 | 8:4 | 180, 182 |
| 89 | 92 | 8:6 | 123, 214 |
| 89:41 [Eng. 40] | 129 | 8:11–12 | 123 |
| 96 | 189 | 8:12 | 123 |
| 97 | 189 | 9:15 [Eng. 16] | 123 |
| 99 | 189 | 10:13-14 | 182 |
| 102 | 92 | 10:20 | 142 |
| 102:14 [Eng. 13] | 125 | 10:24 | 147 |
| 102:15 [Eng. 14] | 135 | 10:25 | 173 |
| 103:20 | 169 | 11:1-10 | 192 |

| | | | |
|---|---|---|---|
| 11:2 | 171 | 56-66 | 157 |
| 13:3 | 139 | 59:21 | 170, 172 |
| 13:13 | 176, 225 | 60 | 186, 188, 189, 192 |
| 13:19 | 165, 268 | 60:1-3 | 194 |
| 14:1 | 232 | 60:1-22 | 260 |
| 14:16 | 176, 177 | 60:3-9 | 193 |
| 14:23 | 224 | 60:4 | 193 |
| 14:28 | 43 | 60:5 | 180, 188, 193 |
| 19 | 189 | 60:5-7 | 194 |
| 19:2 | 188, 224, 226 | 60:6 | 193 |
| 19:16 | 178, 188 | 60:7 | 165, 193 |
| 20:4 | 132 | 60:9 | 193 |
| 21 | 92 | 60:10 | 193 |
| 21:36 | 144 | 60:10-17 | 193 |
| 22:10 | 129 | 60:11 | 193 |
| 23:11 | 224, 225 | 60:12 | 188, 194 |
| 24:17-20 | 188 | 60:14 | 193 |
| 24:18-20 | 179 | 60:16 | 193 |
| 25:6 | 192 | 61:1 | 171 |
| 26:15 | 136 | 63:3 | 199 |
| 28:5 | 142 | 64:10 [Eng. 11] | 165 |
| 28:7 | 132 | | |
| 29:17 | 173 | *Jeremiah* | 43, 48, 92 |
| 30:6 | 182 | 1:1 | 255 |
| 34:10 | 129 | 1:2 | 49 |
| 35:4 | 168 | 1:3 | 49 |
| 37:31 | 164 | 2:30 | 208 |
| 40:7 | 171 | 3:17-18 | 225 |
| 40:13 | 171 | 3:25 | 144 |
| 40:17 | 166 | 4:11 | 123 |
| 41:5 | 178 | 4:26 | 128 |
| 41:6 | 168 | 5:12 | 95 |
| 41:8-9 | 228 | 5:14 | 123 |
| 41:22 | 131 | 6:19 | 123, 214 |
| 42:1 | 135, 172 | 6:21 | 123, 214 |
| 43:5-7 | 193 | 7 | 127, 277 |
| 43:17 | 225 | 7:16 | 123, 214 |
| 44:1 | 228 | 7:23 | 144 |
| 45:14-15 | 186 | 7:28 | 144 |
| 45:14-17 | 193 | 7:33 | 123 |
| 46:3 | 142 | 7:34 | 129 |
| 46:11 | 139 | 8:3 | 165 |
| 48:16 | 170, 172 | 8:16 | 177 |
| 48:20 | 228 | 9:12 | 144 |
| 49:8-21 | 186 | 10:5 | 147, 173 |
| 49:14-21 | 188 | 10:10 | 176, 225 |
| 49:22-23 | 193 | 11:4 | 144 |
| 50:10 | 143 | 11:7 | 144 |
| 51:11 | 193 | 13:1-4 | 213 |
| 51:19 | 198 | 13:10 | 214 |
| 54:16 | 137 | 14:10-11 | 214 |
| 55:5 | 260 | 14:13 | 183, 277 |

| | | | |
|---|---|---|---|
| 14:15–16 | 95 | 30:10 | 228 |
| 15:1 | 200 | 31:4 | 175 |
| 15:13 | 180, 182 | 31:5 | 175 |
| 17:3 | 180, 182 | 31:7–9 | 142 |
| 18:10 | 144 | 31:12 | 140 |
| 18:18 | 203 | 31:23 | 175 |
| 19:1-13 | 213 | 31:31-43 | 278 |
| 20:2 | 118 | 32:2 | 118 |
| 20:16 | 223 | 32:15 | 175 |
| 21:1-24:10 | 231 | 32:23 | 144 |
| 21:6 | 208 | 33:4 | 128 |
| 21:7–9 | 95 | 33:10 | 129 |
| 21:11 | 231 | 33:12 | 129 |
| 22 | 275 | 33:12-13 | 175 |
| 22:5 | 129 | 33:14-16 | 237 |
| 22:8–9 | 138 | 33:15 | 65 |
| 22:14 | 128 | 34:1–2 | 49 |
| 22:21 | 144 | 36 | 245 |
| 22:24 | 144, 229, 230, 231, 238, 277 | 36:9 | 43 |
| | | 36:22 | 43 |
| 22:24-30 | 236 | 36:29 | 140 |
| 23:3 | 142 | 37-41 | 245 |
| 23:5 | 65 | 37:2 | 118 |
| 23:5-6 | 237 | 38:9 | 118 |
| 24:8 | 165 | 38:10 | 118 |
| 25:2 | 118 | 38:14 | 118 |
| 25:9 | 129, 228 | 38:20 | 144 |
| 25:11 | 129 | 39:1 | 43, 45 |
| 25:11–12 | 115 | 39:2 | 43, 45 |
| 25:12–13 | 125 | 40:6 | 165 |
| 25:18 | 129 | 40:9 | 173 |
| 25:29 | 139 | 41 | 89 |
| 26 | 245 | 41:5 | 89 |
| 26:9 | 129 | 41:10 | 165 |
| 27:1-15 | 213 | 42:6 | 144 |
| 27:6 | 228 | 42:11 | 147 |
| 27:8 | 95 | 42:13 | 144 |
| 27:17 | 129 | 42:21 | 144 |
| 28:1 | 43, 45, 49 | 43:4 | 144 |
| 28:5 | 118 | 43:5 | 142 |
| 28:6 | 118 | 43:7 | 144 |
| 28:8 | 225 | 43:10 | 228 |
| 28:9 | 146 | 44:2 | 129 |
| 28:10 | 118 | 44:4 | 146 |
| 28:11 | 118 | 44:6 | 129 |
| 28:12 | 118 | 44:22 | 129 |
| 28:15 | 118, 146 | 44:23 | 144 |
| 28:17 | 43 | 46:1 | 118 |
| 29:1 | 118 | 46:9 | 225 |
| 29:10 | 125 | 46:16 | 224, 226 |
| 29:29 | 118 | 46:21 | 125 |
| 30:4-31:37 | 278 | 47:1 | 118 |

| | | | |
|---|---|---|---|
| 48:8 | 224 | 20:40 | 135 |
| 48:42 | 224 | 20:41 | 135 |
| 49:18 | 223 | 20:43 | 215 |
| 49:21 | 177 | 22:3-4 | 215 |
| 49:34 | 118 | 22:4 | 215 |
| 49:34-39 | 225 | 22:6-16 | 215 |
| 49:38 | 225 | 22:20 | 137 |
| 50:1 | 116, 117, 118 | 22:21 | 137 |
| 50:9 | 151 | 22:26 | 203 |
| 50:15 | 129 | 23:7 | 215 |
| 50:27 | 125 | 23:13 | 215 |
| 50:31 | 125 | 23:17 | 215 |
| 50:40 | 223 | 23:20 | 215 |
| 50:46 | 176, 225 | 23:36-39 | 215 |
| 51:1 | 151 | 24:1 | 45, 48 |
| 51:20-21 | 268 | 24:15-24 | 213 |
| 51:33 | 173 | 25:9 | 165 |
| 52:4 | 43, 45 | 26:1 | 45 |
| 52:5-6 | 43 | 26:9 | 129 |
| 52:6 | 45 | 26:10 | 176, 225 |
| 52:12 | 43 | 26:12 | 180 |
| 52:15 | 165 | 26:15-16 | 178 |
| 52:16 | 95, 262 | 27:3-4 | 165 |
| 52:28-29 | 81 | 27:28 | 177 |
| 52:31 | 45 | 28:22 | 136 |
| | | 28:25 | 228 |
| *Lamentations* | 92 | 29:1 | 45, 49 |
| 1:6 | 165 | 29:17 | 49 |
| 2:15 | 165 | 29:19 | 129 |
| | | 30:2 | 45 |
| *Ezekiel* | 43, 44, 48, 92 | 30:4 | 129 |
| 1:1 | 45, 49 | 30:20 | 49 |
| 1–2 | 43 | 31:1 | 45, 49 |
| 2:6 | 147 | 31:15-16 | 177 |
| 5:1-17 | 213 | 31:16 | 176, 177 |
| 5:11 | 215 | 32:1 | 45, 48 |
| 5:14 | 129 | 32:10 | 178 |
| 6:4-5 | 215 | 32:17 | 45 |
| 7:4 | 206 | 33:23-26 | 215 |
| 7:26 | 203 | 33:23-28 | 95 |
| 8:1 | 45, 49 | 33:24 | 129 |
| 9:7 | 215 | 33:28 | 129 |
| 9:7-9 | 215 | 34:16 | 224 |
| 11:2-11 | 95 | 34:23 | 229, 237 |
| 11:5 | 172 | 36:4 | 129 |
| 11:14-18 | 95 | 36:9 | 200 |
| 14:13 | 140 | 36:10 | 129 |
| 16:39 | 128, 132 | 36:17-18 | 215 |
| 17:21 | 164 | 36:26-32 | 278 |
| 20:1 | 43, 49 | 36:27 | 54 |
| 20:5 | 232 | 36:33 | 129 |
| 20:26 | 215 | 36:35 | 129 |

| | | | |
|---|---|---|---|
| 36:38 | 129 | 2:24 | 140 |
| 37:1 | 171 | 3:3 | 200 |
| 37:9 | 137 | 8:13 | 135, 214 |
| 37:22–25 | 67 | 8:24 [Eng. 22] | 140 |
| 37:24-25 | 229, 237 | 9:11 | 181 |
| 37:25 | 228 | 10:5 | 181 |
| 37:27 | 35, 55 | 11:3 | 228 |
| 38-39 | 179, 186, 191 | 11:6 | 230 |
| 38:15 | 225 | 12:10 [Eng. 9] | 175 |
| 38:17-23 | 191 | 13:15 | 180 |
| 38:19 | 176 | | |
| 38:19-20 | 177, 188 | *Joel* | |
| 38:19-21 | 224, 226 | 1:19–20 | 140 |
| 38:19-23 | 179 | 2-4 | 186 |
| 38:20 | 177, 225 | 2:10 | 225 |
| 38:21 | 139, 188, 191, 219 | 2:11 | 169 |
| 38:22-23 | 188 | 2:20 | 177 |
| 39:6 | 191 | 2:22 | 140 |
| 39:9-10 | 188 | 3:4 [Eng. 3] | 179 |
| 39:13 | 136 | 4 [Eng. 3] | 191 |
| 40–46 | 69 | 4:5 | 182 |
| 40-48 | 191 | 4:5-7 [Eng. 3:5-7] | 188 |
| 40:1 | 45 | 4:9-14 [3:9-14] | 188 |
| 40:4 | 131 | 4:15-16 | |
| 43:5 | 181 |      [Eng. 3:15-16] | 188 |
| 43:7 | 160, 225 | 4:16 [Eng. 3:16] | 176, 188, 225 |
| 43:13-26 | 215 | | |
| 44:3 | 160 | *Amos* | |
| 44:4 | 181 | 1:1 | 43, 49, 176 |
| 44:5 | 131 | 2:11–12 | 155 |
| 44:15 | 120 | 2:16 | 132 |
| 44:19 | 204 | 4:4-6 | 214 |
| 45:17 | 114 | 4:6–13 | 153, 155 |
| 45:18 | 49 | 4:9 | 199, 208, 212 |
| 45:21 | 49 | 4:11 | 223 |
| 45:25 | 49 | 4:12 | 155 |
| 46:16–18 | 68 | 5:10 | 197 |
| 47:1-12 | 183 | 5:19 | 137 |
| 47:17 | 160 | 5:22 | 135 |
| 47:18 | 160 | 6:13 | 224 |
| 47:19 | 160 | 7:2 | 198 |
| 48:3-4 | 188 | 7:4 | 139 |
| 48:7 | 188 | 7:15 | 228 |
| | | 8:5 | 114 |
| *Daniel* | | 8:10 | 223 |
| 1:7 | 66 | 9:1 | 176 |
| 11:8 | 180 | 9:8 | 224 |
| | | | |
| *Hosea* | | *Obadiah* | 92 |
| 1:4 | 173 | | |
| 2:10 | 140 | *Jonah* | |
| 2:11 | 132 | 3:11 | 140, 245 |

*Micah*

| | |
|---|---|
| 2:7 | 171 |
| 2:12 | 142 |
| 3:11 | 203 |
| 4 | 18, 192 |
| 4-6 | 192 |
| 4:1-4 | 186, 188, 189 |
| 4:1-7 | 189 |
| 4:5-6 | 189 |
| 4:7 | 142 |
| 4:9-10 | 189 |
| 4:13 | 180, 188 |
| 5:9 | 188 |
| 6 | 154 |
| 6:7 | 135 |
| 6:13–16 | 153 |
| 6:16b | 155 |
| 7:15-17 | 188 |
| 7:18 | 142 |
| 11:3 | 182 |

*Nahum*

| | |
|---|---|
| 1:5 | 176, 178, 179, 188 |
| 2:9 | 180 |
| 2:10 [Eng. 9] | 180 |

*Zephaniah*

| | |
|---|---|
| 1:1 | 255 |
| 1:3 | 140 |
| 3:12–13 | 142 |

*Haggai*

| | |
|---|---|
| 1:1 | 31, 32, 34, 36, 44, 49, 53, 54, 103, 248, 251, 252, 261, 265, 267 |
| 1:1–2 | 17 |
| 1:1–3 | 35 |
| 1:1–5 | 247 |
| 1:1–11 | 247, 249, 267, 270 |
| 1:1–15 | 34, 246, 248, 250 |
| 1:1-15a | 247 |
| 1:12-14 | 247 |
| 1:2 | 28, 32, 35, 53, 248, 249, 251, 252, 253 |
| 1:2–4 | 33, 248 |
| 1:2–11 | 31, 34, 55, 251 |
| 1:3 | 32, 34, 36, 53, 54, 251, 252, 265, 267 |
| 1:3-9 | 248 |
| 1:3–11 | 34, 37, 267, 272 |
| 1:4 | 253, 267 |
| 1:4-7 | 249 |
| 1:4–8 | 32 |
| 1:4–11 | 35, 249, 251, 253, 254, 271 |
| 1:5 | 53, 104, 248, 252 |
| 1:5–6 | 33, 248 |
| 1:6-9 | 247 |
| 1:6a | 54 |
| 1:7 | 53, 248, 252 |
| 1:7–8 | 33, 214 |
| 1:8 | 53, 55, 89, 249, 252, 253, 265, 267, 278 |
| 1:9 | 35, 253 |
| 1:9a | 253 |
| 1:9b | 253 |
| 1:9–11 | 32, 247 |
| 1:11 | 54, 254 |
| 1:12 | 34, 53, 54, 103, 248, 252, 255, 261, 265, 273, 277 |
| 1:12–14 | 31, 32, 247, 270 |
| 1:12-15 | 247, 249, 250 |
| 1:12a | 36, 54 |
| 1:12b | 36, 37, 54, 265 |
| 1:12b–13 | 35 |
| 1:13 | 53, 252, 253, 254, 255, 266, 268, 273 |
| 1:13-14 | 251 |
| 1:13a | 34, 36 |
| 1:13b | 31, 53 |
| 1:14 | 34, 35, 53, 54, 103, 248, 250, 253, 261, 273, 278 |
| 1:14a | 36 |
| 1:15 | 31, 34, 44, 49, 252 |
| 1:15a | 35, 53 |
| 1:15b–2:2 | 35 |
| 1:15b-2:9 | 247 |
| 2:1 | 31, 34, 36, 44, 49, 53, 54, 103, 248, 252, 265 |
| | 267 |
| 2:1-2 | 17, 249 |
| 2:1–3 | 246, 248, 249, 250, 251, 270 |
| 2:1-9 | 34, 103, 252 |
| 2:2 | 249, 250 |
| 2:2-3 | 31, 248 |
| 2:2–9 | 33, 104, 248, 249, 252, 253, 267 |
| 2:3 | 32 |
| 2:3–5 | |

| | | | |
|---|---|---|---|
| 2:3–9 | 35 | 2:17 | 36, 254 |
| 2:4 | 35, 54, 104, 249, 252, 253, 254 | 2:17a | 253 |
| | | 2:17b | 32, 253 |
| 2:4–5 | 33, 248, 249, 250, 268, 273 | 2:18 | 35, 36, 44, 49, 53, 250, 251, 253, 254 |
| 2:5 | 20, 34, 251, 254, 273, 278 | 2:18-19 | 247, 249, 251, 268, 270 |
| 2:5a | 32, 36, 253 | 2:19 | 36, 253 |
| 2:5b | 54, 253 | 2:20 | 31, 34, 36, 44, 49, 53, 54, 103, 248, 252, 265 |
| 2:6 | 176, 252, 253 | 2:20-21 | 249 |
| 2:6–7 | 33, 248, 268, 271 | 2:20-21a | 267 |
| 2:6–9 | 5, 16, 18, 20, 54, 85, 249, 250, 251, 254, 259, 261, 268, 270, 272 | 2:20–23 | 16, 20, 41, 49, 78, 248, 249, 250, 251, 254, 261, 268 |
| 2:7 | 53, 176, 252, 253 | 2:21 | 36, 103, 176, 252, 253 268, 271 |
| 2:8 | 53 | 2:21-22 | 268, 271 |
| 2:8-9 | 271 | 2:21–23 | 31, 85, 259, 261, 267 |
| 2:9 | 36, 252, 253, 277 | 2:21a | 35 |
| 2:9a | 53 | 2:21b-22 | 159 |
| 2:9b | 32, 53 | 2:21b–23 | 35, 249, 272 |
| 2:10 | 31, 34, 35, 36, 44, 49, 53, 103, 248, 252, 265, 267 | 2:22 | 36, 103, 272 |
| | | 2:22a | 253 |
| 2:10–14 | 4, 25, 55, 247, 267 | 2:23 | 53, 54, 229, 251, 254, 159, 268, 271 |
| 2:10-17 | 247, 267 | | |
| 2:10–19 | 29, 246, 248, 249, 250, 251, 265, 269, 270 | 2:23aa | 253 |
| | | 2:23ab | 253 |
| 2:10-23 | 247 | 2:23b | 253 |
| 2:11 | 53, 252 | *Zechariah* | 41, 43 |
| 2:11–13 | 33, 35, 248, 249, 265 | 1–8 | 29, 36, 37, 39, 40, 44, 49, 56 |
| 2:11–14 | 31, 40 | | |
| 2:11–14a | 32 | 1 | 114 |
| 2:12 | 252, 253, 265 | 1:1 | 57, 118 |
| 2:12–14 | 17 | 1:3 | 133 |
| 2:13 | 36, 53, 252, 253 | 1:7 | 44, 49, 118 |
| 2:14 | 33, 35, 36, 248, 249, 250, 252, 267, 268, 273 | 1:14-16 | 224 |
| | | 1:17 | 174, 232, 233 |
| 2:14-17 | 249 | 2:7 | 82 |
| 2:14b | 32 | 2:16 [Eng. 2:12] | 232, 233 |
| 2:15 | 35, 104, 252, 253 | 2:16b [Eng. 12] | 174 |
| 2:15a | 253 | 3:2 | 232 |
| 2:15b | 253 | 4:6 | 171 |
| 2:15-16 | 253 | 4:6-7 | 209 |
| 2:15-17 | 247, 251 | 4:8-10 | 209 |
| 2:15-18 | 251, 253 | 6:12 | 65 |
| 2:15–19 | 31, 33, 35, 37, 248, 250, 265 | 6:12–13 | 41 |
| | | 7 | 211 |
| 2:16 | 253 | 7:1 | 44, 49 |
| 2:16-17 | 254 | 7:4-7 | 214 |
| | | 7:7 | 160 |
| | | 7:12 | 146 |

| | | | |
|---|---|---|---|
| 8:2 | 65 | 14:18 | 193 |
| 8:4 | 174 | 14:19 | 193 |
| 8:7-8 | 193 | | |
| 8:9 | 209 | *Malachi* | |
| 8:11 | 123 | | 37, 41 |
| 8:17 | 160 | 1:6-14 | 214 |
| 9 | 186 | 1:8–10 | 135 |
| 9-14 | 189 | 1:13 | 135, 137 |
| 9:9-10 | 192 | 2:1–3 | 41 |
| 11:12 | 133 | 3:1–5 | 41 |
| 12-14 | 179, 186 | 3:5 | 132 |
| 14 | 191, 192, 260 | 3:16-18 | 263 |
| 14:1 | 180, 188 | 3:23 | 146 |
| 14:2 | 193 | | |
| 14:3 | 188 | | |
| 14:4 | 193 | New Testament | |
| 14:5 | 176 | | |
| 14:8 | 183, 193 | *Matthew* | |
| 14:9 | 193 | 1:12 | 119 |
| 14:10 | 193 | | |
| 14:12 | 193 | *Luke* | |
| 14:12-13 | 188 | 3:27 | 119 |
| 14:12-15 | 193 | | |
| 14:13 | 188, 191, 226 | Apocrypha and Septuagint | |
| 14:5-6 | 191 | | |
| 14:14 | 193 | *1 Esdras* | |
| 14:16 | 193 | 5:2 | 103 |
| 14:16-17 | 193 | 5:14–16 | 64 |
| 14:16-19 | 189 | | |
| 14:16-20 | 188 | *Tobit* | |
| 14:17 | 188 | 13 | 192 |
| 14:17-19 | 193 | 14 | 192 |

# INDEX OF HEBREW AND ARAMAIC TERMS

אחרון, 252
אל, 116, 203, 220, 265
אמר, 252
את, 170, 160 n. 8, 199 n. 18
בא, 103 n. 7
בוא, 152, 180–81, 248, 253
בחר, 226, 231–33, 241
ביד, 116–17, 164, 203, 220, 265
בית, 248, 253
דבר, 252
דרך, 131 n. 197
הדר, 165
היכל, 253
הנביא, 265
הפך, 221, 223, 225, 239, 253
ועתה, 111, 130, 202
זהב, 182–83
חדש, 48-49
חותם, 229
חזק, 168, 224
חמדה, 179–80
חרב, 89, 128–30
חרד, 178
טמא, 203
יהד, 75
יהוד, 75
יהוה צבאות, 248
יסד, 70, 208, 253
יפי, 165
ירא, 147, 172
ירד, 225
כבד, 134–36
כבוד, 165, 181
כהן, 120
כסא, 219, 223
כסף, 182–83
לקח, 226, 227
מטרם, 252
מלאך, 114, 143, 148–49, 266

מלאכות, 114, 149, 266
ממלכה, 223, 225
מעט, 173–74
מעלה, 207, 252
נחם, 232
נפח, 137
עבד, 226, 228, 241
עוד, 160 n. 11, 173–76, 233, 252
עור, 151
עם הארץ, 168
ענה, 252
עשה, 168, 249
עת, 103–104 n. 7, 123–26, 252
עתה, 198 n. 5, 206, 249
פחה, 68, 77, 77 n. 141
פחוא, 74–77
פחותא, 74
פחרא, 74–77
פחתא, 74
צבי, 165
קדש, 203
ראה, 166
ראשון, 252
רגז, 177
רוח, 152, 171
רחם, 232
רעש, 176–78, 223, 253
רצה, 134–35
שים, 225, 226, 229
שאל, 252
שאר, 164–65
שארית, 141–42, 164
שלום, 183
שלח, 146, 265
שמד, 224
שמע, 142
שנית, 220
תפארה, 165

# INDEX OF SUBJECTS

accession year, 82 n. 161
Achaemenid History Workshop, 26
    n. 146
antedating, 80–85, 82
apocalyptic, 14
Arad ostraca, 45, 65
archeology, 22–23
Asharhaddon, 239
Assyria, 8 n. 46

Babylon, 8 n. 45
Babylonian Empire, 68
Bardiya, 224 n. 36
Beer-Sheba ostraca, 43, 46
Behistun inscription, 45, 45–46 n. 96, 84,
    224, 224 n. 36
Book of the Twelve, 244

calendars and chronology, 80–85
Cambyses, 62, 71, 83, 83 n. 171, 224
    n. 36
    Egyptian campaign *see* Egypt,
        Cambyses' campaign in, 72, 86
charter group, 276
    as model for the sociology of Yehud,
        263
    definition and nature of, 262–263
Christ, 10
Chronicler, 32, 39, 40, 119, 121, 135
    n. 226, 172
Chronistic milieu, 19, 34, 118, 144
continuity, 53–55, 241
continuity motifs, 69, 111, 115, 150, 166,
    170–171, 184–185, 216, 244, 252,
    265
Cyrus, 8, 62, 63, 67, 69
    decree of, 60–63
Cyrus Cylinder, 61, 61 n. 14

Darius I, 44 n. 87, 52, 59, 63, 67, 71, 224,
    259
    Egyptian campaign, 86
Darius II, 59 n. 1
Date formulae, 31, 40, 41–51, 115, 163,
    220
    order of elements, 44
Davidic dynasty, 9, 33, 67, 220, 222,

    229–231, 232 n. 81, 236–239, 248,
    250, 275
day of Yahweh, 225, 227
demography, 90–96, 193
"desire" of the nations, 179–181
Deutero-Isaiah, 4, 14, 16, 92
Deuteronomism, 101
Deuteronomistic History, 92, 101, 118,
    171, 228, 232, 236, 267
Deuteronomistic movement, 10, 34, 52,
    88
Deuteronomistic terminology, 54
Deuteronomistic tradition, 107, 118, 119,
    127, 131, 138, 139, 140, 142–147,
    153, 155, 168, 171, 173, 184, 208
    n. 71, 218, 260, 273
Deuteronomy, 14
Diaspora, 193, 274
direct discourse, 252
Divine Saying Formula, 113, 201, 221,
    227
divine warrior, 186, 225
Dor, 87
double names, 64–66
dramatic conflict, 109, 161–162, 180, 201,
    206, 220, 246, 249, 250, 255
dyarchy, 37, 41, 51 n. 129, 261
dynastic model, 234 n. 92

editorial framework, 34, 37, 38, 244
Egypt, 9
    Cambyses' campaign in, 62
Elnathan, 75
Encouragement Formula, 162
enthronement psalms, 225
epigon, 2, 9
equivalence, hermeneutical tendency in
    Haggai, 273–274
eschatology, 10, 14, 17, 19, 35, 64, 124,
    151, 173, 175, 179, 182–183, 185,
    186, 189, 191, 193, 222, 223, 225–
    227, 233, 238 n. 112, 239, 240, 241,
    242, 243, 248–249, 250, 252–253,
    259, 261
eudaemonism, 156
Ezekiel, 4, 7, 8, 10, 13, 14
Ezra, 4, 9

exile, 8, 230
exiles and returnees, 263
exodus, 225
    from Egypt, 252, 273
    traditions, 239, 241

fear, 172
    of Yahweh, 146–147
focalization, hermeneutical tendency in Haggai, 272
Formula of Assistance, 113, 149, 172
futility curses, 111, 131–132, 153–154, 155, 271, 272
*futurum instans*, 175, 178, 221

Gaumata, 83–84, 224 n. 36
Gedeliah, 91
generalization, hermeneutical tendency in Haggai, 190, 216 n. 121, 223, 235, 237, 239–241, 261, 272
gentile nations, 176, 179, 222, 239, 240, 250, 259, 268, 272
gentiles, 3
*Golah*, 110, 215, 264
governor, Hebrew and Aramaic terms for, 74–80

Haggai, book of
    1:1-15 103–157
    2:1-9 159–195
    2:10-19 197–218
    2:20-23 219–242
    characters and action, 254–255
    critical evaluation of, 2–17
    form, 243
    goals and results, 270
    historical use of, 27–30
    narratives in, 249
    narrative structure, 244–245
    plot, thematic centre, 255–257
    proper names in, 251
    redactional framework of, 19
    redactional history of, 31–57
    role of, 268–269
    structure of, 247–251
    theme of, 256–257
harmonization, hermeneutical tendency in Haggai, 186–190, 240
"Hebraic" versus "Jewish" Religion, 7
hierocracy, 242 n. 130
high priest, 120–121, 141
*historische Kurzgeschichte*, literary genre, 245

Idumea, 87
Idumean ostraca, 43, 46
inclusivist stance, 275
    in Haggai, 195, 263–264
irony, 253

Jehoiachin, 68, 226, 230 n. 73, 231–233, 236, 275
Jeremiah
    attitude to in Haggai, 144–145, 264, 277–278
    redaction of, 236
    traditions, 277
Jerusalem, pilgrimage to, 18
Jerusalem Temple, 6, 9, 264
    destruction of, 33, 88–90, 184
    economic significance of 87, 87 n. 194
    foundations, 69
    in Haggai 2:6-9, 235
    reconstruction of, 17, 28, 50, 127, 134, 167, 195, 253
    rededication of, 52, 59
    refoundation ceremony, 209
    refoundation of, 216–217, 222
    state of, 88–90
Jewish nationalism, 3
Jewish sectarianism, 12
Joshua, 13, 36, 37, 41, 71, 120, 266
Judaism, 2, 268, 275
    post-exilic, 7

*Kalu* ceremony, 209–211, 216

land tenure, 276
legalism, 9
Levites, 15

Messenger Formula, 109, 130, 136, 138, 219 n. 8, 265
messianism, 6, 66, 151, 161 n. 14, 179, 185, 234, 236, 237–238, 237 n. 108, 238 n. 113
Mizpah, 95
monarchy, 261
month, designation of, 48
month names, Babylonian, 49
Moses, 228
"Myth of the Empty Land", 92

Nebuchadnezzar, 11, 228
nationalism, 4, 6

Nehemiah, 4, 11
Neirab, 61, 76

oracles against the nations, 225, 241, 268
OT theology, 7 n. 42

Papyrus Meissner, 46, 47 n. 110
*pax Persica*, 260
peace, eschatological, 183, 189
"People of the Land", 168–169
Persian Empire, 16
    dynastic model, 67, 78
    imperial policy, 64, 87
    internal structure, 79
    rebellions of 522-21, 80
    taxation, 77, 260, 276
    travel in, 62
Persian rule in Yehud, 9 n. 47, 11, 62
    n. 20, 68, 79, 80, 86–88, 219
    n. 4, 220, 226, 259–261, 263, 276
    perception of in Haggai, 260–261
Pharisees, 9
pilgrimage to Jerusalem, 186–187, 192, 240
poetry, Hebrew, 10
postdating, 80–85
priestly terminology, 54
priestly theology, 101
priestly traditions, 52, 118, 218, 269
priests, 9 n. 49, 13
prophecy, 15, 33, 50
    effectiveness of, 254, 256–257
    end of, 9 n. 48, 10, 25
    importance of in Haggai, 255, 275, 276–279
    social location of, 24
    social location of in Haggai, 266–269
    study of, 24
    vocabulary related to, 251, 265
prophetic office, 117–118, 241
    authority of, 267
    view of in Haggai, 265–275
prophetic role, 148
prophetic speech, forms in Haggai, 267
prophetic-symbolic action, 213
prophets, central and peripheral, 266, 268 n. 32
proselytism, 3
purity and impurity, 203
refoundation ceremony, 250, 267, 270

religious anthropology, 97–98
religious traditions *see* traditions, religious
remnant, 141–142, 273
returnees, 276
returnees and non-exiled population, 277
reversal, theme in Haggai, 253

Samaria, 68, 73, 78, 87, 206
Samaritans, 4, 19, 32, 33, 36, 40, 210–213, 268
Second Temple Judaism, 12
Servant of Yahweh, 3, 228 n. 59
shaking of the nations, 176–179
Shallum, 231
Shealtiel, 66
Shelomith, 75
Shenazzar, 63, 64
Sheshbazzar, 63, 63–70
signet, 229–231
    imagery, significance of, 234–239
Sinai covenant, 145, 162, 169, 170–172, 184, 241, 272, 273
    understanding of in Haggai, 252
social sciences, 22

temple vessels, 69
theocracy, 35
theological compromise, 274
theological fiction, hermeneutical tendency in Haggai, 273
time
    concept of in Haggai, 252
    in Haggai 1:2-4, 123
traditions
    eschatological, 186–188
    religious, 18, 19, 21, 97–102, 153–157, 157 n. 367, 183–195, 274, 276
    use in Haggai, 19, 241, 271–275
*Transeuphratène*, 26
Trito-Isaiah, 17, 92

universalism, 6
universalism and particularism, 4, 7, 9

Wadi Dâliyeh, 43, 46, 76, 82
web-sites, 26
wisdom, 101, 126, 130, 156
Word-Event Formula, 109, 220, 248, 251
Word-Reception Formula, 248

Yahweh, activities of in Haggai, 254
Yahweh Sebaoth, epithet, 53, 122
Yehud
    coins, 76
    demography of, 15, 262
    governors of, 68
    independence movement in 522-520,
        5, 11, 35, 85, 152, 270
    land tenure, 262–263
    literary activity in, 94
    Persian rule in *see* Persian rule in
        Yehud, 235, 239, 241
    political status of, 68, 72–80, 234,
        259–261
    political power in, 276
    population of, 90–96, 242
    return to, 8, 63, 69, 72
    sociology of, 262–265

    status of, 241
    structure of communal authority in,
        261

Zadokites, 14, 15
Zechariah, 4, 6, 9, 15, 21 n. 111, 40, 90
Zechariah 1-8, relationship of Haggai to,
    56
Zemah, 65–66
Zerubbabel, 5, 6, 9, 10, 13, 33, 36, 37,
    41, 51, 63, 70–72, 119–120, 231–
    239, 240, 248, 266, 272, 275, 276,
    277
    role of, 261
    theological significance of, 238, 270
Zion theology, 18, 20, 99, 101, 185, 186–
    190, 189, 191, 192, 235, 242, 248,
    259, 260, 271